D1032428

Animal Cognition in Nature

The Convergence of Psychology and Biology in Laboratory and Field

Animal Cognition in Nature
The Convergence of Psychology and Biology in Laboratory and Field

edited by

Russell P. Balda

Department of Biological Sciences,
Northern Arizona University,
Flagstaff, Arizona, USA

Irene M. Pepperberg

Department of Ecology and Evolutionary Biology,
College of Arts and Sciences,
Faculty of Science,
The University of Arizona,
Tucson, Arizona, USA

Alan C. Kamil

School of Biological Sciences,
Manter Hall,
University of Nebraska,
Lincoln, Nebraska, USA

ACADEMIC PRESS

San Diego London Boston
New York Sydney Tokyo Toronto

Academic Press
525 B Street, Suite 1900, San Diego, California 92101-4495, USA
http://www.apnet.com

Academic Press
24–28 Oval Road, London NW1 7DX, UK
http://www.hbuk.co.uk/ap/

ISBN 0-12-077030-X

A catalogue record for this book is available from the British Library

Transferred to digital printing 2006

98 99 00 01 02 03 MP 9 8 7 6 5 4 3 2 1

Contents

Preface

This volume, 'Animal Cognition in Nature', is the result of an ongoing synthesis of several ideas that were considered revolutionary, if not heretical, in the 1960s. At that time, animal behavior, whether studied in field or laboratory, by ethologists or psychologists, was generally interpreted as the result of simple processes relating specific stimuli to specific behaviors. Examples from that time include S–R models, sign stimuli, IRMs, etc. Theoretical constructs such as mental representations, memory or attention were avoided. Today, students of animal behavior work in an entirely different atmosphere. This is the result of several developments.

One of these developments was the aptly named 'cognitive revolution' among psychologists which inspired researchers to adapt the cognitive stance and test a wider range of behaviors, revealing many previously unexpected abilities in their subjects. Simultaneously, behavioral ecology appeared, with a whole set of novel concepts such as optimization models, sociobiology and kin selection. In addition, results from fields as diverse as social communication, navigation and neurobiology suggested that animals remember, process and store large amounts of complex information that allows them to predict outcomes in a variety of situations and thus solve a striking range of problems. For example, two of the editors of this volume have worked on spatial memory in seed-caching birds. In order for long-term spatial memory to occur, an animal must first transform spatial information into some type of neurological code (or representation). This must then be stored, remaining intact in memory for some length of time. Later, this information must be retrieved from long-term memory, decoded and translated into appropriate behavior. This is an example of how cognitive systems involve complexes of neurological and behavioral characteristics. We have long since left the realm where animals are viewed as simple, stimulus-bound responders, passive learners or robotic followers of conditioning regimes.

As we invited the authors of the chapters that constitute this book to participate, we challenged them to approach their research programs from a cognitive perspective. In some cases this required the authors to take an approach that was very novel to them. The reason that the cognitive approach is so novel to many scientists interested in animal behavior can be found in the history of the study of cognition in animals.

Almost a century has passed since scientists first developed concepts, definitions, and experimental paradigms about what would now be called animal cognition. These early studies and ideas were mostly limited to the domain of the experimental psychologist. Cognition consequently was studied in a limited number of species of laboratory animals by scientists looking for homologies to human behavior. Such studies considered neither the ecological setting (or lack thereof) in the laboratory nor the evolutionary history of their subjects. This lack of ecological and evolutionary reasoning often led such studies to seem inappropriate and irrelevant to biologists, who, not surprisingly, tended to ignore the studies. This, we believe, was unfortunate. Even if these experiments seemed to occur in a biological vacuum, the cognitive processes being uncovered by these studies were of fundamental biological importance.

Fortunately, many of the theoretical and empirical problems of the modern study of animal behavior are of great interest to both psychologists and biologists. This has made it relatively easy for concepts and ideas to cross disciplinary boundaries. For example, the results of early studies in behavioral ecology showed that animals are capable of a diversity of adaptive responses to changes in their natural environments. Such complex responsiveness to stimuli is a hallmark of cognitive abilities, and a number of cognitive theories from psychology could be appropriately applied to explain these behaviors.

The growing realization that cognition should be viewed as an evolutionary trait is leading to a paradigm shift. Ecologists, ethologists, and field biologists are beginning to realize and accept the idea that in many instances they are observing, recording, and studying the results of the cognitive abilities of their species. When a new and unique point-of-view is brought to bear on a discipline for the first time, unexpected and stimulating ideas emerge. When disciplines interact and begin to share facts, ideas, methodologies and hypothesis, new interpretations and theories are formulated. These fresh, new viewpoints may be so utilitarian that they are immediately incorporated into existing research programs. The areas of behavioral ecology and comparative psychology offer such a potentially dynamic mix. To some extent, this integration is already occurring. Biologists are beginning to recognize and appreciate that cognitive considerations may play a pivotal role in resolving some problems in field research and natural history. Psychologists are becoming increasingly aware of the importance of ecological and evolutionary factors in determining the nature of cognitive abilities.

As a result of this state of affairs, a number of different books, including this volume, are beginning to appear or are scheduled to appear soon. These books, as well as a number of review articles in major journals, will set the direction of study for the interdisciplinary study of animal cognition in a simultaneously evolutionary and psychological framework. Although the name 'Cognitive Ethology' has been suggested (in this volume) for this new subdiscipline within the Life Sciences, other labels may be just as appropriate. Only time and a spirited dialogue by the participants will resolve the issue. Nevertheless, a new approach is certainly emerging. In putting together this volume, we have used a unique strategy, emphasizing the importance of the study of cognition either under natural conditions or in light of known natural history phenomena.

The authors view cognition as an adaptive trait, shaped largely by the influence of natural selection much as morphological and physiological traits have been so shaped. Cognition is part of the adaptive arsenal with which animals cope with environmental demands and constraints. If this is so, then information-processing abilities must be understood as adaptive traits. This view accepts the idea that the quality and quantity of information an animal has about its environment and neighbors (both conspecifics and others) will be translated into the biological success of the animal. Individuals with varying amounts of information should show differential fitness just as occurs with other biological traits.

In constructing the content of this book, the editors attempted to explore systematically some prominent areas of animal behavior in which cognition most likely plays a dominant role in natural settings, and could be employed to explain the complexity of observed behaviors. Three of the areas in which this integrative approach is proceeding rapidly are animal communication, seed caching and recovery and navigation and orientation. There are also a number of domain-specific cases that are not yet as clearly conceptualized, but hold great promise for future research. These considerations led us to invite a set of leading researchers to participate in this project. Authors of each chapter were challenged to present their most contemporary data, discuss their data in a cognitive framework, considering what advantages and disadvantages such a framework might offer and address potentially fruitful areas of future research within a cognitive perspective. We hope that the resulting volume contributes towards the next generation of integrative research on animal cognition.

About the editors

Balda spent over 20 years studying the natural history, population dynamics, sociobiology and seed-caching behavior of the highly social Pinyon Jay. His years of experience with individually banded (ringed) birds led him to conclude that problem resolution in a social animal requires highly developed mental skills. While observing Pinyon Jays and nutcrackers cache and then recover seeds with high degrees of accuracy he became impressed with the spatial abilities of seed-caching birds. These two areas of interest led him to recognize the importance of bringing these birds into the laboratory for highly controlled experiments. He has cooperated with A. C. Kamil on questions pertaining to spatial abilities, the evolution of cognition and its selective environment for the past 17 years. He is keen on finding natural history traits that indicate cognitive abilities and then attempting to study them in the laboratory. Presently, he is studying the different cognitive abilities of social and asocial jays and sexual differences in spatial memory in Pinyon Jays.

Pepperberg has spent the past 20 years examining the cognitive processes of parrots and the effects of social interactions on vocal learning. Her cognitive studies demonstrate that the capabilities of birds match those of the great apes and marine mammals; her studies on social learning demonstrate intriguing parallels between human and avian vocal development. Her current focus is on the synthesis of these two areas of behavior, and on proposing how this synthesis might provide insights into behavior observed in the field.

Kamil has been a leader in the effort to bring cognitive mechanisms implied by field observations into the laboratory for detailed experimental analysis. He has clearly defined the pros and cons of this approach in a number of provocative articles. Early in his career he found that Blue Jays were capable of complex strategy learning comparable to that found in primates. This led him to consider the implications of cognition as an adaptive trait. Groundbreaking studies included developing a methodology for studying search image in the laboratory and strategy learning in nectar-feeding birds in the field. He and Balda have worked together in an exhaustive series of studies on spatial memory in seed-caching birds. He is presently working on complex geometric learning by seed-caching birds and the effect of cognitive abilities of predators on the evolution of prey appearance.

1

On the Proper Definition of Cognitive Ethology

Alan C. Kamil

School of Biological Sciences and Department of Psychology, Nebraska Behavioral Biology Group, University of Nebraska, Lincoln, NE 68588-0118, USA

Introduction

The last 20–30 years have seen two 'scientific revolutions' in the study of animal behavior: the cognitive revolution that originated in psychology, and the Darwinian, behavioral ecology revolution that originated in biology. Among psychologists, the cognitive revolution has had enormous impact. Similarly, among biologists, the Darwinian revolution has had enormous impact. The major theme of this chapter is that these two scientific research programs need to be combined into a single approach, simultaneously cognitive and Darwinian, and that this single approach is most appropriately called cognitive ethology.

Scientific progress

What constitutes progress in science? At one level, there is substantial agreement: progress consists of the testing of specific alternative hypotheses that results in the rejection of most of these hypotheses. It can be argued that, in the long run, all will be rejected. This is the concept of falsification, perhaps best expressed for the working scientist by the process called strong

ANIMAL COGNITION IN NATURE
ISBN 0-12-077030-X

inference (Platt, 1964), in which multiple hypotheses are generated and experiments designed to disprove as many of them as possible.

However, at another level, the falsificationist position is incorrect. Major high-level theories, such as those of Newtonian physics, Ptolemaic astronomy, Lorenzian ethology or radical behaviorism are not rejected on the basis of one, or even a few, facts or experiments that are inconsistent with them. The process of strong inference does not apply with hypotheses/theories at this level of generality.

Some philosophers (e.g. Kuhn, 1970; Lakatos, 1974) have provided alternative accounts of how scientific progress occurs at these levels. The work of Kuhn is particularly familiar to many scientists. In his book titled *The Structure of Scientific Revolutions*, Kuhn (1970) argued that the falsificationist view is incorrect, demonstrating that changes in broad theories, which he called scientific paradigms, do not occur according to the falsificationist model. Unfortunately, Kuhn failed to specify clearly how the process of change from one paradigm to another, or scientific revolution in his words, takes place. Kuhn makes it sound like a generational or sociological phenomenon, not necessarily related to data at all.

Another philosopher of science, less well known outside philosophical circles, Imre Lakatos (1974), has extended the arguments of Kuhn in a particularly useful way, providing a cogent analysis of how paradigmatic changes that do address the issue of the relationship between broad scientific theories and data take place. Lakatos argues that science is characterized by what he calls research programs, roughly equivalent to Kuhn's scientific paradigms. A research program consists of two parts: a central 'hard core' and a protective belt of specific auxiliary hypotheses. The central core consists of definitions and assumptions that coherently map out directions for research, but this core is not subject to direct test. Instead, the auxiliary hypotheses are used to derive specific models and hypotheses, which are subject to empirical test, revision and rejection.

Lakatos uses an amusing fictional anecdote to illustrate the difference between the hard core of a research program and its surrounding web of auxiliary hypotheses. Imagine a pre-Einsteinian physicist who uses the central core of his scientific program, Newton's mechanics and the law of gravity, to calculate the path of a newly discovered planet, p. However, observation of the planet shows that its orbit deviates from the predicted one. Does the physicist abandon Newtonian physics? No. He revises his auxiliary hypotheses, and calculates that there is another, previously unknown planet, p', which disturbs the orbit of p. This is a new model, which is subjected to test by building a large new telescope to look for p'. Suppose p' is found. It would be considered a great victory for Newtonian physics. Why? – because it would be the discovery of a new, previously unexpected fact, implying that Newtonian physics was a progressive research program. But suppose p' was not observed. The physicist would still not abandon the central core of

Newtonian physics. He might modify his model again, predicting that there is a cloud of dust located so as to obscure the view of supposed planet p′. This new model could then be tested by sending a satellite to collect data to determine if the cloud of dust existed, and so on.

So how does change from one scientific research program to another take place? Lakatos distinguishes two types of programs: degenerate and progressive. A progressive program is one that is resulting in the discovery of new, previously unknown facts. It may also be able to explain facts long known but previously not understood. In contrast, a degenerate program is one that is not producing new discoveries, but only reiterating old ones. Given a choice between these two types of programs, Lakatos argues, most scientists will choose the exciting, progressive program over the dull, degenerate program. The major advantage of Lakatos' approach over Kuhn's is that the formulation of Lakatos specifies a relationship between evidence and scientific revolutions. The paradigm or research program that is leading to exciting new discoveries is the one that will prevail.

This approach to understanding scientific progress suggests that science progresses in two ways. A specific research program is developed and refined through the falsification of specific hypotheses and models that are derived within that program. However, choice of research program is made on a different basis, in terms of the overall usefulness of the research generated by the central core of the program. In this context, usefulness is defined as the discovery of new facts or the novel explanation of phenomena that are known, but have not been previously understood.

Thus, Newtonian physics did not fall because of some experiments that produced results it could not explain (as a falsificationist would have us believe), nor did it fall because Einsteinian physics won some kind of cultural battle (as some naive followers of Kuhn would have us believe). Newtonian physics fell to Einsteinian physics because Einstein's theory predicted a host of new phenomena and explained known, but previously unexplainable, phenomena, and it is in these terms that the cognitive and the Darwinian research programs have come to prevail. Each program has generated new sets of auxiliary hypotheses and, in the process of testing these hypotheses (and discarding and refining them as research proceeded), many new and unexpected phenomena have been uncovered.

The cognitive research program

It is clear that the study of cognitive processes in animals has emerged as a major field of study. There has been an explosion of interest in the approach, as indicated, for example, by the number of books devoted to the subject, beginning with Roitblat *et al.* (1984) through to the present (Vauclair, 1996; Roberts, 1998; Shettleworth, 1998). As the chapters in this volume demonstrate, many phenomena have been approached from the cognitive perspective. These include phenomena traditionally studied by ethologists (e.g. bird song; Kroodsma and Byers, Todt and Hultsch, this volume) as well as those more traditionally associated with psychologists (e.g. timing; Gibbon and Church, 1990). While the approach originated with experimental psychologists, it has also proven to be of great interest to neurophysiologists (e.g. O'Keefe and Nadel, 1978) and biologists (e.g. Real, 1994; Dukas, 1998). As the chapters in this volume demonstrate, it is a very diverse field, with investigators examining phenomena as different as spatial navigation in honey bees, birds and mammals, the perception and production of auditory signals, the comprehension and use of symbolic communication systems. This diversity is a sign of one strength of the approach – the cognitive approach is applicable to a wide variety of phenomena in many different taxa. However, the field of animal cognition also appears to be fragmented, lacking a central definition. This can be seen in the many different labels that are used: animal cognition, comparative cognition, cognitive ecology, cognitive ethology, etc.

Another sign of the fragmentation of the field is the absence of a widely accepted definition of animal cognition. Many texts on animal cognition actually avoid explicit definition, tending to define cognition by example, as the study of certain types of processes such as attention, memory, etc. However, if we apply the lessons of Lakatos, we see that animal cognition is not the study of certain phenomena, it is an approach to a set of problems.

In these terms, then, how should the cognitive research program be characterized? Although it can be phrased in a number of ways, the central assumption of the cognitive program is that organisms possess some type of internal representation of the external world. Examples include cognitive maps, templates or internal images, but simpler ideas such as memories might also be included. These internal representations are related to the external world in two ways: a coding process on the input side and a relationship to behavior on the output side. Many of the alternative hypotheses we test have to do with these input–output relationships between the assumed internal representations and the external world. As Dyer (1994) put it, cognitive approaches, in contrast to noncognitive approaches '. . . postulate processes that organize sensory information into coherent internal models of external events, allowing the animal to respond appropriately to important stimuli even when experiencing them in novel combinations or contexts' (p. 68).

Reasons for fragmentation

Disciplinary diversity

Despite this central theme, the study of animal cognition is, as noted above, fairly fragmented. One of the reasons for this fragmentation is disciplinary diversity. The students of animal cognition come from distinct disciplinary backgrounds. These different disciplines focus on animal cognition in different ways and for different reasons. Furthermore, these disciplines operate within very different research programs or paradigms making different assumptions and having different goals. That is, even in cases where researchers share the central assumptions of the cognitive program, they also are participants in other research programs, which leads to diversity of questions, approaches and goals.

The relationship between human and nonhuman cognition

One large difference among those taking a cognitive approach with animals is whether they are oriented primarily towards understanding humans, using animals as model systems, or are more oriented towards understanding the animals within a biological context. Shettleworth (1993) expressed it well, distinguishing between what she called the 'anthropocentric program' and the 'ecological program' (see Table 1.1).

Specialized vs. general dichotomy

Another problem which has haunted the study of animal cognition is the distinction between specialized and general processes. Historically, this has been a biology–psychology dichotomy. Psychologists tended to emphasize the search for a few general process 'mechanisms' that could explain a very wide

Table 1.1 Comparison of the Anthropocentric and Ecological Programs (after Shettleworth, 1993).

Characteristic	Anthropocentric program	Ecological program
Purpose	Investigate continuity and generality of cognitive processes across species	Investigate impact of evolution on cognition; understand cognition as a biological phenomenon
Phenomena analysed	Animal cognition in tasks modeled on what people do	Cognitive processes that animals use in nature
Species compared	Human vs. nonhuman (often implicit); distantly related species	Close relatives with divergent niches; distant relatives with convergent niches
Relationship to neuroscience	Evidence of continuity needed to justify 'animal models'	Understanding evolution of brain mechanisms; interpreting adaptive specializations as modifications of general processes

variety of phenomena. In contrast, biologists interested in animal cognition tended to be interested in cases where cognitive processing seemed to be devoted to a single (or restricted set of) biological problem(s). The study of imprinting or song learning (at least in the early days) epitomized this approach.

Current state of affairs

In summary, then, the cognitive research program has proved to be an exciting, progressive one. As many of the chapters in this volume make clear, working within the cognitive paradigm has proved quite productive, leading to many exciting, often unexpected results. However, the field is characterized by a number of divisions, mostly related to different investigators working within different traditions and at different levels of analysis in an uncoordinated manner. What is needed is a more comprehensive and inclusive research program which will allow integration across these divisions.

The ethological program

It is interesting to compare this state of affairs with the dilemma facing those studying animal behavior in the 1950s and 1960s. As is the case with animal cognition today, there were many different workers from different disciplines involved, and efforts to understand animal behavior were diverse and diffuse. At least four approaches were present:

1. The 'classical' ethological approach of Lorenz, which emphasizes phylogenetic relationships and genetic contributions to behavior.
2. The 'British' school of ethology, which is oriented more towards adaptation.
3. The American behaviorist tradition, with its emphasis on learning and reinforcement.
4. The Schnierla–Lehrman approach, emphasizing epigenesis and experience in the broad sense.

There was considerable disagreement and confusion about how to reconcile these approaches. Especially problematic was the question of the relationship between evolutionary and mechanistic levels of analysis.

A major event in the resolution of these problems was the publication of Tinbergen's (1963) famous paper 'On aims and methods of ethology'. In that paper, and throughout his work and career, Tinbergen emphasized the necessity of understanding behavior at different levels, in terms of phylogeny (historical), adaptation (function), mechanism (neuroscience) and development (ontogeny). One way to express Tinbergen's position is that it called for the integrated study of these four levels of analysis. Another way to express it is that it encouraged the study of ontogeny and mechanism within a Darwinian perspective, including considerations of phylogeny and adaptation. However it is phrased, it is clear that the integrative, multilevel approach called for by Tinbergen (and others) has been successful. Today, the study of animal behavior, encompassing ethology, behavioral ecology and comparative psychology, is a much more integrated and cohesive field.

This has taken place because students of animal behavior now largely agree on a scientific research program *sensu* Lakatos. The central core of this program is the assumption that every behavior has an evolutionary history, a biological function, an underlying neural mechanism and a developmental history, and that these interact in many ways. This central core has produced a field of study that is a vibrant field, much different than the field of animal behavior of the 1950s and 1960s. Many of the old disciplinary distinctions have largely fallen away. Today, there are biologists in psychology departments, and psychologists in biology departments; there are truly interdisciplinary programs in which departmental or disciplinary affiliation is relatively unimportant, like those at Davis, Indiana and Nebraska. But, most important, it has proven to be a most progressive research program. Any contemporary animal behavior text will give many examples of exciting new findings generated by the multilevel, integrative approach advocated so well by Niko Tinbergen. Examples include research programs incorporating the study of sensory processes into understanding natural and sexual selection (Endler, 1980; Basolo, 1995), programs using comparative and phylogenetic approaches to understand foraging preferences (Arnold, 1981), or sexual behavior (Ryan and Rand, 1995), or programs integrating optimization models based on the concept of adaptedness with the study of behavioral mechanisms (Cuthill and Houston, 1997).

Synthesis

The major theme of this chapter is that the modern ethological approach and the cognitive approach need to be synthesized. On the one hand, the ethological program, strongly evolutionary but emphasizing the importance of mechanism and ontogeny, provides a powerful, pragmatic framework for the study of animal cognition. Those interested in cognition need to view their work in the broad integrative ethological framework. On the other hand, the cognitive research program provides a potent rubric for understanding many of the complexities that are found in the behavior of animals. Those interested in animal behavior can, in many cases, benefit from taking a cognitive approach in trying to understand the behaviors they study.

There are a number of research programs which have adopted this synthetic approach, such as those on spatial memory in seed-caching corvids (Kamil and Balda, 1990; Balda and Kamil, this volume) and parids

(Shettleworth and Hampton, Clayton and Lee, this volume), studies of homing and navigation in birds and bees (Wiltschko and Wiltschko, Bingman *et al.* and Dyer, this volume) and of song learning (Todt and Hultsch, Kroodsma and Byers, DeVoogt and Szekely, this volume). As the chapters in this volume demonstrate, each of the four questions Tinbergen (1963) identified can be asked about animal cognition.

Physiological mechanism

An animal's internal representations of the external world must have their physical bases in the brain, and understanding the neural bases of cognition will be an essential component of fully understanding cognition in animals (and humans). Chapters in this volume, for example, discuss the role of the hippocampus in spatial memory, and the neural bases of song learning and navigation. This work is interesting, with many important implications, but there is a basic problem at present integrating neurobiological techniques and knowledge with behavioral cognitive studies.

The problem is that our behavioral knowledge of cognitive capabilities, rudimentary though it may be in many respects, is still more advanced than our neurobiological knowledge. For example, we know that species differences in hippocampal volume, adjusted for body or total brain size, correlate with dependence on cached food in parids and corvids (Krebs *et al.*, 1989; Sherry *et al.*, 1989), and especially in the case of seed-caching corvids, with performance on a variety of test of spatial cognition (Basil *et al.*, 1996). However, hippocampal volume is a very global, unsatisfactory measure. It would be most helpful if more fine-grained measures could be developed. For example, work with mammals has demonstrated the existence of so-called 'place neurons', neurons which fire only when the animal is in a specific place (different places having different neurons). Do seed-caching birds like nutcrackers and black-capped chickadees have more place neurons than other birds, and is that why their hippocampi are larger?

Recent developments in neurobiology indicate that many new techniques are being developed which will contribute substantially to our understanding of animal cognition by providing more detailed information about the neurobiology of cognition. For example, the positron emission tomography (PET) scans are beginning to reveal much about which parts of the brain are active during different cognitive tasks, such as recall (Schacter, 1996). Also, immunocytochemistry is beginning to provide detailed information about neural circuitry (e.g. Szekely and Krebs, 1996).

Developmental processes

The cognitive processes of animals are strongly influenced by ontogeny. This has been particularly well studied in development of song learning since the pioneering work of Marler (Marler and Tamura, 1964; Todt and Hultsch, Kroodsma and Byers, this volume). Seed caching and navigation provide additional examples (Clayton and Lee; Wiltschko and Wiltschko, this volume). In these cases, the ontogenetic effects seem to have clear targets. That is, the effects of varied experience, at least as they have been studied, are found in relatively specific domains. However, it is possible that ontogenetic effects may have broader, less specific impact.

Perhaps the most suggestive evidence of general effects of ontogeny comes from the work of Rosenzweig and his collaborators (e.g. Bennett and Rosenzweig, 1981). They have shown that differences in early environment have dramatic behavioral and neurobiological effects in rats, including anatomical and biochemical effects on the brain. These results imply that there is much more to be learned about the ontogeny of animal cognition, and that it will pay dividends to combine developmental, behavioral and neurobiological approaches. Clayton and Lee's research (this volume) provides an excellent example of such work. They studied the development of spatial memory and hippocampal growth in storing and nonstoring parids. As they describe in their chapter, they found that hippocampal growth was facilitated by the opportunity to cache, but only in the caching species.

It is possible that these effects found by Clayton and Lee are indicators of more general effects. Consider what we know about ontogeny, neurobiology and spatial memory in seed-caching corvids. Young nutcrackers spend considerable time accompanying their parents recovering seeds, and engage in 'play-like' cache-recovery behavior (Vander Wall and Hutchins, 1983). Dimmick (1993) found that adult, wild-caught nutcrackers recovered their caches more accurately than young nutcrackers under controlled laboratory conditions. This is consistent with the possibility of important ontogenetic effects in the development of spatial memory in nutcrackers. Basil *et al.* (1996) found that nutcrackers have larger hippocampi (adjusted for total brain size) than Pinyon Jays, Scrub Jays or Mexican Jays, which are all corvids less dependent on cached food than nutcrackers. It is possible that the early experience effects suggested by Dimmick's work are expressed in increased hippocampal growth, as suggested by the findings of Basil *et al.*

Comparative experiments suggest even more. Balda and Kamil (1989) found that nutcrackers and Pinyon Jays recover caches more accurately than Scrub Jays. Furthermore, in a series of studies involving noncaching tests of spatial memory, Balda, Kamil and their coworkers have found consistent species differences in spatial memory that parallel the results of the comparative cache-recovery experiment (Olson, 1991; Kamil *et al.*, 1994; Olson *et al.*, 1995). Dimmick's (1993) results suggest that early experience may play an important role in the development of the cache site memory abilities of nutcrackers and other seed-caching corvids. These results may not be limited to cache recovery. It would be most interesting if experiments examining the behavioral and neurobiological effects of differential early experience, and including a battery of tests of spatial memory, were carried out. Such experiments might well reveal general effects of early experience on both spatial memory and hippocampal size.

Adaptive function

The discussion of the analysis of the ontogenetic and neurobiological substrates of cognitive processes has been relatively brief. These approaches are relatively well established and do not need lengthy discussion. However, the analysis of cognition in an evolutionary framework, emphasizing both phylogeny and adaptation, faces some serious unresolved problems. Taking functional analysis first, we know that cognitive processes can have adaptive outcomes: remembering where food has been stored, singing effective songs, finding the way back to the hive. However, there are some special difficulties in the study of behavior as adaptation. It might be worthwhile to review the methods that have been used to test ideas about behavior as adaptation and discuss the potential for the application of these methods within the cognitive paradigm.

Correlational approach

One way to investigate the possible adaptive significance of a trait is to measure biological success (or some correlated variable) as a function of that trait. Most often, the results of such a study are in the form of a correlation. A classic case is provided by studies of the role of avian helpers at the nest. It was well known that in many species of birds, older offspring remained around the nest when subsequent broods were raised, often engaging in what appeared to be helpful behavior, such as feeding the young in the new brood (Skutch, 1961). The question that arose was whether this was actually helping behavior. That is, did the behavior of the helping birds actually increase the number of young raised per nest? The first studies to investigate this issue showed that there was, in many species, a positive correlation between the presence of helpers and the number of young successfully fledged (e.g. Rowley, 1965; see Brown, 1987, esp. pp. 169–173, for review).

As far as I know, this correlational approach has never been attempted with any cognitive trait. The practical problem appears to be the difficulty of obtaining a good measure of cognitive ability without disrupting the animal being studied. For example, it seems quite reasonable to assume that a seed-caching bird that more accurately remembers its cache sites will recover more food when needed and, therefore, survive and reproduce more successfully. However, this idea needs to be tested directly. It would be very interesting to know if individual nutcrackers, Pinyon Jays or Marsh Tits with better cache site memories actually do enjoy higher degrees of biological success than those with poorer memories. However, performing this research would require capturing and testing many birds, then releasing them and collecting data on reproductive success. While possible, this approach would actually be very difficult to carry out successfully.

Another possibility might be found in cases where measures of cognitive ability might be obtainable from free-living animals. For example, Healy and Hurly (1995) have developed a method for testing hummingbirds on a spatial learning and memory task under field conditions. In essence, they used artificial feeders to set up an analog of the radial maze task widely used with rats. The free-flying hummingbirds had to keep track of which feeders in the array they had visited and avoid revisits to these emptied flowers on a subsequent visit. This is quite analogous to a problem that nectar feeders face in nature (Gill and Wolf, 1977). Healy and Hurly found not only that the birds learned the task, but that there were considerable individual differences in performance. Repeat visits to already emptied flowers can have quite significant effects on food intake (Kamil, 1978). It would be particularly interesting to see if the individual differences observed by Healy and Hurly (1995) might correlate with a direct or indirect measure of fitness, such as rate of fat accumulation during pauses in migration.

Experimental approach

Although the correlational approach can produce useful and important information, it has a basic weakness: it only produces a correlation and correlation does not prove causation. The fact that the number of young fledged is correlated with the number of helpers could be due to some third variable which correlates with both variables. For example, territorial quality could influence both factors, causing helpers to stay on better territories, which, by their very nature, also produce more young regardless of the number of helpers. This problem can be avoided by manipulating the variable of interest experimentally, with individual animals assigned to conditions at random. Then, if an effect is found, we can be more certain of the causal relationship between the trait and biological success. Thus, in the case of helpers at the nest, it is possible to identify a set of territories with equivalent numbers of helpers present and then experimentally remove helpers from some nests, selected at random. Such experimental studies have confirmed the hypothesis that, at least in some species, the presence of helpers at the nest does increase the number of young fledged (Brown *et al.*, 1982).

There are three ways that this approach could be applied to cognition.

1. Using neurobiological techniques to interfere with a cognitive ability. One way is to interfere with the cognitive ability by lesioning animals and observing the effects on free-ranging animals. Krushinskaya (1966) performed hippocampal lesions on free-ranging Eurasian Nutcrackers and found that the lesions impaired their ability to relocate their stored food. However, lesions represent a fairly crude manipulation and raise serious ethical concerns. It is possible that, as neurobiological techniques advance, finer and

more detailed methods of interfering with cognitive abilities by disrupting the neural substrate may well become available. If so, these may offer greater promise scientifically as well as reducing the ethical concerns raised by the lesioning techniques.

2. Using a lack of the opportunity to learn as a simulation of inability to learn. For example, Hollis (1984) has examined the effects of associative learning on aggressive behavior. Male Blue Gouramis (*Trichogaster trichopterus*) were conditioned to a red light. Whenever the red light came on, it was followed by the appearance (behind a clear partition) of another male. Control fish received no such conditioning. In the critical test, Hollis placed a conditioned male on one side of an opaque partition; an unconditioned male on the other side. After the red light, which was visible to both fish, came on, the partition was removed. The conditioned fish won most of the ensuing aggressive encounters, showing higher levels of aggressive behavior than the controls. One way of interpreting these data is that the behavior of the control represents the behavior that might be expected from a fish exposed to the same conditioning as the experimental males, but without the ability to learn the association. In this light, these experiments demonstrate an approach to simulating the behavior of animals without specific cognitive abilities to investigate the possible adaptive value of those abilities. More recently, this work has been extended to show that when the conditioned stimulus predicted the appearance of a receptive female, conditioned male gouramis had distinct paternal advantage over nonconditioned males (Hollis *et al.*, 1997).

3. Providing special learning experience to free-ranging animals. Another possibility might be to provide special training experiences and to observe potential effects on biological success. For example, several studies of nectar-feeding birds have shown that they increase foraging efficiency by avoiding flowers which they have already emptied (Gill and Wolf, 1977; Kamil, 1978). Cole *et al.* (1982) found that adult-caught hummingbirds could learn to avoid revisiting artificial flowers more rapidly than they could learn to revisit them. However, Wunderle and Martinez (1987) found that laboratory-raised nectar-feeding bananaquits did not show this bias, although wild-caught adults did. This suggests that the avoidance of visited flowers may be learned. It would be interesting to observe the effects of inexhaustible nectar feeders on the foraging patterns of young free-flying birds.

This approach might be well suited to research with insects. Insects show many types of learning (Papaj and Lewis, 1993) and, with their relatively short life spans, research on the lifetime fitness effects of early experience might be particularly practicable. For example, Heinrich and his collaborators (Heinrich *et al.*, 1977; Waddington *et al.*, 1981) have found experiential effects on flower choice by bumblebees. It might be possible to arrange various early experiences for bees, then observe the effects of these experiences on later foraging success.

Comparative approaches

In this approach, species are chosen for study based upon their natural history and phylogeny, taking advantage of the processes of divergence and convergence. Divergence refers to differences among closely related species owing to differences in their natural histories and adaptations, while convergence refers to similarities among distantly related species owing to similarities in their natural histories and adaptations. There are many examples of the use of these strategies with nonbehavioral and behavioral traits. The classic case in behavior is the study of the effects of cliff nesting in sea birds. Most gulls nest on the ground, but a few, including Kittiwakes, nest on very narrow ledges on steep cliff faces. Many of the behaviors of Kittiwakes differ from those of ground-nesting gulls in ways that seem sensibly related to cliff nesting. For example, Kittiwake adults, unlike other gulls, show weaker reactions to predators, do not remove egg shells and droppings from around nests and do not learn to recognize their young, at least in the first 4 weeks after hatching. Kittiwake chicks do not run when attacked, and show much less movement around the nest (Cullen, 1957). These appear to be reasonable adaptations to cliff nesting, but how is this adaptive hypothesis to be tested?

One way to test it would be to examine the behaviors of other cliff-nesting sea birds. If the hypothesis is correct, many similarities should be found. Studies of the Black Noddy (Cullen and Ashmole, 1963) and the Galapagos Swallow-tailed Gull (Hailman, 1965) generally supported the hypothesis. These two cliff-nesting species also diverged from their close relatives who are ground nesters in a manner similar to those by which the Kittiwake differs from its ground-nesting relatives.

The comparative strategy seems quite appropriate for empirical analysis of questions about the adaptive function of cognitive abilities. However, there is a fundamental problem that confronts the study of cognitive processes in a comparative framework, the learning-performance problem (Kamil, 1988). That is, although we are interested in measuring learning abilities or cognitive abilities in our experiments, all we are ever able to measure directly is behavior, and the behavior we observe is a function of many factors besides cognitive ability. Therefore, whenever we obtain a difference between species in their performance on a cognitive task, how can we be sure that the difference truly represents a difference in cognitive ability?

For example, Balda and Kamil (1989) found that Clark's Nutcrackers and Pinyon Jays recovered their caches more accurately than Scrub Jays in a laboratory situation. This difference might be the result of a species difference in spatial cognition but it might also be due to effects of some parameter of the experiment that was inadvertently ill-suited to Scrub Jays. It is quite possible that, under only slightly different conditions (e.g. different room layouts, motivational conditions, etc.), Scrub Jays would have performed much better.

Bitterman (1965) was the first to point out this problem. He suggested a technique, which he called control by systematic variation, to solve it. The basic idea was to carry out a series of experiments parametrically testing the effects of each potential variable that might have adversely affected the species that performed poorly. These variables were called contextual variables (Macphail, 1985). Although logical, this idea faces a serious problem: it is impossible to test all such variables. A researcher attempting to use control by systematic variation is placed in the position of trying to prove the null hypothesis, that there are no conditions under which the species will be equivalent.

I have suggested an alternative strategy based on the concept of converging operations (Kamil, 1988). The basic idea of this strategy is to test the species in question with a battery of different tests of the same cognitive ability. If a pattern of species differences holds across a wide variety of tasks, involving different environments, this would provide fairly convincing evidence that the difference was due to the aspects that the tasks had in common, namely the cognitive ability under test.

This is the strategy we have followed in comparative studies of spatial memory in seed-caching corvids. After obtaining the species difference in cache-recovery accuracy (Balda and Kamil, 1989), we proceeded to test the species in other settings, including an open room analog of the radial maze (Kamil *et al.*, 1994) and tests in operant chambers (Olson, 1991; Olson *et al.*, 1995). The basic pattern of species differences held across all of these experiments. Although one could still argue for some confounding variable, it would have to be one that was present across all of these very diverse tasks.

In thinking about these results, particularly just how strong an argument they actually present for the existence of differences among these species, two weaknesses in the Kamil (1988) paper have become apparent. The first is that there is an alternative hypothesis that needs to be tested, namely that the species differences observed are not due to a specific difference in cognitive abilities, but rather to some general factor. For example, nutcrackers may simply be more adaptable to the laboratory than other species. The second is that, although the use of converging operations may weaken the argument from contextual variables, it does not eliminate it. These considerations indicate that an additional step is needed.

This additional step might be called differentiation. It involves designing an experiment to be as similar as possible to those demonstrating species differences through converging operations, but testing a different cognitive ability. In the case of the work we have done with seed-caching corvids, there was an obvious possibility, the operant tests. Olson's (1991) original demonstration of differences in an operant setting used a task known as spatial nonmatching to sample. In this task, the animal is required to remember the spatial location of a briefly illuminated spot, then later avoid pecking it. It was relatively easy to design an experiment virtually identical to that of Olson except that the color of the illuminated spot was what needed to be remembered, not its spatial location. When we carried out this experiment (Olson *et al.*, 1995), we found that the ordering of the species was completely different, and that none of the species differences was significant. These data demonstrate that the differences we obtained during spatial tasks are not general across all tasks. They also rule out most contextual variables – if contextual variables were responsible for the differences originally found in spatial tasks, those same variables should have resulted in species differences in this experiment (see Lefebvre and Giraldeau, 1996, for a somewhat different approach).

Taken together, these experiments provide convincing evidence of a set of differences in cognitive abilities that correlate with a feature of natural history, dependence on stored seeds. They also demonstrate one of the major disadvantages of the comparative approach: the necessity to conduct a research program, not one or two experiments. However, hypotheses about the adaptive significance of behavior are never easy to test.

When is cognition adaptive? The problem of cost

One interesting aspect of the analysis of cognition in an adaptive framework is the exploration of the question, 'When does it pay to possess a cognitive ability?'. Relatively little formal theoretical or empirical work has been carried out looking at this basic question. The work that has been done, however, suggests this will be a fruitful area for further exploration. For example, Stephens (1991) has modeled the effects of within and between generational stability on the adaptedness of learning. He did this with a model in which the environment varied between good and bad states within and between generations, and learning genotypes competed with nonlearning genotypes. He found that the learning genotype would prevail only under some circumstances. Furthermore, the range of circumstances under which learners outcompeted nonlearners was more restricted when the learning mechanism had a cost associated with it.

Although the question of the cost of learning has received little formal exploration, one basic piece of information we already have tells us that cognitive abilities have costs. How do we know that? Well, first of all, the cognitive abilities of animals are limited. As Fred Dyer put it in his abstract for the symposium on the evolution of animal cognition held in Flagstaff, AZ, from which many chapters in this volume originated: 'Why do animals not remember more, learn faster, or perform tasks with less error than we observe them doing?'. For example, even the best Clark's Nutcracker forgets some of its cache sites, i.e. its memory ability is limited. This only makes sense if we assume that the ability to perform better, to remember more sites for instance, would entail some costs. Presumably, the development of increased ability would entail carrying around more neural tissue, with an accompanying increased metabolic load. This argument implies that the cost of the extra memory capacity is greater than the cost of storing some extra seeds to compensate for memory loss. Without a method for directly assessing the costs, the concept is difficult to test.

Another sort of evidence that suggests cognitive costs are the biases we find in learning, such as those shown in the well-known phenomenon of taste-aversion learning. It is much easier for many animals to learn an association between certain pairs of stimuli, such as a taste and illness for example, than between other pairs, such as a sound or a light and illness. One way to look at this situation is that the animal experiences a constant stream of stimulation. When a particularly significant event, such as illness, occurs, why does the animal's internal representation of the stimuli preceding the event not include all of the stimuli? One answer would be as suggested above: it is too expensive in terms of the neuronal substrate required. However, another answer is that inappropriate learning could occur. This is, sounds and lights are not usually reliable indicators of illness, and forming such associations might be maladaptive. This example may have broad implications: perhaps one of the costs of learning is that, under some circumstances, if certain kinds of associations, for example, are learned too easily, they will result in behavior that has negative consequences.

An example of this type involves egg recognition in birds that are subject to host parasitism. There are avian species, such as the European Cuckoo (*Cuculus canorus*) or the Brown-headed Cowbird (*Molothrus ater*), that lay their eggs in the nests of other species. Some of these hosts learn what their own eggs look like and then reject eggs that are too different (Lotem *et al.*, 1995). However, there are potential costs associated with rejection. Rejection may result in damage to one's own eggs and there may be mistakes in identification. Therefore, we might expect that decisions of whether or not to reject eggs will be affected by environmental factors, such as the presence of host parasites. This appears to be the case (Davies *et al.*, 1996). Taking the argument a step further, we might reasonably expect egg recognition to evolve only in species that are subject to social parasitism and that would be physically capable of removing the intruding egg from their nest.

Phylogenetic history

Last, and certainly most difficult, is the question of evolutionary history. Recent years have seen an exciting approach to this problem emerge. Interestingly, in a sense, this represents a return to the roots of ethology. One of the most important early papers in gaining acceptance for the study of behavior in biology was Lorenz's comparative study of Anatidae, in which he demonstrated that behavior could be used as a trait in addressing taxonomic issues (Lorenz, 1941). What Lorenz did, in that research, was to use behavioral traits to clarify a phylogeny. However, the opposite approach, using well-accepted phylogeny, in the form of a cladogram, to clarify the evolutionary history of behavioral traits is what we want to emphasize here.

While the comparative approach described above emphasized the selection of species for comparative study on the basis of ecology, the phylogenetic approach uses criteria based on phylogenetic relationship. As spelled out by a number of authors, including Brooks and McLennan (1991; see also Harvey and Pagel, 1991; Martins, 1996), the basic procedure is to map the traits of interest on to an existing phylogeny. Then, using the parsimony assumption, it is possible to draw inferences about the evolutionary history of the trait. This approach has been successfully applied to a number of behavioral traits, including McLennan's (Brooks and McLennan, 1991) work with sticklebacks and Basolo's (1995, 1996) research on sexual selection in Poecilliid fishes.

There are two sets of factors that limit the utility of this approach, one set general and one more specific to cognitive abilities. The general factors have to do with the use of phylogenies. Good phylogenies are often unavailable for specific groups of animals and this, of course, makes any approach that depends on having a phylogeny impossible. In addition, any phylogeny is only a hypothesis, dependent on the characters used to construct it. There are often arguments about which characters are best and there is no universal agreement on the best methods of construction. If a comparative analysis is based on an incorrect phylogeny, and we never know with certainty that any given phylogeny is correct, then it will produce mistaken conclusions.

The other set of problems concerns measurement of the relevant traits. First of all, cladistic analysis is easiest with binary traits and cognitive traits are rarely binary. Secondly, as discussed earlier, there are no standard units for the measurement of cognitive abilities. Therefore, to be even reasonably confident we have found differences in these abilities, we need to use a method of converging operations.

Although there will always be limits on the methods we use for phylogenetic analysis, at least until we have a time machine, we cannot afford to ignore questions of the evolutionary history of cognition. First of all, the results of comparative adaptive studies must be evaluated in light of phylogeny (Balda and Kamil, De Voogd and Szekely, this volume). Secondly, only a broad phylogenetic approach will reveal general trends in the evolution of cognition which can give insight into common constraints and patterns of diversification.

The critical question: integration

The really important point about Tinbergen's (1963) article was not just that all four questions can be asked and are legitimate, a point in little dispute today, at least among behaviorists. Nor is it that they represent different levels of analysis, not competing alternatives in much dispute among behaviorists. However, the really critical point Tinbergen made was that, in the long run, we need to integrate these questions and their answers into a coherent whole. An important corollary is that the questions complement each other in the sense that answers at one level can inform the search for answers at other levels.

There are many examples in the contemporary study of behavior that indicate the power of combining levels of analysis, or using information from one level to inform research at another level. One of the first comprehensive examples was the work of Arnold (1981). This research program combined comparative, developmental, behavior genetic and sensory approaches to develop a comprehensive picture of the evolution, function and behavioral mechanisms of foraging preferences in garter snakes. Another comprehensive example is the work of Endler (1980, 1990) of the relationships between sensory processes and natural selection. The value of the integrative approach for the study of animal cognition is clearly shown in many of the chapters in this book, including work on spatial memory (Clayton and Lee, this volume), on song (De Voogd and Szekely, Kroodsma and Byers, this volume) and migration (Bingman *et al.*, this volume).

The advantages of the synthetic approach

One way we can try to capture the essence of the approach outlined here is to look at a table of its characteristics similar to that used by Shettleworth (1993) to compare the ecological and anthropocentric programs (Table 1.2).

A large advantage of this integrative, Tinbergian approach is that it resolves many of the difficulties that have been discussed earlier in this paper. Clearly, the integrative approach should eliminate many of the problems associated with disciplinary diversity. By including and integrating all four levels of analysis, most questions about cognition can be accommodated.

Another advantage of the synthetic approach is that, when viewed within the broad synthetic and biological context, the specialized vs. general process issue disappears as a divisive issue. In an integrative context, it is clearly a misperception to conceive of the distinction between specialized and general processes as a dichotomy. It is instructive here to look at nonbehavioral systems. In a wide variety of physiological cases, for example, there are general processes, but the exact nature and details of these processes often vary enormously within the animal kingdom, or even within the vertebrates or the mammals. That is, even very general physiological and morphological traits and systems show specialization.

Consider, for example, the problem of oxygen transport. The delivery of oxygen to the cells of the body is an essential, general problem facing many

Table 1.2   Characteristics of the Synthetic Approach.

Characteristic	Synthetic program
Purpose	Use cognitive approach to increase integrative understanding of animals and humans
Phenomena analyzed	Any behavior where cognitive approach is useful
Species compared	Chosen on basis of considerations of adaptation and phylogeny
Relationship to neuroscience	Inclusive

animals. In many invertebrates, oxygen is simply carried in solution in the blood or hemolymph. However, in many animals, and in almost all of the vertebrates, respiratory pigments, special compounds containing metals, are used as oxygen carriers (Schmidt-Nielsen, 1990). There are a number of different respiratory pigments in animals, distributed very systematically across the animal kingdom. In vertebrates, hemoglobin is almost universal, but there are still important differences. For example, the Bohr effect (the acid sensitivity) of hemoglobin varies widely in mammals as a function of body size, and mammals living at higher elevations show greater oxygen dissociation (affinity for oxygen) than those living at lower elevantions. The point here is that, although hemoglobin may represent a general process for oxygen transport, this *does not mean* that it is identical in all animals, all vertebrates or even all mammals. Similar examples are widespread in terms of organs: lungs, hearts, kidneys. Even very general processes show clear evidence of specialization. Therefore, it is not useful to conceptualize biological processes and this includes cognition, as belonging to one of two categories, general or specialized. Even in the case of the most general processes, we should expect some specializations to have evolved.

There are some particularly interesting and difficult problems that need to be resolved around the issue of the relationship between general process on the one hand and specialization, especially in the sense of serving specific function, on the other. One issue is whether or not a cognitive ability that evolved in one context can be expressed in another. On the one hand, selection acts on specific outcomes. Thus, for example, any mechanism that improved the ability of a Clark's Nutcracker to remember its cache locations could be selected for, whether or not that mechanism improved other aspects of the cognitive abilities of nutcrackers, spatial or nonspatial. On the other hand, pleiotropic effects are not uncommon and the results of our comparative studies of spatial memory in seed-caching corvids shows that, in this case at least, selective effects seem to have been general, at least within the domain of spatial memory or cognition.

Another issue is whether or not certain problems are so ubiquitous that, once they have given rise to a process, that process persists. There are physical adaptations, such as warm bloodedness or feathers, whose phylogeny demonstrates that this is quite possible. One of the possible advantages of the cognitive approach is that this approach suggests that, at least at some levels of analysis, this may be the case. As Gallistel (1990) has pointed out, certain problems – representing time and space, and detecting causation in the flow of events, for example – are indeed ubiquitous and this may help understand widespread similarities in spatial information processing and associative learning. In this context, Gallistel (1992) has formulated an interesting model for classical conditioning based on the assumption that treats the classical conditioning process as a computational mechanism evolved to solve a distinct learning problem: extracting information from a multivariate, nonstationary time series.

The place of the anthropocentric approach

One view that is not easily accommodated within the synthetic approach is the 'animal model' anthropocentric view, the approach that is oriented towards using animals as model systems for understanding humans. This view is so nonbiological that it is hard to see how it could fit. Consider this quotation: 'The comparative psychology of cognition follows directly from the theory of evolution. As Darwin (1871) observed, it is "highly probable that with mankind the intellectual faculties have been mainly and gradually perfected through natural selection (p. 160)" ' (Terrace, 1993). This is a very clear statement in favor of taking an evolutionary view of cognition.

However, the peculiar thing about the anthropocentric approach is that, while it accepts the general Darwinian-based point of continuity between humans and other animals, it seems to accept very little else about the Darwinian perspective. For example, Terrace (1993) reviews studies of series learning in pigeons and monkeys. The main reason that Terrace is interested in this paradigm is to discover the properties of serial learning in the absence of language, as if the only important difference between pigeons and humans, or even monkeys and humans, is language. Another indication of the nonbiological thinking typical of this approach is the use of the word phylogeny. Terrace concludes that serial learning '. . . appears to be phylogenetically quite old' (p. 162). However, comparative biologists under- stand the dangers in using comparisons among so few disparate species to make such assertions. Although Terrace's research on serial learning is well executed and clever, and has produced interesting results that are informative about animal cognition, it is clearly not Darwinian in the contemporary sense of the term.

Although the anthropocentric approach may have its successes, it is inherently limited as long as it fails to take into account the biological nature of the animals that are studied. Wasserman (1997) has recently suggested that the anthropocentric and ecological–evolutionary approaches need not be viewed as conflicting with one another because each asks a different question. He argues that '. . . the parallel use of both strategies should make for a powerful and complementary alliance for the future study of animal cognition' (Wasserman, 1997, p. 128). While the potential does exist for such an alliance, it will require both schools to be sophisticated about both evolutionary and proximate, mechanistic factors (just as Tinbergen suggested in 1963).

It is important to realize that, although it is not human-centered, the synthetic approach is relevant to understanding human cognition. Certainly, the study of cognitive processes in animals should contribute to our understanding of human cognition. However, this is more likely to develop if we understand cognition in a broader, more biological framework than that typically used by proponents of the anthropocentric approach. In this context, there is another version of the anthropocentric approach which is more in accord with the synthetic approach. This version uses comparative strategies with humans and closely related primates to try to understand how human abilities evolved (e.g. Povinelli, 1993).

Many examples of the advantages of such a framework can be found. For example, medical research has certainly utilized the 'animal model', anthropocentric approach quite heavily, and with success. None the less, recent work on 'Darwinian medicine' has shown that even more insight can be gained by applying Darwinian ideas to the study of many topics in medicine, including epidemiology, pregnancy, host–parasite interactions and infectious disease (Nesse and Williams, 1991; Ewald, 1994).

Other potential examples come from the emerging field of evolutionary psychology (Barkow *et al.*, 1992). One interesting example of how a broad evolutionary approach might be applied to human cognition comes from studies of social cognition. It has been hypothesized that one of the arenas for the evolution of intelligence has been the social arena (e.g. Humphrey, 1976; Cheney and Seyfarth, 1990). In that case, one might expect that humans could solve social problems most readily. There is also evidence that, when the same logical problem is presented in a social context, people find it easier to solve than when the same logical problem is presented in an abstract, nonsocial context (Cosmides, 1989).

Conclusions

This chapter has outlined a general research program for the study of cognition in animals, an approach which the following chapters of this book demonstate is well under way. This program synthesizes two scientific research programs, the cognitive and the ethological. It applies the approach exemplified by Niko Tinbergen, emphasizing the importance of studying evolutionary and mechanistic levels of explanation in a single, integrative framework, to the study of cognition. What should this approach be called? There are many possibilities, some of which are listed below.

Comparative cognition?

One label that is sometimes used for animal cognitive work is comparative cognition, but it is not appropriate for the approach outlined here. Not all work called for in the synthetic approach needs be comparative; much will not be. Furthermore, current usage of the phrase is inappropriate. It has, for many, come to refer to the anthropocentric approach, emphasizing using information about human cognitive processes in the design of animal studies of cognition.

Cognitive ecology?

Another approach has been labeled cognitive ecology. Real (1993; also Dukas, 1998) has popularized this term, and used it in a manner very similar to much of what has been proposed here. However, the term ecology implies an exclusively adaptive, functional approach, and tends to de-emphasize mechanistic and ontogenetic levels of analysis as well as considerations of phylogeny.

Evolutionary cognition? Cognitive biology?

The potential list goes on and on. However, it seems obvious that, in terms of the basic philosophy of the approach and the methods it gives rise to, there is only one appropriate label for this field: cognitive ethology. This label succinctly captures the two approaches being synthesized, giving appropriate recognition to its historical precursors.

There is only one reason not to adopt this label: it has been pre-empted by Don Griffin and others (e.g. Griffin, 1976, 1978; Ristau, 1991; Bekoff and Allen, 1997), defining cognitive ethology in terms of subjective experience: awareness, consciousness, etc. Many of us working on animal cognition find this term objectionable for many reasons; so objectionable that we completely avoid using the term. One of the reasons it is objectionable is that much of the argument has focused on attempting to prove the existence of these internal states and the nature of some of these arguments is unacceptable. In particular, many of Griffin's arguments are so weak and anecdotal that they remind one of nothing more than Paley's (1851) arguments for the existence of a creator, natural theology based on the argument from design (Blumberg and Wasserman, 1995).

However, this dislike for Griffin's definition does nothing to diminish the fact that cognitive ethology is the most historically appropriate label for the approach outlined here. If workers in this field adopt the term cognitive ethology, a new definition will replace Griffin's. If this takes place, it will challenge those who hold to Griffin's definition to become a subfield of cognitive ethology, confronting the Lakatos definition of a progressive research program. Including postulated internal states in models of behavior is nothing new nor is it objectionable. The test of such models is not truth but usefulness. Do they generate new predictions or insights which have utility? This is the challenge which the proponents of animal awareness must meet. The issue is not proving that animals have minds, it is demonstrating that making the awareness (or consciousness) assumption leads to exciting new questions and discoveries.

Meanwhile, the term cognitive ethology should be adopted to describe the field that synthesizes the Darwinian perspective of Tinbergen and contemporary ethology with the cognitive perspective of psychology. Maybe, in the long run, the difference between assuming animals have internal representations and assuming they have awareness is relatively minor. Future research should determine this issue. Scientists adopting a synthetic approach to animal cognition would do well to settle on the term cognitive ethology for the broad, biological study of cognitive processes. Cognitive ethology is the phrase that most accurately and appropriately describes the science that many of us do.

Acknowledgements

I thank Russ Balda, Jennifer Templeton, Alan Bond, Kristy Gould-Beierle, Brett Gibson and Chris Cink for stimulating discussions and suggestions during the preparation of this manuscript, and Sara Shettleworth for her very insightful comments on an earlier draft of this chapter. Preparation of this paper was supported by NSF grants IBN 9421807 and IBN 9631044.

References

Arnold, S. J. (1981) The microevolution of feeding behavior. In Kamil, A. C. and Sargent, T. D. (eds) *Foraging behavior: Ecological, ethological and psychological approaches*. New York: Garland STPM Press, pp. 409–454.

Balda, R. P. and Kamil, A. C. (1989) A comparative study of cache recovery by three corvid species. *Animal. Behav.* **38**, 486–495.

Barkow, J. H., Cosmides, L. and Tooby, J. (eds) (1992) *The Adapted Mind: Evolutionary Psychology and the Generation of Culture*. New York: Oxford University Press.

Basil, J. A., Kamil, A. C., Balda, R. P. and Fite, K. V. (1996) Differences in hippocampal volume among food-storing corvids. *Brain Behav. Evol.* **47**, 156–164.

Basolo, A. L. (1995) Phylogenetic evidence for the role of a pre-existing bias in sexual selection. *Proc. Roy. Soc. Lond.* B **259**, 307–311.

Basolo, A. L. (1996) The phylogenetic distribution of a female preference. *Syst. Biol.* **45**, 290–307.

Bekoff, M. and Allen, C. (1997) Cognitive ethology: Slayers, skeptics and proponents. In Mitchell, R. W., Thompson, N. S. and Miles, H. L. (eds) *Anthropomorphism, Anecdotes, and Animals*. Albany, NY: State University of New York Press.

Bennett, E. L. and Rosenzweig, M. R. (1981) Behavioral and biochemical methods to study brain responses to environment and experience. In Lahue, R. (ed.) *Methods in Neurobiology*, Vol. 2. New York: Plenum Press, pp. 101–141.

Bitterman, M. E. (1965) Phyletic differences in learning. *Am. Psychol.* **20**, 396–410.

Blumberg, M. S. and Wasserman, E. A. (1995) Animal mind and the argument from design. *Am. Psychol.* **50**, 133–144.

Brooks, D. R. and McLennan, D. A. (1991) *Phylogeny, Ecology, and Behavior*. Chicago: University of Chicago Press.

Brown, J. L. (1987) *Helping and Communal Breeding in Birds*: Ecology and Evolution. Princeton, NJ: Princeton University Press.

Brown, J. L., Brown, E. R., Brown, S. D. and Dow, D. D. (1982) Helpers: effects of experimental removal on reproductive success. *Science* **215**, 421–422.

Cheney, D. L. and Seyfarth, R. M. (1990) *How Monkeys See the World*. Chicago: University of Chicago Press.

Cole, S., Hainsworth, F. R., Kamil, A. C., Mercier, T. and Wolf, L. L. (1982) Spatial learning as an adaptation in hummingbirds. *Science* **217**, 655–657.

Cosmides, L. (1989) The logic of social exchange: Has natural selection shaped how humans reason? Studies with the Wason task. *Cognition* **31**, 187–276.

Cullen, E. (1957) Adaptations in the Kittiwake to cliff-nesting. *Ibis* **99**, 275–302.

Cullen, J. M. and Ashmole, N. M. P. (1963) The black noddy *Anous tenuirostris* on Ascension Island. Part 2, Behavior. *Ibis* **103**, 423–446.

Cuthill, I. C. and Houston, A. I. (1997) Managing time and energy. In Krebs, J. R. and Davies, N. B. (eds) *Behavioural Ecology: An Evolutionary Approach* 4th edn. Oxford: Blackwell, pp. 97–120.

Darwin, C. (1871) *The Descent of Man, and Selection in Relation to Sex*. London: J. Murray.

Davies, N. B., Brooke, M. d. L. and Kacelnik, A. (1996) Recognition errors and probability of parasitism determine whether reed warblers should accept or reject mimetic cuckoo eggs. *Proc. Roy. Soc. Lond.* B **263**, 925–931.

Dimmick, C. R. (1993) Life history and the development of cache-recovery behaviors in Clark's Nutcracker. PhD thesis, Northern Arizona University.

Dukas, R. (ed.) (1998) *Cognitive Ecology: The Evolutionary Ecology of Information Processing and Decision Making.* Chicago: University of Chicago Press (in press).

Dyer, F. C. (1994) Spatial cognition and navigation in insects. In Real, L. A. (ed.) *Behavioral Mechanisms in Evolutionary Ecology.* Chicago: University of Chicago Press, pp. 66–98.

Endler, J. A. (1980) Natural selection on color patterns in *Poecilia reticulata. Evolution* **34**, 76–91.

Endler, J. A. (1990) On the measurement and classification of colour in studies of animal colour patterns. *Biol. J. Linnean Soc.* **41**, 315–352.

Ewald, P. W. (1994) *Evolution of Infectious Disease.* Oxford: Oxford University Press.

Gallistel, C. R. (1990) *The Organization of Learning.* Cambridge, MA: MIT Press.

Gallistel, C. R. (1992) Classical conditioning as a nonstationary, multivariate time series analysis: a spreadsheet model. *Behav. Res. Meth. Instrum. Comput.* **24**, 340–351.

Gibbon, J. and Church, R. M. (1990) Representation of time. *Cognition* **37**, 23–54.

Gill, F. B. and Wolf, L. L. (1977) Nonrandom foraging by sunbirds in a patchy environment. *Ecology* **58**, 1284–1296.

Griffin, D. R. (1976) *The Question of Animal Awareness: Evolutionary Continuity of Mental Experience.* New York: Rockefeller University Press.

Griffin, D. R. (1978) Prospects for a cognitive ethology. *Behav. Brain Sci.* **1**, 527–538.

Hailman, J. P. (1965) Cliff-nesting adaptations in the Galapagos swallow-tailed gull. *Wilson Bull.* **77**, 346–362.

Harvey, P. H. and Pagel, M. D. (1991) *The Comparative Method in Evolutionary Biology.* New York: Oxford University Press.

Healy, S. D. and Hurly, T. A. (1995) Spatial memory in rufous hummingbirds (*Selasphorus rufus*): a field test. *Anim. Learn. Behav.* **23**, 63–68.

Heinrich, B., Mudge, P. and Deringis, P. (1977) A laboratory analysis of flower constancy in foraging bumblebees: *Bombus ternarius* and *B. terricola. Behav. Ecol.* **2**, 247–266.

Hollis, K. L. (1984) The biological function of Pavlovian conditioning: the best defense is a good offense. *J. Exp. Psychol. Anim. Behav. Proc.* **10**, 413–425.

Hollis, K. L., Pharr, V. L., Dumas, M. J., Britton, G. B. and Field, J. (1997) Classical conditioning provides paternity advantage for territorial male blue gouramis (*Trichogaster trichopterus*). *J. Comp. Psychol.* **111**, 219–225.

Humphrey, N. K. (1976) The social function of intellect. In Bateson, P. P. G. and Hinde, R. A. (eds) *Growing Points in Ethology.* Cambridge: Cambridge University Press, pp. 303–318.

Kamil, A. C. (1978) Systematic foraging by a nectar-feeding bird, the Amakihi (*Loxops virens*). *J. Comp. Physiol. Psychol.* **92**, 388–396.

Kamil, A. C. (1988) A synthetic approach to the study of animal intelligence.

In Leger, D. W. (ed.) *Comparative Perspectives in Modern Psychology: Nebraska Symposium on Motivation*, Vol. 35. Lincoln, NE: University of Nebraska Press, pp. 230–257.

Kamil, A. C. and Balda, R. P. (1990) Spatial memory in seed-caching corvids. In Bower, G. H. (ed.) *The Psychology of Learning and Motivation*, Vol. 26. New York: Academic Press, pp. 1–25.

Kamil, A. C., Balda, R. P. and Olson, D. J. (1994) Performance of four seed-caching corvid species in the radial-arm maze analog. *J. Comp. Psychol.* **108**, 385–393.

Krebs, J. R., Sherry, D. F., Healy, S., Perry, V. and Vaccarino, A. (1989) Hippocampal specialization of food-storing birds. *Proc. Natl Acad. Sci. USA* **86**, 1388–1392.

Krushinskaya, N. (1966) Some complex forms of feeding behaviour of nutcracker *Nucifraga caryocatactes*, after removal of old cortex. *Zh. Evol. Biochim. Fisiol.* **II**, 563–568.

Kuhn, T. (1970) *The Structure of Scientific Revolutions*, 2nd edn. Chicago: University of Chicago Press.

Lakatos, I. (1974) *The Methodology of Scientific Research Programs.* Cambridge: Cambridge University Press.

Lefebvre, L. and Giraldeau, L. (1996) Is social learning an adaptive specialization? In Heyes, C. M. and Galef, B. G. (eds) *Social Learning in Animals: The Roots of Culture.* San Diego: Academic Press, pp. 107–128.

Lorenz, K. (1941) Comparative studies on the behaviour of the Anatinae. *J. Ornithologica* **89**, 194–294.

Lotem, A., Nakamura, H. and Zahavi, A. (1995) Constraints on egg discrimination and cuckoo-host co-evolution. *Anim. Behav.* **49**, 1185–1209.

Macphail, E. M. (1985) Vertebrate intelligence: the null hypoithesis. In Weiskrantz, L. (ed.) *Animal Intelligence.* Oxford: Clarendon Press, pp. 37–50.

Marler, P. and Tamura, M. (1964) Culturally transmitted patterns of vocal behavior in sparrows. *Science* **164**, 1483–1486.

Martins, E. P. (ed.) (1996) *Phylogenies and the Comparative Method in Animal Behavior.* New York: Oxford University Press.

Nesse, R. M. and Williams, G. C. (1994) *Why We Get Sick.* New York: Times Books.

O'Keefe, J. and Nadel, L. (1978) *The Hippocampus as a Cognitive Map.* Oxford: Clarendon Press.

Olson, D. (1991) Species differences in spatial memory among Clark's nutcrackers, scrub jays and pigeons. *J. Exp. Psychol. Anim. Behav. Proc.* **17**, 363–376.

Olson, D. J., Kamil, A. C., Balda, R. P. and Nims, P. J. (1995) The performance of four seed-caching corvids in operant tests of nonspatial and spatial memory. *J. Comp. Psychol.* **109**, 173–181.

Paley, W. (1851) *Natural Theology: Or, Evidences of the Existence and Attributes of the Deity, Collected from the Appearances of Nature.* London: Gould & Lincoln.

Papaj, D. R. and Lewis, A. C. (eds) (1993) *Insect Learning: Ecological and Evolutionary Perspectives.* New York: Chapman & Hall.

Platt, J. R. (1964) Strong inference. *Science* **146**, 347–353.

Povinelli, D. J. (1993) Reconstructing the evolution of mind. *Am. Psychol.* **48**, 493–509.

Real, L. A. (1993) Toward a cognitive ecology. *Trends Ecol. Evol.* **8**, 413–417.

Real, L. A. (1994) Information processing and the evolutionary ecology of cognitive architecture. In Real, L. A. (ed.) *Behavioral mechanisms in evolutionary ecology.* Chicago: University of Chicago Press, pp. 99–132.

Ristau, C. A. (ed.) (1991) *Cognitive Ethology: The Minds of Other Animals; Essays in Honor of Don Griffin.* Hillsdale, NJ: Lawrence Erlbaum Associates.

Roberts, W. A. (1998) *Principles of Animal Cognition.* Boston: McGraw-Hill.

Roitblat, H. L., Bever, T. G. and Terrace, H. S. (1984) *Animal Cognition.* Hillsdale, NJ: Lawrence Erlbaum Associates.

Rowley, I. (1965) The life history of the superb blue wren, *Malareus cyaneus. Emu* **64**, 251–297.

Ryan, M. J. and Rand, A. S. (1995) Female responses to ancestral advertisement calls in tungara frogs. *Science* **269**, 390–392.

Schacter, D. L. (1996) *Searching for Memory: The Brain, the Mind, and the Past.* New York: Basic Books.

Schmidt-Nielsen, K. (1990) *Animal Physiology: Adaptation and Environment,* 4th edn. Cambridge: Cambridge Press.

Sherry, D. F., Vaccarino, A. L., Buckenham, K. and Herz, R. (1989) The hippocampal complex of food-storing birds. *Brain Behav. Evol.* **34**, 308–317.

Shettleworth, S. J. (1993) Varieties of learning and memory in animals. *J. Exp. Psychol. Anim. Behav. Proc.* **19**, 5–14.

Shettleworth, S. J. (1998) *Cognition, Evolution and Behaviour.* Oxford: Oxford University Press (in press).

Skutch, A. F. (1961) Helpers among birds. *Condor* **63**, 198–226.

Stephens, D. W. (1991) Change, regularity and value in the evolution of animal learning. *Behav. Ecol.* **2**, 77–89.

Szekely, A. D. and Krebs, Jr (1996) Efferent connectivity hippocampal formation of the zebra finch (*Taenopygia guttata*): an anterograde pathway tracing study using *Phaseolus vulgaris* leucoagglutinin. *J. Comp. Neurol.* **368**, 198–206.

Terrace, H. S. (1993) The phylogeny and ontogeny of serial memory: list learning by pigeons and monkeys. *Psychol. Sci.* **4**, 162–169.

Tinbergen, N. (1963) On aims and methods of ethology. *Z. Tierpsychol.* **20**, 410–433.

Vander Wall, S. B. and Hutchins, H. E. (1983) Dependence of Clark's nutcracker (*Nucifraga columbiana*) on conifer seeds during the postfledgling period. *Can. Field Naturalist* **97**, 208–214.

Vauclair, J. (1996) *Animal Cognition: An Introduction to Modern Comparative Psychology.* Cambridge, MA: Harvard University Press.

Waddington, K. D., Allen, T. and Heinrich, B. (1981) Floral preferences of bumblebees (*Bombus edwardsii*) in relation to intermittent versus continuous rewards. *Anim. Behav.* **29**, 779–784.

Wasserman, E. A. (1997) The science of animal cognition: past, present and future. *J. Exp. Psychol. Anim. Behav. Proc.* **23**, 123–135.

Wunderle, J. M., Jr and Martinez, J. S. (1987) Spatial learning in the nectarivarous bananaquit: juveniles vs. adults. *Anim. Behav.* **35**, 652–658.

2

The Ecology and Evolution of Spatial Memory in Corvids of the Southwestern USA: The Perplexing Pinyon Jay

Russell P. Balda[1] and Alan C. Kamil[2]

[1]*Department of Biological Sciences, Northern Arizona University, Flagstaff, AZ 86011 and* [2]*School of Biological Sciences and Department of Psychology, University of Nebraska, Lincoln, NE 68588, USA*

The ecological stage

It is a cold, crisp morning in mid-September at about 1800 m in the pinyon–juniper woodland in north-central Arizona, on the lower slopes of the San Francisco Peaks. Most Pinyon Pine (*Pinus edulis*) trees bear some green cones and a few bear hundreds, if not thousands. The 'locals' refer to this situation as a 'bumper crop', and the Native Americans will be busy harvesting the pine seeds for food and profit. The cones have spineless scales still tightly closed over large, wingless, highly nutritious seeds. Pitch glistens off the cones as the early morning sunlight strikes. Soft 'kaws' and 'ka-ka-kas' can be heard in the distance. Suddenly the Pinyon Pine trees explode with hundreds of medium-sized light blue birds hopping and flying about, attacking pine cones, some by pecking at the green cones attached to the branch, some by attempting to break cones free of their twigs. Loud 'kaws', 'kraws' and all variations on the crow call are heard continuously. A flock of 150 Pinyon Jays (*Gymnorhinus cyanocephalus*) has just descended on the area to begin their day-long seed harvesting. The birds seem very peaceful

ANIMAL COGNITION IN NATURE
ISBN 0-12-077030-X

and seldon engage in agonistic behaviors while intently harvesting seeds. Within minutes it sounds like the drumming of a hundred woodpeckers as birds hammer at the closed cone scales while standing or hanging on the cones. Birds that have successfully removed cones carry them to forked branches where they wedge the cone securely into the fork. Birds now hack the cone scales to smithereens in their attempt to get at the prized Pinyon Pine seeds. A small pile of empty cones gradually accumulates under these forks. Are these forks tools in the same sense that man uses an anvil? Ripening seeds are extracted with a stout, sharp bill that is curiously feather-free at its base. Through all this frenzy, birds are careful not to smear sticky pitch on to their bills. The feather-free area of the bill certainly aids in this attempt. As harvesting continues, torn cone scales fall like rain drops from the pine trees. Every bird in the flock, males and females, young and old, seem intent on harvesting its share of seeds (Marzluff and Balda, 1992).

This commotion has attracted the attention of other birds. A few rather large gray, black and white birds join in the exploitation of seeds from cones. These birds have massive, sharp-pointed bills with which they can tear open a green pine cone in a matter of minutes. After some time the throats of these birds begin to bulge with seeds, and the birds leave the flock of Pinyon Jays and fly high up onto the nearby San Francisco Peaks with long, strong wings that may carry them up to 22 km from the harvest area. Loud sharp drawn-out 'kaas' often signal their departure. Most often these birds are seen singly or in small groups of 2–5. The Clark's Nutcrackers (*Nucifraga columbiana*) have departed with their share of the bounty.

Another bird attracted to the hustle and bustle of cone opening is a slender, quiet, light-blue bird with a short, rather weak bill, the Western Scrub Jay (*Aphelocoma californica*). This bird's demeanor is just the opposite of the nutcracker and Pinyon Jay, which are both bold and noisy. The Scrub Jay sits inconspicuously hidden in thick vegetation, waiting and watching. When an individual of one of the other species has broken or removed all the cone scales from the cone it has been working on diligently, our silent stalker screams loudly and flies directly at the unsuspecting forager. Invariably, the foraging bird is frightened, drops the cone and flies off. The Scrub Jay retrieves the partly opened cone and proceeds to pry out the partly exposed seeds. This is the only way this species, with its relatively weak bill, can share in the bounty until the cone scales mature and open naturally (Vander Wall and Balda, 1981). After placing 3–5 seeds in its mouth and bill, the Scrub Jay flies a short distance behind some vegetation, to sit quietly on a branch before descending to bury its seeds secretly in subterranean caches.

In areas where Pinyon–Juniper woodland and Ponderosa (*Pinus ponderosa*) Pine forest interdigitate to form an ecotone, Steller's Jays (*Cyanocitta stelleri*) also participate in this seed harvest. This jay has a partially distensible esophagus in which it can carry up to 18 seeds. It is not a strong flier, does not have a particularly strong bill and only carries seeds 2–3 km into the Ponderosa Pine forest (Vander Wall and Balda, 1981).

As the pine seed harvest progresses this morning, casual observation reveals that the throat region of the Pinyon Jay is beginning to swell as well. Soon, a few birds with throats bulging, and then many, appear at the tips of high trees where they perch silently. Shortly thereafter, a rhythmic series of 'kaws' spreads as a loud din throughout the flock and the remaining birds leave the ground and fly up to perches in the low trees. The flock then departs in unison for one of their traditional caching areas that this flock uses every year. Birds usually fly just above tree level on their way to the caching area where the harvested seeds will be stored in subterranean caches. These traditional areas, which may number 8–10 for a flock, will often be some kilometers from the harvest area (Marzluff and Balda, 1992). After the flock departs, the area becomes deadly silent.

We have just witnessed a flock of Pinyon Jays and three flocking associates (Balda *et al.*, 1972) harvesting Pinyon Pine seeds from green cones. This autumnal foraging frenzy by nutcrackers and Pinyon Jays in the southwestern USA will continue from sunrise to sunset every day as long as fresh cones are available and the ground is free of snow. In some areas the species composition will differ but the process is the same. For example, 130 km south of the location described above, no Pinyon Jays exist, but Mexican Jays (*Aphelocoma ultrimarina*) harvest pine seeds there. In areas to the north, Black-billed Magpies (*Pica pica*) are involved in the seed harvest (Balda, personal observation).

The exploitation of pine seeds by species of the family Corvidae is a common occurrence in the western USA. These pine seeds are all nutritious, but the seed of the Pinyon Pine is especially so, containing up to 18% protein and 60% fat (Bodkin and Shires, 1948; Blair *et al.*, 1995). This is powerful fuel to sustain these birds through the long, cold, unproductive winter. The behavior of nutcrackers and Pinyon Jays is immediately altered at the sight of these cones or seeds as they abruptly stop all other behaviors and begin harvesting. These birds spend vast amounts of time and energy harvesting, transporting and caching these seeds. This dramatic change in behavior is a clue that these pine seeds are of special biological significance, at least to some of these corvids. Even when these seeds are placed in conspicuous traps, some Pinyon Jays will allow themselves to be captured 3–4 times in a single day in their attempt to collect these seeds (Marzluff and Balda, 1992). Once, when a trap was set in the snow and placed pine seeds inside the trap, directly on the snow, Clark's Nutcrackers tunneled under the trap in an apparent attempt to get the pine seed without entering the trap (Balda, personal observation). Eurasian Nutcrackers (*Nucifraga caryocatactes*) that had dispersed thousands of kilometers into Germany owing to lack of pine seeds in Siberia immediately began harvesting, eating and caching seeds when presented to them (Conrads and Balda, 1979). We know of no other object or substance that is so addictive to birds as these pine seeds are to these corvids.

The pine tree also has an interesting role in this ecological play. In one out of every five to six years, the Pinyon Pines make it easy for the jays and nutcrackers to harvest their seeds. In these years, every Pinyon Pine tree for kilometers may produce hundreds or even thousands of cones, and the birds do not have to travel far to locate seeds (Ligon, 1978). Seeds are extracted with ease as the pine cones have no sharp spines on their relatively short cone scales to deter extraction. Cones are easily located as they face outward and upward on the tips of branches, and their seeds are held tightly in the cone scale after opening. These traits make it relatively easy for the birds to collect large numbers of seeds (Vander Wall and Balda, 1977). In these years, it is as if the trees are bearing their crop of pine seeds in a manner that facilitates harvesting by jays and nutcrackers (Smith and Balda, 1979; Balda, 1980a). In sharp contrast to these years of bountiful production, there are periodic lean years. In one out of every 5–6 years, trees over a large region may be absolutely barren of cones. In the majority of years, however, pine cones are produced in modest to heavy amounts in small geographic areas or 'hot spots', interspersed with areas of no cone production. Nutcrackers have been observed making long exploratory flights in late summer that appear to be for the purpose of locating these pockets of cones (Vander Wall and Balda, 1977). In autumns when the pine cone crop fails on the home range of a Pinyon Jay flock, the flock sometimes departs its home range in search of these 'hot spots' (Marzluff and Balda, 1992). Thus, during most years, these strong fliers were able to take advantage of cone crops outside of their normal range of occupation. Relatively strong powers of flight may have been a preadaptation for seed-caching behaviors to become fully developed (Vander Wall and Balda, 1981). The Mexican and Scrub Jays are certainly much weaker fliers than nutcrackers and Pinyon Jays, and therefore can not take full advantage of scattered crops of pine cones that occur in most years. These species must 'sit and wait' for a crop of pine seeds to occur where they exist.

The actors

The corvids of the southwest possess many adaptations for the harvest, transport, caching and recovery of pine seeds. However, there is a large degree of between-species variation in the distribution of these traits. These corvids have a well-accepted phylogeny (Hope, 1989), live within close proximity to one another and have relatively well-known natural histories. They therefore present an excellent opportunity to apply the comparative method (Kamil, 1988) to the study of these species differences (Balda *et al.*, 1997). The comparative method for the study of adaptation and evolution of behavioral traits begins with a careful study of the natural histories of the study species which should reveal how a particular trait (or suite of traits) is utilized, and provide some information about the selective pressure and potential fitness which differentially influence the trait in the different species. Species differences (and similarities) in the use of the trait can be attributed to the ecology and/or phylogeny of the species. Two processes are particularly powerful in these types of investigations, convergence and divergence. Convergence leads to similarities among distantly related species owing to the influence of similar ecological constraints. Divergence leads to differences among closely related species that correlate with the influence of different ecological constraints. The strongest support for the evolution of a trait or set of traits is found when one can find patterns of convergence between distantly related groups and divergence between similar groups for a single suite of traits. Here, we examine the natural history of the various southwestern corvids with particular attention paid to the traits involved in seed harvest, caching and cache recovery.

Clark's Nutcracker

This 144–150 g species is a member of the genus *Nucifraga*, which includes only one other species, the Eurasian Nutcracker (*N. caryocatactes*). Clark's Nutcracker is believed to be the more ancient of the two (Goodwin, 1986). Named for Captain Clark of the Lewis and Clark expedition, these birds range from central British Columbia to central Arizona. They live and breed at high elevations within coniferous forest and up to the treeline, where in winter they experience low temperatures, high winds, deep snow and many cloudy days. Primary and secondary productivity is nil in winter and birds depend on their cached food for winter survival and reproduction, using this food for between 80 and 100% of their winter diet (Giuntoli and Mewaldt, 1978). Nutcrackers continue to draw on their caches into the next summer, 9–11 months after they have been made (Vander Wall and Hutchins, 1983). Birds may undertake long-distance irruptions when the pine cone crop fails (Davis and Williams, 1957, 1964; Vander Wall *et al.*, 1981).

   Clark's Nutcrackers are well equipped for the harvest, transport, caching and recovery of hidden pine seeds, which play a major role in the annual cycle of these birds (Fig. 2.1). Nutcrackers have a relatively long, stout, sharp bill which is a very efficient tool for opening green pine cones, extracting seeds and burying seeds in the substrate. Both species of *Nucifraga* possess a sublingual pouch, a unique structure that opens under the tongue, and that can hold up to 90 medium-sized Pinyon Pine seeds (Bock *et al.*, 1973). The sublingual pouch is often full during transport of seeds from harvest area to caching area. These strong flying birds range widely in search of seeds and have been observed carrying pouches full of seeds up to 22 km. In a year when pine cones are superabundant, a single nutcracker will cache between

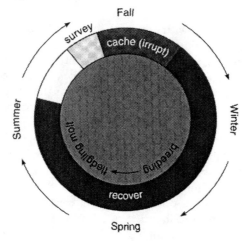

Fig. 2.1 Yearly activity pattern of pine seed use by nutcrackers. The outer circle describes the different behaviors associated with different periods of the year.

22 000 and 33 000 individual seeds in about 6000–8000 subterranean caches. Nutcrackers can distinguish between edible and inedible seeds by 'bill clicking' and 'bill weighing' (Ligon and Martin, 1974) and also by color (Balda, personal observation). Edible seeds have a dark brown seed coat, whereas inedible seeds have a light brown to yellow seed coat.

Birds cache seeds on their breeding territories and also on 'communal' caching areas where winds are strong and snow melts rapidly. These are communal areas in the sense that many birds may intermix caches and the birds do not act aggressively towards each other. Caches, however, are not shared communally with other individuals. In these areas, nutcrackers act very secretively, often perching in a tree for several minutes, peering down intently before swooping to the ground. After a few hops, the bird stops, drives its long bill into the ground with a strong plunge, as if to test the substrate and then proceeds to place up to 14 seeds in a cache, forcing them in with strong, direct thrusts of the head and bill. The seeds in the sublingual pouch are retrieved into the mouth with strong downward strokes of the head. After caching, the bird usually smooths over the soil or places an object such as a leaf, twig, piece of moss, or pine cone on the site. If no object is placed over the cache, it is almost impossible for a human observer to locate the cache. Objects that are placed over the sites seldom remain there for more than a few days (Balda, personal observation). Birds seldom spend more than 30 seconds creating a single cache.

Even at the high elevations inhabited by these birds, they breed in late winter and early spring in large, well-insulated nests. They are also known to feed pine seed to their nestlings (Mewaldt, 1956), a trait shared with few other birds.

Pinyon Jay

Pinyon Jays live and breed from Oregon, Montana and South Dakota to Baja California, central Arizona and New Mexico. These 100–125 g birds inhabit the Pinyon–Juniper woodland and lower reaches of the Ponderosa (*Pinus ponderosa*) Pine forest, where winter conditions can be harsh. This bird is probably the most social bird in North America, living and breeding in permanent flocks of 50–500 individuals on large home ranges. These birds nest colonially, and often use the same traditional areas for nesting year after year and other traditional areas for caching seeds. Seed caching by the Pinyon Jay is a social event, as birds harvest, transport and cache seeds as a collective unit. Upon arriving at a caching area, birds quickly descend to the ground. Flock members usually walk (not hop) in the same direction as they rapidly stick seeds in the ground. Sometimes they move at a brisk pace as they hide seeds singly in caches, either in a straight line or in small circles. Birds spend less than 15 seconds at each cache site and 'a dozen caches could be made in a minute or less' (Stotz and Balda, 1995). Sometimes birds are shoulder to shoulder during these caching bouts. Pinyon Jays rely heavily on pine seeds in winter when they constitute between 70% and 90% of the diet (Ligon, 1978). Pinyon Jays draw upon their caches for 6–7 months after they are created. These jays are known to perform long-distance irruptions when pine cone crops fail (Westcott, 1964; Bock and Lepthien, 1976).

Pinyon Jays possess a relatively long, sharply pointed bill that is featherless at its base. The loss of nasal bristle may be an adaptation to dig more deeply into pine cones without getting pitch on the bill or nasal bristles. Pinyon Jays can readily open green pine cones, and can hold and carry pine seeds in an esophagus that is distensible for about two-thirds of its length. This structure can be expanded to hold up to 39 medium-sized pine seeds (Vander Wall and Balda, 1981). Birds have been observed flying up to 12 km with throats full of seeds. When cones are common, a single Pinyon Jay may cache up to 25 000 seeds in an autumn (Balda, 1987). Ligon (1978) estimated a single flock of Pinyon Jays cached 4.5 million seeds in one autumn. Birds can distinguish between edible and inedible seeds by color, as well as 'bill-weighing' and 'bill-clicking' (Ligon and Martin, 1974). Like the nutcracker, Pinyon Jays began nesting in late winter and early spring, especially when a large crop of seeds occurred the previous autumn. Nestling Pinyon Jays are fed a diet containing between 10 and 32% pine seeds (Ligon, 1978; Bateman and Balda, 1973).

Aphelocoma jays

Western Scrub Jays and Mexican Jays (*Aphelocoma ultramarina*) live at lower elevations and experience much milder winter conditions than either Pinyon Jays or Clark's Nutcrackers (Pitelka, 1951). They are less dependent on stored food for winter survival and concomitantly have few special adaptations for the harvest, transport, caching and recovery of pine seeds. Western Scrub Jays (weighing about 95 g) inhabit the Pinyon–Juniper woodland from Oregon to Baja California, the Mexican plateau and southwestern Mexico. These jays breed in pairs on territories, have short broad wings and are relatively weak fliers, when compared to nutcrackers and Pinyon Jays, although they can maneuver well in dense Pinyon–Juniper stands (Pavlick, Balda and Bednekoff, unpublished data). These birds do not engage in irruptive behavior in years when cone crops fail. They do cache pine seeds, but are noticeably less motivated to do so than are Pinyon Jays and nutcrackers (Hall, unpublished data). Balda (1987) calculated that a single Scrub Jay, in a year with a good cone crop, may cache up to 6000 Pinyon Pine seeds. These jays have no morphological adaptations for carrying seeds and can carry only 3–5 seeds in the mouth and bill. The bill is rather short and broad (Peterson, 1993) and not strong enough for prying open cones with green cone scales. Consequently, Western Scrub Jays must wait for the normal opening of the cones before they can harvest seeds. In years when the cone crop is poor, nutcrackers and Pinyon Jays can harvest the entire crop before the cones open naturally. In these cases Scrub Jays can harvest only the seeds they can steal using their kleptoparasitic behaviors described above. This species usually caches seeds under trees and bushes, although on occasion it will venture into small openings and treeless valleys to cache (Hall, personal observation). Little is known about the caching behavior of the highly social Mexican Jay except that it does spend considerable time and effort caching pine seeds each autumn, and recovers them through the winter and early spring (Gross, 1949; Brown, 1963; J. L. Brown, personal communication). Both *Aphelocoma* species do not breed particularly early, nor do they feed seeds to their nestlings.

A comparison of the characteristics of these four species based on their ability to harvest and cache seeds is presented in Table 2.1. The two species that show the greatest number of behavioral, morphological and ecological adaptations for this behavior, the Clark's Nutcracker and Pinyon Jay, also cache the largest number of seeds each autumn. They are stronger fliers and move pine seeds greater distances from harvest to cache sites. Nutcrackers and Pinyon Jays are highly dependent on cached seeds during the long, cold, harsh winter for survival and reproductive energy. When cone crops fail, they undergo major irruptions, moving hundreds of kilometers out of their normal range (Davis and Williams, 1957, 1964). In contrast, the two *Aphelocoma* jays, which live at lower elevations and in more hospitable winter climates, are less dependent on cached seeds for winter survival because other seeds and berries are available, and some insects and arachnids are active throughout the winter. These two species do not undergo long-distance irruptions when cone crops fail, as alternate foods are available. They breed in spring and do not feed seeds to their young. Thus, these four species show a clear

Table 2.1 Comparison of Physical and Natural History Traits for Harvesting and Caching Seeds by Four Corvid Species.

Trait	Clark's Nutcracker	Pinyon Jay	Scrub Jay	Mexican Jay
Breeding habitat	High coniferous forest (2300–3200 m)	Ponderosa Pine forest/Pinyon–Juniper woodland (1700–2100 m)	Pinyon–Juniper woodland (1700–2000 m)	Pine–Oak woodland (1800–2100 m)
Winter weather conditions	Extremely harsh	Harsh	Moderate	Moderate
Dependence on caches for winter food	Yes	Yes	No	No (?)
Time of breeding	Late winter	Late winter	Spring	Spring
Seeds fed to nestlings	Yes	Yes	No	No
Body mass	150 g	125 g	100 g	140 g
Bill shape	Long, stout, sharp	Moderately long, stout, sharp	Short, broad, hooked	Short, broad, hooked
Seed-carrying structure	Sublingual pouch	Distensible esophagus	Mouth, bill	Mouth, bill
Maximum number of seeds transported	90	39	4–5	4–5 (?)
Maximum distance seeds transported	22 km	11 km	1–2 km	1–2 km (?)
Number of seeds per cache	Many	1	1	1 (?)
Maximum number of seeds cached per season	33 000	22 000	6000	(?)
Social structure during caching and recovery	Single, pairs	Highly social	Single, pairs	Highly social
Duration of cache utilization	9–11 months	8–11 months	6 months	6 months (?)

specialization gradient in both morphological and behavioral traits, from more highly specialized obligate species, to more generalist species that act opportunistically when cone crops are present.

The evolutionary play

How did this particular assemblage of corvids end up in north central Arizona? Where did these birds first appear? Who were their ancestors? How did the seed-caching habit come into being? What is the pine tree and seed doing in this scenario? These are all important questions that need to be explored if we are to understand fully how evolution, ecology, behavior and psychology are interrelated in the development of a set of adaptations. To answer them we need first to consider the taxonomy and biogeography of this group in order to clarify the evolutionary relationships of these species.

Taxonomy and biogeography of the players

There is little doubt that the Clark's Nutcracker is an Old World corvid, a descendent of an ancient, unspecialized relative of the Eurasian Nutcracker (*Nucifraga caryocatactes*) and probably invaded the New World via the Bering Land Bridge during the Pleistocene (1 million years ago) and possibly brought a bird-dispersed species of pine with it (Stegmann, 1934, personal communication; Lanner, 1981; Tomback, 1983)! The coniferous forest of Alaska and the western Canadian mountains probably provided all necessary niche requirements for this species. The extension of this forest type down the west coast of Canada provided a natural corridor for the southward colonization of the nutcracker (Fig. 2.2). Because of their ability to mono-polize conifer seeds and breed early, and because they are strong and aggressive birds, they may have spread rapidly southward. The Cascades, Sierras and Rockies provided excellent corridors for the nutcracker to use to extend its range down into the southwestern USA. In areas from California and Colorado south where Pinyon Pines grew at lower elevations, nutcrackers were quick also to take advantage of that seed source once they encountered them. The seeds of the pinyons are very similar in size and shape to those of *Pinus cembra*, the Old World Stone Pine favored by Eurasian Nutcrackers in the Old World. The above scenario is the most plausible for the invasion and distribution of Clark's Nutcracker into the Nearctic.

The taxonomy of the New World Corvidae has been dealt with by many authors (Amadon, 1944; Pitelka, 1951; Hardy, 1969; Ligon, 1974; Goodwin, 1986; Zusi, 1987; Hope, 1989). There is general agreement about the taxonomy of the New World corvids except for the status of the Pinyon Jay. The question of the origin of the Pinyon Jay has driven avian taxonomists

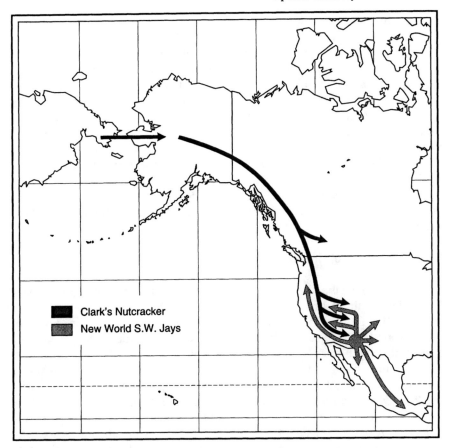

Fig. 2.2 Colonization of North America by nutcrackers and southwestern US jays. Nutcrackers used the Bering Land Bridge and jays differentiated on the Mexican Plateau.

crazy for the past century. This species has been referred to as the Blue Crow, the Pinyon Crow and Maximillian's Crow. While some taxonomists have argued that the Pinyon Jay was of Old World origin, essentially an Old World crow or nutcracker with a mutated blue plumage, others argued that it was of American origin and closely related to the *Aphelocoma* jays. In 1969, Hardy referred to it as 'a jay in color only' (but see Ligon, 1974), and as late as 1970, Mayr and Short (1970) stated that the relationship of the Pinyon Jay was 'obscure'. Others, such as Amadon (1944) and Goodwin (1986), considered the similarity between nutcrackers and Pinyon Jays to be a homoplasy, a case of character convergence owing to intense use of pine seeds for survival and reproduction. Zusi (1987) showed convincingly that the

Pinyon Jay possesses a type of jaw articulation with a peculiar morphological 'buttress' that is present in almost all New World jays and absent in Old World corvids. He argued that Pinyon Jays and nutcrackers were convergent on many aspects of morphology and behavior for the harvest of pine seeds. This hypothesis received strong support from Hope (1989). She used a series of morphological characters and found that the closest relative of the Pinyon Jay was the Mexican Jay. Scrub Jays were also closely related to Pinyon Jays. Thus, it seems reasonable to conclude that the complex of species that includes the Western Scrub Jay, Mexican Jay and Pinyon Jay arose on the Mexican Plateau in the southwestern USA and northern Mexico (Pitelka, 1951; Lanner, 1981, 1996), in an area covered with Madro-Tertiary Flora. As the climate and food sources permitted, these species then colonized new areas to the north and occupied their present distribution by the end of the Pleistocene, 11 000 years ago.

Coevolution by bird and tree

One cannot describe the evolution of food storing in southwestern New World jays without brief mention of the trees that coevolved with them. Without the Pinyon Pines, there would be no modern Pinyon Jay. This information has been reviewed most extensively by Lanner (1981, 1996). The Madro-Tertiary Flora contained a number of tree species that were drought-resistant and able to withstand a climate that was changing from subtropical warm/moist to hot/dry about 60 million years ago. The normal pines with small seeds would have had severe problems becoming established because the seeds provided only a minimal amount of energy and nutrients for the seedlings during the critical time of early growth. Moisture was scarce and the drying winds hot. A larger seed, however, would allow the plants to germinate and successfully establish themselves before depleting all nutrients and energy from the embryonic tissues. These larger-seeded pines would not only be successful at traditional germination sites but also in many more sites because the additional energy and nutrients they contained would allow the tree to penetrate into what had originally been inhospitable areas. Thus, large-seeded plants would leave more offspring than small-seeded ones, and natural selection would have favored the large-seeded individuals.

However, the price for producing these larger seeds was high. The trees had to capture additional, valuable materials and the larger, more conspicuous seeds would be more attractive to predators. Trees now had an 'adaptive choice' to make. They could produce relatively few high-quality seeds each year and gamble that seed predators would not get them, or produce a huge crop of seeds at longer, unpredictable intervals. Short-lived seed predators would die between cone crops and long-lived species would be forced to survive on other sources of energy, and thus not be able to specialize on this seed type. When the ancient pines did produce a mass of seeds in a single season, they could 'swamp' the seed predators. The number of seeds produced would be very high, the number of seed predators would be relatively low and many seeds would survive to germinate. The timing of seed production had to be synchronized among all neighboring pine trees in the area, for a tree out of synchrony would be at a severe disadvantage and have all its seeds consumed by predators (Ligon, 1978).

We can only speculate that the combination of severe climatic conditions and persistent seed predators was responsible for the pattern of seed production seen in Pinyon Pines. These large seeds would not be transported with ease by wind, water or gravity, the usual ways pine seeds are dispersed. Yet, as the Pinyon Pine ancestor(s) left the Mexican Plateau, this species spread rapidly northward through Arizona and New Mexico and into southern California by 25 million years ago, and by 11 000 years ago it had the distributional range we see today. With the advent of the great advances and retreats of the glaciers, the pinyons showed similar movements. After the last glacial retreat, pinyons still continued their active movement into hospitable regions when they became available and out of those areas when they became inhospitable. In fact, paleontologists generally agree that Pinyon Pines, because of their active movement patterns, must be (and have been) moved by a dispersal agent other than wind, water or gravity. The paradox is complete: the seed is large and wingless, yet moves rapidly over the landscape. The most likely scenario is that the seeds did indeed move on wings, the wings of Pinyon Jays.

Our scenario continues with a proposed early response of the Pinyon Jay to the large, periodically abundant seed of the Pinyon Pine. Ancestors of this jay probably lived in the same habitat as the Pinyon Pine and simply ate pine seeds when present and found alternate foods when pine seeds were absent. all corvids are inquisitive and are known to explore nooks, crannies and crevices as part of their daily routine. When crops were large, jays may have carried seeds around in their bill (not an uncommon sight at modern-day bird feeders), occasionaly stopping to deposit one or more in concealed locations. (R. P. Balda and N. Stotz have observed that very young hand-raised jays will frequently store and retrieve objects in their cages.) Maybe the birds first deposited seeds they could not eat in crevices or crotches in the trees near where they had been eating. These seeds were not totally concealed and may have been found by the original storer upon return of the bird to a familiar location when it happened to look into the spot. The use of inconspicuous locations to place seeds would help ensure that they would not be found by other birds.

The use of subterranean caches was probably favored early on, as seeds were then completely hidden from other birds and seed predators. This movement of seeds from trees to ground storage sites was an important aspect of the coevolution of bird and tree, for now seeds were placed in sites where they could germinate and survive. However, now the caching bird had to possess some technique(s) to relocate these caches as they were totally hidden from view. Simply returning to a familiar location to open seeds would not suffice to locate buried ones. The use of subterranean caches and the development of successful recovery techniques probably were linked. In addition to being well concealed, another problem with subterranean caches is that some rodents with a good sense of smell could locate and plunder the caches. Pinyon Jays may have moved caches out of areas where rodent density was high and into areas where it was low, as reported by Mattes (1982) for Eurasian Nutcrackers in Switzerland. Thus, active dispersal within and among habitat types would have occurred. Pinyon Jays could now manage their food supply, storing seeds when supplies were abundant and using them when other foods were in short supply.

However, one important aspect of this system is still absent. How many seeds should a bird cache when seeds are abundant? The answer to that question will always be problematic because of a series of unknowns. Birds cannot predict: (1) the amount of snowfall that could bury caches, making some of them inaccessible; (2) the densities of rodents in areas where seeds were cached which would indicate what proportion of their cached seeds would be plundered; (3) the rate of spoilage of cached seeds and (4) the length or intensity of the long, cold winter. It is also possible that birds will forget the location of some cache sites. These unknowns should lead the bird to cache as many seeds as it possibly can to ensure that, even if all the above occur, the bird still has enough seeds to survive the winter and possibly breed. In average years and in many places this 'insurance policy' would not be necessary and, by mid-summer, thousands of seeds might be left unharvested. This number would be enhanced by the number of seeds cached by birds that perished before having an opportunity to retrieve them.

Now coevolution of the bird and the tree would be complete with both bird and tree receiving benefits from the interaction. The pines could spread rapidly on bird wings to colonize new areas or retreat from inhospitable ones. Numerous seeds would then be available to germinate in subterranean sites and establish themselves. Jays were assured of a food supply for many months after a bumper crop. The nutritious seeds also allowed the birds to uncouple the breeding season from the spring production of food, allowing them to breed very early and giving their young time to grow and mature before the onset of caching and winter weather. Hoarded food also allows birds the possibility to uncouple foraging from eating, as stored food can be eaten directly without extended searching (Sherry, 1984).

At this time, trees and birds were able to disperse rapidly, invading new habitats where terrestrial seed predators had not yet been exposed to these seeds. In their newly invaded habitats, they would have a ready supply of food with a known distribution, simply because they cached it there. As the northward and upward dispersal progressed, the trees eventually came in contact with the Clark's Nutcracker invading from the north (Fig. 2.2). Now both bird species moved the pine and benefited from the high-quality seed. In fact, today, in the San Francisco Peaks just north of Flagstaff, no other pine enjoys the wide altitudinal range of the Pinyon Pine. Because both of these caching species are strong fliers relative to Mexican and Scrub Jays, when cone crops occurred only in 'hot spots', these birds would eventually locate them. In years when crops were absent, both species could undergo long-distance movements in search of alternate foods, returning months later to their home ranges and territories (Vander Wall *et al.*, 1981; Marzluff and Balda, 1992).

Of course, none of this is really plausible if this intense caching behavior is not linked with a successful recovery system. Andersson and Krebs (1978) argued that the fitness of the hoarding individual must exceed that of the nonhoarder, as recovered food must increase survival and/or reproductive output over that of a nonhoarder. If nonhoarders can steal caches made by hoarders, then this is a density-dependent game (Maynard Smith, 1974) in which the payoffs depend on the proportion of hoarders in the population. However, any strategy on the part of hoarders that reduced the probability of a nonhoarder being able to locate caches would reduce the average payoff to nonhoarders.

Recovery of cached seeds in nature

Obviously, in order to receive any benefit from food storage, birds must be able to recover their buried seeds. Early reports in the 1940s through to the 1960s by a host of European workers observing Eurasian Nutcrackers indicate that at times these birds were highly accurate when retrieving seeds from subterranean caches (reviewed by Turcek and Kelso, 1968; Tomback, 1980; Lanner, 1996). Most of these conclusions, however, were based on indirect measures of accuracy. When recovering caches, nutcrackers usually sit silently on a branch, intently peering at the surrounding area below. Birds may then descend with a strong, silent swoop to the ground. After a few hops, the bird stops, looks about and drives its powerful bill into the substrate. Although there are no conspicuous signs that seeds are located at these probe sites, birds often do extract a seed in their bill on the first probe. Nutcrackers may then proceed to extract the remaining seeds from the cache and hold them in their sublingual pouch. Often the bird remains at the extraction site, slowly removing seeds from its pouch and eating them one at a time, either by crushing the seed hull with its powerful bill or puncturing the seed hull with its bill tip while holding the seed in its toes. The seed hulls drop to the ground, next to or in the emptied cache site. It is this extraction by the cache site that most early workers used to try to determine the recovery accuracies of nutcrackers. When nutcrackers have been searching for seeds in an area, it is quite easy to see the holes they have dug and therefore easy to calculate the percentage of such holes with seed hulls nearby. These counts usually revealed that birds were between 60% and 86% accurate when probing for hidden seeds (reviewed in Turcek and Kelso, 1968). However, such indirect estimates must be regarded as lower limit estimates, for at least two reasons. First, nutcrackers often retrieve seeds from more than one cache before opening and consuming seeds. Thus, some probe holes from which seeds were recovered do not have empty seed hulls around. Second, rodents are known to pilfer between 14% and 80% of the seeds cached by nutcrackers (Vander Wall, 1990). A searching nutcracker may dig at a site where it had previously buried seeds and have no way to ascertain that the seeds had been pilfered by a cache robber. These sites would also lack empty seed hulls and would also be counted as errors. Thus, because the goal is to estimate the proportion of probes that are directed at locations where caches had been placed, the above estimates are conservative at best (Balda, 1980b).

There are some reports of direct observations of nutcrackers recovering caches. Five irruptive Eurasian Nutcrackers that had been fed Stone Pine seeds (*Pinus cembra*) one winter for 60+ consecutive days made thousands of caches in a local park in Bielefeld, Germany. These birds were observed directly removing seeds from their caches. They were 86% accurate when recovering their hidden seeds weeks and months later, even through 4–6 cm of snow (Fig. 2.3) (Balda and Conrads, 1990). Vander Wall and Hutchins (1983) directly observed Clark's Nutcrackers recovering buried seeds with accuracies that ranged from 33% to 84% over a 9-month interval. However, these and other field observations lack a great deal of information as we do not know whether the bird retrieving the cache actually made the cache, or when the cache was made relative to when it was recovered, or what techniques the bird used to recover its cache, or how many seeds the bird ordinally placed in the cache, or how many caches this bird had in this vicinity, etc.

These field observations do, however, reveal that nutcrackers are incredibly accurate when locating their caches. This high level of accuracy is truly remarkable when one recalls that nutcrackers: (1) spend about 30 seconds at the site creating a cache; (2) make thousands of caches when pine seeds are available; (3) return to harvest their caches many months after they were created and (4) recover many caches from a substrate that has changed drastically since the caches were made, i.e. birds cache in late summer and fall before snow covers the ground but must recover caches through the snow in fall, winter and early spring (Fig. 2.3).

Less field data on cache recovery are available for Pinyon Jays. Balda and Bateman (1971) reported accurate cache recovery by Pinyon Jays digging through snow to recover seeds. Ligon (1978) also reported a high level of accuracy for Pinyon Jays relocating seed caches. Pinyon Jays must perform under the same four constraints listed above, but also experience additional constraints owing to their social organization. Individual Pinyon Jays do not

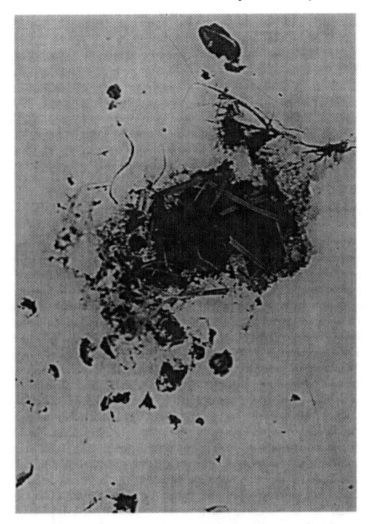

Fig. 2.3 Photograph of hole probed in the snow by a nutcracker to recover a seed cache. Parts of the seed hull are visible around the hole indicating the bird fed on the recovered seeds at this site. (Photograph by Rolf Seebrasse.)

select the general area in which they will create caches because the flock as a whole visits 'traditional areas'. So a bird must use the general area to cache where it landed, relative to the position of the flock. It also appears that birds have little time to deliberate about where to place specific caches once they have landed. The flock as a whole moves in unison and all birds follow this direction. Birds also appear to be very automated when caching, often walking at a steady pace and sticking seeds in the ground at a continuous rate. They must also be constrained by conspecific cache pilferers (Stotz and Balda, 1995; Bednekoff and Balda, 1997).

Little is known about the recovery accuracy of the two *Aphelocoma* species in the field, except that they harvest their caches, appear reasonably accurate, and may do so at least into the beginning of the breeding season (Balda, personal observations; J. R. Brown, personal communication). The hidden food stores of these two jays may provide winter sustenance during those periods when winter weather is unusually severe. Thus, these birds may be able to live on alternate foods most of the time but, during 10–12 days each winter, cached food may provide an important and necessary emergency food.

The evolution of spatial memory

The 'payoff' for caching seeds must be the use of these seeds at a later time. Many alternative mechanisms for cache recovery are possible, including random probing, the use of odor, markings made at cache sites, route reversal and site preferences. The high levels of accuracy observed in field studies argue against random probing but fail to discriminate against most of the other alternatives. A series of controlled laboratory experiments over the past 15 years (Balda, 1980b; Balda and Turek, 1981; Vander Wall, 1982; Kamil and Balda, 1985; Balda *et al.*, 1986; Kamil *et al.*, 1994) have conclusively shown that the use of spatial memory based on visual landmarks is the primary technique employed by all four corvid species that have been studied to date. This makes sense in terms of possible historical competition between hoarders and nonhoarders. The use of spatial memory would provide a method for relocating cached food available to the creator of the caches but not to a noncacher, thus tipping the game in favor of the evolution of caching.

An important historical issue, about which we can currently only speculate, is the question of the evolutionary relationship between general spatial abilities and the special problems faced by seed-caching corvids. Spatial relationships are important to many animals, probably to any animal that can move. A particularly relevant case may be that of migratory birds which are also known to have a keen sense of space. Both migratory and seed-caching birds possess the ability to return to specific locations, migratory birds on a global scale and food-caching birds on a much finer scale (Gallistel, 1990). Perhaps it is more than a coincidence that the two species that recover their caches most accurately (nutcrackers and Pinyon Jays, see below) are the species that are strong fliers, fly many kilometers in search of hot spots of pine cones and irrupt long distances when the pine cone crop fails.

One important mechanism for migratory birds and homing pigeons is the use of a compass. Birds are known to possess a number of different compasses including sun compass, star compass, and magnetic compass which are used during migration and homing (Emlen, 1975; Wiltschko and Wiltschko, 1988).

A compass is a quite general mechanism in the sense that it can be used in many different settings. For example, a compass could be used by animals that had left their territories, as in searching for pine cone hot spots, and now needed to return. Compasses may also play an essential role in cache recovery. Wiltschko and Balda (1989) and Balda and Wiltschko (1992) have demonstrated that the sun compass is used during the relocation of cached seeds by Western Scrub Jays, even when a complex set of landmarks was present and available for their use. Clark's Nutcrackers and Pinyon Jays have recently been shown to use the sun compass when retrieving seeds (Wiltschko *et al.*, unpublished observations).

The landmark/compass system might be a necessary preadaptation to the evolution of seed caching. One can speculate that subterranean seed caching could not evolve without a means of locating hidden seeds. Picture the problem faced by the first bird in an evolutionary lineage to cache. Without a method for relocating the caches, there could be no benefit. A compass-based spatial memory system may have provided this ancestral cacher with the necessary ability. Once this process began, the spatial memory system may well have been selected for intensely, modified and enhanced in species most dependent on hidden food for survival and reproduction (Balda and Kamil, 1989), becoming a key component of the constellation of adaptations that seed-caching animals possess.

The nature of this selection process can be inferred from an analysis of how demands of the seed-caching and recovery problem differ from more global spatial problems. In cases such as migration and homing, there are relatively few specific locations to be remembered, and these often have specific stimuli (e.g. the natal territory, a loft) associated with them. For seed-caching birds such as nutcrackers or Pinyon Jays, thousands of locations must be remembered for up to 9 or 10 months. This clearly implies a memory system of greater capacity and duration. More subtle possibilities exist. For example, there are usually no identifying stimuli located near individual cache sites. A bird who has just made 20 or 30 caches in one end of a meadow may be using one set of landmarks to define the location of each of these cache sites. The use of a compass in this setting would require that each site be identified by a unique set of bearings with respect to the landmarks. This differs markedly from how a compass is used by a migrating bird returning to a single, specific location. One interesting implication of this analysis is the suggestion that nutcrackers and Pinyon Jays may be particularly sensitive to the compass bearings of landmarks.

The evolutionary play: species differences in spatial memory in the laboratory

These birds are strong fliers, wary about being watched and quick to vocalize the approach of an intruder, thus making field studies on seed caching and recovery almost impossible. We have conducted a series of controlled laboratory tests with the southwestern US corvids. Four different comparative tests of seed caching and recovery have been completed. Not all four species participated in all four of the tests, but the results clearly indicate that, although spatial memory is used by all four species to locate caches, there are also important species differences that correlate with ecological differences.

Cache recovery tests of spatial memory

Three species, two conditions test (Balda and Kamil, 1989) This experiment compared the cache recovery performance of Clark's Nutcrackers, Pinyon Jays and Western Scrub Jays under two conditions. The experiment was conducted in an experimental room (3.4 × 3.4 m) with a raised floor that had 180 holes measuring 5.5 cm in diameter, each separated by a center-to-center distance of 23.5 cm. Each hole could be filled with sand for caching or fitted with a wooden plug to prevent caching. The room contained many landmarks on the floor, posters on the walls and a centrally located feeder. During the experiment the cache recovery performance of each bird was tested twice, once with many holes (90) available for cache site selection and once with only a few holes (15) available. The purpose of this design was to assess the accuracy of cache recovery after the birds were given free choice in cache placement so that a cache placement strategy could be employed compared to accuracy of cache recovery after severely limiting the availability of cache sites, so that cache placement strategies would be inhibited. After a 7-day retention interval, birds were released back into the room to recover their caches. The basic measure of accuracy was the proportion of holes probed that contained a seed.

In 40 of the 42 trials the accuracy of the birds was greater than would be expected by chance. Both nonsignificant cases involved Scrub Jays. In general, Scrub Jays performed significantly worse than either nutcrackers or Pinyon Jays, which did not differ from each other. All three species performed better under the 90-hole condition than under the 15-hole condition (Fig. 2.4). Although the species by condition interaction was not significant, the effects of 15 vs. 90 open holes condition appeared to be greatest for Pinyon Jays, who made conspicuous clumps of caches during the 90-hole condition. When the average distance between cache sites was calculated, we found that Pinyon Jays had placed their caches significantly closer together (0.81 m) than either nutcrackers (1.22 m) or Scrub Jays (1.5 m).

These results support the hypothesis that accuracy of cache recovery is a function of some aspect of the ecology of the species being tested. The two species best adapted morphologically for this behavior (and also most dependent on these cached seeds for winter survival and subsequent reproduction) performed significantly better than Scrub Jays. However, the different pattern of space use by Pinyon Jays was unexpected and intriguing.

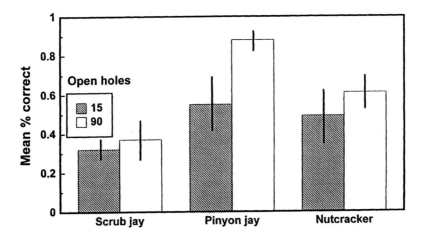

Fig. 2.4 Performance of the three species under the 15- and 90-hole condition.

The clumping of caches may allow the Pinyon Jays to use a nonmnemonic technique, such as area-restricted search, to locate their caches. Recovery of clumped caches could be highly accurate but result from limited memory ability if the jay fills all of the cups with seeds in a relatively small area and then restricts its search to this small, saturated area. Because these birds cache as a social unit, they may also be more inclined to create caches close together owing to the movement restrictions imposed by other members of the group.

Two species, open field (Romonchuk, 1995) This experiment looked more closely at the unexpected clumping of caches by Pinyon Jays. In this study, only individual nutcrackers and Pinyon Jays that were totally unfamiliar with the experimental room and paradigm were used. The experiment was conducted in a $9.1 \times 15.3 \times 2.8$ m room with a raised plywood floor that contained 330 sand-filled holes that were open during both caching and recovery sessions. A number of structures were scattered on the floor and posters lined the walls for visual orientation. Each bird was allowed in the experimental room until it made 25 caches. If a bird stopped caching, it was removed from the room and allowed another session the next day during which previously made caches were capped with wooden plugs. Recovery sessions began 7 days after caching was completed, and birds were allowed to retrieve 25% of their caches during each of four recovery sessions. Sessions were separated by 7 days. The mean intercache distance was measured by averaging the intercache difference between all possible unique pairs of caches. Mean nearest neighbor distance was measured by averaging the distances to a cache's nearest neighbor for all caches.

As in the earlier experiment, the species did not differ in recovery accuracy

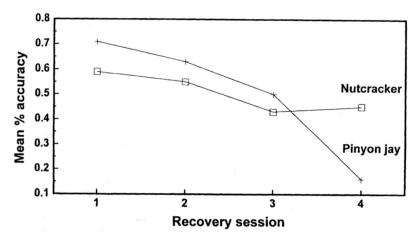

Fig. 2.5 Performance of the nutcracker and Pinyon Jay over four recovery sessions.

(Fig. 2.5). Mean intercache distance was significantly closer for Pinyon Jays ($\bar{x} = 2.66$ m) than for nutcrackers ($\bar{x} = 3.86$ m) (Fig. 2.6). Nutcrackers placed significantly more seeds per cache ($\bar{x} = 2.50$) than did Pinyon Jays ($\bar{x} = 1.12$). These results corroborate the findings of Balda and Kamil (1989) for both recovery accuracy and cache distribution.

Pinyon Jay spacing pattern (Romonchuk, 1995) Can Pinyon Jays accurately find their caches when they are not allowed to cache in clumps? The findings that Pinyon Jays cache in clumps and recover their seeds very accurately do not prove that the clumping is necessary to achieve accurate recovery. Field studies cannot provide an answer because, when given free access to cache sites, Pinyon Jays will always cache in clumps (Stotz and Balda, 1995).

This experiment used two unique sets of cache sites in the large experimental room with 330 holes in the floor. The location of holes for each condition was determined by attempting evenly to distribute the holes throughout the entire room. In one condition, 72 holes were open in the floor and the bird allowed to make 15 caches. With this number of holes open, Pinyon Jays could clump their caches. In the other condition, only 36 holes were open, allowing less opportunity to clump caches. We hypothesized that birds would clump caches under the 72-hole condition but that this would not be possible under the 36-hole condition. If birds used area-restricted search to locate their caches, they should perform with higher accuracy when recovering from the 72-hole condition than from the 36-hole condition.

Unfortunately, this manipulation of number of sites available during caching had no significant effect on intercache distance. Mean intercache

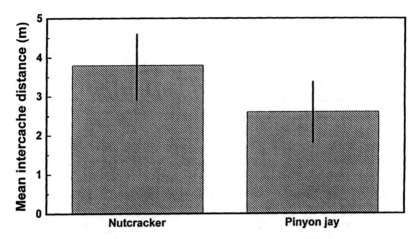

Fig. 2.6 Mean intercache distance for 25 caches made by nutcrackers and Pinyon Jays.

distance was smaller for the 72-hole condition ($\bar{x} = 3.62$ m) than for the 36-hole condition ($\bar{x} = 4.01$ m). However, these intercache distances were greater than those obtained during the Kamil and Balda (1989) study and can reasonably be thought of as representing nonclumped caches.

Accuracy in this experiment was measured using the single cache recovery attempt procedure (SCRAP) developed by Kamil and Balda (1990). Using this procedure, during recovery the bird was presented with a set of clusters, each consisting of a cache site and three empty holes that had not been cached in. The number of errors to find a cache within a cluster could vary between zero (find the cache on the first probe) and three (find the cache after having probed the three noncache holes in the cluster). If birds were probing at random, then each possible outcome, zero through three, should occur with equal frequency and the mean number of errors would be 1.5. For every cluster of holes containing a cache site, a matching cluster was presented that did not contain a cache site. During recovery sessions, birds had a choice of what type of cluster to probe (one that contained a cache or a matching one that did not) and also which hole in a cluster to probe.

There was no significant difference in recovery accuracy between the 36-hole condition and the 72-hole condition. Most importantly, Pinyon Jays performed very accurately, making about 0.75 errors per cluster during both conditions. 'Good' clusters were visited significantly sooner than 'bad' ones. This experiment provides strong evidence that Pinyon Jays do not need to place their caches in clumps and then use area-restricted search to locate them. Birds must have precise spatial information about the exact location of their individual caches.

Comparative long-term spatial memory by four seed-caching corvids (Bednekoff et al., 1997) Are there species differences in the duration of the cache site memory of Clark's Nutcrackers, Pinyon Jays, Western Scrub Jays and Mexican Jays? As reviewed above, in nature, nutcrackers and Pinyon Jays cache greater quantities of pine seeds each fall and rely on them for a longer time period than either Mexican or Western Scrub Jays. In addition, earlier research showed that nutcrackers could remember the location of their caches for at least 285 days (Balda and Kamil, 1992).

We used the large caching room described above, and provided 62 holes as potential cache sites during caching sessions. Birds were allowed to make 24 unique caches. We then allowed birds to recover one-fourth of their caches during each of four recovery sessions conducted 10, 60, 150 and 250 days after caching sessions were completed. During recovery testing, we used the SCRAP procedure (as described in 'Pinyon Jay spacing pattern', above) to assess accuracy. Each cache site was a member of a 2×3 cluster of adjacent holes, so that chance performance was 2.5 errors per recovery.

We used two types of analysis to assess cache recovery accuracy. First, we used *t*-tests to compare accuracy with that expected by chance. When we collapsed data across all retention intervals; each of the four species was more accurate than expected by chance. However, Scrub Jays and Mexican Jays performed only modestly at all retention intervals and did not become less accurate with time. Nutcrackers and Pinyon Jays were very accurate at the 10- and 60-day interval, but only modestly accurate at the 150- and 250-day interval (Fig. 2.7). Second, to assess accuracy, we used a species by interval

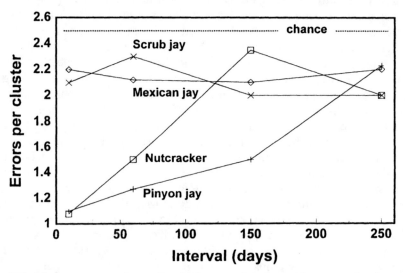

Fig. 2.7 Mean errors per cluster for the four species of corvids at retention intervals of 50, 100, 150, 200 and 250 days.

ANOVA of the mean number of errors. There was a significant main effect of species. Multiple comparisons revealed that nutcrackers and Pinyon Jays did not differ significantly, and that Scrub Jays and Mexican Jays did not differ significantly but that these two pairs of species clearly differed. This result adds further evidence that seed-caching species differ in their ability to locate their hidden seed caches. Again, the species more dependent on seed caches for winter survival and reproduction had the best long-term spatial memory and species with less dependence on this food source had the poorest performance. However, the results of this study fail to clarify any possible species differences in the effects of retention interval. Because the performance of the Scrub and Mexican Jays was so mediocre at all retention intervals, we were unable to detect any effect of retention interval on the performance of these two species.

Other comparative tests of spatial memory

The results of the comparative cache recovery experiments indicate that nutcrackers and Pinyon Jays recover their caches more accurately than either Mexican or Western Scrub Jays. However, does this mean that the species differ in some kind of general spatial memory ability or are these differences limited to tests of cache recovery? It might be argued that these birds are highly specialized for the recovery of seed caches but on other tasks of spatial memory they would perform in an uninteresting or marginal fashion. In addition, differences obtained during any single experiment may be due to differences in spatial cognition or to the effects of contextual variables that may reflect a coincidental effect of some detail of the experimental paradigm (Bitterman, 1965; Macphail, 1982). For example, one species may adapt to laboratory conditions better than another or the rewards could be more suited to one species than to the others. In order to reach a conclusion about these issues, tests with different paradigms are necessary (Kamil, 1988). Therefore, we have conducted a series of spatial memory tasks utilizing procedures quite different from cache-recovery procedures.

Comparative radial maze study (Kamil et al., 1994)   This experiment was carried out with the four species in a small room (3.6 × 3.2 m) with 12 holes arranged in a circle in the floor. The floor contained numerous objects, and the walls were hung with posters. After habituation to the room, members of all four species were given 60 acquisition trials. Each of these trials consisted of two parts, a preretention stage and a postretention stage, separated by a 5-minute retention interval. During the preretention stage, each bird entered the room where four holes chosen at random each day were open and each contained a buried food reward. This stage continued until the bird found and ate the four morsels of food. The bird then left the room and the retention interval began. During the retention interval, four more holes were opened and a food reward placed in each of these newly

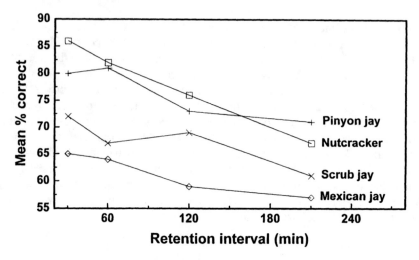

Fig. 2.8 Performance of each species at each interval during an ascending series in the radial maze test.

opened holes. After the 5-minute retention interval the bird was released back into the room that now contained eight open holes, four new holes with seeds and the original four holes that were previously emptied by the bird. The postretention interval continued until the birds either recovered the four rewards or probed six unique holes. Thus, in order to respond accurately, the bird had to remember which four holes it had emptied during the pre-retention phase and visit the newly opened holes.

Although all four species had similar levels of performance at the start of acquisition, they rapidly diverged. Nutcrackers and Pinyon Jays learned the task more rapidly and performed at higher levels than either Western Scrub Jays or Mexican Jays. As retention intervals were increased, all four species declined in accuracy (Fig. 2.8). The results of this experiment are consistent with earlier comparative findings and suggest that the species differences observed during cache recovery are quite robust and are not limited to cache recovery tasks. The selective pressure acting on the spatial memory abilities of these species are general enough to influence performance on a variety of spatial tasks.

Comparative operant spatial and nonspatial memory test (Olson, 1991; Olson et al., 1995)   In an attempt test for memory abilities using procedures as far removed from cache recovery as possible, we have conducted experimental tests of spatial memory with these species in an operant chamber where birds had to peck at lights to receive food rewards (Olson, 1991; Olson *et al.*, 1995). The initial purpose of these experiments was to determine whether these operant procedures would produce the same pattern of species differences in spatial memory as seen during cache recovery and radial maze experiments. In the first of these experiments, Olson (1991) found that nutcrackers performed much better than Western Scrub Jays in this type of task.

We then designed a pair of follow-up experiments. One purpose was to test all four species on an operant task. In addition, we wanted to determine if the species differences we had observed were limited to spatial tasks or would also be found in nonspatial tasks. This experiment was conducted in an operant chamber with a computer monitor at one end and a pecking key and feeder at the other. Each trial began with the illumination of a spot in the center of the monitor. This spot could be red or green; the color illuminated was chosen at random on each trial. A single peck at this sample caused the screen to clear and a yellow light behind the key on the rear panel to be illuminated. One peck at the rear key extinguished that light and two choice stimuli were presented on either side of the monitor, one red and one green. Two pecks directed at either stimulus caused the trial to end. A trial was correct, and followed by delivery of a reinforcer, only if the bird pecked the new color. This procedure required the bird to remember the color it had pecked in the first part of the trial and to avoid that color in the second part. After the birds had learned the task, a titration procedure was employed to assess the duration of nonspatial memory for the sample color. A retention interval was added between the end of the sample presentation and the choice test. If the birds made a correct response, the retention interval increased by 0.1 seconds during the next trial. If the bird made an incorrect response, then the retention interval was decreased by 0.2 seconds. This titration procedure results in a very gradual increase in the retention interval as long as performance is above 67% correct.

The results of this experiment were clear. In stark contrast to the findings of our comparative spatial experiments, the performance of the birds in this nonspatial experiment did not correlate with dependence on stored food and none of the species differences was statistically significant.

Although speed of acquisition and retention interval did not correlate well with dependence on stored food, it seems to correlate with their social organization. Pinyon Jays and Mexican Jays that live in permanent social groups performed better than the more solitary Clark's Nutcracker and Western Scrub Jay (Fig. 2.9). The possible significance of this finding has been discussed elsewhere (Balda *et al.*, 1997).

As soon as this experiment was complete, birds were switched to an almost identical task which required memory for a spatial location rather than a color. Everything remained the same except that in the first stage of each trial, one of two locations, chosen at random for each trial, was illuminated. Then, during the choice phase, two identically colored spots were illuminated, one in the same location as the sample, the other in the novel position. Correct responses were responses to the new location. Titration now

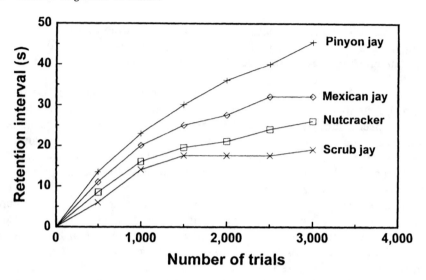

Fig. 2.9 Performance of each species during color memory nonmatching-to-sample titration.

produced very different results. Clark's Nutcrackers performed much better than the other three species, duplicating the finding of Olson (1991) with nutcrackers and Scrub Jays (Fig. 2.10). This is consistent with the results of our cache recovery and radial maze tests. This is the first result from a spatial test in which nutcrackers were clearly superior to Pinyon Jays and the performance of the Pinyon Jays could not be separated from the *Aphelocoma* jays.

The failure to find species differences on the nonspatial test is particularly important. First, it rules out several alternative hypotheses for the species differences we have observed in spatial tasks, such as general intelligence or general adaptability to laboratory test environments. If such general factors were important, then we should have obtained the same species differences in this nonspatial test of memory that we did in spatial tests. Second, they indicate that natural selection can have specific effects on one type of memory while other types are unaffected. This finding substantially increases our confidence that the species differences in dependence on cached food are crucial for the differences in performance on spatial memory tasks.

The evolutionary play: the neural substrate responsible for spatial memory

The pioneering work of Krushinskaya (1966) showed that lesioning the hyperstriatum and hippocampus of Eurasian Nutcrackers impaired their

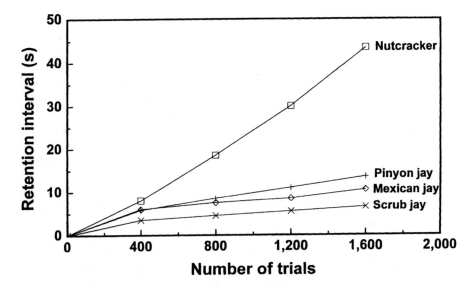

Fig. 2.10 Performance of four species of corvids during spatial memory nonmatching-to-sample titration.

ability to recovery caches accurately. More recently, when Sherry and Vaccarino (1989) lesioned the hippocampus of black-capped chickadees, they could not locate previously made caches, although they continued to make caches and foraged normally. Orientation and recognition of home loft were disrupted when the hippocampus was lesioned in homing pigeons (Bingman *et al.*, this volume). Food-storing birds have a hippocampal complex of greater volume than nonstoring birds, relative to either body size or forebrain volume (Krebs, *et al.*, 1989; Sherry *et al.*, 1989).

We have found differences in the relative size of the hippocampal formation among the nutcracker, Pinyon Jay, Scrub Jay and Mexican Jay (Basil *et al.*, 1996). When the ratio of hippocampal volume to telencephalon volume was calculated for each of these four species and compared on the regression line of this ratio for a wide variety of New and Old World corvids (Krebs *et al.*, 1989; Sherry *et al.*, 1989), nutcrackers had the largest relative hippocampal volume. The three species of southwestern US jays, including the Pinyon Jay, all had small relative hippocampal volumes. Thus, the Pinyon Jay with its excellent spatial memory abilities, especially for cache recovery and radial maze performance, does not follow the pattern whereby a large hippocampus is correlated with excellent spatial memory abilities (Shettleworth and Hampton, this volume).

The evolutionary play: the final act

Vander Wall and Balda (1977, 1981) have described the suite of morphological and ecological adaptations that these birds possess for efficient harvest, transport and caching of the seeds. In general, they concluded that Clark's Nutcrackers and Pinyon Jays are more specialized than either *Aphelocoma* species. The results of our comparative studies of spatial memory lead to the same conclusion, and this buttresses the argument that spatial memory is an adaptation for cache recovery in these animals. In this section, we attempt to integrate this new information with the biogeography, natural history and taxonomy of these species.

When we first began our comparative program of research, we thought of our strategy as the study of divergence among a series of four closely related species. After all, nutcrackers, Scrub Jays, Pinyon Jays and Mexican Jays are all in the same family. Now, however, we think this was too simple. The evidence we have reviewed above is more consistent with the idea that the differences among Scrub Jays, Mexican Jays and Pinyon Jays represent divergence while the similarities between nutcrackers and Pinyon Jays represent convergence. According to this view, the origins of specialized spatial memory and seed-caching behavior are different in the New World jays than in the Old World corvids as this trait has originated more than once in the family Corvidae.

The evidence for the multiple origin of cache site memory is indirect. It seems unlikely that the ancestral *Aphelocoma* jay(s) were very dependent on cached food because of the subtropical habitat in which they lived. This suggests that the spatial abilities of the Pinyon Jay are a relatively recent development. All New World jays examined to date have smaller hippocampuses than many of their Old World relatives that store seeds and retrieve them. This also suggests that New World jays had a noncaching species as an ancestor. Finally, as reviewed above, the biogeography of pine trees with large seeds that do not have wings is consistent with this picture. There appear to have been two distinct historical patterns of distribution. In one, pines have moved north to south, as if transported by invading Clark's Nutcrackers; in the other, the movement has been south to north, as if transported by dispersing Pinyon Jays. The distribution of nutcrackers and Pinyon Jays is consistent with this historical biogeography. While nutcrackers and Pinyon Jays overlap in terms of north–south distribution, nutcrackers range much further to the north than do Pinyon Jays, and Pinyon Jays range farther south.

The details of one of the major adaptations for seed harvesting also fits with the idea that nutcrackers and Pinyon Jays are convergent. The functional similarity of the expandable esophagus of the Pinyon Jay and the sublingual pouch of the nutcrackers is often commented upon (Goodwin, 1986; Marzluff and Balda, 1992). However, analysis of the anatomy of these two adaptations shows that they are completely different in terms of structure (Bock *et al.*, 1973; Marzluff and Balda, 1992). The sublingual pouch is the result of relatively minor modifications of the location and structure of two throat muscles. In contrast, the expandable esophagus is the result of changes in the cell structure of the wall of the esophagus which increases expansibility. These are clearly independently evolved adaptations.

This idea of convergence also helps understand a puzzling aspect of our data on spatial memory and relative hippocampal size. How does the Pinyon Jay recover caches as accurately as the nutcracker, yet have a smaller hippocampal complex? Natural selection works on outcomes and only indirectly on mechanisms (Shettleworth, 1984). In other words, any mechanism that improved the ability to recover caches could be favored by natural selection. The difference in hippocampal volume between nutcrackers and Pinyon Jays suggests that different neural mechanisms may have been involved, but we could only speculate about the location and function of these, as yet unknown, areas. Comparative neuroanatomical studies of the hippocampal complex of nutcrackers and Pinyon Jays may prove very informative.

The results of our comparative operant study also lend support to the idea of different mechanisms in nutcrackers and Pinyon Jays. Pinyon Jays are the equal of nutcrackers in cache recovery accuracy and performance in the radial maze. However, they did not perform nearly as well as nutcrackers in the operant spatial titration task. This may be another indication of different cognitive mechanisms underlying accurate cache recovery in these two species.

At first glance, the Pinyon Jay is truly perplexing. Its subtropical origins suggest that caching is a relatively recent development in its lineage, but it is extremely adept at caching and recovering pine seeds. The taxonomic status of the Pinyon Jay has driven systematists crazy over the years. Its similarities to nutcrackers have suggested one phylogenetic status, as an Old World corvid; other similarities have suggested another classification with the New World jays. We have argued that these perplexities are now largely resolved: that the Pinyon Jay is most reasonably classified with the New World jays, and its adaptations to a caching lifestyle convergent with Old World corvids such as Clark's Nutcrackers. Resolving these perplexities has required consideration of evolutionary history, natural history and even contemporary and historical biogeography. Furthermore, this resolution suggests novel hypotheses about the nature and evolution of the cognitive abilities of animals.

Afterword

Daniel Lehrman was fond of stating that the ultimate reason we study animals in the laboratory is to increase our appreciation of their beauty and sophistication outside of the laboratory, in the field. We know, from personal experience, that the knowledge we have gained through our laboratory research about these wondrous birds has forever changed our perceptions of them. The 'kaws' and 'kraws' will never sound the same; the commotion around the pine trees at harvest time will never seem the same; the sight of a nutcracker or Pinyon Jay arriving at its nest laden with pine seeds will never look the same. Awareness of the cognitive abilities of these animals forever changes our perception of them and their place in nature, and ours.

Acknowledgements

This paper was prepared while both authors were supported by NSF grants DEB-9504105 and DEB-9421807. We thank all our students and colleagues who have contributed to the studies that made this chapter possible. Arla Hile is thanked for her technical assistance in preparing the manuscript of this chapter. The order of authorship correlates with age.

References

Amadon, D. (1944) The genera of Corvidae and their relationships. *Am. Museum Novitates* **1251**, 1–21.
Andersson, M. and Krebs, J. R. (1978) On the evolution of hoarding behavior. *Anim. Behav.* **26**, 707–711.
Balda, R. P. (1980a) Recovery of cached seeds by a captive *Nucifraga caryocatactes. Z. Tierpsychol.* **52**, 331–346.
Balda, R. P. (1980b) Are seed caching systems co-evolved? *Proc. 17th Int. Ornithol. Cong.* **2**, 1185–1191.
Balda, R. P. (1987) Avian impacts on pinyon–juniper woodlands. In Everett, R. L. (compiler) *Proceedings of the Pinyon–Juniper Conference.* Reno, NV: USDA Forest Service General Technical Report, INT-215, pp. 525–533.
Balda, R. P. and Bateman, G. C. (1971) Flocking and annual cycle of the pinyon jay, *Gymnorhinus cyanocephalus. Condor* **73**, 287–302.
Balda, R. P. and Conrads, K. (1990) Freilandbeobachtungen an Siberischen Tannenhahern (*Nucifraga caryocatactes macrorhynchos*) 1977/1978 in Bielefeld. *Ber. Naturwissen Verein Bielefeld Umgegend* **31**, 1–31.
Balda, R. P. and Kamil, A. C. (1989) A comparative study of cache recovery by three corvid species. *Anim. Behav.* **38**, 486–495.
Balda, R. P. and Kamil, A. C. (1992) Long-term spatial memory in Clark's nutcracker, *Nucifraga columbiana. Anim. Behav.* **44**, 761–769.
Balda, R. P. and Turek, R. J. (1984) The cache-recovery system as an example of memory capabilities in Clark's nutcracker. In Roitblat, H. L., Bever, T. G. and Terrace, H. S. (eds) *Animal Cognition.* Hillsdale, NJ: L. Erlbaum Associates, pp. 513–532.

Balda, R. P. and Wiltschko, W. (1992) Caching and recovery in Scrub Jays: transfer of sun-compass direction from shaded to sunny areas. *Condor* **93**, 1020–1023.

Balda, R. P., Bateman, G. C. and Foster, G. F. (1972) Flocking associates of the Piñon Jay. *Wilson Bull.* **84**, 60–76.

Balda, R. P., Kamil, A. C. and Grim, K. (1986) Revisits to emptied cache sites in Clark's nutcrackers (*Nucifraga columbiana*). *Anim. Behav.* **34**, 1289–1298.

Balda, R. P., Kamil, A. C. and Bednekoff, P. A. (1997) Predicting cognitive capacity from natural history: examples from four species of corvids. In Ketterson, E. and Nolan, V. (eds) *Current Ornithology*, Vol. 13. New York: Plenum Press, pp. 33–66.

Basil, J. A., Kamil, A. C., Balda, R. P. and Fite, K. V. (1996) Differences in hippocampal volume among food storing corvids. *Brain Behav. Evol.* **47**, 156–164.

Bateman, G. C. and Bald, R. P. (1973) Growth, development, and food habits of young Piñon Jays. *Auk* **90**, 39–61.

Bednekoff, P. A. and Balda, R. P. (1997) Social caching and observational spatial memory in pinyon jays. *Behaviour* **133**, 807–826.

Bednekoff, P. A., Balda, R. P., Kamil, A. C. and Hile, A. L. (1997) Long term spatial memory in four seed caching corvid species. *Anim. Behav.* **53**, 335–341.

Bitterman, M. E. (1965) Phyletic differences in learning. *Am. Psychol.* **20**, 396–410.

Blair, M., Valenski, T., Sykes, A., Balda, R. P. and Caple, G. (1995) The composition of oils in *Pinus edulis*. In Shaw, D. W., Aldon, E. F. and LoSapio, C. (eds) *Desired Future Conditions for Pinon–Juniper Ecosystems.* Reno, NV: USDA Forest Service General Technical Report, RM-258, pp. 225–226.

Bock, C. E. and Lepthien, L. W. (1976) Synchronous eruptions of boreal seed-eating birds. *Am. Nat.* **110**, 559–571.

Bock, W. J., Balda, R. P. and Vander Wall, S. B. (1973) Morphology of the sunlingual pouch and tongue musculature in Clark's nutcrackers. *Auk* **90**, 491–519.

Bodkin, C. W. and Shires, L. B. (1948) The composition and value of piñon nuts. *New Mexico Exp. Station Bull.* **344**, 2–14.

Conrads, K. and Balda, R. P. (1979) Überwinterungschancen Sibirischer Tannerhäher (*Nucifraga caryocatactes marorhynchos*) im Invasionsgebiet. *Ber. Naturwissen Vereins Bielefeld* **24**, 115–137.

Davis, J. and Williams, L. (1957) Irruptions of the Clark's nutcracker in California. *Condor* **59**, 297–307.

Davis, J. and Williams, L. (1964) The 1961 irruption of the Clark's nutcracker in California. *Wilson Bull.* **76**, 10–18.

Emlem, S. T. (1975) Migration: orientation and navigation. *Avian Biol.* **5**, 129–219.

Gallistel, C. R. (1990) *The Organization of Learning.* Cambridge, MA: MIT Press.

Giuntoli, M. and Mewaldt, L. R. (1978) Stomach contents of Clark's nutcrackers collected in western Montana. *Auk* **95**, 595–598.

Goodwin, D. (1986) *Crows of the World*, 2nd edn. London: British Museum of Natural History Publications.

Hardy, J. W. (1969) A taxonomic revision of the New World jays. *Condor* **80**, 360–375.

Hope, S. (1989) Phylogeny of the avian family Corvidae. Unpublished PhD dissertation, City University of New York.

Kamil, A. C. (1988) A synthetic approach to the study of animal intelligence. In Leger, D. W. (ed.) *Nebraska Symposium on Motivation: Comparative Perspectives in Modern Psychology*, Vol. 35. Lincoln, NB: University of Nebraska Press, pp. 230–257.

Kamil, A. C. and Balda, R. P. (1985) Cache recovery and spatial memory in Clark's nutcrackers (*Nucifraga columbiana*) *J. Exp. Psychol. Anim. Behav. Processes* **11**, 95–111.

Kamil, A. C. and Balda, R. P. (1990) Spatial memory in seed caching corvids. In Bower, G. H. (ed.) *The Psychology of Learning and Motivation*, Vol. 26. New York: Academic Press, pp. 1–25.

Kamil, A. C., Balda, R. P. and Olson, D. J. (1994) Performance of four seed-caching corvid species in the radial-arm maze analog. *J. Comp. Psychol.* **108**, 385–393.

Krebs, J. R., Sherry, D. F., Healy, S. D., Perry, V. H. and Vaccarino, A. L. (1989) Hippocampal specialization of food-storing birds. *Proc. Natl Acad. Sci. USA* **86**, 1388–1392.

Krushinskaya, N. L. (1966) Some complex forms of feeding behavior of nutcracker, *Nucifraga caryocatactes*, after removal of old cortex. *Zh. Evol. Biochem. Fisiol.* **II**, 563–568.

Lanner, R. M. (1981) *The Pinyon Pine, A Natural and Cultural History*. Reno, NV: University of Nevada Press.

Lanner, R. M. (1996) *Made for Each Other: A Symbiosis of Birds and Pines*. New York: Oxford University Press.

Ligon, J. D. (1974) Comments on the systematic relationships of the piñon jay (*Gymnorhinus cyanocephalus*). *Condor* **76**, 468–470.

Ligon, J. D. (1978) Reproductive interdependence of pinyon jays and piñon pines. *Ecol. Monogr.* **48**, 95–110.

Ligon, J. D. and Martin, (1974) Piñon seed assessment by the piñon jay, *Gymnorhinus cyanocephalus. Animal Behav.* **22**, 421–429.

Macphail, E. M. (1982) *Brain and Intelligence in Vertebrates*. Oxford: Clarendon Press.

Marzluff, J. M. and Balda, R. P. (1992) *The Pinyon Jay: Behavioral Ecology of a Colonial and Cooperative Corvid*. San Diego: Academic Press.

Mattes, H. (1982) Die Lebensgemeinschaft von Tannenhäher und Arve. *Swiss Fed. Inst. For. Res. Rep.* **214**, 1–74.

Maynard Smith, J. (1974) The theory of games and the evolution of animal conflicts. *J. Theoret. Biol.* **47**, 209–221.

Mayr, E. and Short, L. L. (1970) *Species Taxa of North American Birds: A Contribution to Comparative Systematics*. Publications of the Nuttall Ornithological Club, Vol. 9. Cambridge, MA.

Mewaldt, L. R. (1956) Nesting behavior of the Clark's nutcracker. *Condor* **58**, 3–23.

Olson, D. J. (1991) Species differences in spatial memory among Clark's nutcrackers, scrub jays, and pigeons. *J. Exp. Psychol. Anim. Behav. Processes* **17**, 363–376.

Olson, D. J., Kamil, A. C., Balda, R. P. and Nims, P. J. (1995) Performance of four seed-caching corvid species in operant tests of nonspatial and spatial memory. *J. Comp. Psychol.* **109**, 173–181.

Peterson, A. T. (1993) Adaptive geographical variation in bill shape of the scrub jay. *Am. Natl.* **142**, 508–527.

Pitelka, F. A. (1951) *Speciation and Ecologic Distribution in American Jays of the Genus* Aphelocoma. University of California Publications in Zoology, Vol. 50.

Romonchuk, W. J. (1995) The role of memory in cache-recovery in Clark's nutcrackers and pinyon jays. Unpublished PhD dissertation, Northern Arizona University, Flagstaff, AZ.

Sherry, D. F. (1984) Food storage by black-capped chickadees: memory for the location and contents of caches. *Anim. Behav.* **32**, 451–464.

Sherry, D. F. and Vaccarino, A. L. (1989) Hippocampal aspiration disrupts cache recovery in black-capped chickadees. *Behavioral Neurosci.* **103**, 308–318.

Sherry, D. F., Vaccarino, A. L., Buckenham, K. and Herz, R. (1989) The hippocamapal complex of food-storing birds. *Brain Behav. Evol.* **34**, 308–318.

Shettleworth, S. J. (1984) Learning and behavioural ecology. In Krebs, J. R. and Davies, N. B. (eds) *Behavioural Ecology: An Evolutionary Approach.* Sunderland, MA: Sinauer Associates, pp. 170–194.

Smith, C. C. and Balda, R. P. (1979) Competition among insects, birds, and mammals for conifer seeds. *Am. Zool.* **19**, 1065–1083.

Stegmann, B. K. (1934) On the ontogeny of the nutcracker (Kedrovka) (trans. L. Kelso). *Dokl. Akad. Nauk. USSR 2* **4**, 267–269.

Stotz, N. G. and Balda, R. P. (1995) Cache and recovery behavior of wild pinyon jays in Northern Arizona. *Southwest. Nat.* **40**, 180–184.

Tomback, D. (1980) How nutcrackers find their seed stores. *Condor* **82**, 10–19.

Tomback, D. F. (1983) Nutcrackers and pines: coevolution or coadaptation? In Nitecki, M. H. (ed.) *Coevolution.* Chicago: University of Chicago Press, pp. 179–223.

Turcek, F. J. and Kelso, L. (1968) Ecological aspects of food transport and storage in the Corvidae. *Comm. Behav. Biol. A* **1**, 277–297.

Vander Wall, S. B. (1982) An experimental analysis of cache recovery in Clark's nutcracker. *Anim. Behav.* **30**, 84–94.

Vander Wall, S. B. (1990) *Food Hoarding in Animals.* Chicago, IL: University of Chicago Press.

Vander Wall, S. B. and Balda, R. P. (1977) Coadaptations of the Clark's nutcracker and the pinyon pine for efficient seed harvest and dispersal. *Ecol. Monog.* **47**, 89–111.

Vander Wall, S. B. and Balda, R. P. (1981) Ecology and evolution of food-storage behavior in conifer-seed-caching corvids. *Z. Tierpsychol.* **56**, 217–242.

Vander Wall, S. B. and Hutchins, H. E. (1983) Dependence of Clark's nutcrackers (*Nucifraga columbiana*) on conifer seeds during the post-fledging period. *Can. Field Nat.* **97**, 208–214.

Vander Wall, S. B., Hoffman, S. W. and Potts, W. K. (1981) Emigration behavior of Clark's nutcracker. *Condor* **83**, 162–170.

Westcott, P. W. (1964) Invasion of Clark's nutcrackers and Piñon jays into southeastern Arizona. *Condor* **66**, 441.

Wiltschko, W. and Balda, R. P. (1989) Sun compass orientation in seed-caching scrub jays (*Aphelocoma coerulescens*). *J. Comp. Physiol. A* **164**, 717–721.

Wiltschko, W. and Wiltschko, R. (1988) Magnetic orientation in birds. *Curr. Ornithol.* **5**, 67–121.

Zusi, R. L. (1987) A feeding adaptation of the jaw articulation in new world jays (Corvidae). *Auk* **104**, 665–680.

3

Adaptive Specializations of Spatial Cognition in Food-storing Birds? Approaches to Testing a Comparative Hypothesis

Sara J. Shettleworth[1] and Robert R. Hampton[2]

[1]Department of Psychology, University of Toronto, Toronto, Ontario M5S 3G3, Canada and [2]Laboratory of Neuropsychology, National Institutes of Mental Health, National Institutes of Health, Bethesda, MD 20892-4415, USA

Introduction

The storing of food, in birds as in other animals, appears to be an adaptation for surviving predictable periods of food shortage (Vander Wall, 1990). Food-storing birds among the parids (chickadees and titmice), corvids (jays, crows and nutcrackers) and sittids (nuthatches) rely on spatial memory to retrieve their caches, though perhaps not exclusively (Petersen and Sherry, 1996; Shettleworth, 1995; Balda and Kamil, this volume). They also have a hippocampus that is larger relative to their brain and body size than the hippocampus of birds that do not store food, and the hippocampus is important for spatial memory in birds, as it is in mammals (Clayton and Lee; Bingman *et al.*, this volume). Thus storing food, an adaptively specialized behavior that engages spatial memory, is accompanied by changes in a part of the brain involved in spatial memory. But is it also accompanied by an adaptive specialization of memory? Here we discuss some of the issues that arise in trying to answer this question, starting with a discussion of what is meant by adaptive specializations in cognition, why they are important and

ANIMAL COGNITION IN NATURE
ISBN 0-12-077030-X

some of the problems in pinning them down. We then outline three ways of formulating hypotheses about adaptation in cognition and illustrate them with recent data from our laboratory.

Adaptive specializations in evolutionary biology and cognitive psychology

Adaptive specializations are morphological, physiological, behavioral or cognitive traits associated with ecological demands particular to a species or group of species. A reliable association between a trait and the specific challenges the species face in making a living indicates that the trait has arisen due to particular selection pressures. There are three general ways to test the hypothesis that a trait has evolved because it contributes to fitness in a particular way: seeing whether the trait can be accounted for by optimality modelling, performing experiments and applying the comparative method (Ridley, 1993). All three have been applied to food storing. A model (Andersson and Krebs, 1978) has helped to stimulate the research on food storing that has been going on for the past 15 years or so. It showed that food storing would evolve only if individuals that invested in storing were more likely to retrieve their stores than conspecifics that did not store. One of the ways in which they could do so would be to remember the locations of their stores. More recently, experiments have shown that storing and retrieving food do contribute to fitness. Nuthatches given extra sunflower seeds to store early in the winter are in better condition later on than those not so provisioned (Nilsson *et al.*, 1993). Field experiments have also established that items stored by a particular jay or tit are more likely to be retrieved by that individual than by other individuals (Brodin and Ekman, 1994; Ekman *et al.*, 1996). However, these findings do not necessarily mean that food storers' memory is any different from other birds' memory. It is possible, for instance, that they have more accurate or detailed spatial perception or that the act of storing engages memory in a particularly effective way. Evidence bearing on possible species differences in memory has come primarily from applications of the comparative method. This involves collecting data from large numbers of species to see whether the trait in question is associated with the ecological conditions to which it is a supposed adaptation. For food-storing birds, the most extensive data of this kind are those showing that a relatively large hippocampus is associated with dependence on stored food.

But surely there is already plenty of evidence for adaptations in behavior, so why is it important or even interesting to test for adaptations in cognition? There are at least two classes of reasons. First, well-supported examples of cognitive adaptations have wide-ranging theoretical implications. In psychology, the notion that cognition (by which we mean information-processing abilities including perception, learning and memory) exhibits species-specific adaptive specializations contrasts with the historically prevalent notion that the properties of learning and cognition generally are the same across species and information-processing domains. As a result of numerous developments in cognitive science, neurobiology and evolutionary biology in the past 25 years or so, there is now substantial support for the view that, instead, cognition consists of a collection of specialized, domain-specific modules that have been shaped by evolution to solve specific information-processing problems (Barkow *et al.*, 1992; Tooby and Cosmides, 1995). This does not mean that cognitive mechanisms have no shared characteristics. Common ancestry and/or common features of the physical environment ensure that there is much in common across even very diverse species, for example, in spatial cognition, timing and the detection of causality (Macphail, 1982; Gallistel, 1990; Bitterman, 1996). In parallel with the ecological or adaptationist approach to cognition in nonhuman species, adaptationist analyses of human cognition have become popular (Barkow *et al.*, 1992). However, such hypotheses are often based on conjectures about situations in distant evolutionary time, in early hominid societies. For really compelling examples of how cognition is shaped by evolution and for models of the kind of data required to back up speculations about evolutionary specializations of cognitive processes, it is necessary to turn to nonhuman species. They can provide particularly clear evidence about what problems a system solves as well as comparative data from large numbers of species.

A second reason for interest in adaptive specializations of cognition is that studying them can contribute to behavioral neuroscience through what has been called *inverse neuropsychology* (Shettleworth, 1995). Rather than attempting to understand brain function by comparing normal to brain-damaged subjects, as is usually done in neuropsychology, investigators taking a comparative approach can look to examples of evolutionarily enhanced function for clues to what specific brain areas do. Comparative studies followed up with lesions or other neuroanatomical manipulations may reveal relationships between structure and function that would not readily be revealed by studies of any one species. In the long run, too, understanding the developmental (see Clayton and Lee, this volume) and genetic mechanisms underlying differences in cognition between closely related species could be an important complement to the genetic engineering approach to the molecular bases of cognition (Gerlai, 1996; Mayford *et al.*, 1995).

When Rozin and Kalat (1971) introduced the term *adaptive specialization* into discussions of learning, they were primarily interested in the notion that some species might exhibit qualitatively specialized kinds of learning for solving species-specific problems. Bird song learning and imprinting are good examples of such species-specific kinds of learning. More generally, however, adaptations consist of quantitative tweakings of traits shared by many species. For instance, the suite of morphological and behavioral adaptations for food storing in Clark's Nutcrackers includes a long sharp beak, used for prying pine seeds out of unripe cones before other birds can reach them, and exceptionally early breeding, made possible by a continuing store of seeds for feeding the young (Vander Wall and Balda, 1981; see Balda and Kamil, this volume). At the level of gross morphology, the hippocampal changes associated with food storing also appear to be quantitative rather than qualitative, although detailed neuroanatomical studies may reveal otherwise (Montagnese *et al.*, 1993; Clayton and Lee; Bingman *et al.*, this volume). A beak, a hippocampus and seasonality in breeding are shared among birds, yet fine tuned in each species.

Researchers studying memory in food-storing species have generally assumed that, by analogy to such adaptations, any cognitive adaptations for food storing can be understood as quantitative enhancements of memory capacity and/or persistence rather than a different memory system devoted to locations of caches. On the whole, the relevant data justify this assumption. For instance, Black-capped Chickadees remember the locations of food 'stored' by the experimenter as well as locations of food they store themselves (Shettleworth *et al.*, 1990), and they remember the same features of both kinds of locations (Brodbeck, 1994). Cross-species comparisons of performance in both corvids and parids tend to produce the same pattern of results in tasks ranging from retrieval of stored food in a large aviary to matching to sample in an operant chamber. This also argues in favor of any specialization of food-storers' memory not being confined to memory for cache locations (Shettleworth, 1995; see also Balda and Kamil).

An old issue in comparative psychology is how to distinguish species differences in performance from species differences in inferred underlying processes such as learning or spatial memory. Two species may perform differently in a test of memory for a variety of theoretically uninteresting reasons. One may be more hungry for the food reward, better habituated to life in captivity, more sensitive to the stimuli being used, less distracted by extraneous features of the testing situation, more adept at the responses required, and so on. The list of potential confounding contextual variables (Macphail, 1987) is nearly endless. In principle, those known to affect a single species' performance in the task in question, such as reward size or amount of prior training, can be varied systematically to see whether they influence species differences in performance (Bitterman, 1975). However, this sort of approach is far from practical for testing sweeping adaptationist hypotheses involving large numbers of species. In the next section of the chapter we discuss three possible ways of making meaningful cross-species comparisons despite the problem of contextual variables.

Defining adaptive specializations in cognition: three approaches

Ecological comparative psychology

After examining data from a large number of vertebrates in standard laboratory learning tasks, Macphail (1982, 1987) concluded there was no firm basis for rejecting the null hypothesis of no differences among species in intelligence, by which he meant learning ability. This startling conclusion arose because Macphail accepted species differences in performance as evidence for species differences in learning only if no contextual variable could reasonably have produced them. However, as Kamil (1988) pointed out, this amounts to saying that the null hypothesis of no species differences can be rejected only if the null hypothesis of no differences due to contextual variables can be proven. In effect, then, the traditional approach to comparing learning ability across species is impotent to find species differences. Kamil's (1988) proposed remedy has two ingredients. First, it is necessary to compare species for which there is some a priori prediction of species difference in cognition based on ecology, as in the case of food-storing birds being discussed in this chapter. This ecological approach (Shettleworth, 1993) generates a principled selection of species to compare and capacities to compare them on. Second, ecologically derived hypotheses about species differences should be tested with a variety of tasks. Convergent evidence from several different tests of the same capacity is compelling as long as it is unlikely that contextual variables affect performance in all of them in the same way. However, some variables that are virtually impossible to eliminate, like species differences in fearfulness, opportunism or compatibility with humans, may facilitate or inhibit performance equally on all laboratory tasks (Lefebvre and Giraldeau, 1996). Therefore, is important to include tests in which different patterns of species abilities are predicted (see Kamil, this volume). In addition, as Kamil (1988) emphasized, the more species that are tested, the less likely that results consistent with the predicted ordering of their abilities have arisen by chance.

Applied to memory in food-storing birds, the ecological approach generates the following hypothesis: if contextual variables are controlled appropriately, then food-storing species will perform better on tests of capacity and/or persistence of spatial memory than species that store less food, and this pattern of species differences will be specific to spatial memory. That is, on a similar procedure testing another kind of memory, the species will not perform differently or the ordering of species by level of performance on the task will be different. Statistically, there will be an interaction of task by species. This simple hypothesis is based on the belief that food-storing species do in fact remember a large number of stored food items for a long time in the field, and has motivated virtually all of the comparative studies of memory in food-storing birds to date (Shettleworth, 1995). Nevertheless, it

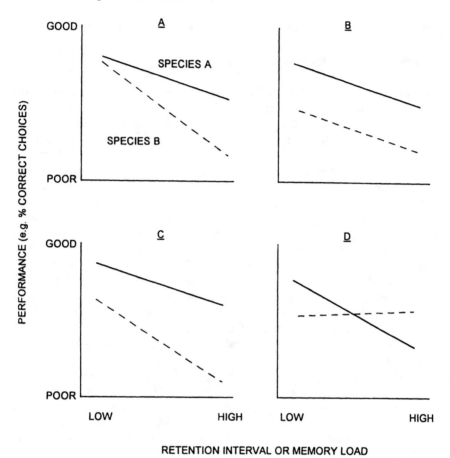

Fig. 3.1 Four possible outcomes of comparing the performance of two species on a test of memory with memory load or retention interval varied. In (A), the two species process and store the information equally well but forget at different rates. In (B), they differ in initial information processing or storage. (C) and (D) represent combinations of differences in both initial processing and retention.

will help to clarify the other approaches we will discuss to consider for a moment what idealized data consistent with this hypothesis might look like.

Figure 3.1 shows some of the possibilities for two hypothetical species whose memory is tested at a range of task difficulties. In easy tasks the animals have only a few items to remember (i.e. a small memory load) or they have to hold those items in memory for only a short time (i.e. a short retention interval). Difficult tasks have a large memory load and/or a long retention interval. (Difficulty could be varied in other ways, for example, by varying the amount of initial exposure to the information to be remembered or the amount of potentially interfering information present.) Example A is the comparative psychologist's dream. When the task is easy, the species both perform well, but not too well. This shows that no animals are prevented by unintended contextual variables from doing well, but since performance could in principle be better than it is, we do not need to worry that a possible species difference is being obscured by a ceiling effect. As the task becomes more difficult, however, the 'unspecialized' species B performs less and less well than the specialized one. Such an interaction is generally accepted as revealing a difference in memory between two groups. An example can be found in Olson's (1991) comparison of operant delayed nonmatching to sample in Clark's Nutcrackers and Scrub Jays with one item to remember at different retention intervals. However, not all comparisons among species thought to differ in spatial memory have revealed this pattern of results, as we will see below.

Example B is more problematical because the species differ consistently at all levels of task difficulty. A pattern like this is found in experiments with a single species when two groups are compared under conditions that differ in how well information to be remembered can be encoded. For instance, in pigeons, longer exposure to the stimulus to be remembered leads to a constant increment in correct choices of that stimulus at all retention intervals (Roberts and Grant, 1976). Thus, in between-species comparisons, the pattern of data in B would be attributed to species differences in initial encoding or processing of information rather than to differences in the ability to retain information once processed. It is arguable whether parallel declines in performance from different starting-points like those in example B should be seen as representing identical rates of forgetting or not. For this reason, behavioral neuroscientists interested in memory typically try to find tasks in which the performance of all their groups can be equated in the easiest version of the task. Equating animals for baseline performance in this way may require training some groups more than others to begin with. However, this introduces problems of its own. For instance, it must be assumed that the rate of forgetting is determined only by the initial level of performance and is not influenced by how much training was required to achieve that level in the first place.

More complex patterns than those in examples A and B can readily be imagined. Example C should warm the heart of a seeker after adaptive specializations, since the performance of one group both starts higher and declines more slowly than that of the other. However, in Example D, the group that performs less well to start with forgets nothing while the group that starts out better forgets almost completely. We dwell on these examples to emphasize that inferences about memory are based not on single measures from one set of conditions but on patterns of performance across variation in memory load, retention interval or the like. The hypothetical data in each example could come from two kinds of tests of the same species such as spatial vs. nonspatial memory tasks or from the same test given to different species.

Of course, any conclusion about adaptative specialization in memory requires data from more than two species. Balda, Kamil and colleagues have compared up to four species of corvids in the same experiment (Kamil *et al.*, 1994; Olson *et al.*, 1995). Clayton and Krebs (1994a) have compared two corvids and two parids within the same experiment. Hilton and Krebs (1990) compared four tit species, but collapsed them into two groups, storers vs. non-storers, and Healy (1995; Healy and Krebs, 1992a) has compared food-storing Marsh Tits to nonstoring Great Tits or Blue Tits. In Toronto we have compared one parid to one nonparid. At present, therefore, attempts to evaluate support for hypotheses about memory in food-storing birds rely on data from several laboratories that are using slightly different procedures. However, although all food-storing species are predicted to show adaptations of spatial memory, there could be differences in the details of those adaptations. For instance, Clark's Nutcrackers might specialize particularly in retaining spatial information for a long time (see Balda and Kamil, this volume), while other species might be successful because they are especially good at spatial discrimination or encoding.

Regression

In general, a large bird has a large hippocampus and a small bird, a small one. Assessments of adaptive specialization of hippocampus and other brain structures (Harvey and Krebs, 1990; Healy, 1996; Sherry *et al.*, 1992) partial out this overall allometric relationship by regressing hippocampal volume against volume of the rest of the brain. Lefebvre (1996; Lefebvre and Giraldeau, 1996) has suggested that, by analogy, in a test of adaptive specialization in spatial memory, a number of species' scores on tests of spatial memory should be regressed against their scores on some 'generalized' test of memory. Data from species thought to be specialized for spatial memory should then lie above the overall 'allometric' relationship between performance on the spatial task and performance on the control task, as in Fig. 3.2A. Alternatively, when two species are each tested on several spatial and nonspatial tasks, performance of the food-storing species can be regressed against performance of the nonstoring species, as in Fig. 3.2B. In this example, the regression line for spatial tasks should lie above that for nonspatial tasks. In the case of two species and two tasks, one of which taps the ability thought to be specialized in one of the species, this approach amounts to looking for a task by species interaction (Lefebvre and Giraldeau, 1996).

This proposal emphasizes comparing species on 'specialized' vs. 'unspecialized' tasks rather than comparing them extensively in tasks assumed to tap

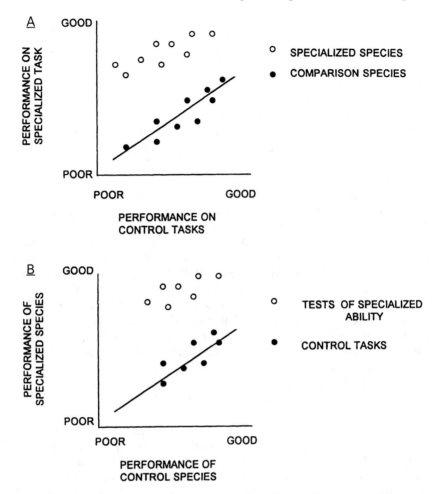

Fig. 3.2 Hypothetical data illustrating the regression approach to species differences in cognition suggested by Lefebvre and Giraldeau (1996). In (A), individuals from each of two species are tested in two tasks that have similar demands except that one ('specialized task') taps an ability that is better developed in the 'specialized' species. Each data point represents a single individual. In (B), groups of animals from two species are tested in a series of tasks, some of which tap the hypothesized specialized ability. Here each data point represents the mean data of a single pair of groups in a single task.

the specialized ability of some of them. Moreover, it points to a concise and heretofore underexploited way of summarizing the results of such comparisons. Most important, like applications of the comparative method to other features of brain or behavior, it prescribes basing conclusions on relative rather than absolute differences between species. However, most of the advantages that Lefebvre and Giraldeau claim for this approach are implicit in existing research on food-storing species. For instance, in a number of cases, the species being compared have been given tests of spatial memory and similar tests of memory for some other feature, generally color (Sherry and Vaccarino, 1989; Hilton and Krebs, 1990; Brodbeck and Shettleworth, 1995; Healy, 1995; Olson et al., 1995; Shettleworth and Westwood, 1998). Including both easy and hard tests of spatial memory within the same experiment achieves a similar end (e.g. Olson, 1991; Hampton and Shettleworth, 1996a; see later), because the species are expected to differ more on harder tests.

A conceptual problem with the regression approach is that it seems to assume there is a good cognitive analogy to the allometric relationship among sizes of structures in different-sized species. Is this analogy 'general intelligence'? That is, are the species in Fig. 3.2 with higher scores on both tests 'more intelligent' than those with lower scores on both tests? Applying the crude notion of general intelligence to nonhuman species is just as suspect as applying it to humans (Mackintosh, 1994). It is also inconsistent with the notion of cognitive modularity that underlies the study of supposed adaptive specializations in cognition. Performance on task A will predict performance on task B only to the extent that they share cognitive, behavioral or motivational demands. There might be no relationship between scores on two tests that reflect two different memory systems. However, something like an allometric relationship between scores on two kinds of tests would arise if this relationship measures the influence of common contextual variables, memory demands, or species characteristics like opportunism or fearfulness.

Lefebvre and Giraldeau (1996) used their approach to assess whether gregarious feral pigeons have a specialized ability to learn socially compared to solitary Zenaida Doves by recording how quickly birds of the two species learned to perform a food-finding task with and without benefit of opportunity to copy a conspecific tutor. It is reasonable to assume a positive correlation between scores on the social and nonsocial tasks, because in both the birds had to learn the same food-finding skill, like opening a container full of grain. Clearly, in the case of social learning, it is critical to take into account the birds' ability to acquire the skills being tested on their own rather than simply comparing how quickly social and nonsocial species learn when exposed to tutors. Evidence consistent with the hypothesis that social living predicts social learning ability would consist of greater relative enhancement from observing the tutor in the social than in the nonsocial species. In principle, the social birds could find the task more difficult than the solitary species, but observing a tutor could double their learning speed while increasing that of the solitary species little or not at all. However, such an outcome would also be obtained if observation improves performance on difficult tasks more than on easy tasks regardless of species. No statistical subtlety can get around the fact that convergent data from several tests are nearly always required for testing hypotheses about cognitive specializations. Moreover, when applied to tests of memory, the regression approach seems to neglect the point of our Fig. 3.1, that inferences about differences in memory across groups of subjects are, of theoretical necessity, based on patterns of data obtained when task variables like memory load and retention intervals change. They cannot readily be summarized in a single value.

With the regression approach, investigators do not need to find absolute superiority of spatial memory in supposedly specialized species. Food-storing species are predicted simply to perform better on spatial tasks relative to some unspecified nonspatial tasks than nonstoring species. This is a weaker hypothesis than the simple hypothesis of food-storers' spatial superiority that has driven most past research in this area (Shettleworth, 1995). On the face of it, it is also less clearly consistent with the observation that food storers seem to remember many items for a long time in the wild. This is an achievement in absolute terms, not relative to some other kind of achievement of these animals. However, testing simply for relative superiority of spatial memory does not have the perhaps unrealistic prerequisite that all species under consideration should perform at the same level on some baseline task. A finding of relative superiority would also be consistent with suggestions (e.g. Healy, 1996) that there may be tradeoffs in the brain between relative enlargement of some structures, such as hippocampus in food-storing species, and relative contraction of others.

Anatomy

It is generally accepted that sensory systems vary adaptively with lifestyle (see Moss and Shettleworth, 1996, for examples). Vision or hearing, for instance, is so well understood that the adaptive fit between structure and function in different species like owls or bats seems immediately obvious. Similarly, if the function of the avian hippocampus were well enough understood, species differences in cognition could be inferred immediately from the well-documented volumetric differences discussed in the chapter by Clayton and Lee. This idea suggests that rather than trying to gather standardized behavioral data from a large sample of species, investigators should focus on understanding what an enlarged hippocampus does by intensively studying a small sample of species (Hampton, 1995; Hampton and Shettleworth, 1996a).

The hippocampus has been much less well studied in birds than in mammals, but it does seem to be involved in spatial memory (Sherry and Vaccarino, 1989; Bingman *et al.*, 1995). Indeed, the fact that species of birds and mammals that have a spatially demanding lifestyle also have a relatively large hippocampus can be taken as lending support to this interpretation of hippocampal function (Sherry *et al.*, 1992; Squire, 1993). This does not mean we know exactly what the hippocampus does, but the three-way relationship of hippocampus, food storing and spatial memory suggests that any cognitive specialization of food-storing species can be characterized as superiority at tasks in which the hippocampus is involved. A direct test of this relationship would consist of examining how hippocampal lesions affect performance on tasks on which food-storing species do and do not differ. We discuss the results of some research of this kind in the next part of the chapter.

The three approaches summarized

Do food-storing species of birds have an adaptive specialization of spatial memory and, if so, how can it best be characterized? Each of the three approaches to answering this question generates an explicit hypothesis. These hypotheses are not necessarily mutually exclusive.

1. The straightforward ecological hypothesis

If contextual variables are controlled appropriately, then food-storing species will perform better on tests of capacity and/or persistence of spatial memory than species that store less food, and the pattern of species differences will be specific to spatial memory.

2. The weaker, regression, hypothesis

Food-storing species perform better on spatial tasks relative to some unspecified nonspatial tasks than nonstoring species. Overall species differences in performance can be removed statistically rather than by manipulating contextual variables.

3. The anatomical hypothesis

Food-storing species will excel at any sort of task that depends on hippocampal function but will perform no differently from other animals on tasks that do not require an intact hippocampus.

Examples from Black-capped Chickadees and Dark-eyed Juncos

Two years ago, an exhaustive survey of comparative studies of memory in food-storing birds (Shettleworth, 1995) concluded that superior spatial memory appeared to be associated with dependence on stored food in corvids, but that this conclusion was less clearly supported by studies involving parids. However, both corvids and parids that are dependent on storing appear to rely on spatial cues more heavily relative to color cues than species thought to store less food in the wild. In addition, there was some evidence that species that are dependent on storing are less susceptible to the effects of interfering information on spatial memory than are species thought to store less food in the wild. We will not systematically review the mass of data contributing to this picture again here, although we will refer to aspects of it in passing. Here we focus on a series of recent experiments in our laboratory that combined comparative studies of memory in several tasks with tests of the effects of hippocampal lesions on performance in those same tasks. This work is therefore primarily an exploration of the anatomical, neurobiological approach to adaptive specialization of memory.

In all of the experiments, just two small passerine species were compared, Black-capped Chickadees (*Parus atricapillus*) and Dark-eyed Juncos (*Junco hyemalis*). Black-capped Chickadees are widely distributed in North America. They store food avidly during the cold months of the year and are thought to retrieve most of it after a few hours or days as Marsh Tits do (Stevens and Krebs, 1986) although as yet there are no good field data to back up this supposition. All North American parids store food (Hampton and Sherry, 1992), so, because we wished to compare a storing to a nonstoring bird, we were forced to choose an unrelated comparison species. Dark-eyed Juncos recommended themselves because they can be found year-round in Southern Ontario in some of the same areas as chickadees, and they perform well in laboratory studies of foraging (Caraco, 1981). Unlike chickadees, juncos forage primarily on the ground and are somewhat migratory. They are about twice as heavy as chickadees (20 vs. 10 g body weight) and, in accordance with their nonstoring status, have a smaller relative hippocampal volume than chickadees (Hampton and Shettleworth, 1996a). The results to date will be reviewed under three headings: spatial memory, interference in spatial memory, and use of spatial vs. color cues. In each case, we have documented species differences in memory similar to those found in other comparative studies of food storers and have used lesion studies to tie the observed differences in performance directly to differences in hippocampal function.

Spatial memory

Natural history and neuroanatomy alike predict that capacity and/or persistence of spatial memory is correlated with reliance on stored food in the wild. For North American corvid species, this prediction has been tested with retrieval of stored food in the laboratory (Balda and Kamil, 1989; Bednekoff, *et al.*, 1997), avoidance of previously visited locations in a radial maze (Kamil *et al.*, 1994), and operant delayed nonmatching to sample (Olson, 1991; Olson *et al.*, 1995). In every case, Clark's Nutcrackers, the birds most reliant on storing in the wild, have performed better than birds of the other species tested. Scrub Jays have always performed less well than nutcrackers, but Pinyon Jays, a species also very reliant on stored food, have sometimes equalled nutcrackers and sometimes performed more like Scrub Jays. Similar tests with European parids have not always produced similarly clear species differences (Hilton and Krebs, 1990; Healy and Krebs, 1992a,b; Healy, 1995).

We tested juncos and chickadees in a spatial memory paradigm that has yielded large and clear differences in corvids, operant spatial delayed nonmatching to sample (Fig. 3.3; Hampton, 1995; Hampton and Shettleworth, 1996a). Unlike parids in previous operant studies (Healy, 1995), birds were trained extensively before being tested with a random mixture of retention intervals. At the start of each trial, one key (the sample) in a chamber with two white pecking keys lit up and the bird pecked it a few times (Fig. 3.3). Then the keys were darkened for the retention interval. Before both keys could light for the test part of the trial, a programmed retention interval had to expire and the bird had to be in the middle of a perch at the back of the cage. This requirement, used in all of our operant tests of memory, ensured that birds could not just wait in front of the correct location on the pecking panel during the retention interval. In the test phase of each trial, birds were reinforced with a bite of powdered sunflower seed for pecking the key not pecked in the sample phase. Eight chickadees and eight juncos were trained for many trials on this procedure with a minimal retention interval and then tested with a random mixture of 5-, 15-, 30- and 60-second retention intervals. Figure 3.4 shows the results. Chickadees performed significantly more accurately than juncos at all retention intervals tested; the species × retention interval interaction was not significant. Thus, the data are like example B in Fig. 3.1, consistent with better processing of the stimuli by the chickadees, but not necessarily with better retention of spatial information.

When the same two locations serve as samples over and over again, about half the trials have the same sample as the trial before, and about half the trials have a different sample (see Fig. 3.3). If the subject inappropriately retains information about the sample and/or the rewarded choice from the previous trial, it will perform better on sample-same trials than on sample-different trials. As Fig. 3.4 shows, the juncos in our experiment did this, whereas the chickadees did not. One way to characterize these results is to say that the chickadees were more resistant to interference from information presented on previous trials than the juncos. Indeed, one might predict that an animal specialized for remembering the locations of large numbers of stored seeds would be especially resistant to interference. Furthermore, some (Shapiro and Olton, 1994) have suggested that one function of the mammalian hippocampus is to allow separate memories to be kept separate, i.e. to resist interference. These results suggest the same might be true of the avian hippocampus.

Chickadees have a larger relative hippocampal volume than juncos and they perform better in delayed nonmatching, but does spatial delayed nonmatching to sample actually involve the hippocampus? The answer is shown in the lower part of Fig. 3.4, which displays the data of juncos and chickadees that were subjected to hippocampal aspiration lesions or to

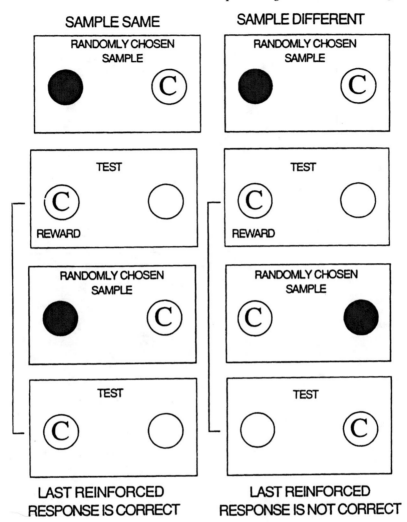

Fig. 3.3 Some of the events in the operant delayed matching to sample procedure used by Hampton and Shettleworth (1996a) to test chickadees and juncos, contrasting sample-same and sample-different trial sequences. Dark disks represent unilluminated pecking keys; white disks represent lighted keys. C = correct, reinforced, choice. A retention interval was programmed between the sample and the test, and at the end of this the bird had to hop on a perch at the end of the cage away from the pecking panel to present the test phase of the trial. A variable intertrial interval intervened between one test and the next sample. Brackets at the side of each column emphasize the critical relationship in each type of trial sequence.

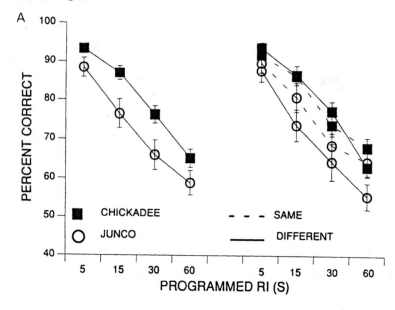

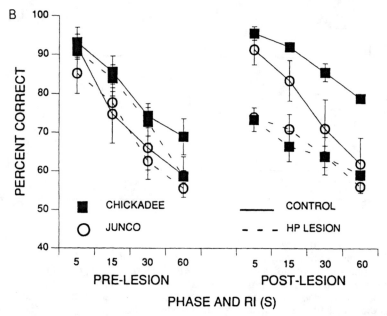

Fig. 3.4 Mean proportion correct choices ($\pm$ s.e.) of chickadees and juncos ($n = 8$) tested on the procedure shown diagrammatically in Fig. 3.3 at four retention intervals (RI), randomly intermixed. (A) The pair of lines to the left shows the overall percentage correct. Data from sample-same and sample-different trials are separated on the right. (B) Data from the same birds, subdivided into groups that received hippocampal lesions vs. control surgery, showing performance before and after surgery. Data from Hampton and Shettleworth (1996a).

control surgery without lesions. Performance of both species declined dramatically after recovery from hippocampal lesions. Performance tended to improve after control surgery, presumably because the birds had not reached asymptotic acquisition of the task before the lesions. Moreover, after lesions both chickadees and juncos performed significantly worse on sample-different than on sample-same trials, i.e. the lesions caused chickadees to perform like juncos in this respect.

The results we have described so far fit the predictions of the anatomical approach to characterizing food-storers' cognitive specializations. However, results of a second, parallel, set of experiments do not (Hampton, 1995; Hampton and Shettleworth, 1996a). In these studies, chickadees and juncos were trained in the same operant chambers as before, with similar methods. The task was similar, too: a bird was reinforced for pecking the key it had not most recently pecked. However, rather than occurring in discrete trials with a sample, retention interval, and choice, followed by an intertrial interval of 30 seconds or so before the next sample, here trials could be described as continuous spatial alternation. Both keys lit up. The bird was reinforced for pecking, say, the left. Then it had to hop to the back to the cage. At the end of the retention interval both keys lit again, and this time the bird would be reinforced for pecking the right one. Each trial continued until the bird pecked the designated correct key. Thus, the requirement was incredibly simple: peck left, hop to the back, peck right, hop to the back, peck left, and so on. Nevertheless, all the birds found alternation much more difficult than nonmatching to sample. More problematically, in three separate experiments with different groups of birds, juncos performed better than chickadees, usually when learning the task, and always when the retention interval was lengthened after acquisition. Clearly, using a procedure that can be described as 'a test of spatial memory' does not guarantee that chickadees will out-perform juncos. Moreover, because choices follow one another in quicker succession, continuous spatial alteration would appear to offer much greater potential for interference than delayed nonmatching to sample. We cannot yet explain why juncos do better than chickadees on alternation. However, the reversal of the species difference on this task is important because it means that contextual variables common to both tasks like the keypecking requirement, the sunflower seed reinforcer, the conditions of captivity, and the like, do not necessarily favor the chickadees. We can be sure that some task-specific features that differ between the two tasks are responsible for the differences in performance we observed.

Despite being spatial and being high in interference, continuous spatial alternation may not be so dependent on hippocampal function in mammals as other spatial working memory tasks (Hampton and Shettleworth, 1996a). To some extent the rigid alternation of responding it requires may be a habit supported by other parts of the brain. Be that as it may, hippocampal lesions in juncos and chickadees decreased accuracy in continuous spatial alternation just as in delayed nonmatching to sample (Hampton and Shettleworth, 1996a). It is not yet clear how to interpret this finding. One possibility is that, while involving the hippocampus, continuous spatial alternation also involves other areas of the brain where juncos might have an advantage over chickadees. Another possibility is that the whole hippocampus is too crude a unit of analysis. The lesion method and the characterization of the anatomical species differences in terms of volume need to be refined so as to focus on specific hippocampal areas, pathways or cell types (Montagnese *et al.*, 1993; Szekely and Krebs, 1993). For instance, more new cells are recruited seasonally to rostral hippocampus than to other areas (Barnea and Nottebohm, 1994). These circumscribed specializations (or peculiarities) of the hippocampus suggest that cognitive specializations may also be more circumscribed than previously thought. We have used only aspiration lesions, which are thought to disrupt fibers of passage; small lesions using chemicals that destroy only cell bodies would permit more accurate localization of the areas underlying effects on memory.

Interference

The finding that chickadees are less affected than juncos by irrelevant information from previous trials is not the only observation suggesting that food-storing species may be especially resistant to interference in memory. Another example comes from experiments in which food-storing Marsh Tits (*Parus palustris*) and nonstoring Blue Tits (*P. caeruleus*) were compared in tests of memory designed to tap into an ability required in remembering locations of stored food (Healy and Krebs, 1992a; see also Brodbeck *et al.*, 1992). In these experiments, a bird was first allowed to find a single half peanut placed in one of several similar sites in an aviary. It was then excluded from the aviary for a short retention interval. When it returned to find and finish the peanut, all the sites – holes in blocks of wood hung on the walls and/or artificial trees – were covered in some way. A bird with perfect memory should go directly to the baited site.

In a comparison of Marsh Tits and Blue Tits, Healy and Krebs (1992a) made it easy for the birds to find the peanut in the first part of each trial by leaving all the holes uncovered and marking the site of the peanut with a distinctively colored sticker. They found no significant differences between the two species. Clayton and Krebs (1993) required birds of the same two species to search for the peanut in the first part of the trial by covering up all the holes. Marsh Tits performed better in the second part of the trial than did Blue Tits. When searching vs. not searching for the peanut in the first part of the trial was compared directly within one experiment, the species differed in accuracy only when they had had to search, just as the earlier results predicted (Clayton and Krebs, 1994b). Searching for the peanut in the first part of the trial requires visiting some empty holes. Marsh Tits apparently discriminate better than Blue Tits between these holes and the hole that held the peanut, i.e. they are more resistant to interference from memories of visits to empty holes.

Having found that chickadees are more resistant than juncos to interference from memories of past rewarded responses, we probed the generality of this species difference by giving the same two species an operant test designed to simulate searching for a peanut (Hampton *et al.*, 1998). Rather than visiting blocks of wood in an aviary, the birds pecked differently colored squares at varying locations on a video monitor. In the first (study) phase of every trial, a bird encountered a rewarded sample, which was different in color and location from the last trial's sample. After a 5-second retention interval, the bird was presented with an array of three colored squares and was rewarded for pecking the one that matched that trial's sample. Trials differed in whether the bird had seen none, one or both of the incorrect stimuli in the first part of the trial, i.e. the sample to be remembered could be preceded by zero, one or two potentially interfering stimuli. The more susceptible an animal is to within-trial interference, the more its performance should fall as the number of extra samples increases. By analogy to the findings with Blue Tits and Marsh Tits, we expected chickadees to be less affected by extra stimuli in the study phase than juncos. However, the results were exactly opposite to this expectation (Fig. 3.5). In fact, juncos were completely unaffected by extra samples, whereas chickadees' performance declined with the addition of distracting samples.

We considered two interpretations of this finding. Maybe juncos' memory is so poor that they forget the extra samples right away and so, in effect, do not experience interference. If so, this would be a situation where food-storers' excellent memory makes them perform worse than nonstorers. However, in other experiments in our laboratory juncos have remembered unrewarded samples with distinctive locations and colors for up to 20 seconds or more, so it is unlikely that they had forgotten the extra samples in this study. A second possibility arises from considering more closely the nature of the interference in the delayed nonmatching to sample experiment. In that experiment, a bird should base its choices on the most recent unrewarded sample, i.e. it should use recognition memory. We described the juncos as suffering from interference because they tended instead to repeat the choice that had been rewarded on the previous trial, i.e. to use associative memory for a recently rewarded stimulus or response. If we describe the difference between juncos and chickadees as a difference in the tendency to use memory for recent rewards rather than as a difference in recognition memory for sample stimuli, we can account for the species differences in the test of interference. An animal that simply repeats a previously rewarded response (pecking the sample) will be confused by the extra samples much less than one that tends to retain information about all the samples. This notion predicts that withholding reward for the sample should cause the juncos to

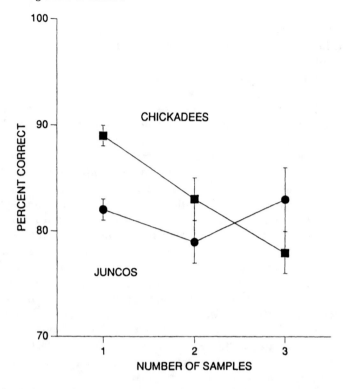

Fig. 3.5 Performance (mean ± s.e.) of chickadees and juncos (*n* = 4) in delayed matching to location plus color samples when the sample to be remembered was preceded by zero, one or two extra, potentially interfering, samples. Birds were reinforced for pecking the sample in the study phase. Chance is 33% correct, since three stimuli were always present in the test phase. If interfering stimuli had been shown, they were among the stimuli present at test. Data from Hampton *et al.* (1998).

perform like chickadees, while leaving chickadees' performance unaffected. We obtained this pattern of results in a further phase of the experiment with unrewarded samples.

But what does repeating rewarded responses or not have to do with the supposed adaptive specialization of food-storing birds? We think it could be related to the fact that birds which store one or a few food items in each cache site should not keep returning to sites they have emptied of food. Indeed, food-storing parids and corvids have the ability to do this (Sherry, 1984; Kamil *et al.*, 1993). However, avoiding emptied caches means, in effect, not returning to a place where reinforcement was obtained. Thus we would predict that scatter-hoarding species in general would be more likely to use recognition memory than associative memory when both possibilities are available. However, this notion does not explain why our results from juncos and chickadees in the operant paradigm are opposite to the results from Marsh Tits and Blue Tits performing a parallel task in an aviary. Differences in the species tested and the experimental paradigms used are obvious candidates for further investigation.

Spatial memory compared to memory for color

Food-storers use spatial cues – landmarks and overall environmental geometry – to relocate their stores (Sherry and Duff, 1996). Reliance on spatial cues makes sense because local cues near a site can change between the time an item is stored and when it is retrieved: leaves fall, snow cover comes and goes, but the spatial relationship of the site to the rest of the environment remains the same. This description of the situation facing food-storers suggests that they might be especially reliant on spatial cues relative to cues like the local color and pattern of a storage site. Brodbeck (1994) first tested this idea with chickadees and juncos trained to return to a peanut in an aviary in a task like the one described in the last section. On each trial a bird was confronted with four new feeders in new locations spread over three walls of the aviary. Once the birds were consistently performing above chance, going to the single-baited site on the first or second look in the test phase of most trials, Brodbeck asked how they were doing it by giving unrewarded tests with the cues altered. The formerly baited feeder was swapped with another feeder and the whole array of feeders was moved along the wall of the aviary in such a way as to dissociate three possible cues to the position of the bait: location relative to the room, location relative to the array of four feeders, and color of the feeder. In a series of such tests interspersed among regular rewarded trials, chickadees nearly always chose first the feeder in the 'correct' position relative to the aviary, second the correct position in the array, and third the feeder of the correct color and pattern. They showed the same pattern of choices if they had stored the peanut themselves rather than having us put it there. In contrast, juncos went first about equally often to each of the three feeders that matched the originally baited feeder in some respect, but seldom visited the fourth feeder first. Chickadees and juncos also showed this pattern of species difference in an operant matching to sample analog to the aviary task, i.e. in a setting that differs dramatically from the aviary in spatial and temporal scale (Brodbeck and Shettleworth, 1995). The methods and results of that experiment are depicted in Fig. 3.6.

A tendency to use spatial cues rather than object-centered cues like color and pattern seems to represent a robust difference between storing and nonstoring species. Clayton and Krebs (1994a) compared Marsh Tits to Blue Tits and European Jays (a food-storing corvid) to Jackdaws (nonstoring corvids), and also found that storers relied on spatial cues to a greater extent

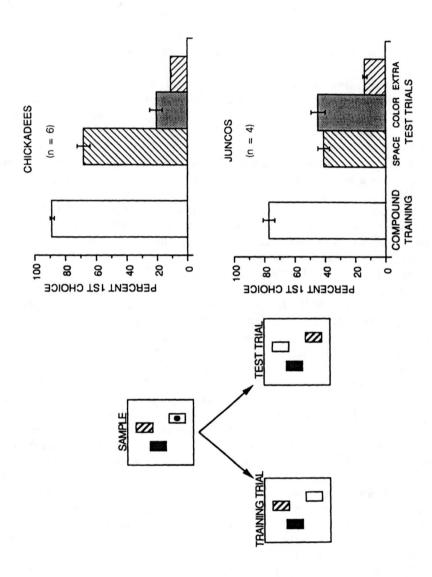

than did nonstorers. Further work with some of these species is reviewed in the chapter by Clayton and Lee, including discussion of the possibility that the relative importance of spatial cues varies seasonally in food-storing species. When Hurly and Healy (1996) gave Rufous Hummingbirds tests of memory for artificial flowers in the field, they found that, like food-storers, these birds also use spatial cues rather than color cues when the two are dissociated. Hummingbirds need accurate spatial memory like food-storers do, but they use it to relocate flowers that are good sources of nectar and avoid flowers recently emptied of nectar, so this result raises the possibility that, in general, animals that rely on accurate spatial memory in the field will be more likely to use spatial than other sorts of cues in controlled tests. Consistent with this suggestion, dissociating cues to the location of a home loft has revealed a similar reliance on spatial over local cues in homing pigeons (see chapter by Bingman *et al.*). However, recent work on Coal Tits by Jolliffe (1996) suggests some caution. Coal Tits store food, but when tested in an aviary in a similar way to Brodbeck's (1994) chickadees, they showed no preference for spatial over color and pattern cues after a 15-minute retention interval. After 24 hours, the Coal Tits had a significant tendency to choose color and pattern over location, suggesting that spatial information is forgotten more quickly in this species. Interestingly, the data from chickadees in Fig. 3.7 suggest the same thing, based on a quite different kind of test.

In the corvids and parids studied by Clayton and Krebs (1994a), tests with a blindfold over one eye or the other revealed that, in common with other birds, both the storers and the nonstorers had a hemispheric asymmetry for processing spatial information as opposed to object-centered information like color. However, when juncos and chickadees were tested with blindfolds in the operant task depicted in Fig. 3.6, only a very small hemispheric asymmetry was found (Brodbeck, Clayton and Shettleworth, unpublished data). In key-pecking tasks, birds use their frontal visual fields, where there is good

---

Fig. 3.6 Procedure and results of experiment 1b in Brodbeck and Shettleworth (1995). Juncos and chickadees were trained in an operant delayed matching to sample procedure with both color and location as relevant cues and three stimuli in the test phase of each trial (left side of figure). The square surrounding the stimuli represents the edges of a 14-inch video monitor, but stimuli are not to scale; the black dot in the sample phase indicates the sample to be remembered for that trial. When birds had achieved 80% correct in this task, occasional test trials occurred with color and location cues dissociated. Mean proportions (± s.e.) of first choices of the three possible stimuli – matching the sample in location ('space') or in color, or the third, 'extra', stimulus – on test trials are shown on the right of the figure, together with proportion of correct choices on the intermixed training trials ('compound training').

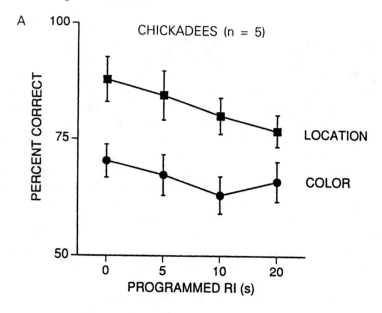

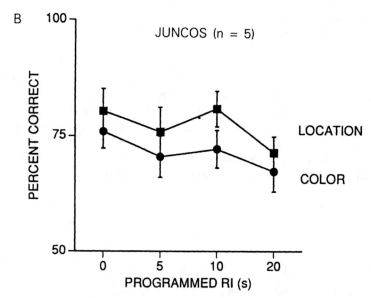

Fig. 3.7 Mean proportion correct choices ($\pm$ s.e.) made by juncos and chickadees performing delayed matching of color and location with randomly mixed retention intervals (RI) of 0–20 seconds. Each bird performed both tasks, on alternate days. Data from Shettleworth and Westwood (1998).

interocular transfer, whereas when moving about in a large space they are more likely to use the lateral fields, where transfer is poor (Goodale and Graves, 1982). If chickadees and juncos use only their frontal fields in our operant task, asymmetry should not have been expected. However, in that case the species difference in choice of color vs. space in Brodbeck and Shettleworth's (1995) operant task could not have reflected a hemispheric asymmetry. Whatever the reason, these findings indicate that food-storers' tendency to use spatial rather than object-centered cues can be obtained in tasks with a variety of demands on the visual system.

Maybe chickadees choose location first because they remember it best, while juncos remember location and object-centered cues about equally well. However, there are other ways in which the results could arise. Brodbeck and Shettleworth (1995) showed that, in the operant task, chickadees are not simply biased to choose location first when presented with conflicting but equally relevant location and color cues. When tested with location or color alone after exposure to samples defined by both color and location, chickadees performed much more accurately with location than with color while juncos performed about equally accurately with either cue. These experiments tell us what the birds do when they can use either spatial or object-centered cues like color to solve a one-trial memory problem, but it is necessary to compare memory for these two classes of cues directly by using a task in which the only cue is either color or location. Shettleworth and Westwood (1998) did this by training individual chickadees and juncos to remember location or color, on alternate days. On Monday, Wednesday and Friday, for example, a bird might be presented with colored disks as samples on the video monitor. After the retention interval, two colored disks appeared, one on each side of the sample's former location. The bird was reinforced for pecking the disk that was the same color as the sample (delayed matching to sample). On Tuesday, Thursday and Saturday, the bird performed the same task in the same apparatus, but samples were white squares that varied in location from one trial to the next, and the test stimuli were both white squares. In these sessions the birds were reinforced for matching the location of the sample. Juncos and chickadees were compared during several thousand trials of acquisition at a minimal retention interval and during three subsequent phases with retention intervals up to 40 seconds. The acquisition phase also included trials with compound color plus location samples in an attempt to discover whether chickadees and juncos divide attention differently between location and color.

Figure 3.7 shows a typical set of results from the tests of memory for location and color after exposure to single cues. Consistent with Brodbeck and Shettleworth's (1995) findings, chickadees performed significantly more accurately with location than with color, and juncos performed about the same with both. However, the chickadees did not actually perform significantly better than the juncos on the tests of spatial memory, nor was there a species × task interaction in an overall ANOVA of the data shown in Fig. 3.7. Notice that because different locations, a total of 20, were used from one trial to the next, the opportunity for between-trial interference was much less in this experiment than in Hampton and Shettleworth's (1996a) delayed nonmatching to sample experiment. This may account for the smaller species difference in spatial performance here, since the species difference in susceptibility to interference could not contribute. Also notice that chickadees performed better with location than with color samples even at the shortest retention interval. Moreover, in the data shown as well as in other parts of the experiment, a significant trial type × retention interval interaction indicated that the chickadees forgot location more quickly than color. However, at every retention interval tested, the chickadees more accurately matched the location of a sample than the color of a sample they were exposed to in an equivalent way. In this sense, they clearly remembered location better than color. However, they may have done so because they encode spatial information more quickly or accurately than color in the first place, not because they retain it better once encoded. The results of the spatial nonmatching experiment (Fig. 3.4) are also compatible with the suggestion that the species difference in performance, at least in these operant tasks, reflects a species difference in initial processing rather than in retention of information.

The results from all our comparisons of memory for location and color are consistent with the prediction of the regression approach, that food-storing species might have better spatial memory relative to some other sort of memory than nonstoring species. Figure 3.8 documents this conclusion informally in two ways with data from all the experiments from our laboratory in which both chickadees and juncos were tested. When individual birds' performance on spatial tasks is plotted against performance on the comparable color tasks (top panel), chickadees and juncos do not form completely separate populations. However, juncos are scattered around the 45° line indicating equivalent performance on location and color whereas all chickadees are above the 45° line, i.e. they all perform better on location than on matched color tests. The same picture emerges when group data are compared across experiments (Fig. 3.8B). Chickadees perform better than juncos on spatial memory tests, whereas the reverse tends to be true on tests of color memory. The one exception to this generalization is spatial delayed alternation, set apart as the triangles in Fig. 3.8. Alternation is also the one procedure for which we do not have comparable data from tests with color rather than spatial cues.

Insofar as the hippocampus is involved specifically in spatial memory as opposed to memory in general, the results summarized in Fig. 3.8 are consistent with the predictions from the species difference in hippocampus. To confirm the connection between species differences in space and color performance and species differences in hippocampus, Hampton and

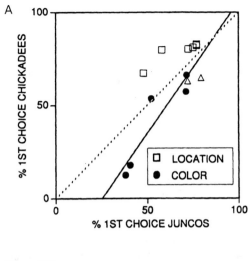

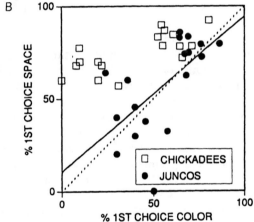

Fig. 3.8 (A) The group mean proportion first choice of location or color from all experiments in our laboratory in which both chickadees and juncos were tested. Included are studies in which the birds chose between location and color, and studies in which they were tested with location or color alone. There were two, three or four alternatives from which to choose, depending on the study. Data are from: Brodbeck (1994), experiments 4 and 5; Hampton and Shettleworth (1996a), experiments 2–4; Shettleworth and Westwood's (1998) data shown in Fig. 3.7; and Brodbeck and Shettleworth (1995). In the latter case, any birds that served in more than one experiment contributed only one data point. Data from any one experiment were averaged over all retention intervals tested. Triangles in the top panel represent spatial delayed alternation (Hampton and Shettleworth, 1996a). (B) Data from individual birds in all the studies represented in the top panel in which each bird was tested with both location and color, thus omitting data from Hampton and Shettleworth (1996a). Each point represents a different bird and is the mean over all retention intervals on which it was tested. Solid lines are regressions for juncos.

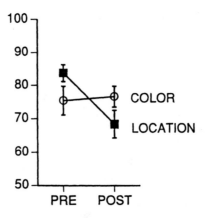

Fig. 3.9   Mean performance (± s.e.) of a group of five juncos and three chickadees matching color or location at a programmed retention interval of 5 seconds immediately before hippocampal aspiration lesions (pre) and after recovery from surgery (post). Data from Hampton and Shettleworth (1996b).

Shettleworth (1996b) performed hippocampal lesions on juncos and chick-adees trained to match both color and location as described above. Figure 3.9 shows the results. After lesioning, every bird performed worse on the test of spatial memory than before surgery, but stayed the same or even improved slightly on the procedurally similar test of memory for color. Because we tested each bird concurrently on two tasks that differed only in the nature of the information to be remembered, these data show more clearly than data from previous experiments (e.g. Sherry and Vaccarino, 1989) that, in passerine birds, the hippocampus is involved specifically in spatial memory. It has less or no involvement in working memory generally. Thus the results concur with the data from intact juncos and chickadees summarized in Fig. 3.8, as well as data from other species (Shettleworth, 1995; Balda and Kamil, Clayton and Lee, this volume) in indicating that the relatively large hippocampus of food-storing species is part of an adaptive specialization for spatial memory.

Conclusions

We started this chapter with an apparently simple question: 'Do food-storing birds have an adaptive specialization of memory?'. We argued that answering such a question is not straightforward because memory and other cognitive processes are inferences from measures of performance, and performance can be affected by many species-specific factors other than memory. Moreover, patterns of species difference in performance that are not attributable to the influence of such contextual variables may reflect a number of theoretically separable cognitive processes. Those that we have mentioned include initial processing of information (itself the outcome of perceptual discrimination abilities and attention, among other processes), susceptibility to interference and memory retentiveness. These distinctions may or may not be important for understanding what food-storing birds accomplish in the field, but they are essential for more detailed analyses of their memory and their brains.

We outlined three ways of framing the hypothesis about species differences in spatial memory: ecological comparative psychology, the regression approach, and the approach via neuroanatomy. The comparisons of chickadees and juncos summarized here have produced results consistent with each one in some respects but not others. For instance, chickadees perform better than juncos in spatial delayed nonmatching to sample and are more resistant to interference from past rewards, and these species differences appear to reflect hippocampal differences. However, in the procedurally very similar spatial delayed alternation task, juncos perform better than chickadees, yet hippocampal lesions still degrade performance in both species. Memory for location as opposed to color or other object-centered cues is becoming a theme in research that has produced results especially consistent with both a regression analysis and the neuroanatomical approach.

Much of the appeal of the kind of research discussed here and in the rest of this volume (see Kamil, this volume) lies in the possibility of tying together natural history, cognitive and neural specializations. With food-storing birds, there has been much progress in doing this, but to progress further we need further to refine our notions about all three elements of this relationship. For example, what exactly are the cognitive requirements of retrieving stored food? We do not know nearly enough about what some of these birds are doing in the wild. There are very few field data on storing and retrieving in Black-capped Chickadees, for example, yet they are used almost exclusively in North American studies of food-storing parids. Refining conceptions about the cognitive differences between species means thinking in terms of more subtle differences than just 'spatial memory', as the research reviewed here illustrates. This can go hand in hand with refining the description of the neuroanatomical species differences, from volumetric ones to differences in hippocampal regions (e.g. Barnea and Nottebohm, 1994), circuits, neurochemistry or cell types (Montagnese *et al.*, 1993). Developmental studies like those described in the chapter by Clayton and Lee are an important part of this enterprise because they show when and how species differences arise during ontogeny. Comparative studies followed up by lesion studies with more precise methods than aspiration may tell us things about the hippocampus that would not be readily revealed by lesion studies in any one species.

Finally, to return to the more general significance of research on evolutionary specializations, the data from brain and behavior in food-storing birds make sense only in the light of a modular approach to cognition. Chickadees are not generally 'smart' or 'birds with good memories' but only good at certain kinds of tasks. In fact they actually performed less well than juncos in some of our tests of memory. For instance, when Brodbeck and Shettleworth (1995) tested memory for location or color alone in birds that had been exposed to a compound of color and location, the chickadees appeared to remember only location, but juncos remembered both location and color to some extent. There is apparently a tradeoff between memory for location and memory for other cues. Similarly, chickadees' relatively poor performance on spatial delayed alternation may reflect the importance of some extrahippocampal area that has been reduced in chickadees in the interests of devoting more brain space to hippocampus. In our studies of interference, we have uncovered a situation where the chickadees' tendency to rely on recognition memory makes them more susceptible to interference than the juncos, with their greater reliance on memory of rewarded stimuli or responses (Fig. 3.7). The generality of all these findings needs to be explored with other species. It has sometimes been pointed out that evolving neural specializations may require tradeoffs, with some brain areas increasing in size at the expense of others (e.g. Healy, 1996). Small birds, with their high metabolism, would be expected to regulate the overall demands from the brain especially closely. The neural and cognitive tradeoffs required for the ability to retrieve large amounts of stored food are another area ripe for future consideration.

Acknowledgements

Preparation of this chapter and the research from our laboratory reviewed in it were supported by a research grant to the first author from the Natural Sciences and Engineering Research Council of Canada. The second author was supported in part by a Graduate Fellowship from the National Science Foundation (USA). We are grateful to Rick Westwood for help with the manuscript and all kinds of help with the experiments. We thank Hilary Broadbent, Nicky Clayton, Sue Healy, Anna Jolliffe, Louis Lefebvre and John Krebs for comments on the manuscript.

References

Andersson, M. and Krebs, J. (1978) On the evolution of hoarding behaviour. *Anim. Behav.* **26**, 707–711.

Balda, R. P. and Kamil, A. C. (1989) A comparative study of cache recovery by three corvid species. *Anim. Behav.* **38**, 486–495.

Barkow, J. H., Cosmides, L. and Tooby, J. (eds) (1992) *The Adapted Mind.* New York: Oxford University Press.

Barnea, A. and Nottebohm, F. (1994) Seasonal recruitment of hippocampal neurons in adult free-ranging black-capped chickadees. *Proc. Natl. Acad. Sci. USA* **91**, 11 217–11 221.

Bednekoff, P. A., Balda, R. P., Kamil, A. C. and Hile, A. G. (1997) Long term spatial memory in four seed-caching corvid species. *Anim. Behav.* **53**, 335–341.

Bingman, V. P., Jones, T. J., Strasser, R., Gagliardo, A. and Ioale, P. (1995) Homing pigeons, hippocampus and spatial cognition. In Alleva, E., Fasolo, A., Lipp, H. P., Nadel, L. and Ricceri, L. (eds) *Behavioral Brain Research in Naturalistic and Semi-naturalistic Settings: Possibilities and Perspectives.* Dordrecht: Kluwer Academic.

Bitterman, M. E. (1975) The comparative analysis of learning. *Science* **188**, 699–709.

Bitterman, M. E. (1996) Comparative analysis of learning in honeybees. *Anim. Learning Behav.* **24**, 123–141.

Brodbeck, D. R. (1994) Memory for spatial and local cues: A comparison of a storing and a nonstoring species. *Anim. Learning Behav.* **22**, 119–133.

Brodbeck, D. R. and Shettleworth, S. J. (1995) Matching location and color of a compound stimulus: comparison of a food-storing and a non-storing bird species. *J. Exp. Psychol. Anim. Behav. Processes* **21**, 64–77.

Brodbeck, D. R., Burack, O. R. and Shettleworth, S. J. (1992). One-trial associative memory in black-capped chickadees. *J. Exp. Psychol. Anim. Behav. Processes* **18**, 12–21.

Brodin, A. and Ekman, J. (1994) Benefits of food hoarding. *Nature* **372**, 510.

Caraco, T. (1981) Energy budgets, risk and foraging preferences in dark-eyed juncos (*Junco hyemalis*). *Behav. Ecol. Sociobiol.* **8**, 213–217.

Clayton, N. S. and Krebs, J. R. (1993) Lateralization in Paridae: comparison of a storing and a non-storing species on a one-trial associative memory task. *J. Comp. Physiol. A* **171**, 807–815.

Clayton, N. S. and Krebs, J. R. (1994a) Memory for spatial and object-specific cues in food-storing and non-storing birds. *J. Comp. Physiol. A* **174**, 371–379.

Clayton, N. S. and Krebs, J. R. (1994b) One-trial associative memory: comparison of food-storing and non-storing species of birds. *Anim. Learning Behav.* **22**, 366–372.

Ekman, J., Brodin, A., Bylin, A. and Sklepkovych, B. (1996) Selfish long-term benefits of hoarding in the Siberian jay. *Behav. Ecol.* **7**, 140–144.

Gallistel, C. R. (1990) *The Organization of Learning.* Cambridge, MA: MIT Press.

Gerlai, R. (1996) Gene targeting studies of mammalian behavior. *Trends Neurosci.* **19**, 177–183.

Goodale, M. A. and Graves, J. A. (1982) Retinal locus as a factor in interocular transfer in the pigeon. In Ingle, D. J., Goodale, M. A. and Mansfield, R. (eds) *Analysis of Visual Behavior.* Cambridge, MA: MIT Press, pp. 211–240.

Hampton, R. R. (1995) Hippocampal complex volume, spatial memory, and food-storing: comparisons between black-capped chickadees and dark-eyed juncos. Ph.D. thesis, Toronto.

Hampton, R. R. and Sherry, D. F. (1992) Food storing by Mexican chickadees and bridled titmice. *The Auk* **109**, 665–666.

Hampton, R. R. and Shettleworth, S. J. (1996a) Hippocampus and memory in a food-storing and in a non-storing bird species. *Behav. Neurosci.* **110**, 946–964.

Hampton, R. R. and Shettleworth, S. J. (1996b) Hippocampal lesions impair memory for location but not color in passerine birds. *Behav. Neurosci.* **110**, 831–835.

Hampton, R. R., Shettleworth, S. J. and Westwood, R. P. (1998) Proactive interference, recency, and associative strength: Comparisons of black-capped chickadees and dark-eyed juncos. *Anim. Learning Behav.* (in press).

Harvey, P. H. and Krebs, J. R. (1990) Comparing brains. *Science* **249**, 140–146.

Healy, S. D. (1995) Memory for objects and positions: delayed-non-matching-to-sample in storing and non-storing tits. *Q. J. Exp. Psychol.* **48B**, 179–191.

Healy, S. D. (1996) Ecological specialization in the avian brain. In Moss, C. F. and Shettleworth, S. J. (eds) *Neuroethological Studies of Cognitive and Perceptual Processes*. Boulder, CO: Westview Press, pp. 84–110.

Healy, S. D. and Krebs, J. R. (1992a) Comparing spatial memory in two species of tit: recalling a single positive location. *Anim. Learning Behav.* **20**, 121–126.

Healy, S. D. and Krebs, J. R. (1992b) Delayed-matching-to-sample by marsh tits and great tits. *Q. J. Exp. Psychol.* **45B**, 33–47.

Hilton, S. C. and Krebs, J. K. (1990) Spatial memory of four species of *Parus*: performance in an open-field analogue of a radial maze. *Q. J. Exp. Psychol.* **42B**, 345–368.

Hurly, T. A. and Healy, S. D. (1996) Memory for flowers in rufous hummingbirds: location or visual cues? *Anim. Behav.* **51**, 1149–1157.

Jolliffe, A. R. (1996) D.Phil. thesis, Department of Zoology, Oxford University.

Kamil, A. C. (1988) A synthetic approach to the study of animal intelligence. In Leger, D. W. (ed.) *Comparative Perspectives in Modern Psychology: Nebraska Symposium on Motivation*, Vol. 35. Lincoln, NE: University of Nebraska Press, pp. 230–257.

Kamil, A. C., Balda, R. P., Olson, D. J. and Good, S. (1993) Returns to emptied cache sites by Clark's nutcrackers, *Nucifraga columbiana*: a puzzle revisited. *Anim. Behav.* **45**, 241–252.

Kamil, A. C., Balda, R. P. and Olson, D. J. (1994) Performance of four seed-caching corvid species in the radial-arm maze analog. *J. Comp. Psychol.* **108**, 385–393.

Lefebvre, L. (1996). Ecological correlates of social learning: problems and solutions for the comparative method. *Behav. Processes* **35**, 163–171.

Lefebvre, L. and Giraldeau, L.-A. (1996) Is social learning an adaptive specialization? In Heyes, C. M. and Galef, B. G. (eds) *Social Learning in Animals: The Roots of Culture*. San Diego, CA: Academic Press, pp. 107–128.

Mackintosh, N. J. (1994) Intelligence in evolution. In Khalfa, J. (ed.) *What is Intelligence?* Cambridge: Cambridge University Press.

Macphail, E. M. (1982) *Brain and Intelligence in Vertebrates.* Oxford: Clarendon Press.

Macphail, E. M. (1987) The comparative psychology of intelligence. *Behav. Brain Sci.* **10**, 645–695.

Mayford, M., Abel, T. and Kandel, E. R. (1995) Transgenic approaches to cognition. *Curr. Opin. Neurobiol.* **5**, 141–148.

Montagnese, C. M., Krebs, J. R., Szekely, A. D. and Csillag, A. (1993) A subpopulation of large calbindin-like immunopositive neurones is present in the hippocampal formation in food-storing but not in non-storing species of bird. *Brain Res.* **614**, 291–300.

Moss, C. F. and Shettleworth, S. J. (eds) (1996) Neuroethological Studies of Cognitive and Perceptual Processes. Boulder, CO: Westview Press.

Nilsson, J.-A., Kallander, H. and Persson, O. (1993) A prudent hoarder: effects of long-term hoarding in the European nuthatch, *Sitta europaea. Behav. Ecol.* **4**, 369–373.

Olson, D. J. (1991) Species differences in spatial memory among Clark's nutcrackers, scrub jays, and pigeons. *J. Exp. Psychol. Anim. Behav. Processes* **17**, 363–376.

Olson, D. J., Kamil, A. C., Balda, R. P. and Nims, P. J. (1995) Performance of four seed-caching corvid species in operant tests of nonspatial and spatial memory. *J. Comp. Psychol.* **109**, 173–181.

Petersen, K. and Sherry, D. F. (1996) No sex difference occurs in the hippocampus, food-storing, or memory for food caches in black-capped chickadees. *Behav. Brain Res.* **79**, 15–22.

Ridley, M. (1993) *Evolution.* Oxford: Blackwell Scientific.

Roberts, W. A. and Grant, D. S. (1976) Studies of short-term memory in the pigeon using the delayed matching to sample procedure. In Medin, D. L., Roberts, W. A. and Davis, R. T. (eds) *Processes of Animal Memory.* Hillsdale, NJ: Lawrence Erlbaum Associates, pp. 79–112.

Rozin, P. and Kalat, J. (1971) Specific hungers and poison avoidance as adaptive specializations of learning. *Psychol. Rev.* **78**, 459–486.

Shapiro, M. L. and Olton, D. S. (1994) Hippocampal function and interference. In Schacter, D. L. and Tulving, E. (eds) *Memory Systems 1994.* Cambridge, MA: MIT Press.

Sherry, D. (1984) Food storage by black-capped chickadees: memory for the location and contents of caches. *Anim. Behav.* **32**, 451–464.

Sherry, D. F. and Duff, S. J. (1996) Behavioural and neural bases of orientation in food-storing birds. *J. Exp. Biol.* **199**, 165–172.

Sherry, D. and Vaccarino, A. L. (1989) Hippocampus and memory for food caches in black-capped chickadees. *Behav. Neurosci.* **103**, 308–318.

Sherry, D. F., Jacobs, L. F. and Gaulin, S. J. C. (1992) Spatial memory and adaptive specialization of the hippocampus. *Trends Neurosci.* **15**, 298–303.

Sherry, D. F., Jacobs, L. F. and Gaulin, S. J. C. (1993) Reply. *Trends Neurosci.* **16**, 57.

Shettleworth, S. J. (1993) Where is the comparison in comparative cognition?

Alternative research programs. *Psychol. Sci.* **4**, 179–184.

Shettleworth, S. J. (1995) Comparative studies of memory in food storing birds: from the field to the Skinner box. In Alleva, E., Fasolo, A., Lipp, H. P., Nadel, L. and Ricceri, L. (eds) *Behavioral Brain Research in Naturalistic and Semi-Naturalistic Settings*. Dordrecht: Kluwer Academic, pp. 159–194.

Shettleworth, S. J. and Westwood, R. P. (1998) Memory for places and colors in black-capped chickadees (*Parus atricapillus*) and dark-eyed juncos (*Junco hyemalis*) (in preparation).

Shettleworth, S. J., Krebs, J. R., Healy, S. D. and Thomas, C. M. (1990) Spatial memory of food-storing tits (*Parus ater* and *P. atricapillus*): comparison of storing and nonstoring tasks. *J. Comp. Psychol.* **104**, 71–81.

Squire, L. R. (1993) The hippocampus and spatial memory. *Trends Neurosci.* **16**, 56–57.

Stevens, T. A. and Krebs. J. R. (1986) Retrieval of stored seeds by marsh tits *Parus palustris* in the field. *Ibis* **128**, 513–525.

Szekely, A. D. and Krebs, J. R. (1993) More hippocampal nitric oxide synthase in food-storing than in non-storing birds. *Society for Neuroscience Abstracts*.

Tooby, J. and Cosmides, L. (1995) Mapping the evolved functional organization of mind and brain. In Gazzaniga, M. (ed.) *The Cognitive Neurosciences*. Cambridge, MA: MIT Press, pp. 1185–1197.

Vander Wall, S. B. (1990) *Food Hoarding in Animals*. Chicago: University of Chicago Press.

Vander Wall, S. B. and Balda, R. P. (1981) Ecology and evolution of food-storage behavior in conifer-seed-caching corvids. *Z. Tierpsychol.* **56**, 217–242.

4

Memory and the Hippocampus in Food-storing Birds

N. S. Clayton and D. W. Lee

Section of Neurobiology, Physiology and Behavior, Division of Biological Sciences, University of California Davis, Davis, CA 95616, USA

Introduction

The relationship between memory and the hippocampus has been of great interest to neuroscientists for many years. Although the hippocampus has been shown to be involved with a number of types of learning, it is clear that this brain region is especially important for the formation of memories about the spatial aspects of the environment (O'Keefe and Nadel, 1978; Nadel, 1991). Much of this research has focused on the mammalian hippocampus. Since most of the animal experiments have used laboratory rodents or primates as models, it is unclear whether theories of hippocampal function derived from these experiments can be generalized to animals which have been tested in more naturalistic settings (see Jacobs, 1995, for an elaboration of this issue). Experiments performed under naturalistic or seminaturalistic conditions are important in establishing what role the hippocampus plays in memory, in the appropriate behavioral, evolutionary and ecological context. As is often the case in behavioral neuroscience, interdisciplinary studies of the brain and natural behavior of animals with highly specialized capacities, such as those of food-storing birds, may add to our general understanding of memory and its neural substrates for two reasons. First, birds are particularly suited for such studies because they show the most sophisticated and complex forms of memory-based spatial behavior

ANIMAL COGNITION IN NATURE
ISBN 0-12-077030-X

including migration, homing and food-storing (Bingman, 1993). Second, the avian brain is remarkably plastic: learning episodes produce dramatic changes in the rates of cell birth and death, and in the overall size of specific brain regions in response to current memory demands.

Recent studies have capitalized on the relationship between spatial memory and the hippocampus by addressing questions about the concomitant development of both the brain and behavior of food-storing birds (Clayton, 1995a). An investigation of the development of the avian hippocampal formation (HF) and memory-based retrieval of caches in food-storing birds sheds considerable light on our understanding of neuronal plasticity and hippocampal function (Clayton and Krebs, 1995a). In this chapter, three basic questions concerning hippocampal function and neuronal plasticity will be addressed. First, how does the hippocampus change as a result of experiences during ontogeny? Second, what types of experiences are necessary to trigger changes in the hippocampus? And third, how do these ontogenetic changes relate to seasonal changes in hippocampal morphology? A brief introduction to avian/mammalian hippocampal homology will be followed by a discussion of each of these questions in turn.

As discussed in detail in the chapters by Balda and Kamil, and Shettleworth and Hampton, food-storing parids (chickadees and titmice), corvids (magpies, crows, nutcrackers and jays) and sittids (nuthatches) have evolved a remarkable feat of memory. Having hidden hundreds to thousands of food caches, each of which is typically hidden in a separate site and scattered throughout their territory, these birds use memory to retrieve their caches when they return hours to months later (e.g. Sherry *et al.*, 1981; Vander Wall and Balda, 1981; Shettleworth and Krebs, 1982; Balda and Kamil, 1989; Petersen and Sherry, 1998). This memory is remarkable in a number of respects: (1) it is based on a single brief visit during which the item was hidden; (2) the spatial location of a large number of items must be remembered and (3) the information must be retained over long periods of time. For example, food-storing birds show accurate retention of large numbers of locations over 285 days in Clark's Nutcrackers (Balda and Kamil, 1992) and 40 days in Willow Tits (Brodin and Eckman, 1994). Observations of food caching in the field allow one to estimate by extrapolation, that an individual bird probably stores somewhere between 10 000 and 100 000 items per year, rarely if ever reusing the same storage sites (Stevens and Krebs, 1986). In the wild, the time-scale over which caches are retrieved is in the range of a few days to a few weeks for members of the parid family (Brodin and Eckman, 1994), whilst in the crow family, some species, e.g. European Jay, *Garrulus glandarius*, retrieve their caches more than 6 months after storage (Bossema, 1979). Long-term storers such as jays and nutcrackers tend to harvest seeds in the autumn and store them for retrieval during the winter or the following spring, while the shorter-term storers in the tit family hoard and retrieve continually, albeit with seasonal peaks of activity.

Food-storing birds also possess an evolutionary specialization of the brain. A region of the dorsomedial cortex, referred to as HF to indicate that it includes both the hippocampus proper and the parahippocampus, tends to be enlarged in species which store and retrieve hidden food caches. This brain region is known to play a role in successful retrieval of stored food since birds with HF lesions continue to store, but cannot remember where they have stored (Krushinskya, 1966; Sherry and Vaccarino, 1989). Comparisons of diverse families of birds show that HF is not only relatively larger but also contains more neurons in species which store food than in those which do not (Krebs *et al.*, 1989; Sherry *et al.*, 1989). Among closely related food-storing species that engage in different amounts of food storing, relative hippocampal volume tends to be correlated positively with the number and/or length of time over which caches are left (Healy and Krebs, 1992; Hampton *et al.*, 1995; Basil *et al.*, 1996). One exception to this is the Pinyon Jay, which caches hundreds of items each autumn and winter, yet appears to possess a relatively small HF (Basil *et al.*, 1996; see Balda and Kamil, and Kamil, this volume).

A number of researchers have speculated that a large HF, relative to telencephalon and body size, is thought to reflect the increased demands on visuospatial cognition that may accompany scatter-hoarding of food (see Shettleworth and Hampton, this volume). This relationship is thought to be an example of a more general correlation between hippocampal volume and the importance of visuospatial cognition in the wild which occurs in several avian and mammalian species (Sherry *et al.*, 1992, 1993; Healy *et al.*, 1996; Reboreda *et al.*, 1996). To summarize, food-storing birds generally have an enlarged HF, and successful cache retrieval is a hippocampally dependent task which relies at least in part on an accurate, long-lasting memory for individual cache sites. These two findings have led to the use of the food-storing system as a model for investigating fundamental questions about the relationship between hippocampus and spatial memory in a naturalistic environment.

The avian hippocampal formation

In order to justify drawing comparisons between the avian HF and mammalian hippocampus, it is important to demonstrate that the two structures are homologous. Despite initial skepticism, there is now a substantial body of evidence to suggest that this is the case (Bingman, 1993). In terms of embryology, the avian and mammalian hippocampi emerge from the same portion of telencephalon (Källen, 1962). Another similarity is that both share the same cell types including pyramidal cells (Molla *et al.*, 1986). Connectivity to other regions of the brain such as the septum, hypothalamus, brainstem nuclei and sensory processing areas show similarities, although there are some differences (Cassini *et al.*, 1986). The presence of the same types of neurotransmitters and transmitter-related enzymes in both the mammalian and avian hippocampus also suggests homology (Erichsen *et al.*, 1991; Krebs *et al.*, 1991). Furthermore, both structures show long-term potentiation of synaptic responses (e.g. Bliss and Lomo, 1973, for mammals; Wieraszko and Ball, 1991, for birds). Finally, and perhaps the most striking similarity of all, both structures have maintained the ability for neurogenesis in adulthood (e.g. Kaplan and Hinds, 1977; Bayer, 1982; Kaplan and Bell, 1984; Kempermann *et al.*, 1997, for mammals; Alvarez-Buylla *et al.*, 1988, 1992; Nordeen and Nordeen, 1990; Patel *et al.*, 1997b, for birds). None the less, there are some marked differences between the avian HF and mammalian hippocampus. For example, the avian HF lacks distinct structures such as the dentate gyrus, Ammon's horn and mossy fibers (Bingman, 1993) and NMDA-dependent long-term potentiation has been found only on homing pigeons and not in nonhoming pigeons (Wieraszko and Ball, 1993; Shapiro and Wieraszko, 1996). Given the 250 million years in which birds and mammals have diverged and evolved independently, it is not surprising that there are some anatomical differences between the two. In summary, the evidence that the avian HF is homologous to the mammalian hippocampus is persuasive.

Although structural differences exist, there appear to be a number of functional similarities between the avian HF and mammalian hippocampus (Nadel, 1991), not least of which is the correlation between food-storing behavior and enlargement of the hippocampal formation. For example, relative hippocampal volume is larger in scatter-hoarding mammals such as the Mirriam's Kangaroo Rat than in larder-hoarders, such as the Bannertail Kangaroo Rat (Jacobs, 1995). Second, lesions of HF in Black-capped Chickadees (Sherry and Vaccarino, 1989; Hampton and Shettleworth, 1996) suggest that the avian HF is involved in spatial memory, but not memory for visual cues, namely the same types of learning shown to be dependent upon an intact hippocampus in rodents (O'Keefe and Nadel, 1978; Olton, 1983; but see Rawlins *et al.*, 1993). Furthermore, small ibotenic acid lesions of the Zebra Finch hippocampus impair spatial but not color one-trial associative learning (Patel *et al.*, 1997a). A third similarity with mammalian studies of hippocampal function is that avian HF seems likely to be involved in consolidation but is probably not the site of memory storage, since lesions impair the acquisition of new information as opposed to the consolidation of established memories, at least in homing pigeons (reviewed by Bingman, 1993). Recent studies on the Zebra Finch hippocampus also indicate that the acquisition of new spatial memories is impaired when birds are given the aromatase inhibitor, fadrozole, but there is no effect on spatial memories that were acquired prior to the drug treatment (Clayton *et al.*, 1997). Interestingly, fadrozole treatment also results in about a 30% shrinkage in hippocampal volume in Zebra Finches (Saldanha *et al.*, 1997). Fourth, studies of hippocampal function in humans and primates have suggested that the hippocampus is important in various forms of long-term memory (LTM), whereas short-term memory (STM) does not depend upon an intact hippocampus (reviewed by Squire *et al.*, 1993). To date, only one study has investigated the effects of lesions on LTM for cache sites in birds (Krushinskya, 1966): when long retention intervals separated the storage of seeds from the opportunity to retrieve them, Eurasian Nutcrackers with lesions of the hyperstriatum (including HF) were significantly impaired in their attempts to retrieve. These results suggest that avian and mammalian hippocampi share striking functional similarities. Since the anatomical organization of HF is markedly different from that of the mammalian hippocampus, this raises the question of whether or not the two do a similar job but in different ways (Clayton, 1995a). Furthermore, since both the mammalian and avian hippocampus undergo neurogenesis even in adulthood, the two key questions may be, first, how does this process differ between the two, if at all?, and second, what role, if any, does the birth of new hippocampal neurons play in memory formation?.

How does ontogeny affect hippocampal change?

Comparative studies of relative hippocampal volume in food-storing and nonstoring species of corvids (Healy and Krebs, 1993) and parids (Healy *et al.*, 1994) show that while adult food-storing and nonstoring species differ in relative hippocampal volume, the nestlings do not. Thus, the species difference in hippocampal volume arises at a relatively late stage in development, after the young birds have fledged from the nest. This result raises the possibility that relative hippocampal growth is associated with some aspect of the experience of food-storing behavior. The hypothesis has been tested in detail by studying the development of food-storing behavior, memory and hippocampal anatomy in hand-raised, postfledging, juvenile Marsh Tits. Food-storing behavior begins around the time of nutritional independence (day 35) and involves a number of behavioral changes which occur rapidly over a period of 10 days: the birds become more dexterous at handling seeds, they leave their caches for longer periods of time before retrieving them, and they become more efficient in how quickly they store seeds and how well they hide them (Clayton, 1992). There is a sudden increase in number of items stored at day 44 (Clayton, 1994). This sudden increase in food caching on day 44 has also been observed recently in two other species of parids, the Coal Tit, *Parus ater* (Jolliffe, 1996; Jolliffe and Clayton, in prep.) and the Mountain Chickadee, *Parus gambeli* (Clayton, 1998). This sudden increase in food caching appears to be age dependent rather than experience dependent (Clayton, 1994), whereas memory-based retrieval performance increases gradually after the onset in food storing. If birds are prevented from storing and retrieving caches until after day 44, the behavior develops rapidly when the opportunity is presented at a later stage.

This result suggests that there is no sensitive period during which experience has to be obtained, at least within the range tested between day 35 and 115, which represents about half the typical life span of a Marsh Tit (Clayton, 1994).

By giving hand-raised Marsh Tits the opportunity to store and retrieve food at different ages, and by measuring the volume of the hippocampal formation, Clayton and Krebs (1994a) showed that the experience of storing and retrieving food results in increased hippocampal volume and neuron number. Age-matched control birds that were prevented from storing and retrieving caches but identical in all other respects had much smaller hippocampal volumes. These control birds also had a higher percentage of apoptotic (dead) cells than did experienced birds. This suggests that one effect of experience is to trigger recruitment of neurons, while the lack of experience may cause cell loss. The experience-dependent hippocampal changes could be triggered rapidly over a period of 24 days in which the birds received only eight food-storing and retrieval tests, once every third day. This effect has also been replicated in Coal Tits (Clayton *et al.*, 1998) and Mountain Chickadees (Clayton, in press) which suggests that the effects of food-storing experience on hippocampal growth are not exclusive to the Marsh Tit.

It would be of great interest to test whether hippocampal growth is also associated with food-storing experience in members of the crow and nuthatch families because food caching has evolved independently in the parids, corvids and sittids. Preliminary results indicate that, while many aspects of the developmental sequence of food storing are similar in parids, corvids and sittids (Clayton, personal observation), the onset of food storing occurs much earlier in corvids than in the sittids and parids. The development of food storing and cache retrieval is being studied in three species of corvid: the Yellow-billed Magpie, *Pica nutalli* (Clayton and Lee, personal observation), the European Magpie, *Pica pica* (Clayton and Jolliffe, personal observation) and the Scrub Jay, *Aphelocoma coerulescens* (Clayton, personal observation). In all three of these corvid species, the young birds begin to cache around the time of fledging by hiding regurgitated food.

It is important to note that experienced birds in the parid developmental studies differed from controls in only two respects: (1) they were provided with whole seeds, not powdered seeds, to eat and store; and (2) they could store and retrieve. Experienced birds did not differ from controls in the number of visits to potential cache sites, nor were there any other obvious differences in motivation or hunger levels. Thus, it would appear that some aspect of the specific experience of storing and retrieving caches is associated with hippocampal growth, while the absence of this experience results in hippocampal attrition. To test whether hippocampal growth precedes or accompanies changes in food-storing behavior, Clayton (1996) sacrificed birds one trial before (day 41), and one trial after (day 47), the sudden increase in food storing and associated increased demands on memory-based retrieval of caches. Experienced birds had larger absolute and relative hippocampal volumes than did controls at all stages of this experiment. Thus, a difference in hippocampal growth between experienced and control birds can be detected by day 41, 3 days before the relatively sudden increase in food-storing intensity. It is not known, however, when this hippocampal growth first appears and how much experience is actually necessary to trigger the increase in volume. Since adult food-storing and nonstoring species differ in relative hippocampal volume, but nestlings do not (Healy and Krebs, 1993; Healy *et al.*, 1994), it would be of interest to determine at what age this difference becomes apparent and whether it corresponds to the actual initiation of storing and memory-based retrieval or whether a critical number of such experiences is needed. Furthermore, since storing in corvids appears before fledging (Clayton, personal observation), the temporal pattern of hippocampal growth and attrition may be very different from that of parids.

These results may be taken to support the hypothesis that hippocampal growth occurs in preparation for food storing, rather than accompanying or following changes in food storing. However, why is HF enlargement and increase in neuron number confined to birds in the experienced groups? Control birds received virtually the same visual stimulation, motor experience and diet as experienced birds, so it seems unlikely that the difference between the groups could be accounted for in terms of a general deprivation vs. enrichment effect. Perhaps the presence of whole seeds, or the opportunity to store and retrieve just one or two seeds, acts as a switch to trigger hippocampal growth. Either way, there appears to be an increase in relative hippocampal volume, and total neuron number, in preparation for the increased memory demands associated with the increase in food storing that does not occur unless some minimal experience with food storing and retrieving is obtained (Clayton, 1996).

These volumetric changes in HF are correlated with changes in total numbers of neurons, rather than with changes in cell size or density (Healy and Krebs, 1993; Healy *et al.*, 1994; Clayton and Krebs, 1994a). A critical question concerns the relative importance of cell birth and programmed cell death since the total number of neurons in HF is a function of the rate of programmed cell death and the rate of cell proliferation within the ventricular zone. Studies by Patel *et al.* (1997b) have tested whether or not the volumetric changes in HF are accompanied by changes in cell birth, and whether cell birth occurs before, after, or at the same time as changes in hippocampal volume. Patel *et al.* (1997b) investigated cell birth and cell death in the hippocampus of the experienced and control birds that were sacrificed either one trial before, or one trial after, the sudden increase in food storing. They found that there was a significantly higher rate of cell proliferation in the ventricular zone adjacent to HF in experienced birds. This effect of experience on rates of cell proliferation was not significant for the ventricular zone adjacent to neostriatum. This result suggests that the effects of experience were localized, rather than having a general effect throughout the brain. Furthermore, these differences between experienced and control birds are evident by day 41, the time at which volumetric changes are apparent. In fact, the effect of experience was greatest after the third trial, at day 41. It is important to determine where new cells migrate and whether they are neurons or glial cells, but these data provide a promising starting-point for future studies. Further work is required to provide a more detailed analysis of the time course of the neurological events and to ascertain: (1) the relative contributions of cell birth and programmed cell death to the morphological changes; (2) the types of experience which trigger these events; (3) whether memory formation is a necessary condition for overall hippocampal change and (4) whether food-storing experience stimulates the same processes of cell birth and cell death as season and photoperiod.

What types of experience trigger hippocampal change?

In another series of experiments, Clayton (1995b) trained both hand-raised Marsh Tits (food storer) and Blue Tits (nonstorer) from day 35 to day 200 on a one-trial associative memory task in which birds were rewarded for returning to the feeder where they had eaten part of a peanut 20 minutes earlier. As described in detail in the chapter by Shettleworth and Hampton, this one-trial associative learning or 'peanut shopping' task does not require the bird to store food, but captures some of the essential aspects of food-storing memory in that the bird has to: (1) learn an association between food and its unique location on the basis of one visit; (2) remember the site using visuospatial cues; and (3) revisit the site 2 hours later in order to obtain the reward. The one-trial associative memory task is therefore a useful tool to assay species differences in the development of memory and HF, and particularly for comparing differences between food-storing and nonstoring species. In Marsh Tits, experience of the one-trial associative memory task triggered hippocampal growth in the same way as food-storing experience (Fig. 4.1), but there was no effect of experience on HF volume in Blue Tits (Fig. 4.2).

These results suggest that memory experiences other than food storing may trigger hippocampal growth, at least in the food-storing species, and that the HF of food storers may differ from that of nonstorers in having the potential to respond to this experience. However, an alternative explanation would be that the species differ in the way they learn to solve the task. For example, Sherry and Vaccarino (1989) have found that the avian HF in Black-capped Chickadees is important for solving spatial tasks but not color-discrimination tasks. Comparative tests of memory in the laboratory suggest that food storers may use predominantly spatial cues whereas nonstorers also use color cues

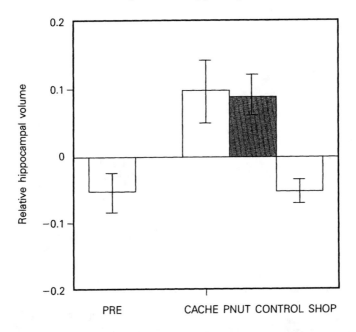

Fig. 4.1 The mean and standard error of the relative hippocampal volume of four groups of juvenile Marsh Tits that were either sacrificed prior to the start of the experiment at 35 days posthatch (PRE) or at 200 days posthatch (CACHE, PNUT SHOP and CONTROL birds) Both the CACHE and PNUT SHOP birds had been trained and tested on the one-trial associative memory task whereas CONTROL birds had not. CACHE birds were allowed to store and retrieve food whereas PNUT SHOP and CONTROL birds were prevented from caching and retrieving seeds by maintaining them on a diet of powdered food. The relative hippocampal volume per bird was calculated by plotting one linear regression of log hippocampal volume and log telencephalon volume, and calculating the deviations from the regression line.

(Brodbeck, 1994; Clayton and Krebs, 1994b). If the task is a spatial, hippocampally dependent one for the food-storing species but not for the nonstoring species, then this might explain why the HF of food storers responds to this experience, whereas the nonstoring HF does not.

What then of memory tasks that do not require the hippocampus? If it is memory formation, rather than nonmemory experiences related to food storing and retrieving, that triggers hippocampal growth, then logically it would follow that memory experiences which do not rely on the hippocampus should not stimulate its growth. It seems clear that experiences which involve the formation of memory for previously encountered food can trigger gross morphological changes in the brains of food-storing birds. To determine whether these changes occur as a result of memory or other nonmemory

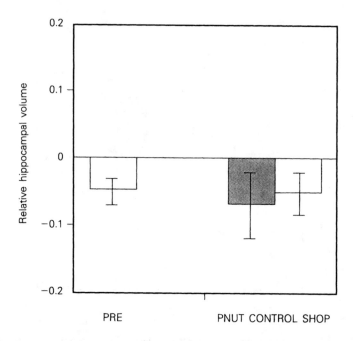

Fig. 4.2 The mean and standard error of the relative hippocampal volume of three groups of juvenile Blue Tits that were either sacrificed prior to the start of the experiment at 35 days posthatch (PRE) or at 200 days posthatch (PNUT SHOP and CONTROL birds). PNUT SHOP birds had been trained and tested on the one-trial associative memory task whereas CONTROL birds had not. For other details, see legend for Fig. 4.1.

factors related to finding food, at least three basic criteria must be met: (1) the morphological changes must be specific to the hippocampus and not involve structures unrelated to the memory task at hand; (2) the formation of these memories must depend upon hippocampal function and (3) memory formation not dependent upon an intact hippocampus should not stimulate growth of this area. One approach which may prove useful in this respect is to design studies which tease out the effects of hippocampally dependent vs. hippocampally independent memory formation on the subsequent growth or attrition of the developing hippocampus.

Previous studies have shown that the developing brain of both birds and mammals, including the mammalian hippocampal region, is plastic in response to specific kinds of sensory input or experience and to hormonal influences, but the results for food-storing birds are unique in having the following combination of features (Clayton and Krebs, 1994a). First, the effect of experience is independent of age within the range tested which represented about one third of their average life span. This is in contrast to effects of visual experience on the development of the visual cortex in mammals (see reviews in Raushecker and Marler, 1987). Second, the effect is specific, both in terms of experience because control and experienced birds did not differ in experience other than the specific task of storing and retrieving food, and in terms of the localization of the effect. It is not an effect following general kinds of environmental enrichment as that resulting in cortical growth in rats (e.g. Rosenzweig *et al.*, 1962; Rosenzweig, 1984; Cramer, 1988; Kempermann *et al.*, 1997). Third, growth of the hippocampus appears to be triggered by some aspect of memory for retrieving previously encountered food.

Specificity of the experience-dependent effects

The experience-dependent effects seem to be specific in that experience triggers growth of the hippocampus but not growth of another telencephalic brain region, the ectostriatum (ECTO), or the telencephalon as a whole (Clayton and Krebs, 1994a). This result suggests that specific kinds of memory experience can stimulate growth of a specific area of the brain. However, to ensure that any volumetric differences are really specific to the HF, other brain regions which do not have connections with HF but may be affected by such complex experience should be measured. Doupe (1994) has suggested that another potential candidate is the paleostriatum.

Work on Zebra Finches using the *Phaseolus vulgaris* leucoagglutin (PHAL) as an anterograde tracer (Székely and Krebs, 1993) has shown that HF has major connections with a number of other brain regions which have been implicated in learning and memory, including the hyperstriatum ventrale (HV), the archistriatum (ARCHI) and the lobus parolfactorius (LPO). Nuclei within these regions are thought to be involved in imprinting and/or passive avoidance learning (Horn, 1985; Rose, 1992). These brain regions also show up-regulation of *c-fos* expression following food storing in Marsh Tits (Székely *et al.*, 1993; Clayton and Krebs, 1995b), which suggests that they form part of a distributed memory circuit in the avian brain. In order to understand how the hippocampus responds to experience, it is crucial that growth and attrition in these other brain regions are investigated.

The extent of brain plasticity

The ontogenetic studies on hippocampal growth in Marsh Tits also raise the possibility that older experienced birds may respond to food-storing experience or the lack thereof in the same way as juveniles during their first food-storing opportunity. If birds are prevented from storing and retrieving caches until after the time period when storing would normally be first observed, the behavior develops rapidly when the opportunity is presented at a later stage (Clayton, 1994). To date only one study has addressed the possibility that adult birds may show similar behavioral and neurobiological plasticity: Cristol (cited in Krebs *et al.*, 1996) compared wild-caught adult Willow Tits which were given intensive experience of food storing and retrieval over a 4-week period with a control group that were prevented from food storing during the same period. The two groups did not differ in relative hippocampal volume. Unfortunately, the Willow Tits used in this study were very old (>4 years) and the sample size was small. The study needs to be repeated to test whether food-storing experience can stimulate hippocampal growth in adult birds or whether the prevention of storing could result in hippocampal regression and, if so, whether or not these changes are irreversible. It would seem fundamental to our understanding of brain plasticity to determine whether morphological changes found in juveniles also occur in adults and, if they do, whether such changes involve the same processes. Volumetric changes in the HF of food-storing birds are correlated with changes in total numbers of neurons, rather than with changes in cell size or density (Healy and Krebs, 1993; Healy *et al.*, 1994); and both cell birth and programmed cell death may be important, but the ratio of the two may vary depending on conditions. For example, volumetric changes in adults might result largely from changes in rates of cell birth, whereas the volumetric changes which occur during the first opportunity to store and retrieve food may result largely from differences in programmed cell death. A related question is whether food-storing experience triggers the same processes of cell birth and death as season and photoperiod.

Developmental vs. seasonal changes in hippocampal morphology

While some aspect of storing and retrieving food undoubtedly triggers hippocampal growth in juvenile birds, there is also some evidence that hippocampal growth and attrition may occur on a seasonal basis. Both field observations and laboratory studies suggest that food-storing behavior has an annual cycle: in parids, it is more marked in autumn and winter than in spring and early summer (Odum, 1942; Haftorn, 1956; Ludescher, 1980) Some corvids (e.g. European Jay) store more food, spend more time hiding caches, and leave them for longer periods in the autumn than in the spring (Bossema, 1979; Clayton *et al.*, 1996). There are also seasonal changes in HF. Smulders *et al.* (1995) found in Black-capped Chickadees that HF was larger, relative to the rest of the brain, in October than at other times of year. Barnea and Nottebohm (1994) reported an increased level of cell birth in wild Black-capped Chickadees during October, when food-storing activity increased. Unfortunately, these two studies did not include a nonstoring control species and, therefore, it is unclear whether the changes are linked to food storing or reflect a more general seasonal effect such as changes in territory use and reproductive status. Seasonal volumetric changes are observed in other brain areas, namely the avian song control nuclei (Nottebohm, 1981). In the case of the song control nuclei, the neuroanatomical alterations probably result from changing levels of circulating steroid hormones associated with reproduction rather than as a direct result of changes in singing behavior or song learning (Brenowitz, 1992). It is not yet clear whether or not the volumetric changes in HF are under the same hormonal control as the song control nuclei. Additional studies need to be performed to test whether or not seasonal changes in hippocampal volume are correlated specifically with the experience of food storing and the formation of new spatial memories, and whether or not they are to be found only in species which store.

In more controlled laboratory experiments, Shettleworth *et al.* (1995) and Krebs *et al.* (1996) manipulated what they termed 'photoperiod' (actually day length and temperature) to create 'autumn' or 'spring' conditions in Black-capped Chickadees. The autumn birds showed much higher levels of food storing than did the spring birds. As both day length and temperature were manipulated it is not clear which factors affected food-storing behavior. Since seasonal changes in food storing are accompanied by hippocampal changes in the wild (Barnea and Nottebohm, 1994; Smulders *et al.*, 1995), Krebs *et al.* (1996) tested whether photoperiodically driven differences in food-storing behavior were accompanied by changes in relative hippocampal volume. No such differences were found. However, birds were allowed to store and retrieve only in their home cages and seeds were visible at all times, so it seems likely that the birds were not using memory to retrieve their caches. Given that the hippocampus plays a role in memory for cache sites rather than in the motivation to store, it is not clear why such manipulations should induce volumetric changes in HF. The critical test would be to allow birds to store in an environment where they use memory to retrieve their caches. An obvious question to ask is if photoperiod-induced changes in food storing are associated with (1) changes in HF, and (2) changes in memory for hippocampally dependent tasks. If so, do these changes result directly from photoperiod manipulations or secondarily from changes in food-storing intensity?

Clayton and Cristol (1996) addressed these questions in adult Marsh Tits by manipulating photoperiod, independent of temperature. Birds were provided with the opportunity to store and retrieve seeds in both the home cage and in an observation chamber where caches were hidden so that they had to rely on memory-based retrieval. Food-storing intensity was recorded in the two conditions. Birds were also tested for their performance on a series of tests of memory for previously encountered food. These memory tests were designed to determine the accuracy of recall for spatial and nonspatial cues, the former being a hippocampally dependent task and the latter being a hippocampally independent task. The prediction was that changes in photoperiod would trigger changes in food-storing intensity and spatial memory but not changes in nonspatial memory. Birds were captured in July and housed individually indoors. After a period of about 2 weeks, during which they were maintained on a natural day length to adjust to captive conditions, they were randomly assigned to one of two rooms which were adjacent and identical in temperature but differed in light:dark cycle. One group received an accelerated autumn photoperiod (decreasing day length) in August, followed by a period of short days (simulated winter) in September and early October, and a sudden onset of long days (simulated summer) in mid-October. The other group was maintained on long days until mid-October, and then suddenly exposed to short days. The results indicate that differences in photoperiod caused differences between treatment groups in food-storing intensity in both the home cage and the observation chamber, and in spatial memory. Birds experiencing short days after an accelerated autumn were more intensive food storers and performed better on a spatial memory test than did those maintained on long days. When the photoperiod was reversed, the difference between groups disappeared. On a very similar test in which subjects could rely only on nonspatial cues (e.g. color), there were no differences between groups, irrespective of photoperiod, indicating that the effects of photoperiod seem to be specific to spatial memory.

There are only a handful of examples of seasonal shifts in behavior that are accompanied by cognitive changes. In some birds, the ability to discriminate between conspecific songs is greatest during the breeding season, the time when birds typically learn new songs (Cynx and Nottebohm, 1992; Calhoun *et al.*, 1993). In two rodent species, sex differences in spatial learning ability have been observed only during the breeding season, simultaneous with the greatest sex differences in spacing behavior (Galea *et al.*, 1994; Jacobs, 1995). In Black-capped Chickadees, food-storing intensity and hippocampal cell birth both increase in autumn, when day length is decreasing (Barnea and Nottebohm, 1994). The result that Marsh Tits on an autumn photoperiod have better recall for spatial cues is consistent with the idea that seasonal neural changes are related to retrieval of stored food and may be the first demonstration that photoperiod manipulations can affect this cognitive ability. The next step is to test if such changes are also accompanied by growth and attrition of HF and, if so, whether or not this occurs as a direct result of changes in photoperiod, or as a consequence of photoperiod-induced changes in food-storing behavior. Hippocampal development and plasticity may then be compared and contrasted to season-mediated hippocampal plasticity, and provide some intriguing answers to questions dealing with memory processes in both the young and old. Does seasonal neurogenesis occur at the same rate as ontogenetic neurogenesis or is it substantially reduced as the animal ages? Do rates of apoptosis differ seasonally as well as during development? Also, perhaps most importantly, can experience modulate the relative contributions of both regardless of age?

Summary

The overall objective of the research described in this chapter is to increase our understanding of the involvement of the hippocampus and other brain regions in memory by using a naturalistic model of memory, namely memory for cache sites in food-storing birds, in order to evaluate hippocampal function in the appropriate behavioral, evolutionary and ecological context. A review of the evidence provides a compelling case for the involvement of HF in memory in food-storing birds, and recent experiments clearly demonstrate that this is an excellent model for investigating how specific environmental influences trigger morphological changes in volume, pro-grammed cell death, and cell birth of a specific region in the fully developed brain, both seasonally and during ontogeny. Investigating the relationship between memory, HF and the associated brain circuitry in food-storing birds may provide a rich framework with which to study the effects of experience on underlying neural mechanisms, brain plasticity and brain repair. As is the case in any program of research, far more questions are asked than are ever answered, and with every answer lie many, many more questions to ponder another day.

Acknowledgements

We thank Sara Shettleworth, Alan Kamil and Russ Balda for helpful comments on an earlier version of the manuscript.

References

Alvarez-Buyulla, A., Theelen, M. and Nottebohm, F. (1988) Birth of projection neurons in the higher vocal center of the canary forebrain before, during, and after song learning. *Proc. Natl Acad. Sci. USA* **85**, 8722–8726.

Alvarez-Buyulla, A., Ling C. Y. and Nottebohm, F. (1992) High vocal center growth and its relation to neurogenesis, neuronal replacement and song acquisition in juvenile canaries. *J. Neurobiol.* **23**, 396–406.

Balda, R. P. and Kamil, A. C. (1989) A comparative study of cache recovery by three corvid species. *Anim. Behav.* **38**, 486–495.

Balda, R. P. and Kamil, A. C. (1992) Long-term spatial memory in Clarke's nutcrackers, *Nucifraga columbiana. Anim. Behav.* **44**, 761–769.

Barnea, A. and Nottebohm, F. (1994) Seasonal recruitment of hippocampal neurons in adult free-ranging black-capped chickadees. *Proc. Natl Acad. Sci. USA* **91**, 11 217– 11 221.

Basil, J. A., Kamil, A. C., Balda, R. P. and Fite, K. V. (1996) Differences in hippocampal volume among food storing corvids. *Brain Behav. Evol.* **47**, 156–164.

Bayer, S. A. (1982). Changes in the total number of dentate granule cells in juvenile and adult rats: a correlated volumetric and ³H-thymidine autoradiographic study. *Exp. Brain Res.* **46**, 315–323.

Bingman, V. (1993). Vision, cognition, and the avian hippocampus. In Zeigler, H. P. and Bischof, H.-J. (eds) *Vision, Brain, and Behavior in Birds.* Cambridge, MA: MIT Press, pp. 391–408.

Bliss, T. V. P. and Lomo, T. (1973) Long-lasting potentiation of synaptic transmission in the dentate area of the anaesthetized rabbit following stimulation of the perforant path. *J. Physiol.* **232**, 331–356.

Bossema, I. (1979) Jays and oaks: an eco-ethological study of a symbiosis. *Behaviour* **70**, 1–117.

Brenowitz, E. (1992) Seasonal changes in avian song nuclei. *Proceedings of the Third International Congress on Neuroethology, Abstracts 1992*, p. 58.

Brodbeck, D. R. (1994) Memory for spatial and local cues: a comparison of a storing and a nonstoring species. *Anim. Learn. Behav.* **22**, 119–133.

Brodin, A. and Ekman, J. (1994) Adaptive long-term hoarding in the boreal willow tit. In Time aspects on food hoarding in the willow tit: an evolutionary perspective, Chapter VI of Brodin, A., Ph.D. thesis, Department of Zoology, Stockholm University.

Calhoun, S., Hulse, S. H., Braaten, R. F., Page, S. H. and Nelson, R. J. (1993) Responsiveness to conspecific and alien song by canaries (*Serinus canaria*) and European starlings (*Sturnus vulgaris*) as a function of photoperiod. *J. Comp. Psychol.* **107**, 235–241.

Cassini, G., Bingman, V. and Bagnoli, P. (1986) Connections of the pigeon dorsomedial forebrain studies with WGA-HRP and 3-H proline. *J. Comp. Neurol.* **245**, 454–470.

Clayton, N. S. (1992) The ontogeny of food-storing and retrieval in marsh tits. *Behaviour* **122**, 11–25.

Clayton, N. S. (1994) The role of age and experience in the behavioural development of food-storing and retrieval in marsh tits, *Parus palustris. Anim. Behav.* **47**, 1435–1444.

Clayton, N. S. (1995a) The neuroethological development of food storing memory: a case of use it, or lose it! *Behav. Brain Res.* **70**, 95–101.

Clayton, N. S. (1995b) Development of memory and the hippocampus: comparison of food-storing and non-storing birds on a one-trial associative memory task. *J. Neurosci.* **15**, 2796–2807.

Clayton, N. S. (1996) Development of food-storing and the hippocampus in juvenile marsh tits (*Parus palustris*). *Behav. Brain Res.* **74**, 153–159.

Clayton, N. S. (in press) Memory and the hippocampus in food storing birds: A comparative approach. *Neuropharmacology.*

Clayton, N. S. and Cristol, D. A. (1996) Effects of photoperiod on memory and food storing in captive marsh tits, *Parus palustris. Anim. Behav.* **52**, 715–726.

Clayton, N. S. and Krebs, J. R. (1994a) Hippocampal growth and attrition in birds affected by experience. *Proc. Natl Acad. Sci. USA* **91**, 7410–7414.

Clayton, N. S. and Krebs, J. R. (1994b) Memory for spatial and object-specific cues in food-storing and non-storing species of birds. *J. Comp. Physiol. A* **174**, 371–379.

Clayton, N. S. and Krebs, J. R. (1995a) Memory in food storing birds: from behaviour to brain. *Curr. Opin. Neurobiol.* **5**, 149–154.

Clayton, N. S. and Krebs, J. R. (1995b) Lateralization in memory and the avian hippocampus in food-storing birds. In Alleva, E., Fasolo, A., Lipp, H.-P. and Nadel, L. (eds) *Behavioural Brain Research in Naturalistic and Semi-naturalistic Settings.* Proceedings of NATO Advanced Study Institute Series Maratea, Italy. The Hague: Kluwer Academic Publishers, pp. 139–157.

Clayton, N. S., Mellor, R. and Jackson, A. (1996) Seasonal patterns of food storing in the jay (*Garrulus glandarius*). *Ibis,* **138**, 250–255.

Clayton, N. S., Sanford, K., Saldanha, C. J. and Schlinger, B. A. (1998). Inhibition of aromatase in zebra finches impairs spatial memory performance and hippocampal structure. I: Behavior. *Neurosci. Abstr.* **23**(2), 826.

Cramer, C. P. (1988) Experience during suckling increases weight and volume of rat hippocampus. *Devel. Brain. Res.* **42**, 151–155.

Cynx, J. and Nottebohm, F. (1992) Role of gender, season, and familiarity in discrimination of conspecific song by zebra finches (*Taeniopygia guttata*). *Proc. Natl Acad. Sci.* **89**, 1368–1371.

Doupe, A. J. (1994) Seeds of instruction: hippocampus and memory in food-storing birds. *Proc. Natl Acad. Sci.* **89**, 7400–7402.

Erichsen, J. T., Bingman, V. P. and Krebs, J. R. (1991) The distribution of neuropeptides in the dorsomedial telencephalon of the pigeon (*Columba livia*): a basis for regional subdivisions. *J. Comp. Neurol.* **314**, 478–492.

Galea, L. A. M., Kavaliers, M., Ossenkopp, K.-P., Innes, D. and Hargreaves, E. L. (1994) Sexually dimorphic spatial learning varies seasonally in two population of deer mice. *Brain Res.* **635**, 18–26.

Haftorn, S. (1956) Contribution to the food biology of tits especially about storing of surplus food. Part III. The willow tit (*Parus atricapillus*). *Det Kgl Norske Videnskabes Selskabs Sckifter* **3**, 1–79.

Hampton, R. R. and Shettleworth, S. J. (1996) Hippocampal lesions impair memory for location but not color in passerine birds. *Behav. Neurosci.* **110**, 946–964.

Hampton, R. R., Sherry, D. F., Shettleworth, S. J., Khurgel, M. and Ivy, G. (1995) Hippocampal volume and food-storing behavior are related in parids. *Brain Behav. Evol.* **45**, 54–61.

Healy, S. D. and Krebs, J. R. (1992) Food-storing and hippocampus in corvids: amount and volume are correlated. *Proc. Roy. Soc. Lond. B* **248**, 241–245.

Healy, S. D. and Krebs, J. R. (1993) Development of hippocampal specialization in a food-storing bird. *Behav. Brain Res.* **53**, 127–131.

Healy, S. D., Clayton, N. S. and Krebs, J. R. (1994) Development of hippocampal specialization in two species of tit (*Parus spp.*) *Behav. Brain Res.* **61**, 23–28.

Healy, S. D., Gwinner, E. and Krebs, J. R. (1996) Hippocampus size in migrating garden warblers: effects of age and experience. *Behav. Brain Res.* **81**, 61–68.

Horn, G. (1985) *Memory, Imprinting, and the Brain.* Oxford: Clarendon Press.

Jacobs, L. F. (1995) The ecology of spatial cognition: adaptive patterns of hippocampal size and space use in wild rodents. In Alleva, E., Fasolo, A., Lipp, H.-P. and Nadel, L. (eds) *Behavioural Brain Research in Naturalistic and Semi-naturalistic Settings*. Proceedings of NATO Advanced Study Institute Series Maratea, Italy. The Hague: Kluwer Academic Publishers, pp. 301–322.

Jolliffe, A. R. (1996) Food storing and memory in the coal tit. D.Phil. thesis, University of Oxford, Oxford.

Joliffe, A. R. and Clayton, N. S. (in prep.) The development of food-storing and hippocampus in coal tits (*Parus ater*): effects of experience and photoperiod. *J. Neurosci.*

Källen, B. (1962) Embryogenesis of brain nuclei in the chick telencephalon. *Ergebnisse Anat. Entwicklung* **36**, 62–82.

Kaplan, M. S. and Bell, D. H. (1984) Mitotic neuroblasts in the 9-day-old and 11-month-old rodent hippocampus. *J. Neurosci.* **4**, 1429–1441.

Kaplan, M. S. and Hinds, J. W. (1977) Neurogenesis in the adult rat: electron microscopic analysis of light radioautographs. *Science* **197**, 1092–1094.

Kempermann, G., Kuhn, H. G. and Gage, F. (1997). More hippocampal neurons in adult mice living in an enriched environment. *Nature* **386**, 493–495.

Krebs, J. R., Sherry, D. F., Healy, S. D., Perry, V. H. and Vaccarino, A. L. (1989) Hippocampal specialization of food-storing birds. *Proc. Natl Acad. Sci. USA* **86**, 1388–1392.

Krebs, J. R., Erichsen, J. T. and Bingman, V. P. (1991) The distribution of choline acetyltransferase-like, glutamic acid decarboxylase-like, serotonin-like and tyrosine hydroxylase-like immunoreactivity in the dorsomedial telencephalon of the pigeon (*Columbia livia*) *J. Comp. Neurol.* **314**, 467–477.

Krebs, J. R., Clayton, N. S., Healy, S. D., Cristol, D., Patel, S. N. and Jolliffe, A. (1996) The ecology of memory and the hippocampus in food-storing birds. *Ibis* **38**, 34–46.

Krushinskya, N. L. (1966) Some complex forms of feeding behaviour of nutcracker, *Nucifraga caryocatactes*, after removal of old cortex. *Zh. Evol. Biochim. Fisiol.* **II**, 563–568.

Ludescher, F.-B. (1980) Fressen und Verstecken von Sämerein bei der Weidermeise Parus montanus im Jahresterlauf unter konstanten Ernährungsbedingungen. *Okol Vogel* **2**, 135–144.

Molla, R., Rodriques, J., Calvet, S. and Garcia-Verdugo, J. (1986) Neuronal types of cerebral cortex of the adult chicken, *Gallus gallus*. A Golgi study. *J. Hirnforschung* **27**, 381–390.

Nadel, L. (1991) The hippocampus and space revisited. *Hippocampus* **1**, 221–229.

Nordeen, E. J. and Nordeen, K. W. (1990) Neurogenesis and sensitive phases in avian vocal learning. *Trends Neurosci.* **13**, 31–36.

Nottebohm, F. (1981) A brain for all seasons: cyclical anatomical changes in song-control nuclei of the canary brain. *Science* **214**, 1368–1370.

Odum, E. P. (1942) Annual cycle of the black-capped chickadee. *Auk* **59**, 499–533.

O'Keefe, J. and Nadel, L. (1978) *The Hippocampus as a Cognitive Map.* Oxford: Clarendon Press.

Olton, D. S. (1983) Memory functions and the hippocampus. In W. Siefert (ed.) *Neurobiology of the Hippocampus.* New York: Academic Press, pp. 335–373.

Patel, S. N., Clayton, N. S. and Krebs, J. R. (1997a) Hippocampal tissue transplants reverse spatial memory deficits produced by ibotenic acid lesions of the hippocampus in zebra finches (*Taeniopygia guttata*) *J. Neurosci.* **17**, 3861–3869.

Patel, S. N., Clayton, N. S. and Krebs, J. R. (1997b). Learning-induced cytogenesis in the avian hippocampus. *Behav. Brain Res.* **89**, 115–128.

Petersen, K. and Sherry, D. F. (1998) Seasonal variation in food storing and the hippocampus in the white-breasted nuthatch (*Sitta carolinensis*) *Behav. Brain Res.* (in press).

Raushecker, J. P. and Marler, P. (1987) *Imprinting and Cortical Plasticity.* New York: Wiley.

Rawlins, J. N. P., Lyford, G. L., Seferiades, A., Deacon, R. M. J. and Cassaday, H. J. (1993) Critical determinants of nonspatial working memory deficits in rats with conventional lesions of the hippocampus. *Behav. Neurosci.* **107**, 420–433.

Reboreda, J. C., Clayton, N. S. and Kacelnik, A. (1996) Species and sex differences in hippocampus size between parasitic and non-parasitic cowbirds. *Neuroreport* **7**, 505–508.

Rose, S. P. R. (1992) On chicks and rosetta stones. In Squire, L. R. and Butters, N. (eds) *Neuropsychology of Memory.* Surrey: Guilford Press.

Rosenzweig, M. R. (1984) Experience, memory, and the brain. *Am. Psychol.* **39**, 365–376.

Rosenzweig, M. R., Krech, D., Bennett, E. L. and Diamond, M. C. (1962) Effects of environmental complexity and training on brain chemistry and anatomy: a replication and extension. *J. Comp. Physiol. Psychol.* **55**, 429–437.

Saldanha, C. J., Clayton, N. S., Sanford, K. and Schlinger, B. A. (1998) Inhibition of aromatase in zebra finches impairs spatial memory performance and hippocampal structure. II: Anatomy. *Neurosci. Abstr.* **23**(2), 826.5.

Shapiro, E. and Wieraszko, A. (1996) Comparative, in vitro, studies of hippocampal tissue from homing and non-homing pigeon. *Brain Res.*, **725**, 199–206.

Sherry, D. F. and Vaccarino, A. L. (1989) Hippocampus and memory for food caches in black-capped chickadees. *Behav. Neurosci.* **103**, 308–318.

Sherry, D. F., Vaccarino, A. L., Buckenham, K. and Herz, R. S. (1989) The hippocampal complex of food-storing birds. *Brain Behav. Evol.* **34**, 308–317.

Sherry, D. F., Jacobs, L. F. and Gaulin, S. J. C. (1992) Spatial memory and adaptive specialization of the hippocampus. *Trends Neurosci.* **17**, 298–303.

Sherry, D. F., Forbes, M. R. L., Khurgel, M. and Ivy, G. O. (1993) Females have a larger hippocampus than males in the brood-parasitic brown-headed cowbird. *Proc. Natl Acad. Sci.* **90**, 7839–7843.

Shettleworth, S. J. and Krebs, J. R. (1982) How marsh tits find their hoards: roles of site preferences and spatial memory. *J. Exp. Psych. Anim. Behav. Proc.* **8**, 354–375.

Shettleworth, S. J., Hampton, R. R. and Westwood, R. P. (1995) Effects of season and photoperiod on food-storing by black-capped chickadees, *Parus atracapillus. Anim. Behav.* **49**, 989–998.

Smulders, T. V., Sasson, A. D. and DeVoogd, T. J. (1995) Seasonal variation in hippocampal volume in a food-storing bird, the black-capped chickadee. *J. Neurobiol.* **27**, 15–25.

Squire, L. R., Knowlton, B. and Musen, G. (1993) The structure and organization of memory. *Ann. Rev. Psychol.* **44**, 453–495.

Stevens, T. A. and Krebs, J. R. (1986) Retrieval of stored seeds by marsh tits *Parus palustris* in the field. *Ibis* **128**, 513–525.

Székely, A. D. and Krebs, J. R. (1993) Target structures of hippocampal projections in the zebra finch brain. *Brain Res. Assoc. Abstr.*, **10**, 21.

Székely, A. D., Clayton, N. S. and Krebs, J. R. (1993) Regional distribution of immediate early gene expression in the avian brain following food storing behaviour. *Eur. J. Neurosci. Suppl.* **5**, 149.48.

Vander Wall, S. B. and Balda, R. P. (1981) Ecology and evolution of food-storage behavior in conifer-seed-caching corvids. *Z. Tierpsychol.* **56**, 217–242.

Wieraszko, A. and Ball, G. (1991) Long-term enhancement of synaptic responses in the songbird hippocampus. *Brain Res.* **358**, 102–106.

Wieraszko, A. and Ball, G. (1993) Long-term potentiation in the avian hippocampus does not require activation of the N-methyl-D-aspartate (NMDA) receptor. *Synapse* **13**, 173–178.

5

Spatial Cognition: Lessons from Central-place Foraging Insects

Fred C. Dyer

Department of Zoology, Michigan State University, East Lansing, MI 48824, USA

Introduction

Spatial orientation has played an extremely important role in the development of ideas about the behavioral capacities of animals. Indeed, as the modern scientific study of animal behavior emerged from its roots in zoology and experimental psychology, studies of spatial orientation figured in the work of many of the pioneering researchers, including Tinbergen (Tinbergen and van Kruyt, 1938), von Frisch (review, 1967), Watson (Carr and Watson, 1908) and Tolman (1948).

In recent years, with the increasing focus on cognitive mechanisms – generally, those processes intervening between the detection of a stimulus and the production of an appropriate response – studies of spatial orientation have continued to play a central role in behavioral science. For example, a fundamental question in the study of cognition concerns the nature of internal representations: neurally encoded records of information about objects or events in the outside world (Roitblat, 1987; Gallistel, 1990). We have only vague hypotheses about how information about environmental patterns might be encoded in the medium of neural tissue and then used to guide subsequent behavior in the same environment. These questions arise regardless of the type of information that animals respond to. One advantage of exploring them within the domain of spatial cognition is the ease with which spatial relationships (in contrast to social or ecological relationships) can be manipulated experimentally.

ANIMAL COGNITION IN NATURE
ISBN 0-12-077030-X

This chapter reviews recent research on spatial orientation in insects, with the aim of showing how these animals provide a model for the development of an integrated theory of spatial cognition. Most of the research that I will discuss concerns orientation by hymenopteran insects (bees, wasps and ants) that provision a central nest, and hence face the task of finding their way repeatedly to a specific point in the environment, sometimes from great distances away (hundreds or even thousands of meters). Some species also face the task of returning repeatedly to rich feeding-sites, and may visit several such feeding-sites during their lifetimes. To solve these navigational problems, insects typically rely upon visual information about landmarks and celestial cues. This in turn entails learning the spatial relationships between these references and locations in the insect's natal habitat. Behavioral evidence has suggested that these learning processes include mechanisms for manipulating internally represented information to compute spatial relationships that the animal has not directly experienced. Thus, insects offer an opportunity to study, in animals with modest-sized nervous systems, the mechanisms underlying such cognitive capacities.

In addition, I believe that research on insect navigation provides an example of how the study of spatial cognition could be broadened and made truly integrative. Consider that most studies of vertebrate spatial cognition by experimental psychologists and neuroscientists employ a restricted set of experimental paradigms, including the radial-arm maze, the Morris water pool, and various other cue-controlled arenas (reviews by Gallistel, 1990; Leonard and McNaughton, 1990; McNaughton *et al.*, 1996). These paradigms all examine only a narrow portion of the spatial tasks that free-ranging animals would be expected to face. There is also a huge zoological literature exploring long-distance migration by birds and other vertebrates (see Wiltschko and Wiltschko, and Bingman *et al.*, this volume), but this work has tended to ignore other navigational problems faced by these animals. By contrast with the literature on vertebrates, studies of insects, especially Honey Bees (*Apis mellifera*; reviews by von Frisch, 1967; Wehner, 1981; Dyer, 1994) and Desert Ants (*Cataglyphis* spp.; review by Wehner *et al.*, 1996), have examined a broad spectrum of navigational mechanisms involved in finding a goal in the environment. This literature therefore provides clues about the integration of mechanisms designed to solve different navigational problems faced by the same animal.

An overview of the main themes that I shall explore in this chapter follows. First, I hope to make clear the specific spatial tasks that are entailed in setting and maintaining a course to a goal, and how different classes of spatial information impose distinct cognitive challenges. We shall see that spatial cognition does not constitute a unitary cognitive domain, but instead involves a diversity of spatial tasks and a corresponding diversity of cognitive solutions.

Second, I hope to show that a full understanding of spatial cognition requires complementary studies of the contents of spatial representations – the information that experienced animals have encoded in memory – and the processes by which these representations are acquired by naive animals. By 'acquisition' I mean more than merely the shape of the learning curve describing the improvement in performance as the animal learns the task. Instead, I am referring to the exploratory strategies by which the animal exposes itself to the patterns that it needs to learn, and to the properties of interim representations that the animal forms as it begins to acquire experience in the environment.

Third, I shall examine a major conceptual challenge that arises in studying cognitive processes: how to interpret the limitations that we observe in the performance of animals solving a particular cognitive task. The question is whether limitations in performance are a consequence of information-processing constraints related to brain size or are adaptive solutions for particular components of a navigational problem.

I shall explore these themes by examining recent research on landmark learning and sun-compass orientation in Honey Bees and other nesting insects. To put this work in context, however, I begin by discussing the challenges involved in goal orientation in a more general way.

Goal orientation: general strategies

Most studies of spatial memory test the ability of animals to return to a specific location, or to a sequence of locations (as in the radial-arm maze and studies of cache retrieval), where they have previously learned to find food, nests or refugia. Goal orientation of this sort – finding a target that is small relative to the area in which the animal is moving – requires that the animal obtain two sorts of information from the environment. First, it must discriminate different body orientations from one another, thus it must have a sense of direction. Second, it must determine the direction that is correct for its current goal, thus it must have a sense of its position relative to the location of the goal. Experiments designed to study spatial memory usually exclude the possibility of obtaining information cues directly emanating from the goal (e.g. odors or visual stimuli), and require instead the use of stimuli that specify the location of the goal only if the animal has previously learned their spatial relationship to the goal.

The most important sources of directional information in the environment are celestial bodies (the sun and stars), the earth's magnetic field, and landmarks (reviews by von Frisch, 1967; Wehner, 1982; Wiltschko and Wiltschko, 1996; Dyer, 1997). In vertebrates, vestibular or proprioceptive cues may provide an internal, or idiothetic, sense of direction (e.g. McNaughton *et al.*, 1996), but such cues are generally regarded as unimportant to the insects considered here.

The directional senses of animals present various puzzles. For example, some animals appear to use directional cues as a frame of reference for learning spatial relationships among landmarks (Gallistel, 1990; Collett and Baron, 1994; Dickinson, 1994; McNaughton *et al.*, 1996; Wehner *et al.*, 1996). It is still very unclear how this integration is achieved. Second, external compasses such as celestial cues or the earth's magnetic field provide accurate directional information only if animals can compensate for latitudinal, seasonal or daily variations in these references. Many animals have to calibrate their responses to compass references to develop a directional sense that is appropriate for current local conditions (reviews by von Frisch, 1967; Wiltschko and Wiltschko, 1990; Wehner and Müller, 1993; Dyer and Dickinson 1994, 1996; Able and Able 1996). Again, the learning processes by which they do this remain very unclear.

An important source of positional information for both vertebrates (Etienne *et al.*, 1996; McNaughton *et al.*, 1996) and invertebrates (reviews by Wehner and Wehner, 1990; Dyer, 1994; Wehner *et al.*, 1996) is path integration. Path integration is an internal process by which an animal measures the directions and distances traveled from a particular point (for example, its nest) and computes its current position in the environment. The animal can then set a homeward course even in the absence of familiar landmarks, for example, if the searching path takes it into unknown terrain, so long as it can continuously measure its angular and linear displacement over the outward path. Desert Ants (*Cataglyphis* spp.), and probably other insects, measure directions in reference to the sun and measure distance from summed optic flow cues (Wehner *et al.*, 1996). Hamsters (Etienne *et al.*, 1996), rats (McNaughton *et al.*, 1996) and human beings (Loomis *et al.*, 1993) can perform path integration and return to their starting-point even in total darkness, because the path integration system can operate on directional and distance information provided by vestibular and proprioreceptive cues. Path integration raises fascinating questions about the mechanisms by which animals store and update a representation of their direction and distance from home, but I will not discuss it in detail here. For reviews, see Gallistel (1990), Wehner and Wehner (1990), Dyer (1994) and McNaughton *et al.* (1996).

If animals are deprived of the information on which the path integration system operates (for example, by displacing them directly so that they cannot record the twists and turns of the outward path), they may still set an accurate homeward course, which implies that they have alternative sources of positional information. For most animals, this is where landmarks play the most important role. Landmarks can be used for homing only if they are familiar to the animal from previous travels in the environment. Thus, path integration, which by definition is performed within an area traveled by the animal, and landmark-based navigation, which requires prior exposure to landmarks, can be regarded as complementary strategies for determining position within a home range (Fig. 5.1).

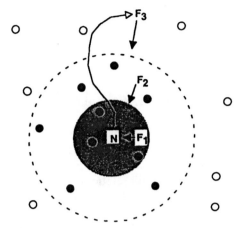

Fig. 5.1 How the task that a nesting insect faces, in determining its position relative to home, varies with the location of the feeding-place. Filled circles are familiar landmarks learned during previous foraging flights; open circles are landmarks in previously unexplored part of the terrain (beyond the boundary described by dotted line). The gray central area is the range over which landmarks visible at the nest (N) are visible to insects on foraging routes. From locations within this range (e.g. F_1), insects can orient toward home using an array of landmarks that is visible during the entire trip. From locations outside this range, but within the previously explored part of the terrain (e.g. F_2), insects can use familiar landmarks to set their initial course, but then would have to switch over to other landmarks to pinpoint the location of the nest. From both F_1 and F_2, insects should be able to set a homeward course in reference to landmarks, even if the insects are displaced there directly and are thus deprived of information about the path that led them there. From locations outside the familiar flight range (e.g. F_3), landmarks cannot provide navigational information. Thus, the insects could set a homeward course only if they have traveled to the site and have performed path integration to compute their position relative to the nest. Adapted from Wehner (1982).

Some animals, however, can set a course when displaced outside a familiar home range, so that neither path integration nor learned landmarks could play a role. Well-studied examples are homing pigeons and various species of migratory birds. The specialized strategies for determining position and direction of travel on this large scale are reviewed by Wiltschko and Wiltschko, and Bingman *et al.* (this volume), and I will not discuss them in detail.

Thus, although much research in spatial memory focuses on landmark learning, it is useful to recognize that animals have evolved multiple strategies for determining their position and direction of travel in the environment. A complete theory of spatial cognition will have to address how these strategies fit together. The topics that I will review here – landmark learning and sun-compass orientation – constitute major components of the navigational repertoire of insects, and allow us to see some of the challenges in developing an integrated theory.

Landmark memory: contents and acquisition

To investigate how animals use landmarks for navigation within a familiar home range, we must consider two criteria for classifying the spatial information encoded by the animal. These criteria are: (1) the spatial scale over which the animal learns spatial relationships among landmarks; and (2) the coordinate system within which landmarks are encoded. These criteria are frequently employed by zoologists as well as psychologists, although they are not always discussed explicitly (see Gallistel, 1990; Poucet, 1993; Collett, 1996; Wehner *et al.*, 1996; Dyer, 1997). The important issue raised by this classification is that theories of landmark learning need to recognize the possible existence of multiple, operationally distinct forms of spatial learning. After discussing each of these two criteria, I shall review our current understanding of the contents and acquisition of spatial representations that insects use for navigation on small and large spatial scales.

Spatial scale

The distance over which an animal has to move to find a particular goal is profoundly important in defining the nature of the navigational task, and hence the cognitive solutions required (see Dyer, 1997, for a comprehensive review). The importance of distance for landmark learning can be appreciated by considering the spatial learning tasks faced by Honey Bees, which may visit feeding sites thousands of meters from home (Visscher and Seeley, 1982; Dyer and Seeley, 1991). Given such flight distances, it is clear that no single set of landmarks could provide navigational information during an entire foraging trip. In fact bees would encounter a sequence of landmarks during a given foraging trip. Furthermore, the task of learning and using landmarks for navigation differs according to how far the bee is from her goal.

When close to the goal, but not so close that she can detect it directly, a bee relies upon surrounding landmarks to narrow her search, making use of memorized information about the appearance of the landmarks and their spatial relationship to the goal (Fig. 5.1). This is more than a matter of simply searching until the array of surrounding landmarks appears the same as it did on a previous visit to the goal. Instead, animals can use surrounding landmarks to set a course to an unseen goal when they start from a displaced position where the view of the landmarks is different. This has led to the general hypothesis that insects obtain information about the course to the goal from view-dependent changes in the appearance of the landmark array (Cartwright and Collett, 1983; reviewed by Dyer, 1994).

The use of a familiar landmark array to pinpoint the location of a goal is a task a bee faces only near the end of her flight to the goal. First, she must reach the part of the terrain where she can see these landmarks. Given their foraging range, however, bees must often start far enough away that they have a view neither of the goal nor of any landmarks near it (Fig. 5.1). Landmarks visible near the starting-point can guide a bee only if she has previously learned the direction relative to these features that leads toward the unseen goal. Then, since these landmarks will be left behind once the animal is underway, she must be able to use other landmarks that come into view during the trip. Clearly, the use of landmarks on this large spatial scale requires the animal to learn several visual scenes that she can experience only sequentially by moving through the terrain. As we shall see, considerable controversy has surrounded the question of how insects integrate spatial information acquired in different parts of a familiar terrain.

Most experimental studies of landmark learning by psychologists and cognitive neuroscientists focus on the small spatial scale, in which the animal's task is to find a goal using landmarks that are visible at every point during the approach to the goal. This is true in experiments involving radial-arm mazes, the Morris water pool and other cue-controlled arenas in which animals are trained to learn the locations of goals (reviews by Gallistel, 1990; Leonard and McNaughton, 1990; McNaughton *et al.*, 1996). It is also true in most studies of cache recovery by food-storing birds (Balda and Kamil, Kamil, and Shettleworth and Hampton this volume). However, most mobile animals would also face the task of using landmarks to travel routes between visually separated parts of the environment. Thus, these primarily laboratory-based studies have potentially overlooked major components of the navigational repertoire of these animals.

Coordinate system for encoding spatial relationships

Learning landmarks is a matter of learning the angles, and possibly the distances, defining the spatial relationships between the landmarks and specific goals or routes in the environment (Gallistel, 1990). An ability to learn angles and distances among objects or locations implies the existence of a coordinate system for measuring and encoding this information. Gallistel (1990) and others (e.g. Schöne, 1984; Poucet, 1993; Wehner *et al.*, 1996) have drawn a major distinction between 'egocentric' and 'allocentric' coordinate systems. An egocentric representation of space encodes the positions of observable points relative to the observer's position and its own body axes. An allocentric representation encodes the positions of objects in a coordinate system external to the observer. For example, we encode locations on maps in reference to a system of latitude and longitude lines, which in turn are defined respectively by the axis of rotation of the earth and the positions of celestial bodies. Also, we can not only estimate the distances and directions of familiar landmarks relative to our present vantage point, but also estimate the positions of landmarks relative to each other.

All experience is initially egocentric; each animal experiences the world from a vantage point centered at its current position, and through sensory organs fixed relative to its body axes. Representing spatial relationships in allocentric coordinates would require internal processes to transfer these egocentrically recorded representations to a reference external to the animal (see Gallistel, 1990). Many animals do refer to external references when learning spatial relationships among landmarks or locations in their environments (Wiltschko and Wiltschko, this volume, for evidence from birds), but the nature of the processes by which they do this remains puzzling. Further complicating the picture, evidence presented below suggests that the distinction between egocentric and allocentric representations is not decided merely by whether external references play a role in landmark learning. Thus this simple dichotomy may need to be re-evaluated.

Landmark learning by insects on a small spatial scale: pinpointing the goal

The preceding sections provide a general and fairly abstract framework for evaluating cognitive processes used in landmark learning. Now I want to establish an empirical foundation for these ideas by discussing how Honey Bees and other nesting insects use landmarks for navigation.

As mentioned, some insect species travel several kilometers in search of food (the Honey Bee's foraging range approaches 10 km; Visscher and Seeley, 1982), and thus face the task of learning the relationships among landmarks on multiple spatial scales. I shall discuss small-scale and large-scale landmark learning separately, although I shall point out some common principles operating on these different spatial scales. In both cases, I shall describe what is known not only about the contents of spatial representations but also about the process by which insects acquire these representations.

Again, the small-scale task is defined as the use of a continuously visible surrounding array of landmarks to pinpoint the location of a goal. The classic example is Tinbergen's experiment showing that Digger Wasps (*Philanthus triangulum*) can learn to find their burrow by referring to an artificial array of landmarks, such as a ring of pine cones around the nest entrance (Tinbergen and Kruyt, 1938). If the array is displaced by a few centimeters when the wasp is away foraging, she will search, on her return, in the location specified by the array and will ignore any olfactory or visual cues still present at the actual location of the nest. Many experiments have proven beyond doubt that wasps, bees and ants pinpoint feeding and nesting sites relative to surrounding landmarks (Fig. 5.2).

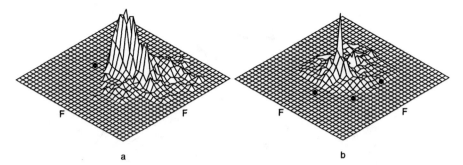

Fig. 5.2 Experimental demonstration that bees use an array of landmarks to pinpoint the location of a feeding place. Circular shapes represent cylindrical landmarks viewed from above. The coordinates of the feeder are indicated by F. Bees were rewarded for several successive visits, then tested in the absence of food. Each distribution shows the relative time spent by a single searching bee in each cell of the grid (lines on the grid are 8.7 cm apart). (a) Search distribution by a bee trained to find food 50 cm from a single landmark; (b) search distribution by a bee trained to find food relative to three landmarks. Reproduced from Cartwright and Collett (1983).

Ideas about how the spatial information provided by such landmarks is encoded and used by insects have consolidated around the following general model, which was first explored in detail by Cartwright and Collett (1983, 1987; see also Wehner, 1981, for an earlier review of this idea) and has since proved remarkably robust as a working hypothesis. The model assumes that the animal records an image in memory of the landmarks from the vantage point of the goal, a sort of neuronal 'snapshot' encoding the spatial pattern that the landmarks present to the eyes. To return to the goal subsequently, the animal somehow steers toward the place where its current view of the landmark array most closely matches the image recorded on previous visits.

A large and still-growing body of experimental work, dealing mostly with Honey Bees, has identified several attributes of the memory images that this snapshot model hypothesizes (see reviews by Wehner, 1981; Gallistel, 1990; Dyer, 1994). The snapshots are panoramic, including most or all of the 360° field of view of the insect's compound eye. They are dominated by features of the visual horizon (rather than by patterns on the ground below the animal). They record the angular sizes of individual landmarks as well as the separations between landmarks; each of these sources of angular information can influence the searching behavior of bees independently. Snapshots also encode distances of landmarks from the goal, in the sense that nearby landmarks have a more powerful influence on searching behavior than do more distant landmarks, even if the apparent size of the landmarks is controlled. Distance is probably measured from motion cues: as the bee moves, the images of nearby landmarks move faster across the eye than the

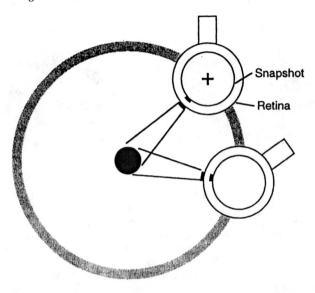

Fig. 5.3 Ambiguity resulting from a simple, retinotopic, pattern-matching strategy. If bees trained to find food at the cross simply learned the appearance of the landmarks from the vantage point of the food, then they would be expected to search in an annulus around the landmark (shaded circle). At all positions on this annulus (one position is shown), bees can find a match between their current and remembered (snapshot) view of the landmark. As shown in Fig. 5.2a, bees appear to have some way of resolving this ambiguity.

images of distant landmarks. The fact that both angular and distance information are encoded means that these snapshots qualify as Euclidean representations of the spatial surround (Gallistel, 1990).

One persistent puzzle has concerned whether insects encode visual images in egocentric or allocentric coordinates. The long-standing assumption by researchers studying insects has been that the brain encodes the retinal positions of different landmarks, which would make the snapshot an egocentric representation. Gallistel (1990) argued, however, that certain evidence was consistent with an allocentric representation referenced to an earth-based coordinate system (e.g. the celestial compass). For example, some landmarks should be ambiguous for a purely egocentric matching process, and yet Honey Bees are not confused when confronted by such landmarks. Bees apparently resolve such ambiguities: they can be trained to find food in a specific location relative to a single cylindrical landmark (Cartwright and Collett, 1983) (Fig. 5.2). A simple egocentric image-matching strategy would cause bees to search in an annulus around the landmark, because their current and remembered views of the landmark would be identical from all viewing directions (Fig. 5.3). One way bees might resolve the ambiguity is to consult an external directional reference such as the sun or the geo-magnetic field, which would seem to imply that their representation is in allocentric coordinates.

Furthermore, when using landmarks to navigate toward a goal, bees seem able to approach from any direction. Since a bee's retinal coordinates are fixed relative to her body axes, researchers have naturally assumed that the direction in which a bee is traveling is the direction she is looking. The ability to use landmarks independent of the direction of approach was therefore interpreted as evidence that the matching mechanism works independently of how the current image of the landmarks falls on the eye. Cartwright and Collett (1983), who used computer simulations to explore various hypothesized image-matching models, had difficulty reproducing the bees' behavior if the snapshot were fixed relative to retinal coordinates (Fig. 5.4). The models that worked best used a snapshot that remained in the same compass orientation in which it was recorded, regardless of the bee's direction of travel. One interpretation of this (see Gallistel, 1990) is that the snap-shot is encoded in reference to an external compass rather than retinal coordinates.

Recent work has confirmed that bees consult external compass references in using an ambiguous landmark to find food. Collett and Baron's (1994) experiments implicated a magnetic compass, Dickinson (1994) studies the sun compass (there is no reason why both compasses could not serve this function). However, Collett and Baron's study also undermined previous suggestions that snapshots are encoded in an allocentric reference frame. This seemingly paradoxical result came from measurements of the bees' body alignment during their final approach to the food (Fig. 5.5). Initially, bees head toward conspicuous landmarks near the goal, as if using them as beacons. When close, however, they adopt a characteristic (usually south-facing) orientation relative to the magnetic compass, even if this requires them to fly sideways to finish their trip to the goal. Thus, it turns out not to be true that the insect's direction of travel is always the direction in which she is looking. This simple observation makes it possible to reconcile the hypothesis that snapshots are encoded in reference to retinal coordinates with Cartwright and Collett's (1983) finding that pattern matching is simplified if the snapshot of the landmark were maintained in a consistent orientation. A consistent alignment of the bee's body would necessarily lead to a consistent orientation of an egocentric, retinally localized snapshot. For this strategy to work, the directional information provided by the external compass reference need not be explicitly integrated with the snapshot of the landmarks. Thus, it does not really make sense to describe the compass reference as providing an allocentric coordinate system within which the positions of the landmarks are encoded. Instead, the compass is used merely to orient the bee so that the egocentric reference frame can be used efficiently.

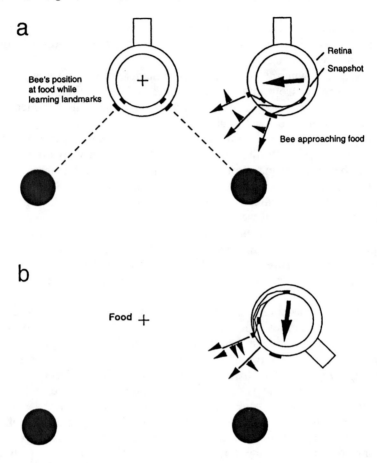

Fig. 5.4 Illustration of the pattern-matching algorithm proposed by Cartwright and Collett (1983). A bee is shown (circle indicating head, rectangle indicating body axis) setting course for a feeding-place (cross) near two cylindrical landmarks (large filled circles). The model assumes that the bee matches elements of the current visual image ('retina') with a memory of the landmarks stored during a previous visit when the bee was at the food ('snapshot'). The positions of and sizes of landmark images on the retina and in the snapshot are shown by the black sectors. The snapshot is encoded in reference to the bee's body axes. For each element in the two images, the brain computes two unit vectors, one translational and one rotational (small arrows); the resultant of these vectors is the direction that the bee steers to reach the food. In computer simulations, this mechanism works quite well to lead a model bee toward the food, but only if the snapshot happened to be aligned in the compass direction in which it was recorded (a). If aligned in other directions (b), the mechanism computes the direction toward the goal incorrectly.

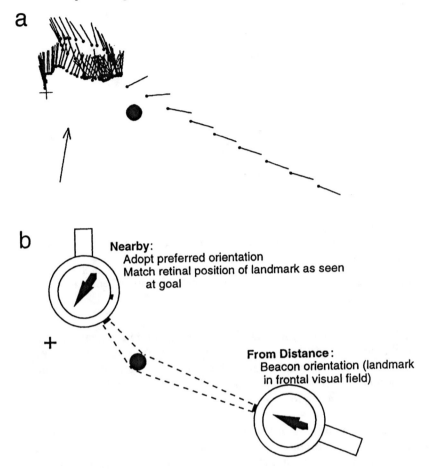

Fig. 5.5 (a) A single bee's approach to a feeding-place marked by a single cylindrical landmark. Each symbol shows the position and orientation (circle shows head; line shows body axis) at 40-millisecond intervals during the search, based on an analysis of videotape recorded from above. The arrow gives the direction of north; the length of the arrow represents 10 cm. Reproduced from Collett (1996). (b) Interpretation. The bee first heads toward the landmark as if using it as a beacon, then, during the last few centimeters of its approach, it adopts a standardized south-facing orientation to compute the final trajectory to the goal (see Fig. 5.4).

The studies discussed so far all focused on the contents of the snapshots used by highly experienced bees, that is, bees that have been exposed to the landmarks on numerous successive trips to a feeding-place. The insights from this work have been extended recently through investigations of the processes by which an insect acquires its snapshots of landmarks during its first few visits to a newly discovered feeding-place.

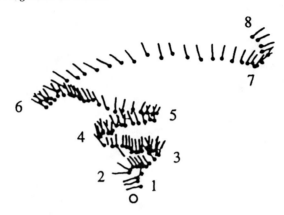

Fig. 5.6 The orientation flight of a single bee viewed from above, showing its side-to-side movements during 'turn-back-and-look' as the bee flies away from the food (indicated by an open circle). The numbers indicate successive positions over time (total duration 2–3 seconds). Note that the bee mainly faces in the same direction during this part of the orientation flight. Reproduced from Lehrer (1996).

At least since the 1930s (Opfinger, 1931), landmark learning has been assumed to take place during a special behavioral episode known as an 'orientation flight', which has been described in numerous species of nesting hymenoptera (reviewed by Wehner, 1981). The orientation flight is performed by an insect just prior to departing from a location to which it will later return. Thus wasps and bees do it just before leaving the nest for a foraging trip, or just before leaving a feeding-place to take a load of food home. Generally, orientation flights are done only during the first few departures, or when the insect is relatively naive; experienced insects depart without doing them.

A typical orientation flight has at least two main phases. First, in what Lehrer (1991) has called the 'turn-back-and-look' (TBL), the departing insect flies backward while facing the target (the nest or the feeding-place), moving its body from side to side as it flies (Fig. 5.6). Then the insect begins to fly in circles of increasing diameter while gaining height, occasionally changing the direction of rotation. Each of these phases lasts roughly 5–10 seconds.

A variety of studies have implicated orientation flights in landmark learning (reviews by Collett, 1996; Lehrer, 1996). One striking finding bears on the question of the coordinate system within which visual-spatial memories are encoded. Collett (1995), studying Yellowjacket Wasps (*Vespula vulgaris*) searching for a feeding-place, observed that the insects tended to adopt a constant orientation during each TBL. Moreover, the orientation adopted during the TBL was highly correlated with the orientation adopted during subsequent arrivals as the insect searched for the food. Thus, the wasps appeared to orient themselves to standardize their view of landmarks both while forming the memory and while using it to return to the goal, at least during the last few seconds of the approach. Indeed, careful measurements from videotape suggest that a conspicuous landmark near the goal falls on the same part of the insect's compound eye during both the TBL and the final approach on returning to the food. This provides strong evidence that the basic representation is encoded in reference to retinal (i.e. egocentric) coordinates and that an external directional reference is used only to standardize the viewing angle.

This coordination of the processes involved in acquiring and using spatial information simplifies what could be a very difficult task. It is tempting to attribute the simplicity of the insect's solution to the information-processing constraints imposed by the small size of the animal's brain: perhaps an egocentric encoding of landmark images is the only feasible option given these constraints. However, it is not only small-brained animals that employ the strategy of standardizing a viewing-angle when trying to recognize familiar patterns. We do it when reading; for example, consider how much faster you read when you hold the page in its standard orientation relative to your field of view than when you rotate it by 45° or 90°. Apparently, there is something fundamental about visual pattern recognition that makes the task easier when images to be recognized fall on the retina in a standard orientation. We can of course recognize familiar patterns that fall on our retinas in different orientations, but recognition of rotated patterns takes more time (reviewed by Kosslyn, 1988). Perhaps, then, a reliance on the use of retinally localized visual images is not an inherently small-brained strategy, but instead is the result of selection for speed of processing in animals that are pressed for time.

Landmark learning by insects: the large spatial scale

Now we consider how insects find their way to parts of the terrain that are not currently in view. Many years ago, Baerends (1941) proposed that they do this through a relatively simple extension of the image-matching process used on a small spatial scale. An insect could, during its forays in the environment, learn sequences of successively encountered visual images along routes connecting the nest with feeding-places. By encoding the appropriate direction of travel relative to the landmarks in each image, the insect would have at its disposal a sort of route map corresponding to its foraging path. Conceivably, a set of such route maps radiating from the nest would allow an insect to navigate with considerable flexibility throughout a large area around the nest.

Baerends (1941) also considered the possibility that insects could form a more comprehensive map of the terrain by integrating the experience on different separately traveled routes. This sort of map would be analogous to the mental maps that we develop when exploring a new city. Having formed such a map, we can deduce spatial relationships among points on different routes, in particular relationships that we have not directly experienced. Among other things, this allows us to estimate the short-cut path connecting any two familiar locations (Byrne, 1982). Baerends, whose studies dealt with Digger Wasps (*Ammophila campestris*), found no evidence for such maps. More recently, Gould (1986) proposed that they do play a role in Honey Bee navigation. His evidence came from experiments in which bees were trained to find a feeding-place about 150 m from the nest, and then captured *en route* to the food and displaced to another location. On their release the bees flew in the short-cut direction toward the food. Gould suggested that they had used a human-like mental map encoding the spatial relationships between the nest, the feeding-place and the location used as the release site.

Unfortunately, Gould's experiment did not provide decisive evidence for such a map. To see why, consider Fig. 5.7, which illustrates how an animal might build up a representation of spatial relationships in the environment. A key premise is that animals experience these large-scale relationships one visual scene at a time; even flying animals cannot fly high enough to take in all of the landmarks in their home range in one glance. Thus, the basic

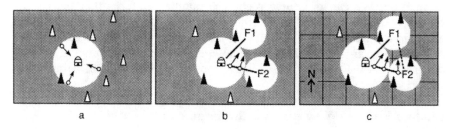

Fig. 5.7 Three ways in which an animal may learn about spatial relationships in its foraging range. The shaded regions are terra incognita, black triangles are known landmarks and white triangles are unknown landmarks. Arrows originating at small circles indicate the paths bees can select toward home (a) or towards the feeding-site F1 (b and c) from various starting-points. (a) Local image, or 'snapshot' of an array of landmarks surrounding a given goal; bees can use such snapshots to approach the nest from a variety of directions. (Reproduced from Cartwright and Collett (1983). (b) Route maps for two feeding-sites, F1 and F2; each route map consists of two local images encountered in sequence along the path to the food. Bees can use such maps to head for an unseen goal (e.g. F1 when it is their current feeding-site) even if they have been displaced so that they see the landmarks associated with the route to their goal from new vantage points (Dyer, 1991). (c) Large-scale metric map, in which bees have encoded the directions and distances separating familiar sites in reference to a common coordinate system (——, experienced; ----, computed). A metric map would allow a bee to set a novel course to F1 even if she found herself near F2, from which she could not see any landmarks associated with the route from the nest to F1. Reproduced from Dyer (1996).

elements of a large-scale representation are the images of visually separated parts of the terrain, akin to the snapshots described by Cartwright and Collett (1983) and others. The first step in developing a larger-scale map is to string together the snapshots taken on successive portions of a given route, as described above. Then, to learn the relationships among routes, the animal must encode the directions and distances traveled on each route in relation to a common reference system. This would produce the sort of map that Gould proposed for bees. In keeping with terminology introduced earlier, it can be classified as a Euclidean (or 'metric'; see Gallistel, 1990) map in allocentric coordinates. Its most important feature is that it allows the animal, by consulting the external reference system, to compute novel routes connecting familiar positions in the terrain.

As Fig. 5.7 shows, flexibility in the routes traveled does not necessarily prove that bees are guided by a metric map in allocentric coordinates. We have already seen that insects guided by a small-scale snapshot can approach the goal from a variety of directions (Cartwright and Collett, 1983), and that this does not necessarily entail an explicit link between an external reference and the memory of the landmarks (Collett and Baron, 1994). It seemed reasonable to suppose that Gould's (1986) bees were using a similar process on a larger spatial scale. In other words, perhaps they could see from the release site landmarks that they had come to associate with their familiar route to the goal, and were setting a trajectory via a process of matching their current view of landmarks with an egocentric memory image stored on previous foraging trips. Gould did not exclude the possibility that such familiar route-based landmarks were visible to bees from the release site.

What was required was an experiment that more clearly prevented bees from seeing such landmarks from the release site. When I performed such an experiment (Dyer, 1991), I found that displaced bees did not set off from the release site in the direction of the food (Fig. 5.8). Instead, they either flew in the compass direction that they were about to travel when caught leaving the hive for the food or they headed homeward. The homeward response was exhibited by bees that I had previously trained to feed at the release site, so I was certain that they had the opportunity to learn this location. The fact that they headed homeward was consistent with the hypothesis that they had developed a route map connecting this location with the nest. Evidently they could not draw upon their previous experience to develop a large-scale metric map encoding the locations of the release site, the nest and the feeding-site used in the experiment.

In a follow-up to these studies, I have examined whether bees could learn the relationship between compass references and the landmarks along a familiar foraging route and have found no evidence that they can do so (Dyer, 1996; unpublished data). This extends the insights of the map experiments by suggesting that bees lack a key ability that would be required to encode familiar route-based memories in a metric map defined by a common

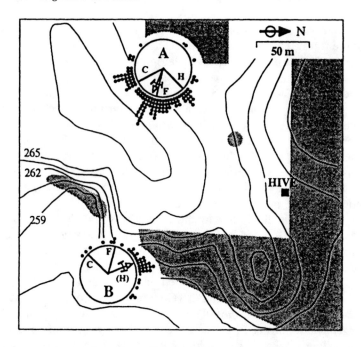

Fig. 5.8 An experimental demonstration that bees can not solve the problem presented in Fig. 5.7c and hence do not have large-scale metric maps of a familiar terrain. The shaded area represents trees and the open area grass. Polar histograms show vanishing bearings at each of two release sites for bees that had been heading from the nest to a feeder placed at the other release site when they were caught. From each release site, bees might fly toward the hive (H), toward the current feeding site (F) or in the compass direction that they were about to fly when they were captured (C). From site A, bees had a view of landmarks that they could see along their current foraging route (from the hive to site B) and they were able to compensate for the displacement by heading directly towards site B. From site B, by contrast, bees could not directly see any landmarks associated with their current foraging route. These bees were unable to compensate for their displacement by selecting a course for the food. They headed homeward instead, suggesting that they were familiar with the landmarks at site B, but had not encoded these landmarks into a metric map of the positions of site A, site B and the hive. See Dyer (1991) for additional data. Reproduced from Dyer (1996).

allocentric coordinate system. Thus, current evidence suggests that the large-scale spatial representations used by experienced bees consist of one or more route maps connecting the nest with feeding-places in the terrain but not a more comprehensive map integrating their experience on separately traveled routes.

Turning to the question of how insects acquire large-scale spatial representations, we face a picture that is considerably less clear than in the case of the memory images used on a small spatial scale. In Honey Bees, orientation flights play an important role for large-scale spatial learning, as they do for the small-scale task. Prior to its first foraging flight, a young bee makes a number of flights from the nest that appear to be for learning only. During each of these exploratory flights, the bee performs the initial stages of the orientation flight described previously, then disappears from the vicinity of the nest for 5–10 minutes, returning without any food. Similar orientation flights are also performed by flight-experienced bees that have moved with their colony to a new nesting site, for example, as members of a reproductive swarm.

These orientation flights are apparently necessary for the development of the ability to use landmarks to find the way home after displacement from the nest. Evidence for this was first provided by Becker (1958; see also Vollbehr, 1975). Becker captured bees on their return to the nest after a single orientation flight in a new terrain, and then displaced them to locations up to 700 m from the nest and recorded what percentage of the bees reached home. As mentioned, bees that have been displaced in this way should be able to find their way home only by using landmarks learned previously, since they have been deprived of the opportunity to perform path integration during the outward trip. Thus, this technique serves as an assay of how well bees had learned about large-scale landmark features during their single orientation flight. Becker found that a substantial fraction (30–80%) of bees could find their way home from locations up to 500 m from the nest. By contrast, bees that had never performed orientation flights arrived home in very low numbers even from release sites <100 m from the nest.

The ability of Becker's bees to reach home from release sites 500 m away does not prove that they had learned about the landmarks this far from the nest. It is possible that they learned only about the landmarks that pinpointed the location of the nest, and relied upon some kind of systematic search strategy to bring them into visual contact with these landmarks after leaving the release site. Such landmarks could be large structural features of the terrain such as hilltops or woodlots, and hence visible from a considerable distance away.

Following up on this question with improved techniques, Capaldi and Dyer (1998) have found that the homing performance of bees that have made a single orientation flight is indeed much higher when the release site offers a view of a landmark panorama that also would be visible during the final approach to the nest. Thus, the orientation may be primarily involved in learning landmarks fairly close to the nest. Under some circumstances, however, bees can orient homeward from release sites that are visually isolated from landmarks near the nest. This implies that they had established a simple route map connecting parts of the terrain containing the release site and the nesting-site during their single brief exploration of the environment. Obviously this learning occurs prior to any reinforcement by food near the release site or anywhere else in the terrain.

We can only speculate about what happens during the orientation flight to allow these large-scale landmark memories to be formed so quickly. Here is a very reasonable general hypothesis. During the orientation flight, the bee guides herself by referring to the sun (landmarks being as yet of no navigational value), and using her path integration system to keep track of her position relative to home. As she flies she records images of landmarks seen along the way, and somehow links to these images information about the direction that leads homeward. What needs to be resolved is how this linkage takes place.

To summarize this discussion of large-scale landmark learning, I would like to reiterate that much of the performance of insects can be accounted for by the hypothesis that egocentrically encoded visual images, or snapshots, form the building-blocks of landmark learning. Large-scale landmark learning appears to involve the learning of sequences of such snapshots. On both small and large spatial scales, external references (e.g. the sun compass) play a role in encoding spatial features of landmarks, but there is still no evidence that the bees encode landmarks in an allocentric coordinate system frame defined by these references.

The inability of insects to form large-scale metric cognitive maps raises the possibility that they are constrained in the ability to carry out the necessary computations, perhaps because of neural limitations related to their small brain size. Consider, however, that the formation of such maps might require, in addition to such computations, more extensive exploration of the environment to acquire the necessary information. Such a time cost would be incurred by any animal regardless of its brain size; simply it takes more time to cover more ground. Even in human beings, accurate large-scale cognitive maps develop only after extensive exploration of a novel environment (Pailhous, 1984), and are preceded by the development of route maps. Perhaps, as in the case of their reliance on egocentrically encoded images of small-scale landmark arrays, the bees' use of route maps rather than large-scale metric maps is not a result of neural constraints, but is a design feature favored by their need to develop spatial competence quickly.

The insect sun compass: contents and acquisition

Many species, both vertebrate and invertebrate, have evolved the ability to use the sun as a compass (reviews by von Frisch, 1967; Schmidt-Koenig *et al.*, 1991). As mentioned earlier, the sun plays an important role in allowing insects to navigate when landmarks are unfamiliar. It serves as the directional reference for their system of path integration and, once they have set a course for a particular goal, allows them to hold their course. We have also seen that bees consult their sun compass during the process of using landmarks to pinpoint the location of a goal. Then, of course, there is their dance language, which communicates the direction of food relative to the current position of the sun (von Frisch, 1967). The dance consists of a repeated series of movements in which the bee runs in a straight direction on the vertical sheet of comb, while waggling her body from side to side. The orientation of these repeated waggling runs relative to gravity correlates with the direction of the foraging flight relative to the solar azimuth.

The sun defines fixed directions on the earth's surface only if an animal can compensate for the movement of the sun relative to earth-bound features, such as landmarks and the locations of nests and food. From a cognitive perspective, the most intriguing aspect of sun compass orientation concerns the fact that animals generally learn the sun's pattern of movement. Certain features of solar movement essentially preclude the possibility of using an innate rule for sun compensation, such as compensating at the average rate of solar movement (15°/hour). For one thing, the sun's azimuth, which is the component of the sun's position that specifies directions in the horizontal plane, changes at a variable rate over the day. The rate is relatively slow as the sun is rising in the morning and setting in the evening, and relatively rapid as the sun crosses the local meridian at midday (Fig. 5.9a). Furthermore, the pattern of change of the azimuth over the day, or the solar ephemeris function, itself varies with season and with latitude (Fig. 5.9b). The most dramatic example of this variation is that the direction of movement of the azimuth is different in the northern and southern temperate regions. In the north the azimuth moves left to right across the southern horizon. In the south it moves right to left across the northern horizon. Within the tropics, both patterns are seen at different times of year. Clearly, a fixed compensation rule would ill-suit animals with the potential to live at a wide range of latitudes and seasons. Thus, it is not surprising that most species that rely upon the sun as a compass, including insects (von Frisch, 1967; Wehner, 1982; Dyer, 1987), have been shown to learn the current local ephemeris function.

An ability to learn the sun's course implies that the animal has a mechanism for integrating visual measures of the sun's changing position relative to earth-bound features with information about time of day (from the animal's internal clock). A long-standing puzzle, however, is how this integration takes place during the development of the sun compass by a naive animal. An early study of Honey Bees by Lindauer (1957, 1959) eliminated the obvious possibility that the animal simply encodes a list of time-linked positions of the sun's azimuth, thus forming a sort of 'look-up table' in memory. Instead, he found that bees reared in an incubator and then exposed only to the afternoon portion of the sun's course could nevertheless use the sun for compass orientation when they saw it for the first time in the morning. Thus, they had apparently filled in this gap in their experience of the sun's course. Similar abilities have been observed in a variety of vertebrate and invertebrate species (reviews by von Frisch, 1967; Schmidt-Koenig *et al.*, 1991; Dyer and Dickinson, 1994).

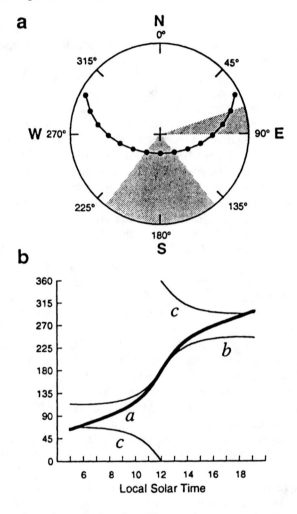

Fig. 5.9 The solar ephemeris function. The sun moves at constant rate of 15°/hour along its arc (symbols show sun's position at hourly intervals starting at 05.00 on the June solstice in East Lansing, MI, ≈43°N) but the azimuth, or the compass direction of the sun, changes at a variable rate during the day. Shaded sectors show the change in azimuth for two 2-hour time intervals, one early in the morning when the azimuth changes relatively slowly (≈7°/hour) and one spanning noon when the azimuth changes quickly (≈40°/hour) (b) An alternative method for representing the sun's pattern of movement, illustrating seasonal and latitudinal variation in the ephemeris function. The thick line (a) shows the ephemeris function for East Lansing, MI, on the June solstice. Other lines show functions for the equator on two dates: (b) the June solstice, when the azimuth shifts right to left (counterclockwise relative to cardinal compass coordinates) along the northern horizon; (c) the December solstice, when the azimuth shifts left-to-right (clockwise) along the southern horizon. Function c appears in two segments, with the break occurring at noon when the azimuth is in the north. Reproduced from Dyer and Dickinson (1996).

Over the three decades following Lindauer's discovery, various explanations were proposed for the ability of insects to estimate unknown portions of the sun's course. The general assumption has long been that the brain employs some sort of mechanism that computes the sun's position as if assuming that the azimuth moves at a uniform rate during times of day when it has not yet been observed. Different computational models have been proposed, each invoking a different process for determining the appropriate compensation rate on the basis of solar positions that the animal has observed. Each model was supported by experimental evidence; no one model could account for all of the available data.

Recent studies of Honey Bees (Dyer and Dickinson, 1994, 1996) and Desert Ants, *Cataglyphis* spp. (Wehner and Müller, 1993) have suggested that none of the previous hypotheses is correct, and have led to a new model that explains most if not all of the previous data. Here I shall discuss the experiments of Dyer and Dickinson (1994). We employed Lindauer's (1959) method of rearing Honey Bees in an incubator and then exposing them to a restricted portion of the sun's course. In our case the bees could see the sun from about 15.00 onward, which represented only about 20% of the diurnal course of the azimuth. During the afternoon flight period, we trained bees to a feeding station and labeled them individually, so that we knew that they had had the opportunity to record time-linked positions of the sun relative to landmarks around the hive. After giving the bees several days of afternoon flight experience, we considered how they would estimate the sun's position during the morning and the middle of the day. To do this we observed dances performed by bees after their return from the food at these times of day. The dance encodes the direction the dancer has flown relative to the solar azimuth on her way to the food (Fig. 5.10a). Since we knew where the food was, we could infer from the dances where the dancers had determined the sun to be relative to the line of flight.

A further crucial feature of our experimental design was that we allowed bees to make their first morning and midday flights only when the sky was completely overcast, which deprived them of any direct information about the location of the sun (Dyer, 1987). To set a dance angle on a cloudy day, bees must estimate the sun's position relative to landmarks visible during the flight. Bees with experience throughout the day can draw upon a memory of the sun's position relative to landmarks, compensated for its movement over time (Dyer and Gould, 1981; Dyer, 1987). By testing afternoon-experienced bees on a cloudy day, we challenged bees to show us, via their dances, how they computed unknown portions of the sun's course.

Previous models of sun compensation each predicted that afternoon-experienced bees would compensate at a specific, uniform rate to fill in portions of the sun's course outside the training period. Our data decisively eliminated all of these previous models (Fig. 5.10b). In the morning, bees used a solar azimuth 180° from the azimuth during the afternoon training

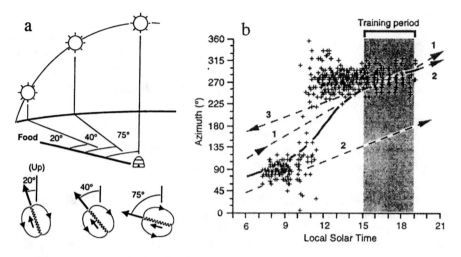

Fig. 5.10 Studies of how bees complete unknown portions of the sun's course. (a) The communication of the flight direction relative to the sun in waggle dances. The dancing bee repeatedly turns a figure-eight pattern in which the orientation of the straight 'waggling run' relative to gravity indicates the angle of the food relative to the solar azimuth. As the azimuth changes during the day, bees dancing to a given feeding-site change their orientation by a corresponding amount. (b) Solar positions inferred from dances to the same feeding-place by incubator-reared bees that had previously seen the sun only from 15.00 until sunset ('training period') on days prior to the test. The data shown are from 554 dances performed over the day by 44 different bees. Bees were tested on a cloudy day, so they could not base their dances on a direct perception of the sun during the flight to the food but had to estimate the sun's position based on their experience on previous afternoons. The thick line is actual solar ephemeris function at the time of the experiment. Lines 1–3 show the predictions of previous computational models proposed to explain the ability of insects to fill gaps in their experience of the sun's course: (1) the linear interpolation of the sun's position at times between sunset and the beginning of the daily training period; (2) the forward extrapolation (through the night and into the next day) of the rate of solar movement measured during the training time; (3) the backward extrapolation of the rate observed during the daily training period to earlier times during the day. All three do a poor job of accounting for the bees' behavior. The data can be described by a step function in which the azimuth used in the morning is 180° from the azimuth the bees experienced on previous afternoons. This figure excludes the data from two bees that used the afternoon angle in the morning and the morning angle in the afternoon (see Dyer and Dickinson, 1994, for these data).

period. They continued to use angle until a brief period near midday, when they switched to the afternoon azimuth. Thus, the afternoon-experienced bees appeared to have developed an internal representation of the sun's course that approximated its actual course. In both the internal ephemeris and the actual ephemeris, the azimuth in the morning is opposite its position in the afternoon, and the rate of change of the azimuth is relatively slow in the morning and afternoon and relatively quick at midday.

In one of our experiments, we showed that bees with more extensive flight experience throughout tracked the sun's course fairly accurately by memory, as previous studies of fully flight-experienced bees have shown (Dyer, 1987). We concluded that the approximate ephemeris developed by afternoon-experienced bees is modified as bees incorporate measurements of the sun's actual position at different times of day.

Following is a summary of our current understanding of how the insect sun compass develops, based on the results of Dyer and Dickinson (1994), on similar findings in Desert Ants by Wehner and Müller (1993), and on various other data. To begin with, naive insects are equipped with an innate representation of the general pattern of solar movement, which they link through learning to features of the local terrain. This allows them not only to remember observed positions of the sun but also to estimate the sun's course throughout the rest of the day. The internal function that produces these estimates has the following properties, all of which are also properties of any actual solar ephemeris function: (1) it is continuous – although the function developed by our partially experienced bees could be modeled as a 180° step-function, the transition from the morning angle to the afternoon angle at midday is actually progressive (if rapid) rather than discrete (Dyer and Dickinson, 1994; Dickinson, 1996); (2) it is cyclic, spanning 24 hours and 360° of azimuth, which allows insects to estimate the sun's position at night (Lindauer, 1957; Wehner, 1982; Dyer, 1985); (3) it is symmetric around noon, such that the rate of movement of the azimuth and its distance from the local meridian are matched at equivalent times before and after noon. Finally, the bees' innate function is modifiable with experience, so that it can be reconfigured to match the pattern of solar movement actually observed. A major challenge ahead will be to determine what sort of neural processes could produce an internal representation with these various properties (see Dickinson, 1996; Dickinson and Dyer, 1996).

In addition to yielding insights into mechanisms underlying the internal representation of a complex environmental pattern, studies of sun compensation offer an opportunity to examine the adaptive design of a representational process. For example, two intriguing insights emerge from the resemblance between the approximate ephemeris function developed by partially experienced bees, which we modeled as a 180° step-function, and actual patterns of solar movement. First, the 180° step-function very closely resembles ephemeris functions observed at tropical latitudes, where the azimuth stays

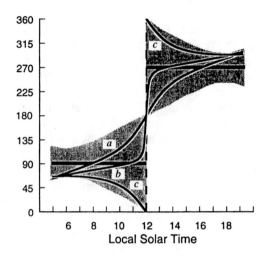

Fig. 5.11   A comparison of the 180° step-function with actual ephemeris functions. Curving lines show the ephemerides for three latitudes on the June solstice: (*a*) 43°N (East Lansing, MI, USA); (*b*) 25°N; (*c*) 15°N. The shaded region covers all the possible solar ephemeris functions that could be observed on the earth's surface (i.e. all latitudes and all days of the year). The mean of all these functions is a 180° step-function resembling that used by the bees. Reproduced from Dyer and Dickinson (1996).

relatively constant as the sun ascends toward the zenith before noon, changes by 180°, and then stays constant again as the sun descends toward the horizon in the afternoon (Fig. 5.11). Even at higher latitudes the approximate ephemeris deviates from the actual ephemeris by more than 45° of azimuth for only an hour or so at midday. An important consequence of this is that bees with limited flight experience would be able to navigate using the sun with relatively little error throughout much of the day, and thus could carry on with their foraging tasks before they had extensively sampled the sun's course at different times of day.

Second, if one calculates the average of all possible actual ephemeris functions observable on the earth's surface, the result would be a 180° step-function (Fig. 5.11). Thus, a neural network that by default encodes a 180° step-function would have to change relatively little to converge on a more accurate representation of the ephemeris function at a particular season and latitude. This might allow faster recalibration of the internal ephemeris than if the bees were not equipped with innate information about the sun's general pattern of movement (Dickinson, 1996).

Both of these observations suggest that the learning mechanisms underlying sun compensation should allow bees rapidly to develop competence in using the sun for navigation. The advantage of speed is clear when we consider that Honey Bee workers have only about 10 days in which to collect food for their colony before they die. Shortening the time spent learning about the sun and other navigational references presumably leaves more time for food collection.

The results discussed here also bear on more general questions about the adaptive value of developing behavioral capacities through learning rather than through processes not dependent on experience. Stephens (1993) has proposed that learning is advantageous when relevant features of the environment are sufficiently variable that the appropriate behavioral responses cannot be reliably specified in a hard-wired design. In addition, however, the environment should not vary so rapidly that a response learned at time t would be inappropriate at time $t + 1$. A hard-wired developmental program would be favored either when the environment is stable, and hence highly predictable, or when it varies rapidly (favoring a fixed response appropriate for long-term average conditions).

Stephens developed this argument for a simple case in which a phenotype that learns a particular response is compared with a phenotype that develops the behavior without experience. The general argument applies quite well, however, to the learning of the sun compass by Honey Bees, in which the memory of the sun's course develops under the influence of both innate and individually acquired information. What seems to be wired-in are certain features of solar movement that are universal, and hence would be useful at any point on the earth's surface and any time of the year. What is left for the individual bee to learn are the details of the current local ephemeris function, including the rate of change of the azimuth at different times of day and whether it moves across the southern or northern horizon at midday. Once these details are learned, they are almost certain to be valid for the bee's entire life, since a bee's life span is short and the pattern of solar movement observed at a particular location changes relatively slowly. Thus, a bee might have no need to learn a new ephemeris function as she ages, as long as she does not move from her current location.

The situation might be different in migratory populations, such as the African Bee, *Apis mellifera scutellata* (Schneider and McNally, 1994), and the Asian Giant Honey Bee, *Apis dorsata* (Dyer and Seeley, 1994) in which colonies undertake movements long enough to transport individuals to a latitude at which the sun's pattern of movement differs from that learned early in life. Also, longer-lived animals such as birds, even if they are relatively sedentary, may be confronted with the need to relearn the sun's pattern of movement as it changes seasonally (Schmidt-Koenig *et al.*, 1991).

In summary, the long tradition of work on the insect sun compass has arrived at a sharpened understanding of how visual and temporal information is integrated to form a representation of the sun's pattern of movement over the day. Most important are the new insights into the long-puzzling observation (Lindauer, 1957, 1959; New and New, 1962; Wehner, 1982; Dyer,

1985) that insects can fill in gaps in their experience of the sun's course. This ability at first glance seems to involve a sophisticated mathematical computation in which the insect's brain calculates unknown positions of the sun based on portions of the sun's course previously seen. The new results suggest, however, that bees and ants are equipped with an innate 'template' encoding general features of solar movement, analogous to the auditory templates that aid some birds in learning species-specific songs (Marler, 1976). The learning of the sun's course can, therefore, be seen as a process of linking this innate, generalized ephemeris function to the local terrain (which provides the reference for measuring changes in the sun's position) and then reshaping it through further experience so that the internal ephemeris resembles the actual local ephemeris function. The major questions now are: (1) how the innate ephemeris is encoded in the nervous system; and (2) how the insect's measurements of the sun's actual position are integrated with the information specified in the innate ephemeris function, leading to a more accurate representation of the sun's course (see Dickinson and Dyer, 1996).

General considerations

Spatial cognition and cognitive maps

At least within the tradition of experimental psychology, research in spatial cognition has been dominated by investigations of the much debated hypothesis that animals form 'cognitive maps' of familiar environments. This hypothesis, first articulated by Tolman (1948), has engendered both controversy and confusion, in large part because both components of the term 'cognitive map' are open to multiple interpretations. Indeed, the term is often used metaphorically to refer to any internal ordering of information, including nonspatial information (for examples, see Bennett, 1996).

Even when discussed in reference to spatial memory, however, cognitive maps are defined in a variety of ways, if they are defined at all. Some authors regard a cognitive map as any internal representation of spatial relationships that function to guide movements in the environment encoded in the map. This is the definition used by Gallistel (1990), who then suggests that cognitive maps (e.g. of different species) may exhibit a wide range of properties depending upon the kinds of spatial relationships that they encode, and the complexity of the behavior that they support. Other authors favor restricting the term to behavioral phenomena that meet certain narrower criteria. One such criterion that is commonly invoked is the ability to follow novel routes in a familiar environment, for example, to follow a never-traveled short cut between two familiar locations that have previously been visited from other directions (O'Keefe and Nadel, 1978; Byrne, 1982; Gould, 1986). The implication is that the map allows the animal to compute spatial relationships that it has not directly experienced.

As we have seen, in using familiar landmarks, insects appear to exhibit the sort of navigational flexibility that has been taken as evidence for cognitive maps. Close scrutiny of the behavior suggests, however, that this flexibility is achieved in the absence of mechanisms that compute spatial relationships not previously experienced (Dyer, 1991). This raises the question of whether the map concept should apply not merely to certain behavioral capabilities but to specific mechanistic accounts of such capabilities. In light of such difficulties, some skeptics recommend abandoning the term 'cognitive map' altogether and focusing directly on the mechanisms that allow animals to find their way (e.g. Bennett, 1996; Wehner *et al.*, 1996).

I sympathize with the skeptics to a large extent. The cognitive map concept has had considerable heuristic value by focusing attention on the internal mechanisms by which animals memorize information about the spatial arrangement of objects and locations, and use this information to guide their movements. Thus, it has provided an invaluable antidote to behaviorist descriptions of spatial behavior. On the other hand, whether cognitive maps are defined broadly, as in Gallistel (1990), or by narrow operational criteria, the map concept remains a metaphor that provides little guidance as to the underlying neural mechanisms.

Furthermore, a major source of confusion arises from the failure to acknowledge the sorts of distinctions that I described earlier about the contents of spatial memory. For example, the map concept is commonly invoked for both the small-scale task of finding a goal amidst a surrounding landmark array and the large-scale task of setting a course to a distant part of the terrain (Gallistel, 1990; Poucet, 1993). As the experiments with insects have shown, however, navigational tasks on these different spatial scales involve very different challenges. Whereas the map concept applied so broadly implies a unitary set of processes for encoding spatial relationships among landmarks, these animals have actually evolved a diversity of representational processes to meet these different challenges. Using the map concept in such a broad sense tends to restrict research by obscuring the divergent challenges that animals face in learning landmarks.

The map concept has been restrictive also because it has led to a preoccupation with landmark learning among researchers studying spatial cognition, especially within the large and active psychological community that employs rodents in laboratory mazes. By contrast, zoological studies of spatial orientation by zoologists, who have mainly studied birds (Wiltschko and Wiltschko, and Bingman *et al.*, this volume) and insects (this chapter; see also Collett, 1996; Dyer, 1996; Wehner *et al.*, 1996), have shown that processes of path integration and compass orientation play an integral role in navigation and yet involve computational problems quite distinct from those imposed by the use of landmarks. Thus, a comprehensive theory of spatial cognition must encompass these other processes as well as landmark learning (see Gallistel, 1990). It is a welcome sign that a major effort is now underway to understand the relationship between path integration and landmark learning in the rodent brain (McNaughton *et al.*, 1996).

Constraints on spatial cognition

A major conceptual and empirical challenge in animal cognition is to account for the limitations that we observe in the performance of animals solving a particular cognitive task. Why do animals not remember more, learn faster or perform tasks with less error than we observe them doing? This is a general issue, arising even for human beings, although our limitations are less immediately apparent to us than are those of animals whose abilities are evaluated in comparison with us. A commonly invoked hypothesis is that cognitive limitations are a result of information-processing constraints related to brain size. This hypothesis is invoked any time we assume that an animal could perform at a higher level if only its brain, or a particular region of its brain, were larger, for example, when we correlate species or sex differences in performance with species or sex differences in brain volume (Wehner, 1991; Clayton and Lee; and DeVoogd and Szekely, this volume).

Rigorous application of this hypothesis, however, requires specifying exactly how a larger brain (or brain region) would lead to an improvement in performance. Although it is eminently reasonable to suppose that brain size limits performance, in no case can we determine exactly why brain size might matter. Furthermore, evidence from insects, which are often assumed to be constrained behaviorally by their small brain sizes, suggests that some behavioral limitations may actually reflect design solutions for particular components of a navigational problem.

The studies discussed in this chapter illustrate these points nicely. First we can consider the learning of landmarks by honey bees, both for the small-scale task of pinpointing the location of food relative to surrounding landmarks and for the large-scale task of following a familiar foraging route. We have seen that bees encode landmarks as retinally localized snapshots and employ these egocentric representations by means of various tricks that spare them the need to encode a richer allocentric representation. This might be because their brains are too small to encode an allocentric representation, a hypothesis that could be tested only by showing how much more brain tissue (and in what configuration) would be required to encode spatial information in this way. Alternatively, it might be because an egocentric representation is an intrinsically faster recognition of familiar patterns than an allocentric encoding, and because it can be acquired with less extensive experience. These speed advantages of the egocentric strategy would not be limited to small-brained animals; I have pointed out that even human beings may employ techniques to facilitate matching of visual patterns by placing the pattern to be recognized in a standard orientation relative to retinal coordinates. Speed would be especially useful, however, for a short-lived animal like a Honey Bee, which, as mentioned, lives only about 10 days after it commences its life as a forager. Thus, the apparent constraints might actually represent adaptive design features of the learning mechanism.

Similar considerations apply to the development of the sun compass. The fact that bees are innately informed of general features of solar movement might be taken as evidence of size-related constraints on the capacity of individuals to acquire this information on their own. However, it seems more likely that the critical issue is the time that would be required to acquire through individual experience the information that bees are born with. Thus, even a large-brained animal might benefit from having an innate ephemeris function, if there were some advantage to develop a competent sun compass quickly. By the way, the evidence is equivocal as to whether birds, for which a time-compensated sun compass plays an important role in navigation, are innately informed of the overall pattern of solar movement and can estimate portions of the sun's course not previously seen. At least one study of pigeons showed that afternoon-experienced birds failed to demonstrate an ability to use a sun compass when first tested in the morning (Wiltschko and Wiltschko, 1981). On the other hand, both starlings and pigeons have been shown to exhibit sun-compass orientation under the arctic midnight sun, even if they had previously seen only the daytime course of the sun at temperate latitudes (reviewed by Schmidt-Koenig *et al.*, 1991).

A final example that supports this basic argument comes from the study of path integration, which foraging insects (and many other animals) use to keep track of their position while foraging. The output of the path integration mechanism is a continually updated estimate of the direction and distance to the nest. As Müller and Wehner (1988) first showed in Desert Ants, *Cataglyphis fortis*, this estimate deviates systematically from the true homeward direction. Specifically, ants consistently veer right of the homeward direction if they have made a sharp right-hand turn (or more right-hand turns than left-hand turns) on the outward trip, and they veer left of the homeward direction if they have made a sharp left-hand turn on the outward trip. The bias is more pronounced the sharper the turns on the outward trip. Similar systematic biases have been found in the path-integration systems of other invertebrate species, and were initially ascribed to a 'small-brained' information-processing strategy (Wehner, 1991). More recently, however, an advantage of these biases has become apparent (Hartmann and Wehner, 1995; Dyer, 1997). The effect of the systematic bias in the estimate of the homing direction is that the ant is overly conservative in closing the polygon traced out by its round-trip foraging path. The biased estimate, if not corrected, would lead the ant across the initial portion of its outward searching path. The advantage of this may be to counteract the effects of random error in the path-integration system. Random error in an estimate of the true homing direction might result in some ants failing to close the polygon altogether and hence missing the nest. By crossing the initial segment of the outward path, ants will be more likely to encounter familiar landmarks that could allow them to correct their homeward course. Thus, what appears to be 'inaccuracy' in the ant's computation might actually reflect an adaptive bias shaped by circumstances that have little to do with the intrinsic limitations on the ability of the nervous system to produce unbiased solutions to the path-integration problem.

These various examples offer a general lesson regarding apparent performance limitations in animal cognition. Although it is no doubt true that brain size does constrain performance in some way, we need to understand better how such constraints arise. Furthermore, even if brain size does constrain behavior, we must remain open to the possibility that the less constrained strategies would actually be an inferior solution to the problem the animal faces.

Functional incompatibility of spatial learning mechanisms

Considerable attention has been paid over the past 25 years to the question of whether learning mechanisms are adaptively specialized to achieve specific behavioral ends. Various chapters in this volume reflect this concern. Studies of spatial cognition in insects illustrate a particularly dramatic form of adaptive specialization (see Sherry and Schacter, 1987; Gallistel, 1990; Shettleworth, 1993): the demands of different cognitive tasks may require fundamentally different systems for organizing and encoding sensory information. Thus, the learning of landmarks entails a fundamentally different problem than the learning of the sun's course, which requires not only the storing of visual–spatial patterns but also the highly structured integration of this visual information with information from the circadian clock. Landmark learning and sun-compass learning are both fundamentally different learning tasks from path integration, which entails the rapid assimilation of compass and distance information to produce a continuously updated representation of the homing vector (reviewed by Dyer, 1994; Wehner *et al.*, 1996). In Sherry and Schacter's terminology, these various learning tasks appear to be 'functionally incompatible', requiring distinct neural architectures to encode the appropriate representation.

It is possible that these different types of spatial learning share some common processes. Furthermore, whatever functional incompatibility exists, it must not interfere with the integration that is required in learning the course of the sun relative to landmarks, or in using the sun as a directional reference for path integration. Given the likely differences in the core mechanisms, however, further studies of these learning processes offer an exciting opportunity for comparing different forms of learning within the same species.

References

Able, K. P. and Able, M. A. (1996) The flexible migratory orientation system of the savannah sparrow (*Passerculus sanwichensis*). *J. Exp. Biol.* **199**, 3–8.

Baerends, G. P. (1941) Fortpflanzungsverhalten und Orientierung der Grabwaspe *Ammophila campestris* Jur. *Tijdschr. Ent. Deel* **84**, 68–275.

Becker, L. (1958) Untersuchungen über das Heimfindevermögen der Bienen. *Z. vergl. Physiol.* **41**, 1–25.

Bennett, A. T. D. (1996) Do animals have cognitive maps? *J. Exp. Biol.* **199**, 219–224.

Byrne, R. W. (1982) Geographical knowledge and orientation. In Ellis, A. W. (eds) *Normality and Pathology in Cognitive Functions*. London: Academic Press, pp. 239–264.

Carr, H. and Watson, J. B. (1908) Orientation of the white rat. *J. Comp. Neurol. Psychol.* **18**, 27–44.

Cartwright, B. A. and Collett, T. S. (1983) Landmark learning in bees. *J. Comp. Physiol.* **151**, 521–543.

Cartwright, B. A. and Collett, T. S. (1987) Landmark maps for honeybees. *Biol. Cybern.* **57**, 85–93.

Collett, T. S. (1995) Making learning easy: the acquisition of visual information during the orientation flights of social wasps. *J. Comp. Physiol. A* **177**, 737–747.

Collett, T. S. (1996) Insect navigation en route to the goal: multiple strategies for the use of landmarks. *J. Exp. Biol.* **199**, 227–235.

Collett, T. S. and Baron, J. (1994) Biological compasses and the coordinate frame of landmark memories in honeybees. *Nature* **368**, 137–140.

Collett, T. S., Dilmann, E., Giger, A. and Wehner, R. (1992) Visual landmarks and route following in desert ants. *J. Comp. Physiol. A* **170**, 435–442.

Dickinson, J. A. (1994) Bees link local landmarks with celestial compass cues. *Naturwissenschaften* **81**, 465–467.

Dickinson, J. A. (1996) How do honey bees learn the sun's course? Alternative representations. Dissertation, Michigan State University.

Dickinson, J. A. and Dyer, F. C. (1996) How insects learn about the sun's course: alternative modeling approaches. In Maes, P., Mataric, M., Meyer, J.-A., Pollack, J. and Wilson, S. W. (eds) *From Animals to Animats 4: Proceedings of the Fourth International Conference on Simulation of Adaptive Behavior*. Cambridge, MA: MIT Press (in press).

Dyer, F. C. (1985) Nocturnal orientation by the Asian honey bee, *Apis dorsata. Anim. Behav.* **33**, 769–774.

Dyer, F. C. (1987) Memory and sun compensation in honey bees. *J. Comp. Physiol. A* **160**, 621–633.

Dyer, F. C. (1991) Bees acquire route-based memories but not cognitive maps in a familiar landscape. *Anim. Behav.* **41**, 239–246.

Dyer, F. C. (1994) Spatial cognition and navigation in insects. In Real, L. A. (ed.) *Behavioral Mechanisms in Evolutionary Ecology*. Chicago: University of Chicago Press, pp. 66–98.

Dyer, F. C. (1996) Spatial memory and navigation by honeybees on the scale of the foraging range. *J. Exp. Biol.* 199, 147–154.

Dyer, F. C. (1997) Cognitive ecology of navigation. In Dukas, R. (ed.) *Cognitive Ecology.* Chicago: University of Chicago Press.

Dyer, F. C. and Dickinson, J. A. (1994) Development of sun compensation by honeybees: how partially experienced bees estimate the sun's course. *Proc. Natl Acad. Sci. USA* 91, 4471–4474.

Dyer, F. C. and Dickinson, J. A. (1996) Sun-compass learning in insects: representation in a simple mind. *Curr. Dir. Psychol. Sci.* 5, 67–72.

Dyer, F. C. and Gould, J. L. (1981) Honey bee orientation: a backup system for cloudy days. *Science* 214, 1041–1042.

Dyer, F. C. and Seeley, T. D. (1991) Dance dialects and foraging range in three Asian honey bee species. *Behav. Ecol. Sociobiol.* 28, 227–233.

Dyer, F. C. and Seeley, T. D. (1994) Colony migration in the tropical honey bee *Apis dorsata* F. (Hymenoptera: Apidae). *Insect Soc.* 41, 129–140.

Etienne, A. S., Maurer, R. and Séguinot, V. (1996) Path integration in mammals and its interactions with visual landmarks. *J. Exp. Biol.* 199, 201–209.

Frisch, K. von (1967) *The Dance Language and Orientation of Bees.* Cambridge, MA: Harvard University Press.

Frisch, K. von and Lindauer, M. (1954. Himmel und Erde in Konkurrenz bei der Orientierung der Bienen. *Naturwissenschaften* 41, 245–253.

Gallistel, C. R. (1990) *The Organization of Learning.* Cambridge, MA: MIT Press.

Gallistel, C. R. (1996) Brains as symbol-processors: the case of insect navigation. In Sternberg, S. and Osherson, D. (eds) *An Invitation to Cognitive Science,* Vol. 4: *Conceptual and Methodological Foundations.* Cambridge, MA: MIT Press.

Gould, J. L. (1986) The locale map of honey bees: do insects have cognitive maps? *Science* 232, 861–863.

Hartmann, G. and Wehner, R. (1995) The ant's path integration system – A neural architecture. *Biol. Cybern.* 73, 483–497.

Kosslyn, S. M. (1988) Aspects of a cognitive neuroscience of mental imagery. *Science* 240, 1621–1626.

Lehrer, M. (1991) Bees which turn back and look. *Naturwissenschaften* 78, 274–276.

Lehrer, M. (1996) Small-scale navigation in the honey bee – active acquisition of information about the goal. *J. Exp. Biol.* 199, 253–261.

Leonard, B. and McNaughton, B. L. (1990) Spatial representation in the rat: conceptual, behavioral, and neurophysiological perspectives. In Kesner, R. P. and Olton, D. S. (eds) *Neurobiology of Comparative Cognition.* Hillsdale, NJ: L. Erlbaum Associates, pp. 363–422.

Lindauer, M. (1957) Sonnenorientierung der Bienen unter der Aequatorsonne und zur Nachtzeit. *Naturwissenschaften* 44, 1–6.

Lindauer, M. (1959) Angeborene und erlernte Komponenten in der Sonnenorientierung der Bienen. *Z. vergl. Physiol.* 42, 43–62.

Loomis, J. M., Klatzky, R. L., Golledge, R. G., Cicinelli, J. G., Pelligrino, J. W. and Fry, P. A. (1993) Nonvisual navigation by blind and sighted:

assessment of path integration ability. *J. Exp. Psychol. Gen.* **122**, 73–91.

Marler, P. (1976) Sensory templates in species–specific behavior. In Fentress, J. (ed.) *Simpler Networks and Behavior.* Sunderland, MA: Sinauer, pp. 314–329.

McNaughton, B., Barnes, C. A., Gerrard, J. L., Gothard, K., Jung, M. W., Knierem, J. J., Kudrimoti, H., Qin, Y., Skaggs, W. E., Suster M. and Weaver, K. L. (1996) *J. Exp. Biol.* **199**, 173–185.

Müller, M. and Wehner, R. (1988) Path integration in desert ants, *Cataglyphis fortis. Proc. Natl Acad. Sci. USA* **85**, 5287–5290.

New, D. A. T. and New, J. K. (1962) The dances of honey-bees at small zenith distances of the sun. *J. Exp. Biol.* **39**, 279–291.

O'Keefe, J. and Nadel, L. (1978) *The Hippocampus as a Cognitive Map.* Oxford: Oxford University Press.

Opfinger, E. (1931) Über die Orientierung der Biene an der Futterquelle. *Z. vergl. Physiol.* **15**, 431–487.

Pailhous, J. (1984) The representation of urban space: its development and its role in the organisation of journeys. In Raff, R. and Moscovi, S. (eds) *Social Representations.* Cambridge: Cambridge University Press, pp. 311–327.

Poucet, B. (1993) Spatial cognitive maps in animals: new hypotheses on their structure and neural mechanisms. *Psychol. Rev.* **100**, 163–182.

Roitblat, H. L. (1987) *Introduction to Comparative Cognition.* New York: W. H. Freeman.

Schmidt-Koenig, K., Ganzhorn, J. U. and Ranvaud, R. (1991) The sun compass. In *Orientation in Birds*, Berthold, P. (ed.) Basel: Birkhauser, pp. 1–15:.

Schneider, S. S. and McNally, L. C. (1994) Waggle dance behavior associated with seasonal absconding in colonies of the African honey bee, *Apis mellifera scutellata. Insect Soc.* **41**, 115–127.

Schöne, H. (1984) *Spatial Orientation.* Princeton, NJ: Princeton University Press.

Sherry, D. F. and Schacter, D. L. (1987) The evolution of multiple memory systems. *Psychol. Rev.* **94**, 439–454.

Shettleworth, S. J. (1993) Varieties of learning and memory in animals. *J. Exp. Psychol. Anim. Behav. Proc.* **19**, 5–14.

Stephens, D. W. (1993) Learning and behavioral ecology: incomplete information and environmental unpredictability. In Papaj, D. R. and Lewis, A. C. (eds) *Insect Learning: Ecological and Evolutionary Perspectives.* New York: Chapman and Hall, pp. 195–218.

Tinbergen, N., and van Kruyt, W. (1938) Über die Orientierung des Bienenwolfes (*Philanthus triangulum* Fabr.) III. Die Bevorzugung bestimmter Wegmarken. *Z. vergl. Physiol.* **25**, 292–334.

Tolman, E. C. (1948) Cognitive maps in rats and men. *Psychol. Rev.* **55**, 189–208.

Visscher, P. K. and Seeley, T. D. (1982). Foraging strategy of honeybee colonies in a temperate deciduous forest. *Ecology* **63**, 1790–1801.

Vollbehr, J. (1975) Zur Orientierung junger Honigbienen bei ihrem ersten Orientierungsfliug. *Zool. Jb. allg. Zool. Physiol.* **79**, 33–69.

Wehner, R. (1981) Spatial vision in arthropods. In Autrum, H. (ed.) *Handbook of Sensory Physiology*, Vol. VII/6C. Berlin: Springer, pp. 287–616.

Wehner, R. (1982) Himmelsnavigation bei Insekten. Neurophysiologie und Verhalten. *Vierteljahrsschr. Naturforsch. Ges. Zürich* **5**, 1–132.

Wehner, R. (1991) Visuelle Navigation: Kleinstgehirn-Strategien. *Verh. dt. zool. Ges.* **84**, 89–104.

Wehner, R. and Müller, M. (1993) How do ants acquire their celestial ephemeris function? *Naturwissenschaften* **80**, 331–333.

Wehner, R. and Wehner, S. (1990) Insect navigation: use of maps or Ariadne's thread? *Ethol. Ecol. Evol.* **2**, 27–48.

Wehner, R., Bleuler, S., Nievergelt, C. and Shah, D. (1990). Bees navigate by using vectors and routes rather than maps. *Naturwissenschaften* **77**, 479–482.

Wehner, R., Lehrer, M. and Harvey, W. R. (eds) (1996a) Navigation. *J. Exp. Biol.* **199**(1).

Wehner, R., Michel, B. and Antonsen, P. (1996b) Visual navigation in insects: coupling of egocentric and geocentric information. *J. Exp. Biol.* **199**, 129–140.

Wiltschko, R. and Wiltschko, W. (1981) The development of sun compass orientation in young homing pigeons. *Behav. Ecol. Sociobiol.* **9**, 135–141.

Wiltschko, W. and Wiltschko, R. (1996) Magnetic orientation in birds. *J. Exp. Biol.* 199, 29–38.

6

The Navigation System of Birds and its Development

Wolfgang Wiltschko and Roswitha Wiltschko

Fachbereich Biologie der J. W. Goethe-Universität, Zoologie, Siesmayerstrasse 70, D-60054 Frankfurt a.M., Germany

Moving on the wing

As a result of their ability to fly, birds can move faster than other animals, and this ability affects almost all aspects of their life. Rapid changes in location do not pose any problems. This is most obvious when spectacular phenomena such as annual migrations of birds from northern breeding grounds to subtropical and tropical wintering areas are considered – journeys which may involve thousands of kilometers. However, the distances normally covered every day by birds within their home range also exceed those of other animals. Their home ranges are considerably larger than those of mammals of comparable size. The size of the home ranges varies widely between species, from less than a kilometer to a few kilometers in most small passerines, up to 20 km in birds such as rock doves or gulls, and it may reach hundreds of kilometers in some pelagic seabirds. The regular travels within the home range are of crucial importance, as they represent the task which the birds have to master every day. The movements from one site to the next must be fast and efficient, without unnecessary delay, detours, etc., in order to save time and energy and to escape predation.

'*There is a universal need for orientation*'. With this statement, Adler (1970, p. 322) underlined the general necessity to optimize one's movements in space. It is these flights within the home range that we see as a major cause

ANIMAL COGNITION IN NATURE
ISBN 0-12-077030-X

for the development of a powerful orientation system in birds because it is in everyday life that the selective forces are strongest and even minute advantages will be profitable and will pay off in the long run.

What is the orientation system of birds like? For animals moving through the air at speeds of about 40–90 km/h, the general conditions are rather different from those encountered by animals moving on foot. Hence the mechanisms used must be adapted to the mode and the speed of motion. By moving in the 'third dimension', birds can disregard most obstacles that force walking animals to go round and detour. For flying animals, any kind of obstacle is of far less importance than it is for nonflying animals. As a consequence, flying animals can travel on more or less straight routes. However, in the case of extended flights, the potential effect of wind drift has to be considered. Their height above the ground allows the birds a wide view of the landscape as well as the sky. This means that celestial cues are much more easily accessible to birds than they are to animals, moving on foot through vegetation in structured terrain. Furthermore, their speed of flight allows birds to cover distances of 600 m or more within a minute, which means that they cross the space directly accessible to their sensory organs in a comparably short time. Where visual landmarks are concerned, this leads to fast parallactic shifts. The most important difference between birds and nonflying animals, however, lies in the distances they travel.

Birds rarely have direct contact with their destination which means that, in most cases, they cannot be guided by cues emitted by the goal itself (Fig. 6.1, left). They must, therefore, establish contact with their goal indirectly. This can only be done by using an external reference (Fig. 6.1, right).

In this chapter, we describe the navigational system of birds as we see it today. Emphasis lies on the ontogeny of the orientation mechanisms as well as on the birds' general view of space, which we believe differs from our own view by being organized around an external directional reference, a compass.

With map and compass

When an animal wants to travel from a site A to a distant site B, the position of B with respect to A must be defined. This means that the sites must be represented in such a way that the animal can derive information to lead it from A to B. One might spontaneously think of landmarks characterizing this relationship. However, for birds that move over extended distances, this hardly seems feasible as it would require remembering a very large number of landmarks and their spatial relationship. It appears much more economic to define the position of potential goals in terms of their directional relationship to each other. This relationship cannot be expressed in terms of 'right' or 'left', but requires the use of an external reference system based

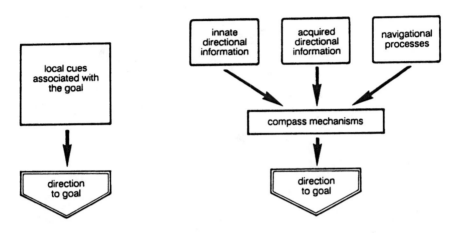

direct orientation

orientation via an external reference

Fig. 6.1   Schema illustrating two different modes of orientation. Left: Direct orientation by local cues emitted by or associated with the goal that indicate the direction to the goal directly in the sense of 'this way'. Right: Indirect orientation which established the direction to the goal via an external reference in a two-step process. The direction is first represented as a compass course, which is then located with help of a compass and thus transformed into a specification like 'this way'. (After R. Wiltschko and Wiltschko, 1995.)

on cues accessible from site A as well as from B. This leads to specifications that are equivalent to our own use of compass directions, for example, when we say: 'B lies *east* of A'.

The vast literature on bird orientation indicates that birds indeed navigate in this way. Kramer, who discovered the sun compass in 1950, was the first to realize that birds generally rely on an external reference provided by a compass. As a consequence, he described avian navigation as a two-step process: in the first step, the bird determines the compass course leading to the goal, then, in the second step, it uses a compass to locate this course (Kramer, 1959). For example, a bird that has been displaced to the north determines its home direction in terms equivalent to '180° south', then it uses a compass to find out where 180°S lies, obtaining a specification such as 'this way' or 'go there', thus transforming the compass course into an actual direction of flying (Fig. 6.1 right).

Kramer's (1959) so-called 'map and compass' model represents the basic theoretical concept in avian orientation. It was originally proposed specifically for characterizing the processes involved in the home orientation of displaced birds, as in the above example. However, the model can be

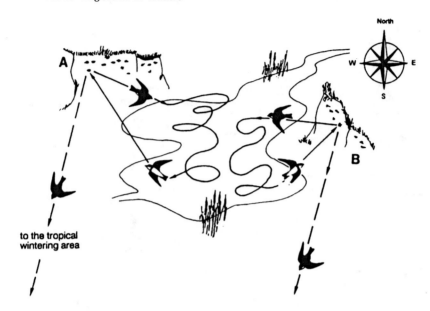

Fig. 6.2 Courses of various origin can be located with a compass: courses remembered from previous flights when the birds leave the colony on a foraging trip; courses determined by a navigational process when the birds decide to return to the colony; and the population-specific migratory course when the birds leave for their winter quarters in autumn. (After R. Wiltschko and Wiltschko, 1995.)

generalized to cover other avian orientation processes as well. The first step defining the direction to the goal as a compass course, which in the case of homing is a navigational process, is then replaced by other sources of information on the appropriate course (Fig. 6.2; cf. Fig. 6.1 right). If a bird wants to visit a favorite feeding-site, it may remember the course from previous foraging flights, i.e. in this case, the course is acquired by experience and stored in memory. During migration, when the bird moves to its wintering area in a distant part of the world, it relies on genetic information specifying the migratory course (Helbig, 1991).

The fact that the 'map and compass' model takes an external reference provided by a compass to be an integrated component of the various orientation and navigation processes has an important implication: spatial information is organized in a directionally oriented way. This is especially true for the navigational 'map' that allows birds to head to distant goals directly, in particular – the case studied most extensively by scientists – to head *home* from distant, completely unfamiliar sites (Schmidt-Koenig, 1961; Keeton, 1974; R. Wiltschko *et al.*, 1994). It seems to apply also for a bird's representation of its home range in the vicinity of the home site (e.g. Graue, 1963; Keeton, 1974; Schmidt-Koenig, 1979). Recent evidence suggests that compass orientation may even be involved in small-scale tasks within the limited space of just a few meters (W. Wiltschko and Balda, 1989; Balda and Wiltschko, 1991; Sherry and Duff, 1996).

Compass mechanisms providing the reference direction

Owing to the extent of the home range of birds, coding the directional relationship of various sites in memory requires directional cues that are independent of any specific location, being accessible from everywhere within the home range and beyond. Pardi and Ercolini (1986) termed such cues 'global cues', in contrast to 'local cues' which emerge from the local situation and usually indicate the direction to a goal area directly. Two types of factor possess the required characteristics: the *geomagnetic field*, and *celestial cues* – the same cues that humans use for direction finding. Birds also make use of both: they can locate directions with the help of the geomagnetic field and with the help of the sun; migratory birds that migrate at night additionally use the stars for this purpose. The birds thus have two or even three compass mechanisms at their disposal.

The magnetic compass and the sun compass are general mechanisms available to all birds for their various orientation tasks. The star compass, in contrast, has only been demonstrated in night-migrating birds and might be a special adaptation for their extended nocturnal flights (see Able and Bingman, 1987, for details).

The magnetic compass

Magnetic-compass orientation in birds was first demonstrated and analysed in connection with migratory orientation. An analysis of its functional mode revealed some surprising differences from the technical compass used by humans: (1) the birds' magnetic compass is an 'inclination compass', i.e. it ignores the polarity of the field, using instead the axial course of the field lines and their inclination in space; and (2) it functions only within a physiological window that is narrowly tuned to the total intensity of the ambient magnetic field, but can be enlarged by exposing the birds to other intensities for a certain interval of time (for details, see R. Wiltschko and Wiltschko, 1995).

A magnetic compass has been demonstrated in 18 species of migrants with various migration habits (W. Wiltschko and Wiltschko, 1996). Evidence of the use of the magnetic compass in homing is less clear, mainly owing to methodical problems: in homing experiments, birds are released and fly free so that the magnetic information available to them cannot be easily manipulated. A first approach was to disturb the magnetic field with magnets, which was found to be effective under overcast skies (Keeton, 1971; Ioalè

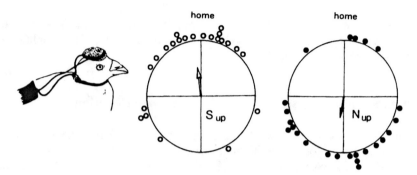

Fig. 6.3 Evidence for a magnetic 'inclination compass' in pigeons. Under overcast skies, the direction of current in a small set of coils around the pigeon's head affects the orientation of homing pigeons. Left: arrangement of the coils, wiring and the battery (black). Right: Pigeons oriented homeward when the polarity of the induced field pointed downward (S_{up}), but reversed their headings when it pointed upward (N_{up}) resulting in a resultant field with an upward inclination. (Data from Walcott and Green, 1974.)

1984; W. Wiltschko *et al.*, 1987a). Direct evidence for magnetic-compass orientation in homing is provided by the data of Walcott and Green (1974) and Visalberghi and Alleva (1979): when pigeons were released under overcast skies with a small pair of coils around their head, they roughly reversed their headings when north, induced by the coils, pointed upward (Fig. 6.3). In this case, the resultant field was directed roughly northward-upward; the pigeons' response indicates that they also use a magnetic 'inclination compass' for direction finding when the sun compass is not available (see below).

The magnetic compass appears to be a fairly simple mechanism based on the ability to detect magnetic fields. For a bird which is able to perceive the course of the field lines, the axis of the field lines defines a prominent reference direction. *North* and *south* or, considering the functional mode of the birds' magnetic compass as an 'inclination compass', *poleward* and *equatorward*, can be distinguished. With respect to these directions, any other direction can be defined. The mere perception of the geomagnetic field in this way leads to an anisotropy in the horizontal, just as perception of gravity, by defining 'up' and 'down', leads to an anisotropy in the vertical.

The sun compass

Any animal using the sun as a compass faces the problem that the sun moves across the sky during the course of the day. In order to obtain meaningful directional information, this apparent movement must be compensated for

Fig. 6.4 Shifting the birds' internal clock to 6 hours slow and its effect on orientation. Left: The photoperiod for the control and for 6 hours slow-shifted pigeons, where the photoperiod begins and ends 6 hours after sunrise and sunset. Right: The orientation behavior at a site 40 km N of the loft; the control birds (open symbols) head homeward, the 6 hours slow-shifted pigeons (solid symbols) show a typical clockwise deflection which roughly corresponds to the difference in the sun's azimuth between the time of the day and the time indicated by their internal clock. Symbols at the periphery of the circle indicate vanishing bearings of individual birds, the arrows represent the mean vectors proportional to the radius of the circle = 1. The home direction, 192°, coincides with the control vector.

by estimating the sun's current azimuth with help of an internal clock, i.e. a bird intending to fly a southerly course on the northern hemisphere must head 90° to the right of the sun during early morning, towards the sun at noon, and 90° to the left of the sun during late afternoon, etc.

This important role of an internal clock in sun-compass orientation allows us to demonstrate the use of the sun compass by an easy manipulation. In the now classic clock-shift experiments, first introduced by Schmidt-Koenig (1958a), the internal clock of pigeons is reset by subjecting them for a few days to an artificial light regime, with the light/dark period corresponding in length to the natural day, but with the beginning and end of the light period shifted, usually by 6 hours (for details see, Schmidt-Koenig, 1958b). This causes the birds to misjudge the time of the day and, as a result, the azimuth of the sun. When such pigeons are released away from their home, they show a predictable deviation from the direction taken by untreated controls; this deviation indicates that the sun compass is used (Fig. 6.4).

Clock-shift experiments also illustrate the general importance of the sun compass in the orientation of birds. Manipulating the internal clock interferes only with the sun compass, leaving the magnetic compass intact. The fact that pigeons are misled by their shifted internal clock, although their magnetic compass could have given them correct directional information, clearly demonstrates the dominant role of the sun compass. As long as the sun is visible, compass information from the sun is preferred over corresponding information from the magnetic field. Under overcast conditions, however, the orientation of pigeons is equally good (Keeton, 1969; R. Wiltschko, 1992), indicating that, when information from the sun is not available, the sun compass can be replaced by the magnetic compass without apparent loss.

Sun-compass orientation has been experimentally demonstrated in a few species only; they include feral pigeons (Edrich and Keeton, 1977), Mallards (*Anas plathyrhynchos*; Matthews, 1963) and Scrub Jays (*Aphelocoma coerulescens*; W. Wiltschko and Balda, 1989). In these cases, spontaneous behavior within the home region was tested, and the birds showed the typical deflection when clock-shifted. In a few more passerine species, sun-compass orientation has been suggested by directional training (e.g. Hoffmann, 1954; von Saint Paul, 1954, 1956; Able and Dillon, 1977; Sherry and Duff, 1996), but such conditioning experiments can be problematic where orientation mechanisms are concerned (Kramer, 1957; Schmidt-Koenig, 1958b; for discussion, see R. Wiltschko, 1980). Nevertheless, we may safely assume that the sun compass is widespread among birds and that all day-active species use this mechanism to orient their foraging flights and other flights within the home range.

The processes establishing the sun compass in pigeons

Compared to the magnetic compass, the sun compass represents a much more complex mechanism. A view of the sun alone is not sufficient for indicating directions; compensation for the sun's apparent movement, involving an internal clock, is required. The situation is even more difficult than it may seem because the sun's progress is not constant during the day. Different rates of change in sun azimuth have to be considered, which vary greatly with geographic latitude, being most uneven in the tropics. Additionally, they change with the seasons. For a bird using the sun compass, this means that the compensation mechanism must be tuned to the local sun's arc and adjusted to seasonal changes. In view of this, it is not surprising that the sun compass is not genetically fixed but established by individual experience.

A mechanism based on experience

The nature of the sun compass as a learned mechanism was first indicated by experiments with young pigeons that were raised under the conditions of a permanent 6-hour slow shift, i.e. for them, the photoperiod always began 6 hours after sunrise and ended 6 hours after sunset (W. Wiltschko *et al.*, 1976). A control group lived in a photoperiod synchronized with the natural day. In the afternoon, during the overlap time between the natural and the artificial day, both groups were set free to fly around at their loft. Later, they

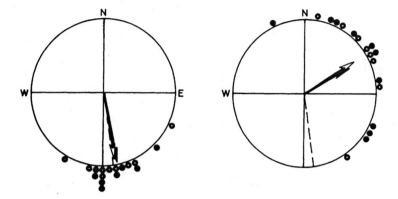

Fig. 6.5 The behavior of pigeons during and after being subjected to a permanent clock-shift reveals that the sun compass is established by experience. Left: During the phase of permanent shift, 6 hours slow-shifted pigeons (solid symbols) orient like untreated controls (open symbols). Right: When their internal clock was shifted to be synchronized with the natural day, the formerly shifted pigeons (solid symbols) showed a counterclockwise deflection that corresponded to that of 6 hours fast-shifted control birds (open symbols). For details, see text. The home direction, 172°, is indicated by a dashed radius; other symbols as in Fig. 6.4.

performed training flights together as a flock. When these birds we released singly in critical tests, the orientation of experimental birds and controls did not differ (Fig. 6.5, left).

This result, however, did not provide any conclusion about the sun compass because orientation by the magnetic compass was also possible. To find out what mechanism the experimental pigeons relied on, they were subjected to a clock-shift procedure that advanced their internal clock by 6 hours, thus synchronizing it with the natural day. As a result, the experimental birds now showed the deviation from the mean direction of controls that is typical for a fast shift; in fact, their orientation was identical with that of control pigeons whose internal clock had been shifted 6 hours fast (Fig. 6.5, right). This clearly showed that the experimental pigeons used a sun compass that had been adapted to the experimental situation: because of the 6-hour slow-shifted photoperiod, they had learned that the sun was in the south during their 'morning' and in the west at their 'noon' (W. Wiltschko *et al.*, 1976).

When is the sun compass learned?

After understanding that the relationship between sun azimuth, time and geographic direction that makes up the sun compass is based on experience, learning processes became of interest. The first question, namely, 'When do they occur?', was answered by a series of experiments with young pigeons of various age and experience (R. Wiltschko and Wiltschko, 1981).

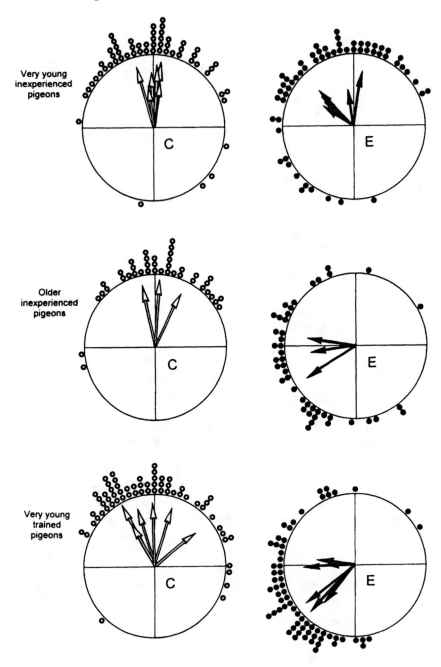

Normally, young pigeons begin to fly when they are about 5 weeks old. After a short phase of clumsiness, they circle around their home loft as a coordinated flock that gradually begins to range further and further away. These spontaneous flights offer young pigeons a first opportunity to gain flying experience and normally precede training releases away from the loft.

When such young, untrained birds were released in clock-shift experiments, those that were younger than 12 weeks did not respond significantly to clock-shifting (Fig. 6.6, top), whereas those older than 12 weeks showed the typical deflection indicating sun compass use (Fig. 6.6, center). These results seemed to suggest that the sun compass is spontaneously established at some time in the third month of life. It is impossible to give a more precise estimate, since considerable differences between individuals are indicated. The data for the clock-shifted younger pigeons show marked scatter, and a certain deviation to the expected side might be attributed to the bearings of a small number of birds that departed as if fully clock-shifted. Apparently, some advanced young pigeons develop their sun compass earlier than others, which is not unusual when spontaneous learning processes are concerned.

The experiments described above involved a third group of pigeons, namely birds younger than 12 weeks that had, in contrast to the first group, participated in a training program with up to ten releases from distances up to 10 km. These birds already showed the full response to clock-shifting at an age where the untrained members of their age group did not yet respond (Fig. 6.6, bottom). The typical deflection could be observed even in pigeons only 8–9 weeks old when these birds had homed from a few short training flights (R. Wiltschko and Wiltschko, 1981). This finding documents that the establishment of the sun compass can be considerably advanced by early flying experience. Flying experience appears to be more important than age for determining when the sun compass is established, which indicates a crucial role of flying experience for the development of the navigational system. On their first more extended flights, young pigeons face the necessity to orient and this may initiate the processes establishing the sun compass.

Fig. 6.6 The development of sun-compass orientation in young pigeons and the effect of flying experience. Left: Control birds living in the natural photoperiod; right: experimental birds whose internal clock had been shifted 6 hours fast. Top: Data from pigeons *younger than 12 weeks* whose only experience was spontaneous flights at the loft. Center: Data from young pigeons *older than 12 weeks* with only spontaneous flying experience. Bottom: Data from pigeons *younger than 12 weeks* that had homed as a flock for up to ten training releases not exceeding 10 km. For pooling data from various sites, the home direction is set upwards. Symbols as in Fig. 6.4; the various arrows indicate the vectors of individual releases. (Data from R. Wiltschko and Wiltschko, 1981.)

The time schedule for establishing the sun compass outlined here applies to homing pigeons; other species will have their own schedule depending on when they begin to fly. In young passerines, dispersal sets in shortly after fledging. Many young migrants leave for migration less than 3 months after hatching. In these cases, the development of the sun compass is expected to be considerably faster.

This leaves the question concerning the mechanisms used by young birds before their sun compass has developed. The oriented behavior of the very young pigeons (Fig. 6.6, top) clearly shows that they were in command of a well-functioning navigational system. An obvious possibility is that they use the magnetic field as a compass. This view is supported by data showing that very young, untrained pigeons were disoriented by small bar magnets under the sun, i.e. under conditions where older and more experienced pigeons are not affected (Keeton, 1971). The magnetic compass, which does not require any learning processes, appears to precede the sun compass and ensures compass orientation during the first weeks of flying before the sun compass is established. Experiments with young pigeons that were raised without ever seeing the sun also indicate the important role of the magnetic field: these birds developed a functioning orientation system relying exclusively on the magnetic compass (W. Wiltschko *et al.*, 1987a).

How is the sun compass learned?

The mode of learning was the subject of further analyses. Young pigeons were allowed to observe the sun only in the afternoon after culmination, but never before. When clock-shifted and released in their subjective morning, they departed in the same directions as untreated controls, not showing the deflection indicating sun compass use (R. Wiltschko and Wiltschko, 1980). Also, in the morning, these birds were disoriented by magnets even when the sun was visible. Together, these findings show that pigeons that were familiar only with the afternoon sun did not use the sun compass in the morning, but used the magnetic compass instead (R. Wiltschko *et al.*, 1981).

These observations indicate the inability of pigeons to extrapolate the entire arc of the sun from a limited portion and thus reveal an important feature of the processes establishing the sun compass. Apparently, they are not a mere linking together of innate components in the correct manner the way circadian rhythms are synchronized with the natural day. Instead, the birds must observe the entire sun's arc or at least extended portions at various times of the day and associate sun azimuth, time and direction in order to be able to use the sun compass at all times of the day. On the other hand, this type of learning, by relying entirely on experience, guarantees that the sun compass is everywhere adapted to the situation in which the birds have to orient, as the compensation mechanisms are perfectly tuned to the local sun's arc.

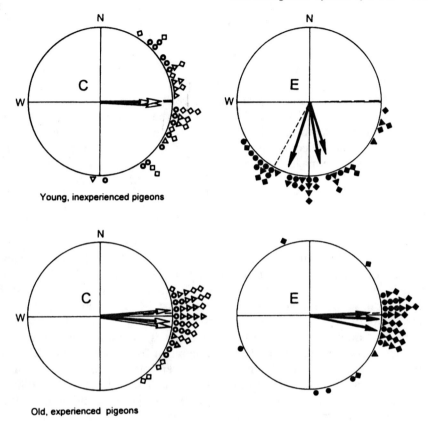

Fig. 6.7 The different responses shown by young and adult pigeons to observing the sun from an altered magnetic field suggests that there is a sensitive period. Left: Control pigeons housed in the local geomagnetic field (open symbols); right: experimental pigeons housed for 10 sunny days in a magnetic field with north turned by 120° to ESE (solid symbols). The home direction, 88°, is indicated by a dashed radius; the other dashed radius in the upper right diagram marks 208°, the home direction plus 120°. The different symbols and arrows indicate the data of individual releases. (After R. Wiltschko and Wiltschko, 1990.)

This leads to the question of how pigeons calibrate the sun's movement, namely, how, in this case, 'direction' is defined for them. Obviously, they could measure the sun's progress against the magnetic field, observing that the sun rises in the morning in the magnetic east and culminates at noon in the magnetic south, etc. In order to test this hypothesis, young pigeons were exposed to the sun with an altered directional relationship with the magnetic field. For this purpose, they were housed in a small loft enclosed in a coil system that deflected magnetic north 120° clockwise to ESE. Staying inside this field, they could observe the sun from an aviary on the roof. The first tests of this kind were performed with young pigeons raised in such a loft (W. Wiltschko *et al.*, 1983; cf. R. Wiltschko, 1983); however, it proved sufficient to move young birds into the coil loft only temporarily during the stage when their sun compass was developing (R. Wiltschko and Wiltschko, 1990). After being exposed to the altered relationship between sun azimuth and magnetic north for about 10 sunny days, the experimental birds showed a deviation from the direction of the controls to the side in which magnetic north had been deflected (Fig. 6.7, top). This is in agreement with the hypothesis that the magnetic compass serves as reference for establishing the sun compass (W. Wiltschko *et al.*, 1983; R. Wiltschko and Wiltschko, 1990).

Imprinting-like learning?

When early learning shapes an important mechanism that is of great significance in later life, it seems to suggest the possibility that the learning processes involved might represent imprinting *sensu* Lorenz (1935; see also Immelmann, 1975) rather than ordinary learning processes. To distinguish between these alternatives, two questions must be answered: (1) is there a sensitive period?; and (2) is the result irreversible?

The first question, with due caution, receives a positive answer. In the last-mentioned experiments, adult pigeons aged 2 or more years had been subjected to the same treatment, i.e. they were also exposed for 10 sunny days to the abnormal relationship between the sun and the magnetic field. The subsequent behavior of these birds, however, did not differ from that of untreated controls (Fig 6.7, bottom). This means that a treatment that markedly altered the orientation of young pigeons in their third month of life failed to affect the orientation of older, more experienced pigeons. It indeed suggests the existence of a sensitive period, in which the directional relationship between sun and magnetic field is of special significance (R. Wiltschko and Wiltschko, 1990). However, all that is known about this sensitive period is that in pigeons, it comprises the third month of life; other details, like its onset, duration, etc., are unknown.

Concerning the question of the persistence of the result of such learning, however, the answer is clearly negative. The sun compass established by young pigeons is not fixed and can be modified by later experience. This was clearly shown by a series of experiments in which adult pigeons, more than a year old and shown to have a well-developed sun compass, were transferred to conditions of a permanent 6-hour slow shift (W. Wiltschko *et al.*, 1984). After a few days of flying in the overlap time between the natural and their experimental photoperiod, and thus experiencing an altered relationship of sun azimuth, direction and time, the birds adjusted to the new situation and ceased to show an orientation difference compared to untreated controls. When, after more than 2 months, their internal clock was reshifted to the natural day, they showed the same deflection as had been observed in young birds raised under the conditions of a permanent 6-hour slow shift (cf. Fig. 6.5 right). This indicates that they had changed their original sun compass reading and had adapted their sun compass to the experimental situation (W. Wiltschko *et al.*, 1984).

In summary, the learning processes establishing the sun compass share with imprinting a sensitive period, yet the result is not irreversible. This leaves the question of the significance of the sensitive period, which is characterized by an alertness towards the relationship between sun, time of day and magnetic field. The occurrence of such a sensitive phase indicates preprogrammed learning, probably associated with specific neuronal correlates. What may be established during this sensitive period are the general principles of sun-compass orientation, namely linking sun azimuth, internal clock and direction. It may be that this connection must be formed during that phase in order to achieve functioning compensation mechanisms. The early learning processes, of course, also provide first specifications on *how* azimuth, time and direction are to be linked, but this association remains flexible and open to modification by experience.

In view of what is learned, such flexibility is not surprising. The compass mechanism which is established makes use of celestial factors and such a mechanism must remain flexible to cope with seasonal changes. This is essential to keep the orientation system at a high level of efficiency. In migratory birds, even greater flexibility is required, as they face the additional problem that the sun's arc changes with latitude. Northern migrants crossing the equator into the southern hemisphere must be expected to develop two totally different sun compass mechanisms, one compensating for clockwise movements of the sun in their northern breeding-ground and one compensating for counterclockwise movements in their southern winter quarters (cf. R. Wiltschko and Wiltschko, 1990).

Determining the homeward course from distant sites

The ability of pigeons to return from totally unfamiliar locations has always posed a problem for scientists and stimulated discussions on possible mechanisms. Several fundamentally different types of navigational strategies have been suggested. They may be divided into roughly two categories, namely those based on route-specific information collected during the outward journey, and those based on site-specific information collected at the starting point of the return flight. Considerable experimental effort has been invested in attempts to distinguish between the various possibilities. For this type of analysis, the birds' preference of the sun compass over the magnetic compass provides an important methodological tool, because sun compass orientation can easily be demonstrated in free-flying birds (see 'The sun compass'). By indicating sun compass use, clock-shift experiments offer an easy means of demonstrating a general involvement of compass orientation. This, in turn, is crucial for deciding whether or not the orientation strategy used in a given case follows the so-called 'map and compass' model described by Kramer (1959).

Positive results of clock-shift experiments thus exclude procedures like dead-reckoning in the sense of path integration based only on internal representations of the route, as has been suggested by Barlow (1964) and was demonstrated, for example, in small mammals moving within the limited area of an arena (Etienne *et al.*, 1985). Likewise, a response to clock-shifting excludes homing based solely on familiar landmarks, as was proposed by Griffin (1955), and has recently been reconsidered as a strategy at familiar sites under certain conditions (e.g. Papi, 1986). This leaves mainly two types of strategies, namely the use of route-specific information based on an external reference, and navigation by site-specific factors whose directional relationship to the goal is familiar to the birds (W. Wiltschko and Wiltschko, 1982).

The available evidence indicates a basic difference between young, inexperienced and older, experienced pigeons. Experienced pigeons, in contrast to young, inexperienced ones (see 'The orientation of untrained pigeons'), were largely unaffected by various manipulations which interfered with their access to navigational information during the outward journey, like transporting them on irregularly rotating turntables (e.g. Matthews, 1951; Keeton, 1974), distorting the magnetic field (e.g. Kiepenheuer, 1978; R. Wiltschko and Wiltschko, 1985) or a combination of various treatments, including olfactory deprivation (e.g. Wallraff, 1980; Wallraff *et al.*, 1980). Even when pigeons were transported to the release site under deep anesthesia, they headed home as soon as they had recovered (e.g. Exner, 1905; Walcott and Schmidt-Koenig, 1973). These findings speak against orientation by information collected *en route* and indicate that experienced birds mainly rely on local, site-specific information for determining their home course. This leads to the concept of a directionally oriented navigational 'map'.

The navigational 'map'

The concept of a navigational 'map' was inspired by the commonly used geographic map with its world-wide grid of coordinates and dates back to the last century (Viguier, 1882). However, a world-wide 'map' is certainly not the only theoretical possibility. Except during migration, most birds move around within a limited area, and their spontaneous flights seldom exceed 10 or 20 km. Even displacement experiments with pigeons usually take place within a radius of less than 200 km. Thus, factors of only regional distribution might also be enlisted for navigation, provided they are available within an area of sufficient range.

Wallraff (1974) discussed the various possibilities based on data on pigeon homing in the literature. One point becomes evident: celestial cues, like the sun or stars – which at one time were suggested as being suitable (e.g. Matthews, 1953; Sauer, 1957) – are, in fact, not suitable as components of the navigational 'map' because the rotation of the earth and the movements of the earth around the sun cause complex apparent movements. The use of celestial factors in the 'map' would require an extremely exact internal clock and highly complex compensation mechanisms, much more complex than the use of the sun as compass. Furthermore, the results of clock-shift experiments clearly show that the sun is used as compass only (cf. Kramer, 1959; Keeton, 1974). This leaves geophysical factors – factors that originate in the earth itself, rotate with the earth and thus do not need sophisticated additional mechanisms.

The model

The present model of the avian navigational system has been described in detail by Wallraff (1974, 1991) and by W. Wiltschko and Wiltschko (1978, 1982, 1987).

The navigational 'map' or 'grid map' (Papi, 1990) is assumed to be a directionally oriented mental representation of the spatial distribution of navigational factors. These factors – of which there must be at least two – have the nature of *gradients*, i.e. their values vary continously in space, and they must not intersect at very acute angles (Fig. 6.8). Birds know in what direction the respective values increase and decrease, and can thus derive their home course by comparing the local scalar values at their present location with the ones remembered from home. In the example in Fig 6.8, the birds know that one gradient increases to the east and another to the south. If they find themselves at a location where the local values of both are lower than the home values (P_1 in Fig. 6.8), they know that they are in the northwest of home and have to head towards the southeast.

So far, the navigational 'map' is described as an open system. The number of factors is not limited so that any suitable gradient extending over a large enough area might be incorporated and serve as a navigational factor. Several such factors are under discussion, including magnetic and gravitational cues, odors, infrasound, the view of a distant landscape feature, etc. (see Fig. 6.20). Here, however, we are not concerned with the specific nature of navigational factors, but focus on how such information may be represented and processed.

In the vicinity of home, the 'grid map' based on environmental gradients is supplemented by a 'mosaic map' of landmarks, which is discussed in more detail on page 186.

Observations and findings

Clock-shift experiments with homing pigeons have produced the typical deflection in all directions from the loft and at distances ranging from less

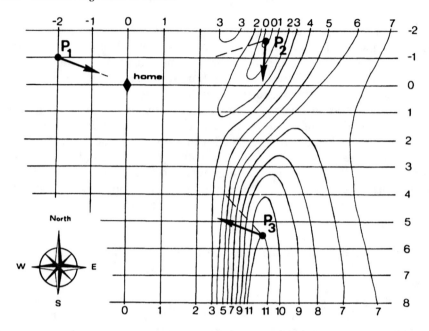

Fig. 6.8 A model of the navigational 'map' or 'grid map' which is assumed to be a *directionally oriented* mental representation of the spatial distribution of environmental gradients. The isolines of two such gradients are given in relative units. Left side: at site P_1, where the gradients show a regular distribution, the birds determine their home course correctly; right side: irregularities in the distribution of gradients at P_2 and P_3 lead to *release-site biases*, initial errors, which are later corrected. (After W. Wiltschko and Wiltschko, 1982.)

than 1.5 km to 167 km (e.g. Schmidt-Koenig, 1965; Keeton, 1974). Thus, navigation follows the 'map and compass' model within the entire range studied so far and we may conclude that the relation to home is generally established via a directional reference. The next step is to compare the model of the 'map' with the actual data on pigeon navigation.

Any model of the navigational 'map' should be able to account for the following findings:

1. Birds are able to determine their home direction at totally unfamiliar, distant sites far beyond the range of immediate experience.
2. The directions in which pigeons depart rarely coincide with the true home direction; however, the deviations are mostly small, seldom exceeding 30° to 45°, and they are typical for a given site (for a summary, see R. Wiltschko, 1992).
3. Pigeons set off immediately, i.e. in less than 20 seconds (e.g. Pratt and Thouless, 1955), in the direction in which they finally depart.

The latter observation means that the navigational process does not require an extended searching flight, thus excluding the possibility that pigeons need to scan local gradients to learn gradient directions. What is more, pigeons have at least a rough idea about their home direction before they even start flying. Released from a cage with several openings, they tended to choose the ones pointing towards the direction in which they will later vanish from sight (e.g. Chelazzi and Pardi, 1972; Kowalski, 1994). The model of the navigational 'map' explains these findings by assuming that birds know in which direction the values increase and decrease, and have this information incorporated in their 'map'. The following section will describe how this knowledge is obtained.

The first two observations – orientation at unfamiliar sites and headings deviating from the home course – are explained by the assumption that the 'map' is based on environmental gradients. There is no direct proof for the use of gradients as navigational factors; however, it is unclear how such evidence might be obtained. Pigeons are able to head more or less directly home from distant sites where all local features are unfamiliar to them, and they can do this even when they have been deprived of all known navigational information during the outward journey. This can only be explained by the use of factors indicating position which the birds can read because they know them from other locations. It points to factors such as gradients, which can be extrapolated beyond the range of direct experience.

At such distant sites, birds have to base extrapolation on their 'map' as it is formed by the gradient directions within the familiar area. If the navigational factors are not completely regularly distributed, this might cause birds to misjudge their position and, as a consequence, depart in directions deviating from the home course (see Fig. 6.8, sites P_2 and P_3). The model of the navigational 'map' thus attributes the frequently observed deviations from the true home course to unexpected irregularities in the distribution of navigational factors (cf. Keeton, 1973; W. Wiltschko and Wiltschko, 1982). This appears to be the most parsimonious explanation, since it is based only on two assumptions, namely, that navigational factors can be extrapolated and that they may not be totally regular. Other assumptions are not necessary.[1]

The observation that these deviations are characteristic for a given site (e.g. Wallraff, 1959, 1970; Schmidt-Koenig, 1963; Keeton, 1973) is in agreement with this interpretation. There may be considerable variability, but, at certain sites, the pigeons depart almost always to the right of home, while at others, they tend to depart to the left. The size of the deviations and the amount of scatter are likewise characteristic (Fig. 6.9; for more examples, see R.

---

[1]A totally different explanation for deviations from the home course, based on the assumption of a 'preferred compass direction', has been proposed by Wallraff (e.g. 1978, 1986).

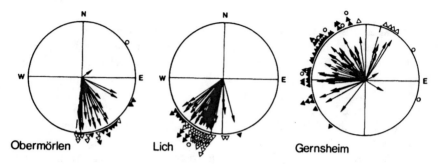

Fig. 6.9 Examples for the initial orientation of pigeons from our Frankfurt loft at three frequently used release sites. Obermörlen is 30 km N; Lich is 40 km N and Gernsheim is 40 km S of the loft. The home directions, 185°, 192° and 16°, respectively, are indicated by a dashed radius. The arrows represent the mean vectors of individual releases; the symbols at the periphery give the direction of these vectors and indicate whether the group of pigeons released together was homeward oriented (open triangles), showed a *bias* or a significant deviation from the home direction (solid triangles), or did not show a significant directional preference (open circles). (After R. Wiltschko, 1993; for details on the definition of the various categories of initial orientation, see W. Wiltschko *et al.*, 1987b.)

Wiltschko, 1992, 1993). Apparently, at many locations, not the true home direction, but a direction regularly deviating from it is indicated by the navigational system. The phenomenon is referred to as 'release-site bias' (Keeton, 1973), as a translation of the German terms 'Ortsmißweisung' by Schmidt-Koenig (1958b) and 'Ortseffekt' by Wallraff (1959). The bias direction and not the home direction also represents the baseline for clock-shift responses (Schmidt-Koenig, 1958b; Keeton, 1973; R. Wiltschko, 1993; see also Fig. 6.16, right).

Release-site biases are not restricted to pigeons, but are observed in other species of birds as well. In the case of Bank Swallows, *Riparia riparia*, the similarity of biases to those of pigeons could be demonstrated directly: birds from a colony near the pigeon loft showed the same deviations from the home course as pigeons when they were released at the same sites (Fig 6.10; Keeton, 1973). The factors causing these deviations act on the various bird species in a similar way, as must be expected if they are part of the 'map'.

The processes establishing the navigational 'map'

The navigational 'map' is established by learning processes. This is true for regional and for world-wide factors alike. None of the known environmental gradients is completely regular, so that the birds in any case have to familiarize themselves with the distribution of these factors within their home region. These learning processes, on the other hand, allow birds to include

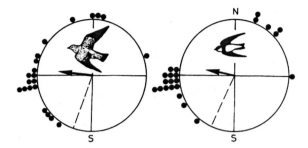

Fig. 6.10 The similar behavior shown by carrier pigeons (left) and Bank Swallows (right) from the same home region at a site 145 km NNE shows that release-site biases are not restricted to pigeons, but involve other species in a similar way. (Data from Keeton, 1974.) Symbols as in Fig. 65.

all suitable factors into the 'map' and guarantee that the navigational 'map' is perfectly adapted to the situation in the birds' home area.

Very little is known about the respective learning process because, in this case, the relevant information cannot be manipulated as easily as in the case of the sun compass. However, some details may be inferred from the behavior of pigeons with varying experience, and certain parallels to the development of the sun compass may be assumed.

Spontaneous experience

It appears safe to assume that pigeons begin to establish their 'map' during the first months of life. When young Rock Doves, *Columba livia* (the species from which the carrier pigeons originate), start to fly, they join their parents on extended foraging flights and thus have an opportunity to establish their 'map' under their parents' guidance. Young carrier pigeons normally do not undertake such foraging flights. When released, they circle around their loft as a flock and, after reaching a certain level of flying skill, they venture farther and farther away, thus becoming familiar with the vicinity of their home. Later, on more extended flights, the young pigeons explore an increasing area of their home region and begin to incorporate the distribution of local gradients into their 'map'.

An alternative hypothesis suggested that the navigational 'map' may instead be established during long-term exposure at the home loft (e.g. Wallraff, 1974, 1983; Papi, 1976, 1982). However, this appears possible only with a certain type of factor, e.g. odors carried by the wind; in this case, the birds might associate specific odors with wind direction. Local values of gradients, in contrast, do not convey any information on gradient directions. Hence, the distribution of gradients can only be realized during extended flights where young pigeons directly experience an increase or decrease in gradient values.

The importance of flying for the development of the navigational system is amply documented. Pigeons will consider as their 'home' the location where they flew around during the first months of life. It is well known among pigeon-breeders that settling new birds at one's loft works well only if the young birds have not yet flown around; otherwise, they might return to their previous loft. Findings from wild birds also emphasize the crucial role of free flying for establishing the 'map': only birds that had been allowed to fly freely in an area were able to return to that area after migration; migrants were never found to return to a place that they knew only from staying in an aviary (Löhrl, 1959, for Collared Flycatchers, *Ficedula albicollis*; Berndt and Winkel, 1980, for Pied Flycatchers, *Ficedula hypoleuca*; Sokolov *et al.*, 1984, for Chaffinches, *Fringilla coeleps*). These observations have often been interpreted in view of imprinting on a specific area; however, they also suggest that extended flights are necessary to obtain the crucial information enabling birds to return to a specific home area. Baker (e.g. 1982; 1993) also points out the importance of spontaneous exploratory trips as the basis for establishing the navigational system.

Considering this, establishing the navigational 'map' might take place in the following way. While flying around, young pigeons register the direction in which they are flying with the help of their compass mechanisms; at the same time, they register changes in gradient values encountered *en route*. These two pieces of information are linked together and incorporated in the 'map' by associating changes in gradients with the current direction of flight. This gradually leads to a mental representation of the navigational factors which reflects the distribution of gradients within the home region in a realistic way.

Experiences gathered on spontaneous flights are difficult to assess, since they escape control. One can never tell where the birds went and precisely what places they visited. Also, among young pigeons, there is considerable variability in the willingness to fly; some individuals as well as some groups are much more ready to undertake extended flights than others. Altogether, we can only assume that experience and the familiarity with the area around the loft increase with increasing age, while, at the same time, enormous differences between individuals and groups must be expected. The latter may result in differences in the way the distribution of the navigational factors is interpreted.

A chance observation shows that experience in the vicinity of the loft can indeed shape the navigational 'map'. From a group of young pigeons allowed to fly at their loft, about two-thirds took off and stayed out of sight for about 1 hour 15 minutes; the ones that stayed at home were identified. When released the next day at a site 66 km from the loft, there was a significant difference in orientation between the two subgroups (Fig. 6.11). At a leisurely flying speed, the birds may have covered about 60 km on their excursion. It is unlikely that they went straight out and straight back, but even in this case,

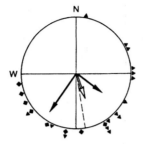

Fig. 6.11 The effect of a spontaneous experience near the loft on the orientation of untrained young pigeons at a site in 66 km distance. One group of pigeons had gone for a spontaneous flight that took them out of sight for more than an hour on the day before release (diamonds), the others had stayed at home (triangles). The home direction, 170°, is indicated by a dashed radius. The two solid arrows represent the mean vectors of the two subgroups, the open arrow gives the mean vector of the joint samples. (After R. Wiltschko, 1991.)

they never approached the future release site. The data in Fig. 6.11 are the only documented case so far that an experience on a spontaneous flight may have consequences for navigation at a distant location. This experience caused the pigeons to extrapolate their 'map' differently, resulting in a different interpretation of the navigational factors at the distant release site.

The orientation of untrained pigeons

The development of the navigational 'map' must be assumed to be a continuous process, promoted by spontaneous experiences and, if the pigeons are released for training flights away from their loft, by experiences gathered during these flights. The behavior of untrained birds indirectly reveals some details on how the 'map' develops.

Figure 6.12 shows how the vector length and the deviation from home of untrained pigeons vary with increasing age. The data show a pronounced trend: very young birds are well oriented homewards. Between 9 and 10 weeks of age the agreement between birds is best; in most cases, the bearings are close to the home course. Between 10 and 11 weeks of age, the agreement between birds is still very good, but larger deviations from home are now more frequent; in about half the releases, release-site biases are observed. When the birds grow older, their behavior is characterized by decreasing agreement within the group. Vector length and deviation from home show more and more variability, which is still true for untrained yearlings, i.e. pigeons in their second year of life (R. Wiltschko, 1991). This great variability seems to be typical for the final stage of a navigational system based only on spontaneous experience.

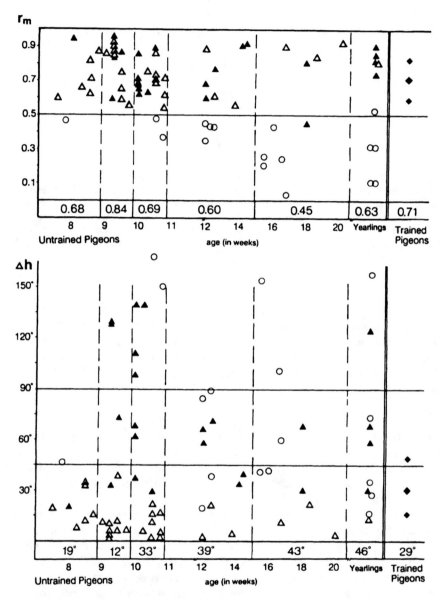

Fig. 6.12 The initial orientation of inexperienced pigeons of various ages. The upper diagram gives the vector length, r_m, the lower the deviation from home, Δh, of untrained young pigeons from the Frankfurt loft arranged according to increasing age. Medians of the data between the dashed lines are given as numerical values above the abscissae. The various symbols refer to the category of orientation (see Fig 6.9): open triangles, homeward oriented; solid triangles, bias; open circles, no significant orientation. The median and the quartiles of the data from trained Frankfurt birds are given for comparison as diamonds on the right. (From R. Wiltschko, 1991.)

At first glance, the observed trend – initally excellent homeward orientation followed by an apparent deterioration – seems odd. However, it reflects
different phases in the development of the navigational system, involving a
change in strategy. When very young, untrained pigeons were displaced in
a distorted magnetic field, they were no longer oriented. The same magnetic
treatment after arrival at the release site had no effect (Fig. 6.13), which
clearly shows that the treatment itself does not affect orientation, but only
its application during displacement (R. Wiltschko and Wiltschko, 1978). This
suggests a crucial role of route-specific information from the magnetic field.
Apparently, young pigeons determine their homeward course by reversing
the direction of the outward journey – a strategy that may be characterized
as *route reversal* (Schmidt-Koenig, 1975; W. Wiltschko and Wiltschko,
1982);[2] twists, turns and detours of the outward journey are apparently
integrated.

The effect shown in Fig. 6.13 is restricted to very young, untrained pigeons.
Untrained birds older than about 12 weeks were no longer found to be
affected by displacement in a distorted magnetic field and neither were
trained pigeons (R. Wiltschko and Wiltschko, 1985). This indicates a change
in navigational strategy at about the pigeons' third month of life: the initial
phase of excellent homeward orientation in Fig. 6.12 may be interpreted as
a stage during which the young birds rely exclusively on information collected
during the outward journey. The increasing number of release-site biases
observed from the tenth week onward marks the onset of a gradual transition
to the use of the navigational 'map', at the same time indicating that some
groups start to use 'map' information earlier than others. In the beginning,
experience within the groups is still rather uniform, which is reflected by long
vectors. The decrease in vector lengths observed later appears to indicate

---

[2]There is an unfortunate confusion of terms concerning this navigational strategy of integration
of the route using a compass as external reference. The term 'route reversal' was introduced
by Schmidt-Koenig (1975) in order to designate this strategy first described in foraging ants and
bees (e.g. Jander, 1957; von Frisch, 1965; Wehner, 1972). We adopted this term for the analogous
strategy in young pigeons (e.g. W. Wiltschko and Wiltschko, 1982, 1987; R. Wiltschko and
Wiltschko, 1995), emphasizing the crucial role of compass orientation, which, in birds, involves
the magnetic compass, whereas social hymenoptera seem to rely exclusively on the sun compass.
Papi, in an attempt to characterize the various possible types of strategies based on route-specific
information, suggested the term 'route reversal' for a very different strategy, namely for
orientation following sequences of landmarks (e.g. 1990). Orientation involving a compass as
directional reference was termed 'course reversal', but integration was explicitly excluded in the
definition. For the integration of directions and distances, Papi proposed the term 'path
integration'. Unfortunately, the term 'path integration' has been used frequently in connection
with orientation based entirely on internal signals from self-produced movements, without
external cues (e.g. Etienne *et al.*, 1985, 1991), which is just the opposite of the strategy applied
by young pigeons, so that this term might lead to confusion. We will continue to use the
traditional term 'route reversal' for navigational strategies based on information obtained during
the outward journey, and specify what type of 'route reversal' we mean – in the present case,
a strategy that is based on integrating directional information with a compass as external
reference.

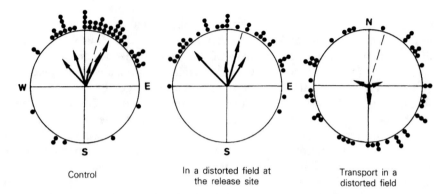

Fig. 6.13   The displacement in a distorted magnetic field results in disorientation in very young, untrained pigeons, indicating that these birds rely on information collected *en route* during the outward journey. Symbols as in Fig. 6.6. (Data from R. Wiltschko and Wiltschko, 1978.)

growing differences between individuals, probably caused by differences in individual experience. The example in Fig. 6.11 illustrates this: part of the group had by chance been observed to fly out of sight, and thus the difference in orientation owing to this incident could be recognized as such. Yet normally, one would not be aware of spontaneous flights, and the wide scatter caused by specific differences in experience might simply be misinterpreted as 'poor orientation' (see open arrow in Fig. 6.11).

Why change strategy?

The excellent initial orientation during the phase of route reversal and the often rather poor orientation when the pigeons begin to use their 'map' leads to the question why the birds change their strategy at all, particularly as it appears to change for the worse. However, the reasons are quite obvious when the advantages and the disadvantages of the two strategies are compared. Route reversal has one crucial advantage: it does not require any foreknowledge. The relevant information is obtained during the outward journey; all that is needed is a functioning compass and the ability to record and process directional information, including the integration of detours. The basic computations may be complex, but they seem to represent an innate ability, thus being carried out automatically without requiring any learning. Yet any strategy based entirely on route-specific information has one crucial disadvantage: there is no possibility to correct for errors. The accuracy of navigation depends strongly on how accurately birds can measure and process directional information. Errors may balance each other to some extent, but absolute accuracy cannot be expected. Any initial mistake, however, bears the danger that the birds pass their home at a certain distance, and this might become of crucial importance when the young pigeons begin to venture farther away. The navigational 'map', on the other hand, allows the birds to redetermine their home course from any site as often as they feel necessary. This increases the safety of getting home. However, the use of the 'maps' requires detailed knowledge on the spatial distribution of the factors involved – knowledge that is not immediately available but which must be gathered by learning processes that require a certain amount of time.

When the young birds begin to fly, they have only one option: without knowledge of the distribution of the navigational factors, they can only rely on route-specific information. This is sufficient for the first short flights. Yet when the birds extend their flights, the inability to correct for errors becomes an increasing risk. Any system that allows such corrections appears advantageous. The change in strategy from using route information to the use of the navigational 'map' appears to take place, with considerable variability, at some time within the third month of life (see Fig. 6.12), at approximately the same time as the sun compass is established and possibly in a similar fashion. Like the development of the sun compass, it might be promoted by early flying experience. As soon as the 'map' is used, initial errors are no longer of importance. Also, if wind drift leads to a certain lateral displacement, this can be easily compensated for by redetermining the homeward course. The increased safety resulting from the use of site-specific information must be assumed to be the primary reason for changing from route-based navigation to navigation with help of the 'map' (W. Wiltschko and Wiltschko, 1982, 1987).

Figure 6.12 appears to suggest that the initial orientation of the older untrained birds now using their 'map' is not particularly good – an apparent weakness that must be attributed to the untrained birds' limited experience, which may provide an insufficient basis for extrapolating navigational factors at greater distances. At this point, however, one should be aware that displacement experiments often overchallenge the untrained pigeons by forcing them to home from distances much farther away than they would spontaneously fly. Figure 6.14 shows that a navigational system based only on spontaneous experience is sufficiently powerful for orientation within the area around the loft – larger deviations and increased scatter become frequent only at distances of more than 25 km, far beyond the range of spontaneous flights (R. Wiltschko, 1991).

For a more detailed discussion of the processes establishing the navigational 'map', see W. Wiltschko and Wiltschko (1987) and R. Wiltschko (1991).

Updating the 'map'

At most lofts, young pigeons are released in flocks away from their loft to simulate some of the experiences their wild ancestors gathered on extended

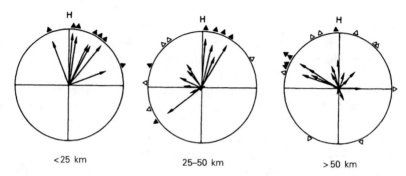

Fig. 6.14 The orientation of untrained pigeons at various distances from the loft indicate a deterioration with increasing distances. The home direction is upward. The arrows represent the mean vectors of individual releases, the triangles at the periphery give the mean directions and indicate whether the samples were significantly oriented (solid triangles) or not (open triangles).

foraging flights. Such systematic training usually involves birds that are 3–6 months old; it makes experience within the group more uniform and enlarges the area of immediate experience considerably. As a consequence, birds become familiar with the true distribution of the navigational factors in a more extended area. This is reflected in the generally improved orientation of trained pigeons, which is indicated at the right-hand side of Fig. 6.12 for comparison (R. Wiltschko, 1991).

The experience young pigeons gather during their first months of life seems to set general rules for the use of the navigational 'map', specifying how navigational factors are to be extrapolated. However, the 'map' remains flexible and later experiences are regularly included. This is demonstrated by a series of experiments at distant sites 120–200 km from the loft (Grüter and Wiltschko, 1990). The test birds were old, experienced pigeons. The flying experience of all groups was similar, but involved different regions, i.e. one group had been trained in the N, another in the SE of the loft. Figure 6.15 documents a continuous improvement of orientation with increasing familiarity. Pigeons that had homed from a distant site in a previous release (Fig. 6.15, right) were much better oriented than birds that had the same flying experience, but in a different region (Fig. 6.15, left). The most interesting point, however, is that even birds that had covered 60–80% of the route from the test site on a previous homing flight (Fig. 6.15, center) were better oriented than the birds that had their entire experience in a different region. This suggests that knowing parts of the terrain between the distant site and home had already helped their orientation at the distant site. This can best be explained by the assumption that their extended knowledge on the true distribution of navigational factors in the region between home and the future

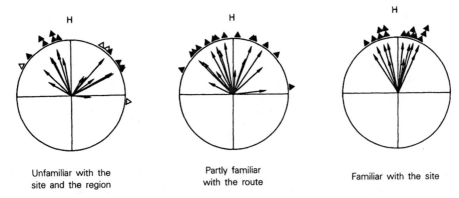

| | | |
| Unfamiliar with the site and the region | Partly familiar with the route | Familiar with the site |

Fig. 6.15 The influence of regional and local experience on the initial orientation of experienced pigeons. All birds had similar flying experience but in different regions. The home direction is upward. The arrows represent the mean vectors of individual releases; the triangles at the periphery give the mean directions (open: non-significant samples). (After Grüter and Wiltschko, 1990.)

release site helped them with interpreting these factors at the distant site (Grüter and Wiltschko, 1990).

The findings described above show that even pigeons several years old extended their 'map' and included new information when they found themselves in a region where they had never been before. Details on the processes updating the navigational 'map' are not known; one would tend to assume that they are similar to those establishing the 'map' during the birds' first year. However, there is one important difference: the processes updating the 'map' only modify the 'map' locally. This was pointed out by the experiments mentioned above, when some birds had been released in the unfamiliar region before their second flight from the distant site in their training region. The experience in a new region did not affect their behavior within the familiar region.

Local modifications of the 'map' are also suggested by experiments with adult pigeons that were transferred to conditions of a permanent clock-shift (W. Wiltschko *et al.*, 1984). After their sun compass had adapted to the experimental situation (see 'The processes establishing the sun compass in pigeons'), they continued to show small deviations in the range of 30° from their controls, which may be attributed to an involvement of temporally varying map factors. Permanently shifted birds always showed these deviations when they were released *for the first time* from a given site but not on their second flight. Interestingly, these deviations at new sites were still observed after more than 2 months, at a time when they had long disappeared from other, familiar sites. Here, too, the experience of homing from a specific location seemed to change the reading of the 'map' for that location only (and maybe the immediate vicinity), without affecting the pigeons' interpretation at other sites (for a detailed presentation of the relevant data and a more detailed discussion, see W. Wiltschko *et al.*, 1984).

In summary, the processes originally establishing the 'map' appear to set up general rules for reading and extrapolating the navigational 'map', rules that are, for the time being, valid everywhere. Beyond the range of immediate experience, the birds seem to use these rules until direct experience tells them that the distribution of gradients in a particular region differs from the one represented in the 'map'. Then they modify the 'map' locally according to this new experience. This difference between establishing and updating the 'map' is of great importance because it seems to guarantee the formation of a differentiated, highly effective 'map' for an extended area. Birds can even deal with some of the irregularities in the distribution of environmental gradients this way: it is helpful to adapt the regional part of the 'map' to the specific distribution of the navigational factors in the respective region, at the same time leaving untouched the rules for extrapolation in other regions, where the distribution of navigational factors may be different and where the old rules may work quite successfully.

Orientation at familiar sites and within the home range

The behavior at familiar sites is of special interest because it was repeatedly hypothesized that birds might change their navigational strategy and rely solely on familiar landmarks. This would correspond to Type I orientation as proposed by Griffin (1955), later referred to as 'piloting'. It means that birds follow sequences of landmarks until they reach their goal. 'Piloting' at familiar sites was again suggested by Benvenuti *et al.* (1973), Hartwick *et al.* (1977), Papi (1986) and others.

At familiar sites

The available data, however, clearly argue against such a sole use of landmarks. Pigeons respond to clock-shifting also at familiar sites, which means that, at familiar sites, the direction of flight is also determined as a compass course (e.g. Luschi and Dall'Antonia, 1993; R. Wiltschko *et al.*, 1994). This is not only true for release sites that birds just cursorily know from one or two previous releases, but also for sites that are extremely familiar to them from more than 60 homing flights. At those sites, they should be well acquainted with surrounding landmarks, especially with those along the route on which they normally depart. Yet when clock-shifted, they showed the typical deviation from their previous course and departed on a different route, seemingly ignoring all landmarks (Fig. 6.16; Füller *et al.*, 1983; R. Wiltschko, 1991). Thus, even at extremely familiar sites, pigeons continue

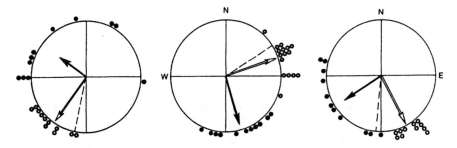

Fig. 6.16 The effect of clock-shifting at extremely familiar sites from which the pigeons had homed more than 60 times before. The home directions are given as a dashed radius. Open symbols, untreated controls; solid symbols, pigeons whose internal clock had been shifted 6 hours slow. (From R. Wiltschko, 1991.)

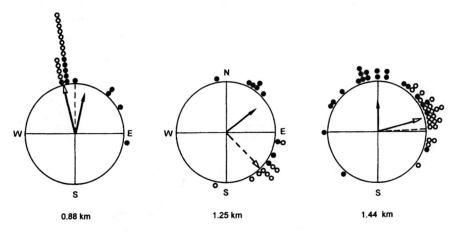

Fig. 6.17 The effect of clock-shifting in the vicinity of the loft. The home directions are given as dashed radius. Open symbols, untreated controls; solid symbols, pigeons whose internal clock had been shifted 6 hours fast. (From Keeton, 1974.)

to establish the relationship to the goal by a compass; they do not change their navigational strategy in this respect.

The above examples refer to sites 30–60 km from the home loft. However, the same principles seem to apply also to navigation within the home range. Responses to clock-shifting have been observed as close as 1–1.5 km from the loft, i.e. in an area where familiarity with the terrain and the landmarks might be inferred (Fig. 6.17; Graue, 1963; Keeton, 1974; Schmidt-Koenig, 1979). Apparently, the 'map and compass' model is valid also in the immediate vicinity of the home loft. Clock-shift experiments thus clearly indicate that even near the loft, 'piloting', or Type I navigation based exclusively on landmarks as suggested by Griffin (e.g. 1955; see also Papi, 1990), does not exist.

The 'mosaic map'

These clock-shift responses observed close to the loft show that the area around the loft is also represented in a directionally oriented way. This led to the model of the 'mosaic map', which supplements the 'grid map' in the vicinity of home where the local gradient values can no longer be distinguished from the home values.

The 'mosaic map' is assumed to be a *directionally oriented representation* of the lay of the land with the positions of prominent local features (Fig. 6.18; Wallraff, 1974, 1991; W. Wiltschko and Wiltschko, 1982). It largely corresponds to the 'grid map'; yet instead of a few continuous gradients, the 'mosaic map' involves numerous separate entities whose directional relationship is familiar to the birds. The features involved need not be restricted to visual landmarks but may include marks of other sensory qualities (cf.

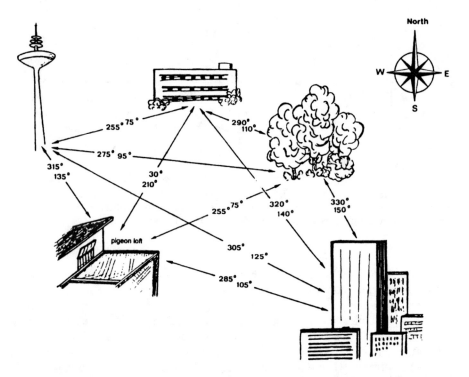

Fig. 6.18 A model of the 'mosaic map' which is assumed to be a *directionally oriented* mental representation of the distribution of landmarks in the vicinity of home. (After W. Wiltschko and Wiltschko, 1982.)

Kreithen, 1978), like local sources of infrasound, magnetic anomalies, etc. These landmarks indicate *locations*, not routes. The directional relationship of these locations to the goal is known in terms of a compass, so that the navigational system here also gives the direction to the goal as a compass course (cf. Graue, 1963; Wallraff, 1974; W. Wiltschko and Wiltschko, 1982, 1987). In this respect, there seems no difference between nearby and distant sites and between 'mosaic map' and 'grid map'. Only the view of the loft itself could occasionally override the use of the sun compass (Graue, 1963; Keeton, 1974), suggesting that this view of the loft may function as a cue indicating the direction to the goal directly (see Fig. 6.1 left).

The establishment of the 'mosaic map' largely escapes experimental analysis. It must be assumed to occur during early flights, maybe even a little earlier than the establishment of the sun compass and the navigational 'map', because knowledge of the immediate vicinity of home is essential. Young pigeons visit landmarks and other prominent features around their loft, and store the positions of these features in their memory, together with the directional relationships among these marks and home. When they extend their flights, new landmarks may be added so that the 'mosaic map' also increases with increasing experience to some extent. As a consequence of being based on distinct local features, however, the 'mosaic map' includes only terrain that birds know from direct experience and perhaps a small area beyond – see Baker's (1982) concept of the 'familiar area map'.

Small-scale orientation

The finding that even the view of the vicinity of home is directionally oriented leads to the question about representations of space of even smaller sizes. For the analysis of how birds proceed in small-scale orientation tasks, it was important to find behaviors that include precisely locating sites within the radius of a few meters. A behavior that proved most helpful is caching and recovery of food items. Some species of corvids, like the nutcrackers (genus *Nucifraga*) and several jays, are known to harvest seed in autumn, store them in caches and retrieve them weeks or months later (for details, see Vander Wall and Balda, 1981). These birds also show this behavior in captivity so that the mechanisms involved can be analyzed. Two species of parids (*Parus atricapillus* and *P. palustris*) also cache food for hours or days, and have been tested in the laboratory (see Sherry, 1985). In order to find out what strategies were involved, the birds were forced to use only specific sites determined by the experimentalist for caching (e.g. Kamil and Balda, 1985). The rate of relocating cache sites even under these conditions was very high – so high that it could only be explained by assuming that the birds precisely remember the locations where they stored their seeds or, in other words, they use 'spatial memory' (for reviews, see Balda *et al.*, 1987; Sherry, 1987).

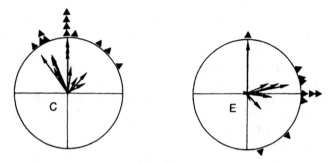

Fig. 6.19 The effect of clock-shifting on the search activity of Scrub Jays, *Aphelocoma coerulescens*, in an aviary. Left: Control – the birds cached and later recovered pine seeds while living in the natural day; right: the same jays had been clock-shifted 6 hours slow between caching and recovering the seed. The cache sectors are set upward. The arrows represent the distribution of the search activity of individual birds; the symbols at the periphery mark the mean directions. (Data from W. Wiltschko and Balda, 1989.)

Compass orientation as a component of 'spatial memory'

Most of the early experiments analyzing how birds locate specific sites within an area of a few meters were performed in closed rooms, i.e. in a situation where only certain cues were available. The question of the mechanisms involved in spatial memory was addressed by focusing attention mainly on the role of landmarks (e.g. Vander Wall, 1982; Herz *et al.*, 1994). However, tests in an outdoor aviary indicated that compass orientation is also a component in remembering cache sites.

In such tests, Scrub Jays (*Aphelocoma coerulescens*) were allowed to cache pinyon seeds in 12 sand-filled cups within a 90° sector of an octagonal aviary devoid of landmarks. A few days later, during recovery, 48 sand-filled holes symmetrically arranged in all four quadrants were open. The birds clearly concentrated their probing efforts in the sectors where they had cached their seeds. However, when their internal clock was shifted between caching and recovery, they mostly probed in the adjacent 90° (Fig. 6.19), thus showing the typical shift that indicates the use of the sun compass (W. Wiltschko and Balda, 1989; Balda and Wiltschko, 1991). These results are remarkable insofar as the aviary, which was 4.90 m in diameter, stood in a square courtyard bordered by buildings and containing shrubs and various trees as distant landmarks. The surroundings were neither uniform nor symmetrical; nevertheless, the Scrub Jays clearly responded to clock-shifting. This suggests that the landmark array outside the aviary did not provide the framework for memorizing cache sites, but compass information together with the aviary (W. Wiltschko and Balda, 1989). This dominance of the sun compass over the distant landmarks might reflect a general disposition to rank compass orientation high in all spatial orientation tasks, and suggested that even the small-scale environment of an aviary is also represented in a directionally oriented way, like the lay of the land around a bird's home in the 'mosaic map'. In case of the experiments mentioned above, the birds might have memorized their caches in terms equivalent to 'in the *northern sector*' or '*north from* the center pole'.

Meanwhile, sun compass use in caching and recovery has also been demonstrated in two more species of corvids using the same aviary (Wiltschko and Balda, unpublished observations). Tests with Black-capped Chickadees (*Parus atricapillus*) also indicated that the sun compass is involved in locating food items. In this case, however, the birds had not cached their own food, but had been trained to search for seeds at the edge of an octagonal cage (Sherry and Duff, 1996). The response of the chickadees was markedly smaller than expected. Smaller deflections have also been observed in European Jays (*Garrulus glandarius*) and Carrier Pigeons trained to search for food at specific places within an aviary (Hagmann *et al.*, 1994; Chappell and Guilford, 1995).

Forming a mental picture of the environment

In their experiments with Black-capped Chickadees, Sherry and Duff (1996) observed an interesting phenomenon: the birds responded to clock-shifting with a deflection only when they were tested in a familiar location where they were at home with the surrounding landmarks. In unfamiliar surroundings, the clock-shifted birds appeared to be disoriented. The authors point out that directions derived from the sun compass must be combined with information from a familiar landmark array. This corresponds to the model of the 'mosaic map', as this 'map' is assumed to be constituted by such a combination of compass directions and landmarks. Apparently, the birds realized that they were in strange, unfamiliar surroundings not included in their 'mosaic map' and felt insecure. Only when the birds have familiarized themselves sufficiently with their environment and formed a coherent representation of the environment are they ready to make use of their sun compass in the normal way. There is an interesting parallel in pigeon homing: clock-shifted experienced pigeons often show smaller deflections than expected; at very familiar sites, however, their deflections are significantly larger than at unfamiliar or only vaguely familiar sites (R. Wiltschko *et al.*, 1994).

The phenomenon that birds need to familiarize themselves with their surroundings before they are ready to perform spatial tasks in the normal way was also indicated by the behavior of corvids in caching experiments. When these birds were allowed into the test aviary for the first time, they hesitated to cache; only after additional sessions, adding up to more than 2 hours for most birds, did they begin to cache seeds. The next cachings occurred after continuously shorter intervals. However, caching time increased significantly again after the birds had been clock-shifted (Wiltschko and Balda, unpublished observations). In this situation, the birds obviously hesitated once more, probably because they realized that something was odd. They might have felt that their picture of the environment was no longer correctly oriented and needed some time to readjust it to the experimental situation. This suggests that the surrounding landmarks, even if they do not indicate directions to the birds, form an integrated part of their representation of the environment, their 'mosaic map'.

The birds' view of space

The findings on avian orientation discussed above show that compass orientation forms the backbone of the birds' representation of space. Equipped with a magnetic compass that is available spontaneously, the birds establish, through early learning processes, the complex mechanisms they preferentially use for navigation later in life: the sun compass and the 'maps'.

Learning processes form the navigational system

The sun compass as well as the 'mosaic map' and the 'grid map' form essential parts of the avian navigational system, but these mechanisms cannot be based on innate information because they make use of factors whose existence is reliable, but whose specific manifestation cannot be anticipated. It is absolutely certain that birds will see the sun and will encounter landmarks and suitable factors to be incorporated into the 'maps'. However, neither the local arc of the sun, nor the specific nature and the position of landmarks, nor the regional distribution of gradients can be predicted. To make use of these factors, animals have to obtain the relevant information by individual experience.

A highly efficient way to do this are preprogrammed learning processes during the animals' early youth. Preprogrammed learning is facilitated by a sensitive period and by specific brain areas prepared to store information that is relevant for important behaviors that promote survival and fitness. In this sense, establishing navigational mechanisms might represent a parallel to song learning (cf. Marler, 1983).

Figure 6.20 briefly summarizes the ontogeny of the navigational system (open arrows) and its use in experienced birds (solid arrows). The directional reference provided by the magnetic compass forms the basis of the learning processes, linking together cues of various different natures that form the complex learned mechanisms used by adult, experienced birds.

Preprogrammed learning thus guarantees that the respective mechanisms

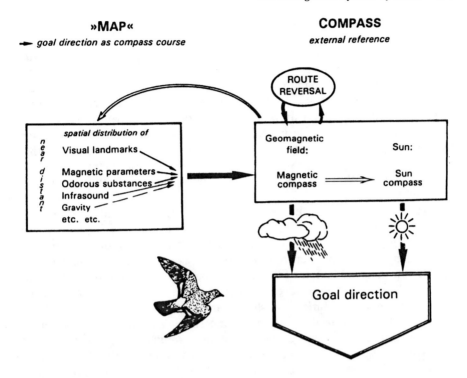

Fig. 6.20 A model of the navigation system of birds. The magnetic compass is a central element; open arrows indicate learning processes establishing the complex mechanisms preferentially used by experienced birds, the sun compass and the 'maps'. Solid arrows indicate the actual use of information during homing. (After W. Wiltschko *et al.*, 1991.)

are perfectly tuned to the situations in the bird's home region: the sun compass compensates for the local sun's arc, the 'mosaic map' will be a true picture of the lay of the land around home and the navigational 'map' a realistic representation of the local distribution of gradients. This means that there are differences in the compensation mechanisms of the sun compass according to latitude and regional differences in the navigational 'map', which may involve the nature of the gradients used and how the various navigational factors are rated and ranked. Such differences in the 'map' of pigeons have been documented. They are reflected by different responses to identical experimental treatments (e.g. W. Wiltschko *et al.*, 1987b) or by different behavior in birds of different origin at certain sites (e.g. Walcott and Brown, 1989). Most of the observed differences may be attributed to differences in experience (W. Wiltschko *et al.*, 1991). Occasionally, genetic differences may also be involved (e.g. Benvenuti and Ioalè, 1988).

Characteristics of the birds' representation of space

In the general discussions on mental representations of space, findings in birds have received little attention so far. When cases are discussed, they predominantly involve mammals (e.g. Ellen, 1987) or, more recently, insects such as Honey Bees and ants (e.g. Wehner, 1992). If birds are mentioned at all, the emphasis is mostly on small-scale orientation within the limited space of a room or an aviary (e.g. Vauclair, 1987; Gallistel, 1990; Wehner and Menzel, 1990). Homing of displaced birds is seldom considered in this context. This is surprising insofar as theoretical models of the 'map' are well developed (e.g. Wallraff, 1974, 1991; Lednor, 1982; W. Wiltschko and Wiltschko, 1982, 1987).

Certain differences between our model of avian 'maps' and the currently discussed concepts of spatial representations in other animals become obvious. The most striking aspect is distance: the discussion on how animals represent space usually refers to orientation tasks in the range of a few meters up to a few hundred meters at the most in contrast to avian navigation which involves distances of up to several hundred kilometers. This adds a different dimension when landmarks, snapshot memory of landscape (see Cartwright and Collett, 1983), routes, etc. are concerned. The essential difference, however, is that any 'map' discussed for other animals is taken to consist of separate entities like landmarks, and the relationships between these landmarks; in this way, they show parallels to the 'mosaic map'. The navigational 'map' of birds, in contrast, is assumed to be based on environmental gradients, i.e. continuous factors whose distribution varies in space. This permits the use of the navigational 'map' at distant locations beyond the area of immediate experience and gives the avian 'map' a quality that maps based on landmarks can never reach.

A third important difference is the role of compass information. The discussions on animal maps emphasize that the relationship between landmarks is represented but it is not always clear in what terms this relationship is specified. It might be entirely in an animal-centered system, or in relation to other landmarks or the walls of the enclosure. Specifications in terms of compass direction have also been discussed (e.g. Gallistel, 1990), but have not received very much attention so far. In the 'mosaic map' as well as in the 'grid map' of birds, directional information is an essential component. Both 'maps' generate compass courses and require a compass to transform these courses into an actual heading for the flights. Thus, in birds, 'mosaic map' cues such as landmarks and compass orientation do not represent alternatives as they seem to do in insects (e.g. von Frisch and Lindauer, 1954; Dyer and Gould, 1981). However, the analysis of the spatial representation of bees and ants has only just begun; the difference in the role of compass orientation might turn out smaller than it appears at the moment.

The organization of space based on an external reference ensures that birds, with their great motility and their ability to move faster and farther than other animals, have a highly efficient navigational system at their disposal. Surprisingly, the same principle seems also to apply to spaces of only a few meters. For birds, spatial information seems to be represented in a directionally oriented way over the entire range of distances, from several hundred kilometers, where the benefit of such a representation is obvious, to a few meters within the home range, where an advantage is less evident to us humans. It might mean that birds have just one standard way to code space – that they generally use an external reference may be the result of their ability to fly and the large distances they cover.

References

Able, K. P. and Bingman, V. P. (1987) The development of orientation and navigation behavior in birds. *Q. Rev. Biol.* **62**, 1–29.

Able, K. P. and Dillon, P. M. (1977) Sun compass orientation in a nocturnal migrant, the White-throated Sparrow. *Condor* **79**, 393–395.

Adler, H. E. (1970) Ontogeny and phylogeny of orientation. In Aronson, L. R., Tobach, E., Lehrmann, D. S. and Rosenblatt, J. S. (eds) *Development and Evolution of Behavior: Essays in Memory of T. C. Schneirla*. San Francisco: W. H. Freeman, pp. 303–336.

Baker, R. R. (1982) *Migration – Path Through Time and Space*. London: Hodder and Stoughton.

Baker, R. R. (1993) The function of post-fledging exploration: a pilot study of three passerines ringed in Britain. *Orn. Scand.* **24**, 71–79.

Balda, R. P. and Wiltschko, W. (1991) Caching and recovery in Scrub Jays: transfer of sun-compass direction from shaded to sunny areas. *Condor* **93**, 1020–1023.

Balda, R. P., Bunch, K. G., Kamil, A. C., Sherry, D. F. and Tomback, D. F. (1987) Cache site memory in birds. In Kamil, A. C., Krebs, J. and Pulliam, H. R. (eds) *Foraging Behavior*. New York, London: Plenum, pp. 645–668.

Barlow, J. S. (1964) Inertial navigation as a basis for animal navigation. *J. Theoret. Biol.* **6**, 76–117.

Benvenuti, S. and Ioalè, P. (1988) Initial orientation of homing pigeons: different sensitivity to altered magnetic fields in birds of different countries. *Experientia* **44**, 358–359.

Benvenuti, S., Fiaschi, V., Fiore, L. and Papi, F. (1973) Homing performance of inexperienced and directionally trained pigeons subjected to olfactory nerve section. *J. Comp. Physiol.* **83**, 81–92.

Berndt, R. and Winkel, W. (1980) Field experiments on problems of imprinting to the birthplace in the Pied Flycatcher *Ficedula hypoleuca*. In Nöhring, R. (ed.) *Acta XII Congressus Internationalis Ornithologici*. Berlin: Deutsche Ornithologen-Gesellschaft, pp. 851–854.

Cartwright, B. A. and Collett, T. S. (1983) Landmark learning in bees. *J. Comp. Physiol.* **151**, 521–543.

Chappell, J. and Guilford, T. (1995) Homing pigeons primarily use the sun compass rather than fixed directional visual cues in an open-field arena food-searching task. *Proc. Roy. Soc. Lond. B* **260**, 59–63.

Chelazzi, G. and Pardi, L. (1972) Experiments on the homing behaviour of caged pigeons. *Monit. Zool. Ital. (N.S.)* **6**, 11–18.

Dyer, F. C. and Gould, J. L. (1981) Honeybee orientation: a back-up system for cloudy days. *Science* **214**, 1041–1042.

Edrich, W. and Keeton, W. T. (1977) A comparison of homing behavior in feral and homing pigeons. *Z. Tierpsychol.* **44**, 389–401.

Ellen, P. (1987) Cognitive mechanisms in animal problem-solving. In Ellen, P. and Thinus-Blanc, C. (eds) *Cognitive Processes and Spatial Orientation in Animal and Man*, Vol. 1. Dordrecht: Martinus Vijhoff Publishers, pp. 20–38.

Etienne, A. S., Teroni, E., Maurer, R., Portenier, V. and Saucy, F. (1985) Short distance homing in a small mammal: the role of exteroreceptive cues and path integration. *Experientia* **41**, 122–125.

Etienne, A. S., Hurni, C., Maurer, R. and Séguinot, V. (1991) Twofold path integration during hoarding in the Golden Hamster? *Ethol. Ecol. Evol.* **3**, 1–11.

Exner, S. (1905). Über das Orientierungsvermögen der Brieftauben. *Sitzungsber. Akad. Wiss. Wien, Math.-Naturwiss. Kl. III* **114**, 763–790.

Füller, E., Kowalski, U. and Wiltschko, R. (1983) Orientation of homing pigeons: compass orientation vs. piloting by familiar landmarks. *J. Comp. Physiol.* **153**, 55–58.

Gallistel, C. R. (1990) *The Organisation of Learning.* Cambridge, MA: Massachusetts Institute of Technology Press.

Graue, L. C. (1963) The effect of phase shifts in the day–night cycle on pigeon homing at distances of less than one mile. *Ohio J. Sci.* **63**, 214–217.

Griffin, D. R. (1955) Bird navigation. In Wolfson, A. (ed.) *Recent Studies in Avian Biology.* Urbana: University of Illinois Press, pp. 154–197.

Grüter, M. and Wiltschko, R. (1990). Pigeon homing: the effect of local experience on initial orientation and homing success. *Ethology* **84**, 239–255.

Hagmann, K., Ledda, A. P., Weber, C. and Wiltschko, W. (1994) The role of sun compass and near landmarks in memorizing sites in an aviary. *J. Ornithol.* **135** (Sonderheft), 91.

Hartwick, R. F., Foa, A. and Papi, F. (1977) The effect of olfactory deprivation by nasal tubes upon homing behavior in pigeons. *Behav. Ecol. Sociobiol.* **2**, 81–89.

Helbig, A. J. (1991) Inheritance of migratory direction in a bird species: a cross-breeding experiment with SE- and SW-migrating blackcaps (*Sylvia atricapilla*). *Behav. Ecol. Sociobiol.* **28**, 9–12.

Herz, R. S., Zanette, L. and Sherry, D. F. (1994) Spatial cues for cache retrieval by Black-capped Chickadees. *Anim. Behav.* **48**, 343–351.

Hoffmann, K. (1954) Versuche zu der im Richtungsfinden der Vögel enthaltenen Zeitschätzung. *Z. Tierpsychol.* **11**, 453–475.

Immelmann, K. (1975) Ecological significance of imprinting and early learning. *Ann. Rev. Ecol. Syst.* **6**, 5–37.

Ioalè, P. (1984) Magnets and pigeon orientation. *Monit. Zool. Ital. (N.S.)* **18**, 347–358.

Jander, R. (1957) Die optische Richtungsorientierung der Roten Waldameise (*Formica rufa* L.). *Z. Vergl. Physiol.* **40**, 162–238.

Kamil, A. C. and Balda, R. P. (1985) Cache recovery and spatial memory in Clark's Nutcrackers (*Nucifraga columbiana*). *J. Exp. Psychol. Anim. Behav. Processes* **11**, 95–111.

Keeton, W. T. (1969) Orientation by pigeons: is the sun necessary? *Science* **165**, 922–928.

Keeton, W. T. (1971) Magnets interfere with pigeon homing. *Proc. Natl. Acad. Sci. USA* **68**, 102–106.

Keeton, W. T. (1973) Release-site bias as a possible guide to the 'map' component in pigeon homing. *J. Comp. Physiol.* **86**, 1–16.

Keeton, W. T. (1974) The orientational and navigational basis of homing in birds. *Adv. Study Behav.* **5**, 47–132.

Kiepenheuer, J. (1978) The effect of magnetic fields inversed during displacement on the homing behavior of pigeons. In Schmidt-Koenig, K. and Keeton, W. T. (eds) *Animal Migration, Navigation, and Homing*. Berlin: Springer Verlag, pp. 135–142.

Kowalski, U. (1994) Das Richtungsverhalten verfrachteter Brieftauben (*Columba livia*) im Orientierungskäfig. *J. Ornithol.* **135**, 17–35.

Kramer, G. (1950) Weitere Analyse der Faktoren, welche die Zugaktivität des gekäfigten Vogels orientieren. *Naturwissenschaften* **37**, 377–378.

Kramer, G. (1957) Experiments in bird orientation and their interpretation. *Ibis* **99**, 196–227.

Kramer, G. (1959) Recent experiments on bird orientation. *Ibis* **101**, 399–416.

Kreithen, M. L. (1978) Sensory mechanisms for animal orientation – can any new ones be discovered? In Schmidt-Koenig, K. and Keeton, W. T. (eds) *Animal Migration, Navigation and Homing*. Berlin: Springer Verlag, pp. 25–34.

Lednor, A. J. (1982) Magnetic navigation in pigeons: possibilities and problems. In Papi, F. and Wallraff, H. G. (eds) *Avian Navigation*. Berlin: Springer Verlag, pp. 109–119.

Löhrl, H. (1959) Zur Frage des Zeitpunkts einer Prägung auf die Heimatregion beim Halsbandschnäpper (*Ficedula albicollis*). *J. Ornithol.* **100**, 132–140.

Lorenz, K. (1935) Der Kumpan in der Umwelt des Vogels. *J. Ornithol.* **83**, 137–213, 289–413.

Luschi, P. and Dall'Antonia, P. (1993) Anosmic pigeons orient from familiar sites by relying on the map-and-compass mechanism. *Anim. Behav.* **46**, 1195–1203.

Marler, P. (1983) Some ethological implications for neuroethology: the ontogeny of birdsong. In Ewert, J.-P., Capranica, R. R. and Ingle, D. J. (eds) *Advances in Vertebrate Neuroethology*, NATO Advanced Sciences Institutes Series A, Life Sciences, Vol. 56. New York: Plenum Press, pp. 2–52.

Matthews, G. V. T. (1951) The experimental investigation of navigation in homing pigeons. *J. Exp. Biol.* **28**, 508–536.

Matthews, G. V. T. (1953) Sun navigation in homing pigeons. *J. Exp. Biol.* **30**, 243–267.

Matthews, G. V. T. (1963) The astronomical bases of 'nonsense' orientation. In Sibley, C. (ed.) *Proceedings of the XIIIth International Ornithological Congress*, Ithaca 1962. American Ornithological Union, pp. 415–429.

Papi, F. (1976) The olfactory navigation system of the homing pigeon. *Verhand. Deutsch. Zool. Ges.* **69**, 184–205.

Papi, F. (1982) Olfaction and homing in pigeons: ten years of experiments. In Papi, F. and Wallraff, H. G. (eds) *Avian Navigation*. Berlin: Springer Verlag, pp. 149–159.

Papi, F. (1986) Pigeon navigation: solved problems and open questions. *Monit. Zool. Ital. (N.S.)* **20**, 471–517.

Papi, F. (1990) Homing phenomena: mechanisms and classifications. *Ethol. Ecol. Evol.* **2**, 3–10.

Pardi, L. and Ercolini, A. (1986) Zonal recovery mechanisms in talitrid crustaceans. *Boll. Zool.* **53**, 139–160.

Pratt, J. G. and Thouless, R. H. (1955) Homing orientation in pigeons in relation to opportunity to observe the sun before release. *J. Exp. Biol.* **32**, 140–157.

Sauer, F. (1957) Die Sternorientierung nächtlich ziehender Grasmücken, *Sylvia atricapilla, borin* und *curruca*. *Z. Tierpsychol.* **14**, 29–70.

Schmidt-Koenig, K. (1958a) Der Einfluß experimentell veränderter Zeitschätzung auf das Heimfindevermögen von Brieftauben. *Naturwissenschaften* **45**, 47.

Schmidt-Koenig, K. (1958b) Experimentelle Einflußnahme auf die 24-Stunden-Periodik bei Brieftauben und deren Auswirkung unter besonderer Berücksichtigung des Heimfindevermögens. *Z. Tierpsychol.* **15**, 301–331.

Schmidt-Koenig, K. (1961) Die Sonne als Kompaß im Heim-Orientierungssystem der Brieftauben. *Z. Tierpsychol.* **18**, 221–244.

Schmidt-Koenig, K. (1963) On the role of the loft, the distance and site of release in pigeon homing (the 'cross loft experiment'). *Biol. Bull.* **125**, 154–164.

Schmidt-Koenig. K. (1965) Current problems in bird orientation. *Adv. Study Behav.* **1**, 217–276.

Schmidt-Koenig, K. (1975) *Migration and Homing in Animals*. Berlin: Springer Verlag.

Schmidt-Koenig, K. (1979) *Avian Orientation and Navigation*. London: Academic Press.

Sherry, D. F. (1985) Food storage by birds and mammals. *Adv. Study Behav.* **15**, 153–188.

Sherry, D. F. (1987) Spatial memory in food-storing birds. In Ellen, P. and Thinus-Blanc, C. (eds) *Cognitive Processes and Spatial Orientation in Animal and Man*, Vol. 1. Dordrecht: Martinus Vijhoff Publishers, pp. 305–322.

Sherry, D. F. and Duff, S. J. (1996) Behavioral and neural basis of orientation in food-storing birds. *J. Exp. Biol.* **199**, 165–171.

Sokolov, L. V., Bolshakov, K. V., Vinogradova, N. V., Dolnik, T. V., Lyuleeva, D. S., Payevsky, V. A., Shumakov, M. E. and Yablonkevich, M. L. (1984) The testing of the ability for imprinting and finding the site of future nesting in young Chaffinches. *Zool. J. (Moscow)* **43**, 1671–1681 (in Russian).

Vander Wall, S. B. (1982) An experimental analysis of cache recovery in Clark's Nutcracker. *Anim. Behav.* **30**, 84–94.

Vander Wall, S. B. and Balda, R. P. (1981) Ecology and evolution of food-storage behavior in conifer-seed-caching. *Z. Tierpsychol.* **56**, 217–242.

Vauclair, J. (1987) A comparative approach to cognitive mapping. In Ellen, P. and Thinus-Blanc, C. (eds) *Spatial Orientation in Animal and Man*, Vol. 1. Dordrecht: Martinus Vijhoff Publishers, pp. 89–96.

Viguier, C. (1882) Le sens de l'orientation et ses organes chez les animaux et chez l'homme. *Rev. Phil. France l'Étranger* **14**, 1–36.

Visalberghi, E. and Alleva, E. (1979) Magnetic influences on pigeon homing. *Biol. Bull.* **125**, 246–256.

von Frisch, K. (1965) *Tanzsprache und Orientierung der Bienen.* Heidelberg: Springer Verlag.

von Frisch, K. and Lindauer, M. (1954) Himmel und Erde in Konkurrenz bei der Orientierung der Bienen. *Naturwissenschaften* **41**, 245–253.

von Saint Paul, U. (1954) Nachweis der Sonnenorientierung bei nächtlich ziehenden Vögeln. *Behaviour* **6**, 1–7.

von Saint Paul, U. (1956) Compass directional training of Western Meadow Larks (*Sturnella neglecta*). *Auk* **73**, 203–210.

Walcott, C. and Brown, A. I. (1989) The disorientation of pigeons at Jersey Hill. In *Orientation and Navigation – Birds, Humans and Other Animals.* Royal Institute of Navigation, Cardiff 1989, paper 8.

Walcott, C. and Green, R. P. (1974) Orientation of homing pigeons altered by a change in the direction of an applied magnetic field. *Science* **184**, 180–182.

Walcott, C. and Schmidt-Koenig, K. (1973) The effect on homing of anesthesia during displacement. *Auk* **90**, 281–286.

Wallraff, H. G. (1959) Örtlich und zeitlich bedingte Variabilität des Heimkehrverhaltens von Brieftauben. *Z. Tierpsychol.* **16**, 513–544.

Wallraff, H. G. (1970) Über die Flugrichtungen verfrachteter Brieftauben in Abhängigkeit vom Heimatort und vom Ort der Freilassung. *Z. Tierpsychol.* **27**, 303–351.

Wallraff, H. G. (1974) *Das Navigationssystem der Vögel. Ein theoretischer Beitrag zur Analyse ungeklärter Orientierungsleistungen.* Munich, Vienna: Schriftenreihe 'Kybernetik', R. Oldenbourg Verlag.

Wallraff, H. G. (1978) Preferred compass direction in initial orientation of homing pigeons. In Schmidt-Koenig, K. and Keeton, W. T. (eds) *Animal Migration, Navigation, and Homing.* Berlin: Springer Verlag, pp. 171–183.

Wallraff, H. G. (1980) Does pigeon homing depend on stimuli perceived during displacement? I. Experiments in Germany. *J. Comp. Physiol.* **139**, 193–201.

Wallraff, H. G. (1983) Relevance of atmospheric odours and geomagnetic field to pigeon navigation: what is the 'map' basis? *Comp. Biochem.*

Physiol. **76A**, 643–663.

Wallraff, H. G. (1986) Directional components derived from initial orientation data of inexperienced homing pigeons. *J. Comp. Physiol.* **159**, 143–159.

Wallraff, H. G. (1991) Conceptual approaches to avian navigation systems. In Berthold, P. (ed.) *Orientation in Birds.* Basel: Birkhäuser, pp. 128–165.

Wallraff, H. G., Foa, A. and Ioalè, P. (1980) Does pigeon homing depend on stimuli perceived during displacement? II. Experiments in Italy. *J. Comp. Physiol.* **139**, 203–208.

Wehner, R. (1972) Visual orientation performances of desert ants (*Cataglyphis bicolor*) toward astromenotactic directions and horizon landmarks. In Galler, S. R. *et al. Animal Orientation and Navigation.* Washington, DC: NASA SP-262, US Government Printing Office, pp. 421–436.

Wehner, R. (1992) Homing in arthropods. In Papi, F. (ed.) *Animal Homing.* London: Chapman and Hall, pp. 45–144.

Wehner, R. and Menzel, R. (1990) Do insects have cognitive maps? *Annu. Rev. Neurosci.* **13**, 403–414.

Wiltschko, R. (1980) Die Sonnenorientierung der Vögel. I. Die Rolle der Sonne im Orientierungssystem und die Funktionsweise des Sonnenkompaß. *J. Ornithol.* **121**, 121–143.

Wiltschko, R. (1983) The onotogeny of orientation in young pigeons. *Comp. Biochem. Physiol.* **76A**, 701–708.

Wiltschko, R. (1991) The role of experience in avian navigation and homing. In Berthold, P. (ed.) *Orientation in Birds.* Basel: Birkhäuser Verlag, pp. 250–269.

Wiltschko, R. (1992) Das Verhalten verfrachteter Vögel. *Vogelwarte* **36**, 249–310.

Wiltschko, R. (1993) Release site biases and their interpretation. In *Orientation and Navigation – Birds, Humans and Other Animals.* Proceedings of the Conference of the Royal Institute of Navigation, Oxford, 1993, paper no. 15.

Wiltschko, R. and Wiltschko, W. (1978) Evidence for the use of magnetic outward-journey information in homing pigeons. *Naturwissenschaften* **65**, 112.

Wiltschko, R. and Wiltschko, W. (1980) The process of learning sun compass orientation in young homing pigeons. *Naturwissenschaften* **67**, 512–514.

Wiltschko, R. and Wiltschko, W. (1981) The development of sun compass orientation in young homing pigeons. *Behav. Ecol. Sociobiol.* **9**, 135–141.

Wiltschko, R. and Wiltschko, W. (1985) Pigeon homing: change in navigational strategy during ontogeny. *Anim. Behav.* **33**, 583–590.

Wiltschko, R. and Wiltschko, W. (1990) Zur Entwicklung der Sonnenkompaßorientierung bei jungen Brieftauben. *J. Ornithol.* **131**, 1–19.

Wiltschko, R. and Wiltschko, W. (1995) *Magnetic Orientation in Animals.* Berlin: Springer Verlag.

Wiltschko, R., Nohr, D. and Wiltschko, W. (1981) Pigeons with a deficient sun compass use the magnetic compass. *Science* **214**, 343–345.

Wiltschko, R., Kumpfmüller, R., Muth, R. and Wiltschko, W. (1994) Pigeon homing: the effect of clock-shift is often smaller than predicted. *Behav. Ecol. Sociobiol.* **35**, 63–73.

Wiltschko, W. and Balda, R. P. (1989) Sun compass orientation in seed-caching Scrub Jays (*Aphelocoma coerulescens*). *J. Comp. Physiol.* **164**, 717–721.

Wiltschko, W. and Wiltschko, R. (1978) A theoretical model for migratory orientation and homing in birds. *Oikos* **30**, 177–187.

Wiltschko, W. and Wiltschko, R. (1982) The role of outward journey information in the orientation of homing pigeons. In Papi, F. and Wallraff, H. G. (eds) *Avian Navigation*. Berlin: Springer Verlag, pp. 239–252.

Wiltschko, W. and Wiltschko, R. (1987) Cognitive maps and navigation in homing pigeons. In Ellen, P. and Thinus-Blanc, C. (eds) *Cognitive Processes and Spatial Orientation in Animal and Man*. Dordrecht: Martinus Nijhoff Publishers, pp. 201–216.

Wiltschko, W. and Wiltschko, R. (1996) Magnetic orientation in birds. *J. Exp. Biol.* **199**, 29–38.

Wiltschko, W., Wiltschko, R. and Keeton, W. T. (1976) Effects of a 'permanent' clock-shift on the orientation of young homing pigeons. *Behav. Ecol. Sociobiol.* **1**, 229–243.

Wiltschko, W., Wiltschko, R., Keeton, W. T. and Madden, R. (1983) Growing up in an altered magnetic field affects the initial orientation of young homing pigeons. *Behav. Ecol. Sociobiol.* **12**, 135–142.

Wiltschko, W., Wiltschko, R. and Keeton, W. T. (1984) The effect of a 'permanent' clock-shift on the orientation of experienced homing pigeons. I. Experiments in Ithaca, New York. *Behav. Ecol. Sociobiol.* **15**, 263–272.

Wiltschko, W., Wiltschko, R., Keeton, W. T. and Brown, A. I. (1987a) Pigeon homing: the orientation of young birds that had been prevented from seeing the sun. *Ethology* **76**, 27–32.

Wiltschko, W., Wiltschko, R. and Walcott, C. (1987b) Pigeon homing: different effects of olfactory deprivation in different countries. *Behav. Ecol. Sociobiol.* **21**, 333–342.

Wiltschko, W., Beason, R. and Wiltschko, R. (1991). Introduction and concluding remarks to the symposium 'Sensory Basis of Orientation'. In Williamsson, M. (ed.) *Acta XX Congressus Internationalis Ornithologici, Christchurch 1990*. Christchurch, New Zealand, pp. 1803–1850.

7

Neuroethology of Avian Navigation

Verner P. Bingman[1]*, Lauren V. Riters[2], Rosemary Strasser[1] and Anna Gagliardo[3]

[1] *Department of Psychology, Bowling Green State University, Bowling Green, Ohio 43403, USA*
[2] *Laboratory of Biochemistry, University of Liege, 17 Place Delcour, Bat. L1, B-4020, Liege, Belgium, and*
[3] *Dipartimento di Etologia, Ecologia e Evoluzione, Universitá di Pisa, Via A. Volta 6, I-56126 Pisa, Italy*

Introduction

Ethological investigations into mechanisms of spatial orientation and navigation in animals have revealed a rich array of environmental stimuli and behavioral strategies that animals can employ to navigate through space (Able, 1980). This observation is probably most strikingly demonstrated in birds, whose complex and often baffling navigational ability allows them to find relatively restricted goal locations often from very long distances. From both a behavioral and neurobiological perspective, the homing pigeon (*Columba livia*) has been the most extensively studied species. This chapter will focus almost exclusively on exploring the relationship among specific regions of the avian forebrain, homing-pigeon navigational performance and navigational learning processes.

*To whom all correspondence should be addressed.

ANIMAL COGNITION IN NATURE
ISBN 0-12-077030-X

Maps and compasses in homing pigeons

In their chapter, Wiltschko and Wiltschko offer an extensive summary of the current knowledge of navigation and orientation behavioral mechanisms in homing pigeons, and a personal perspective on this same issue has been written recently (Bingman, 1998). Therefore, I will summarize only the most salient aspects of these behavioral mechanisms.

When returning home from a distant, unfamiliar release site, homing pigeons rely on what Kramer (1959) described as a map-and-compass mechanism. Briefly, a homing pigeon would use its 'navigational map' to determine its position in space or direction of displacement with respect to home (i.e. north of home). The environmental stimuli used in the operation of the navigational map have been controversial (Able, 1996; Wallraff, 1996; Wiltschko, 1996), although it is clear that atmospheric odors are often used (Papi, 1991; Wallraff, 1991). Having established the direction of displacement with respect to home with the use of the navigational map, a pigeon would then rely on an independent compass mechanism to identify the direction home. Continuing the example, after determining its position is north of home, a pigeon would use its compass to identify south and fly off in that direction. Two types of compasses have been described: a sun compass (Schmidt-Koenig, 1979) and a geomagnetic compass (Wiltschko and Wiltschko, 1988).

The navigational map is used by pigeons from unfamiliar locations where they have never been before and where they are beyond sensory contact with familiar environmental stimuli. However, closer to the loft, where a bird would be in contact with familiar environmental stimuli, homing pigeons can additionally rely on an independent navigational mechanism based on familiar landmarks to determine their location with respect to the home loft (Wallraff, 1991; Wallraff *et al.*, 1993).

It should be emphasized that our behavioral understanding of homing pigeon navigation has progressed substantially, and research in this area is an example of how ethological research can reveal fundamental insights into naturally occurring cognitive processes. It is this ethological framework which sets the foundation for meaningful research into the neural mechanisms of homing-pigeon navigation that is the focus of this chapter.

Brain regions and their role in homing-pigeon navigation

Neuroethological investigations examining the brain regulation of spatial behavior have traditionally focused on the processing of what we prefer to call perceptual space: the spatial domain that includes all environmental stimuli that are currently accessible to sensory systems. Examples include electrolocation in fish (Heiligenberg, 1991), sound localization in owls

Table 7.1 Participation in Homing Pigeon Navigation.

	Navigational map		Familiar landmark (local) navigation	
	Learning	Operation	Learning	Operation
Hippocampal formation	Yes	No	Yes	Yes
Piriform cortex	Yes	Yes	No(?)	No(?)
Caudolateral neostriatum	Probably(?)	Yes	?	No(?)
Dorsal wulst	No	No	Yes(?)	No

(Knudson and Brainard, 1991) and echolocation in bats (Suga, 1984). However, homing in pigeons operates in cognitive space, where goal locations are beyond sensory contact, and, consequently, some type of memory-based information is needed for goal navigation. Therefore, pigeon homing offers an exciting opportunity to use a neuroethological perspective to understand the relationship among the brain, representational organization of cognitive space and behavior (Bingman *et al.*, 1995).

The first step taken to examine the relationship between brain regions and homing-pigeon navigation was an empirical attempt to determine the effects of lesions to specific brain regions on homing performance. Specifically, I will summarize the observed effects of restricted brain lesions on the learning (acquisition) and operation (retention) of a navigational map and familiar landmark navigation (Table 7.1). In summarizing these effects it should be kept in mind that none of the brain regions discussed has been found to impair compass orientation. Further, it is assumed that behavioral effects recorded at unfamiliar release sites distant from the loft serve as evidence for an effect on the navigational map while behavioral effects recorded near the loft or in familiar areas serve as evidence for an effect on familiar landmark navigation.

Hippocampal formation

Owing to the well-known importance of the hippocampal formation for spatial cognition in rodents (O'Keefe and Nadel, 1978; Morris *et al.*, 1982), the avian hippocampal formation (Fig. 7.1) was the first and remains the most extensively studied brain region investigated for its importance in homing-pigeon navigation. An extensive review of the effects of hippocampal lesions on homing performance has been published recently (Bingman *et al.*, 1995); therefore, only a brief summary will be given here.

Hippocampal lesions in young homing pigeons that have yet to learn a navigational map strongly impair navigational map learning (Bingman *et al.*, 1990). It also appears that hippocampal lesions in adult, experienced birds impair navigational map learning when pigeons are transferred to a new loft and need to learn a new navigational map (Bingman and Yates, 1992). Surprisingly, hippocampal lesions in adult, experienced birds have no effect on the operation of an already learned navigational map; such birds orient home from distant, unfamiliar release sites in a manner indistinguishable from intact birds (Bingman *et al.*, 1984, 1988).

In summary, the hippocampal formation plays a critical role in navigational map learning/acquisition but no necessary role in operation/retention. However, one word of caution is warranted. The experiments described above took place in Italy, where it is known that the navigational map is based on atmospheric odors (Papi, 1991), and Ohio, USA, where it is strongly suspected that the navigational map is based on atmospheric odors (Bingman and Mackie, 1992). Given the possibility that a navigational map could be based on nonolfactory, currently unidentified environmental stimuli (see Wiltschko and Wiltschko, this volume), it remains unknown whether the hippocampal formation would be similarly involved in such a map.

With respect to familiar landmark navigational learning, hippocampal lesions in young pigeons strongly impair their ability to learn to navigate in the vicinity of the loft, indicating a deficit in familiar landmark navigational learning (Bingman *et al.*, 1994a). Also, hippocampal lesions in adult experienced birds impair the operation/retention of a previously learned ability to use familiar landmarks to navigate near the loft (Bingman and Mench, 1990). The hippocampal formation is critical for all aspects of familiar landmark navigation when familiar landmarks are thought to be encoded as a map-like representation that can be used flexibly to navigate among goal locations (see Bingman *et al.*, 1995; Bingman, 1998).

Piriform cortex

The piriform cortex (Fig. 7.1) is a recipient of a large projection from the olfactory bulb (Reiner and Karten, 1985; Bingman *et al.*, 1994b) and piriform cortex lesions in young pigeons impair their ability to learn/acquire a navigational map based on atmospheric odors (Gagliardo *et al.*, 1997). Further, piriform cortex lesions in adult experienced pigeons impair the operation/retention of an already learned navigational map based on atmospheric odors (Papi and Casini, 1990).

Therefore, the piriform cortex is a critical olfactory processing region whose integrity is necessary for both the learning and operation of an olfactory navigational map. From a developmental perspective, it is worth noting that there are several other telencephalic brain regions that receive a projection from the olfactory bulb (Reiner and Karten, 1985), and that none of these alternative olfactory bulb recipient areas can functionally replace the piriform cortex in navigational map learning.

Young homing pigeons given piriform cortex lesions successfully navigate

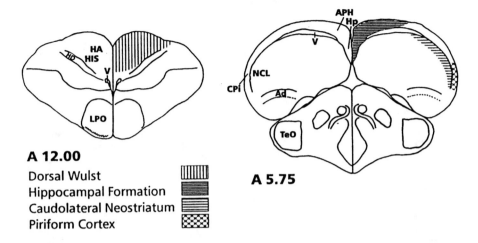

A 12.00

Dorsal Wulst
Hippocampal Formation
Caudolateral Neostriatum
Piriform Cortex

A 5.75

Fig. 7.1 Two coronal sections through the avian telencephalon, adapted from the atlas of Karten and Hodos (1967), identifying the location of the hippocampal formation (Hp, hippocampus; APH, area parahippocampalis), piriform cortex (CPi), caudolateral neostriatum (NCL) and dorsal wulst (HA, hyperstriatum accessorium; HIS, hyperstriatum intercalatus superior). Ad, Archistriatum, pars dorsalis; HD, hyperstriatum dorsale; LPO, lobus parolfactorious; TeO, tectum opticum; V, ventriculus.

in the vicinity of the loft (Gagliardo *et al.*, 1997). Thus the existing data suggest that the piriform cortex plays no necessary role in learning to navigate by familiar landmarks. In adult experienced birds, unimpaired operation/retention of familiar landmark navigation following piriform cortex lesions has also been suggested (Papi and Casini, 1990). Although this question needs to be examined more thoroughly, the existing data indicate that the piriform cortex plays no necessary role in familiar landmark navigational learning/acquisition or operation/retention.

Caudolateral neostriatum

The caudolateral neostriatum is a large telencephalic region that lies ventral and medial to the lateral ventricle (Fig. 7.1) and shares a number of similarities with portions of prefrontal cortex in mammals (Mogensen and Divac, 1982; Divac *et al.*, 1985; Waldmann and Güntürkün, 1993; Gagliardo *et al.*, 1996b). Caudolateral neostriatum lesions in adult experienced birds impair navigational map operation/retention, at least when the map is based on atmospheric odors (Gagliardo and Divac, 1993). In contrast, the same treatment does not seem to impair the operation/retention of familiar landmark navigation (Riters and Bingman, unpublished data; Fig. 7.2).

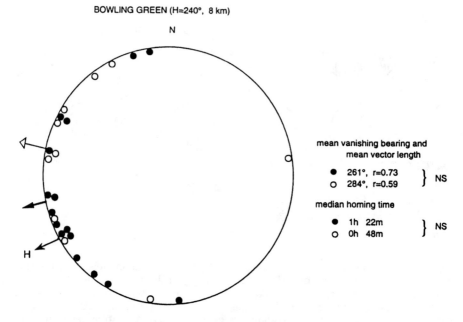

Fig. 7.2 Homing performance of intact control and caudolateral neostriatum-lesioned (lesioned as experienced birds) pigeons during a short-distance release. The solid circles identify the vanishing bearings of control birds and the open circles the vanishing bearings of caudolateral neostriatum-lesioned birds. Outside the circle, the arrow with the adjacent H identifies the direction home, the arrow with closed head the mean vanishing bearing of the control birds, and the arrow with the open head the mean vanishing bearing of the caudolateral neostriatum-lesioned birds. N identifies north. Reproduced from Riters and Bingman (unpublished data).

Experienced homing pigeons were subjected to lesions of the caudolateral neostriatum, allowed to recover and then released from a location 8 km from home where familiar landmarks would be used to guide the return home. Control and caudolateral neostriatum-lesioned birds displayed similar homeward orientation and took the same time to return home (Fig. 7.2), indicating no necessary role of the caudolateral neostriatum for the operation/retention of familiar landmark navigation. It should be noted that a previous report of a deficit in the operation/retention of familiar landmark navigation following caudolateral neostriatum lesions (Leutgeb *et al.*, 1995) may have been a consequence of associated damage to the dorsolateral cortex, a brain region related to the hippocampal formation.

Lesions to the caudolateral neostriatum have not been performed in young pigeons and, therefore, the role this brain area may play in the learning/acquisition of a navigational map and familiar landmark navigation is unknown. However, given the known participation of the caudolateral neostriatum in olfactory navigational map operation, it seems reasonable to assume that this brain region is also necessary for olfactory navigational map learning.

Dorsal wulst

The dorsal wulst is an anterior forebrain region consisting primarily of the hyperstriatum accessorium and hyperstriatum intercalatus, but does not include the hyperstriatum dorsale. The brain regions involved are generally considered sensory processing areas particularly with respect to visual and somatosensory stimuli (Delius and Bennetto, 1972; Karten *et al.*, 1973; Bagnoli and Burkhalter, 1983). This is an interesting region because it has been used regularly as a control region in experiments examining the role of the hippocampal formation. Indeed, dorsal wulst lesions in young birds do not impair navigational map learning (Bingman *et al.*, 1990) nor navigational map operation in experienced birds (Bingman *et al.*, 1984). The dorsal wulst also does not seem to play any necessary role in the operation/retention of familiar landmark navigation (Bingman *et al.*, 1984). It is somewhat surprising, therefore, that there is some evidence indicating that the dorsal wulst does participate in the learning/acquisition of familiar landmark navigation (Bingman *et al.*, unpublished data; Fig. 7.3).

During two research seasons, young homing pigeons were subjected to lesions of the dorsal wulst. After a 3-month, free-flight training period, the birds were tested for their navigational ability. For each season, the first release was from a relatively short distance where familiar landmarks are presumably important (sites at Campaldo and La Costanza, Fig. 7.3). From there, the dorsal wulst-lesioned birds were observed to orient poorly and take more time to return home compared to intact controls. This was particularly striking from Campaldo, only 9 km from home. In contrast, when subsequently released from farther away (sites at Fornacette and San Donato, Fig. 7.3), where the navigational map would be important, the dorsal wulst-lesioned birds behaved in the same way as the controls.

Any interpretation of these data must be considered tentative. However, they are at least consistent with the hypothesis that the dorsal wulst participates in learning to navigate by familiar landmarks and consequently inspire further investigation. The participation of the dorsal wulst in visual processing adds support to the hypothesis. However, this interpretation of the data is confounded by the fact that the first releases were nearer to the loft than the later releases. This leaves open the possibility that the effect may have nothing to do with distance or the navigational mechanism employed, but rather result from some unspecified effect of homing experience.

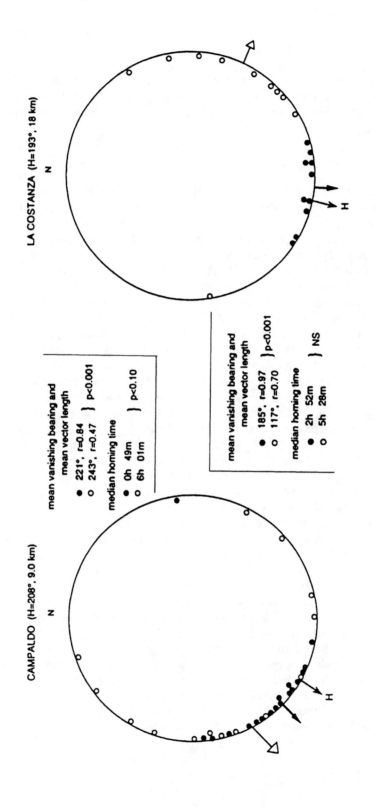

LA COSTANZA (H=193°, 18 km)

N

H

mean vanishing bearing and
mean vector length

● 185°, r=0.97 } p<0.001
○ 117°, r=0.70

median homing time

● 2h 52m } NS
○ 5h 28m

CAMPALDO (H=208°, 9.0 km)

N

H

mean vanishing bearing and
mean vector length

● 221°, r=0.84 } p<0.001
○ 243°, r=0.47

median homing time

● 0h 49m } p<0.10
○ 6h 01m

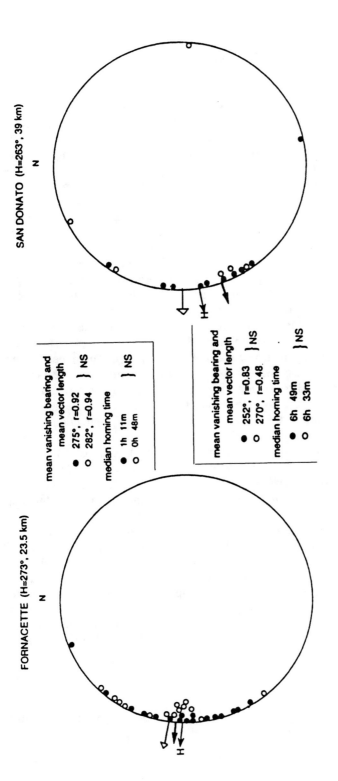

Fig. 7.3 The homing performance of intact control (●) and dorsal wulst-lesioned (○; lesioned as young, inexperienced birds) pigeons on their first experimental release (Campaldo and La Costanza) and a later release (Fornacette and San Donato). The explanation is as in Fig. 7.3 except that the open circles now identify the vanishing bearings of dorsal wulst-lesioned pigeons. Reproduced from Bingman, Gagliardo, Ioalé, Casini and Bagnoli (unpublished data).

Navigational map and familiar landmark navigation: building neural circuits

There is reason to believe that all four brain regions discussed participate at some level in homing-pigeon navigation. However, their roles in navigational map and familiar landmark navigation are not identical (Table 7.1), emphasizing the behavioral complexity of homing-pigeon navigation and associated richness in brain areas that participate in the regulation of some aspect(s) of navigation. (It should be mentioned here that the *caudomedial* neostriatum does not seem to participate in any aspect of homing.)

Bingman *et al.* (1995) proposed that learning an olfactory navigational map involved a neural circuit consisting in part of the piriform cortex, hippocampal formation, caudolateral neostriatum and the hyperstriatum dorsale of the ventral wulst; brain areas that share a variety of anatomical connections. The piriform cortex was hypothesized to operate as an olfactory sensory processing region, the hippocampal formation constructed a directional framework in which the distribution of odors in space could be associated with directions in space determined by the sun compass (see later), and the caudolateral neostriatum was one location where a neural representation of the distribution of odors in space (the navigational map) would be stored. The hyperstriatum dorsale was included to provide a neural pathway connecting the piriform cortex and hippocampal formation with the caudolateral neostriatum (Leutgeb *et al.*, 1996). The need to incorporate the hyperstriatum dorsale in this circuit may be superfluous because there may be a direct connection between the piriform cortex and caudolateral neostriatum, which is not revealed in the pathway connectivity study of Bingman *et al.* (1994b) because of their close proximity to each other (Fig. 7.1) and possible functional relatedness (Veenman *et al.*, 1995). In any event, once the map is learned, the hippocampal formation becomes dissociated from this circuit for the operation of the map, which continues to require the integrity of the piriform cortex and caudolateral neostriatum. This model circuit remains consistent with the existing data.

With respect to familiar landmark navigation, modeling a neural circuit for how the map is acquired and used is premature. What can be said is that the hippocampal formation participates in both aspects and perhaps visual processing in the wulst, reaching the hippocampal formation via the hyperstriatum dorsale (Casini *et al.*, 1986), is important at least during learning. The piriform cortex and caudolateral neostriatum do not appear to participate, indicating differences at the neural level between familiar landmark navigation and the navigational map.

Compasses

Although considerably more certainty is associated with our behavioral understanding of compass mechanisms, it is interesting that how the sun and geomagnetic compass are regulated at the neural level remains somewhat of a mystery. Because compasses operate in the domain of perceptual space, they are used to perceive directions associated with sensory accessible environmental stimuli; therefore, only a brief summary will be offered here.

Compass studies have primarily relied on migratory birds whose orientation can be conveniently studied in experimental cages isolated from confounding influences of the navigational map (Wiltschko and Wiltschko, this volume). The first work in this area (the references for which we have sadly lost and we are unaware of any secondary references) was carried out by Russians and suggested that the optic tectum (superior colliculus) of the midbrain was critical for sun-compass orientation. Confirmation of this result would not be surprising as many orientation responses to environmental stimuli take advantage of the topographical organization found in the tectum (e.g. electric fish and owls, cited previously). However, it should be kept in mind that the optic tectum may play a primarily sensory processing role, perhaps like piriform cortex and olfaction, and not participate directly in the more complex aspects of the sun compass, such as compensation for the apparent motion of the sun by some circadian rhythm and incorporation of the sun-compass orientation into learning processes. Recent research suggests that, in fact, the hippocampal formation may play some role in these more interesting aspects of the sun compass (see later).

Beason and Semm (1991) have carried out numerous electrophysiological investigations identifying potential brain regions that could participate in the regulation of the geomagnetic compass. A variety of brainstem structures that also participate in visual or somatosensory (trigeminal) processing have been implicated, and this work is nicely summarized in Beason and Semm (1991).

Hippocampal formation and caudolateral neostriatum: functional properties

Hippocampal formation

The previous discussion identifying what aspects of homing are regulated by specific brain regions was primarily an empirical account of what homing pigeons can and cannot do without certain brain areas. It serves as a first step, which should be followed by investigations into the perhaps more interesting question of why damage to the hippocampal formation, or any brain region, should impair navigational learning. What specific learning and memory processes does the hippocampal formation participate in such that, following hippocampal lesions, homing pigeons can not learn a navigational map?

Although the navigational map and familiar landmark navigation are distinct spatial mechanisms, it is interesting that the hippocampal formation participates in the learning of both and is the only brain region known to do so (Table 7.1). Therefore, it is a reasonable first assumption that navigational map and familiar landmark navigational learning share some specific learning process(es) and that this learning process(es) requires an intact hippocampal formation. Although speculative, it is very likely that, when learning an olfactory navigational map, homing pigeons must rely on some directional reference to learn the distribution of atmospheric odors in space (Wallraff, 1974; Ioalé *et al.*, 1990). To learn that a specific odor profile is principally north of the loft, a pigeon must be able to identify north. Similarly, in learning the distribution of familiar landmarks in space, a directional reference system is probably used to learn that landmark A is north of home and landmark B is south (Wiltschko and Wiltschko, 1987). These two navigational mechanisms probably share a learning process in which pigeons learn the distribution of stimuli in space by using some directional reference. However, what is this directional reference? The sun compass is the principal (although not the only) directional reference used by pigeons as well as most diurnal animals (Able, 1991) to identify directions and orient themselves in space. Is the functional role of the hippocampal formation in navigational learning a reflection of its participation in a learning process in which the sun compass establishes a directional framework, within which pigeons can learn the distribution of stimuli in the environment and thus form map-like spatial representations?

To test this possibility, Bingman and Jones (1994) trained control and hippocampal-lesioned birds to use the sun compass to learn the directional location of a food reward in an experimental arena. The arena, covered with a clear plexiglass roof, allowed pigeons to view the sun and sky, but prevented any view of surrounding landmarks. Pigeons were simply trained to orient and move in a specific compass direction to locate a food reward held in a cup hung outside the arena wall. The logic of the experiment was the following. Associating a food goal with a sun compass-determined direction was assumed to be similar to associating an odor profile or local landmark with a sun compass-determined direction during navigational learning. If the reason hippocampal-lesioned pigeons are impaired at navigational learning is because they cannot integrate sun compass directional information with environmental features, then hippocampal-lesioned pigeons should not be able to associate a food goal with a direction defined by the sun compass.

Hippocampal-lesioned homing pigeons were found to be unable to learn the directional location of a food goal using the sun compass. However, hippocampal-lesioned pigeons quickly learned to locate the food goal in the arena when it was associated with a color landmark (Bingman and Jones, 1994) or was found at a fixed angular distance from the sun (Bingman *et al.*, 1995). The failure of hippocampal-lesioned birds to use the sun compass for spatial learning supports the hypothesis that the role of the hippocampal formation in navigational learning reflects its participation in a process in which a directional reference, in this case the sun compass, is used to learn the distribution of stimuli in space.

The results of this first experiment raised a number of interesting questions that have been pursued in more recent experiments. The first question is related to the operation of the sun compass itself. Is the hippocampal formation necessary for sun-compass operation (orientation) or does the hippocampal formation specifically mediate spatial learning that uses the sun compass as a directional reference? Bingman *et al.* (1996) recently examined the orientation of phase-shifted homing pigeons that were subjected to hippocampal lesions as experienced adults and therefore continued to possess a fully operational navigational map (Table 7.1). If these birds displayed the characteristic shift in orientation following phase-shift that proves sun compass use (Schmidt-Koenig, 1979), then hippocampal-lesioned birds can be said to possess an operational sun compass that can be used for orientation.

The phase-shifted hippocampal-lesioned pigeons displayed the characteristic shift in orientation identifying intact sun-compass orientation. Therefore, the failure of hippocampal-lesioned pigeons to use the sun compass for spatial learning appears to be a specific consequence of an inability to integrate the sun compass into learning processes and not a general loss of sun-compass orientation ability. However, although displaying appropriate orientation shifts, the clock-shifted hippocampal-lesioned pigeons consistently showed a more exaggerated shift in orientation compared to control birds. This is a remarkable finding because a difference in orientation between similarly treated pigeons is never seen in nonphase-shifted birds (Bingman *et al.*, 1984, 1988).

What might the difference in the magnitude of the shift mean? Bingman *et al.* (1996) speculate that hippocampal lesions may alter a process in which a circadian rhythm, which regulates the sun compass, re-entrains to a new photoperiod. There are other explanations for the data (an impairment in the magnetic compass is one; for details, see Bingman *et al.*, 1996). However, if this hypothesis is correct, it would support the surprising suggestion that the hippocampal formation participates in the control of a circadian rhythm, or at least its re-entrainment response to an altered photoperiod, that regulates sun compass orientation.

Hippocampal-lesioned homing pigeons are not able to use the sun compass but can use a color landmark to locate goal locations (Bingman and Jones, 1994). It is interesting to note that intact pigeons (Chappell and Guilford, 1995) as well as Scrub Jays (*Aphelocoma coerulescens*) (Wiltschko and Balda, 1989) preferentially rely on the sun compass to locate a goal location in an experimental arena when both the sun compass and landmark features are available simultaneously. But what about hippocampal-lesioned birds? When allowed to locate a goal with both sun compass and landmark features available simultaneously, do they also prefer to rely on the sun compass, and necessarily fail, or do they not even attend to the sun compass and immediately use landmark features to locate the goal?

Gagliardo *et al.* (1996a) examined the ability of intact and hippocampal-lesioned homing pigeons to locate a goal in an outdoor experimental arena where they could use the sun compass and/or different pattern features along the walls of the arena to locate a food goal. Both groups of birds learned the location of the goal equally fast. The birds were subsequently subjected to a phase-shift procedure, i.e. day starts 6 hours before sunrise and ends 6 hours before sunset. After the phase shift, the pigeons were retested. If the birds were relying on their sun compass to locate the goal, then following the phase shift, they should have shown an approximate 90° shift in orientation. Indeed, intact controls displayed a shift in orientation. Although the shift was not as large as one would expect if they were relying exclusively on the sun compass, as also found in Chappell and Guilford (1995), the change in behavior after phase shift clearly demonstrates that the controls were using, in part, directional information from the sun compass to locate the goal. In contrast, the directional choices of the hippocampal-lesioned pigeons did not change after the phase shift indicating that their goal localization strategy did not involve the sun compass.

After the phase shift, the pigeons were subjected to a second manipulation in which the pattern features were rotated in the arena. If the pigeons were relying on the patterns, then they should have shown a shift in directional responses that paralleled the shift in the pattern features. Intact control pigeons did not change their directional responses following the shift of the features, indicating that their representation of the goal location was entirely based on directional cues outside the arena. In contrast, the hippocampal-lesioned pigeons changed their responses following the shift in the pattern features. This finding indicates that the hippocampal-lesioned pigeons located the goal using the pattern features on the walls of the arena, effectively ignoring directional information from outside the arena.

In summary, the intact controls and hippocampal-lesioned pigeons learned the location of the goal equally well, although they relied on very different stimuli to identify the goal. The fact that the hippocampal-lesioned birds learned as quickly as controls suggests that the preferred directional strategy (sun compass) of intact birds did not interfere with hippocampal-lesioned pigeons learning to associate a feature pattern with the goal. As such, the data are at least consistent with the idea that hippocampal-lesioned birds do not try and are possibly unaware of using directional cues such as the sun compass to learn about locations or build map-like representations of the environment.

The previous summary of experiments examining the failure of hippocampal-lesioned birds to use the sun compass to learn environmental locations is consistent with a role of the hippocampal formation in learning spatial relationships among stimuli. However, might the hippocampal formation only be necessary when the sun compass is used as a directional reference or does it play a more general role in learning spatial relations? For example, the sun compass need not be used to learn a navigational map (Wiltschko *et al.*, 1987), suggesting that another directional reference, presumably the geomagnetic compass, could also be used to learn the distribution of atmospheric odors or any other environmental stimulus that could be part of the navigational map. Would the hippocampal formation be necessary if the geomagnetic compass was used as a directional reference?

To address this general question, Strasser and Bingman (1997) trained intact and hippocampal-lesioned homing pigeons to locate a food goal in a laboratory room with a variety of stimuli that could be used to locate the food. The food was located in one of four uniquely colored bowls that were always present. Next to the goal bowl was a black cylinder (landmark beacon) and the goal bowl could also be located with the use of room cues (location in room), such as the door, overhead lamps and ventilation ducts. Simplistically, a pigeon could rely on a feature cue (bowl color), a proximal spatial cue (black cylinder) and/or distal spatial cues (room cues) to locate the food goal. There is a considerable amount of literature suggesting that these cues are viewed as distinct (Brodbeck, 1994; Clayton and Krebs, 1994; Strasser and Bingman, 1996; see Clayton and Lee, and Shettleworth and Hampton, this volume) but we can think of no a priori reason why they should be (see later). After learning to locate the bowl containing food, the environment was manipulated occasionally (probe trials were introduced among the training trials) to examine how the stimuli were used to locate the goal. The manipulation that we shall highlight here involved removing the landmark beacon from the test room and moving the color bowl rewarded during training trials to another location in the room. This probe trial resembles the manipulation in the Gagliardo *et al.* (1996a) experiment when the feature-pattern cues were shifted. Ideally, the room manipulation described here was designed to reveal whether the birds relied primarily on the color of the bowl or room cues to locate the food goal.

The control and hippocampal-lesioned birds rapidly learned to locate the food, but surprisingly, the hippocampal-lesioned birds performed better (learned more quickly) during the early training sessions. However, the most remarkable finding emerged from the probe trials (Fig. 7.4). During the probe trials, the hippocampal-lesioned birds consistently selected the color bowl that contained the food during training trials. This suggests, like the Gagliardo *et al.* (1996a) study, that hippocampal-lesioned birds readily use color or patterns to recognize goal locations. Surprisingly, the control birds randomly chose among the four bowls present, showing no preference for the color or room location that was previously associated with the food. It should be emphasized that three other types of probe trials were employed and, in two

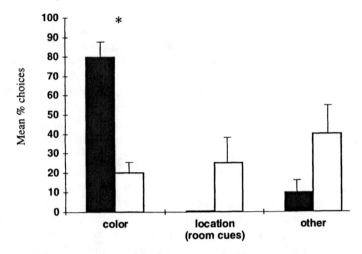

Fig. 7.4　The bowl selection of intact control (□) and hippocampal-lesioned (■) birds on probe trials when the landmark beacon was removed from the room and the color of bowl associated with the food goal during probe trials was moved to another position in the room. Hippocampal-lesioned pigeons overwhelmingly preferred to choose the color of the bowl associated with the food goal during training, significantly (*) more so than intact controls. Indeed, the controls chose randomly, showing no preference for the color or room location of the bowl associated with the food goal during training compared to the two other bowls in the room. Means represent the average performance of five birds/group tested four times each on this probe trial. Percentages do not quite add up to 100 for each group because occasionally no choice would be made on a probe trial. Data from Strasser and Bingman (1997).

of those (two out of four total), the controls chose randomly among the bowls, while hippocampal-lesioned birds always preferred a bowl that was previously associated with the food reward even when color was removed and all the bowls were white.

How can these results be explained? The hippocampal-lesioned birds behaved quite predictably. They apparently learned to associate each of the available cues with the food goal and did so in a manner suggesting that they learned three distinct, nonrelational associations, i.e. food is next to red, food is next to the landmark beacon, and food is in a particular room location. Further, they preferred to respond to color. The general failure of the intact controls to select a bowl that was associated with a stimulus that was associated with food during training trials suggests that what they learned was not three distinct, separate stimulus response associations. Rather, they behaved as if they learned to represent the goal location by its relationship to several if not all of the available cues. In other words, they seemed to have formed a relational association in the sense of Eichenbaum *et al.* (1994) in which the available stimuli were integrated into a relational whole. When the cues were manipulated during the probe trials, the test environment no longer resembled the training environment (the relations among the stimuli had been substantially altered) and, therefore, the relational representation that coded for the goal location could not be activated (context) and/or not be used.

Although not yet compelling, these data suggest that, at least under some test conditions, birds do not treat stimulus categories such as features and spatial location as distinct entities, but attempt to integrate these various stimuli into holistic-like relational representations. If true, the hippocampal formation would be necessary for the formation of such holistic representations as described by Eichenbaum *et al.* (1994). [It should be pointed out, however, that this experiment has no bearing on the more substantial claim by Eichenbaum *et al.* (1994) that the hippocampal formation is important for all types of relational learning including those that are nonspatial.] Hippocampal-lesioned pigeons are, therefore, limited to forming single stimulus–response associations, which, bizarrely, makes them more likely to choose a bowl that was previously associated with food during the probe trials. As such, the hippocampal formation is not simply a structure that regulates spatial learning only when the sun compass is used as a directional reference, but whenever relationships among different stimuli are integrated to form spatial representations.

Although some of these experiments examine behavioral phenomena that are somewhat remote from homing and navigation, they have considerable implications for the cognitive processes that require the participation of the hippocampal formation. Again, they support the general conclusion that a hippocampal formation is necessary for the learning of spatial relations among stimuli. This would include learning that odor profile X is north of home during navigational map learning, which would require the presence of a directional reference (e.g. sun compass), as well as the spatial distribution of stimuli in an experimental room perhaps using asymmetries in room geometry to establish a directional framework. The important point is that it is the hippocampal formation that permits multiple stimuli to be integrated into holistic, spatial representations.

Caudolateral neostriatum

Although still in the early stages, a number of studies have attempted to explore the specific role of the caudolateral neostriatum in homing. Laboratory studies have shown that, with lesions of the caudolateral neostriatum, pigeons display a striking deficit in behavioral alternation tasks reminiscent of prefrontal cortex lesions in mammals (Mogensen and Divac, 1982; Gagliardo *et al.*, 1996b). This was complemented by experiments showing that caudolateral neostriatum lesions in homing pigeons impaired navigational map performance (Gagliardo and Divac, 1993), while seemingly leaving familiar landmark navigation unaffected (Riters and Bingman, unpublished data; Fig. 7.2). However, in the context of homing, what might caudolateral neostriatum be doing? Is it involved in learning spatial relations based on some directional reference together with the hippocampal formation? Might its role be more limited to some type of sensory processing, like olfaction and the piriform cortex, or a motor transformation mechanism by which the cognitive processes that regulate navigation are converted into a motor signal? Anatomical connections between caudolateral neostriatum, and both telencephalic sensory processing regions and motor areas (archistriatum) suggest that both of these are possible (Leutgeb *et al.*, 1996). Alternatively, because of its proximity to the piriform cortex, is the caudolateral neostriatum one location where a neural representation (memory) of the spatial distribution of atmospheric odors is stored?

In a first attempt to examine these alternatives, Riters and Bingman (unpublished data) tested pigeons in the sun compass, spatial learning paradigm described earlier for hippocampal-lesioned pigeons, in which birds are trained to use the sun compass to identify the direction of a food goal in an outdoor arena. The behavior of the caudolateral neostriatum-lesioned birds was different from that which was expected. As seen in Fig. 7.5, during early training sessions, they learned the task in a manner similar to controls, a task that hippocampal-lesioned birds just do not learn. Therefore, it seems that the caudolateral neostriatum does not participate in the same spatial learning process that involves the hippocampal formation. However, it should be mentioned that, although no difference in the rate of learning during early training sessions was found between control and caudolateral neostriatum-lesioned pigeons, the caudolateral-neostriatum-lesioned birds took significantly more sessions than controls to reach a criterion of 3 days (sessions) in a row at better than 80% correct. Interpreting this finding is not easy. However, given the obvious learning of the caudolateral-neostriatum-lesioned birds (Fig. 7.5), we consider the difficulty in reaching criterion as a possible reflection of an inability to withhold responses to unrewarded stimuli because: (1) a similar delay in reaching the criterion was observed when the caudolateral neostriatum-lesioned pigeons were trained to respond to a color landmark; and (2) the prefrontal cortex-lesioned mammals, which resemble caudolateral neostriatum-lesioned pigeons, are known to have difficulty withholding responses to unrewarded stimuli (Sakurai and Sugimoto, 1985).

If either the sensory processing or motor transformation hypothesis is correct, it would be expected that homing pigeons with lesions in the caudolateral neostriatum would have difficulty navigating home from locations where they could use familiar landmark navigation similar to that used at more distant sites where the navigational map would be used. Both navigational systems require the animals to interpret sensory conditions at the release site in the context of a stored spatial representation, then based

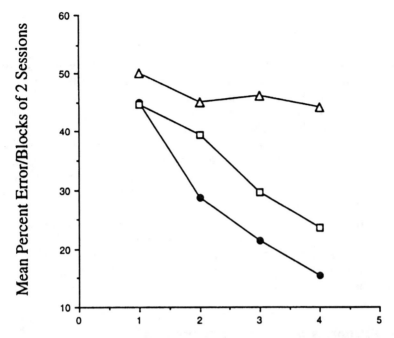

Fig. 7.5 Learning curves examining the performance of intact control (●), caudolateral neostriatum (□) and hippocampal-lesioned (△) pigeons on the task where the sun compass needs to be used to identify the direction of a food goal in an outdoor experimental arena. Performance is plotted over the first eight training sessions in blocks of two sessions. Note the reduced number of errors, and consequently learning by the intact control and caudolateral neostriatum-lesioned pigeons and the consistently bad performance of the hippocampal-lesioned birds. Intact control and caudolateral neostriatum data from Riters and Bingman (unpublished data). *Hippocampal data adapted from Bingman and Jones (1994).

on that interpretation, compute a motor response guided by the sun compass. However, as described earlier (Fig. 7.2), homing pigeons with lesions in the caudolateral neostriatum home in a manner indistinguishable from controls from a location where familiar landmark navigation would be used, suggesting sensory processing and motor transformation processes are intact.

Caution is necessary in interpreting the results from the homing experiments conducted with caudolateral neostriatum-lesioned pigeons. Although the data in Fig. 7.2 are clear, they represent only one release and it would be imprudent to draw any firm conclusion from one release. Also, it is not certain that the lesions that produced navigational map impairments (Gagliardo and Divac, 1993) are identical to the lesions that did not produce a familiar landmark navigation deficit. Indeed, a recent characterization of neurotransmitters, neuropeptides and transmitter-related enzymes found in the caudolateral neostriatum (Riters *et al.*, unpublished data) indicates the presence of two subdivisions. A ventral subdivision characterized by higher levels of vasoactive intestinal polypeptide (VIP) and a dorsal subdivision characterized by higher levels of tyrosine hydroxylase, choline acetyltransferase and substance P. These neurochemically defined subdivisions may correspond to differences in the participation of the two regions in navigation. It would not be surprising that, if one group of lesions primarily damaged one subdivision while another primarily damaged the other, different effects on homing would be found.

None the less, the existing behavioral evidence supports as a working hypothesis that caudolateral neostriatum contributes to homing-pigeon navigation by acting as a storage site for the spatial representation of atmospheric odors that guides the navigational map. Damage to this area impairs the performance of the navigational map (Gagliardo and Divac, 1993) while apparently leaving other aspects of homing-pigeon navigation more or less intact, including hippocampal-mediated spatial learning. However, the observation that lesions of the caudolateral neostriatum impair spatial alternation in the laboratory in addition to the olfactory navigational map suggests that this hypothesis may be overly simplistic.

Generalization to other vertebrate groups

This chapter has primarily focused on neural mechanisms that may control aspects of homing-pigeon navigation. We have done so because the homing pigeon has served as the primary neuroethological model species for investigations into the neural control of navigational behavior in cognitive space. However, it is important to consider the extent to which conclusions from homing pigeons generalize to other bird species and vertebrates in general. In attempting to draw generalizations from homing pigeons to other vertebrate groups, we are necessarily limited to a discussion of the hippocampal formation. Although some comparisons can be drawn between mammalian prefrontal cortex and caudolateral neostriatum, so little is known about their functional characteristics that it would be premature to identify any generalizations.

A variety of passerine bird species are known to store and later recover food, and the same species are consistently found to have a larger hippocampal formation than related species (Krebs *et al.*, 1989; Sherry *et al.*, 1989; Healy and Krebs, 1992; see Clayton and Lee, and Shettleworth and Hampton, this volume). Food-storing parids generally prefer to identify goal locations by relying on spatial relations rather than feature cues (Brodbeck, 1994; Clayton and Krebs, 1994) and impairments in recovering stored food result from hippocampal lesions (Sherry and Vaccarino, 1989). These observations suggest that the hippocampal formation participates in a cognitive representation of space that allows the animals later to recover food they have previously stored. However, what is unknown is the nature of the spatial representation these animals would use under natural conditions. The work on the homing pigeon would suggest that some directional reference, which is likely to be the sun compass but possibly also the geomagnetic compass, would be used to learn the spatial distribution of stimuli in the environment that would guide food recovery. Scrub Jays that recover cached seeds have in fact been shown to rely on the sun compass (Wiltschko and Balda, 1989).

The importance of the mammalian hippocampal formation for the learning of cognitive representations of space has been known for a long time (O'Keefe and Nadel, 1978). However, only recently have researchers considered the nature of the spatial representations that are critically dependent on the hippocampal formation. Two observations are noteworthy. First, hippocampal-lesioned rats readily learn to form single associations with environmental stimuli that allow the recognition of goal locations, but they are unable to form relational, holistic representations involving multiple stimuli for the same purpose (Eichenbaum *et al.*, 1990). This is reminiscent of the hippocampal-lesioned pigeons used in the room experiment described earlier. Second, McNaughton and his colleagues (1996) have recently argued that, in rats, learning a cognitive map is critically dependent on egocentric, spatial behavior guided by path integration. Essentially, path integration would serve as an egocentric spatial reference that is used to learn the spatial relations among stimuli in the environment ultimately leading to the formation of a cognitive map. Hypothetically, the hippocampal formation serves to integrate path-integration information with information from stimuli in the environment in much the same way that the avian hippocampal formation is hypothesized to integrate sun-compass directional information with environmental stimuli in learning navigational mechanisms. It would appear, therefore, that at a very basic functional level the mammalian and avian hippocampal formations participate in very similar spatial cognitive processes.

The functional similarity between the avian and mammalian hippocampal formations may also extend to other vertebrate groups. In a recent study (Rodriguez *et al.*, 1994), it was found that fish could learn a cognitive representation of space very similar to that which birds and mammals acquire in laboratory settings. Although anatomical identification of a hippocampal formation in fish is not easy, these same researchers found that telencephalic lesions, which would include a hippocampal formation, disrupted the learning of the cognitive representation of space. To the extent one can interpret this last result, the data suggest that a hippocampal-like structure is a universal feature of the vertebrate telencephalon, that this hippocampal-like structure universally participates in the learning of cognitive representations of space, and, therefore, cognitive representations of space are an ancient vertebrate characteristic.

In any event, at the level of the brain, the hippocampal formation has proved to be the most important structure in the neural control of spatial cognitive representations. The challenge now is to explore more fully how the hippocampal formation interacts with other brain regions to regulate the various features of vertebrate spatial cognition.

Acknowledgements

We gratefully thank Meliha Duncan for her help in preparing the manuscript. Much of the research presented in this chapter was generously supported by grants to VPB from the National Science Foundation and the National Institutes of Health, and a NATO Collaborative Research Grant (CRG 950084) to VPB and Floriano Papi of the University of Pisa, Italy. Al Kamil was instrumental in completing the final draft of the manuscript, and we thank him for his help.

References

Able, K. P. (1980) Mechanisms of orientation, navigation and homing. In Gauthreaux, S. A. (ed.) *Animal Migration, Orientation, and Navigation.* New York: Academic Press, pp. 283–373.

Able, K. P. (1991) Common themes and variations in animal orientation systems. *Am. Zool.* **31**, 157–167.

Able, K. P. (1996) The debate over olfactory navigation by homing pigeons. *J. Exp. Biol.* **199**, 121–124.

Bagnoli, P. and Burkhalter, A. (1983) Organization of the afferent projections to the Wulst in the pigeon. *J. Comp. Neurol.* **214**, 103–113.

Beason, R. C. and Semm, P. (1991) Neuroethological aspects of avian orientation. In Berthold, P. (ed.) *Orientation in Birds.* Basel: Birkhäuser Verlag, pp. 106–127.

Bingman, V. P. (1998) Spatial representations and homing pigeon navigation. In Healy, S. D. (ed.) *Spatial Representation in Animals.* Oxford: Oxford University Press (in press).

Bingman, V. P. and Jones, T.-J. (1994) Hippocampal lesions disrupt sun compass directional learning in homing pigeons. *J. Neurosci.* **14**, 6687–6694.

Bingman, V. P. and Mackie, A. (1992) Importance of olfaction for homing pigeon navigation in Ohio, USA. *Ethol. Ecol. Evol.* **4**, 395–399.

Bingman, V. P. and Mench, J. (1990) Homing behavior of hippocampus and parahippocampus lesioned pigeons following short-distance releases. *Behav. Brain Res.* **40**, 227–238.

Bingman, V. P. and Yates, G. (1992) Hippocampal lesions impair navigational learning in experienced homing pigeons. *Behav. Neurosci.* **106**, 229–232.

Bingman, V. P., Bagnoli, P., Ioalè, P. and Casini, G. (1984) Homing behavior in pigeons after telencephalic ablations. *Brain Behav. Evol.* **24**, 94–106.

Bingman, V. P., Ioalè, P., Casini, G. and Bagnoli, P. (1988) Hippocampal ablated homing pigeons show a persistent impairment in the time taken to return home. *J. Comp. Physiol. A* **163**, 559–563.

Bingman, V. P., Ioalè, P., Casini, G. and Bagnoli, P. (1990) The avian hippocampus: evidence for a role in the development of the homing pigeon navigational map. *Behav. Neurosci.* **104**, 906–911.

Bingman, V. P., Ioalè, P., Casini, G., Bagnoli, P. and Strasser, R. (1994a) Critical importance of the hippocampus for local navigational learning in young homing pigeons. *Soc. Neurosci. Abst.* **20**, 1012.

Bingman, V. P., Casini, G., Nocjar, C. and Jones, T.-J. (1994b) Connections of the piriform cortex of the homing pigeon *Columba livia* stained with Fast-Blue and WGA-HRP. *Brain Behav. Evol.* **43**, 206–218.

Bingman, V. P., Jones, T.-J., Strasser, R., Gagliardo, A. and Ioalè, P. (1995) Homing pigeons, hippocampus and spatial cognition. In Alleva, E., Fasolo, A., Lipp, H.-P., Nadel, L. and Ricceri, L. (eds) *Behavioural Brain Research in Naturalistic and Semi-Naturalistic Settings*. Dordrecht: Kluwer Academic Publishers, pp. 207–238.

Bingman, V. P., Gagliardo, A. and Ioalè, P. (1996) Hippocampal participation in the sun compass orientation of phase-shifted homing pigeons. *J. Comp. Physiol. A* **179**, 695–702.

Brodbeck, D. R. (1994) Memory for spatial and local cues: a comparison of a storing and non-storing species. *Anim. Learning Behav.* **22**, 119–133.

Casini, G., Bingman, V. P. and Bagnoli, P. (1986) Connections of the pigeon dorsomedial forebrain studies with WGA-HRP and (3H)-proline. *J. Comp. Neurol.* **245**, 454–470.

Chappell, J. and Guilford, T. (1995) Homing pigeons primarily use the sun compass rather than fixed directional visual cues in an open-field arena food-searching task. *Proc. Roy. Soc. Lond. B* **260**, 59–63.

Clayton, N. A. and Krebs, J. R. (1994) Memory for spatial and object-specific cues in food-storing and non-storing birds. *J. Comp. Physiol. A* **174**, 371–379.

Delius, J. D. and Bennetto, K. (1972) Cutaneous sensory projections to the avian forebrain. *Brain Res.* **37**, 205–221.

Divac, I., Mogensen, J. and Bjorklund, A. (1985) The prefrontal 'cortex' in the pigeon: biochemical evidence. *Brain Res.* **332**, 365–368.

Eichenbaum, H., Stewart, C. and Morris, R. G. M. (1990) Hippocampal representation in place learning. *Neuroscience* **10**, 3531–3542.

Eichenbaum, H., Otto, T. and Cohen, N. J. (1994) Two functional components of the hippocampal memory system. *Behav. Brain Sci.* **17**, 449–518.

Gagliardo, A. and Divac, I. (1993) Effects of ablation of the presumed equivalent of the mammalian prefrontal cortex on pigeon homing. *Behav. Neurosci.* **107**, 280–288.

Gagliardo, A., Mazzotto, M. and Bingman, V. P. (1996a) Hippocampal lesion effects on learning strategies in homing pigeons. *Proc. Roy. Soc. Lond. B* **263**, 529–534.

Gagliardo, A., Bonadonna, F. and Divac, I. (1996b) Behavioural effects of ablations of the presumed 'prefrontal cortex' or the corticoid in pigeons. *Behav. Brain Res.* **78**, 155–162.

Gagliardo, A., Mazzotto, M. and Bingman, V. P. (1997) Piriform cortex ablations block navigational map learning in homing pigeons. *Behav. Brain Res.* **86**, 143–148.

Healy, S. D. and Krebs, J. R. (1992) Food-storing and the hippocampus in corvids: amount and volume are correlated. *Proc. Roy. Soc. Lond. B* **248**, 241–245.

Heiligenberg, W. (1991) *Neural Nets in Electric Fish*. Cambridge, MA: MIT Press.

Ioalè, P., Nozzolini, M. and Papi, F. (1990) Homing pigeons do extract directional information from olfactory stimuli. *Behav. Ecol. Sociobiol.* **26**, 301–305.

Karten, H. and Hodos, W. (1967) *A Sterotaxic Atlas of the Brain of the Pigeon Columba livia*. Baltimore: Johns Hopkins University Press.

Karten, H., Hodos, W., Nauta, W. J. H. and Revzin, A. M. (1973) Neural connections of the 'visual Wulst' of the avian telencephalon: experimental studies in the pigeon (*Columba livia*) and owl (*Speotyto cunicularia*). *J. Comp. Neurol.* **150**, 253–278.

Knudson, E. I. and Brainard, M. S. (1991) Visual instruction of the neural map of auditory space in the developing optic tectum. *Science* **253**, 85–87.

Kramer, G. (1959) Recent experiments on bird orientation. *Ibis* **101**, 399–416.

Krebs, J. R., Sherry, D. F., Healy, S. D., Perry, V. H. and Vaccarino, A. L. (1989) Hippocampal specialization of food-storing birds. *Proc. Natl Acad. Sci. USA* **86**, 1388–1392.

Leutgeb, S., Husband, S., Riters, L. V., Bingman, V. P. and Shimizu, T. (1995) Afferent connections and cognitive function of the pigeon neostriatum caudolaterale. *Soc. Neurosci. Abst.* **21**, 431.

Leutgeb, S., Husband, S., Riters, L. V., Shimizu, T. and Bingman, V. P. (1996) Telencephalic afferents to the caudolateral neostriatum of the pigeon. *Brain Res.* **730**, 173–181.

McNaughton, B. L., Barnes, C. A., Gerrard, J. L., Gothard, K., Jung, M. W., Knierim, J. J., Kudrimoti, H., Qin, Y., Skaggs, W. E., Suster, M. and Weaver, K. L. (1996) Deciphering the hippocampal polyglot: the hippocampus as a path integration system. *J. Exp. Biol.* **199**, 173–185.

Mogensen, J. and Divac, I. (1982) The prefrontal 'cortex' in the pigeon: behavioral evidence. *Brain Behav. Evol.* **21**, 60–66.

Morris, R. G. M., Garrud, P., Rawlins, J. and O'Keefe, J. (1982) Place navigation impaired in rats with hippocampal lesions. *Nature* **297**, 681–683.

O'Keefe, J. and Nadel, L. (1978) *The Hippocampus as a Cognitive Map*. Oxford: Clarendon Press.

Papi, F. (1991) Olfactory navigation. In Berthold, P. (ed.) *Orientation in Birds*. Basel: Birkhäuser Verlag, pp. 52–85.

Papi, F. and Casini, G. (1990) Pigeons with ablated piriform cortex home from familiar but not from unfamiliar sites. *Proc. Natl Acad. Sci USA* **87**, 3783–3787.

Reiner, A. and Karten, H. (1985) Comparison of olfactory bulb projections in pigeons and turtles. *Brain Behav. Evol.* **27**, 11–27.

Rodriguez, F., Duran, E., Vargas, J. P., Torres, B. and Salas, C. (1994) Performance of goldfish trained in allocentric and egocentric maze procedures suggests the presence of a cognitive mapping system in fishes. *Anim. Learning Behav.* **22**, 409–420.

Sakurai, Y. and Sugimoto, S. (1985) Effects of lesions of prefrontal cortex and dorsomedial thalamus on delayed go/no-go alternation in rats. *Behav. Brain Res.* **17**, 213–219.

Schmidt-Koenig, K. (1979) *Avian Orientation and Navigation*. New York: Academic Press.

Sherry, D. F. and Vaccarino, A. L. (1989) The hippocampus and memory for food caches in black-capped chickadees. *Behav. Neurosci.* **103**, 308–318.

Sherry, D. F., Vaccarino, A. L., Buckenham, K. and Herz, R. S. (1989) The hippocampal complex of food-storing birds. *Brain Behav. Evol.* **34**, 308–317.

Strasser, R. and Bingman, V. P. (1996) The relative importance of location and feature cues for homing pigeon (*Columba livia*) goal recognition. *J. Comp. Psychol.* **110**, 77–87.

Strasser, R. and Bingman, V. P. (1997) Goal recognition and the homing pigeon (*Columba livia*) hippocampal formation. *Behav. Neurosci.* **111**, 1245–1256.

Suga, N. (1984) Neural mechanisms of complex-sound processing for echolocation. *Trends Neurosci.* **7**, 20–27.

Veenman, C. L., Wild, J. M. and Reiner, A. (1995) Organization of the avian 'corticostriatal' projection system: a retrograde and anterograde pathway tracing study in pigeons. *J. Comp. Neurol.* **354**, 87–126.

Waldmann, C. and Güntürkün, O. (1993) The dopaminergic innervation of the pigeon caudolateral forebrain: immunocytochemical evidence for a 'prefrontal cortex' in birds? *Brain Res.* **600**, 225–234.

Wallraff, H. G. (1974) *Das navigationssystem der Vögel*. Munich: R. Oldenburg.

Wallraff, H. G. (1991) In Berthold, P. (ed.) *Orientation in Birds*. Basel: Birkhäuser Verlag, pp. 128–165.

Wallraff, H. G. (1996) Seven theses on pigeon homing deduced from empirical findings. *J. Exp. Biol.* **199**, 105–111.

Wallraff, H. G., Kiepenheuer, J. and Streng, A. (1993) Further experiments on olfactory navigation and non-olfactory pilotage by homing pigeons. *Behav. Ecol. Sociobiol.* **32**, 387–390.

Wiltschko, R. (1996) The function of olfactory input in pigeon orientation: does it provide navigational information or play another role? *J. Exp. Biol.* **199**, 113–119.

Wiltschko, W. and Balda, R. P. (1989) Sun compass orientation in seed-caching Scrub Jays (*Aphelocoma coerulescens*). *J. Comp. Physiol A* **164**, 717–721.

Wiltschko, W. and Wiltschko, R. (1987). In Ellen, P. and Thinus-Blanc, C. (eds) *Cognitive Processes and Spatial Orientation in Animal and Man*. Dordrecht: Martinus Nijhoff, pp. 201–216.

Wiltschko, W. and Wiltschko, R. (1988) Magnetic orientation in birds. In Johnston, R. F. (ed.) *Current Ornithology*, Vol. 5. New York: Plenum Press, pp. 67–121.

Wiltschko, W., Wiltschko, R., Keeton, W. T. and Brown, I. A. (1987) Pigeon homing: the orientation of young birds that had been prevented from seeing the sun. *Ethology* **76**, 27–32.

8

Cognitive Implications of an Information-sharing Model of Animal Communication

W. John Smith

Department of Biology, University of Pennsylvania, Philadelphia, Pennsylvania, USA

Introduction

In social communication, one animal signals and another responds. Several cognitive steps are involved as the second animal selects its responses; these steps can be described as follows in terms of an informational model. First, the responding individual must evaluate the information made available by the signaling on the basis of other information, available from sources contextual to the signal. Second, the respondent must fit all of the relevant information into patterns generated from recall of past events (conscious recall is not generally required; pattern fitting is a fundamental skill). Third, conditional predictions must be made; and fourth, the individual must test and modify any of these predictions for which significant consequences exist. Many vertebrate animals appear to respond to signaling with considerable flexibility. Communicative events are thus complex but are by no means intractable. Indeed, communication provides us with excellent opportunities to investigate animal cognition.

Animals, particularly those of relatively social species, often communicate to coordinate their activities. Moreover, when competing they often negotiate resolution of their differences. Yet, in the last few decades, most biologists have focused more on conflict and gamesmanship than on interacting for

ANIMAL COGNITION IN NATURE
ISBN 0-12-077030-X

mutual advantage. This focus has largely missed the truly interesting point that social interactions typically offer something to each participant, even though the payoffs may be of different coin and unequal value. Certainly, individuals have different and inherently selfish needs and agendas. The core of social behavior, however, is that individuals do adjust and accommodate to one another, coordinate with each other and, yes, cooperate. They act together and profit. This profit is the basic reason why individuals signal, sharing information with one another, and why they respond to signaled information. What is shared is shared selectively, of course, but nonetheless facilitates orderly, useful, social interactions.

Among the most interesting challenges for cognitive ethologists is thus to determine how each participant uses signaled information to anticipate events and to choose its interactional moves. Given the diversity of interactions, whether categorized by functions or complexity, there is considerable scope within which to seek both generalized and more narrowly focused cognitive processes. The main tasks with respect to communication are to determine how animals categorize and process information from signals, evaluate it in the context of information from other social and nonsocial sources, and make conditional, probabilistic predictions within the limits of their incomplete knowledge.

Social communication is the process of sharing information between individuals, but what is information? As I use the term 'information' is not a material thing, but a property of entities and events (Smith 1977, 1997). Acquisition of information reduces an individual's uncertainty about those things and events. Having information enables the individual to choose how to behave, and information is essential for coping with the inconstant world in which the individual lives. That information is not lost or depleted by being shared, as material things would be, implies that, in analyses, information is an intervening concept and not a causative agent as some biologists hold (discussed further by Smith, 1997). For the present purposes, the important issues are simply that having information helps individuals select among options and that signaling shares information.

'Signaling', herein, denotes behavior that has been specialized to make information available. The basic signals studied by ethologists are usually termed 'displays' (Moynihan, 1955). That several repertoires (Smith, 1986a) of signaling specializations with distinctive properties and kinds of information exist in addition to displays, and are available to most individual animals (especially vertebrates), is a distinction not crucial to this chapter. The term 'signal' is used here to encompass all such specialized actions, and the focus is on events in which such signals are performed. Because of their specialization, signals should usually be among the more pertinent sources of information as animals interact. Signals are thus an obvious focus for cognitive studies.

Determining the kinds of information made available by signaling (the 'messages' of signaling) is a first step. That determination is accomplished largely by discovering the various correlates of signal performance. (What regularly correlates with a signal is what you acquire information about when you detect a performance of the signal.) Seeing how recipients of the signal exploit its information differently in different circumstances, including experimentally altered circumstances, reveals some of the relevant kinds of information animals obtain from sources contextual to the signal. It also reveals ways in which animals discriminate among sources of information, how they can be flexible and how they use communication to mediate various tasks. The more we learn about information obtained and used from all sources, the better we will be able to understand how animals categorize things, actions and events, and how they combine information of different sorts in the process of selecting their responses. Perhaps more importantly, we may begin to grasp the cognitive operations underlying animals' expectations of events.

Information

Discovering the information made available by animals' signaling can reveal the kinds of uncertainties that can be reduced as communication facilitates social encounters. The numbers of kinds of uncertainties, and the extents to which they can be reduced, are highly constrained by the limited numbers of signals and signaling procedures available to the members of any one species (Smith, 1977). Presumably, natural selection has honed animal communication to focus on especially pertinent issues. Also, because signaling evolved both to be salient and to provide pertinent information, its study is an obvious way in which to begin inquiries into social cognition. [Claims that much animal signaling is almost endlessly redundant are spurious. Originators of these claims (e.g. Dawkins and Krebs, 1978) fail to grasp the tasks that signaling accomplishes (Smith, 1997).] Signals are never, however, the only sources of information that affect social behavior. We must be very attentive to the circumstances in which signaling occurs, and to the properties that individual animals bring with them to their interactions.

Signaled information

An animal's signals can provide information about its behavior, identity and location, and the classes of external stimuli to which it is responding. To a considerable extent, animals as different as birds and mammals, and animals living in different ecological and social environments, appear to make available at least grossly similar sorts of information by signaling.

No signaling is done at random, that is, each performance occurs in correlation with particular classes of a signaler's behavior. The number of classes that characterize the basic signals of any species is small, perhaps fewer than a dozen (Table 8.1). Some correlations are relatively narrow, linking a signal to attack, escape or other activity. Others are much broader. For instance, a signal may correlate with interactional behavior of all kinds or with a wide functional range of locomotory activities.

Animals signal when selecting between alternative actions. As a result, each kind of signal correlates with more than one kind of behavior and with the indecisive behavior that occurs during the process of choosing. For instance, when choosing whether to attack or flee, and pausing or making false starts toward and away from an opponent, an animal's signaling provides information about the relative (and conditional) probabilities of all three classes: attack, escape and behaving indecisively. Our understanding of widespread behavioral 'messages' was summarized earlier (Smith, 1977) and recently updated in Smith (1997). Therefore, it will not be reviewed further in this chapter.

Features of the physical forms of signals can be specific to an individual, a local population, a species or even a matriline (e.g. *Macaca nemestrina*, see Gouzoules and Gouzoules, 1990). Such features make available information that identifies each signaler. In addition, the physical forms of audible signals provide clues to a signaler's direction relative to a recipient and, as modified by the environment through which they pass, clues to distance. Some signals, perhaps used primarily when signaler and recipient are not close to each other, provide information about external referents such as a source of danger or resource to which a signaler is reacting. Many signals have broad classes of external referents, in that attack behavior requires: an object of attack; escape, something from which to escape; association, someone with whom to associate; and the like.

For cognitive studies we must determine what kinds of information animals process in different kinds of events. In close interactions, participants commonly have similar information available to them about the situation. Unless something of great moment, e.g. an approaching predator, is suddenly detected by only one participant, what each individual needs most is information (private, unless signaled) about actions the other may take. When relatively far apart, individuals may be less quickly affected by each other's behavior. One may have even greater need of information about that predator, especially if unable to see its companion's alarmed reaction. Either might use information about its companion's need for help in, say, a fight. A member of a group might need to attract its traveling companions if it stops because it has found a significant amount of some resource (Smith, 1977). Conversely, it might need to turn them away in order to reduce overlap in an area where it is foraging (Boinski and Campbell, 1996).

To be efficient, individuals responding to a signal may not fully process all of its information, especially in rapidly developing events. They may rank the messages and focus on the most pertinent, with experience and current

Table 8.1 Most basic signals ('displays') of most species of at least birds and mammals make available primarily the kinds of information about behavior listed in IA, as well as supplemental information of at least categories IB1 and IB2. All signals provide some information about a signaler's identity (IIA) and all sounds provide some clues to the signaler's location (IIB). Less is known, as yet, about the provision of information about external stimuli ('external referents').

I. Behavioral information

A. Information about selections from the subject's behavioral repertoire. Many different species signal primarily about the following:

1. Interact
2. Attack
3. Associate ⎫ These three are related in that each is a way of interacting
4. Copulate ⎭
5. Escape
6. Incompatible alternatives
7. Indecisive
8. Locomotory
9. Attentive
10. Remaining with site

B. Information supplemental to the behavioral selections:

1. Probability
2. Intensity
3. Relative stability
4. Extent of initiative (from active to deferring)
5. Direction

II. Nonbehavioral information about attributes of subjects

A. Identity, e.g. species, sometimes infraspecific group, individual

B. Location: direction, distance

III. Information about external stimuli to which the subject is responding

A. Things:

1. Resources (some more narrowly specified, such as food, or a territory or other site).
2. Sources of danger, such as predators (some more narrowly specified, to particular classes of predators).
3. Objects of interactional behavior of all kinds, and attentive monitoring; elicitors of escape; sites at which a signaler remains.

B. Events: classes of interactional circumstances

context as guides. Perhaps a vulnerable individual responds more to the probability of attack that can be predicted from a signal and a less vulnerable individual more to the prediction of indecisive behavior.

Information from contextual sources

A single individual responds differently to a particular signal in different circumstances. Different individuals respond differently to that same signal in a single circumstance. Responses are thus based on more than just the information in the signal. Sources of information that exist in both a situation and in the animals themselves (e.g. as memories or hormonal states) are perceived to invest the signal with customized implications as cognitive processes work to select a response. For example, the speed and direction of a signaler's movements are often pertinent sources of information, as are the presence or absence of other individuals, a responding individual's history with the signaler, the location of the event relative to social features (e.g. territorial boundaries) and resources (such as food or cover), the point in a seasonal cycle of behavior, and so on. No occurrence of a signal is ever context free. In principle, everything can be informative. Necessarily, perception is selective. Some sources of information are treated as focal and others as background, partly pertinent and partly irrelevant. The task for cognitive ethologists is to determine how such categories are deployed and how categorization changes as situations differ.

If repertoires of signals are as small as they now appear to be, each signal should be used as effectively as possible. To the extent that responses to a signal must be quick and precise, the information provided by a signal must be narrowly predictive. Conversely, when responses can be selected over appreciable intervals and adjusted as needed, the information provided by a signal can be only broadly predictive, and applicable in a relatively wide array of events (Smith, 1977). The cognitive processes involved in responding to broadly predictive information must to some degree be flexible and open to novelty. The world has a great potential for novelty.

Broadly predictive information about behavior (see Table 8.1) is usable because sources of information contextual to signals help recipients narrow their predictions to those most appropriate for each event. Indeed, in the absence of crucial or expectable contextual sources of information, an individual responding to a signal may resort to special tactics. It may seek further information before committing to any other response, perhaps using vocal signals as probes to elicit information. The individual may begin to respond on the basis of the most probable course of events and adjust as it acquires more information. It may play safe and respond as if the worst that could be expected were about to happen, even when that is relatively improbable. For instance, hearing a vocalization that indicates the signaler is very probably fleeing, but being unable to see the signaler's situation, a responding individual might immediately seek cover. If already in or near cover, it might instead alertly scan for further information (Smith, 1991).

An animal's responses to an event thus do not always tell us what information has been acquired. Sometimes, responses depend more on what information the individual still needs to acquire. Research in which 'alarm calls' are played back to animals from hidden speakers has usually failed to address the latter issue.

Categorizing information

Our representations of information that animals process cognitively must differ from theirs. One obvious difference is that we generally represent the information in words and they can not. Yet it is the power that signaled information gives animals to make predictions that is crucial, not the mode in which descriptions of the information are represented. Our task is to describe the information in ways that enable us to predict animal behavior, even if we cannot specify the form in which their cognitive operations represent that information.

Much of our own processing of information as we interact with one another never emerges in our consciousness as words. We do not, in casual events, represent to ourselves the information in a friend's smile or grimace in words. (Indeed, it is not obvious that we readily could.) Yet we do use that information as we respond. Two colleagues and I once studied a facial expression of humans and other primates, a visible protrusion of the tongue (Smith *et al.*, 1974). Through observations and experiments, we found that tongue showing provides information that the signaler will tend to eschew social overtures from other individuals, at least while signaling. Subsequently, Dolgin and Sabini (1982) showed experimentally that human subjects respond appropriately, initiating necessary interactions much less quickly and assertively, when faced with a tongue-showing individual than with one who is not. Significantly, the experimental subjects were not consciously aware of their tongue showing when they responded, and were surprised when told about it after the trials. Thus, even humans, when responding to a nonverbal signal, may do so without conscious awareness. Presumably, nonhuman animals always deal with signaled information by cognitive procedures that do not require language-like representations and need not always require awareness.

If we have studied the behavioral (and other) correlates of an animal's signals in detail, we can describe the behavior in classes framed to fit the signals' uses. Our representations should shed light on categories important to the animals. The categories indicate some of what is relevant (in the sense of Pepperberg, 1996) and usable for the cognitive operations of communicating animals. Such categories as interactional behavior or initiative-taking (Table 8.1), for instance, show how animals must depend on information gleaned from contextual sources if they are to formulate relatively precise expectations. Further, knowing the signaled information and the overt responses of recipient individuals in different circumstances, we can speculate about the contextual sources and their information, and can design experiments to test our hypotheses.

Animals do appear to make predictions about each other's behavior, and so they must be able to classify actions. In contrast, no evidence has been found that individuals, even monkeys and (perhaps) apes, attribute mental states to one another (Cheney and Seyfarth, 1990), although it is not clear that fully appropriate research procedures have been used (Heyes, 1993). If animals do not make attributions of mental states, then there may be little reason to presume that they categorize and communicate about motivations or emotions, and even less reason to describe the activities as 'mind-reading' (Dawkins and Krebs, 1978). For now, they appear to operate at the less abstract level of making predictions about behavior, and appear to divide behavior into at least the sorts of classes shown in Table 8.1. What we know about their signaling also suggests that responding must involve cognitive processes that incorporate competing alternatives, probability assessments, conditionally, and influence from sources of information contextual to signals.

To the extent that animals' signals inform about external referents, such as classes of predators, and that the information involves classification into fuzzy sets (Gouzoules *et al.*, 1995), the capacity of animals to assess probability is again pertinent. The probabilities here are the likelihood of particular items being members of a set. Fuzzy sets include items that may be members only to some degree, or only at some times.

Flexibility

Context-dependent responding entails multiple kinds of responses to each type of signal. Such diversity does not necessarily lead to flexible responding, in the sense of nonreflexive choices and unprogrammed options. However, fully programmed responses to all stimulus conditions would be seriously inefficient for active animals who encounter situations that cannot be anticipated in detail. Learning to respond to novel events and to use information from memory sets the stage for flexibility; that is, an animal has become flexible when it can process individually acquired knowledge, seek further information and hold a range of options open as it works to anticipate the course of an event. Such an individual can fine-tune and modify its responses. It can evaluate unexpected information and cope better with variable environments than can the 'releaser'-driven individuals posited by early ethologists. Yet flexibility must always have limits and is in various ways channeled by cognitive constraints.

Conditionality is also a factor. The conditionality of predictions that can be made on receipt of a signal is, for signaling individuals, a necessary limitation of commitment. For individuals responding to signals, conditional predictions are another reason to be attentive to changing circumstances, another task requiring flexibility.

Openness of responding can involve several tactics, often concurrently. An individual may tentatively try various moves and assess their effects. It may respond to inconclusive information by adopting a 'typical case scenario' (Smith, 1991) and correcting course as an event unfolds, in effect responding by means of rules ordered in a default hierarchy (Waldrop, 1992) and devising new rules as experience allows. It may act to obtain information from sources not initially used or apparent, and even try to elicit information by probing in various ways. It may skeptically refuse to accept information being made available, testing a signaler in ways that can reveal the extent to which the signaling is reliable. It may calibrate individuals with whom it interacts, adjusting to idiosyncrasies in the relative probabilities of the choices each may make when performing particular signals (Smith, 1986b).

Calibrating is a particularly interesting cognitive procedure, not just for coping with a companion's idiosyncrasies or a competitor's suspect reliability, but also for dealing with inevitable changes. For instance, immature individuals may initially signal at times that are at best only marginally appropriate (e.g. Seyfarth and Cheney, 1986; Roush and Snowdon, 1994), although such signaling often is appropriate for the youngsters' developmental stages (e.g. Hersek and Owings, 1994). Immature animals' signals can mislead unwary responders, for instance, into expecting danger in events that are actually innocuous. Yet responding individuals can adapt. Ontogenetic development is broadly predictable as an individual's social relationships, bonds, needs and competencies change. The details are determined by multiple forces, however (West and King, 1996), leading to somewhat divergent trajectories for different individuals. Unless each individual is calibrated continually by other group members, the implications of its behavior will become relatively uncertain. Indeed, change continues throughout life. Individuals who interact with each other repeatedly must expect occasional changes, and must recalibrate their expectations and accommodate to new conditions.

Animals cope with unanticipated novelty. We know little about the process and its limits, but some striking cases have been reported. For instance, Richards (1979) found that conspecific neighbors of a towhee (*Papilo erythrophthalmus*) who sang not only songs typical of his species, but also a very different song apparently learned from a Carolina Wren (*Thryothorus ludovicianus*), learned to identify this individual even by hearing just its wren-like song. Specifically, his neighbors both distinguished this Towhee from local wrens and accepted it as their own species. They had the flexibility to cope with a discordance in visible and audible clues that was outside their previous experience with towhees.

Birds' flexibility in categorizing a situation in which major sources of information are at variance is also revealed during experimental playbacks of songs to territorial birds. Interactive playback simulates intrusion of a competitive stranger into a bird's territory, making some response almost mandatory. When subjects approach playback they find no singing bird. They cannot be prepared for such an event. Most briefly search and attempt to challenge with vocal and visible signaling (Smith, 1996; Smith and Smith, 1996a,b,c). If playback is timed to answer subjects' songs, and moved to simulate an intruder's jockeying for position, subjects can be enticed to approach repeatedly and continue to signal. Although the absence of a visible intruder violates important expectations, the careful timing and local movements of the playback stimuli are undeniably responses to a subject's own moves. Usually considerable differences exist among subjects in persistence, however. Some individuals are sufficiently concerned to keep trying to find an invisible singer that they appear to treat the human with the playback speaker merely as an aversive obstacle. Others appear to accept the dissonance as indicating irrelevance, and waste less time responding.

Comparable results are often obtained if a stuffed bird or model is used as a simulated intruder. Subjects are unable to make this visible stimulus respond to them, a situation that must violate very basic expectations. Again, some subjects appear to adopt a worst-case scenario, such as: 'I see the red feathers I'd expect on an intruder, so I'll treat this odd stimulus as I'd treat an intruder'. In Lack's (1940, 1953) studies, some European Robins, *Erithacus rubecula*, responded to a decoy from which all parts except the red breast feathers had been removed; other subjects ignored such abstracted stimuli.

Experiments like Lack's indicate considerable flexibility. The results should not be overinterpreted as indicating tendencies to reflexive responding, as Krebs and Dawkins (1984, p. 385) did: 'that animals are susceptible to being "tricked" by the crude dummies of ethologists . . . makes it likely that natural selection will favor similar exploitation by other animals'. In real events stimuli are not isolated. Animals trying to 'trick' other individuals will inevitably supply information from many sources, some of which may be contradictory. Natural selection will have opposing effects, favoring exploitation on the one hand and flexible coping procedures on the other.

Surely one of the hardest questions about flexibility is: to what extent can signalers anticipate responses to their signaling and control that signaling to influence the behavior of other individuals? Can they choose whether to signal, and perhaps even what signal to use, based on expectations of the responses they may elicit? The parrot Alex can, with English words (e.g. Pepperberg, 1990), but can birds have similar control over their species-specific signaling? Evidence of such effects is inconclusive.

So-called 'audience effects' are sometimes cited as evidence of volitional control of signaling; some may well be. In many if not most cases, however, plausible alternative explanations have not been ruled out (Smith, 1990, pp. 211–214). For instance, does an individual ground squirrel (e.g. *Spermophilus beldingi*) behave differently on detecting a predator if it is near or not near its close relatives? It is more likely to utter trills when near close relatives (Sherman, 1977), but is this because in such a situation it is more likely alertly to monitor a predator, or because its audience elicits the calls? If the former, then the audience effect does not influence signaling directly. The influence is indirect, through an effect on the signaler's monitoring behavior. If a high probability of staying attentive is part of the information that the vocalization provides about the signaler's behavior, then the presence of relatives may be simply a condition for the monitoring rather than a basis for a decision to vocalize. The point is that we can not learn whether animals make decisions about whether to signal until we have fully grasped the requisite conditions (and thus the regular correlates) of signaling. If an individual retains freedom with respect to those correlates, then its signaling can be modulated by audience effects and the like. However, if the correlates are regular and thus represented by the 'messages' of the signal, there is little opportunity to signal electively. Signaling behavior is useful for cognitive research only when the referents of signals have been carefully studied.

Surprisingly, a signaler can also be its own audience. An unanticipated effect of an individual's vocal signaling on its own hormonal states was discovered by Cheng (1992). The ovarian follicles of female Ring Doves, *Streptopelia risoria*, who cannot coo because of experimental brain lesions, severed syringial nerves or deflated air sacs do not mature. If the doves are exposed to playback of their own previously recorded coos, the follicles do mature. Cheng proposed that 'vocal self-stimulation' might also be important in physiological responses to other signaling – a male passerine's singing, for instance, or a human's crying, talking or singing in the dark. Any such physiological changes would alter the bases for cognitive processing, and thus for social responsiveness as well.

The contributions of signaled information to social processes

Social behavior is useful for studies of cognition because it provides us with events in which individual animals must adjust their behavior to one another, and because it is the arena for signaling. We can recognize the sorts of information with which interacting animals must deal, can search for the ways in which communication makes a portion of this information available, and can ask how each individual influences and is influenced by the others. Signals can serve in many ways, for example, to confirm other individuals' expectations, to reassure, alert, update, challenge or appease, and to probe for informative responses. Explorations of how signaled information contributes to such tasks will show us much about basic social cognition. In many events, one animal may signal as a simple move, largely adequate in itself to influence another animal. At other times signaling is incorporated into interactional patterns that are managed jointly by two or more individuals. The most pervasive joint task is surely negotiating.

Negotiating occurs when interacting individuals keep their options open rather than trying to resolve an issue by immediately taking or relinquishing control. The ability to negotiate helps animals adjust to one another, restrain themselves and resolve issues efficiently. Negotiation also lets each participant operate for extended periods on the verge of missteps without usually committing serious tactical errors. Negotiating individuals run the risks that have to be taken to uncover and pursue the best available opportunities. The escalation that could occur in the absence of sufficient information (Maynard Smith and Parker, 1976) is forestalled as negotiators gradually make selected information available.

In many interactions, each participant initially lacks sufficient information to be able to assess the extent to which it can control the event. Neither individual initially commits to decisive action. Instead, each provides some information about how it may behave, indicating that the immediate probabilities of most actions are low relative to the probability of continued indecisive behavior (that is, pausing, vacillating or remaining poised, usually with further signaling). Decisions are delayed while information is both provided and elicited, often within a formal pattern to which both participants adhere (a formalized interaction; Smith, 1977). The delaying actions themselves provide information pertinent to the process of negotiating.

Information about the class I have termed indecisive behavior is made available by signaling in a great range of circumstances, from face-to-face confrontations and mobbing to group travel, pair formation, pair-bond maintenance and caring for offspring. The striking prevalence of information about indecisive behavior is further evidence of negotiating. Further, provision of such information suggests that negotiating may be central to diverse interactions. Learning what additional kinds of information are provided and acquired during negotiations should reveal to us aspects of the cognitive processes with which animals develop their expectations, deal with uncertainty and missing information, assess their level of confidence in interpreting an event, and select among alternative activities.

Negotiations are often continuous, prolonged and obvious in competitive events in which much is at stake (Smith, 1977, 1997). Newly met competitors negotiate to establish dominance ranks, territorial borders and other relationships with minimal expenditures. Negotiating lessens dependence on outright fighting, an effect recognized by early ethologists. The early ethological tradition was to interpret signaling opponents as expressing emotional states such as aggression and fear. Hinde (1985a,b), in a discussion of difficulties with concepts of emotion, distinguished between signaling that is primarily expressive and that which is primarily concerned with negotiation. More simply, we might recognize that some functions of signaling can follow just from making information (whether about emotions or behavior, or other referents) available, whereas other functions depend on the two-way informational exchange of the process of negotiating.

Many behavioral ecologists (e.g. Caryl, 1979, 1982), assuming that indications of aggression should make acts of attack predictable, became concerned that, in encounters with a great deal of signaling, few or no attacks occurred. Because signaling makes attack behavior predictable only as one option, and conditional upon events that are typically forestalled by negotiating, the concerns were unfounded. None the less, the paucity of attacks was widely accepted as revealing that much signaling was bluff, functioning to mislead rather than to inform reliably about probable behavior (e.g. Dawkins and Krebs, 1978). Some bluffing may occur, although it has rarely been shown (for a well-studied case involving stomatopod crustaceans, see Caldwell, 1986). However, bluffing over serious issues should be difficult between animals who are familiar with each other as individuals and who interact frequently (Smith, 1986b).

The assumption that two individuals, who meet and then signal copiously while competing, should also attack frequently lacks observational support. Indeed, such encounters often persist for long periods with neither fighting nor fleeing. The signaling instead predicts that continued indecisive confrontational behavior is by far the most probable choice of both participants. They are negotiating: each reveals that it will stay in the encounter, and each assesses the other's commitment to staying (sometimes with occasional brief feints, probing the other's defenses, as in fighting fish, *Betta splendens*; Simpson, 1968). The focus of the interaction is on persistence. Decisive acts such as attacking or fleeing are relatively improbable until the persistence of one or both participants wanes. If neither participant triumphs, both may continue to accept the status quo (e.g. see the challenge rituals of Wildebeest, *Connochaetes taurinus*; Estes, 1969).

Negotiating is common in mundane, repeated interactions that are much less dramatic than faceoffs over a limited resource. The basic features of negotiating are actually evident in all jointly managed interactions. At some level, joint control requires compromise. Each participant in some ways accommodates to the other's behavior, although yielding no more control than it must. Consider, for instance, birds (e.g. Carolina chickadees, *Parus carolinensis*) or primates (e.g. savanna baboons, *Papio cynocephalus*) that forage while they move through their territory in a cohesive group. Individuals can keep track of the group's progression by watching one another. Yet visual surveillance is difficult when cover is dense, and costly in taking time and attention away from searching for food. Group coherence can also be maintained using audible clues. An individual can simply travel in the direction in which it hears vocal companions. Less passively, the individual can also get some measure of control over the timing and direction of group movements by vocalizing and influencing its companions. At any moment, the individuals most ready to move on may vocalize differently from those most inclined to stay put, simple differences that provide the basis for simple negotiations that determine the travel patterns of the group as a whole.

Negotiations need not be face-to-face. In many species of birds, an individual can sing one kind of song when actively trying to initiate interaction with other individuals, and another kind when more preoccupied with noninteractional behavior, yet in the latter case can still be responsive to overtures from, say, a neighbor (e.g. Smith and Smith, 1992, 1996a,b,c). The difference may seem small, because the singer would interact in either case. However, the difference should affect the efficiency of conducting territorial business enormously. What does such communication suggest about cognitive processes? First, that males on neighboring territories may categorize an event in terms of its relevance to maintenance of the status quo largely by discriminating between two song types. Further, as a singer's ratio of one song type to the other shifts, predictions can be modified. By replying with song, a neighbor might negotiate with the initial singer even while they remain apart from each other.

Negotiating can be subtle. Subtlety may be prevalent when, for instance, animals live continuously in social groups and members share long-term social bonds. Changes in relationships among individuals may be slow, the cumulative result of any interactions in which small effects become trends. Dramatic events, such as the forceful usurpation of a dominance rank, can be much less common than are repeated, indirect tests such as those described by Simpson (1973) during a dominance reversal of two chimpanzees. Perhaps even more common are minute jockeyings for social position, or the continual limitation of setbacks to small losses and victories to small gains. Simple encounters may be conducted as minute, intermittent steps in what amounts to an extended negotiation.

Animals negotiate as they adjust and coordinate their activities in a wide range of social events. Cognitive ethologists thus have abundant opportunities to assess the information that is provided by signaling, the influence of information from nonsignal sources, the tactics animals employ and the processes by which decisions are reached.

Conclusions

Given the range and complexity of animal communication, our ability to dissect the process into interrelated but distinct components presents many opportunities to cognitive ethologists. Because all animals have quite limited repertoires of signals, the information provided by each signal should be fundamentally important in their management of social events. This information is accessible to us when we study specialized signaling. Such studies reveal that animals provide one another with information about who and where they are, behavioral options that are likely to be exercised, and even certain external stimuli to which they are responding. The different ways in which an animal responds to a signal suggest the kinds of information that are gleaned or sought from sources other than signals as recipients assign significance to particular events. By controlling the information available from different sources, we can learn how animals construct categories, deal with competing interpretations and assess conditional probabilities. We can explore their cognitive flexibility and ways in which it is constrained. We can learn the many ways in which animals negotiate with one another, and explore the kinds of information and cognitive operations that contribute to negotiating and other social tasks.

Acknowledgements

For discussions of cognition and help with this manuscript, I thank Anne Marie Smith, Irene Pepperberg, Benson Smith, Paul Rozin and Lorraine Palita.

References

Boinski, S. and Campbell, A. F. (1996) The huh vocalization of white-faced capuchins: a spacing call disguised as a food call? *Ethology* **102**, 826–840.

Caldwell, R. L. (1986) The deceptive use of reputation by stomatopods. In Mitchell, R. W. and Thompson, N. S. (eds) *Deception. Perspectives on Human and Nonhuman Deceit.* Albany, NY: State University of New York Press, pp. 129–145.

Caryl, P. G. (1979) Communication by agonistic displays: what can games theory contribute to ethology? *Behaviour* **68**, 136–169.

Caryl, P. G. (1982) Telling the truth about intentions. *J. Theoret. Biol.* **97**, 679–689.

Cheney, D. L. and Seyfarth, R. M. (1990) *How Monkeys See the World.* Chicago: University of Chicago Press.

Cheng, M. F. (1992) For whom does the female dove coo? A case for the role of vocal self-stimulation. *Anim. Behav.* **43**, 1035–1044.

Dawkins, R. and Krebs, J. R. (1978) Animal signals: information or manipulation? In Krebs, J. R. and Davies, N. B. (eds) *Behavioural Ecology. An Evolutionary Approach.* Sunderland, MA: Sinauer, pp. 282–309.

Dolgin, K. G. and Sabini, J. (1982) Experimental manipulation of a human non-verbal display: the tongue-show affects an observer's willingness to interact. *Anim. Behav.* **30**, 935–936.

Estes, R. D. (1969) Territorial behavior of the wildebeest (*Connochaetes taurinus* Burchell, 1823). *Z. Tierpsychol.* **26**, 284–370.

Gouzoules, H. and Gouzoules, S. (1990). Matrilineal signatures in the recruitment screams of pigtail macaques, *Macaca nemestrina. Behaviour* **115**, 327– 347.

Gouzoules, H., Gouzoules, S. and Ashley, J. (1995) Representational signaling in non-human primate vocal communication. In Zimmerman, E., Newman, J. D. and Jurgens, U. (eds) *Current Topics in Primate Vocal Communication.* New York: Plenum Press, pp. 235–252.

Hersek, M. J. and Owings, D. H. (1994) Tail flagging by young California ground squirrels, *Spermophilus beecheyi*: age-specific participation in a tonic communicative system. *Anim. Behav.* **48**, 803–811.

Heyes, C. M. (1993) Anecdotes, training, trapping and triangulating: do animals attribute mental states? *Anim. Behav.* **46**, 177–188.

Hinde, R. A. (1985a) Was 'the expression of the emotions' a misleading phrase? *Anim. Behav.* **33**, 985–992.

Hinde, R. A. (1985b) Expression and negotiation. In Zivin, G. (ed.) The *Development of Expressive Behavior.* New York: Academic Press, pp. 103–116.

Krebs, J. R. and Dawkins, R. (1984) Animal signals: mind-reading and manipulation. In Krebs, J. R. and Davies, N. B. (eds) *Behavioural Ecology*, 2nd edn. Oxford: Blackwell, pp. 380–402.

Lack, D. (1940) The releaser concept of bird behaviour. *Nature* **145**, 107–108.

Lack, D. (1953) *The Life of the Robin.* London: Pelican.

Maynard Smith, J. and Parker, G. A. (1976) The logic of asymmetric contests. *Anim. Behav.* **24**, 159–175.

Moynihan, M. (1955) Types of hostile display. *Auk* **72**, 247–259.

Pepperberg, I. M. (1990) Some cognitive capacities of an African grey parrot. *Adv. Study Behav.* **19**, 357–409.

Pepperberg, I. M. (1996) Categorical class formation by an African grey parrot (*Psittacus erithacus*). In Zentall, T. R. and Smeets, P. M. (eds) *Stimulus Class Formation in Humans and Animals.* New York: Elsevier, pp. 71–90.

Richards, D. G. (1979) Recognition of neighbors by associative learning in rufous-sided towhees. *Auk* **96**, 688–693.

Roush, R. S. and Snowdon, C. T. (1994) Ontogeny of food-associated calls in cotton-top tamarins. *Anim. Behav.* **47**, 263–273.

Seyfarth, R. M. and Cheney, D. L. (1986) Vocal development in vervet monkeys. *Anim. Behav.* **34**, 1640–1658.

Sherman, P. W. (1977) Nepotism and the evolution of alarm calls. *Science* **197**, 1246–1253.

Simpson, M. J. A. (1968) The display of the Siamese fighting fish, *Betta splendens. Anim. Behav. Monogr.* **1**, 1–73.

Simpson, M. J. A. (1973) The social grooming of male chimpanzees. In Michael, R. P. and Crook, J. H. (eds) *Comparative Ecology and Behaviour of Primates*. New York: Academic Press.

Smith, W. J. (1977) *The Behavior of Communicating. An Ethological Approach*. Cambridge, MA: Harvard University Press.

Smith, W. J. (1986a) Signaling behavior: contributions of different repertoires. In Schusterman, R. J., Thomas, J. A. and Woods, F. G. (eds) *Dolphin Cognition and Behavior: A Comparative Approach*. Hillsdale, NJ: Erlbaum, pp. 315– 330.

Smith, W. J. (1986b) An 'informational' perspective on manipulation. In Mitchell, R. W. and Thompson, N. S. (eds) *Deception: Perspectives on Human and Nonhuman Deceit*. Albany, NY: State University of New York Press, pp. 71–86.

Smith, W. J. (1990) Communication and expectations: a social process and the cognitive operations it depends upon and influences. In Bekoff, M. and Jamieson, D. (eds) *Interpretation and Explanation in the Study of Animal Behavior* Vol. 1. Boulder, CO: Westview, pp. 234–253. Reprinted in Bekoff, M. and Jamieson, D. (eds) *Readings in Animal Cognition*. Cambridge, MA: MIT Press, pp. 243–255.

Smith, W. J. (1991) Animal communication and the study of cognition. In Ristau, C. (ed.) *Cognitive Ethology. The Minds of Other Animals*. Hillsdale, NJ: Erlbaum, pp. 209–230.

Smith, W. J. (1996) Using interactive playback to study how songs and singing contribute to communication about behavior. In Kroodsma, D. E. and Miller, E. H. (eds) *Ecology and Evolution of Acoustic Communication in Birds*. Ithaca, NY: Cornell University Press, pp. 375–397.

Smith, W. J. (1997) The behavior of communicating, after twenty years. In Owings, D. H., Beecher, M. D. and Thompson, N. S. (eds) *Perspectives in Ethology*, Vol. 12. New York, London: Plenem, pp. 7–53.

Smith, W. J., Chase, J. and Lieblich, A. K. (1974) Tongue showing: a facial display of humans and other primate species. *Semiotica* **11**, 201–246.

Smith, W. J. and Smith, A. M. (1992) Behavioral information provided by two song forms of the eastern kingbird, *T. tyrannus. Behaviour* **120**, 90–102.

Smith, W. J. and Smith, A. M. (1996a) Information about behaviour provided by Louisiana waterthrush, *Seiurus motacilla* (Parulinae), songs. *Anim. Behav.* **51**, 785–799.

Smith, W. J. and Smith, A. M. (1996b) Vocal signaling of the great crested flycatcher, *Myiarchus crinitus* (Aves, Tyrannidae). *Ethology* **102**, 705–723.

Smith, W. J. and Smith, A. M. (1996c) Playback interactions with great crested flycatchers, *Myiarchus crinitus* (Aves, Tyrannidae). *Ethology* **102**, 724–735.

Waldrop, M. (1992) *Complexity. The Emerging Science at the Edge of Order and Chaos*. New York: Simon and Schuster Touchstone Books.

West, M. and King, A. (1996) Eco-gen-actics: a systems approach to avian communication. In Kroodsma, D. E. and Miller, E. H. (eds) *Ecology and Evolution of Acoustic Communication in Birds*. Ithaca, NY: Cornell University Press, pp. 20–38.

9

Cognitive Processes in Avian Vocal Acquisition

Luis F. Baptista[1], Douglas A. Nelson[2] and Sandra
L. L. Gaunt[2]

[1]Department of Ornithology and Mammalogy, California Academy of Sciences,
Golden Gate Park, San Francisco, CA 94118-4599, USA
[2]Borror Laboratory of Bioacoustics, Department of Zoology, 1735 Neil Avenue,
The Ohio State University, Columbus, OH 43210-1293, USA

Introduction

A comparative study of vocal acquisition by birds provides insight into avian cognitive capacities in the realm of communication, i.e. memory, information processing and categorization. Variation exists within and between avian taxa in the representation of sound information in memory, i.e. cognitive content, and when those memories are obtained, processed and organized, i.e. cognitive structure–function (*sensu* Yoerg and Kamil, 1991). Recognition of this variation can aid in elucidating the development and evolution of avian vocal communication systems.

The cognitive functions of 'selective attention, information processing, decision processing and choice between alternative strategies' (Lassalle, 1996, p. 7) direct behavioral responses to ranges of environmental stimuli such as temperatures, food types, mates, etc. In vocal communication the animal must attend to, select from and/or respond to sounds that may range from noninformative background noise to information-rich and species-typical signal(s). Thus, animals must have mechanisms that facilitate recognition of appropriate signals at one level and decision processes concerning response to and/or production of signals at another. Signal recognition as well as vocal expression may be directed wholly or in part by pre-existing, heritable representations within the nervous system. Cognitive processes, however, can influence even such stereotypic (Pepperberg, 1991) and/or nonconscious (Yoerg and Kamil, 1991) signals and signaling responses, as we will discuss below.

Behavioral plasticity can also increase fitness and survivorship in a changing environment. Vocal learning, both of signals to recognize and to produce, can impart such plasticity. Thus, vocal learning has long-term consequences, but plasticity in behavior may also be achieved by shorter term shifts between alternative patterns of behavior such as in matched counter-singing in birds (Krebs *et al.*, 1981; Adret-Hausberger, 1982) that involves the cognitive process of categorization. Such categorization enables birds to distinguish between song themes and choose appropriate behaviors with which to respond (Hausberger and Cousillas, 1996).

How animals obtain and retain information and later use those retained memories is general cognition or intelligence, whereas vocal learning is one of several 'specialized' or 'domain specific' cognitive processes (Kamil, 1994; Moscovitch, 1995) covered in this book. A cognitive account of vocal development must consider how and when song memories are acquired, and what factors influence the timing and outcome of song ontogeny. In this review we survey studies illustrating how birds recognize what to sing through the interaction of innately specified predispositions and learning, and what variation there is in the mode and timing of vocal acquisition.

Vocal development in nonoscines

With the exception of parrots and hummingbirds (Baptista and Schuchmann, 1990; Baptista, 1993; Pepperberg, 1993; Gaunt *et al.*, 1994), most nonoscines recognize and produce sound signals independent of sensory experience with the sounds. The heritability of dispositions to produce species-typical sounds in such species is evident from isolation, deafening, breeding, cross-fostering and hybridization experiments.

Roosters (*Gallus gallus*), Ring Doves (*Streptopelia roseogrisea*) and tyrant flycatchers (Tyrannidae) raised in isolation or deafened produce species-typical sounds (Konishi, 1963; Konishi and Nottebohm, 1969; Nottebohm and Nottebohm, 1971; Kroodsma and Konishi, 1991). Data from deafening experiments indicate that, unlike songbirds (oscines), nonoscines do not require audiosensory feedback in order for normal vocalizations (motor output) to develop. Vocalizations in these groups are dependent almost entirely on internal signal representations ('innate auditory templates', Marler and Peters, 1977; Searcy and Marler, 1987) that are tuned to and impart a predisposition to attend to, allow recognition of, direct responses to, and dictate vocal output of species-specific vocalizations.

In the breeding of domesticated strains of chicken, pigeon (*Columba livia*) and Zebra Doves (*Geopelia striata*), various voice characteristics with varying complexities have been selected (Darwin, 1868; Baptista and Abs, 1983; Layton, 1991; Kuwayama *et al.*, 1996). In addition, cross-fostering various dove species indicate that advertising coos of columbiforms develop in the absence of experience with conspecific adult tutors (Whitman, 1919; Lade and Thorpe, 1964; Layton, 1991). Further, although doves will respond to playback of conspecific coos, they do not respond to playback of coo calls from other species (Blockstein and Hardy, 1989). Similarly, Bobwhite Quail (*Colinus virginianus*), when cross-fostered or when raised as naive young in groups comprised of quail from different geographic origins, develop their assembly ('hoy-poo') call, a call that varies in frequency and temporal characteristics between populations, without imitation (Goldstein, 1978; Baker and Bailey, 1987a,b).

Component characteristics of a vocal signal such as tonal quality, temporal pattern and frequency may be inherited separately as demonstrated by crosses between various species of galliforms and pigeons (Baptista, 1996). Moreover, hybrids between closely related pigeon species produce calls with at least some characteristics of one or the other parental form, whereas hybrids between distantly related species produce vocalizations with characteristics resembling neither parent. Hybrids between distantly related species presumably have more genetic incompatibility than hybrids between closely related species indicating a correlation between degree of genetic incompatibility and disruption of expression of the end products, namely the coo calls (review in Baptista, 1996).

Thus, the operative cognitive function of categorization can be independent of vocal learning as exemplified by recognition of conspecific calls in species that inherit vocal repertoires. In addition, learning to recognize and respond to signals of individuals or other species, i.e. learning to discriminate, is also found in groups that inherit vocalizations as developed below.

Learning

Selective attention

Oscines raised in acoustic isolation do not express species-typical vocalizations. Given a rich acoustic environment that includes conspecific vocalizations, oscines, for the most part, select to incorporate into memory only species-typical signals. Thus, when species-typical vocal signals are learned rather than inherited in oscines (and presumably also in hummingbirds and parrots), there remain filtering mechanisms that predispose them selectively to attend to specific portions of the acoustical environment. Thus focused, the learner or 'pupil' selects the 'correct' signals to be acquired into memory (an acquired vocal template, Konishi, 1985).

Experiments exposing naive, isolated individuals to tape-recorded songs of conspecific and a variety of heterospecifics have demonstrated that this disposition to focus on species-typical sounds is innate (e.g. Marler, 1970; Konishi, 1985; review in Baptista, 1996) and presumably is a derived character from the similar condition in nonoscines. Some species of songbird may recognize conspecific song by sound alone as demonstrated when isolated songbirds learn from tape-recorded stimuli played to them (Konishi, 1985).

How an observer discovers what signals a bird has memorized has historically been achieved by monitoring behavioral responses to different stimuli and more recently by monitoring neural responses in brain centers and pathways (see DeVoogd and Székely, this volume). The behavioral response most often observed is the song type(s) that an adult bird chooses to produce after exposure as a juvenile to an array of stimuli. Konishi (1985) presented naive, isolated White-crowned Sparrows (*Zonotrichia leucophrys*) with tape recordings containing songs of White-crowned Sparrows and those of several potentially sympatric oscines. In all but one case, the White-crowned Sparrows selected conspecific sounds as models to memorize and later produce. An even more persuasive example of innate recognition of conspecific song is illustrated by the studies of Marler and Peters (1977) on Swamp Sparrows (*Melospiza georgiana*). Naive and isolated fledgling Swamp Sparrows presented with synthesized songs containing mixtures of Swamp and Song Sparrow syllables extracted conspecific syllables out of these acoustic 'cocktails' and constructed species-typical songs from them.

Because precocial, nonoscine birds are known to be primed to recognize conspecific sounds while still in the egg (review in Johnston, 1988; see also Tschanz, 1968), it might be argued that the oscine chicks are similarly primed prior to hatching. However, both Swamp and White-crowned Sparrows were reared in the laboratory from the egg prior to 'pipping' (Marler and Peters, 1977; Konishi, 1985) precluding experience with adult conspecific sounds prior to hatching.

Stimulus preference at the juvenile rather than adult stage of development has more recently been demonstrated (Nelson and Marler, 1993a). Fledgling sparrows of both sexes respond to adult songs with begging calls. When naive isolated fledgling White-crowned Sparrows were presented with tape-recorded conspecific and heterospecific songs, they responded by giving more begging calls to the conspecific songs than to alien song. These data indicate that fledglings 'possess a perceptual predisposition to respond to conspecific song' at the beginning of the impressionable phase (Nelson and Marler, 1993a, p. 807). Adult females can also be assayed for stimulus preference by using the copulation solicitation display (reviewed in Nelson and Marler, 1993b).

If naive juveniles can interact with live adult models, the juveniles' attention may be focused on conspecific vocalizations and learning is thus facilitated (review in Baptista and Gaunt, 1997). For example, fledgling Bullfinches (*Pyrrhula pyrrhula*), Zebra Finches (*Taeniopygia guttata*) and various Galapagos finches (*Geospiza* spp.) are fed by their fathers and form a social bond with them (Nicolai, 1959; Grant, 1984; Gibbs, 1990; Zann, 1990, 1993). In most cases, sons sing the same song type as their father. Male fledgling European Starlings (*Sturnus vulgaris*) bond with adult males and fledgling females bond with adult females. Thus, adult females pass song tradition to fledgling females and adult males to male progeny, and vocal tradition is along sexual lines (Hausberger, 1993). Another example of gender-based song tradition has been demonstrated in the duets sung by the Tropical Bay Wrens (*Thryothorus nigricapillus*). A duet is initiated by the female. Females have many songs and all of the female's songs are shared with at least one other female in the population, whereas males use several nonshared, unique songs in duets (Levin, 1996a,b).

Birds exposed to a variety of conspecific and heterospecific avian vocalizations may, however, commit these signals to memory, categorize them, but eventually choose conspecific sounds to vocalize or, occasionally, express heterospecific signals (review in Catchpole and Baptista, 1988; see below). Thus, a heritable filtering mechanism in some species may be modified or overridden. Further, some birds must employ information and decision processing, two attributes of cognition, to resolve which signals in it's learned repertoire will be actively expressed at maturity and which are simply stored in memory.

Memory and recognition

Historically only the ability of adult birds to vocalize sounds presented to them as naive juveniles was taken as evidence of learning (e.g. Mulligan, 1966; Marler, 1970). However, various lines of evidence indicate that 'sensory learning' or storage without vocal production occurs in many oscine and nonoscine species, and in different age and sex classes.

As mentioned above, precocial chicks of various nonoscine species are primed to recognize and imprint on maternal vocalizations before hatching. Typically precocial chicks vocalize 2 or 3 days prior to hatching during the stage when the egg shell is first breached or 'pipped'. Incubating mothers vocalize in response to these prenatal sounds, and, by so doing, impress upon the hatching chick the image of the maternal calls. This enables the chick to respond to and approach or follow the mother after hatching.

Male Mourning Doves (*Zenaida macroura*) will often call when feeding older nestlings (Luther, 1979). Nestlings apparently store the characteristics of their father's call and, as fledglings, will discriminate between a playback of the father's and a stranger's calls (Hitchcock *et al.*, 1989). Common Murres (*Uria aalge*) learn the characteristics of the parents' calls while still in the egg (Tschanz, 1968; see review in Falls, 1982, for parent–young recognition in other colonial sea birds). Conversely, adults of the highly colonially breeding Bank Swallow (*Riparia riparia*) learn to recognize the voices of their young, which fledge when they are about 18 or 19 days old. Adults will accept and rear unrelated nestlings if the nestlings are younger than 15 days; older chicks are rejected (Beecher *et al.*, 1981).

Neighbor–stranger discrimination is well documented in oscines that learn songs (review in Falls, 1982); however, Blue Grouse (*Dendrogapus obscurus*) discriminate between a playback of neighbor vs. stranger calls, indicating that this nonoscine can learn to recognize individuals by sound. In response to a playback of a neighbor's call, the target grouse faced the direction of the speaker and countersang. In response to a stranger's call, the grouse approached the speaker and performed various displays (Falls and McNicholl, 1979), i.e. the response to the stranger's call is stronger than to that of the neighbor.

Species with similar feeding ecologies may defend interspecific territories in sympatry (and syntopy) and will often respond to playback of heterospecific song. This principle was developed as the 'character convergence' model by Cody (1973), and this may occur even in species, such as North American flycatchers, that do not learn song. For example, the 'fitz-bew' song of the Willow Flycatcher (*Empidonax traillii*) and the 'fee-bee-o' of the Alder Flycatcher (*E. alnorum*) developed normally when fledglings were raised in isolation (Kroodsma, 1984). The alternate playback of each song type to individuals of both species living sympatrically in one locale in Ontario indicated that both species would respond to both song types. Similar playback studies conducted in allopatry, however, revealed that each species only responded to playback of conspecific song (Prescott, 1987).

This phenomenon may be observed even between unrelated species. For example, Bewick's Wrens (*Thryomanes bewickii*) and Song Sparrows (*Melospiza melodia*) will respond to a playback of each other's songs in an area of sympatry, but will ignore a playback of heterospecific song in areas of allopatry (Gorton, 1977). On the island of Eigg, off the coast of Scotland, where territories of Great Tits (*Parus major*) and Chaffinches (*Fringilla coelebs*) are packed together, both species will respond to a playback of both species' songs. On the mainland, where their territories are more dispersed, each species will respond only to playback of conspecific song (Reed, 1982).

Naive, fledgling White-crowned Sparrows store and later sing tape-recorded conspecific songs but will not, as adults, vocalize presented recordings of heterospecific Song Sparrow songs. As discussed above, this finding has been interpreted as a rejection of the alien sound model (Marler, 1970), i.e. birds memorize and produce only conspecific sounds. However, although most White-crowned Sparrows in the wild will respond to only a playback of conspecific song, a subset of White-crowned Sparrows sympatric with Song Sparrows respond to playback of both conspecific and Song Sparrow song (Catchpole and Baptista, 1988) and vice versa (Baptista and Catchpole, 1989; Fig. 9.1). Similarly, a White-crowned Sparrow with a territory adjacent to a Lincoln's Sparrow (*M. lincolnii*) responded to that species' songs (Baptista *et al.*, 1981; Baptista, 1990; Fig. 9.2). These data indicate that even though White-crowned Sparrows preferentially memorize stimuli from their own species, they will, under certain circumstances, memorize the song of the other sparrows though they do not express these songs. Rather, the song memories are used to recognize competitors and the response is aggression.

Song learning by males

By selective attention and memory, birds acquire a bank of sounds used in communication. However, there are within-species differences, including gender and geography, and between-species differences in what is learned and when learning occurs. Here we treat song learning in the more vocal and thus more intensively studied gender – males. Females are treated in a later section.

1. What is learned?

It is well documented that males of oscines, hummingbirds and parrots learn, store and produce vocalizations. However, it must be emphasized that, even in these groups, not all aspects of song are necessarily learned. White-crowned Sparrows and Anna's Hummingbirds (*Calypte anna*) learn details of syllable structure, syntax and rhythm in their songs (Marler, 1970; Cunningham and Baker, 1983; Baptista and Petrinovich, 1984, 1986; Baptista and Schuchmann 1990). In contrast, song syllables in Short-toed Treecreepers (*Certhia brachydactyla*) develop from begging calls with little or no modification, and it is only the syntax that is learned (Thielcke, 1970). Eurasian Greenfinches (*Carduelis chloris*) may learn heterospecific syllables from Canaries (*Serinus canarius*) but these are always sung in a greenfinch rhythm (Güttinger, 1979). Even White-crowned Sparrows and Song Sparrows that learn most details of their song have one feature, total duration of song, that develops independently of learning experience (Baptista, 1996).

Although, the frequency component, as measured in kilohertz, of a vocalization can be learned in some species, it can also be a nonlearned function of body mass alone in others. In those species, frequency is often negatively correlated with body mass for both nonoscines and oscines (review in Baptista, 1996). For example, frequency in vocalizations of nonoscines, juvenile *Coturnix* quail and various geese (*Anser* spp.) decrease gradually as mass increases with age (Wündinger, 1970; Schleidt and Shalter, 1973; ten Thoren and Bergman, 1987). Frequency in vocalizations of *Calypte* hummingbirds and various oscines who learn sounds is also inversely correlated

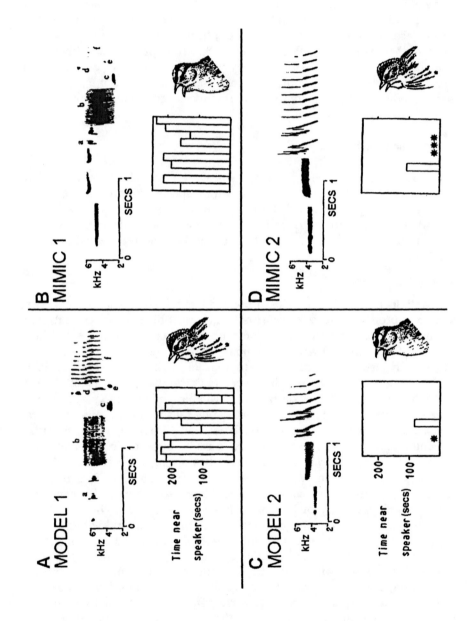

A
MODEL 1

B
MIMIC 1

C
MODEL 2

D
MIMIC 2

kHz

SECS 1

Time near
speaker (secs)

200

100

with mass (Schubert, 1976; Wells *et al.*, 1978, Bowman, 1979; Ryan and Brenowitz, 1985; Clayton, 1990a,b).

Mundinger (1988, 1995) studied various breeds of domestic canaries and found that the smaller 'roller' breed had a lower-pitched song than that of the larger 'border' breed. Songs of isolates were simpler in structure, but they retained the same frequencies as tutored individuals. Although low frequency may also be due to modifications in syringeal membranes, as has been found in *Otus* owls (Miller, 1934), Mundinger (personal communication) has found that juveniles of roller and border breeds may produce vocalizations of both strains during subsong, but as adults only vocalize syllables of their own breed. Thus, it is neural rather than syringeal constraints that control vocal behavior of canary breeds. This case may be the first known demonstration of genetic control of acoustic frequency in vocalizations of an oscine. These examples indicate that many, possibly interacting, aspects of a species' biology may place limits on what is open to modification by cognitive processes.

2. When is sound learned?

Thorpe (1958) showed experimentally that Chaffinches learned songs during a fixed time window that closes after their first spring. This time window when sensory input takes place has been termed the 'sensitive phase'. Sensitive phases have since been demonstrated in a number of bird species raised under both isolate and social conditions, e.g. Zebra Finches, White-crowned Sparrows, Song Sparrows (Immelmann, 1969; Marler, 1970, 1987; Slater *et al.*, 1988) and others. Birds with short sensitive phases have been called 'age-limited' learners.

In contrast, some oscine species and parrots appear to learn vocalizations well into adulthood and perhaps throughout their lives. Open-ended song learning most probably occurs in European Starlings and cardueline finches (Mundinger, 1970; Adret-Hausberger *et al.*, 1990; Chaiken *et al.*, 1994;

Fig. 9.1 (A) Song of a Song Sparrow sung by a Song Sparrow, the model. (B) Mimicked elements (a–f) of a Song Sparrow song sung by a White-crowned Sparrow. (C) Song of a White-crowned Sparrow sung by a White-crowned Sparrow, the model. (D) Mimic of a White-crowned Sparrow song sung by a Song Sparrow. These 4 songs were played to groups of 10 naive Song Sparrows each; histograms beneath each song indicate the number of seconds each Song Sparrow spent near the speaker playing that song. All 10 Song Sparrows responded to model Song Sparrow song (A) and 8 responded to the mimic Song Sparrow song (B). Two Song Sparrows responded to White-crowned Sparrow model song (C) and 4 to the mimic White-crowned Sparrow song (D). Of these birds responding to the White-crowned Sparrow song, 4 approached the speaker and then attacked the White-crowned Sparrows that also approached the speaker [asterisks in (C) and (D)]. Adapted from Baptista (1990).

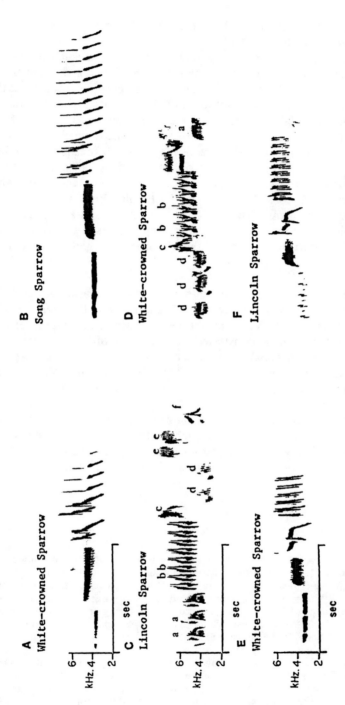

Fig. 9.2 Song mimesis by Emberizine Finches in the wild. (A) The song of a White-crowned Sparrow from San Francisco, California. (B) A Song Sparrow imitation of a sympatric White-crowned Sparrow song. (C) The song of a Lincoln's Sparrow from Tioga Pass, California. (D) A White-crowned Sparrow imitation of a sympatric Lincoln's Sparrow song. (E) The song of a White-crowned Sparrow from Tioga Pass, California. (F) A Lincoln's Sparrow imitation of a sympatric White-crowned Sparrow song. Adapted from Baptista (1990).

Mountjoy and Lemon, 1995) and possibly in Canaries, Red-winged Black-birds and Indigobirds (*Vidua chalybeata*) (Yasukawa *et al.*, 1980; Payne, 1985; Nottebohm, 1993). However, for most species of oscines studied to date, sound experiences of juveniles are unknown and thus expression of memories stored early in life can not be ruled out when songs are first detected late in life (and see below).

3. The role of a live tutor

It has been shown that the sensitive phase in White-crowned Sparrows may be extended if live birds are used rather than tape-recorded song as tutor stimuli (Baptista and Petrinovich, 1984, 1986). Birds tutored with tape recordings beyond 50 days of age did not vocalize the model songs the following spring. Birds presented with living tutors after 50 days of age in most cases vocalized the live model's songs as adults. All birds presented with a living tutor for 50 days and then given a living tutor singing a different dialect beyond 50 days sang normal adult songs; about half the birds sang the song of the second tutor (Petrinovich and Baptista, 1987).

It has been argued that the tutor plays a role as instructor and as motivator (Pepperberg and McLaughlin, 1996; Pepperberg, 1997). Nelson *et al.* (1995, 1996a) presented tape-recorded songs to naive White-crowned Sparrows at various ages beyond 50 days and found that fledglings vocalized many of those sounds during the practice stage, but dropped most of them as adults. This indicates that sensory learning takes place well beyond what was interpreted as a short time window, but much of it did not progress to permanent motor output (see below). It would appear then that between 50 and 100 days both tape and live tutors are still able to effect 'instruction', but only the live tutor may be effective enough to motivate the subject into vocalizing the stored information until this material crystallizes.

4. Expression of stored song memory

At temperate latitudes, various songbirds learn songs from adult models as juveniles (the sensory phase). As photoperiods shorten with the approach of fall, gonads in adults regress and the amount of singing decreases. There then follows a silent period during the winter months and a resumption of singing the following spring as photoperiods increase (Davis, 1958; Bezzel, 1988). During this time, yearlings come into subsong, which gradually passes into rehearsed or plastic song, and finally terminates in crystallized or full song (the motor phase).

The sensory phase, when syllables are experienced and memorized, is often separated from the motor phase, when songs are expressed, by a long period of silence. The intervening silent phase in temperate regions occurs during the fall and winter months. Thus, birds are capable of singing from memory (Marler and Peters, 1982). In some species, e.g. Zebra Finches, sensory and motor phases may overlap (Immelmann, 1969). Sensory and motor phases are separated in the Nuttall subspecies of White-crowned Sparrow (*Z. l. nuttalli*) raised in the laboratory (Konishi, 1965; Marler, 1970; Baptista and Petrinovich, 1984) but not in the wild. Great variation exists in the age at which juveniles begin practicing song (subsong) in the wild (Fig. 5 in DeWolfe *et al.*, 1989); however, fledglings have been known to sing rehearsed (plastic) song by 28 days of age while still being fed by the parent, and one fledgling sang fully crystallized song and defended a territory (Baptista *et al.*, 1993a). Wingfield (personal communication) also found juvenile Song Sparrows singing crystallized songs and defending territories in the fall.

These data indicate that the temporal separation of sensory and motor phases during song development may be an artifact of the deficient social environment in laboratory experiments with captive birds in contrast to learning in the field or under more natural laboratory conditions. Possibly selective attention is lost owing to habituation to invariant signals and/or the absence of visible motor activity of live adults (Petrinovich, 1988). Hatching-year White-crowned Sparrows of the *pugetensis* subspecies from northern latitudes arrive in the San Francisco Bay area in mid-September and already sing fully adult (crystallized) or almost crystallized song, indicating that this finding also applies to this migratory subspecies (DeWolfe and Baptista, 1995).

The differences in singing behavior in studies of White-crowned Sparrows under laboratory and field conditions parallel differences in the volume of brain nuclei associated with singing. Two such centers in the brains of wild, White-crowned Sparrows grew in volume in the spring and regressed in the fall. However, captive White-crowned Sparrows of the subspecies *gambelii* and *nuttalli* do not show these neural cycles (Smith *et al.*, 1995; Brenowitz *et al.*, 1998). Two lines of evidence suggest that these results may be attributable to differences in hormone levels: laboratory-kept birds had lower titers of testosterone as compared to field birds, and captives treated with testosterone in spring increased the volumes of these same brain centers (Smith *et al.*, 1995).

5. Learning of heterospecific song

We have reviewed some of the literature illustrating that many songbirds have a preference to learn conspecific song and that acquisition of heterospecific sounds occurs only under special circumstances. However, several families of birds are known to incorporate a variety of sounds into their advertising song; i.e. they are habitual mimics. These include lyrebirds (*Menura* spp.), mimids, bowerbirds and various starlings (Robinson, 1975; Brenowitz, 1982; Loffredo and Borgia, 1986; Hausberger *et al.*, 1991).

Darwin (1871) theorized that complexity in male song is driven by intersexual selection; i.e. females tend to select males with more complex songs as external cues of their fitness. Song complexity may be achieved by imitating conspecific sounds (e.g. Catchpole *et al.*, 1984) or heterospecific sounds (Hartshorne, 1961). It has been shown that female Satin Bowerbirds (*Ptilonorhynchus violaceus*) and European Starlings do indeed prefer males with more mimicked sounds over those with fewer mimicked sounds, lending credence to Darwin's (1871) theory of runaway sexual selection (Loffredo and Borgia, 1986; Eens *et al.*, 1991).

Parasitic Viduine Finches (*Vidua* spp.) incorporate songs and calls of their hosts apparently as cues for females to recognize conspecific males and identify their hosts (Nicolai, 1964; Payne, 1973a,b). This behavior is especially important when several sibling species occur together and must lay eggs in the nest of the correct foster species.

A special case of interspecific vocal acquisition has been described for the Thick-billed Euphonia (*Euphonia laniirostris*). This tanager imitates calls of the most common passerine in the area and by so doing may attract them in order to mob predators in dangerous situations (Morton, 1976).

These are yet more examples of categorization: females choose between males based on song complexity, choose between hosts based on species specificity of vocal characters, and euphonias choose among passerine models to mimic based on their frequency of occurrence.

6. Which factors affect how many songs a bird memorizes?

We have discussed one constraint on the song-learning process: males preferentially learn species-typical songs for production. Given that appropriate stimuli are available, how many songs are actually committed to memory (learned) for potential production later in life? There are two basic approaches to the question of what factors influence a male bird's memory capacity for song.

One approach is illustrated by the works of Todt and Hultsch discussed in this volume. Their elegant series of experiments examines how variation in an individual's experience, such as the temporal interval between songs, influences an individual male's ability to memorize tutor songs. A second approach is comparative and asks what evolutionary forces have led populations or species to differ in the number of songs they sing. A comparative approach conducted within an appropriate experimental framework can identify genetic contributions to differences in song memorization. The contribution of Kroodsma and Byers to this volume explores what factors influence the size of the adult song repertoire in different species. Here we shall compare different populations of one species, the White-crowned Sparrow.

First, however, we must consider how memory capacity for song can be measured in a bird. The size of the adult song repertoire may underestimate memory as it is not necessarily the same as the number of song types held in production memory (e.g. McGregor and Avery, 1986). A more accurate estimate of memory capacity can be obtained from an intermediate stage in song development, plastic song, wherein males practice singing the song(s) memorized earlier (Konishi, 1965; Marler and Peters, 1982) before reducing the repertoire to the adult crystallized song. Thus, the plastic song repertoire is usually considerably larger than the adult repertoire (Marler and Peters, 1982; Nelson *et al.*, 1996a).

Plastic song has been studied in most detail in several emberizine species in which adult males retain the same song(s) from one year to the next (Swamp Sparrow, Marler and Peters, 1982; White-crowned Sparrow, Petrinovich, 1985). Other species may change their song repertoire from year to year (Great Tit, McGregor and Krebs, 1989; American Redstart, *Setophaga ruticilla*, Lemon *et al.*, 1994) or, within a breeding season (Yellow Warbler, *Dendroica petechia*, Cosens and Sealy, 1986). It is not known whether these changes to the adult repertoire represent acquisition of novel songs in adults or recall of songs previously learned. In at least one species, the European Starling, males in laboratory experiments can add novel songs to the production repertoire up to at least 18 months of age (Chaiken *et al.*, 1994). This demonstrates that the age-related increases in repertoire size observed in a wild population of European Starlings (Mountjoy and Lemon, 1995) are the likely result of song acquisition in adulthood. In the European Starling then, the plastic song repertoire would not provide an accurate estimate of memory capacity for song.

The size of the plastic song repertoire has been measured as an assay of song memory in recent work with White-crowned Sparrows that usually sing one song type in their crystallized adult repertoire (Baptista and King, 1980; Chilton and Lein, 1996a). The goal of this work was to demonstrate how genetic predispositions and experience with song interact to affect the number of songs a male bird memorizes for production. This series of comparative studies suggests how different life histories, exemplified in sedentary versus migratory annual cycles, may influence the timing and amount of song memorization.

Vocal development was compared in three subspecies of White-crowned Sparrows: the sedentary Nuttall's White-crowned Sparrow, *Z. l. nuttalli*, which breeds along the central California coast; and two migratory taxa: the Mountain White-crowned Sparrow, *Z. l. oriantha*, and Puget Sound White-crowned Sparrow, *Z. l. pugetensis*. Nuttall's White-crowned Sparrow, inhabiting the chaparral of the central California coast, has a relatively long breeding season, and pairs frequently raise two or three broods in a single season (Blanchard, 1941; Mewaldt and King, 1977; DeSante and Baptista, 1989). Young males often disperse 100–300 m from their hatch place to their first breeding territory, and are known to occupy and defend territories with song in their hatching year (DeWolfe *et al.*, 1989). In contrast, the Mountain White-crowned Sparrow vacates the breeding-grounds in late summer and early fall to migrate south, and natal dispersal distances are apparently one to two orders of magnitude larger than in *nuttalli*. Mountain White-crowned Sparrows almost never rear two broods during the short breeding season at high altitudes (Morton *et al.*, 1972).

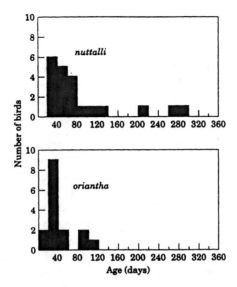

Fig. 9.3 Nuttall's White-crowned Sparrows learn significantly later than do Mountain White-crowned Sparrows. Adapted with permission from Nelson *et al.* (1995).

On the basis of these differences in the annual cycle, Nelson *et al.* (1995) reasoned that Nuttall's White-crowned Sparrow, with its long breeding season, might display a relatively long sensitive period for song acquisition compared to the Mountain White-crowned Sparrow, which spends a short period on the breeding grounds. Nestling males of both subspecies were collected, hand-reared in the laboratory and subjected to a tutoring regime in which novel pairs of songs were introduced every 10 days throughout the first year of life. By recording the imitations of tutor song that pupil birds produce during the plastic song stage, they determined when during that stage the birds memorized the songs. As predicted, the sedentary Nuttall's males memorized their crystallized songs at a significantly later age (median = 71 days), and over a broader range of ages than did the migratory Mountain White-crowned Sparrow males (median = 31 days, Fig. 9.3). The majority of the song material imitated was memorized prior to 120 days of age.

Unexpected, however, was a significant difference between the subspecies in the number of different song types produced during the stage of vocal rehearsal. The production of a number of song types in plastic song beyond that retained in the final crystallized repertoire is termed 'overproduction' (Marler and Peters, 1982). The *oriantha* males produced twice as many song types as did the *nuttalli* males. This finding led Nelson *et al.* (1995, 1996a) to hypothesize that overproduction is associated with a migratory annual cycle.

To explain this prediction we must consider evidence for a form of vocal learning that differs from the familiar sensorimotor process of learning based on imitation. This form of song learning has been termed 'action-based learning' (Marler and Nelson, 1993) or 'selective attrition'. The selective attrition process has two components: first, males learn to produce several distinct song types (overproduce) by the sensorimotor process. They then selectively discard one or more song types from their overproduced repertoire based on interactions with other birds. One form of interaction is 'matched countersinging', in which neighboring males exchange similar songs. This might be a mechanism by which local song dialects arise (Marler, 1960), as several studies have demonstrated a tendency for territorial males to use similar song types in their adult repertoires during countersinging (e.g. Baptista, 1975; Falls *et al.*, 1982; Weary *et al.*, 1990; Stoddard *et al.*, 1992). In a laboratory study, Nelson and Marler (1994) examined whether matched countersinging would occur during plastic song, and thereby lead to vocal convergence between males. Playback of one tutor song type that matched one of the song types in yearling males' overproduced repertoires led them to crystallize selectively the matching song type and discard the other song types. There is evidence that selective attrition via matched countersinging occurs in wild sparrow populations (Baptista and Morton, 1982, 1988; DeWolfe *et al.*, 1989; Nelson, 1992).

The selective attrition model assumes that memorization of songs for production is restricted to an early sensitive phase, that males visit several dialects and that they memorize the song types therein during their first summer and/or fall migration. Young *oriantha* males are known to wander widely at the time when songs are being memorized (Morton *et al.*, 1991; Morton, 1992). If they encounter males with alien dialects, as has been documented (Baptista and Morton, 1982), they may learn from tutors in several different dialects. By rearing wild-tutored *oriantha* fledglings in the laboratory, Baptista and Morton (1988) found that two of four males overproduced, thereby demonstrating that young males do experience several dialects early in life.

A fledgling male who had visited and memorized the songs of several dialects would benefit from this experience because he could occupy unpredictable territory vacancies the next year. Nelson *et al.* (1996a) argued that yearling *oriantha* males face greater uncertainty in where they will set up their first territories: they may settle several dialects away from their birthplace. This greater uncertainty is a consequence of the smaller patches of suitable habitat in the montane environment (DeWolfe and DeWolfe, 1962; Banks, 1964; Baker, 1975; Orejuela and Morton, 1975), annual variation in habitat availability owing to snow cover and the subspecies' migratory habits. In contrast, *nuttalli* males with their short dispersal distances and more contiguous dialect areas, may often be able to settle within the natal dialect or an adjacent one, thus there would appear to be less selective pressure to acquire a large repertoire.

Given that the ability to acquire songs is limited to early in life in studied sparrow species (Marler, 1970; Baptista *et al.*, 1993a; Nelson *et al.*, 1995), then an *oriantha* male must learn his repertoire in his first summer and autumn if he is to match song types the next spring with his territorial rivals. Note that if memorization of novel songs were routinely possible in yearlings, then males could 'fit in' to the local dialect wherever they settle to breed, and we would not expect any relationship between overproduction and migratory habits. Thus, the limitation of memorization to an early sensitive phase is a second, important constraint on song learning in this species.

To test the proposed relationship between increased overproduction and a migratory annual cycle, Nelson *et al.* (1996b) studied vocal development in a third subspecies of White-crowned Sparrow. The Puget Sound White-crowned Sparrow breeds from northern California to coastal British Columbia and is, by all accounts, the sister taxon of *Z. l. nuttalli*. It differs from *nuttalli*, and resembles *oriantha*, in that northern populations are strongly migratory (Blanchard, 1941; Lewis, 1975). Although *pugetensis* dialects, as defined by the terminal trill, are large, there is considerable variation in other parts of the song within dialects (Baptista, 1977; Nelson, personal observation). The presence of this local variation might favor overproduction by male *pugetensis*. Nelson *et al.* (1996a) predicted that, if recency of common ancestry determines the degree of overproduction during plastic song, and that the correlation between overproduction and migration is spurious, then *pugetensis* should closely resemble *nuttalli*. Alternatively, if the degree of overproduction is evolutionarily responsive to differences in migratory habits, then *pugetensis* should overproduce to the same extent as in *oriantha*.

Hand-reared males of the three subspecies were tutored in the first 3 months of life with a rich regime of tape-recorded tutor songs, on the expectation that this procedure would maximize opportunities for overproduction. Beginning shortly after fledging, males heard 16 different tutor songs daily for 40 days, before changing to a set of 16 different songs for 40 additional days. All of the males were tutored again the next spring but no songs were imitated. Nelson *et al.* (1996a) recorded the young males' imitations of tutor songs in plastic song and counted the number of different tutor song types imitated.

In agreement with the hypothesis that an increased degree of song overproduction is associated with a migratory annual cycle, male *pugetensis* overproduced significantly more than male *nuttalli*, and were statistically indistinguishable from male *oriantha* (Fig. 9.4). Relative recency of common ancestry is not a good predictor of the amount of song overproduction. These comparative studies of song memorization demonstrate that genetic differences between the 3 subspecies of White-crowned Sparrow contribute to subspecific differences in the number of tutor songs memorized and subsequently reproduced during plastic song.

It is also possible to examine how variation in tutor experience within a

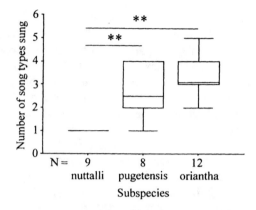

Fig. 9.4 A box plot of the number of distinct song types produced during plastic song by males from 3 subspecies of White-crowned Sparrow. Migratory male *pugetensis* and *oriantha* sang significantly more song types than did sedentary male *nuttalli*. **$P < 0.025$. Adapted with permission from Nelson *et al.* (1996a).

subspecies contributes to differences in memorization ability, as has been studied in the Nightingale, *Luscinia megarhynchos* (Todt and Hultsch, this volume). The work on White-crowned Sparrows can also contribute some insight to this question. The first study described above used what we term a 'lean' tutoring regime (Nelson *et al.*, 1995, 1996b). Male *nuttalli* and *oriantha* were presented with pairs of tutor songs for 10-day-long periods successively throughout the first year of life. The second study used a 'rich' regime in which males heard 16 song types daily for 40 days before changing to a different set of 16 types for 40 additional days (Nelson *et al.*, 1996a,b).

Male *oriantha* responded significantly to this variation in early tutor experience while *nuttalli* males seemed unaffected (Fig. 9.5). When given the chance to learn from a large repertoire of tutor songs, *oriantha* males increased the size of their plastic song repertoire by almost 400%. In contrast, *nuttalli* males overproduced the same on both lean and rich tutor regimes. This result demonstrates that the number of songs male White-crowned Sparrows memorize and produce, i.e. their cognitive capacity to learn, is a product of the interaction between their genetic endowment and experience, i.e. the number of songs available during the sensitive phase.

Song learning by females

Early studies often reported that, in most cases, only male oscines learn songs. This conclusion was based on the inability of female birds to reproduce songs presented to them from tape-recorded tutor song. There is, however,

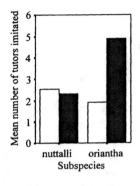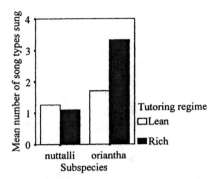

Fig. 9.5 The mean number of tutors imitated (left) and number of song types sung in plastic song (right) varied between subspecies and tutoring regimes. Male *oriantha* overproduced significantly more when tutored with a 'rich' regime of tutor song (■) than with a 'lean' regime (□). Male *nuttalli* overproduced the same on both tutor treatments. Adapted with permission from Nelson *et al.* (1996b).

accumulating evidence that female oscines often store in memory songs heard as juveniles, although they usually do not vocalize them.

Much has been written on song learning in the male Zebra Finch (Immelmann, 1969; Slater *et al.*, 1988; Clayton, 1990a,b). Females not only do not sing, but do not have the brain centers associated with storage and production of song (Gurney, 1981; Pohl-Apel and Sossinka, 1984). Yet, playback studies have demonstrated that females can distinguish their father's song from those of other males (Miller, 1979). Similar results have been found in female White-rumped Munias (*Lonchura striata*, Dietrich, 1980). Female Zebra Finches implanted with silastic tubes containing estradiol will solicit preferentially to playback of insular versus mainland songs (Clayton, 1990a,b), indicating that they are capable of discriminating between songs of different subspecies.

Efforts to teach female White-crowned Sparrows male song have not been successful (Baptista and Petrinovich, 1986). Yet, wild-caught females treated with testosterone in the laboratory will vocalize recognizable song dialects (Konishi, 1965; Kern and King, 1972; Baptista, 1974; Baptista and Morton, 1982; Tomback and Baker, 1984). Females treated with estradiol will solicit preferentially to specific dialects based on early experience (Baker, 1983; but see Chilton and Lein, 1996b). This indicates that, although females do not normally sing during the breeding season (Baptista *et al.*, 1993b), they do learn and store male dialects, and may distinguish between different song forms. Female White-crowned Sparrows of some subspecies express songs prior to or following the breeding season presumably to defend territories (Baptista *et al.*, 1993a; Chilton and Lein, 1996b). Thus, females must recognize, memorize and categorize vocalizations.

Conclusions

Cognition in its broadest sense refers to neural processes that bridge environmental events impinging on an animal and the behavioral response of the animal. These are 'processes by which sensory input is transformed, elaborated, stored, recovered and used' (Neisser, 1967). Clearly, cognitive processes in avian vocal systems vary between species and within species at the population and individual level. Primitively, in nonoscines the cognitive content or nature of represented sound information was inherited neural circuitry. Normal vocalizations develop independently of specific experience with adult models. As we have shown, however, even these 'innate memory templates' are influenced by and under the control of cognitive processes.

Vocal learning in most birds, although imparting more plasticity to communicative behavior, is similarly constrained by genetically based predispositions to learn species-typical signals. Throughout this review we have emphasized the need to distinguish between stored memory of sound and motor expression of these signals. This difference is important in interpreting sensitive phase and stimulus-filtering phenomena. Thus, when a bird does not vocalize a (crystallized) conspecific or heterospecific signal as an adult it, does not mean that the signal has not been processed and/or stored in memory.

Rather, storage of sound signals to be used in recognition appears to be a widespread phenomenon among many avian taxa and is found in species that learn to sing as well as those that do not. Detailed studies of song ontogeny through the subsong and plastic song stage have been few and are confined almost exclusively to laboratory studies. Certainly such studies are highly desirable and need to be expanded to include studies under more natural settings in order to understand the evolution of avian communication systems.

References

Adret-Hausberger, M. (1982) Social influences on the whistled songs of starlings. *Behav. Ecol. Sociobiol.* **11**, 241–246.

Adret-Hausberger, M., Güttinger, H.-R. and Merkel, F. W. (1990) Individual life history and song repertoire changes in a colony of starlings (*Sturnus vulgaris*). *Ethology* **84**, 265–280.

Baker, J. A. and Bailey, E. D. (1987a) Sources of phenotypic variation in the separation call of northern bobwhite (*Colinus virginianus*). *Can. J. Zool.* **65**, 1010–1015.

Baker, J. A. and Bailey, E. D. (1987b). Ontogeny of the separation call in northern bobwhite (*Colinus virginianus*). *Can. J. Zool.* **65**, 1016–1020.

Baker, M. C. (1975) Song dialects and genetic differences in white-crowned sparrows (*Zonotrichia leucophrys*). *Evolution* **29**, 226–241.

Baker, M. C. (1983) The behavioral response of female Nuttall's white-crowned sparrows to male song of natal and alien dialects. *Behav. Ecol. Sociobiol.* **12**, 309–315.

Banks, R. C. (1964) Geographic variation in the white-crowned sparrow *Zonotrichia leucophrys*. *Univ. Calif. Publ. Zool.* **70**, 1–123.

Baptista, L. F. (1974) The effects of songs of wintering white-crowned sparrows on song development in sedentary populations of the species. *Z. Tierpsychol.* **34**, 147–171.

Baptista, L. F. (1975) Song dialects and demes in sedentary populations of the white-crowned sparrow (*Zonotrichia leucophrys nuttalli*). *Univ. Calif. Publ. Zool.* **105**, 1–52.

Baptista, L. F. (1977) Geographical variation in song and song dialects of the migratory white-crowned sparrow, *Zonotrichia leucophrys pugetensis*. *Condor* **79**, 356–370.

Baptista, L. F. (1990) Song learning in white-crowned sparrows (*Zonotrichia leucophrys*): sensitive phases and stimulus filtering revisited. *Proceedings of the International 100 Deutchues Ornithologen Gesellschaft Meeting, Current Topics in Avian Biology*, Bonn, pp. 143–152.

Baptista, L. F. (1993) El estudio de la variacion geografico usando vocalizaciones y las bibliotecas de sonidos de aves neotropicales. In Escalante-Pliego, P. (ed.) *Curación Moderna de Colecciones Ornitológicas*. Washington, DC: American Ornithologists' Union, pp. 15–30.

Baptista, L. F. (1996) Nature and its nurturing in avian vocal development. In Kroodsma, D. E. and Miller, E. H. (eds) *Ecology and Evolution of Acoustic Communication in Birds*. Ithaca, NY: Cornell University Press, pp. 39–60.

Baptista, L. F. and Abs, M. (1983) Vocalizations. In Abs, M. (ed.) *Behavior and Physiology of the Pigeon*. New York: Academic Press, pp. 309–325.

Baptista, L. F. and Catchpole, C. K. (1989) Vocal mimicry and interspecific aggression in songbirds: experiments using white-crowned sparrow imitation of song sparrow song. *Behaviour* **109**, 247–257.

Baptista, L. F. and Gaunt, S. L. L. (1997) The role of social interaction on vocal development in birds. In Hausberger, M. and Snowdon, C. (eds) *Social Influences on Vocal Development*. London: Cambridge University Press, pp. 23–40.

Baptista, L. F. and King, J. R. (1980) Geographical variation in song and song dialects of montane white-crowned sparrows. *Condor* **82**, 267–284.

Baptista, L. F. and Morton, M. L. (1982) Song dialects and mate selection in montane white-crowned sparrows. *Auk* **99**, 537–547.

Baptista, L. F. and Morton, M. L. (1988) Song learning in montane white-crowned sparrows: from whom and when. *Anim. Behav.* **36**, 1753–1764.

Baptista, L. F. and Petrinovich, L. (1984) Social interaction, sensitive phases and the song template hypothesis in the white-crowned sparrow. *Anim. Behav.* **32**, 172–181.

Baptista, L. F. and Petrinovich, L. (1986) Song development in the white-crowned sparrow: social factors and sex differences. *Anim. Behav.* **34**, 1359–1371.

Baptista, L. F. and Schuchmann, K.-L. (1990) Song learning in the Anna hummingbird (*Calypte anna*). *Ethology* **84**, 15–26.

Baptista, L. F., Bell, D. A. and Trail, P. W. (1993a) Song learning and production in the white-crowned sparrow: parallels with sexual imprinting. *Neth. J. Zool.* **43**, 17–33.

Baptista, L. F., Trail, P. W., DeWolfe, B. B. and Morton, M. L. (1993b) Singing and its functions in female white-crowned sparrows. *Anim. Behav.* **29**, 95–101.

Baptista, L. F., Morton, M. and Pereyra, M. E. (1981) Song mimesis in a Lincoln sparrow. *Wilson Bull.* **93**, 265–267.

Beecher, M. D., Beecher, I. M. and Hahn, S. (1981) Parent–offspring recognition in bank swallows (*Riparia riparia*): II Development and acoustic basis. *Anim. Behav.* **29**, 95–101.

Bezzel, E. (1988) Die Gesangszeiten des Buchfinken (*Fringilla coelebs*): eine regionalstudie. *J. Ornithol.* **129**, 71–81.

Blanchard, B. D. (1941) The white-crowned sparrows (*Zonotrichia leucophrys*) of the Pacific seaboard: environment and annual cycle. *Univ. Calif. Publ. Zool.* **46**, 1–178.

Blockstein, D. E. and Hardy, J. W. (1989) The Grenada dove (*Leptotila wellsi*) is a distinct species. *Auk* **106**, 339–340.

Bowman, R. I. (1979) Adaptive morphology of song dialects in Darwin's finches. *J. Ornithol.* **120**, 353–389.

Brenowitz, E. A. (1982) Aggressive response of red-winged blackbirds to mockingbird song imitation. *Auk* **99**, 584–587.

Brenowitz, E. A., Baptista, L. F., Lent, K. and Wingfield, J. C. (1998) Seasonal plasticity of the song control system in wild Nuttall's white-crowned sparrows. *J. Neurobiol.* **34**, 69–82.

Catchpole, C. K. and Baptista, L. F. (1988) A test of the competition hypothesis of vocal mimicry, using song sparrow imitations of white-crowned sparrow song. *Behaviour* **106**, 119–128.

Catchpole, C. K., Dittami, J. and Leisler, B. (1984) Differential responses to male song repertoires in female songbirds implanted with oestradiol. *Nature* **312**, 563–564.

Chaiken, M., Böhner, J. and Marler, P. (1994) Repertoire turnover and the timing of song acquisition in European starlings. *Behav.* **128**, 25–30.

Chilton, G. and Lein, M. R. (1996a) Song repertoires of Puget Sound white-crowned sparrows *Zonotrichia leucophrys pugetensis*. *J. Avian Biol.* **27**, 31–40.

Chilton, G. and Lein, M. R. (1996b) Songs and sexual responses of female white-crowned sparrows (*Zonotrichia leucophrys*) from a mixed dialect population. *Behaviour* **133**, 173–198.

Clayton, N. S. (1990a) Subspecies recognition and song learning in zebra finches. *Anim. Behav.* **40**, 1009–1017.

Clayton, N. S. (1990b) Assortative mating in zebra finch subspecies (*Taeniopygia guttata guttata*) and (*T. g. castanotis*). *Phil. Trans. Roy. Soc. Lond. B* **330**, 351–370.

Cody, M. L. (1973) Character convergence. *Ann. Rev. Ecol. System.* **4**, 189–211.

Cosens, S. E. and Sealy, S. G. (1986) Age-related variation in song repertoire size and repertoire sharing of yellow warblers (*Dendroica petechia*). *Can. J. Zool.* **64**, 1926–1929.

Cunningham, M. A. and Baker, M. C. (1983) Vocal learning in white-crowned sparrows: sensitive phase and song dialects. *Behav. Ecol. Sociobiol.* **13**, 259–269.

Darwin, C. (1868) *The Variation of Animals and Plants under Domestication.* London: John Murray.

Darwin, C. (1871) *The Descent of Man and Selection in Relation to Sex.* London: John Murray.

Davis, J. (1958) Singing behavior and the gonad cycle of the rufous-sided towhee. *Condor* **60**, 308–336.

DeSante, D. and Baptista, L. F. (1989) Factors affecting termination of breeding in Nuttall's white-crowned sparrows. *Wilson Bull.* **101**, 120–124.

DeWolfe, B. B. and DeWolfe, R. H. (1962) Mountain white-crowned sparrows in California. *Condor* **64**, 378–389.

DeWolfe, B. B. and Baptista, L. F. (1995) Singing behavior, song types on their wintering grounds and the question of leap-frog migration in Puget Sound white-crowned sparrows (*Zonotrichia leucophrys pugetensis*) *Condor* **97**, 376–389.

DeWolfe, B. B., Baptista, L. F. and Petrinovich, L. (1989) Song development and territory establishment in Nuttall's white-crowned sparrows. *Condor* **91**, 397–407.

Dietrich, K. (1980) Vorbildwahl in der Gesangsentwicklung beim Japanischen Mövchen (*Lonchura striata* var. *domestica*), Estrildidae. *Z. Tierpsychol.* **52**, 57–76.

Eens, M., Pinxten, R. and Verheyen, R. F. (1991) Male song as a cue for mate choice in the European starling. *Behaviour* **116**, 210–238.

Falls, J. B. (1982) Individual recognition by sound in birds. In Kroodsma, D. E. and Miller, E. H. (eds) *Acoustic Communication in Birds*, Vol. 2. New York: Academic Press, pp. 237–278.

Falls, J. B. and McNicholl, M. K. (1979) Neighbor–stranger discrimination by song in male blue grouse. *Can. J. Zool.* **57**, 457–462.

Falls, J. B., Krebs, J. R. and McGregor, P. (1982) Song-matching in the great tit: the effect of song similarity and familiarity. *Anim. Behav.* **30**, 997–1009.

Gaunt, S. L. L., Baptista, L. F., Sánchez, J. E. and Hernandez, D. (1994) Song learning as evidenced from song sharing in two hummingbird species (*Colibri coruscans* and *C. thalassinus*) *Auk* **111**, 87–103.

Gibbs, H. L. (1990) Cultural evolution of male song types in Darwin's medium ground-finches (*Geospiza fortis*). *Anim. Behav.* **39**, 253–263.

Goldstein, R. B. (1978) Geographic variation in the 'hoy' call of the bobwhite. *Auk* **95**, 85–94.

Gorton, R. E., Jr (1977) Territorial interactions in sympatric song sparrows and Bewick's wren populations. *Auk* **94**, 701–708.

Grant, B. R. (1984) The significance of song variation in a population of Darwin's finches. *Behaviour* **89**, 90–116.

Gurney, M. E. (1981) Hormonal control of cell form and number in the zebra finch song system. *J. Neurosci.* **6**, 658–673.

Güttinger, H.-R. (1979) The integration of learnt and genetically programmed behavior: a study of hierarchical organization in songs of canaries, greenfinches and their hybrids. *Z. Tierpsychol.* **49**, 285–303.

Hartshorne, C. (1961) Sketch of a theory of imitative singing. *The Oriole* **26**, 23–27.

Hausberger, M. (1993) How studies on vocal communication in birds contribute to a comparative approach of cognition. *Etología* **3**, 171–185.

Hausberger, M. and Cousillas, H. (1996) Categorization in birdsong: from behavioural to neuronal responses. *Behav. Process.* **35**, 83–91.

Hausberger, M., Jenkins, P. F. and Keene, J. (1991) Species-specificity and mimicry in bird song: are they paradoxes? A reevaluation of song mimicry in the European starling. *Behaviour* **117**, 53–81.

Hitchcock, R. R., Mirarchi, R. E. and Lishak, R. S. (1989) Recognition of individual male parent vocalizations by nestling mourning doves. *Anim. Behav.* **37**, 517–520.

Immelmann, K. (1969) Song development in the zebra finch and other Estrildid finches. In Hinde, R. A. (ed.) *Bird Vocalizations*. London: Cambridge University Press, pp. 61–74.

Johnston, T. D. (1988) Developmental explanation and the ontogeny of birdsong: nature nurture/redux. *Behavior Brain Sci.* **11**, 617–630.

Kamil, A. C. (1994) A synthetic approach to the study of animal intelligence. In Real, L. A. (ed.) *Behavioral Mechanisms in Evolutionary Ecology*. Chicago: University of Chicago Press, pp. 11–45.

Kern, M. D. and King, J. R. (1972) Testosterone-induced singing in female white-crowned sparrows. *Condor* **74**, 204–209.

Konishi, M. (1963) The role of auditory feedback in the vocal behaviour of the domestic fowl. *Z. Tierpsychol.* **20**, 346–367.

Konishi, M. (1965) The role of auditory feedback in the control of vocalization in the white-crowned sparrow. *Z. für Tiërpsychol.* **22**, 770–783.

Konishi, M. (1985) Bird song: from behavior to neuron. *Annual Review of Neuroscience* **8**, 125–170.

Konishi, M. and Nottebohm, F. (1969) Experimental studies in the ontogeny of avian vocalizations. In Hinde, R. A. (ed.) *Bird Vocalizations*. London: Cambridge University Press, pp. 29–48.

Krebs, J. R., Ashcroft, R. and van Orsdol, K. (1981) Song matching in the Great Tit (*Parus major* L.). *Anim. Behav.* **29**, 918–923.

Kroodsma, D. E. (1984) Songs of the alder flycatcher (*Empidonax alnorum*) and willow flycatcher (*Empidonax traillii*) are innate. *Auk* **101**, 13–24.

Kroodsma, D. E. and Konishi, M. (1991) A suboscine bird (eastern phoebe, *Sayornis phoebe*) develops normal song without auditory feedback. *Anim. Behav.* **191**, 477–487.

Kuwayama, T., Ogawa, H., Munechika, I., Kono, T. and Ichinoe, K. (1996) Crowing characteristics of jungle fowls, Japanese native breeds and white leghorn breed of chicken. *Jap. Poultry Sci.* **33**, 89–95.

Lade, B. I. and Thorpe, W. H. (1964) Dove songs as innately coded patterns of specific behaviour. *Nature* **202**, 366–368.

Lassalle, J. M. (1996) Neurogenetic basis of cognition: facts and hypotheses. *Behav. Process.* **35**, 5–18.

Layton, L. (1991) *Songbirds in Singapore, the Growth of a Pastime*. New York: Oxford University Press.

Lemon, R. E., Perreault, S. and Weary, D. M. (1994) Dual strategies of song development in American redstarts, *Setophaga ruticilla. Anim. Behav.* **47**, 317–329.

Levin, R. N. (1996a) Song behaviour and reproductive strategies in a duetting wren, *Thryothorus nigricapillus*: I. Removal experiments. *Anim. Behav.* **52**, 1093–1096.

Levin, R. N. (1996b) Song behaviour and reproductive strategies in a duetting wren, *Thryothorus nigricapillus*: II. Playback experiments. *Anim. Behav.* **52**, 1107–1117.

Lewis, R. A. (1975) Reproductive biology of the white-crowned sparrow (*Zonotrichia leucophrys pugetensis* Grinnell) I. Temporal organization of reproductive and associated cycles. *Condor* **77**, 46–59.

Loffredo, C. A. and Borgia, G. (1986) Male courtship vocalizations as cues for mate choice in the satin bowerbird (*Ptilonorhynchus violaceus*). *Auk* **103**, 189–195.

Luther, D. M. (1979) An intensive study of parental behavior in the mourning dove. *Indiana Audubon Q.* **54**, 209–232.

Marler, P. (1960) Bird songs and mate selection. In Lanyon, W. E. and Tavolga, W. N. (eds) *Animal Sounds and Communication*. Washington, DC: American Institute of Biological Science, pp. 348–367.

Marler, P. (1970) A comparative approach to vocal learning: song development in white-crowned sparrows. *J. Comp. Physiol. Psychol. Monograph* **71**, 1–25.

Marler, P. (1987) Sensitive periods and the role of specific and general sensory stimulation in bird song learning. In Rauschecker, J. P. and Marler, P. (eds) *Imprinting and Cortical Plasticity*. New York: John Wiley and Sons, pp. 99–135.

Marler, P. and Nelson, D. A. (1993) Action-based learning: a new form of developmental plasticity in bird song. *Neth. J. Zool.* **43**, 91–103.

Marler, P. and Peters, S. (1977) Selective vocal learning in a sparrow. *Science* **198**, 519–521.

Marler, P. and Peters, S. (1982) Developmental overproduction and selective attrition: new processes in the epigenesis of birdsong. *Devel. Psychobiol.* **15**, 369–378.

McGregor, P. K. and Avery, M. I. (1986) The unsung songs of the great tit (*Parus major*): learning neighbor's songs for discrimination. *Behav. Ecol. Sociobiol.* **18**, 311–316.

McGregor, P. K. and Krebs, J. R. (1989) Song learning in adult great tits (*Parus major*): effects of neighbours. *Behaviour* **108**, 139–159.

Mewaldt, L. R. and King, J. R. (1977) The annual cycle of white-crowned sparrows (*Zonotrichia leucophrys nuttalli*) in coastal California. *Condor* **79**, 445–455.

Miller, A. H. (1934) The vocal apparatus of some North American owls.

Condor **36**, 204–213.

Miller, D. B. (1979) Long-term recognition of father's song by female zebra finches. *Nature* **280**, 389–391.

Morton, E. S. (1976) Vocal mimicry in the thick-billed euphonia. *Wilson Bull.* **88**, 485–487.

Morton, M. L. (1992) Effects of sex and birth date on premigration biology, migration schedules, return rates and natal dispersal in the mountain white-crowned sparrow. *Condor* **94**, 117–133.

Morton, M. L., Horstmann, J. L. and Osborn, J. M. (1972) Reproductive cycle and nesting success of the mountain white-crowned sparrow (*Zonotrichia leucophrys oriantha*) in the central Sierra Nevada. *Condor* **74**, 152–163.

Morton, M. L., Wakamatsu, M. W., Pereyra, M. E. and Morton, G. A. (1991) Postfledging dispersal, habitat imprinting, and philopatry in a montane, migratory sparrow. *Ornis Scand.* **22**, 98–106.

Moscovitch, M. (1995) Models of consciousness and memory. In Gazzaniga, M. S. (ed.) *The Cognitive Neurosciences*. Cambridge, MA: MIT Press, pp. 1341–1356.

Mountjoy, D. J. and Lemon, R. E. (1995) Extended song learning in wild European starlings. *Anim. Behav.* **49**, 357–366.

Mulligan, J. A. (1966) Singing behavior and its development in the song sparrow (*Melospiza melodia*). *Univ. Calif. Publ. Zool.* **81**, 1–76.

Mundinger, P. C. (1970) Vocal imitation and individual recognition of finch calls. *Science* **168**, 480–482.

Mundinger, P. C. (1988) Conceptual errors, different perspectives, and genetic analysis of song ontogeny. *Behav. Brain Sci.* **11**, 643–644.

Mundinger, P. C. (1995) Behaviour-genetic analysis of canary song: inter-strain differences in sensory learning, and epigenetic rules. *Anim. Behav.* **50**, 1491–1511.

Neisser, U. (1967) *Cognitive Psychology*. New York: Appleton-Century-Croft.

Nelson, D. A. (1992) Song overproduction and selective attrition lead to song sharing in the field sparrow (*Spizella pusilla*). *Behav. Ecol. Sociobiol.* **30**, 415–424.

Nelson, D. A. and Marler, P. (1993a) Innate recognition of song in white-crowned sparrows: a role in selective learning? *Anim. Behav.* **46**, 806–808.

Nelson, D. A. and Marler, P. (1993b) Measurement of song-learning behavior in birds. In Conn, P. M. (ed.) *Methods in Neurosciences*, Vol. 14: *Paradigms for the Study of Behavior*. New York: Academic Press, pp. 447–463.

Nelson, D. A. and Marler, P. (1994) Selection-based learning in bird song development. *Proc. Natl Acad. Sci. USA* **91**, 10498–10501.

Nelson, D. A., Marler, P. and Palleroni, A. (1995) A comparative approach to vocal learning: intra-specific variation in the learning process. *Anim. Behav.* **50**, 83–97.

Nelson, D. A., Marler, P. and Morton, M. L. (1996a) Overproduction in song development: an evolutionary correlate with migration. *Anim. Behav.* **51**, 1127–1140.

Nelson, D. A., Whaling, C. S. and Marler, P. (1996b) The capacity for song memorization varies in populations of the same species. *Anim. Behav.* **52**, 379–387.

Nicolai, J. (1959) Familientradition in der Gesangsentwicklung des Gimpels (*Pyrhula pyrrhula* L.). *J. Ornithol.* **100**, 39–46.

Nicolai, J. (1964) Brutparasitismus der Viduinae als ethologische Problem. *Z. Tierpsychol.* **21**, 129–204.

Nottebohm, F. (1993) The search for neural mechanisms that define the sensitive period for song learning in birds. *Neth. J. Zool.* **43**, 193–234.

Nottebohm, F. and Nottebohm, M. E. (1971) Vocalizations and breeding behaviour of surgically deafened ring doves (*Streptopelia risoria*). *Anim. Behav.* **19**, 313–327.

Orejuela, J. E. and Morton, M. L. (1975) Song dialects in several populations of mountain white-crowned sparrows (*Zonotrichia leucophrys oriantha*) in the Sierra Nevada. *Condor* **77**, 145–153.

Payne, R. B. (1973a) Behavior, mimetic songs and song dialects, and the relationships of the parasitic indigobirds (*Vidua*) of Africa. *Ornithol. Monogr.* **11**, 1–333.

Payne, R. B. (1973b) Vocal mimicry of paradise whydahs (*Vidua*) and response of male whydahs to song of their hosts (*Pytilia*) and their mimics. *Anim. Behav.* **21**, 762–771.

Payne, R. B. (1985) Behavioral continuity and change in local song populations of village indigobirds *Vidua chalybeata. Z. Tierpsychol.* **70**, 1–44.

Pepperberg, I. M. (1991) A communicative approach to animal cognition: a study of conceptual abilities of an African grey parrot. In Ristau, C. A. (ed.) *Cognitive Ethology: The Minds of Other Animals.* Hillsdale, NJ: Lawrence Erlbaum Associates, pp. 153–186.

Pepperberg, I. M. (1993) A review of the effects of social interaction on vocal learning in African grey parrots (*Psittacus erithacus*). *Neth. J. Zool.* **43**, 104–124.

Pepperberg, I. M. (1997) Social influences on the acquisition of human-based codes in parrots and nonhuman primates. In Snowdon, C. T. and Hausberger, M. (eds) *Social Influences on Vocal Development.* Cambridge: Cambridge University Press, pp. 157–177.

Pepperberg, I. M. and McLaughlin, M. A. (1996) Effect of avian–human joint attention on allospecific vocal learning by grey parrots (*Psitacus erithacus*) *J. Comp. Psychol.* **110**, 286–297.

Petrinovich, L. (1985) Factors influencing song development in the white-crowned sparrow (*Zonotrichia leucophrys*). *J. Comp. Psychol.* **99**, 15–29.

Petrinovich, L. (1988) The role of social factors in white-crowned sparrow song development. In Zentall, T. R. and Galef, B. G., Jr (eds) *Social Learning: Psychological and Biological Perspectives.* Hillsdale, NJ: Lawrence Erlbaum Associates, pp. 255–278.

Petrinovich, L. and Baptista, L. F. (1987) Song development in the white-crowned sparrow: modification of learned song. *Anim. Behav.* **35**, 961–974.

Pohl-Apel, G. and Sossinka, R. (1984) Hormonal determination of song capacity in females of the zebra finch: modification of learned song. *Z.*

Tierpsychol. **64**, 330–336.

Prescott, D. R. C. (1987) Territorial responses to song playback in allopatric and sympatric populations of alder (*Empidonax alnorum*) and willow (*E. traillii*) flycatchers. *Wilson Bull.* **99**, 611–619.

Reed, T. M. (1982) Interspecific territoriality in the chaffinch and great tit on islands and the mainland of Scotland: playback and removal experiments. *Anim. Behav.* **30**, 171–181.

Robinson, F. N. (1975) Vocal mimicry and the evolution of bird song. *Emu* **75**, 23–27.

Ryan, M. J. and Brenowitz, E. A. (1985) The role of body size, phylogeny, and ambient noise in the evolution of bird song. *Am. Nat.* **126**, 87–100.

Schleidt, W. M. and Shalter, M. D. (1973) Stereotypy of a fixed action pattern during ontogeny in *Coturnix coturnix coturnix*. *Z. Tierpsychol.* **33**, 35–37.

Schubert, M. (1976) Über die variabilität von Lockrufen des Gimpels *Pyrrhula pyrrhula*. *Ardea* **64**, 62–71.

Searcy, W. A. and Marler, P. (1987) Response of sparrows to songs of deaf and isolation reared males; further evidence for innate auditory templates. *Dev. Psychobiol.* **20**, 509–519.

Slater, P. J. B., Eales, L. A. and Clayton, N. S. (1988) Song learning in zebra finches (*Taeniopygia guttata*). *Adv. Study Behav.* **18**, 1–34.

Smith, G. T., Brenowitz, E. A., Wingfield, J. C. and Baptista, L. F. (1995) Seasonal changes in song nuclei and song behavior in Gambel's white-crowned sparrows. *J. Neurobiol.* **28**, 114–125.

Stoddard, P. K., Beecher, M. D., Campbell, S. E. and Horning, C. L. (1992) Song type matching in the song sparrow. *Can. J. Zool.* **70**, 1440–1444.

ten Thoren, A. and Bergman, H.-H. (1987) Die Entwicklung der Lautäusserungen bei der Graugans (*Anser anser*). *J. Ornithol.* **128**, 181–207.

Thielcke, G. (1970) Lernen von Gesang als möglicher Schrittmacher der Evolution. *Z. Zool. System. Evolutionfors.* **8**, 309–320.

Thorpe, W. H. (1958) The learning of song patterns by birds, with especial reference to the song of the chaffinch (*Fringilla coelebs*). *Ibis* **100**, 535–570.

Tomback, D. F. and Baker, M. C. (1984) Assortative mating by white-crowned sparrows at song dialect boundaries. *Anim. Behav.* **32**, 465–469.

Tschanz, B. B. (1968) Trottellummen, die Entstehung der persönlichen Beziehungen zwischen Jungvögel und Eltern. *Z. Tierpsychol. Beiheft* **4**, 1–100.

Weary, D. M., Falls, J. B. and McGregor, P. K. (1990) Song matching and the perception of song types in great tits, *Parus major. Behav. Ecol.* **1**, 43–47.

Wells, S., Bradley, R. and Baptista, L. F. (1978) Hybridization in *Calypte* hummingbirds. *Auk* **96**, 537–549.

Whitman, C. O. (1919) *The Behavior of Pigeons*. Posthumous Works, Vol. III. Washington, DC: Carnegie Institute.

Wündinger, I. (1970) Erzeugung, Ontogenie und Funktion der Lautäusserungen bei vier Gänsearten. *Z. Tierpsychol.* **27**, 257–302.

Yasukawa, K., Blank, J. L. and Patterson, C. B. (1980) Song repertoires and sexual selection in the red-winged blackbird. *Behav. Ecol. Sociobiol.* **7**, 233–238.

Yoerg, S. I. and Kamil, A. C. (1991) Integrating cognitive ethology and cognitive psychology. In Ristau, C. A. (ed.) *Cognitive Ethology: The Minds of Other Animals.* Hillsdale, NJ: Lawrence Erlbaum Associates, pp. 273–289.

Zann, R. (1990) Song and call learning in wild zebra finches in south-east Australia. *Anim. Behav.* **40**, 811–828.

Zann, R. (1993) Variation in song structure within and among populations of Australian zebra finches. *Auk* **110**, 716–726.

10

Hierarchical Learning, Development and Representation of Song

Dietmar Todt and Henrike Hultsch

Institut für Verhaltensbiologie, Freie Universität, D-12163 Berlin, Germany

Introduction

The singing of birds is a special form of communication. Because this singing is very often a learned behavior, what birds sing and how they sing are likely to tell us something about how they learn and how they retrieve stored information. In this chapter, we shall describe how singing can be characterized by a structural hierarchy, how performances of this behavior can be further characterized according to a procedural hierarchy, what training with altered hierarchies tells us about birds' cognitive processes, and how certain aspects of vocal learning in birds have parallels with human behavior patterns.

How we characterize song

The concept basic to singing is that of 'song' ('strophe') as the specific signal pattern used in singing interactions. Our analyses suggest that a 'song' is a significant chunk of information stored in a bird's brain. Most direct support for this idea has been collected through learning experiments and much of our chapter will deal with this issue. To begin, however, we define a 'song' in a more operational manner, that is, as an acoustical compound that, for most species, lasts for only a brief period, typically 2–4 seconds. Such compounds seem to be optimal units of vocal interaction (citations in Todt

ANIMAL COGNITION IN NATURE
ISBN 0-12-077030-X

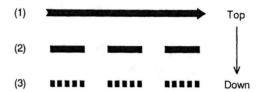

Fig. 10.1   Schema of a structural hierarchy. The bar on top (1) refers to an episode of singing that encompasses (2) acoustical patterns called 'songs' (strophe) and, on a lower level, (3) phonological units that compose the songs (term: 'elements'). The concept of *structural* hierarchy is used to address formal relationships between different *levels* of behavioral organization.

and Hultsch, 1996). In many species, singing interactions are seasonal, linked to gender and take place between territorial neighbors. Constraints on song duration seem to be shaped by constraints within a bird's information-processing systems, e.g. working memory. Also, constraints on song duration seem to facilitate vocal interaction: the signal is long enough to convey a distinct message but, at the same time, not so long that auditory checking for a potential answer or reply is delayed.

The hierarchical nature of singing

Once we have defined songs, we can describe singing by a structural hierarchy (Fig. 10.1). The highest level, singing behavior, is the actual sequence of songs used by the bird (the intersong level). The individual songs form an intermediate level. On the lowest or basic level, one can distinguish elements or notes that compose the songs (the intrasong level). Usually, this basic level is subjected to an analysis in which units are compared and classified according to parametric cues, i.e. values assessed by spectrographic analysis. The pool of classified units is then used to categorize the songs and so assess the repertoire of song types. Such analyses are part of a traditional approach to studying avian vocal behavior and have shown that the complexity of songs varies greatly across species (Todt, 1968; Lemon and Chatfield, 1971; Shiovitz, 1975; Bondesen, 1979; Kroodsma, 1982; Thompson *et al.*, 1994).

The singing of birds can, however, also be described by a set of rules that concern the sequential position of element types within a given song. We introduce the term *procedural hierarchy* for this second form of hierarchical ordering (Fig. 10.2). The procedural hierarchy found within songs of some members of the thrush family, such as the Eurasian Blackbird (*Turdus merula*) or the Common Nightingale (*Luscinia megarhynchos*) can be specified as follows (Fig. 10.3). First, particular types of elements occur only at a particular song position. Second, some element-type combinations are

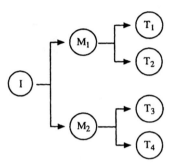

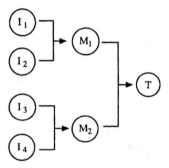

Fig. 10.2 Typical versions of a procedural hierarchy. The schema shows simple cases only, i.e. sequences with three different positions (initial, medial, terminal). Circles with symbols refer to units that occupy these positions. Such units may be, for instance, element types that constitute a short song or song types that compose a short episode of singing. Top: a model of a solofluent flow chart. It represents a sequence that is initiated by unit-type 'I', continued by 'M' and terminated by 'T'. Middle: a model of a diffluent flow chart. Here, it represents four different sequences that start with the same type of initial unit (I). Two of the sequences also share their middle part (M_1 or M_2), but differ in terminal unit types. Bottom: a model of a confluent flow chart. Here, it represents four different sequences that end with a same type of terminal unit (T). Two of the sequences also share their middle part (M_1 or M_3), but differ in initial unit types. The *procedural* hierarchy concept is used to address formal relationships between different *positions* that particular types of units can hold within a given stream of behavior.

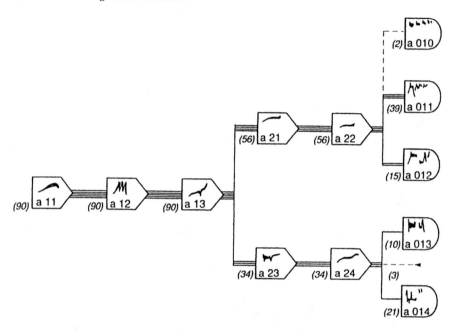

Fig. 10.3 An illustration of how a Eurasian Blackbird (*Turdus merula*) connected 12 phonological units (element types) in his songs. The beginning of songs is at the left, and the end at the right. Unit types are represented by cells that give their ID-number and their sonogram. To the left of each cell is the number of times that unit occurred in our sample (500 songs that the bird produced during one singing episode). According to our definition of song types, this graph mirrors five different types of songs that all share the same type of initial element (a11). The repertoire of our bird also contained 43 other song types that formed ten separate flow charts ('element syngraphs'); these are not included in this figure. Note: the graph documents a procedural hierarchy that concerns the intrasong level and shows a combination of solofluent and diffluent flow charts. After Todt (1968); see also Fig. 10.2.

produced in a predictable manner, whereas others reflect certain degrees of permutational freedom. Third, elements occurring at the beginning of songs are more frequent than others at later positions. Viewed from another perspective, the third rule means that many songs share initial elements, but differ in subsequent ones. This hierarchy means that a bird has a number of options for continuing a song after the first element has been produced (Todt, 1970; Hultsch, 1980; Naguib and Kolb, 1992).

A procedural hierarchy can also be found at the intersong level, where it concerns, for example, a string of songs in a given episode of singing. In contrast to the sequencing of song elements, however, the sequencing of songs reflects a remarkably higher degree of freedom, i.e. in principle, song types can occur in any order. Nevertheless, one can find preferred sequential combinations of particular types of songs. According to their specific singing styles, song bird species have been classed as either eventually versatile (singing A,A,A, . . . B,B,B . . .) or immediately versatile songsters (singing A,B,C,D . . .; Hartshorne, 1973; Kroodsma, 1977; Ince and Slater, 1985).

For both procedural hierarchies, therefore, a sequence of units (e.g. songs or song elements) can be described as a sequence of behavioral decisions. In such sequences, a given unit or unit compound can be examined as a point of decision about the next unit in the sequence. Rules governing the flow of decisions within songs have been studied mainly in species of the European biosphere; thus the examples given here may not cover the complete range of procedural rules encoded in the singing of birds.

The detection of such formal rules should prompt questions about both their scientific significance and their biological relevance (Dawkins, 1976; Todt and Hultsch, 1980; Nelson, 1990; Pepperberg, 1994). Answering such questions is essential for showing that the hierarchy principles are indeed relevant for the songsters themselves and are not just a reflection of our own cognitive strategies for recognizing such formal rules. Such skepticism is reasonable because humans tend to organize phenomena in a hierarchical manner, particularly when they must deal with large amounts of information (Anderson, 1983; Greenfield, 1991). Therefore, we examine whether birds that acquire and use especially large amounts of song material also invoke hierarchical rules to organize their singing behavior.

Hierarchy dimensions in the song acquisition of nightingales

Testing for the presence of hierarchical rules requires a subject that has both a truly complex repertoire and a system of song acquisition and development that is well described in terms of different levels of song organization. These criteria are partially fulfilled by species such as the Song Sparrow (*Melospiza melodia*; Marler and Peters, 1982a), Marsh Wren (*Cistothorus palustris*; Kroodsma, 1979), Canary (*Canarius serinus*; Nottebohm *et al.*, 1986), Starling (*Sturnus vulgaris*, Chaiken *et al.*, 1993) and Common Nightingale (*Luscinia megarhynchos*). Systematic studies on the learning of information encoded on the intersong level, however, are available only for the Common Nightingale. Therefore, we focus on this bird.

The nightingale is renowned for its outstanding vocal virtuosity. The repertoire of an adult individual comprises about 200 different types of songs, and these are performed with an immediate versatility. As in most other species, singing is the domain of the territorial male. We began our nightingale studies in the field (review in Todt and Hultsch, 1996), obtaining data on how a nightingale uses its vocalizations. We then proceeded to investigate these birds' song acquisition and development. Our research allowed us to uncover a number of properties of the nightingales' memory mechanisms.

Methodological aspects

Three characteristics of nightingales made them good candidates for studying song learning in the laboratory. First, the early period of auditory song acquisition begins around day 15 posthatching and continues for at least the first 3 months of life, thus providing an extended time span in which to conduct learning experiments. Second, young nightingales readily accept as their social tutor a human caretaker (Todt *et al.*, 1979; Todt and Boehner, 1994), thus enabling us to standardize variables and to control for factors that affect the acquisition process. Third, nightingales develop excellent copies of conspecific songs presented in a laboratory learning program, which may be a problem in some other oscine species.

To prepare a learning program, which is played to the bird through a loudspeaker, particular songs are selected at random from our catalogue of song types and recorded on tape to form a particular string of master songs. In the standard design, each song in a string is a different song type and, likewise, each of the different strings to which a subject is exposed during the period of tutoring consists of a unique set of song types. We thus label a particular tutoring situation or regime by its particular string. The subsequent vocal output of the tutored males allows us to infer whether and how their singing is influenced by exposure to the particular variables that we manipulate. We also evaluate the effect of variables by analysing audiovisual recordings, which enable us to see, for example, an individual bird's motility (movements around in the cage) during a tutoring experiment (Müller-Bröse and Todt, 1991).

Beyond a certain point, the song acquisition of nightingales is remarkably resilient to changes in variables such as exposure frequency or list length; such findings have interesting implications for theories of learning. For example, birds imitate around 75% of song types that they hear only 15 times and additional exposure does not significantly increase the number of songs that are acquired. Only after exposure is decreased to five times per song does learning decrease to about 30% of the songs that are heard. Also, the birds copy equally well when the number of songs in a string is increased considerably (e.g. from 20 to 60 song types), even when we do not raise exposure frequencies accordingly (Hultsch and Todt, 1989a). These results contrast with paradigms from learning theory, which state that for learning to occur, exposure frequency must increase proportionally with the number of stimuli to be acquired (review in Crowder, 1976). Implications of our findings are also relevant to the issue of song acquisition as a special process or template learning (Marler, 1976), and any inquiry into the memory

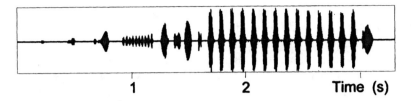

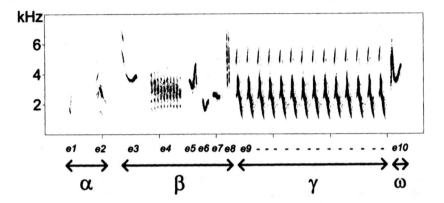

Fig. 10.4 Amplitude wave form (top) and frequency spectrogram (bottom) of a nightingale song. The pattern is composed by ten types of element (e1–e10). The symbols α, β, γ and Ω refer to the four song sections that are typical for this species.

mechanisms that are involved must take into account specific adaptations that are involved in the learning process.

Information encoded within songs

Typical nightingale songs are characterized by their division into several sections (Fig. 10.4). The α-section holds 1–3 elements that are low in volume and short in duration. The β-section is louder, and typically consists of note complexes or motifs, which give that song part a tonal or melodic structure. In contrast, the γ-section is clearly rhythmical (trill section). Most songs also have a final section (Ω) that is filled by one unrepeated element. Other types of syntax features become clear when song sections are compared across different song renditions and flow charts of elements are inspected. Successive songs, for instance, often begin with the same type of α-element. In addition, the transition between α- and β-sections, as well as between β- and γ-sections, usually coincides with a number of 'decision points'. Here, flow charts of elements show a kind of branching that results from alternative continuations of song patterns (= diffluent flow schema; see Fig. 10.2).

The accuracy of song imitations in hand-raised nightingales with respect to syntax is remarkably high, even when males experience a given song type only 10–20 times (Hultsch, 1993a). To examine whether this accomplishment requires exposure to normal nightingale songs, we tested the effect of modifying the syntax in a way that violated the species-typic rules of song composition. Our investigations showed that young nightingales are indeed able to cope successfully with a number of challenges when they are exposed to experimental modifications of the syntactical rules described above. The majority of modifications were 'accepted' by the birds and produced as imitations during the early stages of song ontogeny. At the end of song development, however, such atypical song versions were either corrected or dropped from the final repertoire (see section on 'Repertoire modification during development'). In particular, we found the following effects after specific modifications:

1. Modifications to α-sections. We omitted the introductory song elements. The modified songs were acquired at a rate comparable to that of normal songs. During song development, however, the birds often invented α-sections that were consistent with their species-typical patterns.
2. Modifications to α-sections. We repeated the normally unrepeated element complexes of the α-sections. The modified songs were not acquired by the birds.
3. Modifications to γ-sections. We tripled the length of γ-sections by increasing the number of syllable repetitions. These songs were acquired at a rate comparable to that of normal songs, but the birds reduced the number of syllable repetitions to the species-typical range.
4. Modifications to Ω-sections. We repeated the normally unrepeated terminal element. These songs were acquired at a rate that was comparable to that of normal songs. During the early stages of song ontogeny (plastic singing), the birds imitated the modifications. During adult singing, however, the birds corrected their imitations and produced only a single terminal element.

To examine further whether the birds have an idea about the general patterning of a species-typical song, we exposed nightingales to a learning program composed of artificial 'supersongs'. These supersongs were generated by experimentally erasing the silent intersong interval that normally segregates two successive master songs in a given string. Although birds initially acquired the modified master songs as a sort of supercompound, they were found to split these compounds into two different song types during their adult song performances. In other words, the nightingales clearly can identify the boundaries between the tutored super patterns. Our results suggest that the birds have access to a 'concept' of a species-typical song.

The findings invite us to inquire how these subjects would cope with information encoded at a hierarchically higher level of song organization.

Information encoded between songs

Analyses of song performances recorded from tutored nightingales revealed that birds had acquired information about the serial succession of master song types presented during the training (Hultsch and Todt, 1989a,b,c, 1992, 1996; Hultsch, 1991a). Such learning is evident, for example, from the formation of what we define here as packages and context groups, or from the imitation of the serial order of song types in a master string.

1. The package effect. This effect documents that a large body of serial data, here information from a string of master songs, is segmented into subsets of sequentially associated items. Such subsets show two particularly striking features. First, strong sequential associations exist among members of a given package, here the learned song types. As a rule, these relationships are not unidirectional, but bi- or multidirectional. Second, subsets have a limited size: the distribution of package sizes shows a prominent peak between three and four song types. In other words, a limited number of learned song types occurs in sequential association, and these association groups are termed packages.
2. The context effect. This effect documents that nightingales obviously learn a given master string as a sort of superunit that they sequentially separate from another superunit, i.e. from songs learned from another master string. These units are context groups. In contrast to the package groups, context groups are not limited in size and are determined by the length of a tutored song string.
3. The serial order effect. This effect documents the extent to which nightingales are able to learn and memorize serial information encoded in a string of master song types. The strength of this effect is, in contrast to the packaging of song types, related to the presentation frequency of a master string, and the birds must hear the string sufficiently often in order to learn the ordering. When birds are exposed to high presentation frequencies (e.g. 100 times), serial order learning can modify consequences of the package effect, for instance, by changing multidirectional relationships among package members to unidirectional ones or by blurring the boundaries between different packages.

These findings thus reveal the existence of two hierarchy levels above the level of individual songs. Thus the traditional hierarchy presented in Fig. 10.1 must be revised and extended. The first hierarchy level now involves the packages, composed of songs; the next involves the context groups, composed of packages. Both song order and context groups clearly reflect the serial organization of input during auditory learning and can be characterized as

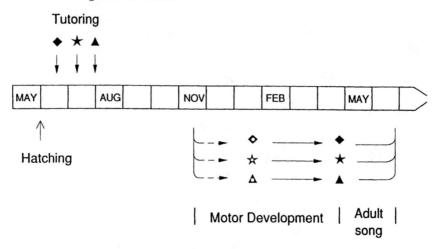

Fig. 10.5   Time schedule of song learning and development in nightingales.

'exposure-induced' associations. These combinations can thus be distinguished from the package groups that originate from systems constraints (e.g. constraints on short-term memory) and that we thus characterize as 'self-induced' associations.

A crucial question concerning the formation of exposure-induced song-type associations is whether they simply reflect the memorization of stimulus chains or whether they are based on cognitive accomplishments, such as 'categorization'. For the context groups such categorical cues would be, for instance, song types 'heard from a particular individual', 'heard at a particular location or time' or 'specified by a particular quality'. Preliminary evidence suggests that birds are indeed using such cues, and experiments that systematically examine this matter are under way.

The song development of nightingales

The general pattern of song development in nightingales is similar to that described for the Song Sparrow and other well-known subjects of developmental research. Thus, the nightingales' early phase of auditory learning is segregated from the phase of vocal production by an interval of several weeks (Fig. 10.5). Furthermore, the tripartite model introduced by Marler and Peters (1982a), which distinguishes subsong, several stages of plastic song and crystallized song, also applies to nightingales (Fig. 10.6).

Song development thus proceeds in the following typical manner. Males begin to produce subsong at about 6 months of age and then have a short winter hiatus. The first precursors of acquired imitations can be discerned

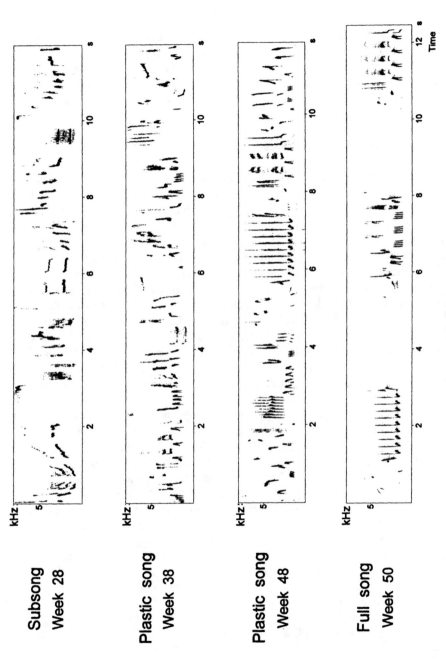

Fig. 10.6 Frequency spectrogram of vocalizations produced by a young nightingale during four stages of song development.

in January. Vocal ontogeny then proceeds through several stages of plastic singing and, after about 4 months, performance characteristics are crystallized into adult song. As a rule, the adult song of first-year males lasts for approximately 4 weeks. Song learning and song development, however, occur not only in a nightingale's first year of life, but also contribute to repertoire modifications found in the second and third years. Thus, according to a classification of Marler and Peters (1987), this species belongs to the 'age-independent learners' among oscine birds.

Periods of vocal performances

The singing of young nightingales is, very much like other kinds of behavior, delivered in a bout-wise manner or during particular performance periods. We examined these activity periods for the effect of variables such as time of the day, duration and composition. Usually, we proceeded by analysing recordings in a retrograde direction, i.e. backwards from crystallization until we reached the phonologically amorphous material of subsong. The procedure allowed us to identify the ontogenetic trajectories of several performance rules. At an early age, for instance, the birds' singing periods were short and occurred predominantly around noon. Beginning at week 42, the timing of vocalizing shifted gradually so that periods of vocalization occurred in the morning, after light onset. Then, after a clear decline in overall singing activity, which coincided with the time of migration and ended after week 49, the nightingales reached a new stage of development: their circadian singing activity showed a bimodal shape with a major peak in the early morning, and with some individuals starting to vocalize during the dark (nocturnal singing). Concurrently, singing bouts increased in both number and duration. Eventually, the total amount of time spent singing ranged between 4 and 12 hours per day (Kopp, 1996; see Fig. 10.7).

In our analyses, we compare a male's vocalizations during development to both the tutor songs and the song patterns that he produces during adult singing. If his vocalizations match either the tutor songs or his own crystallized songs, or significant parts of these patterns, we class them as identified patterns or IPA. The remaining portions of the vocalizations then are classed as unidentified patterns or UPA. During ontogeny, nightingales generally alternate between bouts of IPA and bouts of UPA; the duration of IPA bouts progressively increases with age, whereas the duration of UPA bouts concurrently decreases.

We hypothesize that bouts of IPA reflect periods of vocal activity in which a male is retrieving information from his memory (Hultsch, 1989). We developed this hypothesis after rejecting an earlier hypothesis that examined whether the production of UPA reflects a kind of search strategy for retrieving information acquired during auditory learning. In other words, we initially used the IPA/UPA distinction to examine whether birds would

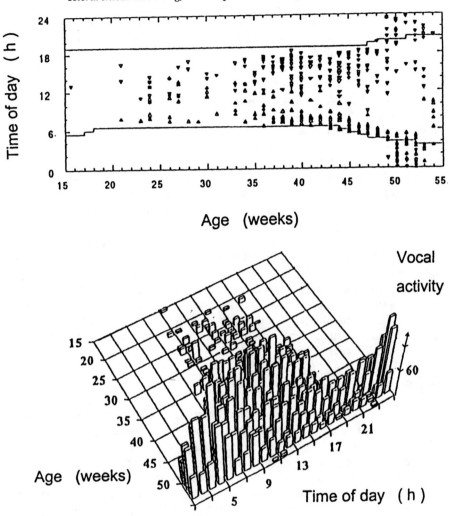

Fig. 10.7 The singing activity of male nightingales plotted against their age (week 15–week 50) and time of day (automatic registration; data pooled from $n = 5$ males). Top: lines within the distribution show the start and the end of the light phase. Bottom: the height of columns indicates the amount of time (minutes; pooled data) that the birds spent singing. After Kopp (1996).

randomly 'invent' vocal patterns and be reinforced (by some unspecified kind of feedback) for producing those that matched stored information. That is, if the invented vocal pattern was by chance a UPA, it would not be reinforced and be dropped, whereas if it was an IPA, it would be reinforced and retained. One implication of the rejected hypothesis was that we would find precursors of a final pattern randomly embedded in the stream of UPA vocalizations. Our analyses showed that such behavior exists only in the very early stage of development. Later, IPAs do not occur in a random distribution. Rather they are temporally clumped and new precursors emerge embedded in bouts of IPAs. Thus, the initial hypothesis had to be rejected.

The ontogenetic development of temporal structure of nightingale song can be characterized as an increase in the amount and duration of discontinuous singing (Wendtland and Todt, 1995; Kopp, 1996). Like other oscines, nightingales are continuous songsters early in life, and only after crystallization occurs (around week 47; see Fig. 10.6) do the birds develop the pattern of discontinuous singing that is typical of the adult males in this species. In discontinuous singing, structurally stereotyped songs are segregated by conspicuous silent intersong intervals. The transition from continuous to discontinuous singing does not involve prolonging the silent intersong intervals. Rather, during the period in which temporal patterns are crystallizing, both continuous and discontinuous performance phases may be produced on a given day or even alternate within a single song bout. Interestingly, however, the ontogenetically most advanced (i.e. discontinuous) singing is produced during the early morning hours right after light onset. Song bouts recorded later in the day, then, have either a continuous or 'mixed' characteristic. A similar result has been obtained for the Song Thrush (*Turdus philomenos*; Heupel, 1996).

Trajectories of song development

Trajectories of song development can be found on two hierarchy levels, that is, within or between songs. With the beginning of plastic singing, the number of song-type precursors that can be distinguished (IPAs) increases gradually, and complete acquisition of the repertoire of song-type precursors takes about 6 weeks in nightingales. Development at the intersong level, that is, with respect to formation of packages and context groups, also occurs over time and according to specific rules, and the temporal order of song-type acquisition does not reflect the temporal order of auditory input.

Ontogenetic trajectories at the intrasong level appear to involve syntax and phonology. During early stages of ontogeny, birds often sing incomplete songs, i.e. some song constituents may be missing. In addition, the serial succession of song sections may be inverted, so that the final trill section of a song may be produced ahead of the normally preceding note complex. Thus, the intrasong syntax is not initially stereotyped. Song crystallization in these birds appears to occur in two stages with pattern (e.g. note) phonology crystallizing first and intrasong syntax crystallizing later. Interestingly, the syntactical and phonological quality of song precursors produced relatively late in ontogeny is not inferior to that of precursors produced earlier. Specifically, the early precursors are initially rather poor in quality and improve over time, whereas the later precursors are, at the time of incorporation, equal in quality to the improved versions of the early precursors. This result suggests a developmental trajectory that does not build on vocal 'experience' with a particular output, but concerns a general progression in motor competence or skill (Hultsch, 1991b).

At the intersong level, trajectories are characterized by the following rules. First, the temporal order of song precursor occurrence does not reflect the temporal order of auditory input. In other words, imitations of master songs that the birds heard early in life do not emerge earlier than imitations of others that they heard later. Second, imitations that, in the adult performance, are identified as members of the same package emerge quite consistently together in time (Fig. 10.8). In addition, throughout ontogeny, these precursors are sequentially associated in the same way as in adult singing. The association of different packages, i.e. the development of context groups, in contrast, is delayed until development is nearly complete. The adult form of context groups can thus be assessed only after all song-type precursors of a nightingale have been identified. However, the temporal structure of singing gives some indication that context groups, even during ontogeny, are significant in terms of behavioral organization. During the phase of continuous vocal production, for example, the intervals between imitations acquired from the same master string or context group were significantly shorter than the intervals we observed when the birds switched to imitations of another context group (Fig. 10.9).

In conclusion, learning trajectories exist on intrasong and intersong levels and, on the intersong level, ontogeny indeed reflects properties of the song-type association groups to which we referred earlier (see section 'Information encoded between songs'). The trajectories do not only substantiate the view that these groups are memorized and encoded as higher-level units of song organization, but also suggest that retrieval of material from memory may follow similar hierarchical mechanisms.

Repertoire modification during development

Ontogeny is not simply the time in which a bird improves the quality of acquired song material by vocal rehearsal. At least two additional behavior patterns that occur during this period merit a short discussion. One enlarges the repertoire of a bird, whereas the other has the opposite effect. In nightingales, an increase in repertoire size is much more likely than a decrease. Repertoire enlargement is achieved by acquiring additional song types, developing new recombinations or, finally, inventing novel songs (Freyschmidt *et al.*, 1984; Wistel-Wozniak and Hultsch, 1993). How nightingales decrease their repertoire is particularly interesting because the mechanism that they seem to use has not previously been described for song birds.

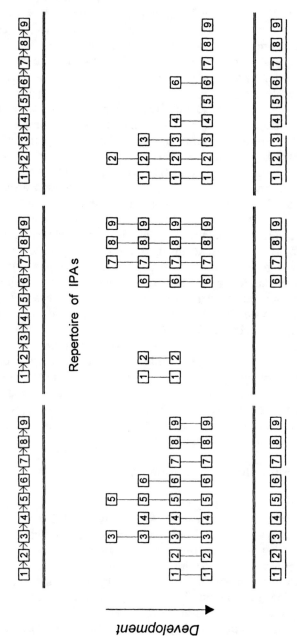

Fig. 10.8 Song development in nightingales. Top: an illustration of three tutored strings of master songs (songs = cells with ID numbers). Middle: the ontogenetic ordering observed for the precursors of imitations observed in one male's repertoire (IPA = identified patterns). Bottom: the final repertoire of that bird. Here, lines below cells indicate which imitations were associated with a song-type package. Note: this bird did not learn three of the tutored master songs and discarded two other imitations from his final repertoire.

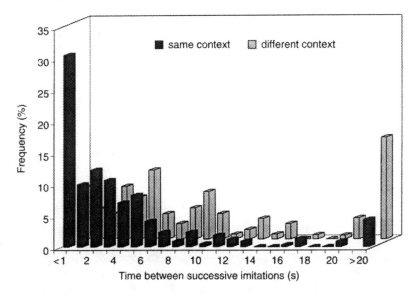

Fig. 10.9 The frequency distribution of intervals observed between successive imitations (abscissa) developed by a nightingale. Intervals between imitations belonging to the same context group were shorter (black columns) than intervals between imitations of different context groups (hatched columns).

Further learning can occur either during the phase of plastic singing or later in life. When 9-month-old nightingales (i.e. those currently in the plastic song stage) were exposed to a master string with a familiar portion (heard by the birds during the first period of song acquisition) and a novel portion (containing new song types), we observed the following two effects. First, the renewed exposure to the familiar song types raised the performance frequency of imitations that the birds had acquired earlier. A similar finding was reported for White-crowned Sparrows (*Zonotrichia leucophrys*; Nelson, 1992), pointing to a process coined as 'action-based learning' by Marler and Nelson (1993). Second, the birds acquired the novel song types and performed them as an integral part of that context group from which the familiar song-type sequence was taken (Hultsch, 1991b; Todt and Hultsch, 1996).

The effect is in line with data from birds that, instead of being housed in isolation, were housed together, thus allowing them to interact vocally with each other (Table 10.1). The development of song repertoires in these socially housed birds was clearly influenced by their preference to perform shared song types. Thus, additional learning coupled with a shaping of performance towards convergence can lead to a sharing of at least parts of repertoires among conspecific neighbors (Hultsch and Todt, 1981; Payne, 1981; Slater, 1989; Lemon *et al.*, 1994).

Table 10.1 Effects of social housing on trajectories of song development (control: acoustic isolation after tutoring).

Variables	Effects
Time of crystallization	
Pattern phonology and syntax	No difference
Time structure	Preterm
Song-type repertoire	
Composition	Converging
Preferred song types	Converging

A different strategy of repertoire enlargement, which enhances the vocal individuality of a songster, is the development of new recombinations or novel inventions of songs. Nightingales are able to generate individual specific song types by recombining parts of imitated songs in a novel way. Interestingly, such recombinations (termed 'acquired imitations') are predominantly limited to material from song types within the same package group (Hultsch, 1993b). In addition, nightingales may devise song types that do not contain material from the learning experiments, and so are completely new (termed 'novel inventions'). Both during development and in adult singing, genuine inventions occur as coherent subsets, which result in an alternation of performance periods containing acquired imitations or novel inventions. Males classified as poor learners (acquisition success, related to presented master song types, <40%) develop a larger proportion of inventions than those classified as good learners (acquisition success >60%). Because hand-raised birds that are exposed to a small number of master song types (~30) likewise develop more inventions than birds exposed to a larger number of song types (~90), invented songs point to a strategy for increasing the repertoire, at least in hand-raised nightingales. Nevertheless, the occurrence of inventions raises a number of questions. The most puzzling one concerns their origin. Analyses are under way, for instance, that examine whether birds generalize acoustic features of master song phonology and use them when inventing novel song patterns (Hughes and Hultsch, 1997).

Like some other species, nightingales may reduce their song-type repertoire when they reach the final stage of song development. However, the amount of material discarded is much smaller than, for instance, in the Swamp Sparrow or the White-crowned Sparrow (Marler and Peters, 1982b; Nelson *et al.*, 1995), and involves only about 5–8% of the imitations identified in the course of song development (Hultsch, 1991c). Nevertheless, the process of repertoire constriction is quite fascinating in nightingales. Evidence exists that repertoire constriction reflects a selection process that results in an omission of only particular song types. During plastic singing, song types that are eventually discarded show both a low-performance frequency (see also Marler and Peters, 1982a) and a poor copy quality. In nightingales, these two variables seem interrelated. In addition, an even more advanced variable can affect the selection process.

Birds may also select what to keep and what to discard based on rules related to the 'procedural hierarchy' discussed above. We derive this conclusion from a recent experiment in which we tutored birds with input designed to violate the rule that two songs that differ in their first part should not share the pattern of their second part (Fig. 10.10). Remember that a partial phonological similarity of song types is quite common in the repertoire of the individual nightingale, but is constrained to a sharing of initial parts such as the α- and the β-sections (= diffluent branching within element flow charts; Fig. 10.2). To examine the significance of this rule, we presented young nightingales with pairs of master songs that were different in their first part (α- + β-section), but shared the pattern of their second part (γ- + Ω-section). Because such pairs do not occur in a male's normal repertoire, we synthesized the test songs experimentally. As a control, birds also heard pairs of master songs which shared the pattern of their first part, but were different in their second part and so followed the species-typic rule of intrasong organization.

We observed two outcomes. First, males in the control situation developed imitations of both of the tutored master song versions. The pair-wise similar imitations were performed at about equal rates throughout song ontogeny and all persisted in the birds' repertoires. Second, the majority of males in the test situation also developed imitations of both of the tutored master song versions. During ontogeny, however, in this group there was a marked decline in the performance rate of one of the pairwise similar imitations. In most cases, then, only one song version 'survived' to the end of song crystallization.

We explain the latter result as an example of a rule-bound selection process induced by prescriptions from the species-typic organization of song patterns. An important aspect of our findings relates to the fact that repertoire constriction occurred only rather late in ontogeny. Thus constraints from species-typic song organization did not restrict acquisition during auditory exposure or early vocal practice. Only after a certain amount of vocal practice had occurred did 'analysis' arising from structure-dependent knowledge come into play to set performance parameters according to species-typic rules. Interestingly, such knowledge concerns a syntactical rule that refers to the composition of song repertoires and that poses constraints on possible song variants (allowing for diffluent branching only). Such a mechanism was hitherto unknown for the song development of birds.

Conclusions and perspectives

The singing behavior of many birds reflects a structural hierarchy that, in a bottom-up order, is given by the units that compose a song pattern (intrasong

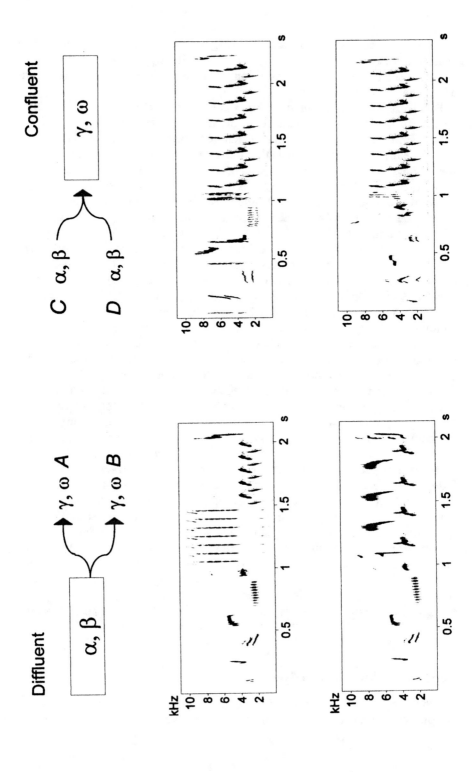

level), by the songs, and finally by sequences in which songs are produced (intersong level). Each of these levels reveals a specific organization and dynamics that we address by another kind of hierarchy, termed procedural. The procedural hierarchy involves two sets of rules: one set for sequencing elements within songs and another for sequencing songs within an episode of singing. For the versatile songster, these rules may reflect the hierarchical mechanisms a bird uses during song retrieval and when choosing among the various elements that compose a given song.

The fact that bird song is a learned behavior allows us to use the hierarchy concept to ask questions about the role that individual experience plays in the implementation of singing rules. Our results from learning experiments and studies of song development revealed a close link between both hierarchy domains, and confirmed that both play a biologically relevant role. Birds like nightingales, which acquire large vocal repertoires, for example, develop two categories of song-type associations. These are the packages composed of about 3–5 song types and the context groups that incorporate all packages derived from a given learning context. Such associations not only reflect a hierarchical representation of the memorized information (Fig. 10.11), but their characteristics also allow us to trace the properties of the underlying memory mechanisms.

Acquisition mechanisms and memory properties

Auditory song acquisition by nightingales has been explained as a co-ordinated operation of three mechanisms: 'short-term memory', 'recognition memory' and a battery of 'submemories' (Hultsch and Todt, 1989c). Short-term memory is constrained by limited capacity and the length of time over which information can be stored (Hultsch, 1992). To accommodate these constraints, short-term memory cuts a serially coherent master string into segments of 3–5 songs (i.e. the prospective 'packages') and stores this

---

Fig. 10.10 The frequency spectrogram of four master songs to which nightingales were exposed during a learning experiment. Songs given on the left are congruent in their α- and β-section, but differ in their further parts, thus complying with the species-typic decision flow (diffluent branching). Songs given on the right, in contrast, differ in their first part, but are congruent in their γ- and Ω-section. Since this form of song-type similarity does not occur in a nightingale's normal song composition, these test songs were experimentally synthesized (confluent branching). Pairs of such song patterns were used to examine whether a violation of species-typic rules would impair song learning. Our results showed that the birds did acquire both versions of the artificial song pairs, but there was a marked decline in the performance rate of one version of a pair during ontogeny. We explain this effect as an example of a rule-bound selection process that leads to repertoire constriction towards the end of song development.

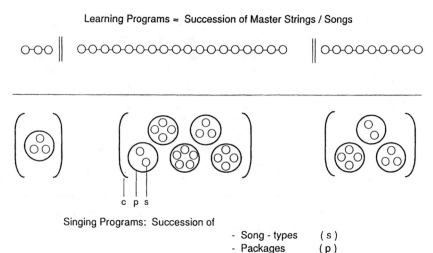

Fig. 10.11 An illustration of the hierarchy levels (packages, context groups) found in the singing of trained birds. Top: a bird was tutored with three master strings that were composed by different song types (small circles). Bottom: schematic illustration of the results. Songs developed from different master strings are performed as members of different context groups (large brackets) and the size of these groups depends on the length of the tutored strings. The number of song-type packages (large circles) developed from a master string also depends on this length, whereas their size does not. There is evidence suggesting that these hierarchy levels have a representation in a bird's song memory.

material. If recognition memory classifies all incoming song types composing a given segment (i.e. the material in short-term memory) as novel (i.e. as stimulus patterns that have never before been in short-term memory), these data are transferred from the short-term memory to a submemory that further processes these song data as a particular package of information. If recognition memory classifies the next string segment as novel, another submemory will be installed. Thus, hearing a long string of master song types for the first time will lead to the establishment of a battery of submemories, each of which stores information about one single string segment or one package on a long-term basis. If, in contrast, recognition memory classifies all incoming songs in a string (i.e. the material in short-term memory) as familiar (i.e. part of what was at some point previously in short-term memory but is now in a submemory), then the information in short-term memory will be transferred to the appropriate existing submemory. Thus, hearing a given song type again would improve or supplement the information stored in a submemory. Because long master strings are learned as effectively as short ones, even when heard only 10–20 times, we assume that data processing in the battery of submemories takes place in a parallel manner. However, because each submemory holds information from one string segment only, an additional process must be postulated that somehow links those submemories that have been established during the same learning context and thereby assigns the song-type packages stored in these submemories to the same context group. We assume that such an additional process is also initiated by the recognition memory.

Support for the proposed acquisition system comes from recent experiments in which the serial succession of song types in a master string was altered during subsequent exposures. The sequencing of imitations observed in the birds' adult singing revealed that the first exposure to a master string played a key role in the acquisition of serial information on song-type sequencing. In addition, a single exposure was sufficient for subjects to acquire this information; the phenomenon was termed 'primer effect' (Hultsch and Todt, 1996). Nevertheless, accuracy in reproducing a sequence improved with increasing exposure to a master string. The findings suggest that initial learning of some features in the song learning of birds operates in a discontinuous, 'all or none' manner and, at the same time, overall learning is enhanced gradually, i.e. through an incremental process.

Viewed from a biological perspective, the proposed mechanisms appear clearly adaptive. During song acquisition in a natural context, birds would not be exposed to stereotyped sequences. Instead, considerable variability exists in the song delivery of a natural tutor in the field. To acquire the various song patterns from such tutor, it seems feasible to start a memory trace right from the first exposure ('reference') and use information acquired during further exposures to update and/or ameliorate memory contents. Behavioral support for the particular salience of the first exposure(s) for a bird's perceptual attention comes from the experiments of Müller-Bröse and Todt (1991). They showed that the motility of birds (perch changes) during the tutoring was low during the first exposure and increased with more frequent string presentations. Interestingly, this motility dropped again when a sequence of new song types, i.e. a novel master string, was presented.

Both the particular salience of the first exposure and the incremental effects of exposure frequency on the serial performance of acquired imitations are relevant to neurobiological concepts of the song acquisition system (reviewed in Konishi, 1989; Doupe, 1992; Nottebohm, 1993). Morphological correlates of acquisition processes, as first demonstrated by Scheich and coworkers for both imprinting and song learning (reviewed in Scheich and Braun, 1988) can be outlined as a decline in synaptic connectivity (reduction of spine synapses) along with learning-related neuronal activity. According to their arguments for imprinting, specific information from the first stimulation would induce synaptic selection or regression. Concurrently functional (i.e. active) synapses would be consolidated by repeated input (Hebbian type of learning; Hebb, 1949). It seems premature, however, to elaborate further on the neurological basis of the findings described above.

Retrieval rules document a hierarchical representation of song data

Evidence exists that the representation of memorized information about songs is organized hierarchically. Our analyses of song performance uncovered specific rules of song retrieval. Some of these rules can be identified even during the ontogeny of singing. Thus, trajectories of the three hierarchy levels that, in a top-down order, were described as context groups, packages and song types, develop in a way that allows early detection of their particular features. To recall one example, the temporal diversity of intervals within and between context groups (shorter duration within, than at switches between, context groups) presumably points to properties of intrinsic pattern choice or retrieval. The effect could imply that access to the stored representation of song types is quick or delayed depending on whether a retrieval 'program' from a given context group is already 'on' (i.e. a nonswitch) or not yet 'on' (i.e. a switch). Alternatively, the differences in intervals could reflect decision times for retrieving patterns acquired from same or different contexts (Hultsch, 1993b).

In the adult birds, a hierarchically prestructured repertoire could be a mechanism to facilitate retrieval in situations demanding rapid vocal responses, e.g. during interactive countersinging. Here, centrally or auditorily mediated decisions on 'what to sing next' would not have to be made among the entire pool of developed song types. Rather, decision steps and decision time would both be reduced by using a search routine that subsequently addresses a particular subset of patterns only. We assume that such a strategy makes sense not only above the level of songs, but also within songs. This assumption is derived from features of the procedural hierarchy described for the intrasong level. To recall two aspects that seem to matter here: (1) even versatile songsters may start successive songs with initial elements of the same type, which may reflect an easier access to a particular set of song units (see section 'The hierarchical nature of singing'); and (2) after the decision about introductory elements has been made, only a limited number of alternatives need next be considered, and their retrieval is achieved without causing any reduction in the versatility among successive songs.

In species that, like the nightingale, manage large repertoires, the adaptive value of a hierarchically organized representation format of song data is quite conclusive. During vocal interactions, songsters may respond to each other by sophisticated rules, i.e. by pattern-specific and time-specific relationships between the mutually exchanged songs. For example, in a reply category termed rapid matching, a male has to identify a neighbor's song and at the time also select and retrieve songs of the same types from his own repertoire within a latency of approximately one second (Hultsch and Todt, 1982;

Wolffgramm and Todt, 1982). In contrast, species in which individual males develop and use only one particular song type need not cope with the same type of retrieval and decision problems during interactional challenges.

Summary and comparative aspects

From a comparative perspective, the vocal development of birds may show parallels with language development of humans. Such parallels were postulated for the role of interactional variables (Pepperberg, 1993; this volume), or for predispositions and sensitive phases to guide the acquisition process (Marler and Peters, 1981). Our findings on learning mechanisms allow us to add further parallels to such a comparative framework. One parallel is the hierarchical organization of memory, which facilitates the administration and use of large amounts of learned information. Another parallel is in the domain of acquisition mechanisms, where the formation of song-type packages shows striking similarities to the chunking of information in human serial learning (Bower, 1970; Simon, 1974). In humans, chunking is related to cognitive processes that define a chunk as a unit of sense, given, for example, by a term or a sentence, or more. In the song acquisition of birds, a chunk equivalent is given by a song (strophe), and a song can be regarded as a unit of sense as well. Our conclusion arises from the fact that songs are units of interaction that play a particular role, for example, during vocal communication between neighbors. On formal grounds, 'songs' have been compared to 'sentences' (Todt and Hultsch, 1996).

It seems expedient, therefore, to suggest that cognitive capacities are involved in the development and use of bird song (see also Pepperberg, 1993; this volume). An interesting case pointing to such mental operations occurs when the birds' performance is organized according to categorical cues that are acquired during exposure to stimuli. Such cues may be temporal, spatial or social ones. Straightforward examples are the studies of Kroodsma (1988) and Spector *et al.* (1989), which demonstrate that warbler species learn the situations in which to use their songs. The exposure-induced song-type associations developed by our nightingales, the context groups, reflect such accomplishments on a higher level of song organization. Another example is the performance of invented songs that might be categorized as 'patterns that are specific to individuals'. Currently, however, the cues upon which such categorization would rely are unclear, thus challenging us to address this issue explicitly in future research on birds with large repertoires.

Acknowledgements

We thank a number of people for their dedication and skillful involvement in hand raising birds and conducting experiments, among them, H. Brumm,

C. Fichtel, N. Geberzahn, M. Hoffmann, F. Schleuß, G. Schwartz-Mittelstädt and A. Wistel-Wozniak. Irene Pepperberg and Don Kroodsma made most valuable suggestions for an improvement of the manuscript. The work was supported by the Berlin-Brandenburgische Akademie der Wissenschaften and the Deutsche Forschungsgemeinschaft.

References

Anderson, J. R. (1983) *The Architecture of Cognition.* Cambridge, MA: Harvard University Press.

Bondesen, P. (1979) The hierarchy of bioacoustic units expressed by a phrase formula. *Biphon* **6**, 2–6.

Bower, G. H. (1970) Organizational factors in memory. *Cognitive Psychol.* **1**, 18–46.

Chaiken, M., Böhner, J. and Marler, P. (1993) Song acquisition in European starlings, *Sturnus vulgaris*: a comparison of the songs of live-tutored, tape-tutored and wild-caught males. *Anim. Behav.* **46**, 1079–1090.

Crowder, R. G. (1976) *Principles of Learning and Memory.* Hillsdale, NJ: Lawrence Erlbaum Associates.

Dawkins, R. (1976) Hierarchical organization: a candidate principle for ethology. In Bateson, P. P. G. and Hinde, R. A. (eds), *Perspectives in Ethology.* Cambridge: Cambridge University Press, pp. 7–54.

Doupe, A. (1992) A neural circuit specialized for vocal learning. *Curr. Opin. Neurobiol.* **3**, 104–111.

Freyschmidt, J., Kopp, M. L. and Hultsch, H. (1984) Individuelle Entwicklung von gelernten Gesangsmustern be Nachtigallen. *Verh. Dtsch. Zool. Ges.* **77**, 244.

Greenfield, P. M. (1991) Language, tools and brain: the ontogeny and phylogeny of hierarchically organized sequential behavior. *Behav. Brain Sci.* **14**, 531–551.

Hartshorne, C. (1973) *Born to Sing.* Bloomington, IN: Indiana University Press.

Hebb, D. O. (1949) *The Organization of Behavior.* New York: Wiley and Sons.

Heupel, K. (1996) Ontogenese und tageszeitliche Variation der Zeitstruktur im Gesang der Singdrossel (*Turdus Philomelos*). Diplom-thesis, Faculty of Biology, Freie Universität, Berlin.

Hughes, M. and Hultsch, H. (1997) Is stereotypy in the song of the nightingale (*Luscinia megarhynchos*) learned? *Adv. Ethol.* **32**, 116.

Hultsch, H. (1980) Beziehungen zwischen Struktur, zeitlicher Variabilität und sozialem Einsatz im Gesang der Nachtigall, *Luscinia megarhynchos*. Ph.D. thesis, Freie Universität, Berlin.

Hultsch, H. (1989) Ontogeny of song patterns and their performance mode in nightingales. In Erber, J., Menzel, R., Pflüger, H. J. and Todt, D. (eds) *Neural Mechanisms of Behaviour.* Stuttgart: Thieme, p. 113

Hultsch, H. (1991a) Early experience can modify singing styles – evidence from experiments with nightingales, *Luscinia megarhynchos. Anim. Behav.* **42**, 883–889.

Hultsch, H. (1991b) Correlates of repertoire constriction in the song ontogeny of nightingales (*Luscinia megarhynchos*). *Verh. Dtsch. Zool. Ges.* **84**, 47.

Hultsch, H. (1991c) Song ontogeny in birds: closed or open developmental programs? In Elsner, N. and Penzlin, H. (eds) *Synapse, transmission, modulation.* Stuttgart: Thieme, p. 576.

Hultsch, H. (1992) Time window and unit capacity: dual constraints on the acquisition of serial information in songbirds. *J. Comp. Physiol. A* **170**, 275–280.

Hultsch, H. (1993a) Ecological versus psychobiological aspects of song learning in birds. *Etologia* **3**, 309–323.

Hultsch, H. (1993b) Tracing the memory mechanisms in the song acquisition of birds. *Neth. J. Zool. A.* **43**, 155–171.

Hultsch, H. and Todt, D. (1981) Repertoire sharing and song post distance in nightingales. *Behav. Ecol. Sociobiol.* **8**, 182–188.

Hultsch, H. and Todt, D. (1982) Temporal performance roles during vocal interactions in nightingales. *Behav. Ecol. Sociobiol.* **11**, 253–260.

Hultsch, H. and Todt, D. (1989a) Song acquisition and acquisition constraints in the nightingale (*Luscinia megarhynchos*). *Naturwissenschaften* **76**, 83–86.

Hultsch, H. and Todt, D. (1989b) Memorization and reproduction of songs in nightingales (*Luscinia megarhynchos*): evidence for package formation. *J. Comp. Physiol. A* **165**, 197–203.

Hultsch, H. and Todt, D. (1989c) Context memorization in the learning of birds. *Naturwissenschaften* **76**, 584–586.

Hultsch, H. and Todt, D. (1992) The serial order effect in the song acquisition of birds. *Anim. Behav.* **44**, 590–592.

Hultsch, H. and Todt, D. (1996) Discontinuous and incremental processes in the song learning of birds: evidence for a primer effect. *J. Comp. Physiol A*, 291–299.

Ince, S. A. and Slater, P. J. B. (1985) Versatility and continuity in the songs of thrushes *Turdus* spp. *Ibis* **127**, 455–364.

Konishi, M. (1989) Bird song for neurobiologists. *Neuron* **3**, 541–549.

Kopp, M. L. (1996) Ontogenetische Veränderungen in der Zeitstruktur des Gesangs der Nachtigall, *Luscinia megarhynchos.* PhD. thesis, Faculty of Biology, Freie Universität, Berlin.

Kroodsma, D. E., (1977) Correlates of song organization among north American wrens. *Am. Nat.* **11**, 995–1008.

Kroodsma, D. E. (1979) Vocal dueling among male Marsh Wrens: evidence for ritualized expressions of dominance/subordinance. *Auk* **98**, 506–515.

Kroodsma, D. E. (1982) Song repertoires: problems in their definition and use. In Kroodsma, D. E. and Miller, E. H. (eds) *Acoustic Communication in Birds*, Vol. 2. New York: Academic Press, pp. 125–146.

Kroodsma, D. E. (1988) Song-types and their use: developmental flexibility of the male blue-winged warbler. *Ethology* **79**, 235–247.

Lemon, R. E. and Chatfield, C. (1971) Organization of song in Cardinals. *Anim. Behav.* **19**, 1–17.

Lemon, R. E., Perrault, S. and Weary, D. M. (1994). Dual strategies of song development in American redstarts, *Setophaga ruticilla*. *Anim. Behav.* **47**, 317–329.

Marler, P. (1976) Sensory templates in species-specific behaviour. In Fentress, J. C. (ed.) *Simpler Networks and Behavior*. Sunderland, MA: Sinauer Associates, pp. 314–329.

Marler, P. and Nelson, D. (1993) Action-based learning: a new form of developmental plasticity in bird song. *Neth. J. Zool.* **43**, 91–101.

Marler, P. and Peters, S. (1981) Birdsong and speech: evidence for special processing. In Eimas, P. and Miller, J. (eds) *Perspectives on the Study of Speech*. Hillsdale, NJ: Erlbaum, pp. 75–112.

Marler, P. and Peters, S. (1982a) Structural changes in song ontogeny in the Swamp Sparrow, *Melospiza georgiana*. *Auk* **99**, 446–458.

Marler, P. and Peters, S. (1982b) Developmental overproduction and selective attrition: New processes in the epigenesis of birdsong. *Dev. Psychobiol.* **15**, 369–378.

Marler, P. and Peters, S. (1987) A sensitive period for song acquisition in the song sparrow, *Melospiza melodia*: a case of age limited learning. *Ethology* **76**, 89–100.

Müller-Bröse, M. and Todt, D. (1991) Lokomotorische Aktivität von Nachtigallen (*Luscinia megarhynchos*) während auditorischer Stimulation mit Artgesang, präsentiert in ihrer lernsensiblen Altersphase. *Verh. Dtsch. Zool. Ges.* **84**, 476–477.

Naguib, M. and Kolb, H. (1992) Vergleich des Strophenaufbaus und der Strophenabfolgen an den Gesähgen von Sposser (*Luscinia luscinia*) und Blaukehlchen (*Luscina svecica*). *J. Ornithol.* **133**, 133–145.

Nelson, D. A. (1992) Song overproduction, song matching and selective attrition during development. In McGregor, P. K. (ed.) *Playback and Studies of Animal Communication*. New York: Plenum Press, pp. 121–133.

Nelson, D. A., Marler, P. and Palleroni, A. (1995) A comparative approach to vocal learning: intraspecific variation in the learning process. *Anim. Behav.* **50**, 83–97.

Nelson, K. (1990) Hierarchical organization revisited. *Neth. J. Zool.* **40**, 585–616.

Nottebohm, F. (1993) The search for neural mechanisms that define the sensitive period for song learning in birds. *Neth. J. Zool.* **43**, 193–234.

Nottebohm, F., Nottebohm, M. E. and Crane, L. A. (1986) Developmental and seasonal changes in canary song and their relation to changes in the anatomy of song control nuclei. *Behav. Neurol. Biol.* **46**, 445–471.

Payne, R. B. (1981) Song learning and social interaction in indigo buntings. *Anim. Behav.* **29**.

Pepperberg, I. M. (1993) A review of the effects of social interaction on vocal learning in African grey parrots (*Psittacus erithacus*). *Neth. J. Zool.* **43**, 104–124.

Pepperberg, I. M. (1994) Language and cognition: the interesting case of subjects 'P'. *Behav. Brain Sci.* **17**, 359.

Scheich, H. and Braun, K. (1988) Synaptic selection and calcium regulation:

common mechanisms of auditory and filial imprinting and vocal learning in birds? *Verh. Dtsch. Zool. Ges.* **81**, 77–95.

Shiovitz, K. A. (1975) The process of species-specific song recognition by the indigo bunting (*Passerina cyanea*). *Behaviour* **55**, 128–179.

Simon, H. A. (1974) How big is a chunk? *Science* **183**, 482–468.

Slater, P. J. B. (1989) Bird song learning: causes and consequences. *Ethol. Ecol. Evol.* **1**, 19–46.

Spector, D. A., McKim, L. K. and Kroodsma, D. E. (1989) Yellow warblers are able to learn songs and the situations in which to use them. *Anim. Behav.* **38**, 723–725.

Thompson, N. S., LeDoux, K. and Moody, K. (1994) A system for describing bird song units. *Bioacoustics* **5**, 267–279.

Todt, D. (1968) Zur Steuerung unregelmässiger Verhaltensabläufe. In Mittelstaedt, H. (ed.) *Kybernetik*. Munich: Oldenbourg, pp. 465–485.

Todt, D. (1970) Zur Ordnung im Gesang der Nachtigall (*Luscinia megarhynchos*). *Verh. Dtsch. Zool. Ges.* **64**, 249–252.

Todt, D. and Böhner, J. (1994) Former experience can modify social selectivity during song learning in the nightingale (*Luscinia megarhynchos*). *Ethology* **97**, 169–176.

Todt, D. and Hultsch, H. (1980) Functional aspects of sequences and hierarchy in bird song. *Acta XVII. Congr. Int. Orn. Berlin* 663–670.

Todt, D. and Hultsch, H. (1996) Acquisition and performance of repertoires: ways of coping with diversity and versatility. In Kroodsma, D. E. and Miller, E. H. (eds) *Ecology and Evolution of Communication*. Ithaca, NY: Cornell University Press, pp. 79–96.

Todt, D., Hultsch, H. and Heike, D. (1979) Conditions affecting song acquisition in nightingales (*Luscinia megarhynchos*). *Z. Tierpsychol.* **51**, 23–25.

Wendtlandt, S. and Todt, D. (1995) Ontogeny of time structure in the nightingale song. *Proc. 14. IBAC, Potsdam*, p. 46.

Wistel-Wozniak, A. and Hultsch, H. (1993) Konstante und altersabhängig veränderte Gesangsmerkmale bei handaufgezogenen Nachtigallen. *Verh. Dtsch. Zool. Ges.* **86**, 281.

Wolffgramm, J. and Todt, D. (1982) Pattern and time specificity in vocal responses of Blackbirds, *Turdus merula*. *Behavior* **81**, 264–286.

11

Songbird Song Repertoires: an Ethological Approach to Studying Cognition

Donald E. Kroodsma and Bruce E. Byers

Department of Biology, University of Massachusetts, Amherst, MA 01003, USA

Introduction

In our studies of the singing behavior of song birds, our goal is to understand song repertoires at as many levels of explanation as possible. We want to understand how a bird acquires its songs (ontogeny), how the neural and endocrine systems enable a bird to learn and produce those songs (mechanism), how repertoires are used to influence fitness (function, or current utility), and how repertoires have been modified to match particular life histories (evolution). Our four-part approach has been decidedly ethological (Tinbergen, 1963).

Perhaps because of our ethological bias, the word 'cognition' has not been part of our everyday vocabulary. We know, however, that birds can remember, categorize, discriminate and even recognize number (Pepperberg, 1991; Wiley, 1994; Horn and Falls, 1996). We often implicitly assume the presence of cognitive mechanisms that are required to support our explanations of function. Our informal conversations are also replete with language that implies cognition. We observe that the birds are behaving *as if* they have desires, intentions, goals and emotions, and these 'as if' attributions often help clarify our descriptions of behavioral function. Our ultimate goal is really

ANIMAL COGNITION IN NATURE
ISBN 0-12-077030-X

to understand how the avian mind works; perhaps most of all we would love to know what mental processes occur in our birds' brains as they use vocal communication to establish their social relationships. We believe that Griffin (1992) is correct, that the study of communication will provide a window on the minds of our birds.

We are thus wholeheartedly interested in cognition and animal intelligence (*sensu* Kamil, 1994; this volume), but our approach is not the traditional one of the laboratory psychologist. Rather, our approach is ethological and ecological, born and nourished out of doors. We are fascinated by how song birds in nature acquire information about vocal signals, how they use memory to store those signals, and how they decide to use those memories either minutes or a year later. Furthermore, we relish what we can learn from different song bird evolutionary lineages; we are fascinated by how ancestral mental processes are modified over evolutionary time so that they can succeed in the context of a particular life history (i.e. cognitive ecology; R. Dukas, personal communication). In the form of different song bird species, literally thousands of cognitive, evolutionary designs lie before us, just begging to be described. In this ethological and ecological approach to studying cognition, we find tremendous opportunities.

Using this approach, we here focus on two groups that illustrate particularly well the complex vocal communication systems that have evolved among song birds. Male Marsh Wrens (*Cistothorus palustris*), especially in western North America, have repertoires of 100–200 different songs, all of which are learned from other males; neighbors race through their song repertoires, interacting with each other in fascinating ways (Verner, 1976). Comparisons with other *Cistothorus* wrens help us to appreciate how specialized their signaling systems are (Kroodsma, 1996). Our second example is the paruline warblers, with a focus on the Chestnut-sided Warbler (*Dendroica pensylvanica*). These warblers have smaller repertoires than do the wrens, but warbler repertoires are specialized into two categories, with one category used primarily with males and the other more with females (Spector, 1992). Particularly fascinating to us are how these warblers learn their songs, why they have song repertoires that are partitioned into two categories and what 'games' they play as they use these songs to interact with each other.

For each species, we first provide a brief account of the basic natural history that illustrates several aspects of what we find so fascinating about each system. We then address function and evolution, and ontogeny and mechanism; we conclude each section by comparing behaviors of close relatives. Last, we list several other examples of song bird communication that offer excellent opportunities for understanding how avian minds grapple with the day-to-day negotiations in social networks.

The Marsh Wren

Natural history

The Marsh Wrens at Turnbull National Wildlife Refuge, just outside Spokane, Washington, are typical of western wrens (Verner, 1965a,b, 1976; Kroodsma and Verner, 1997). Males defend small territories (about 0.05–0.06 hectares) in the cattail fringe around the small lakes. At dawn's first light, males begin to sing, perhaps at the rate of 10 songs/minute, but as more and more males interact, rates escalate, up to 25 songs/minute. Each male delivers song after song, each one different from the preceding one. Careful analysis of tape recordings reveals that each male has over 100 different song types in his repertoire and that he sings them in a fairly predictable sequence. Thus, after 5–6 minutes, he begins to repeat himself. To a human listener, the overall vocal display seems extraordinarily energetic as the male presents an enormous variety of songs.

Each of these energetic vocal displays by a male is part of a larger community affair (see Fig. 11.1). Males are clearly listening to each other, because neighbors tend to alternate songs, or take turns, so that they either do not interfere with each other or can take note of what the other is singing. Sometimes two neighbors engage one another and exchange songs, each racing through his repertoire, but each in step with the other so that, over a period of 15–30 seconds, a sequence of 5–10 songs is exchanged, A for A (i.e. males countersing with the same type 'A' song), B for B, with one male echoing the other up to ten times in a row. At other times, it is clear that several males within earshot are engaging in these interactions, with multiple males using the same song types at the same time. Clearly each male has learned the song types and sequences from other males in the neighborhood, and, as he sings, he is aware of which songs his neighbors are using and is capable of matching his neighbors, song for song, in these vocal displays.

Function and evolution

Questions on these subjects abound! Matched countersinging requires a leader and a follower (Fig. 11.2a), and in these vocal duels, who leads and who follows? Who plays which role? Does age, dominance or some other factor dictate the roles? Do roles reverse and, if so, when? Does a male actively choose to follow or not to follow? Just how complex is the information-processing algorithm required to interact with these songs? Can simple rules describe the roles that males take in these interactions or are far more complex rules required? How much do males weigh (i.e. think about) past encounters, current situations and future opportunities as they engage one another? Can they deceive or cheat in these exchanges? And, of course, what is the function of the exchange? What is being negotiated

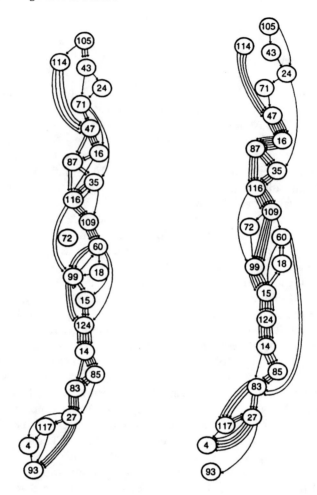

Fig. 11.1   Representative transition flow diagrams of song types from two Marsh Wren males at Turnbull National Wildlife Refuge, E. Washington, showing a highly regular pattern of song-type sequences [on the left is male 5 in Fig. 11, and on the right male 2 in Fig. 12 of Verner (1976)]. Each circled number (ranging from 1 to 127 in the original figures) designates a song type found in the repertoires of six males studied in the Turnbull population. Each arrow designates one transition. Multiple arrows between song types reveal favorite sequences, and a comparison of the two transition flow diagrams shows how neighboring males use their shared, learned song types in similar sequences, often as they countersing with each other. After Verner (1976); from Kroodsma and Verner (1997), reprinted with permission of Birds of North America.

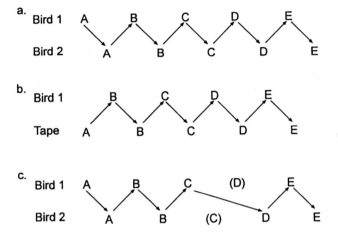

Fig. 11.2 Matched countersinging by Marsh Wrens. (a) Bird 1 leads and bird 2 follows in this stylized sequence of matched countersinging. (Time runs from left to right.) (b) Certain song sequences are commonly used within a population, and Verner (1976) discovered that a resident territorial male typically anticipates the next song and sings it in advance of a sequence played from a tape recorder. (c) If a follower (e.g. bird 2) skips a song (song C) in an expected sequence, the leader (here bird 1) becomes a follower, unless he also skips one or more songs; such adjustments suggest that males maneuver for leader roles, or perhaps to avoid follower roles (Kroodsma, 1979).

during this matched countersinging (Smith, 1977)? Do the males engage one another solely for territorial rights, which give indirect access to females who might choose males based on the quality of their territory, or do females listen directly and make mating decisions based on what they hear? Exactly how is fitness related to what these males are doing?

What we know so far

Over 20 years ago, Verner (1976) discovered that, using a tape recorder and loudspeaker, he could countersing with the wrens in his eastern Washington population (Fig. 11.2b). By playing a commonly used sequence of songs in the center of a territory, Verner found that the resident male often matched the recorder, song for song, up to nine times in a row. Intriguingly, however, the resident male typically led the interaction: he anticipated the next song type from the tape recorder and sang that type in advance of the recorder. The resident male was thus the leader in the duel, and the simulated intruding male the follower.

A laboratory experiment provides some additional support for the hypothesis of a dominant leader and subordinate follower (Fig. 11.2c; Kroodsma, 1979). Two males from a New York population were trained with a reduced repertoire of nine song types (50 is more typical for this population) that were presented in a consistent sequence. During solo singing, each male tended to sing the same sequence of songs that he had heard from the tutor tape. When both birds were singing, however, their interactions affected their song sequences. Bird B was routinely the follower in the countersinging sequences, with A singing a type and B echoing that type. If B did not match but instead skipped one song in the sequence, bird A then had a choice. If he ignored bird B and continued singing his usual sequence, he would become the follower, with bird B the leader. Alternatively, bird A could avoid the follower role by also skipping at least one song in the sequence. Bird A seemed to choose the nonfollower role actively, advancing in the song sequence so that he matched bird B no more often than expected by chance. On one occasion when songs of bird B were amplified, bird A matched B's songs more often than on any other occasion. Perhaps not coincidentally, bird A was the healthier of the two birds; he had completed his song development earlier than bird B and was dominant in physical interactions.

These glimpses from the field and the laboratory suggest the potential for complex countersinging gamesmanship. Data from both sources suggest that dominant birds lead and subordinate birds follow. The laboratory data suggest a maneuvering for position, that choice of song by one bird influences the choice by the other and that who sings what must have some significance.

What to do next

We would like to know more about how Marsh Wrens process signals from their neighbors and choose an appropriate response. We see opportunities to study complex interactions that encode important information about status and current or future behavior. We stop short, however, because we really do not know what the birds are doing (Table 11.1).

Before addressing some of the most intriguing questions, we realize that we must return to the field (see also Smith, 1991). Throughout a season, from the time of first arrival of the males to when they fall silent in July or August, we must *describe* how males use their large song repertoires to interact with each other. What are the favored song sequences when a male sings without the influence of neighbors, and how does singing of neighbors influence the choice of the next song to be delivered? When and under what circumstances do males match one another or avoid matching one another? How are signals varied in other ways to encode additional information? To study these phenomena, we must know our birds well. It is best if the birds are faithful to a site and restrict their activities to a relatively small area throughout their adult lives, so that individuals can be identified and their life histories known. Only then can we evaluate the importance of factors such as age, prior experiences and familiarity with neighbors. Such a field study is a tall order but fundamentally important.

Table 11.1 A checklist for understanding the function of song repertoires (or other aspects of communication). To begin, one must describe the behavior and its use. Eventually, one must manipulate and experiment in an attempt to identify cause-and-·effect relationships.

1. Describe the behavior throughout the season
2. Document how the behavior is correlated with fitness
3. Use interactive playback to study how birds use behaviors
4. Assess cognitive constraints to determine limits of learning and memory
5. Manipulate and experiment to determine cause and effect

In our descriptive efforts, we would pay special attention to rare events, because countersinging during such events could be disproportionately important and informative. During periods of territorial instability, for example, vocal exchanges seem especially intense. Territorial stability could be experimentally reduced by removing a male from his territory, thereby creating a situation in which new social relationships must be established as males vie for ownership of the vacated territory. Manipulating territorial boundaries can thus create a situation in which countersinging could be profitably studied.

Included in these descriptions must be a thorough understanding of how various countersinging behaviors correlate with mating success. Birds (and other animals) use vocalizations to manage their social environments for personal fitness gains (Smith, 1977). Who or what is being managed, however, and for what purpose? As males countersing, we assume they are negotiating a relationship with each other, which in turn probably dictates who owns which part of the marsh. Females probably listen directly to these counter-singing duels, though they are also undoubtedly capable of evaluating the quality of territories that males hold. So, directly or indirectly, the singing must be about mating opportunities.

We must also describe how birds respond to selected playback signals. Interactive playbacks can be a powerful means for exploring how the wrens choose their countersinging roles (Nielson and Vehrencamp, 1995; Smith, 1996; McGregor and Dabelsteen, 1996). The large repertoires of Marsh Wrens represent a challenge, because intelligent interactions with the birds will require that we recognize which of the 100+ song types the bird has just sung. Nevertheless, with practice, a good listener can learn to recognize a number of especially distinctive songs, even from a repertoire of 100–200 songs, and interactive playbacks will be especially feasible as computers are programmed to recognize song types in large repertoires.

Fundamental to all of these efforts is knowing the memory capacity of both the male and female wrens. As demonstrated by their response to playbacks, males have a remarkable ability to memorize and recall each element in their large vocabularies. Can they also discriminate subtle nuances of each song type from different neighbors, so that they can identify their neighbors based on any one of their hundred or so songs (Stoddard *et al.*, 1992; Stoddard, 1996)? With 3–4 neighbors, identifying neighbors on the basis of a single song would require memorizing 300–400 songs, but work with males of other species with simpler song repertoires suggests that such cognitive abilities might not be unreasonable (Stoddard, 1989; Stoddard *et al.*, 1992). The memory capacity of the nonsinging female is also important. Understanding the abilities of both males and females, as can be explored in standard laboratory tests of cognitive psychologists, would help us understand the potential function(s) of these large repertoires and their use.

Well-executed field descriptions and interactive playbacks must be followed by additional work under more controlled conditions, either in the field or the laboratory. If correlations can be established between countersinging behaviors and the number of offspring fathered, for example, some aspect of the system needs to be manipulated so that cause-and-effect relationships can be verified (Kroodsma and Byers, 1991). In the laboratory, for example, both the repertoire size and the particular song types learned can be dictated (within limits; Kroodsma, 1979). Interactions between males that are randomly assigned to different repertoire size groups can then be staged under controlled conditions. This more controlled approach would be especially valuable for understanding the range of behaviors possible among these countersinging wrens, especially if seminaturalistic marsh habitat could be provided, with males on territories and factors such as male density and mating status controlled. A multifaceted approach, including description and interactive playback under free-ranging conditions in the field, but also including similar description and playback under a more controlled, seminaturalistic setting, would be ideal for revealing how these wrens use their large song repertoires to manage one another.

Ontogeny and mechanism

Selection acts on adult wrens, presumably favoring a fully developed communication system, appropriate for a given life history, that somehow enhances fitness. Young wrens begin working on their vocal abilities almost as soon as they leave the nest, and how a young wren acquires his adult signals and gains competence in their use is especially intriguing.

We know most about eastern Marsh Wrens. They are superb imitators. A young (eastern) male is capable of imitating Yellow Warblers (*Dendroica petechia*), Sedge Wrens (*Cistothorus platensis*) and other species, but when given a choice he prefers to imitate songs of Marsh Wrens (Kroodsma and Pickert, 1984a). He seems to learn best between days 20 and 70, but by using live tutors instead of tutor tapes that learning period can be extended to the next spring, when the bird is about a year old (Kroodsma and Pickert, 1984b).

If he hears only five song types, he will learn only those five types, but if he hears more, up to about 50, he will also learn all of those (Brenowitz *et al.*, 1995). If he hears fewer than five, he may improvise a larger repertoire, as if he knows he needs more. He attends to the sequence of songs that he hears, too, and faithfully favors the sequence he learned from his tutors (Kroodsma, 1979). If he hears nothing appropriate to imitate, he will delay his learning period, but eventually improvise 15–20 odd songs that only vaguely resemble normal songs. Although day length at hatching drastically affects molt and migration schedules, it has far less of an effect on the timing of the sensitive period for learning songs (Kroodsma and Pickert, 1980). Male Marsh Wrens are thus primed to learn, during either their hatching year or the next year, the songs that they will use in their interactions with other males.

Far less is known about the female. She does not sing, although if she is treated with testosterone, she delivers a burst of buzzes of roughly the appropriate duration for a song, but unlike anything a normal male would do. Because she does not learn songs and sing them, we have no convenient means to determine whether she has memorized or can recognize male songs that she heard at a particular place or time. Her knowledge of male songs could be tested, of course, using appropriate techniques in the laboratory (e.g. Stoddard *et al.*, 1992).

Many issues remain unstudied, especially in nature (Beecher, 1996). *From whom* does a young male learn? Does he concentrate on one adult tutor or does he choose the most common songs he hears, or the most common sequences? *Where* does he learn those songs relative to his natal territory and his eventual breeding territory? He is capable of learning songs while still on his father's territory, but does he disperse and, like Bewick's Wrens (*Thryomanes bewickii*; Kroodsma, 1974), reject his father's songs in favor of the songs at his future breeding location? *When* does this learning occur? Birds that hatch early in the season can disperse and still have time to learn songs during the hatching year at some distant location; some young hatch after adults have stopped singing for the year, however, and these young undoubtedly wait until the next spring to learn their songs (Kroodsma and Pickert, 1980). Also, *how much* must the young male learn? He clearly learns which songs to sing, but how does he become competent in the use of those songs (West and King, 1996)? How much does he model his behavior after other males? Exactly how these young wren minds acquire large, learned, fully functional song repertoires is, to us, one of the wonders of the natural world.

Our knowledge of how the endocrine and neural systems enable young males to learn and use songs is only fragmentary (Arnold, 1994; Brenowitz and Kroodsma, 1996). Castrating a young male marsh wren does not prevent song learning, although the reduced testosterone levels appear to prevent him from progressing from plastic to full song the next spring (Kroodsma, 1986).

Western males, which have song repertoires roughly three times the size of eastern males, also have larger neural centers than do eastern males. Within either the eastern or western wren groups, males with larger repertoires tend to have larger song control nuclei (Canady *et al.*, 1984). The size of the song control nuclei, however, apparently is not influenced by how many songs a male learns. Rather, it seems that the size of the song control nuclei with which a young bird is endowed must dictate, to some extent, the number of song types that he will be able to learn (Brenowitz *et al.*, 1995).

Overall, we find it remarkable how natural selection has modified the brains of these wrens to guide the learning, memory and use of these large song repertoires. A comparison with other *Cistothorus* wrens, discussed below, helps to place these abilities in an evolutionary context.

Evolution among *Cistothorus* wrens

We are particularly intrigued at how an ancestral cognitive ability is modified over evolutionary time to exploit a particular ecology. In different evolutionary lineages, signals are modified, repertoire sizes adjusted and styles of development change. The function(s) of signals may diverge. Mental capacities for memory and recall can be revised. The western Marsh Wren discussed above, for example, is but one extant population of several *Cistothorus* species (Monroe and Sibley, 1993). How do other *Cistothorus* populations differ from the western Marsh Wren, and how do their life history strategies seem to affect how signals are acquired and used? Perhaps we can learn more about why Marsh Wrens behave the way they do by exploring some of these other species that have solved their evolutionary problems in slightly different ways.

Ideally, when using the comparative method, one first establishes a phylogeny for the particular group and then maps the behaviors on to that phylogeny (Brooks and McLennan, 1991). Without a phylogeny for *Cistothorus* wrens (Fig. 11.3), we can at best make only selective comparisons. Among the *Cistothorus* populations, then, we compare close relatives, searching for relationships between ecology and signaling systems. The identified correlations are transformed to hypotheses that must then be tested within other groups of birds. In that spirit, we here take a brief glimpse of the evolutionary alternatives among *Cistothorus* communication systems.

Density, mating system and complexity of vocal behavior

We compare first the eastern and western Marsh Wrens (Table 11.2). The Marsh Wren, as described in field guides, occurs from the Atlantic to the Pacific; in reality, however, this one 'species' comprises two evolutionary groups, an eastern and a western form. These two sister taxa were separated from each other during Pleistocene glaciations, and the ranges of these two groups now meet in the central Great Plains (Kroodsma, 1989). In Sas-

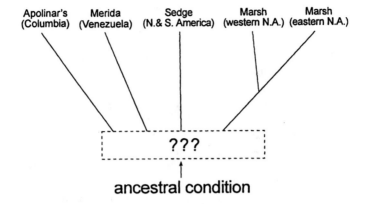

Fig. 11.3 The vocal behaviors of *Cistothorus* wrens must be mapped on to a phylogeny. Four species are currently recognized. The Marsh Wren (*C. palustris*) consists of a western and an eastern group, each of which probably warrants species status (Kroodsma, 1989). The Apolinar's Wren (*C. apolinarae*, in Columbia) and the Merida Wren (*C. merida*, in Venezuela) appear to be close relatives of the Sedge Wren (*C. platensis*), which occurs throughout the Americas (Traylor, 1988). The Sedge Wren itself may consist of several species, given its regional differences in vocal behavior.

Table 11.2 The two lineages of Marsh Wrens differ from each other in vocal behavior, neural control and life histories. Among *Cistothorus* wrens, breeding density appears correlated with song repertoire size.

	Western Marsh Wren	Eastern Marsh Wren
Song repertoire size	100–200	30–60
Rate at which song types are presented	Higher	Lower
Forebrain song control centers	Larger	Smaller
Breeding density	Higher	Lower
% males polygynous	Higher	Lower

katchewan marshes the two forms often occur together and mating appears to be largely assortative.

During the period of separation, aspects of both vocal behavior and its neural control diverged markedly. Compared to eastern wrens, western wrens have larger song repertoires and race through their repertoires far more rapidly, thus presenting a far greater diversity of songs per unit time. To manage these larger repertoires, crucial song control centers in the forebrain are also much larger in western males. When young wrens of each kind are raised under identical conditions in the laboratory, the brain and behavioral differences persist: western birds develop larger song control centers, learn more songs and deliver their songs more rapidly, showing that these two wrens differ substantially in both their neural control of singing and their ability to learn and use complex signal repertoires (Canady *et al.*, 1984; Kroodsma and Canady, 1985).

Do current ecological differences between eastern and western wrens suggest a reason for these superior abilities and more frenzied singing behaviors among western wrens? No simple answers are available, in part because both eastern and western populations are themselves ecologically diverse. Furthermore, the current interglacial period has undoubtedly allowed expansion of eastern and western populations into ecological circumstances in which the current brains and behaviors did not evolve. Any attempt to match ecology with signal system is thus beset with several problems.

Our hunch, however, is that the more complex vocal behaviors among western males have evolved in response to high competition for resources, both territories and mates. Western populations tend to have smaller territories and higher levels of polygyny than do eastern populations (see Kroodsma and Verner, 1997). Also, many western populations are non-migratory or have longer breeding seasons. Nonmigratory status means that males come to know their neighbors in relatively stable neighborhoods. With the high density, these neighboring males are countersinging with one another at close range; overall, the potential for both success and failure is higher for western males, which have a high variance in reproductive success among males. With the stakes high, the vocal behaviors by which males acquire and defend territories and mates have also escalated.

If this evolutionary scenario for Marsh Wrens is correct, one would then predict that, among *Cistothorus* wrens, a monogamous population or species with a low density should have a relatively simple vocal communication system. A test species for this idea is the Merida Wren (*C. merida*), endemic to the high paramo of the Venezuelan Andes. Apparently monogamous, males of this species have large territories of 10 hectares or more, 100 times the size of western Marsh Wren territories. Intense vocal exchanges with neighbors are certainly not routine as they are in western Marsh Wrens (D. E. Kroodsma, R. P. Muradian and V. P. Salas, unpublished data).

The signaling system is also far simpler. Each male sings only 20–25 different songs; of all *Cistothorus* populations that have been studied so far, this repertoire size is the smallest. Each of these songs is relatively simple, too, consisting of 2–4 simple notes modulated in amplitude or frequency. Also, the style of song delivery is simplest. Unlike other *Cistothorus* wrens, each song type is repeated many times before another song type is introduced.

The simplicity of the signaling system of the Merida Wren thus supports the idea that high-density or polygynous mating systems, or both, promote evolution of complex communication systems. Data from these wrens suggest that large repertoires, a rapid delivery of highly contrasting signals and frequent vocal exchanges with neighbors must all be involved in minute-to-minute negotiations with females and other males.

Song development and population stability

Because Marsh Wrens are songbirds, we expect them to imitate (Slater, 1988; Catchpole and Slater, 1995). We also expect dialects, because dispersal from the site of learning is usually limited and dispersal of the learned songs is therefore also limited (Baker and Cunningham, 1985). These features of the communication system are routine among song birds and we begin to take them for granted. However, not all songbirds fit this pattern and the exceptions are especially helpful in understanding how evolution has shaped songbird communication systems to match particular ecologies.

When a mixed group of young Marsh and Sedge Wrens from North America was presented with the same learning task in the laboratory, the outcomes were remarkably different (Kroodsma and Verner, 1978; Kroodsma and Pickert, 1984a). The training tape consisted of a mixture of pure Marsh and Sedge Wren songs, combinations of their songs and songs of a few other species, too. As expected, the Marsh Wrens imitated, producing good copies of many songs from the tape. In contrast, Sedge Wrens imitated little, if anything! Rather, they improvised and invented, generating a considerable repertoire of songs that seemed fairly normal. Although the Sedge Wrens did learn some from each other, suggesting that social tutoring might increase the amount of imitation, most songs of each individual's repertoire (about 80%) were unique to that individual. The brains of these two closely related, *Cistothorus* wrens have thus been organized very differently: one imitates, the other improvises.

How might the communication systems of these two wrens match their ecologies? The Marsh Wren inhabits wet marshes with standing water, the Sedge Wren moist meadows to drier upland habitat. In their overall breeding biology, the two species are similar in many ways. Each is polygynous (some populations more than others) and each occurs in relatively high density in habitats with relatively few other species. Also, repertoire sizes for males of both species are relatively large, ranging from 50 to 150 or even 200 per male (Kroodsma, 1977).

Perhaps the difference in song development is a consequence of the seminomadic population movements of the North American Sedge Wren (Bedell, 1996; see Fig. 11.4). Sedge Wrens are known for their unpredictability throughout their geographic range. All breeding populations are migratory and appear to be opportunistic, taking advantage of appropriate habitat where it exists, as available habitat depends on unpredictable rainfall. Males on adjacent territories during one part of the breeding season may never see

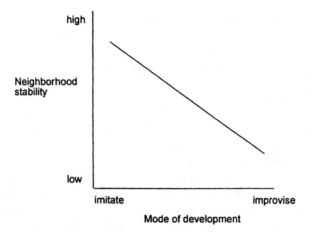

Fig. 11.4 A proposed relationship between the style of song development and population biology, as suggested by *Cistothorus* wrens. If neighborhoods are stable, so that neighboring males countersing with the same individuals over most of their lifetime, imitation of the neighbors' songs is favored; if, however, neighborhoods are not stable, and males are somewhat nomadic, then song improvisation is favored.

each other again. Population movements have not been studied in detail, but it is possible that males 1000 km apart one year could be neighbors the next. In contrast, site fidelity in most populations of the Marsh Wren is far greater (Verner, 1971; Kroodsma and Verner, 1997).

The strategy of Sedge Wren song development seems appropriate for these population movements. By improvising large repertoires of unique but species-typical songs, males increase individual variation in songs; by so doing, they decrease the amount of geographic variation in the songs. In an initial survey, for example, we could find no difference in the degree of song sharing among neighbors and more distant individuals (Kroodsma and Verner, 1978). The style of song development thus seems to guarantee that males and females, regardless of their natal area and regardless of where they acquired their songs, will share a common vocal code.

This scenario appears consistent with our current data but we would like to know more. We would like to understand Sedge Wren song development better and how it differs from that of Marsh Wrens. Vocal signals in nature are acquired in a rich social milieu but those in the laboratory are acquired in an impoverished environment. By enhancing the social environment, perhaps we can find conditions under which Sedge Wrens will imitate more. We would also like to know more about population movements of these Sedge Wrens. How site faithful are male and female wrens in different habitats throughout their range? Perhaps the amount of movement can be detected indirectly, by surveying the genetic structure of populations (Avise *et al.*, 1987).

If the style of song development and population biology are truly related in this fashion, then the nonmigratory, resident Central and South American populations of the Sedge Wren offer an intriguing test case. Based on distributional maps and migratory habits (or the lack thereof), we believe that many of these populations are well isolated from each other, and especially from the North American population (Traylor, 1988). The distribution of song forms also suggests isolation: songs are similar throughout the North American population (Kroodsma and Verner, 1978) and other unique song forms in other regions suggest other isolated populations (D. E. Kroodsma, unpublished data).

Male Sedge Wrens in resident populations might therefore be expected to imitate, thus behaving more like Marsh Wrens than like their conspecific Sedge Wrens in North America. Preliminary data (D. E. Kroodsma, unpublished data) show that song sharing is high among neighbors in certain Sedge Wren populations, thus confirming the importance of song imitation. In Brasilia National Park, Brazil, two males were recorded countersinging in Marsh Wren-style with one another, using three song types to match each other ten songs in a row, thus revealing that they learn their songs from each other. Males in Costa Rica, Argentina, and the Falkland Islands also share many song types with their neighbors and such sharing with large repertoires can be accomplished only through song imitation. All three of these populations are believed to be resident, with little dispersal or population movement.

These selective comparisons are intriguing and warrant further testing of the proposed relationship between the style of song development and site fidelity. Other species, especially those with seminomadic population movements, need study. The Eastern Towhee (*Pipilo erythrophthalmus*) may also be a good test case (Ewert and Kroodsma, 1994). In Florida, resident birds in stable neighborhoods imitate each other and share large portions of their song repertoire with each other. In migratory birds of New England, however, repertoires are smaller and song sharing is much reduced. Perhaps the Florida towhees are better at imitating precise details of songs, and the New England towhees are more prone to improvise. Have the minds of the ancestral towhee been adapted so that signals are acquired in a way that maximizes their ability to manage females and other males in local neighborhoods of differing stability?

Overview

These vignettes reveal striking differences in song development, song repertoire size, style of song delivery and extent of microgeographic variation among *Cistothorus* wrens. The ancestral *Cistothorus* communication system has clearly been modified in various ways. We assume that natural selection has optimized the management potential for these communication systems in diverse life histories, and that selection has led to the current differences among populations and species. We emphasize that hypotheses developed from these wren species must be tested within other song bird groups.

Other song bird groups provide other kinds of opportunities for understanding how communication systems have been modified over evolutionary time. The paruline warblers of North America, featured in the next section, provide such an opportunity. In contrast to the wrens, which have developed large song repertoires of multipurpose songs, these warblers have developed two-parted song repertoires, with particular songs used in particular contexts.

The Chestnut-sided Warbler

Natural history

In Savoy State Forest, high in the Berkshire hills of western Massachusetts, dense populations of Chestnut-sided Warblers inhabit old fields, forest clearings and powerline rights-of-way. At about 4.30 on a typical June morning, the males begin their singing day. The singing starts with a few tentative warbles, but the pace gradually quickens until each male repeats his song perhaps every 5 seconds. During the short gap between songs, each male utters staccato bursts of chip notes. Territories are small, so each male can hear three to four other Chestnut-sided Warblers on nearby territories. Neighbors are sometimes singing within a few meters of one another. The combination of tightly packed birds, rapid singing and constant chipping creates an impression of frenzy; the birds seem to devote every iota of energy to their dawn outburst.

After about 40 minutes of this intense dawn performance, one male abruptly switches to a different kind of song, a song so different that an unsuspecting observer might mistake it as coming from a different species. Instead of the chipping and warbling sounds that he has been repeating over and over since 4.30 am, he now sings the more familiar 'please, please, pleased to *meet*cha' that field guides describe. Within minutes, as if by mutual agreement, all of the other Chestnut-sided Warblers within earshot have also shifted to the new song type. The dawn frenzy is over, and singing rates decrease as the males mix bouts of singing with their daily routines of foraging and patrolling their territories.

Singing persists throughout the day and each male uses both kinds of songs as he goes about his business. Conformity has broken down, however. At any given time, some individuals are singing the 'dawn' songs but others are singing the 'field guide' songs. None the less, a given bird's choice of song is not random. Instead, as careful listening and observation have revealed, the birds are singing according to a pattern or set of rules that divides their song repertoires into two parts.

Function and evolution

The daily singing pattern of the Chestnut-sided Warbler raises a number of questions. Why do the males sing two different kinds of songs? What does it mean to listening birds when a singer switches from one type to another? Are the brains of Chestnut-sided Warblers in some way specialized for acquiring and processing two different kinds of signals? More generally, what is the purpose of the idiosyncratic singing patterns of Chestnut-sided Warblers? How was this function shaped by natural selection?

What we know so far

Like Marsh Wrens, each Chestnut-sided Warbler has a repertoire of different song types, but the repertoires are much smaller: 3–12 song types per bird. The warblers also use their repertoires in a distinctly different manner. Instead of a wren's rapid switching among a large variety of song types, a warbler usually repeats a single song type over and over for long periods. Moreover, this repeated song is usually selected from among only two or three predominant types. The other types in the warbler's repertoire are sung only rarely. Thus, it takes a few months of daily listening to hear all of a Chestnut-sided Warbler's songs, and each male essentially hides most of his song repertoire (Byers, 1995).

A more readily apparent aspect of Chestnut-sided Warbler repertoires is that they include two distinctly different kinds of songs: the warbled unaccented-ending (UE) songs heard at dawn and the distinctive accented-ending (AE) songs that occur at the close of the dawn bout (Ficken and Ficken, 1965; Lein, 1978). When a bird sings a UE or an AE song, it reveals information about its social situation and impending behavior. On the basis of song category alone, a human listener can determine if a bird is mated, whether and in what direction the bird is likely to move, if the bird is likely to interact with a female or with another male, if the bird is near the center or near the edge of its territory, and if the bird is near its mate or one of its male neighbors. Each song category is correlated with a different set of behavioral contexts, so a singer's choice of song category enables any listener to infer the singer's social circumstances and predict his behavior (Byers, 1996a).

Among the different social and behavioral circumstances that are associated with the two Chestnut-sided Warbler song categories, many show an interesting gender bias. AE songs are preferentially sung by unmated males, by males in close proximity to their mates and by birds who are about

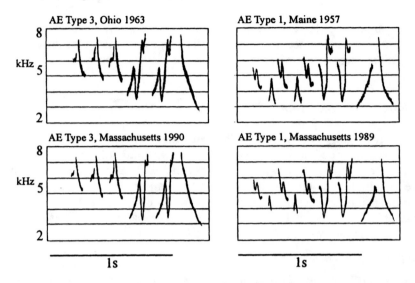

Fig. 11.5 Chestnut-sided Warbler accented-ending (AE) songs show extraordinary stereotypy over large distances and long time periods. Illustrated are examples of two of the five known AE song types, type 3 in the left column and type 1 in the right column.

to chase a female. UE songs are preferentially sung by males in close proximity to other males, by males who are close to a territorial border and by males who are about to fight with other males. Overall, AE singing appears to be specialized for male–female communication; UE singing functions in male–male communication.

AE and UE songs differ not only in what information they contain but also in their patterns of variation in form. AE songs are extraordinarily stereotyped (Fig. 11.5). Any AE song recorded across the range of the species will be one of only five different types. UE songs, however, vary considerably over geographic distance. UE and AE songs also differ in how they are shared among birds in a local neighborhood. AE song types appear to be distributed among individuals in a random manner. In contrast, the UE repertoires of territorial neighbors overlap considerably, so that UE song types are likely to be shared by nearby birds (Byers, 1996b).

The sharp contrast between the highly stereotyped form of AE songs and the variable form of UE songs suggests that each kind of signal is optimized for a different set of functions. Stereotyped, redundant signals are useful because they reduce signal ambiguity and minimize errors in signal detection (Wiley, 1983). In addition, a highly stereotyped signal provides a fixed, readily identifiable standard against which to distinguish differences in phenotypic quality among signalers (Zahavi, 1980). Stereotyped signals, however, have only limited potential for encoding information. Variable signals are much better for encoding a number of different messages, such as indicators of short-term changes in moment-to-moment behavior. Such variable signals are therefore the most effective vehicle for the numerous, rapidly changing messages of social negotiation. So, signals are under selection pressure to be both stereotyped *and* variable (Morris, 1957). One viable solution to this evolutionary conundrum is to evolve a partitioned signal repertoire. In partitioned repertoires, each signal category can evolve independently, free from the evolutionary compromises that would be required to serve both kinds of functions with a single kind of signal.

The preferential use of AE songs during male–female interactions and the corresponding bias towards UE songs in male–male interactions suggest to us that the distinction between Chestnut-sided Warbler AE and UE songs arose because selective forces were partitioned along sexual lines. Females, who choose mates from among singing, territorial males, are likely to benefit from rapid, accurate assessment of male phenotypic quality. Female choice may thus serve to enforce AE song stereotypy, which facilitates comparisons among males. Male reproductive success is, however, also influenced by contests among males for territories (and, therefore, access to females). These contests have probably generated selection for variable and flexible singing. UE songs, with their wide diversity of forms and plasticity sufficient to enable song-type sharing among neighbors, may represent the outcome of this intrasexual component of selection.

What to do next

Our path to a better understanding of Chestnut-sided Warbler song function will in many respects parallel our approach to the Marsh Wren. As with the wrens, we begin by recognizing that we cannot explain a communication system until it is adequately described. Even though we have spent thousands of hours observing and recording Chestnut-sided Warblers, we have only just begun the process of fully documenting their singing behavior. We need to know more details about how songs are used in male–male and male–female interactions, and about the connection between variability in singing and variability in male fitness. We must also extend our model of song use to encompass information that is encoded in signal variation at levels finer than that of song category. Song category actually sits at the top of a hierarchy of signal variation. Within each song category, each bird has multiple song types, some predominant and others rare. Additional dimensions of variability are nested within each song type. These dimensions include song amplitude (each type can be sung along a continuum from very soft to very loud); song length (each type can be uttered in full or in varying degrees of completeness); and song frequency (other parulines are known to shift the frequency at which a particular type is sung). The information-encoding potential of these additional kinds of variability could be revealed by a model-building process similar to the one we performed at the level of song category.

Behavioral description is necessary but not sufficient to evaluate function. We must also learn how receivers respond to songs; we need to know how the signals actually *work*. If, for example, we find that male reproductive success is correlated with particular aspects of song variability, we must next ask which of those aspects actually affect fitness by affecting the outcomes of social interactions. The only way to answer this question is to 'ask' the birds how they respond to different aspects of song variability. As with the Marsh Wren, well-designed, preferably interactive playback experiments are the most practical and effective method for testing receiver responses.

Receiver responses are often difficult to interpret because we do not know the cognitive constraints on receivers. For example, we have no idea of the degree to which the cognitive algorithms of a Chestnut-sided Warbler can match the performance of our statistical testing algorithms, which revealed that many different kinds of information are simultaneously encoded in song category. We do not know if the birds can make the interpretive adjustments that our multivariate models make (e.g. a UE song at dawn means something different from a UE song at noon; an AE song at a territorial border is different from an AE song in the territory center). Similarly, we cannot easily determine which dimensions of song variability are responsible for an observed response of a receiver. If we knew more about what kind of information warbler receivers can remember and what signal components they can discriminate, we would know more about limits on the range of possible meanings to receivers. We would be able to limit our search for the functionally important aspects of song repertoires to those that can actually be perceived, remembered and discriminated by the birds.

For example, one of the most puzzling aspects of Chestnut-sided Warbler repertoires is the rarity with which most songs in a male's repertoire are uttered. The standard hypotheses for repertoire function are precluded if repertoires are not normally revealed to listeners. One can develop a number of alternative hypotheses to explain the persistence of 'hidden' repertoires, but it would be much easier to distinguish among them if we knew more about how receivers perceived rare songs. Are Chestnut-sided Warblers capable of remembering rarely heard songs? If so, can they also remember the identity of the individual whose repertoire contains the rare song? If this kind of memory is *not* part of the bird's cognitive ability, then explanations involving song or repertoire matching (e.g. Beecher *et al.*, 1996) would be much less viable. We might then ask whether the message of a rare song is related simply to its rarity, i.e. its status as a novel or surprising vocalization. The plausibility of this class of explanations could be tested by experiments to determine if Chestnut-sided Warblers can distinguish between 'routine' and novel sounds associated with a particular source.

Ontogeny and mechanism

The extreme stereotypy of AE songs over long stretches of time and geographic distance presents an intriguing developmental puzzle. Given the typical plasticity of song bird song development, how are the same AE song forms passed with little or no modification from generation to generation? How can a young Chestnut-sided Warbler in Massachusetts during the 1990s acquire the exact same song as did a bird in Ohio during the 1950s? A fixed (no external song models required) developmental program for AE songs would be an appealing explanation but does not apply; a Chestnut-sided Warbler that hears no adult songs during its hatch year will not grow up to sing normal, species-typical songs. Still, AE songs are in some sense more easily learned than are UE songs. In the laboratory, hand-reared birds learn UE songs only if they are sung by visible, live adults, but these same birds can imitate AE songs that they hear only from loudspeakers (Byers and Kroodsma, 1992). So, young birds seem somehow predisposed to imitate AE (but not UE) songs with a minimal stimulus and are therefore more likely to acquire the AE portion of their repertoires early in life.

The mechanism of cultural transmission for AE and UE songs remains unknown. How does a hatch-year bird know, for example, that its AE songs must conform to some species-wide standard, a cultural tradition maintained from generation to generation over broad geographic expanses? How does it know that UE songs are exempt from those standards, and that cultural traditions of UE songs are transmitted only within specific locales? Is the predisposition for precise imitation of AE songs somehow in place at birth and then triggered by the stimulus of hearing some feature of the stereotyped AE song form, or is AE stereotypy enforced by the responses of conspecifics to a singer's earliest vocalizations? These questions are, in essence, questions about information processing. We know, roughly, what the auditory inputs are and what the vocal outputs are. We need to know more about the nature of what occurs between those inputs and outputs, about the features that cause AE and UE song inputs to be processed differently. This general problem can be decomposed into a series of more one-dimensional questions, each of which is amenable to investigation by a series of controlled experiments.

One such question is: at exactly what temporal stage of the developmental process does the ability to discriminate between AE and UE develop? The answer to this question would tell us something about whether the developmental split occurs on the input or output side of the learning process. If, for example, birds cannot discriminate song categories very early in life, then it would be less likely that the two kinds of inputs enter different developmental channels, and subsequent developmental investigation could focus on processes that modify vocal outputs. An effective experimental approach to isolating the onset of discrimination ability might involve a playback protocol that tests whether birds of various ages (nestling through age of first breeding) respond differentially to AE vs. UE songs.

We would also like to know if precise imitation of AE songs is triggered by any particular embedded feature of AE songs. The answer to this question would tell us something about whether the developmental split is tied to an endogenous program that is triggered by a predictably occurring audio input. An effective experimental approach might involve tutoring hand-reared birds with artificial songs in which various potential 'trigger' sounds (drawn from AE songs) were embedded. If any embedded trigger sound truly plays a role in fixing AE song development, we would expect that birds would imitate any altered songs containing it.

The persistence of AE stereotypy is remarkable, but even more remarkable is that the narrowly constrained development of AE songs takes place within a developmental system that simultaneously permits flexible, open-ended development of UE songs. Development of these songs is sufficiently flexible that birds are able to match the idiosyncratic song forms of nearby birds. Territorial neighbors in the wild share distinctive UE song types, which suggests that UE repertoires are modified in response to the vocal behavior of other birds. In the laboratory, Chestnut-sided Warblers retain the ability to modify their UE songs at least into the first breeding season and have a strong tendency to copy the songs of other birds singing nearby at that time.

The flexible component of Chestnut-sided Warbler song development raises questions about the social and cognitive processes that guide the developmental 'choice' of UE songs to include in a repertoire. Exactly what kinds of social interactions determine if an individual will use a previously memorized UE song, copy a neighbor's song or improvise a new song? Must an individual be able to recall past interactions in order to distinguish between neighbors whose songs should be copied and neighbors whose songs need not be matched? Such questions seem amenable to investigation by experimental manipulation of the social environment in which development occurs.

Developing Chestnut-sided Warblers acquire not only songs but also the ability to use them to communicate. Adult males must be able to sing the appropriate song for any circumstance, and both males and females must be able quickly and accurately to decode the information contained in songs. Are these abilities learned? Must developing birds observe and interact with adults in order to discover and memorize the rules that govern the two-category communication system? Some tantalizing clues come from experimental studies of Blue-winged Warblers (*Vermivora pinus*; Kroodsma, 1988) and Yellow Warblers (*Dendroica petechia*; Spector et al., 1989). In both of these species, experimenters raised birds under tutoring regimes in which the ambient light conditions normally associated with each song category were reversed. This treatment caused corresponding reversals in the charac-

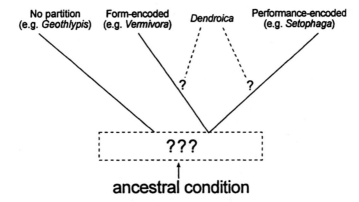

Fig. 11.6 The cognitive mechanisms associated with particular methods of song-repertoire partitioning may be too complex to evolve repeatedly within a lineage. If so, wood-warbler taxonomy will require revision to reflect three monophyletic clusters of genera: one with unpartitioned repertoires (typically with a single song type), one with form-encoded repertoire partitioning and one with performance-encoded partitioning. The genus *Dendroica* is currently problematic, as it includes both form-encoding and performance-encoding species.

teristics of songs that the experimental males later used at dawn and during the daytime. Apparently, simple associative learning plays a role in ensuring that the correct song category is used during the dawn bout. It is unlikely that all of the complexities of species-typical song use are acquired by this simple learning mechanism, but the experimental results certainly suggest that development of song usage is influenced by experiential inputs.

Evolution among paruline warblers

The comparative approach that is so promising among *Cistothorus* wrens is less immediately informative when applied to *Dendroica* wood-warblers. All *Dendroica* species thus far studied have bipartite song repertoires, as do species in the closely related paruline genera *Vermivora*, *Parula*, *Mniotilta* and *Setophaga* (reviewed in Spector, 1992). These species include both tropical and temperate region breeders, both migrant and sedentary populations, and residents of both forested and open habitats. So, the presence of partitioned repertoires within these paruline genera is not correlated with any obvious ecological parameter. Rather than being an adaptation to a particular ecological circumstance, partitioned repertoires may simply be an innovation that arose early in the evolution of this lineage. If so, partitioning may be a character that unites this cluster of genera and that distinguishes it from the parulines that make do with a single song type per individual (e.g. Common Yellowthroat, *Geothlypis trichas*).

Although bipartite repertoires are common in the Parulinae, the warblers seem to implement this communication strategy in two different ways. In some wood-warbler species (e.g. the Chestnut-sided Warbler), song categories are encoded in two distinct song forms. However, in other species (e.g. the American Redstart, *Setophaga ruticilla*), the categories are distinguished by two different patterns of performance (repeating the same song type over and over versus rapid switching from type to type; e.g. MacNally and Lemon, 1985). The differences between form-encoded and performance-encoded categories would seem to require differences in development, perception and cognitive processing. We might expect that the two encoding strategies represent two distinct variants of the ancestral wood-warbler condition, but the current taxonomic organization of the Parulinae is at odds with the idea that form-encoding and performance-encoding define two different branches of the wood-warbler genealogy. For example, *Dendroica* includes both form-encoding and performance-encoding species, but each strategy also occurs in other paruline genera (Fig. 11.6). If, as we suspect, form-encoding mental processing and performance-encoding mental processing are each too uniquely specialized to be likely to have evolved multiple times independently, it may be necessary to revise paruline taxonomy.

Other examples

The songbird literature is replete with examples of how song birds process and use vocal signals in their daily lives. We believe this kind of signal processing provides an excellent window on avian cognitive processes (see also Hausberger, 1993) and we therefore provide here just a few additional examples that we think offer excellent opportunities for exploring song bird cognition.

Dawn contests

Individuals of many species engage in intense vocal interactions at dawn, often over a period of 45–60 minutes, during the 'dawn chorus' (Staicer *et al.*, 1996). For example, during dawn singing, beginning roughly 45 minutes before sunrise, male Chipping Sparrows (*Spizella passerina*) often sit on the ground, sometimes just centimeters away from each other, delivering their songs in rapid bursts, alternating or overlapping with their immediate neighbor. These displays are rapid-fire, response and counter-response. Interactions are probably not limited to two individuals, either, because an entire community, consisting of numerous participants and eavesdroppers, can be involved (McGregor and Dabelsteen, 1996). For Chipping Sparrows, this dawn frenzy contrasts sharply with daytime singing, when males typically sing a roughly 2-second song from a high perch, often with no obvious interactions with other individuals.

For these intense dawn behaviors, we again ask who, what, when, where and why. How do males acquire their songs? What is important about the particular song acquired? How does the intensity of the dawn effort vary with ecology and mating system? What is being negotiated during these interactions (e.g. see Smith, 1996)? Do males weigh the consequences of past and current behaviors and respond in some way that maximizes future opportunities for success? If we are to understand how and why these birds engage one another intensely at dawn, this profusion of questions must yield to the methodical attack outlined in Fig. 11.2.

Polyterritoriality (and deception?)

A typical male songbird has a single territory to which he attracts a female and on which he raises a family. Unpaired males continue to sing most of the day, but males who pair typically abort their nonstop daytime singing shortly thereafter. In some species, however, an occasional male flies some distance to advertise for a female on a second territory. There he behaves as if he is unpaired, singing throughout the daytime hours (e.g. American Redstart; Secunda and Sherry, 1991). The seasonal song cycle is thus not rigid. Males must evaluate the potential for intersexual interactions and future matings, and make short-term decisions, depending on territorial context, as to how to sing.

In other contexts, too, males act as if they know what they want or are doing. A male who loses his mate (experimentally or naturally) begins his nonstop daytime singing almost immediately. A male Marsh Wren, having accommodated one female on one part of his territory, flies to a distant portion of his territory and immediately renews his singing and nest building (Verner, 1965a). The functions of these behaviors are clear: to attract another female, to raise another brood. What is unclear are the factors that the male must perceive and the mental processes involved in making decisions about how to behave.

Polyterritoriality also raises questions of deception (Stenmark *et al.*, 1988; Temrin and Arak, 1989). By their singing behavior at new locations, males seem to act as if they are unpaired, 'promising' to a female that she will receive his undivided help throughout the nesting cycle. In fact, however, he may desert her when she has committed herself (e.g. Alatalo *et al.*, 1982). What mental processes are involved in the seemingly deceptive behavioral changes?

Socially mediated, alternative vocal behaviors?

Throughout most of the North American range of the Black-capped Chickadee (*Parus atricapillus*), from Maine to British Columbia, males use a single song form, the 'fee-bee-ee' (Hailman, 1989; Kroodsma *et al.*, 1995). Each male uses his song over a range of frequencies, singing first on one frequency, then another, then another (Horn *et al.*, 1992). In the laboratory, however, each male develops a repertoire of different songs, each one sung on its own frequency, and songs vary from group to group (i.e. room to room), in dialectal fashion.

These laboratory chickadees behave much like male chickadees in outlying parts of the species' geographic range. On Martha's Vineyard, an island off the coast of Massachusetts, males typically have two different song forms, one on a high and one on a low frequency. Males on Chappaquiddick Island, just a stone's throw from Martha's Vineyard, have up to five songs apiece, all different from the Vineyard songs. Males in Oregon and Washington also have a repertoire of at least two song forms apiece. Males in these outlying regions also have dialects, so that the predominant song forms change over only short geographic distances.

How chickadees come to sing their particular songs is a mystery. Presumably, some social constraints among intermixing populations maintain the stereotyped form of the 'fee-bee-ee' from the Atlantic to the Pacific. However, why or how are these constraints released in the laboratory and in outlying populations? Black-capped Chickadee singing behavior is far more flexible than one would surmise from the stereotyped 'fee-bee-ee' of North America, and what is acceptable at any given geographic location undoubtedly depends to some extent on what neighboring males can agree upon. The processes involved may be simple, but the variability provides a small window on how the mind of the chickadee works. Just how does social behavior, intrasexual or intersexual or both, dictate these alternative mental states? Who sets the standards, and why?

Repertoire matching

During countersinging, male songbirds often match each other, singing the same song type at the same time. These interactions could be simple responses, such as 'hear A, sing A'. Games that the Marsh Wrens seem to play suggest a higher level of interplay, however, such as 'hear A, sing C, because my neighbor will sing B next, and I do not want to follow him' (see above). Song Sparrows (*Melospiza melodia*) add yet another dimension to these vocal duels (Beecher *et al.*, 1996). Because young male sparrows settle in a neighborhood and learn the songs of the adults there, neighboring territorial males tend to have the same song types in their repertoires. Male sparrows often choose to countersing not with the same song that the neighbor is singing, but rather with another song in his repertoire (Beecher, 1996). They thus match repertoires, but not necessarily particular song types. Neighboring male Chestnut-sided Warblers also 'repertoire-match'; they share many song types, but the predominant song of one bird tends to be a more rarely used song of the neighbor. This indirect matching (or repertoire matching) suggests an additional layer of complexity in how males must choose which signal with which to reply to a neighbor. The process involves 'hear A, sing D, which I know to be another song that my neighbor can sing'.

Conclusions

From our biological perspective, we believe that the greatest impediment to understanding nonhuman minds is our ignorance of how those minds are used in the real world. For every system (see Table 11.1), we desperately want thorough, solid descriptions of how birds behave, and we must know the fitness consequences of those behaviors. We must, to begin, describe carefully the behaviors of our subjects (Marler and Peters, 1982). After describing and identifying correlations, we must manipulate conditions, establishing causes and effects. Ideally, we would like to use the taped vocalizations of the birds to interact with them, so as to establish a conversation, a dialogue that will let our mind glimpse how the avian mind functions.

In thinking about issues of cognition and song bird vocal communication systems, we initially asked how studying 'cognition' might help us understand song repertoires in birds. Study of animal cognition is, after all, a rapidly developing field, one receiving much attention (e.g. Ristau, 1991a). After a brief identity crisis, we realized, however, that we were already cognitive ethologists or cognitive ecologists, or perhaps just cognitive biologists. We have been studying how avian brains grapple with acquiring signals, how they store the signals, how they control the signals, and the change in the signal-processing apparatus over evolutionary time. We have become increasingly convinced that an evolutionary approach, with a focus on understanding the diversity of communication systems among species in nature, has much to offer in our efforts to understand nonhuman cognitive abilities. Those of us in the biological tradition also have much to learn about cognition from those in more psychological and philosophical traditions. We must agree with Ristau (1991b, p. 124), that those of us who study animal minds from different viewpoints have much 'to learn from each other', and that only a multifaceted approach to studying animal cognition will be successful.

Acknowledgements

We thank Russ Balda, Al Kamil and Irene Pepperberg for their invitation and editorial efforts. Kroodsma thanks Fabian Gabelli, Roldan Muradian, Viviana Salas, Julio Sanchez, Dave Stemple, Jacques Vielliard and Robin Woods for collaborative efforts on surveying Sedge Wren vocal behaviors.

We also thank the National Science Foundation for a predoctoral fellowship for Byers and continued grant support for Kroodsma (IBN-9408520).

References

Alatalo, R. V., Lundberg, A. and Stahlbrandt, K. (1982) Why do Pied Flycatcher females mate with already-mated males? *Anim. Behav.* **30**, 585–593.

Arnold, A. P. (1994) Critical events in the development of bird song: what can neurobiology contribute to the study of the evolution of behavior? In Real, L. A. (ed.) *Behavioral Mechanisms in Evolutionary Ecology*. Chicago: University of Chicago Press, pp. 219–237.

Avise, J. C., Arnold, J., Ball, R. M., Bermingham, E., Lamb, T., Neigel, J. E., Reeb, C. A. and Saunders, N. C. (1987) Intaspecific phylogeography: The mitochondrial DNA bridge between population genetics and systematics. *Ann. Rev. Ecol. Syst.* **18**, 489–522.

Baker, M. C. and Cunningham, M. A. (1985) The biology of bird-song dialects. *Behav. Brain Sci.* **8**, 85–133.

Bedell, P. A. (1996) Evidence of dual breeding ranges for the Sedge Wren in the central Great Plains. *Wilson Bull.* **108**, 115–122.

Beecher, M. D. (1996). Birdsong learning in the laboratory and field. In Kroodsma, D. E. and Miller, E. H. (eds) *Ecology and Evolution of Acoustic Communication in Birds*. Ithaca, NY: Cornell University Press, pp. 61–78.

Beecher, M. D., Stoddard, P. K., Campbell, S. E. and Horning, C. L. (1996) Repertoire matching between neighbouring song sparrows. *Anim. Behav.* **51**, 917–923.

Brenowitz, E. A. and Kroodsma, D. E. (1996) The neuroethology of birdsong. In Kroodsma, D. E. and Miller, E. H. (eds) *Ecology and Evolution of Acoustic Communication in Birds*. Ithaca, NY: Cornell University Press, pp. 269–281.

Brenowitz, E. A., Lent, K. and Kroodsma, D. E. (1995) Brain space for learned song in birds develops independently of song learning. *J. Neurosci.* **15**, 6281– 6286.

Brooks, D. R. and McLennan, D. A. (1991) *Phylogeny, Ecology, and Behavior*. Chicago: University of Chicago Press.

Byers, B. E. (1995) Song types, repertoires, and song variability in a population of Chestnut-sided Warblers. *Condor* **97**, 390–401.

Byers, B. E. (1996a) Messages encoded in the songs of chestnut-sided warblers. *Anim. Behav.* **52**, 691–705.

Byers, B. E. (1996b) Geographic variation of song form within and among Chestnut-sided Warbler populations. *Auk* **113**, 288–299.

Byers, B. E and Kroodsma, D. E. (1992) Development of two song categories by Chestnut-sided Warblers. *Anim. Behav.* **44**, 799–810.

Canady, R. A., Kroodsma, D. E. and Nottebohm, F. (1984) Population differences in complexity of a learned skill are correlated with the brain space involved. *Proc. Natl Acad. Sci. USA* **81**, 6232–6234.

Catchpole, C. K. and Slater, P. J. B. (1995) *Bird Song. Biological Themes and Variations*. Cambridge: Cambridge University Press.

Ewert, D. N. and Kroodsma, D. E. (1994) Song sharing and repertoires among migratory and resident Rufous-sided Towhees. *Condor* **96**, 190–196.

Ficken, M. S. and Ficken, R. W. (1965) Comparative ethology of the chestnut-sided warbler, yellow warbler, and American redstart. *Wilson Bull.* **77**, 363–375.

Griffin, D. R. (1992) *Animal Minds*. Chicago: University of Chicago Press.

Hailman, J. P. (1989) The organization of major vocalizations in the Paridae. *Wilson Bull.* **101**, 305–343.

Hausberger, M. (1993) How studies on vocal communication in birds contribute to a comparative approach of cognition. *Etologia* **3**, 171–185.

Horn, A. G. and Falls, J. B. (1996) Categorization and the design of signals: the case of song repertoires. In Kroodsma, D. E. and Miller, E. H. (eds) *Ecology and Evolution of Acoustic Communication in Birds*. Ithaca, NY: Cornell University Press, pp. 121–135.

Horn, A. G., Leonard, M. L., Ratcliffe, L., Shackleton, S. A. and Weisman, R. G. (1992) Frequency variation in the songs of Black-capped Chickadees (*Parus atricapillus*). *Auk* **109**, 847–852.

Kamil, A. C. (1994) A synthetic approach to the study of animal intelligence. In Real, L. A. (ed.) *Behavioral Mechanisms in Evolutionary Ecology*. Chicago: University of Chicago Press, pp. 11–45.

Kroodsma, D. E. (1974) Song learning, dialects, and dispersal in the Bewick's Wren. *Z. Tierpsychol.* **35**, 352–380.

Kroodsma, D. E. (1977) Correlates of song organization among North American wrens. *Am. Nat.* **111**, 995–1008.

Kroodsma, D. E. (1979) Vocal dueling among male Marsh Wrens: evidence for ritualized expressions of dominance/subordinance. *Auk* **96**, 506–515.

Kroodsma, D. E. (1986) Song development by castrated Marsh Wrens. *Anim. Behav.* **34**, 1572–1575.

Kroodsma, D. E. (1988) Song types and their use: Development flexibility of the male Blue-winged Warbler. *Ethology* **79**, 235–247.

Kroodsma, D. E. (1989) Two North American song populations of the Marsh Wren reach distributional limits in the central Great Plains. *Condor* **91**, 332–340.

Kroodsma, D. E. (1996). Ecology of passerine song development. In Kroodsma, D. E. and Miller, E. H. (eds) *Ecology and Evolution of Acoustic Communication in Birds*. Ithaca, NY: Cornell University Press, pp. 3–19.

Kroodsma, D. E. and Byers, B. E. (1991) The function(s) of song. *Am. Zool.* **31**, 318–328.

Kroodsma, D. E. and Canady, R. A. (1985). Differences in repertoire size, singing behavior, and associated neuroanatomy among Marsh Wren populations have a genetic basis. *Auk* **102**, 439–446.

Kroodsma, D. E. and Pickert, R. (1980) Environmentally dependent sensitive periods for avian vocal learning. *Nature* **28**, 477–479.

Kroodsma, D. E. and Pickert, R. (1984a) Repertoire size, auditory templates, and selective vocal learning in songbirds. *Anim. Behav.* **32**, 395–399.

Kroodsma, D. E. and Pickert, R. (1984b) Sensitive phases for song learning: effects of social interaction and individual variation. *Anim. Behav.* **32**, 389–394.

Kroodsma, D. E. and Verner, J. (1978) Complex singing behaviors among *Cistothorus* wrens. *Auk* **95**, 703–716.

Kroodsma, D. E. and Verner, J. (1997) The Marsh Wren (*Cistothorus palustris*). In Poole, A. and Gill, F. (eds) *The Birds of North America*, No. 308. Philadelphia, PA: The Academy of Natural Sciences; Washington, DC: The American Ornithologists' Union.

Kroodsma, D. E., Albano, D. J., Houlihan, P. W. and Wells, J. A. (1995) Song development by Black-capped Chickadees (*Parus atricapillus*) and Carolina Chickadees (*P. carolinensis*). *Auk* **112**, 29–43.

Lein, M. R. (1978) Song variation in a population of chestnut-sided warblers (*Dendroica pensylvanica*): its nature and suggested significance. *Can. J. Zool.* **56**, 1266–1283.

MacNally, R. C. and Lemon, R. E. (1985) Repeat and serial singing modes in American redstarts (*Setophaga ruticilla*): a test of functional hypotheses. *Z. Tierpsychol.* **69**, 191–202.

Marler, P. and Peters, S. (1982) Subsong and plastic song: their role in the vocal learning process. In Kroodsma, D. E. and Miller, E. H. (eds) *Acoustic Communication in Birds*. New York: Academic Press, pp. 25–50.

McGregor, P. K. and Dabelsteen, T. (1996) Communication networks. In Kroodsma, D. E. and Miller, E. H. (eds) *Ecology and Evolution of Acoustic Communication in Birds*. Ithaca, NY: Cornell University Press, pp. 409–425.

Monroe, B. L., Jr and Sibley, C. G. (1993) *A World Checklist of Birds*. New Haven, CT: Yale University Press.

Morris, D. (1957) 'Typical intensity' and its relation to the problem of ritualization. *Behaviour* **11**, 1–12.

Nielsen, B. M. B. and Vehrencamp, S. L. (1995) Responses of Song Sparrows to song-type matching via interactive playback. *Behav. Ecol. Sociobiol.* **34**, 109–117.

Pepperberg, I. M. (1991) A communicative approach to animal cognition: a study of conceptual abilities of an African Grey Parrot. In Ristau, C. A. (ed.) *Cognitive Ethology. The Minds of Animals*. Hillsdale, NJ: Erlbaum Associates, Inc., pp. 153–186.

Ristau, C. A. (1991a) Aspects of the cognitive ethology of an injury-feigning bird, the Piping Plover. In Ristau, C. A. (ed.) *Cognitive Ethology. The Minds of Animals*. Hillsdale, NJ: Erlbaum Associates, Inc., pp. 91–126.

Ristau, C. A. (ed.) (1991b) *Cognitive Ethology. The Minds of Animals*. New York: The Rockefeller University Press.

Secunda, R. C. and T. W. Sherry (1991) Polyterritorial polygyny in the American Redstart. *Wilson Bull.* **103**, 190–203.

Slater, P. J. B. (1988) Bird song learning: causes and consequences. *Ethol. Ecol. Evol.* **1**, 19–45.

Smith, W. J. (1977) *The Behavior of Communicating*. Cambridge, MA. Harvard University Press.

Smith, W. J. (1991) Animal communication and the study of cognition. In Ristau, C. A. (ed.) *Cognitive Ethology. The Minds of Animals.* Hillsdale, NJ: Erlbaum Associates, Inc., pp. 209–230.

Smith, W. J. (1996) Using interactive playback to study how songs and singing contribute to communication and behavior. In Kroodsma, D. E. and Miller, E. H. (eds) *Ecology and Evolution of Acoustic Communication in Birds.* Ithaca, NY: Cornell University Press, pp. 377–397.

Spector, D. A. (1992) Wood-warbler song systems: a review of paruline singing behaviors. *Curr. Ornithol.* **9**, 199–238.

Spector, D. A., Mckim, L. K. and Kroodsma, D. E. (1989) Yellow Warblers are able to learn songs and situations in which to use them. *Anim. Behav.* **38**, 723–725.

Staicer, C. A., Spector, D. A. and Horn, A. G. (1996) The dawn chorus and other diel patterns in acoustic signaling. In Kroodsma, D. E. and Miller, E. H. (eds) *Ecology and Evolution of Acoustic Communication in Birds.* Ithaca, NY: Cornell University Press, pp. 426–453.

Stenmark, G., Slagsvold, T. and Lifjeld, J. T. (1988) Polygyny in the Pied Flycatcher, *Ficedula hypoleuca*: a test of the deception hypothesis. *Anim. Behav.* **36**, 1646–1657.

Stoddard, P. K. (1989) Song repertoire use and perception by male Song Sparrows (*Melospiza melodia*) in the Puget Sound region. Ph.D. dissertation, University of Washington, Seattle, WA.

Stoddard, P. K. (1996) Vocal recognition of neighbors by territorial passerines. In Kroodsma, D. E. and Miller, E. H. (eds) *Ecology and Evolution of Acoustic Communication in Birds.* Ithaca, NY: Cornell University Press, pp. 339–355.

Stoddard, P. K., Beecher, M. D., Campbell, S. E. and Horning, C. L. (1992) Song-type matching in the Song Sparrow. *Can. J. Zool.* **70**, 1440–1444.

Temrin, H. and Arak, A. (1989) Polyterritoriality and deception in passerine birds. *Trends Ecol. Evol.* **4**, 106–109.

Tinbergen, N. (1963) On aims and methods of ethology. *Z. Tierpsychol.* **20**, 410–433.

Traylor, M. A., Jr (1988) Geographic variation and evolution in South American *Cistothorus platensis* (Aves: Troglodytidae). *Fieldiana* **48**, 1–35.

Verner, J. (1965a) Breeding biology of the Long-billed Marsh Wren. *Condor* **67**, 6–30.

Verner, J. (1965b) Time budget of the male Long-billed Marsh Wren during the breeding season. *Condor* **67**, 125–139.

Verner, J. (1971) Survival and dispersal of male Long-billed Marsh Wrens. *Bird-Banding* **42**, 92–98.

Verner, J. (1976) Complex song repertoire of male Long-billed Marsh Wrens in eastern Washington. *Living Bird* **14**, 263–300.

West, M. and King, A. (1996) Eco-gen-actics: a systems approach to the ontogeny of avian communication. In Kroodsma, D. E. and Miller, E. H. (eds) *Ecology and Evolution of Communication in Birds.* Ithaca, NY: Cornell University Press, pp. 20–38.

Wiley, R. H. (1983) The evolution of communication: information and manipulation. In Halliday, T. R. and Slater, P. J. B. (eds) *Animal Behaviour*, Volume 2. Oxford: Blackwell Scientific Publications, pp. 82–113.

Wiley, R. H. (1994) Errors, exaggeration, and deception in animal communication. In Real, L. A. (ed.) *Behavioral Mechanisms in Evolutionary Ecology*. Chicago: University of Chicago Press, pp. 157–189.

Zahavi, A. (1980) Ritualization and the evolution of movement signals. *Behaviour* **72**, 77–81.

12

Causes of Avian Song: Using Neurobiology to Integrate Proximate and Ultimate Levels of Analysis

Timothy J. DeVoogd[1] and Tamás Székely[2]

[1]Department of Psychology, Uris Hall, Cornell University, Ithaca, NY 14853, USA
[2]Department of Zoology, Kossuth University, Debrecen, H-4010, Hungary

Overview

It is increasingly clear that the vocabulary and constructs of cognition can be used productively in integrating observations on behavioral interactions within and between species (Bekoff, 1995). High-order mental processes such as categorization, inference and expectation can be powerful tools for summarizing behaviors that would otherwise appear too complex for adequate description. Others in this volume (Baptista, Pepperberg) present ways in which cognitive concepts can be linked to avian vocalization. Frequently, such accounts refer back to neural or evolutionary bases for higher-order cognition. The present chapter does not discuss mental processes associated with singing, but looks instead at these prior issues – at the question of why a song bird sings.

Why does a bird sing a song? This question is not easy to answer – it is not even one question. There are elements of 'why sing a song that sounds like its species and not like another species?', of 'why sing a song that is different from other individuals of this species' and of 'why sing now and not at some other time?'. Tinbergen (1963) pointed out that 'why' questions in biology generally can be answered in four ways. The four ways relate to

ANIMAL COGNITION IN NATURE
ISBN 0-12-077030-X

aspects of the causes of behavior from mechanism and developmental course (often called proximate cause) to present function and evolutionary history (often called ultimate or evolutionary cause) (Alcock and Sherman, 1994; Krebs and Davies, 1991). Answers from one of these perspectives complement answers from others (reviewed by Mayr, 1982; Dewsbury, 1992). Behavioral biologists have pointed out that many disagreements in biology result from treating answers to different aspects of the 'why' question as if they were exclusive alternatives rather than complementary facets of knowledge (Sherman, 1988). One of the essential lessons of training in biology then is to be clear about what is being asked and answered in a 'why' question, and to keep the levels of analysis distinct. Many biologists choose to study either proximal or ultimate causes of behavior and are very careful to avoid mixing the other into their experiments.

However, in his original description, Tinbergen went further than merely describing the distinction between these levels. He pointed out that the goal of the biologist is to ask all four questions, and to try to integrate the answers. This synthesis and integration remain uncommon in biology. In this chapter, we shall discuss the question 'why does a bird sing a song' from the four perspectives of Tinbergen. We shall present a description of key behavioral findings at each of these levels of analysis together with what is known of neurobiological attributes associated with the behavior. Others have cited avian song as an example of a behavior whose cause can be viewed at multiple levels of analysis (Sherman, 1988; Krebs and Davies, 1991). We shall go further and show that neurobiological analysis is providing answers or insights in each of the four perspectives. Finally, we shall suggest that findings in neurobiology can be seen as a common currency with which to evaluate and relate the four sorts of answers. Thus, by analysis of attributes of neural connectivity and physiology, it is now possible to relate evolution of song to its implementation within an individual.

Mechanism

Song characteristics

The first way in which to answer the question 'why does a bird sing a song?' is by describing the neural mechanism for song production. This research is most easily understood in the context of patterns of behavior characterizing song production in adult birds.

There are more than 4500 oscine (song bird) species, comprising at least 870 genera in 35 families (Monroe and Sibley, 1993). Individuals in these species sing as adults; for many, the songs are an important part of the bird's behavior and are striking to human observers [many of the issues mentioned below are extensively reviewed in Kroodsma and Miller (1996)]. Consequently, singing has been casually observed throughout human history and has been systematically studied since early in this century. While there is immense variation across these species in song complexity and organization, several features are characteristic of those species that have been studied intensively. The first is that males sing more than do females. In many species, adult females do not sing at all. In others, females sing less often than males or sing a song that is much less elaborate than that of males. In some species such as canaries, adult females begin to sing if given testosterone; in others such as Zebra Finches, even this does not induce song.

The second feature of song is that it is usually produced in phase with reproduction throughout the bird's life. The pattern of song production varies with the species' pattern of reproduction. Thus, Zebra Finches, native to arid regions of Australia, sing and reproduce continually when sufficient food and humidity levels are maintained (Immelmann, 1969; Zann and Straw, 1984). In temperate latitudes where reproduction occurs in the spring, most of the singing is done in late winter and early spring, and relatively little in other seasons. Thus, canaries begin singing vigorously in winter as day length increases. They continue to sing throughout the period of reproduction in spring. They then decrease the amount of singing in late summer and fall, or stop altogether. Year after year, the cycle repeats. Typically, as singing resumes in late winter, the song is variable and unstable and resembles plastic song (a late stage of song learning in young adults). This winter phase is brief and is followed by stereotyped production of song elements for that reproductive season. In summer, as singing ceases, song may also be unstable (Nottebohm et al., 1986, 1987). For species that modify or augment their song as adults, the changes to the song most often occur between singing seasons rather than within them (Nottebohm et al., 1986; Kirn et al., 1989). In such species, the signal for resumption of song typically is increasing day length.

The third feature of song is its predictability. A song contains qualities specific to the species producing it. For example, a White-crowned Sparrow song can always be identified and distinguished from the song of a Red-winged Blackbird. Even species capable of mimicry use conspecific sounds in their songs. A song may resemble the songs of nearby conspecifics and be distinct from the songs of conspecifics in other places – subspecies of White-crowned Sparrow have been identified on the basis of their song (see Baptista et al., this volume). Typically, a song also contains qualities that are specific to the individual producing it. For some species, the individual variation consists of variation in note structure within a song whose overall structure is quite similar across conspecifics (Kroodsma, 1996). For other species, especially those with a repertoire of songs, individual variation may also be quantitative: differences between individuals in how many songs are produced (Catchpole, 1986; Hasselquist et al., 1996). For many species, song is stereotyped: it is produced with very little change throughout a singing season and may be produced without substantial change for the bird's life.

A final feature typical of song across oscines is that it is learned. Aspects of song are affected by auditory experience in every oscine species in which it has been studied. Many experiments have shown that birds often have songs that are similar to nearby conspecifics and, especially, that the songs of young birds resemble those of the older adults from which they had heard songs during development (reviewed by Kroodsma and Byers; Baptista *et al.*, this volume; Marler, 1991a). Song learning will be explored further in the section on development (below).

Neurobiology of brain regions involved in song

Nottebohm *et al.* (1976) described the major brain nuclei that control song production (Fig. 12.1). Many of the subsequent advances in relating learning and endocrine changes to neurobiology have been possible because the brain areas involved in song production are easily visualized and have relatively few major projections (song system anatomy; reviewed by Konishi, 1989; Williams, 1990b; DeVoogd, 1991). The high vocal center (HVC) is a telencephalic nucleus that receives input from the medial magnocellular nucleus of the anterior neostriatum (m-MAN), from Uva, a diencephalic structure, from NIf, a telencephalic structure, and indirectly from a high auditory center (Field L) (Kelley and Nottebohm, 1979; Nottebohm *et al.*, 1982; Vates *et al.*, 1996). In addition, several areas have recently been described that receive inputs from Field L or auditory thalamus, project to HVC, NIf or nearby areas, and seem to be involved in perception of songs of conspecifics (Chew *et al.*, 1996; Vates *et al.*, 1996, 1997). HVC projects to the robust nucleus of the archistriatum (RA) and to Area X in the lobus parolfactorius. Area X projects via the medial portion of the dorsolateral nucleus of the thalamus (DLM) to the lateral magnocellular nucleus of the anterior neostriatum (l-MAN) which projects to RA and adjacent areas (Johnson *et al.*, 1995), as well as back to Area X (Vates and Nottebohm, 1995). RA in turn projects directly and through the dorsomedial nucleus of the intercollicular complex (DM) to the caudal portion of the hypoglossal nucleus (nXIIts) and to a brainstem area involved in respiration (Wild, 1993; Vicario, 1993). Motoneurons in nXIIts innervate the syrinx. This organ, comprised of muscles and cartilage at the base of the trachea, is activated to produce song. Thus, put most basically, oscine birds sing because they have a network of brain areas that receive input from auditory areas and ultimately project to the muscles that produce the sounds of song.

If HVC or RA is lesioned bilaterally, singing ceases and never resumes (Nottebohm *et al.*, 1976). If these nuclei are stimulated while a bird is producing song, either the overall pattern of the song or the characteristics of the current note are disrupted (Vu *et al.*, 1994). Such results indicate that

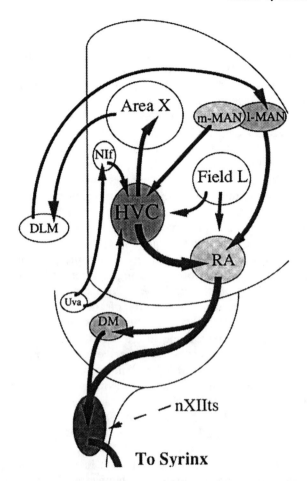

Fig. 12.1 Schematic representation of the major nuclei and projections comprising the avian song system. All nuclei occur in both hemispheres. Shading indicates relative number of cells in the nuclei that concentrate androgens. Field L is a complex auditory area that projects to areas adjacent to HVC and RA, that may be important for song perception. There appear to be two functionally distinct paths in the song system: caudal projections necessary to song production (HVC→ RA →nXIIts) and rostral projection necessary to song acquisition (HVC→ Area X→DLM→ l-MAN→ RA). Abbreviations are explained in text.

there is a caudal circuit within the song system that directly stimulates song production (HVC→ RA → nXIIts). If l-MAN or Area X is lesioned in adult males that are singing, singing continues with little change (Nottebohm *et al.*, 1976; Bottjer *et al.*, 1984). If l-MAN is lesioned in adults during a season in which they are not singing, the song is modified when singing resumes (Benton *et al.*, 1998). However, if l-MAN or Area X is lesioned in juveniles prior to song crystallization, large lasting deficits occur in subsequent song production (Bottjer *et al.*, 1984; Sohrabji *et al.*, 1990; Scharff and Nottebohm, 1991). These findings suggest that there is also a rostral circuit in the song system that may be involved in learning or song modification, but not directly in production (HVC→Area X→DLM→MAN→HVC or RA). The findings hint that the representation of a song may be distributed across the nuclei of the song system such that the different nuclei are dedicated to discrete aspects of perception or production.

Neurons in song-system nuclei are both motor and sensory. Many neurons in HVC and RA show activity correlated with aspects of the sounds being produced (McCasland, 1987; Doupe and Konishi, 1991; Lewicki, 1996). Neurons in all major nuclei including nXIIts show sound-evoked activity (Katz and Gurney, 1981; Williams and Nottebohm, 1985). Many neurons in HVC are activated by conspecific song, and some seem to be specifically activated by the bird's own song (Margoliash, 1987; Doupe and Konishi, 1991; Margoliash and Fortune, 1992), indicating that some perceptual aspects of song are transmitted throughout the song system. Why should neurons throughout the song system respond to *hearing* a song? Perhaps the bird uses these perceptions to monitor the quality of the song it is producing, or perhaps it uses the neural activity generated by its own song as the standard by which the songs of other conspecifics are evaluated.

Neurons in song-system nuclei also receive input from the endocrine system. Many in HVC, RA and MAN, and more caudally in DM and nXIIts, concentrate androgens (Arnold *et al.*, 1976; Nordeen *et al.*, 1986; Brenowitz and Arnold, 1992). There are high levels of androgen receptors in each of these sites (Harding *et al.*, 1984; Balthazart *et al.*, 1992). In addition, there are neurons in HVC, l-MAN and DM that concentrate estradiol or have estradiol receptors (K. W. Nordeen *et al.*, 1987; Gahr and Konishi, 1988; Brenowitz and Arnold, 1989). These receptors in the song system allow it to be exquisitely sensitive to endocrine changes such as those caused by changing day length.

Sex differences

One of the striking attributes of song is the general tendency for it to be produced exclusively or predominantly by males. Why is most song produced by males? – because of sex differences in neural mechanism (reviewed by Ball *et al.*, 1994; DeVoogd, 1994b; Brenowitz and Kroodsma, 1996). One of the more dramatic discoveries in the song system was the finding that there are large sexual dimorphisms in most of the song-system nuclei. These differences range from 80% (nXIIts) to 275% (HVC) larger in Nissl-stained tissue sections from male canaries than in sections from females. Sex differences in Zebra Finches are even larger – Area X cannot even be distinguished in adult female finches. In both species, other nuclei outside the song system are not dimorphic (Nottebohm and Arnold, 1976; Nottebohm, 1981; DeVoogd *et al.*, 1991). Subsequent analysis has shown that the sex differences in the volumes of song-system nuclei result from differences in their neuronal constituents. Thus, males have more neurons than females in all the major telencephalic song-system nuclei (Arnold, 1980; Gurney, 1981; Bottjer and Dignan, 1988; Kirn *et al.*, 1989). In addition, dendrites are longer and have more spines in males than in females for HVC, RA and l-MAN (DeVoogd and Nottebohm, 1981a; Nixdorf *et al.*, 1989; Wallhausser-Franke *et al.*, 1995b). Other characteristics are also dimorphic. For example, in Zebra Finches, a greater proportion of HVC and l-MAN neurons concentrate androgens in males than in females (Arnold, 1980), and the projection from HVC to RA is virtually absent in females (Konishi and Akutagawa, 1985; Williams, 1985).

Seasonality

A second attribute of song production is that it is linked to the cycles of reproduction. Why do birds sing during some seasons and not others? The answer in terms of mechanism is because of seasonal changes in endocrinology and in song-system neurobiology. Testosterone levels in males may be orders of magnitude higher at the time of reproduction than at other times (Wingfield and Farner, 1993). As indicated above, most of the song-system nuclei have receptors for gonadal steroids. In adult song birds of temperate latitudes, phasic production of song has been related to a variety of changes in song-system neurobiology as well. The overall volumes of HVC, RA, nXIIts and Area X are larger in spring than in fall in both males and females (Nottebohm, 1981; Kirn *et al.*, 1989; Brenowitz *et al.*, 1991; Smith *et al.*, 1995). This oscillation is associated with a 40% shift in the number of dendritic spines on one neuronal class in RA in male Red-winged Blackbirds (Hill and DeVoogd, 1991). While the absolute magnitude of the changes is small in females, the percentage shift is greater than in males (Kirn *et al.*, 1989). Ultrastructural studies in females have shown that the number and size of synapses, and the number of transmitter vesicles of synapses in RA and nXIIts, also vary with season (DeVoogd *et al.*, 1985; Clower *et al.*, 1989).

The major cue for the onset of regrowth in the song system appears to be increasing day length. Increased day length stimulates a huge increase in the size of the gonads and in the levels of the steroids that they produce (reviewed by Wingfield and Farner, 1993). Manipulating steroid levels in adult birds results in anatomical shifts similar to those found after a change in season or day length (reviewed by DeVoogd, 1994b). This suggests that the seasonal changes in steroid levels are the direct cause of many of the associated neural changes in the song system. Because of the speed of action and the level of control offered by laboratory manipulations, more is known about effects on song-system anatomy of direct hormonal manipulation in adult birds than about natural anatomical changes. Thus, Nottebohm (1980a) found that giving testosterone to adult female canaries results in onset of singing and an increase of more than 50% in the volumes of HVC and RA. Treating female canaries that had been ovariectomized in infancy with estradiol or dihydrotestosterone causes dendrites in RA to grow about 20% longer, to the size found in intact females. Giving testosterone to adult females ovariectomized in infancy causes singing and dendritic growth nearly to the size found in males (DeVoogd and Nottebohm, 1981b). Giving testosterone to intact females causes increases in the size of synapses and in the number of synapses in RA and nXIIts, and in the number of transmitter vesicles they contain (DeVoogd *et al.*, 1985; Clower *et al.*, 1989). This treatment also increases the weight of the female's syrinx and the level of activity of acetylcholinesterase in the syringeal muscles (Luine *et al.*, 1980). In each of these experiments, treated females begin to sing, using song-system nuclei and syringeal muscles. Co-occurrence of song and anatomical change in these experiments have made it difficult to determine cause and effect – it is possible: (1) that the new behavior is caused by neural growth that is directly or indirectly induced by the steroid; (2) that increased use of the system leads to the neural growth; or (3) that there is interaction between the two through reciprocal stimulation.

Stereotypy and learning

A third attribute of song is that it typically is constant for an individual (at least within a singing season and often over a lifetime) and distinct from other individuals. Why does a bird produce a particular song? The mechanism responsible for individual variation in song is poorly understood. Clearly, neurons in major song system nuclei are selectively responsive to particular songs and are used to generate particular aspects of the bird's own song (Margoliash and Fortune, 1992; reviewed by Margoliash *et al.*, 1994). However, neural algorithms for auditory analysis or song synthesis remain elusive. Several experiments have found neural correlates for individual differences in song that are quantitative. Nottebohm *et al.* (1981) found that the volumes of HVC and RA are greater in male canaries that produce many syllables in their songs than in males that produce few. The volume of HVC in female canaries also appears to be correlated with the number of syllables they produce when induced to sing by testosterone (Nottebohm, 1980b). Similarly, there are significant positive correlations between syllable repertoire size and HVC volume within males of two populations of Marsh Wrens (Canady *et al.*, 1984). However, in Red-winged Blackbirds, a species in which individual males may produce from four to ten song types, no significant correlations were found between repertoire size and the volumes of the major song system nuclei (Kirn *et al.*, 1989). To date, individual variation has been studied in too few species for any strong hypotheses to be proposed about why the association with gross song-system anatomy occurs in some species but not others. When differences in song-system anatomy that are related to song are found, these differences could be due to a differential genetic heritage or to a differential opportunity to learn. Recent research suggests that in Marsh Wrens, different amounts of song learning as juveniles does not affect the adult volumes of the major song-system nuclei (Brenowitz *et al.*, 1995) but does result in different numbers of dendritic spine synapses within the HVC (Airey *et al.*, 1994).

Together, these data indicate that it is possible to relate song-system neurobiology to each of the attributes of song described above, even if at this point the relations are simplistic. From the perspective of the mechanism, birds sing because they have a song system that can generate a song. Singing is done by males in the spring because males have an enhanced song system that expands and adds capacity for production and perhaps enhanced perception in response to the steroid surge induced by increasing day length. Finally, at least in some species, individuals sing more songs because they have more of the neural components needed for producing a song.

Development: how is a song put together?

Behavioral development

The second way in which to answer the question 'why does a bird sing a song?' is developmental. Briefly, a bird sings a song because the ability to form some aspects of song is genetically encoded into the development of the nervous system, and the bird learns to form other aspects of song. Both sorts of features are used in the song that the bird will produce as an adult. Extensive research has shown that there are clear stages of song acquisition and has enumerated the neural changes in the song system that are associated with each stage. Furthermore, numerous studies have described consequences of altered vocal or auditory experience during the stages of song learning. As described below, these interventions affect song-system anatomy in intriguing ways that may account for many of the capacities and limitations of song learning.

For a very long time, it has been known that song birds learn aspects of the song they produce. Typically some or all of the song that a bird produces can be related to songs that it heard as a juvenile (reviewed by Kroodsma, 1996). Thus, for example, the song of a canary is very similar to the songs of canaries it had heard and is different from the songs of canaries it did not hear (Marler and Waser, 1977; Waser and Marler, 1977). The process can be studied experimentally – juveniles of many species will learn song elements from tape recordings that are later incorporated into a song (Marler, 1970; Marler and Peters, 1982; Marler, 1990).

There are large differences between species in the optimal timing and duration of song models, the timing and content of plastic song, and the extent and form of transfer into eventual full song (reviewed by Marler, 1987; Todt and Hultsch, this volume). For example, Zebra Finches assemble fragments from several models into a single song (Williams and Staples, 1992). This song is then retained throughout adult life with little or no change in the structure or ordering of the sound elements (Price, 1979; Nordeen and Nordeen, 1992). Canaries practice a large number of syllables during plastic song. Twenty to thirty of these are retained for use in full song (Nottebohm and Nottebohm, 1978). In contrast to the Zebra Finches, the ordering of the elements in a canary's song can vary and, each year, some of the syllables in song are discarded and others are added (Nottebohm *et al.*, 1986). It remains unclear whether this change represents completely new learning (either by improvisation or by novel auditory learning), or whether the birds are selecting for production from a somewhat larger sample of songs learned and practiced as a juvenile. White-crowned Sparrows practice several songs that closely resemble song models they have heard and eventually produce a single song to which they return annually without substantial change (Marler, 1970; Baptista and Morton, 1988; Baptista *et al.*, this volume). Other species modify or augment their adult songs to such an extent that it is hard to decide whether this behavior reflects extremely sophisticated learning, improvising or deficient memory for past coordinations.

Infancy

Little is known of behavioral interactions in the first few weeks after hatching that contribute to song learning. Quite soon after hatching, young birds of both sexes make begging calls that help elicit feeding by the parents. Later, the young begin making other sorts of calls. No research has yet determined either whether these are a necessary prerequisite to eventual song production. In addition, there is no information on whether these calls are produced by the same neural network that will be used to produce song. Some species learn visual characteristics of their caretaker during this time that appear to be used later in selecting a source for song learning (Hultsch and Todt, personal communication). This suggests that, from its inception, song learning is integrated with other sensory and social cues.

Auditory song learning

In most song birds that have been studied, the auditory model on which they will base their song is learned during a sensitive period early in development. (In general, experiments reviewed below on the stages of song learning have studied males; very little research has examined whether aspects of song learning also occur in females.) In Zebra Finches, auditory learning begins around 30 days after hatching (Immelmann, 1969; Price, 1979; Clayton, 1987). Learning is subject to constraints that vary substantially between species. In many species, there is a perceptual selective process that determines how suitable an environmental sound is as a potential song component. Typically, if an acceptable song model is present and is learned, sensitivity to other subsequent song models ends. Zebra Finches that have been exposed to Zebra Finch song learn little from songs they hear after about 60 days. The bounds of the sensitive period can be modulated by experience – birds are able to learn from a live tutor with whom they are interacting for a longer interval than from a tape recording (Payne, 1981; Kroodsma and Pickert, 1984; Petrinovich and Baptista, 1987). Indeed, some species seem unable to learn a song without social interactions (Hultsch and Todt, 1989b; Williams, 1990a; Hultsch, 1992). If a bird does not hear an acceptable model for song, the sensitive period may remain open for a couple of months (Eales, 1985, 1987; Slater *et al.*, 1992; Jones *et al.*, 1996), or even until the next reproductive season (Kroodsma and Pickert, 1980). However, even in the complete absence of a song model the sensitive period eventually ends. Young males from most species that have been studied eventually form a song of their own and become unable to learn from external models (Marler, 1970; Price, 1979; Marler and Sherman, 1985). This 'isolate' song has rhythmic and compositional characteristics of learned songs of the species. These similarities to learned song indicate that some aspects of song production are determined by developmental programs that do not require external information, and suggest that acquisition of a song model is also guided by endogenous perceptual specifiers or constraints (discussed by Marler, 1987, 1991a; DeVoogd, 1994a).

Motor song learning

In many species, auditory song learning is followed by several stages of motor song learning (i.e. learning to produce stereotyped vocalizations that are based on an auditory memory) (Marler, 1987, 1990). The first stage is subsong in which vocalizations are produced that have characteristics of the species' song, but are soft, highly variable and difficult to relate to the particular song models to which the birds have been exposed. Both sexes produce subsong (Marler *et al.*, 1988). This behavior is followed by plastic song in which many vocalizations are produced that are variable and unstable, but results of learning can be discerned. The vocalizations can be matched to songs that the bird has heard and can be related to the accomplished ('full') song that the bird will eventually sing.

Song production and modification in adulthood

Recently, Marler (1990, 1991b) has proposed 'action-based learning' as a further selective stage of song learning that happens in young adulthood, (Marler and Nelson, 1992). Frequently, birds will practice many songs during the plastic phase of song learning. These are then winnowed down to one or a few songs that will comprise the adult repertoire (Marler and Peters, 1982). Marler and Nelson suggest that the attrition process is not random – it is learned, based to a large degree on social cues. Thus, as young male White-crowned or Field Sparrows first try to establish a territory, they selectively retain the song(s) that most resemble those being sung near them by older males (DeWolfe *et al.*, 1989; Nelson, 1992). In contrast to earlier stages of learning, this process involves either actively inhibiting or forgetting well-learned songs.

It is unknown how this selective process is related to endocrinology. The young males are sexually mature, with high androgen levels, although they may not attract a mate or be able to defend a territory during this first reproductive season. It is also unknown whether the process occurs at the perceptual as well as the motor level. Perhaps the inhibition occurs only at the motor or production level, and there continue to be neurons throughout the song system selectively responsive to songs that are no longer sung. If so, this would provide a powerful tool that a bird could use throughout adult life to classify and evaluate the songs of other birds.

Neural development

Early development of song-system nuclei

Substantial research has attempted to relate changes in anatomy or physiology of song-system nuclei to the stages of song acquisition. Much of the initial formation of these nuclei seems to occur in both sexes. Early development is independent of auditory experience. Thus, soon after hatching, telencephalic song-system nuclei cannot be distinguished in either sex in Zebra Finches. At about 10 days, HVC, l-MAN and RA can be resolved as distinct nuclei. For about 15 days more, these nuclei grow larger in both sexes as additional cells are incorporated into the nuclei and the size of the cells and the amount of neuropil in the nuclei increase. Neurons in HVC, RA and l-MAN form elaborate dendritic trees densely covered with spines (reviewed in DeVoogd, 1991). The initial growth is similar in males and females. A major projection grows from l-MAN to RA and makes large numbers of synapses with RA neurons (Herrmann and Arnold, 1991). Projections between rostral nuclei in the song system reach their targets as early as 15 days after hatching and rapidly expand thereafter (Johnson and Bottjer, 1992). In contrast, the majority of HVC axons do not enter RA until about day 35 (Konishi and Akutagawa, 1985). One interpretation of these results is that the rostral pathway becomes functional earlier than the caudal. If this were true, it might indicate that song-related actions of the rostral circuit commence before those of the caudal circuit, but further study of formation of song-system connections is needed to confirm this hypothesis.

Another interpretation is that the caudal pathway is also active early in development by means of projections that have not been extensively studied. RA may receive functionally important inputs from parts of the telencephalon that immediately surround it. Also, there are early projections from HVC to areas near RA (Konishi and Akutagawa, 1985), and from areas near

HVC to RA (Margoliash *et al.*, 1994). These projections could influence formation of circuits within HVC and RA, and could participate in later song learning and production.

Recently, we have found that high levels of NADPH-diaphorase are present in many areas of the telencephalon in the first month after hatching (Wallhausser-Franke *et al.*, 1995a). Levels of this enzyme in HVC, RA and Area X drop substantially at later ages. NADPH-diaphorase is used in synthesizing nitric oxide, a molecule that has been associated with retrograde synaptic and short-distance communication and with subsequent neural plasticity (reviewed by Garthwaite, 1991; Zorumski and Izumi, 1993). Together, the findings on early expression of NADPH-diaphorase, and early growth of dendrites and synapses, indicate that the first month after hatching is a time when many of the connections between nuclei are established and patterns of connections within nuclei are organized.

During the third and fourth weeks after hatching, cell death increases in HVC, RA, l-MAN and Area X. The rate of cell death becomes much greater in females than in males, resulting in shrinkage of HVC, RA and l-MAN in females, and leading to the appearance of dimorphic anatomy for these nuclei (E. J. Nordeen and Nordeen, 1988; Kirn and DeVoogd, 1989; Nordeen *et al.*, 1992). Further divergence in the morphology of RA occurs as dendrites in females regress back to a fraction of the extent found in males (DeVoogd, 1991).

The role of gonadal steroids in the early formation of the song system remains one of the major puzzles in this research area. Neurons in DM, MAN and in HVC, and a zone medial to it, concentrate estradiol in young finches (K. W. Nordeen *et al.*, 1987). Giving estradiol to female Zebra Finches for an interval in the first 18 days after hatching prevents the augmented cell death found in the song system of untreated females. This results in development of a masculinized song system and the ability to sing a male-like song (Gurney, 1981, 1982; Pohl-Apel and Sossinka, 1984; Adkins-Regan *et al.*, 1994). These results suggest that organization of dimorphic features of the song system and of the capacity to produce song follow a pattern similar to that seen with development of dimorphic reproductive behaviors in mammals: an estradiol pulse in males sets off a series of 'organizational' changes that result in development of neuroanatomy and neuroendocrinology in a male-typical direction – and confer a capacity for male-typical behaviors. However, in the experiments that manipulated early levels of estradiol in baby Zebra Finches, complete masculinization of the song system and of the ability to sing a full song was difficult to achieve. It came only when the steroid levels remained elevated for at least 10 days that included the third week after hatching (Pohl-Apel and Sossinka, 1984; E. J. Nordeen *et al.*, 1987; Konishi and Akutagawa, 1988). Furthermore, steroid levels during early development of Zebra Finches are quite similar in the two sexes: careful developmental endocrine studies have found no differences in serum levels of estradiol (or any other gonadal steroid) large enough or long enough to account for the natural development of anatomical and behavioral dimorphisms in this species (Adkins-Regan *et al.*, 1990; Schlinger and Arnold, 1992a; Arnold, 1992). How then could sex differences in anatomy and function of the song system be organized? Perhaps there are sex differences that have not yet been described in the song systems of very young birds that confer differential reactions to similar steroid levels after hatching. These critical sex differences could include, for example, sex differences in number, steroid affinity or timing of activation of steroid receptors. Schlinger and Arnold (1992b, 1993) have shown that high levels of aromatase are present in the brains of Zebra Finches. Perhaps the pulse of estradiol that normally induces male-typical differentiation is synthesized and metabolized locally in the brain, and therefore is not evident in serum assays. Either of these possibilities would require substantial revision to our assumptions about the brain's understanding of its sex (from steroids as messengers to the brain to direct neural access to sex chromosomes) (see Arnold and Schlinger, 1993).

Neural changes leading up to song learning

As indicated above, many changes occur in song-system anatomy in the weeks leading up to the opening of the sensitive period for song learning. These changes are likely to be essential prerequisites for learning but have not yet been related to the specific capacities and constraints with which the young bird begins to learn songs. For example, prior to the sensitive period, the song system must be forming the perceptual specificity that will allow it to select conspecific songs for auditory learning, even if the songs of many species are present in the auditory environment. It must also be organizing species-specific motor patterns that would eventually be built into a learned song. Even if raised in isolation, birds of many species form songs that contain recognizable characteristics of normal song (Konishi, 1965; Marler, 1970; Marler, 1976). The term 'innate templates' (Konishi, 1965, 1985; Marler, 1976) has been used to indicate the behavioral selectivity that exists before both auditory and motor learning. One way of studying how these qualities are formed and interact is through physiological recording in young birds. However, there has been little research on response properties of neurons from song-system nuclei during the first month after hatching.

Neural changes during song acquisition

Much of auditory learning occurs in the second month after hatching in Zebra Finches. Neural and behavioral development is extremely rapid in Zebra Finches and this is an interval in which many systems are changing. So much is changing that it has been difficult to determine whether specific anatomical changes are associated with specific behavioral changes. Even in nuclei that appear to be stable, it is likely that complementary neural changes (like simultaneous addition and subtraction of synapses) are occurring. During this interval, HVC and RA become slightly larger in males, apparently because of continued neurogenesis in HVC and net growth of dendrites, and an increase in the amount of neuropil in both nuclei (Bottjer *et al.*, 1986; K. W. Nordeen and Nordeen, 1988; Kirn and DeVoogd, 1989). In contrast, l-MAN appears to shrink substantially and loses many of its synapses in RA during this interval (Herrmann and Arnold, 1991).

Lesioning l-MAN or Area X prior to plastic song results in profound deficits in later song performance (Bottjer *et al.*, 1984; Sohrabji *et al.*, 1990; Scharff and Nottebohm, 1991). Such observations have led to the hypotheses that the rostral nuclei of the song system play a special role in song learning, and that the apparent shrinkage of l-MAN is associated with the loss of this function (Bottjer and Arnold, 1986). Although the role of l-MAN is not yet understood either in development or in adulthood, several findings indicate that this hypothesis is incomplete. First, even after auditory song learning and anatomical regression, l-MAN does not become unimportant for song production. Several experiments have indicated a major continuing role for l-MAN in monitoring or initiating song (e.g. Benton *et al.*, 1998). Second, if large volume for l-MAN were associated with the special function of auditory learning, one would predict that the decrease in volume would occur when the special need ended. However, the shrinkage of l-MAN and its loss of synapses occur during auditory learning, not afterward.

Recently, we have proposed a contrasting hypothesis to account for relations between these structural changes and aspects of early song learning (Nixdorf-Bergweiler *et al.*, 1995; Wallhausser-Franke *et al.*, 1995b). As described above, song-system nuclei grow and elaborate their connections very early – apparently before the bird begins to acquire auditory information related to song. For several nuclei, there appears to be neuronal or synaptic regression as song learning occurs. Perhaps this stage of song learning is based on mechanisms that select between existing synapses rather than instructing the formation of new ones. Several behavioral and anatomical findings support this hypothesis. We have raised Zebra Finches in a colony environment from which adult males have been removed, thereby removing the sources for song models. At 55 days, near the end of the normal sensitive period for auditory song learning, song-deprived males have 30% more spine synapses in l-MAN than do normally reared males (Wallhausser-Franke *et al.*, 1995b). Perhaps the bird is able to identify sounds that could be learned and incorporated into song because acceptable sounds activate neurons within the song system in addition to neurons in more purely auditory areas such as Field L (Doupe,. 1997). Thus, the 'innate template' as described from behavioral experiments would be equivalent to the specificity, caused by the pattern of auditory system connections to the song system, song-system local circuits and motor projections, that is formed prior to song learning (discussed by DeVoogd, 1994a; Hogan, 1994). As a result of selective activation of these circuits which happens when the bird hears a particular model song, a process is initiated by which the activated components are strengthened or preserved, whereas those that have not been activated atrophy and die. When no acceptable song model is present, the animal remains open to auditory learning. On the neural side, when there is no activation of the perceptual network in the song system, the network remains plastic and loss of synapses in HVC and l-MAN (and potentially other areas not yet assessed) is slowed or delayed.

Many aspects of this hypothesis require further research. In some species, auditory learning can be extremely fast – as few as eight exposures to a cluster of songs are enough for a nightingale to acquire the songs and subsequently make use of them in assembling its own song (Hultsch and Todt, 1989a,b; Hultsch, 1992). Does this mean that the assortative synaptic process can be initiated extremely rapidly in such species, giving a life-or-death advantage to the elements of the song-system circuitry that participate in the perceptions? What neural mechanisms are used in these processes? NMDA receptors are used in processes like LTP to reinforce or strengthen synapses in which there is sustained coincident presynaptic and postsynaptic activation (reviewed by Morris *et al.*, 1990). Synapses from l-MAN afferents on to RA neurons have NMDA receptors (Kubota and Saito, 1991; Mooney and Konishi, 1991; Mooney, 1992). Could these be used in preserving the synapses that are activated by exposure to a song model? Conversely, what mechanism condemns synapses that are not activated by song exposure, but preserves them for months if no part of the circuitry is activated? Under natural conditions, young birds of many species hear many different examples of song, but practice only a few and end up producing fewer still (Marler, 1970; Marler and Peters, 1982; Williams, 1990a; Nelson, 1992). Are these stages of selection random or guided by social and perceptual cues (see, e.g. Eales, 1985)? On the neural side, how does the neural network responsible for song learning incorporate specific songs when it is being activated by many acceptable songs? Alternatively, if the hypothesis proposed is correct, why should parts of the network regress that are receiving appropriate stimulation? Finally, what are the relations between the synapses activated by perception and those used for song production? – the possibility that these are essentially the same is discussed by Williams (1989, 1990b). Each of these questions deserves further study that integrates behavioral and neurobiological observations.

The interval during which auditory learning occurs is a time of major changes in endocrine interactions with the song system. In Zebra Finches, the proportion of cells in song-system nuclei that concentrate androgens increases substantially (Bottjer, 1987). In l-MAN, this increase seems to be due to selective loss of cells insensitive to the steroid (E. J. Nordeen *et al.*, 1987). It is unclear what initiates these brain changes. At least until day 54, estradiol levels are similar in male and female Zebra Finches. Androgen levels during the second month after hatching are similar in the two sexes or are higher in females (Adkins-Regan *et al.*, 1990). High levels of aromatase are present in the telencephalon of Zebra Finches including the regions of major song-system nuclei at ages from hatching into adulthood (Vockel *et al.*, 1998, 1990; Schlinger and Arnold, 1992a, 1993). This enzyme is used to convert testosterone into estradiol. High levels of 5-α-reductase, the enzyme that catalyzes the conversion of testosterone into dihydrotestosterone, are found in HVC, RA, Area X and MAN. The latter enzyme is higher in males than in females, a difference that was not altered by male castration or female treatment with testosterone (Vockel *et al.*, 1990). The presence of these enzymes suggests that major changes in local levels of particular steroids could occur within the brain without necessarily showing up as changes in blood levels.

Neural changes during motor song learning

In many song-bird species, motor song learning occurs during an interval distinct from the period of auditory song learning (reviewed by Marler, 1987, 1990). However, neurobiology of song-system development has been studied most completely in Zebra Finches, a species in which motor learning begins during the second half of auditory learning and continues to about 90 days. During this interval, sex differences in song-system anatomy become larger, primarily due to continued growth of neurons in males and persistence of the regressed state in females (reviewed by DeVoogd, 1991). Synapses in RA achieve their full size in males (Herrmann and Arnold, 1991); ultrastructural changes in other areas have not yet been studied. Volman (1993) finds that neurons in HVC now begin to show a preference for the bird's own songs. Less neuronal activity is elicited by the tutor song in the instances in which the two differ. This result indicates that song perception and production overlap in the same nuclei and potentially in the same neurons, supporting the theory that the two are necessarily intertwined (Williams and Nottebohm, 1985; Williams, 1989). The neuronal selectivity could be caused by two sorts of mechanisms: either auditory learning of external song models is followed by synthesis of a variant that will be the bird's own song; or the initial process of auditory learning is one of selection between alternative 'preformed' or endogenously organized behavioral possibilities. The latter mechanism could result in organizing a song that is close but not identical to the song model; these learning models are discussed by Changeux (1985) and Hogan (1988, 1994).

Gonadal steroids appear to play an important role in this phase of song development. If young males are castrated and treated with an antiandrogen or an antiestrogen, their songs fail to become stereotyped both in the structure of individual syllables and in the linkage of syllables as they do in normal males (Bottjer and Hewer, 1992). In contrast, augmenting testosterone levels near the beginning of plastic song results in formation of a stereotyped song that contains an abnormally small number of syllables (Korsia and Bottjer, 1991). Together, these findings suggest that the song system's function early in motor learning is to add motor programs for new song elements to the bird's repertoire (although without high precision), and that rising androgen levels cause a shift in function to one of increasing the precision with which song elements are produced that have already been learned. The rise in androgen levels at puberty may then be the signal which not only brings reproductive maturity, but also a fully formed stereotyped song. Focused anatomical study is needed to determine where and how the androgens act, and what the effects are for song system anatomy and function.

Neurobiology of action-based learning

Very little is known of neural mechanisms responsible for action-based learning in which a young adult bird selects between several songs it has learned. The mechanisms are likely to be distinct from the selective processes proposed for auditory song learning or the synaptic growth proposed for early phases of motor learning, given that it happens in adulthood when androgen levels are high. We have found hints that the process involves inhibition rather than literal loss of the memories. Thus, some adult, male, White-crowned Sparrows respond to bilateral lesions of l-MAN by modifying their song so as to reincorporate song elements that were practiced during plastic song and then dropped (Benton *et al.*, 1998). Whether songs once practiced during the plastic phase and then lost retain a special meaning for unlesioned birds remains to be studied.

Changes in song-system neurobiology have been associated with many of the behavioral changes that occur during development of singing. Put simply, birds sing because a neural system develops that links audition to vocal production. This system is specialized to be selectively responsive to conspecific song. It appears to encode initial stages of song learning by selectively reinforcing some neural circuits and eliminating others. Throughout development, as well, changes in steroid receptors and in song-system circuits in response to steroids create a neural system that acts differently in the two sexes and that can change function dynamically in response to changes in circulating steroids. The close links between behavioral and neural development can be studied further in many ways. Electrophysiology and anatomy can be used to study development of song representation in the brain – how prefunctional perceptual and motor elements needed for song are created and how these are distributed across the song system, for example.

Function

The third approach to answering the question 'why does a bird sing a song?' is to study the function of song, looking both at the general effects of song in a species and at differences in the effects of the songs of different individuals within a species. This approach assesses the current effects of singing, for both the sender and the receiver. Frequently, researchers studying function then try to determine whether these effects confer a reproductive advantage (reviewed by Searcy and Andersson, 1986; Kroodsma and Byers, 1991; McGregor, 1991; Andersson, 1994; Catchpole and Slater, 1995). The linkage to reproductive advantage is based on the assumptions that: (1) current selective pressures resemble those that have operated in the past; and (2) song is now elicited by stimuli that are similar to stimuli that elicited it as its form was shaped by selective forces. There is good evidence for two major functions of song that confer reproductive advantages.

Behavioral functions of song

Male song as a signal to conspecific males

First, males may sing to defend their territories against other males. Song may signal the presence of a male on a territory and gives a 'keep out' warning directed to conspecific males. This function has been demonstrated in a number of ways. For example, males often countersing with each other and respond aggressively to encounters simulated by song playbacks (reviewed by Kroodsma and Byers, 1991; Falls, 1992). Also, vacated territories are quickly occupied and such invasion can be prevented or delayed by broadcasting song (Krebs, 1977; Krebs *et al.*, 1978; Yasukawa, 1981; Falls, 1988). Finally, muted males are slower to gain territories than unmanipulated or sham-operated ones, and they are more likely to lose their territories in territorial disputes (Peek, 1972; Smith, 1979; McDonald, 1989; Westcott, 1992). Possession of a territory, in turn, may help a male to find food, to hide from predators and to attract a female. The latter may be particularly important, because territory is a prerequisite for breeding in a number of song birds such as the Great Tit (*Parus major*).

Male song as a signal to conspecific females

Second, males may sing to attract, guard or stimulate a mate. Effects of song on females have been demonstrated in several song bird species (reviewed by Searcy, 1992; Searcy and Yasukawa, 1996; Stacier *et al.*, 1996). Female Pied Flycatchers and European Starlings are attracted to nestboxes that broadcast male song, whereas they pay less attention to silent nestboxes (Eriksson and Wallin, 1986; Mountjoy and Lemon, 1991). Unmated males spend a large proportion of time singing. However, song output drops after pairing in Sedge Warblers, Reed Warblers and Bluethroats, for example (Catchpole, 1973; Merila and Soonen, 1994). The high level of singing behavior returns when the female of mated males is experimentally removed (Catchpole, 1973; Wasserman, 1977; Krebs *et al.*, 1981; Cuthill and Hindmarsh, 1985; Spector, 1991; Searcy and Yasukawa, 1995).

Males may sing not only to attract mates but to guard them from other males (Møller, 1991). The peak fertile period of many female song birds is before initiation of egg laying (Birkhead and Møller, 1992). According to the mate-guarding hypothesis, males should guard their mates most intensively during the females' fertile periods. Guarding has been found in several song bird species in which song output peaked shortly before or during egg laying (Catchpole, 1973; Slagsvold, 1977; Lampe and Espmark, 1987). In other species, however, the highest song rate and longest songs are found after the fertile period, in contrast to what would be predicted by the mate-guarding hypothesis (Hiett and Catchpole, 1982; Rodriguez, 1996).

Males may sing to increase the receptivity of their females. Female canaries exposed to male song built nests more actively than females having no song or a simpler song (Hinde and Steele, 1976; Kroodsma, 1976). Male Great Tits and Willow Tits sing more at times of peak female fertility than at others (Mace, 1987; Welling *et al.*, 1995). Male song also stimulates ovarian growth (Morton *et al.*, 1985).

Why do some males have larger repertoires than others?

For many species, males differ in the number of songs in their repertoire. Several experiments have found that these individual differences in singing are correlated with the male's reproductive success. Hiebert *et al.* (1989) demonstrated that song repertoire size is positively correlated with lifetime reproductive success (LRS) in the Song Sparrow. Estimating LRS is difficult – very few direct measures of LRS are available. Researchers, therefore, often investigate some attribute believed to contribute to LRS, such as pairing dates, number of mates and number of young fledged. For example, males with larger repertoires pair up sooner than males with small repertoires (Howard, 1974; Catchpole, 1980; Eens *et al.*, 1991). Males with large repertoires may attract females that lay their eggs sooner than mates of males with smaller repertoires (Wright and Cuthill, 1992). The number of mates or harem size may increase with song repertoire size (Payne and Payne, 1977; Yasukawa *et al.*, 1980; Møller, 1983; Eens *et al.*, 1991). In Great Tits and Red-winged Blackbirds, a large repertoire is more effective than a small one at repelling rival males (Krebs *et al.*, 1978; Yasukawa, 1981). Finally, song-repertoire size in some species is positively correlated with the number of offspring that are produced in a breeding season or with the number of young who survive until breeding (McGregor *et al.*, 1981; Lambrechts and Dhondt, 1986; Eens *et al.*, 1991). Other studies, however, do not find a relation between repertoire size and male mating success (Searcy *et al.*, 1985; Alatalo *et al.*, 1986).

Why do females pay attention to males?

Females may gain two sorts of benefits by listening to males sing. First, singing behavior and song may indicate the resources of the male. Such resources could include the territory or the male's ability to provide parental care. Male Willow Warblers spend more time singing on territories that provide abundant food than on poor territories (Radesater *et al.*, 1987) and males on good territories attract females earlier than males on poor territories. Male Stonechats that sing frequently spend more time feeding and defending their young (Greig-Smith, 1982), thus the males' song output is an honest advertisement of their parental abilities.

Second, better singers may advertise their superior genes. Male Great Tits with larger repertoires survive better and produce more young than males with small repertoires (Lambrechts and Dhondt, 1986). Thus, females may mate with better singers because the offspring of such males are more likely to survive. Attractive male Zebra Finches spend more time in singing than less attractive ones, and the amount of singing is a good indicator of their offspring's body mass at fledging (Houtman, 1992). Hasselquist *et al.* (1996) find that postfledging survival of young correlates positively with the song repertoire of the genetic father (whether or not he is paired with their mother), suggesting that a male's song is a good predictor of his fitness and that females are able to make use of this information.

Separating these two sorts of explanations is difficult (Searcy and Andersson, 1986). For example, song repertoire size, territory quality and male paternal care may all increase with the age of males. These changes could happen because males become more experienced or because those males survive in adulthood who possess many features that are better than average. In line with the latter explanation, Lambrechts and Dhondt (1986) showed young Great Tits with small repertoires are more likely to die when young than ones with large repertoires.

If females use song as an index of male quality, they must be capable of discriminating small differences in song performance – fidelity in reception is as important as in production in a communication system. Although reception has not been systematically studied, females in many species do appear to make precise discriminations of conspecific song (Miller, 1979a,b; Baker, 1983; McGregor and Avery, 1986; Wiley *et al.*, 1991; Cynx and Nottebohm, 1992), sometimes more accurately than do males (Searcy and Brenowitz, 1988).

What are the costs of singing?

Males typically do not sing throughout the year and singing may gradually diminish during the breeding season. This pattern suggests that singing must be associated with some costs. The costs of singing have received much less attention than the benefits. In males such costs may include energetic expenditure, time lost from other activities, provoking aggression from conspecific males or increased predation risk (Reid, 1987; Eberhardt, 1994). Singing makes a male more conspicuous to predators as well as conspecifics. The tradeoff between singing and foraging was investigated in Pied Flycatchers, Dunnocks and Red-winged Blackbirds (Searcy, 1979; Davies and Lundberg, 1984; Alatalo *et al.*, 1990). These studies showed that males on food-supplemented territories spend less time on feeding, sing more and have higher mating success than males on unsupplemented territories.

In females, too, there is a tradeoff between searching for the best mate and such costs as the time lost from breeding, the chance of dying during mate search and the possibility that a good male will have been chosen by another female and no longer available should she be unsuccessful in searching for a better one. Prolonged searching may decrease the available time for the breeding season. Female behavior reflects a balance between a rapid choice and a perfect choice. Female Pied Flycatchers visit up to nine males before choosing one (Dale *et al.*, 1992). Female Great Reed Warblers visit approximately six territories over 1–3 days while searching for a mate (Bensch and Hasselquist, 1992). Females may increase benefits and decrease costs in these decisions by continuing to search even while paired: females in many species seek extrapair copulations (Birkhead and Møller, 1992). In Great Reed Warblers, the males chosen invariably have larger repertoires than the female's 'social mate' (Hasselquist *et al.*, 1996).

Neurobiological basis for song functions

There has been relatively little research on the physiological basis for these functional attributes of song. Each could be better understood by relating behavioral data to mechanism. For example, a territorial male will respond aggressively to a novel song or to a familiar song from a novel location, but not to a familiar song from a familiar location. Thus, the male maintains memories of songs, locations and associations between the two; such findings suggest that there must be neural links between brain regions responsible for auditory and spatial processing. These links have not yet been described. Similarly, modulation in song production associated with the presence of a female suggests neural links between high-order visual processing and the endocrine system or the song system.

As described above, females pay attention to male song because it can be a reliable indicator of a male's resources or genetic fitness. Thus, a female must be able to assess the quality of the song that the male produces. Brenowitz (1991) has shown that doing so requires an intact HVC. It is not known which brain nuclei are required for such assessments, or whether there are individual differences in the ability of females to make such discriminations and in the anatomy of the brain systems she uses to do so.

What are the links between a male's song and aspects of fitness as described above? Across song-bird species, an elaborate song requires an elaborate neural song system (DeVoogd *et al.*, 1993; Székely *et al.*, 1996), which in turn may be linked to augmented anatomy and function in other neural systems (Airey *et al.*, 1996). However, within a species, it is not known whether formation and maintenance of a song system that is able to produce especially complex songs are necessarily tied to special capabilities for other brain components.

Evolutionary history: toward comparative study of song learning

There is no typical song bird. There are more than 4500 species in the oscine suborder and they show immense variation in song composition as well as in the details of acquisition and expression. Most song bird species live for several years; some live for many years. Typically, they continue to sing throughout life, in reproductive and agonistic contexts. There is immense natural variation in the pattern of song production in adulthood. Species differ in the focus or context for song, the degree to which song elements are produced in a fixed order, the extent to which song is modified or augmented either in day-to-day interactions or across the bird's lifetime. As described above, adult song is a mix of attributes that are innately specified, learned and specific to the individual. However, the weighting of the mix differs greatly between species. Although learning contributes to adult song in all species studied to date, some species may learn one song that is retained throughout life with little or no subsequent alteration (Zebra Finches, White-crowned Sparrows). Others may learn as many as 2000 distinct songs (Brown Thrasher) (Kroodsma and Parker, 1977). In most species, the learning results in a song that is idiosyncratic and is more complex than would occur without access to an outside model. In contrast, wild Black-capped Chickadees appear to learn a song that is simpler than the song produced if there is no model, and the song is expressed similarly by all members of the species (Kroodsma *et al.*, 1995). Some species may learn complex songs exclusively and accurately from a model (Marsh Wren), while others use a model as the basis for improvising and elaborating their songs (Catbirds). The song of an individual may be composed of two or three sounds (White-throated Sparrow) or hundreds (Nightingale). This variation can be seen as an unfortunate barrier to an inclusive account of the neurobiology of song. Alternatively, the variation can be seen as an immense natural experiment: natural selection has modified the song system so as to produce thousands of different patterns for a learned behavior. Comparative study of brain–behavior relations then can be a powerful tool for understanding the neural algorithms used in song learning and expression, and can provide a window through which to view how a particular behavioral pattern evolved. Ultimately, comparative approaches can be used to study evolution of higher-order behavioral processes and of their neural substrates.

Focal study

The simplest comparative approach is focal study: suggesting a relation between a behavioral or ecological attribute and a characteristic of the song system, and then testing the correspondence by focusing on another species selected because the behavioral characteristic is different. For example, song-system nuclei are much larger in male Zebra Finches than in females. In this species, females never sing, which suggests that the additional cells and connections in the males may enable the additional functional capacities of the males. One way of assessing this relation is to study the song system in species in which females also sing. In neotropical wren species in which females sing duets with their mates, the neuroanatomical sex differences are smaller or absent throughout the song system (Brenowitz and Arnold, 1986; DeVoogd et al., 1988). In another example of focal study, Nottebohm (1981, 1984) noted that large seasonal shifts in song-system anatomy are found in canaries but not Zebra Finches, and suggested that this might be related to the canary's capacity to modify its song annually. However, further study found seasonal changes as large or larger in Red-winged Blackbirds, a species that shows minor changes in the song repertoire from one year to the next (Kirn et al., 1989), and in Orange-bishop Birds and Rufous-sided Towhees in which the song is stable (Arai et al., 1989; Brenowitz et al., 1991).

The focal approach has been useful in supporting or disconfirming hypotheses, but has major problems. It is always possible to find alternative behavioral or ecological variables that appear to covary with brain measures, since each bird species differs in many ways from others. Also, it is not possible to quantify the degree of confidence that an association in a single species is consistent or meaningful. In other words, finding that a species with a particular song pattern also has a particular neuroanatomical attribute by itself predicts little about the nature of brain–behavior associations in the next species or more generally. Fortunately, alternative, more powerful comparative techniques are now available because of recent advances in the theory of comparative analysis and in molecular techniques for determining phylogeny.

Phylogenetic analyses of song and the song system

Novel approaches to comparative study derive from two central assumptions of evolutionary theory. First, although there is immense variation in song acquisition and expression, it is not random. Individuals within a species tend to be alike as are species within a genus, and to a degree, genera within a family (phylogenetic inertia; Harvey and Purvis, 1991). Indeed, similarities in morphology and behavior have been the basis for inferring degrees of relatedness. Second, evolutionary modification, including brain and behavioral modification, is assumed to be parsimonious; for discussion of potential limitations of this assumption, see Sober (1988), Stewart (1993), and Frumhoff and Reeve (1994). Thus, the presence of a trait in several conspecific species is best explained by a single evolutionary change in a species ancestral to the group rather than by several independent, convergent evolutionary events (Harvey and Krebs, 1990; Harvey and Purvis, 1991).

Several methods have been developed that analyze variation in a trait across species. A major problem for past analyses has been phylogenetic nonindependence – seeing a trait in two species does not provide two data points if the trait evolved in a common ancestor and is present in the two species simply because of common descent. The new methods control for phylogenetic nonindependence, such that correlations between anatomy and behavior can be tested in a way that is unbiased, rigorous and quantitative (Felsenstein, 1988; Harvey and Pagel, 1991; Harvey and Purvis, 1991; Gittleman and Luh, 1992; Garland *et al.*, 1992). Such approaches require an adequate sampling of variation across a phylogeny – inferences about the most likely timing of evolution of a trait may be skewed if the species that are sampled do not include the range of variation present in the entire phylogeny.

We have used one of these techniques, the method of independent contrasts (Felsenstein, 1985; Garland *et al.*, 1992; Purvis and Rambaut, 1994), to study relations between aspects of song and gross anatomy of song-system nuclei. In this method, a phylogeny is partitioned into all its branching points (or nodes), each of which is used for a comparison (or contrast) of the trait in question. Data from pairs of contemporary sibling species would be used for one set of contrasts. Using rules of parsimony, estimates of the trait are derived for the species ancestral to the contemporaneous pairs. These estimates then are used for another set of contrasts between closely related pairs of ancestral species. Trait estimates are then derived for species ancestral to each member of these secondary contrasts and the process continues until the highest contrast within the phylogeny is reached (these higher-order contrasts could also be thought of as contrasts between related genera, between subfamilies, and finally between families). These contrasts are scaled by the time intervals between nodes, since the distant nodes have had more time to accumulate character change. The entire set of contrasts are statistically independent and can then be used as data for conventional regression or correlation analyses. This technique is most robust and powerful if a phylogeny is sampled extensively and is reconstructed accurately. In recent years, huge improvements in the latter have come with the advent of molecular techniques for determining patterns of relatedness.

In an initial survey, we measured telencephalon volume and the volumes of HVC and Area X in the brains of males from 41 species representing eight diverse oscine families (DeVoogd *et al.*, 1993). We derived estimates for the song repertoire typical for a male in each species (an index of learning capacity) and for the number of syllable types typically found in a song bout.

We found that differences in song repertoire are significantly correlated with differences in the relative volume of HVC – and are not significantly correlated with differences in the relative volume of Area X. The number of syllable types per song bout is not significantly correlated with either brain measure. These results suggest that there is distribution of function within the song system – selection for enhanced learning capacity has not affected gross anatomy throughout the entire song system. Furthermore, these data suggest conservation of function across evolutionary time. The pattern of association between song repertoire and relative HVC volume is present across bird species that have not had a common ancestor for millions of generations.

Relating brain and behavior across a diverse phylogeny diversity gives findings that are general, but also has major theoretical and practical problems. Song is so diverse across song birds that there are no indices of amount of learning or of pattern of production that can be applied to all. It is possible that, over the evolutionary time represented by the entire oscine phylogeny, the representation of song and the algorithms for song construction in the song system may have diverged, such that there are now different patterns of brain–behavior associations in different branches of the oscines. Each of these problems can be reduced by examining a limited group of related species in which songs are organized in similar ways and, because of more recent divergence, functions of brain nuclei are less likely to have diverged.

One such group is the *Acrocephalus* and *Locustella* warblers. These species are small and inconspicuous. They look alike, live in similar habitats (marshes, meadows and streams), and have similar diets (insects). They sing bouts of song containing stereotyped syllables. There is substantial variation between species in the number of syllables used in song. *Locustella* species average from one to four syllables in the repertoire of males; *Acrocephalus* species from 20 to 90. For several of the *Acrocephalus* species, there is good evidence that females select their mates on the basis of their song (Catchpole, 1980, 1986; 1987; Bensch and Hasselquist, 1992). Across males from five *Acrocephalus* and three *Locustella* species, there is a significant correlation between the number of syllables typical of a male's song and the relative volume of HVC (Fig. 12.2b; Székely *et al.*, 1996), but not the relative volumes of RA, Area X or l-MAN. As in the earlier, more general study, these results suggest that neural instantiation of the capacity for producing a learned song is focal. They raise the intriguing possibility that other song-system nuclei may be especially concerned with representation of other aspects of song representation or production. This is supported by preliminary data comparing females of these species in which there is a significant correlation between the relative volume of l-MAN in the females and the number of different song syllables typically produced by males of the species (DeVoogd *et al.*, 1996). Thus, female choice may be possible because the females who are

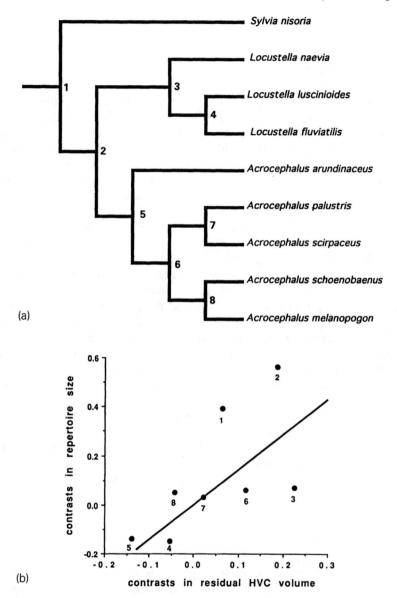

Fig. 12.2 (a) A reconstructed phylogeny of *Acrocephalus* and *Locustella* warblers based on their taxonomy (Glutz von Blotzheim, 1991), which is supported by a recent molecular phylogeny (Leisler *et al.*, unpublished data). *Sylvia nisoria* was selected as an outgroup, as *Sylvia* warblers belong to the same family as *Acrocephalus* and *Locustella* warblers. (b) Correlation between syllable repertoire size and residual volume of HVC ($r = 0.685$, $p < 0.05$, $n = 8$). The phylogenetically independent contrasts were based upon the phylogeny in (a) and the numbers refer to the particular contrasts used in the analysis. Reproduced from Székely *et al.* (1996).

making sophisticated choices have a sophisticated neural system for song perception.

Evolutionary history

Evolutionary comparative approaches offer an additional advantage in that they can infer the sequence of evolution of variation in neuroanatomy and behavior in a contemporary group of related species (Purvis, 1990; Garland *et al.*, 1992; Maddison and Maddison, 1992). These approaches involve reconstructing a phylogenetic tree and using rules of parsimony to suggest how traits or characters may have evolved (Swofford and Olsen, 1990; Brooks and McLennan, 1991). This sort of reconstruction of past state suggests, for example, that the capacity for song learning evolved at or after the evolutionary divergence of the oscines and the suboscines (Nottebohm, 1972), and that vocal learning evolved independently in parrots, hummingbirds and oscines (Brenowitz, 1991). The more precise phylogenetic trees generated by current analysis suggest that evolutionary changes in song-system anatomy have not been monotonic. Using parsimonious models of evolutionary change, the relative size of HVC has tended to increase in *Acrocephalus* warblers and this increase is most pronounced in the Marsh and Reed Warblers. However, the reconstruction also indicates that there have been repeated instances in which this nucleus has become smaller than in an ancestral species (Fig. 12.3). Such evolutionary changes need not be parallel among the nuclei of song system. For example, l-MAN has not tended to change much in *Acrocephalus* warblers but has increased in relative volume in *Locustella* warblers (Fig. 12.3b). If female choice has been conserved in these warbler lineages, these results suggest that females have sometimes shifted in the behavior they are choosing, ultimately resulting in the *Locustella* genus that shows little song learning but amazing volume and endurance in song production, and the closely related *Acrocephalus* genus that is renowned for song complexity.

Interrelations between levels of analysis

Why does a bird sing a song? This chapter indicates that four distinct sorts of answer are possible. Some behavioral data related to each are reviewed; more complete descriptions of behavioral data related to development and function are presented in the chapters in the present volume by Kroodsma and Byers, and by Todt and Hultsch. As argued above, each of these behavioral answers can be related to capacities and limitations of the neural network responsible for song perception and production. We would argue that, by understanding this neural system and how it produces or makes possible each of these behavioral answers, we create bridges between them.

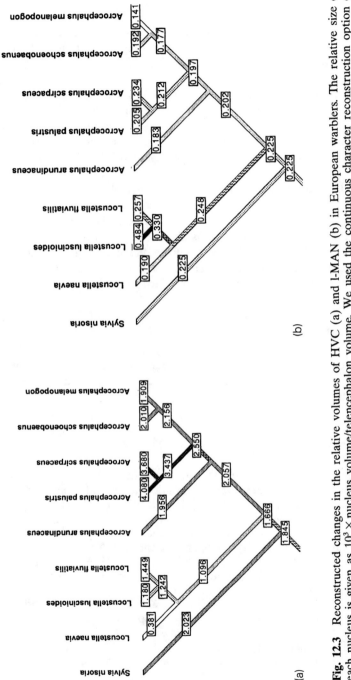

Fig. 12.3 Reconstructed changes in the relative volumes of HVC (a) and l-MAN (b) in European warblers. The relative size of each nucleus is given as $10^3 \times$ nucleus volume/telencephalon volume. We used the continuous character reconstruction option of MacClade 3.04 (Maddison and Maddison, 1992). When rules of parsimonious change are applied to neural data from contemporary species, it is clear that nuclei have increased in relative size in some lineages (filled lines) and decreased in others (clear lines) – and that the sequence of changes can be different for different nuclei in the song system.

Thus, it is possible to determine which aspects of the structures and connections of the song system are determined by genetic information without reference to auditory or vocal experience, and the kinds of capacities that this gives the animal – capacities for learning, for stereotyped production, or for synchronizing use of the system with endocrine shifts. This initial neural circuitry sets constraints on the sorts of song that can be perceived or learned, and on the amount of learning. It is possible to determine how exposure of this neural system to hormonal and experiential influences during development works within these constraints to create a system capable of species-appropriate song perception and production. It is possible to study how use of this neural system varies in individuals and species that show differences in the function of song. Finally, with behavioral traits that differ between individuals linked to the morphology and physiology of this neural system, it is possible to determine neural consequences of selection based on behavioral characters. This then allows inferences about evolutionary history of singing behaviors and predictions about evolutionary consequences. Thus, neurobiology of the song system may be the common language that ties together the different answers to Tinbergen's four 'whys', making it possible to go beyond distinguishing the answers to synthesizing them.

Acknowledgements

Thanks to Sarah Newman, Mark Hauber and Paul Sherman for helpful suggestion, and to NATO (CRG 931542) and the US-Hungary Joint Fund (117/91) for support.

References

Adkins-Regan, E., Abdelnabi, M., Mobarak, M. and Ottinger, M. A. (1990) Sex steroid levels in developing and adult male and female zebra finches (*Poephila guttata*). *Gen. Comp. Endo.* **78**, 93–109.

Adkins-Regan, E., Mansukhani, V., Seiwert, C. and Thompson, R. (1994) Sexual differentiation of brain and behavior in the zebra finch: critical periods for effects of early estrogen treatment. *J. Neurobiol.* **25**, 865–877.

Airey, D. C., DeVoogd, T. J. and Kroodsma, D. E. (1994) Morphology of song control neurons in differentially tutored eastern marsh wrens (*Cistothorus palustris*). *Soc. Neurosci. Abst.* **20**, 164.

Airey, D. C., Niederer, J. K., Nelson, A. K., DeVoogd, T. J. and Finlay, B. L. (1996) High vocal center and encephalization: specialization and developmental constraints. *Soc. Neurosci. Abst.* **22**, 1402.

Alatalo, R. V., Lundberg, A. and Glynn, C. (1986) Female pied flycatchers choose territory quality and not male characteristics. *Nature* **323**, 152–153.

Alatalo, R. V., Glynn, C. and Lundberg, A. (1990) Singing rate and female attraction in the pied flycatcher an experiment. *Anim. Behav.* **39**, 601–603.

Alcock, J. and Sherman, P. (1994) The utility of the proximate-ultimate dichotomy in ethology. *Ethology* **96**, 58–62.

Andersson, M. (1994) *Sexual Selection*. Princeton, NJ: Princeton University Press.

Arai, O., Taniguchi, I. and Saito, N. (1989) Correlation between the size of song control nuclei and plumage color change in orange bishop birds. *Neurosci. Lett.* **98**, 144–148.

Arnold, A. P. (1980) Quantitative analysis of sex differences in hormone accumulation in the zebra finch brain: methodological and theoretical issues. *J. Comp. Neurol.* **189**, 421–436.

Arnold, A. P. (1992) Developmental plasticity in neural circuits controlling birdsong: sexual differentiation and the neural basis of learning. *J. Neurobiol.* **23**, 1506–1528.

Arnold, A. P. and Schlinger, B. A. (1993) Sexual differentiation of brain and behavior: the zebra finch is not just a flying rat. *Brain Behav. Evol.* **42**, 231–241.

Arnold, A. P., Nottebohm, F. and Pfaff, D. W. (1976) Hormone accumulating cells in vocal control and other brain regions of the zebra finch (*Poephila guttata*). *J. Comp. Neurol.* **165**, 487–512.

Baker, M. C. (1983) The behavioral response of female Nutthall's white-crowned sparrows to male song of natal and alien dialects. *Behav. Ecol. Sociobiol.* **12**, 309–315.

Ball, G. F., Casto, J. M. and Bernhard, D. J. (1994) Sex differences in the volume of avian song control nuclei: comparative studies and the issue of brain nucleus delineation. *Psychoneuroendocrinology* **19**, 485–504.

Balthazart, J., Foidart, A., Wilson, E. M. and Ball, G. F. (1992) Immunocytochemical localization of androgen receptors in the male songbird and quail brain. *J. Comp. Neurol.* **317**, 407–420.

Baptista, L. F. and Morton, M. L. (1988) Song learning in montane white-crowned sparrows: from whom and when. *Anim. Behav.* **36**, 1753–1764.

Bekoff, M. (1995) Cognitive ethology and the explanation of nonhuman animal behavior. In Roitblat, H. L. and Meyer, J.-A. (eds) *Comparative Approaches to Cognitive Science*. Cambridge, MA: MIT Press, pp. 119–150.

Bensch, S. and Hasselquist, D. (1992) Evidence for active female choice in a polygynous warbler. *Anim. Behav.* **44**, 301–311.

Benton, S., Nelson, D. A., Marler, P. and DeVoogd, T. J. (1998) Anterior forebrain pathway is needed for stable song expression in adult male white-crowned sparrows (*Zonotrichia leucophrys*). *Behav. Brain Res.* (in press).

Birkhead, T. R. and Møller, A. P. (1992) *Sperm Competition in Birds: Evolutionary causes and consequences*. London: Academic Press.

Bottjer, S. W. (1987) Ontogenetic changes in the pattern of androgen accumulation in song-control nuclei of male zebra finches. *J. Neurobiol.* **18**, 125–139.

Bottjer, S. W. and Arnold, A. P. (1986) The ontogeny of vocal learning in songbirds. In Blass, E. M. (ed). *Handbook of Behavioral Neurobiology*, Vol. 8. New York: Plenum, pp. 129–161.

Bottjer, S. W. and Dignan, T. P. (1988) Joint hormonal and sensory stimulation modify neuron number in adult canary brains. *J. Neurobiol.* **19**, 624–635.

Bottjer, S. W. and Hewer, S. J. (1992) Castration and antisteroid treatment impair vocal learning in male zebra finches. *J. Neurobiol.* **23**, 337–333.

Bottjer, S. W., Miesner E. and Arnold, A. P. (1984) Forebrain lesions disrupt development but not maintenance of song in passerine birds. *Science* **224**, 901–903.

Bottjer, S. W., Glaessner, S. L. and Arnold, A. P. (1985) Ontogeny of brain nuclei controlling song learning and behavior in zebra finches. *J. Neurosci.* **5**, 1556–1562.

Bottjer, S. W., Miesner E. and Arnold, A. P. (1986) Changes in neuronal number, density and size account for increases in volume of song-control nuclei during song development in zebra finches. *Neurosci. Lett.* **67**, 263–268.

Brenowitz, E. A. (1991) Altered perception of species-specific song by female birds after lesions of a forebrain nucleus. *Science* **251**, 303–305.

Brenowitz, E. A. and Arnold, A. P. (1986) Interspecific comparisons of the size of neural song control regions and song complexity in duetting birds: evolutionary implications. *J. Neurosci.* **6**, 2875–2879.

Brenowitz, E. A. and Arnold, A. P. (1989) Accumulation of estrogen in a vocal control brain region of a duetting song bird. *Brain Res.* **480**, 119–125.

Brenowitz, E. A. and Arnold, A. P. (1992) Hormone accumulation in song regions of the canary brain. *J. Neurobiol.* **23**, 871–880.

Brenowitz, E. A. and Kroodsma, D. E. (1996) The neuroethology of birdsong. In Kroodsma, D. E. and Miller, E. H. (eds) *Ecology and Evolution of Acoustic Communication in Birds*. Ithaca, NY: Cornell University Press, pp. 285–304.

Brenowitz, E. A., Nalls, B., Wingfield, J. C. and Kroodsma, D. E. (1991) Seasonal changes in avian song nuclei without seasonal changes in song repertoire. *J. Neurosci.* **11**, 1367–1374.

Brenowitz, E. A., Lent, K. and Kroodsma, D. E. (1995) Brain space for learned song in birds develops independently of song learning. *J. Neurosci.* **15**, 6281– 6286.

Brooks, D.R. and McLennan, D.A. (1991) *Phylogeny, ecology and behavior: A research program in comparative biology*. Chicago: University of Chicago Press.

Canady, R. A., Kroodsma, D. E. and Nottebohm, F. (1984) Population differences in complexity of a learned skill are correlated with the brain space involved. *Proc. Natl Acad. Sci. USA* **81**, 6232–6234.

Catchpole, C. K. (1973) The functions of advertising song in the sedge warbler (*Acrocephalus schoenobaenus*) and reed warbler (*A. scirpaceus*). *Behaviour* **46**, 300–320.

Catchpole, C. K. (1980) Sexual selection and the evolution of complex songs among European warblers of the genus *Acrocephalus. Behaviour* **74**, 149–166.

Catchpole, C. K. (1986) Song repertoires and reproductive success in the great reed warbler *Acrocephalus arundinaceus. Behav. Ecol. Sociobiol.* **19**, 439–445.

Catchpole, C. K. (1987) Bird songs, sexual selection and female choice. *Trends Evol. Ecol.* **2**, 94–97.

Catchpole, C. K. and Slater, P. J. B. (1995) *Bird Song: Biological Themes and Variations.* Cambridge: Cambridge University Press.

Changeux, J.-P. (1985) *Neuronal Man: the Biology of Mind.* New York: Pantheon.

Chew, W. J., Vicario, D. S. and Nottebohm, F. (1996) A large capacity memory system that recognizes the calls and songs of individual birds. *Proc. Natl Acad. Sci.* **93**, 1950–1955.

Clayton, N. S. (1987) Song learning in cross-fostered zebra finches: a re-examination of the sensitive phase. *Behavior* **102**, 67–81.

Clower, R. P., Nixdorf, B. E. and DeVoogd, T. J. (1989) Synaptic plasticity in the hypoglossal nucleus of female canaries: structural correlates of season, hemisphere and testosterone treatment. *Behav. Neural Biol.* **52**, 63–77.

Cuthill, I. and Hindmarsh, A. (1985) Increase in starling song activity with removal of mate. *Anim. Behav.* **33**, 326–328.

Cynx, J. and Nottebohm, F. (1992) Role of gender, season, and familiarity in discrimination of conspecific song by zebra finches (*Taeniopygia guttata*). *Proc. Natl Acad. Sci. USA* **89**, 1368–1371.

Dale, S., Rinden, H. and Slagsvold, T. (1992) Competition for a mate restricts mate search of female pied flycatchers. *Behav. Ecol. Sociobiol.* **30**, 165–176.

Davies, N. B. and Lundberg, A. (1984) Food distribution and a variable mating system in the dunnock (*Prunella modullaris*). *J. Anim. Ecol.* **53**, 895–912.

DeVoogd, T. J. (1991) Endocrine modulation of the development and adult function of the avian song system. *Psychoneuroendocrinol.* **16**, 41–66.

DeVoogd, T. J. (1994a) The neural basis for the acquisition and production of bird song. In Bolhuis, J. and Hogan, J. (eds) *Causal Mechanisms in Behavior Development.* Cambridge: Cambridge University Press, pp. 49–81.

DeVoogd, T. J. (1994b) Interactions between endocrinology and learning in the avian song system. *Ann. N.Y. Acad. Sci.* **743**, 19–43.

DeVoogd, T. J. and Nottebohm, F. (1981a) Sex differences in dendritic morphology of a song control nucleus in the canary: a quantitative Golgi study. *J. Comp. Neurol.* **196**, 309–316.

DeVoogd, T. J. and Nottebohm, F. (1981b) Gonadal hormones induce dendritic growth in the adult brain. *Science* **214**, 202–204.

DeVoogd, T. J., Nixdorf, B. E. and Nottebohm, F. (1985) Formation of new synapses related to acquisition of a new behavior. *Brain Res.* **329**, 304–308.

DeVoogd, T. J., Brenowitz, E. A. and Arnold, A. P. (1988) Small sex differences in song control dendrites are associated with minimal differences in song capacity. *J. Neurobiol.* **19**, 199–209.

DeVoogd, T. J., Pyskaty, D. J. and Nottebohm, F. (1991) Lateral asymmetries and testosterone induced changes in the gross morphology of the hypoglossal nucleus in adult canaries. *J. Comp. Neurol.* **307**, 65–76.

DeVoogd, T. J., Krebs, J. R., Healy, S. D. and Purvis, A. (1993) Evolutionary correlation between repertoire size and a brain nucleus amongst passerine birds. *Proc. Roy. Soc. Lond. B.* **254**, 75–82.

DeVoogd, T. J., Cardin, J. A., Székely, T., Buki, J. and Newman, S. W. (1996) Relative volume of L-MAN in female warbler species varies with the number of songs produced by conspecific males. *Soc. Neurosci, Abs.* **22**, 1401

DeWolfe, B. B., Baptista, L. F. and Petrinovich, L. (1989) Song development and territory establishment in Nuttall's white-crowned sparrows. *Condor* **91**, 397–407.

Dewsbury, D. A. (1992) On the problems studied in ethology, comparative psychology, and animal behavior. *Ethology* **92**, 89–107.

Doupe, A. J. (1997) Song- and order-selective neurons in the songbird anterior forebrain and their emergence during vocal development. *J. Neurosci.* **17**, 1147– 1167.

Doupe, A. J. and Konishi, M. (1991) Song-selective auditory circuits in the vocal control system of the zebra finch. *Proc. Natl Acad. Sci. USA* **88**, 11 339– 11 343.

Eales, L. A. (1985) Song learning in zebra finches: some effects of song model availability on what is learnt and when. *Anim. Behav.* **33**, 1293–1300.

Eales, L. A. (1987) Song learning in female-raised zebra finches: another look at the sensitive phase. *Anim. Behav.* **33**, 1356–1365.

Eberhardt, L. S. (1994) Oxygen consumption during singing by male Carolina wrens (*Thryothorus ludovicanus*). *Auk* **111**, 124–130.

Eens, M., Pinxten, R. and Verheyen R. F. (1991) Male song as a cue for mate choice in the European starling. *Behaviour* **116**, 210–238.

Eriksson, D. and Wallin, L. (1986) Male bird song attracts female – a field experiment. *Behav. Ecol. Sociobiol.* **19**, 297–299.

Falls, J. B. (1988) Does song deter territorial intrusion in white-throated sparrows (*Zonotrichia albicollis*)? *Can. J. Zool.* **66**, 206–211.

Falls, J. B. (1992) Playback: a historical perspective. In McGregor, P. K. (ed.) *Playback and Studies of Animal Communication*. New York: Plenum Press, pp. 11–33.

Felsenstein, J. (1985) Phylogenies and the comparative method. *Am. Nat.* **125**, 1–15.

Felsenstein, J. (1988) Phylogenies and quantitative characters. *Ann. Rev. Ecol. Syst.* **19**, 445–471.

Frumhoff, P.C. and Reeve, H.K. (1994) Using phylogenies to test hypotheses of adaptation: A critique of some current proposals. *Evolution* **48**, 172–180.

Gahr, M. and Konishi, M. (1988) Developmental changes in estrogen-sensitive neurons in the forebrain of the zebra finch. *Proc. Natl Acad. Sci, USA* **85**, 7380–7383.

Garland, T., Harvey, P.H. and Ives, A.R. 1992 Procedures for the analysis of comparative data using phylogenetically independent contrasts. *Syst. Biol.* **41**, 18–32.

Garthwaite, J. (1991) Glutamate, nitric oxide and cell-cell signalling in the nervous system. *Trends Neurosci.* **14**, 60–67.

Gittleman, J.L. and Luh, H.K. (1992) On comparing comparative methods. *Annual Rev. Ecol. Syst.* **23**, 383–404.

Glutz von Blotzheim, U.N. (1991) *Handbuch der Vögel Mitteleuropas, Vol. 12/1,* Wiesbaden: Akademische Verlagsgesellschaft.

Greig-Smith, P. W. (1982) Song-rates and parental care by individual male stonechats (*Saxicola torquata*). *Anim. Behav.* **30**, 245–252.

Gurney, M. (1981) Hormonal control of cell form and number in the zebra finch song system. *J. Neurosci.* **1**, 658–673.

Gurney, M. (1982) Behavioral correlates of sexual differentiation in the zebra finch song system. *Brain Res.* **231**, 153–172.

Harding, C. F., Walters, M. J. and Parsons, B. (1984) Androgen receptor levels in hypothalamus and vocal control nuclei in the male zebra finch. *Brain Res.* **306**, 333–339.

Harvey, P. H. and Krebs, J. R. (1990) Comparing brains. *Science* **249**, 140–146.

Harvey, P. H. and Pagel, M. D. (1991) *The Comparative Method in Evolutionary Biology.* Oxford: Oxford University Press.

Harvey, P.H. and Purvis, A. (1991) Comparative methods for explaining adaptations. *Nature* **351**, 619–624.

Hasselquist, D., Bensch, S. and von Schantz, T. (1996) Correlation between male song repertoire, extra-pair paternity and offspring survival in the great reed warbler. *Nature* **381**, 229–232.

Herrmann, K. and Arnold, A. P. (1991) The development of afferent projections to the robust archistriatal nucleus in male zebra finches: a quantitative electron microscopic study. *J. Neurosci.* **11**, 2063–2074.

Hiebert, S. M., Stoddard, P. K. and Arcese, P. (1989) Repertoire size, territory acquisition and reproductive success in the song sparrow. *Anim. Behav.* **37**, 266–273.

Hiett, J. C. and Catchpole, C. K. (1982) Song repertoires and seasonal song in the yellowhammer *Emberiza citrinella. Anim. Behav.* **30**, 568–574.

Hill, K. M. and DeVoogd, T. J. (1991) Altered daylength affects dendritic structure in a song-related brain region in red-winged blackbirds. *Behav. Neural. Biol.* **56**, 240–250.

Hinde, R. A. and Steel, E. (1976) The effect of male song on an oestrogen dependent behaviour in the female canary, *Serinus canarius. Horm. Behav.* **7**, 293–304.

Hogan, J. A. (1988) Cause and function in the development of behavioral systems. In Blass, E. M. (ed.) *Handbook of Behavioral Neurobiology, Vol. 9, Developmental Psychobiology and Behavioral Ecology.* New York: Plenum Press, pp. 63–106.

Hogan, J. A. (1994) Development of behavior systems. In Bolhuis, J. and Hogan, J. (eds) *Causal Mechanisms in Behavior Development.* Cambridge: Cambridge University Press, pp. 242–264.

Houtman, A. (1992) Female zebra finches choose extra-pair copulations with genetically attractive males. *Proc. Roy. Soc. Lond. B* **249**, 3–6.

Howard, R. D. (1974) The influence of sexual selection and interspecific competition on mockingbird song (*Mimus polyglottos*). *Evolution* **28**, 428–438.

Hultsch, H. (1992) Time window and unit capacity: dual constraints on the acquisition of serial information in songbirds. *J. Comp. Physiol. A* **170**, 275–280.

Hultsch, H. and Todt, D. (1989a) Memorization and reproduction of songs in nightingales (*Luscinia megarhynchos*): evidence for package formation. *J. Comp. Physiol, A* **165**, 197–203.

Hultsch, H. and Todt, D. (1989b) Song acquisition and acquisition constraints in the nightingale, *Luscinia megarhynchos*. *Naturwissenschaften* **76**, 83–85.

Immelmann, K. (1969) Song development in the zebra finch and other estrildid finches. In Hinde, R. A. (ed.) *Bird Vocalizations*. Cambridge: Cambridge University Press, pp. 61–74.

Johnson, F. and Bottjer, S. W. (1992) Growth and regression of thalamic efferents in the song control system of male zebra finches. *J. Comp. Neurol.* **326**, 442–450.

Johnson, F., Sablan, M. M. and Bottjer, S. W. (1995) Topographic organization of a forebrain pathway involved with vocal learning in zebra finches. *J. Comp. Neurol.* **358**, 260–278.

Jones, A. E., ten Cate, C. and Slater, P. J. B. (1996) Early experience and plasticity of song in adult male zebra finches. *J. Comp. Psychol.* **110**, 354–369.

Katz, L. C. and Gurney, M. E. (1981) Auditory responses in the zebra finch's motor system for song. *Brain Res.* **221**, 192–197.

Kelley, D. B. and Nottebohm, F. (1979) Projections of a telencephalic auditory nucleus – Field L – in the canary. *J. Comp. Neurol.* **183**, 455–470.

Kirn, J. R. and DeVoogd, T. J. (1989) The genesis and death of vocal control neurons during sexual differentiation in the zebra finch. *J. Neurosci.* **9**, 3176–3187.

Kirn, J. R., Clower, R. P., Kroodsma, D. E. and DeVoogd, T. J. (1989) Song-related brain regions in the red-winged blackbird are affected by sex and season but not repertoire size. *J. Neurobiol.* **20**, 139–163.

Konishi, M. (1965) The role of auditory feedback in the control of vocalization in the white-crowned sparrow. *Z. Tierpsychol.* **22**, 770–783.

Konishi, M. (1985) Birdsong: from behavior to neuron. *Ann. Rev. Neurosci.* **8**, 125–170.

Konishi, M. (1989) Birdsong for neurobiologists. *Neuron* **3**, 451–460.

Konishi, M. and Akutagawa, E. (1985) Neuronal growth, atrophy and death in a sexually dimorphic song nucleus in the zebra finch brain. *Nature* **315**, 145–147.

Konishi, M. and Akutagawa, E. (1988) A critical period for estrogen action on neurons of the song control system in the zebra finch. *Proc. Natl Acad. Sci. USA* **85**, 7006–7007.

Korsia, S. and Bottjer, S. W. (1991) Chronic testosterone treatment impairs vocal learning in male zebra finches during a restricted period of development. *J. Neurosci.* **11**, 2362–2371.

Krebs, J. R. (1977) Song and territory in the great tit *Parus major*. Stonehouse, B. and Perrins, C. (eds) *Evolutionary Ecology*. London: Macmillan, pp. 47–62.

Krebs, J.R. and Davies, N.B. (Eds.) (1991) *Behavioural Ecology, An Evolutionary Approach, third edition*. Oxford, UK: Blackwell Science.

Krebs, J. R., Ashcroft, R. and Webber, M. (1978) Song repertoires and territory defence in the great tit. *Nature* **271**, 539–542.

Krebs, J. R., Avery, M. and Cowie, R. J. (1981) Effect of removal on the singing behaviour of great tits. *Anim. Behav.* **29**, 635–637.

Kroodsma, D. E. (1976) Reproductive development in a female song bird: differential stimulation by quality of male song. *Science* **192**, 574–575.

Kroodsma, D. E. (1996) Ecology of passerine song development. In Kroodsma, D. E. and Miller, E. H. (eds) *Ecology and Evolution of Acoustic Communication in Birds*, Ithaca. NY: Cornell University Press, pp. 3–19.

Kroodsma, D. E. and Byers, B. E. (1991) The function(s) of bird song. *Am. Zool.* **31**, 318–328.

Kroodsma, D. E. and Miller, E. H. (eds) (1996) *Ecology and Evolution of Acoustic Communication in Birds*. Ithaca, NY: Cornell University Press.

Kroodsma, D. E. and Parker, L. D. (1977) Vocal virtuosity in the Brown Thrasher. *Auk* **94**, 783–785.

Kroodsma, D. E. and Pickert, R. (1980) Environmentally dependent sensitive periods for avian vocal learning. *Nature* **288**, 477–479.

Kroodsma, D. E. and Pickert, R. (1984) Repertoire size, auditory templates, and selective vocal learning in songbirds. *Anim. Behav.* **32**, 395–399.

Kroodsma, D. E., Albano, D. J., Houlihan, P. W. and Wells, J. A. (1995) Song development by Black-capped Chickadees (*Parus atricapillus*) and Carolina Chickadees (*P. carolinensis*). *Auk* **112**, 29–43.

Kubota, M. and Saito, N. (1991) NMDA receptors participate differently in two synaptic inputs in neurons of the zebra finch robust nucleus of the archistriatum in vitro. *Neurosci. Lett.* **125**, 107–109.

Lambrechts, M. and Dhondt, A. A. (1986) Male quality, reproduction, and survival in the great tit (*Parus major*). *Behav. Ecol. Sociobiol.* **19**, 57–64.

Lampe, H. M. and Espmark, Y. O. (1987) Singing activity and song pattern of the redwing *Turdus iliacus* during the breeding season. *Ornis Scand.* **18**, 179–185.

Lewicki, M. S. (1996) Intracellular characterization of song-specific neurons in the zebra finch auditory forebrain. *J. Neurosci.* **16**, 5854–5863.

Luine, V. N., Nottebohm, F., Harding, C. F. and McEwen, B. S. (1980) Androgen affects cholinergic enzymes in songbird syringeal motor neurons and muscle. *Brain Res.* **192**, 89–107.

Mace, R. (1987) The dawn chorus in the great tit *Parus major* is directly related to female fertility. *Nature* **330**, 745–746.

Maddison, W.P. and Maddison, D,.R. (1992). *MacClade: Analysis of phylogeny and character evolution. Version 3.0*. Sunderland, Massachusetts: Sinauer Associates.

Margoliash, D. (1987) Neural plasticity in birdsong learning. In Rauschecker, J. P. and Marler, P. (eds) *Imprinting and Cortical Plasticity*. New York: Springer-Verlag, pp. 289–309.

Margoliash, D. and Fortune, E. S. (1992) Temporal and harmonic combination-sensitive neurons in the zebra finch's HVc. *J. Neurosci.* **12**, 4309–4326.

Margoliash, D., Fortune, E. S., Sutter, M. L., Yu, A. C., Wren-Hardin, B. D. and Dave, A. (1994) Distributed representation in the song system of oscines: evolutionary implications and functional consequences. *Brain Behav. Evol.* **44**, 247–264.

Marler, P. (1970) A comparative approach to vocal learning: song development in white-crowned sparrows. *J. Comp. Physiol. Psychol. Mono.* **71**, 1–25.

Marler, P. (1976) Sensory templates in species-specific behavior. In Fentress, J. (ed.) *Simple Networks and Behavior*. Sunderland, MA: Sinauer, pp. 314–329.

Marler, P. (1987) Sensitive periods and the roles of specific and general sensory stimulation in birdsong learning. In Rauschecker, J. P. and Marler, P. (eds) *Imprinting and Cortical Plasticity*. New York: Springer-Verlag, pp. 99–135.

Marler, P. (1990) Song learning: the interface between behaviour and neuroethology. *Phil. Trans. R. Soc. Lond. B* **329**, 109–114.

Marler, P. (1991a) Differences in behavioural development in closely related species: birdsong. In Bateson, P. (ed.) *The Development and Integration of Behaviour: Essays in Honour Robert Hinde*. Cambridge: Cambridge University Press, pp. 41–70.

Marler, P. (1991b) Song learning behaviour: the interface with neuroethology. *Trends Neurosci.* **14**, 199–206.

Marler, P. and Nelson, D. A. (1992) Action-based learning: a new form of developmental plasticity. *Neth. J. Zool.* **43**, 91–103.

Marler, P. and Peters, S. (1982) Developmental overproduction and selective attrition: new processes in the epigenesis of birdsong. *Develop. Psychobiol.* **15**, 369-378.

Marler, P. and Sherman, V. (1985) Innate differences in singing behaviour of sparrows reared in isolation from adult conspecific song. *Anim. Behav.* **33**, 57–71.

Marler, P. and Waser, M. S. (1977) Role of auditory feedback in canary song development. *J. Comp. Physiol. Psychol.* **91**, 8–16.

Marler, P., Peters, S., Ball, G. F., Dufty, A. M. and Wingfield, J. C. (1988) The role of sex steroids in the acquisition and production of birdsong. *Nature* **336**, 770–772.

Mayr, E. (1982) *The Growth of Biological Thought*. Cambridge, MA: Harvard University Press.

McCasland, J. S. (1987) Neuronal control of bird song production. *J. Neurosci.* **7**, 23–39.

McDonald, M. V. (1989) Function of song in Scott's seaside sparrow, *Ammodramus maritimus peninsulae*. *Anim. Behav.* **38**, 468–485.

McGregor, P. K. (1991) The singer and song: on the receiving end of bird song. *Biol. Rev.* **66**, 57–81.

McGregor, P. K. and Avery, M. I. (1986) The unsung songs of great tits (*Parus major*): learning neighbour's songs for discrimination. *Behav. Ecol. Sociobiol.* **11**, 311–316.

McGregor, P. K., Krebs, J. R. and Perrins, C. M. (1981) Song repertoires and lifetime reproductive success in the great tit (*Parus major*). *Am. Natur.* **118**, 149–159.

Merilä, J. and Sorjonen, J. (1994) Seasonal and diurnal patterns of singing and song-flight activity in bluethroats (*Luscinia svecica*). *Auk* **111**, 556–562.

Miller, D. B. (1979a) The acoustic basis of mate recognition by female zebra finches (*Taeniopygia guttata*). *Anim. Behav.* **27**, 376–380.

Miller, D. B. (1979b) Long-term recognition of father's song by female zebra finches. *Nature* **280**, 389–391.

Møller, A. P. (1983) Song activity and territory quality in the corn bunting *Miliaria calandra*; with comments on mate selection. *Ornis Scand.* **14**, 81–89.

Møller, A. P. (1991) Why mated songbirds sing so much: mate guarding and male announcement of mate fertility status. *Am. Nat.* **138**, 994–1014.

Monroe, B. L., Jr and Sibley, C. G. (1993) *A World Checklist of Birds*. New Haven, CT: Yale University Press.

Mooney, R. (1992) Synaptic basis for developmental plasticity in a birdsong nucleus. *J. Neurosci.* **12**, 2464–2477.

Mooney, R. and Konishi, M. (1991) Two distinct inputs to an avian song nucleus activate different glutamate receptor subtypes on individual neurons. *Proc. Natl Acad. Sci. USA* **88**, 4075–4079.

Morris, R. G. M., Davis, S. and Butcher, S. P. (1990) Hippocampal synaptic plasticity and NMTA receptors: a role in information storage? *Phil. Trans. Roy. Soc. Lond. B* **329**, 187–204.

Morton, M. L., Pereyra, M. E. and Baptista, L. F. (1985) Photoperiodically induced ovarian growth in the White-crowned sparrow (*Zonotrichia leucophrys gambelii*) and its augmentation by song. *Comp. Biochem. Physiol.* **80**, 93–97.

Mountjoy, D. J. and Lemon, R. E. (1991) Song as an attractant for male and female European starlings, and the influence of song complexity on their response. *Behav. Ecol. Sociobiol.* **28**, 97–100.

Nelson, D. A. (1992) Song overproduction and selective attrition during song development in the field sparrow (*Spisella pusilla*). *Behav. Ecol. Sociobiol.* **30**, 415–424.

Nixdorf, B.E., Davis, S.E. and DeVoogd, T.J. (1989) Morphology of Golgi-impregnated neurons in hyperstriatum ventralis, pars caudalis (HVc) in adult male and female canaries. *J. Comp. Neurol.* **284**, 337–349.

Nixdorf-Bergweiler, B. E., Wallhausser-Franke, E. and DeVoogd, T. J. (1995) Regressive development in neuronal structure during song learning in birds. *J. Neurobiol.* **27**, 204–215.

Nordeen, E. J. and Nordeen, K. W. (1988) Sex and regional differences in the incorporation of neurons born during song learning in zebra finches. *J. Neurosci.* **8**, 2869–2874.

Nordeen, E. J., Nordeen, K. W. and Arnold, A. P. (1987) Sexual differentiation of androgen accumulation within the zebra finch brain through selective cell loss and addition. *J. Comp. Neurol.* **259**, 393–399.

Nordeen, E. J., Grace, A., Burek, M. J. and Nordeen, K. W. (1992) Sex-dependent loss of projection neurons involved in avian song learning. *J. Neurobiol.* **23**, 671–679.

Nordeen, K. W. and Nordeen, E. J. (1988) Projection neurons with a vocal motor pathway are born during song learning in zebra finches. *Nature* **334**, 149–151.

Nordeen, K. W. and Nordeen, E. J. (1992) Auditory feedback is necessary for the maintenance of stereotyped song in adult zebra finches. *Behav. Neural Biol.* **57**, 58–66.

Nordeen, K. W., Nordeen, E. J. and Arnold, A. P. (1986) Estrogen establishes sex differences in androgen accumulation in zebra finch brain. *J. Neurosci.* **6**, 734–738.

Nordeen, K. W., Nordeen, E. J. and Arnold, A. P. (1987) Estrogen accumulation in zebra finch song control nuclei: implications for sexual differentiation and adult activation of behavior. *J. Neurobiol.* **18**, 569–582.

Nottebohm, F. (1972) The origins of vocal learning. *Am. Nat.* **106**, 116–140.

Nottebohm, F. (1980a) Testosterone triggers growth of brain vocal control nuclei in adult female canaries. *Brain Res.* **189**, 429–437.

Nottebohm, F. (1980b) Brain correlates of a learned motor skill. *Verh. Dtsch. Zool. Ges.* **1980**, 262–267.

Nottebohm, F. (1981) A brain for all seasons: cyclical anatomical changes in song-control nuclei of the canary brain. *Science* **214**, 1368–1370.

Nottebohm, F. (1984) Birdsong as a model in which to study brain processes related to learning. *Condor* **86**, 227–236.

Nottebohm, F. and Arnold, A. P. (1976) Sexual dimorphism in vocal control areas of the song bird brain. *Science* **194**, 211–213.

Nottebohm, F. and Nottebohm, M. E. (1978) Relationship between song repertoire and age in the canary, *Serinus canarius. Z. Tierpsychol.* **46**, 298–305.

Nottebohm, F., Stokes, T. M. and Leonard, C. M. (1976) Central control of song in the canary. *J. Comp. Neurol.* **165**, 457–468.

Nottebohm, F., Kasparian, S. and Pandazis, C. (1981) Brain space for a learned task. *Brain Res.* **213**, 99–109.

Nottebohm, F., Kelley, D. B. and Paton, J. A. (1982) Connections of vocal control nuclei in the canary telencephalon. *J. Comp. Neurol.* **207**, 344–357.

Nottebohm, F., Nottebohm, M. E. and Crane, L. A. (1986) Developmental and seasonal changes in canary song and their relation to changes in the anatomy of song-control nuclei. *Behav. Neural Biol.* **46**, 445–471.

Nottebohm, F., Nottebohm, M. E., Crane, L. A. and Wingfield, J. C. (1987) Seasonal changes in gonadal hormone levels of adult male canaries and their relation to song. *Behav. Neural Biol.* **42**, 197–211.

Payne, R. B. (1981) Song learning and social interaction in indigo buntings. *Anim. Behav.* **29**, 688–697.

Payne R. B. and Payne, K. (1977) Social organisation and mating success in local song populations of village indigobirds *Vidua chalybeata. Z.*

Tierpsychol. **45**, 133–173.

Peek, F. W. (1972) An experimental study of the territorial function of vocal and visual display in the male red-winged blackbird. *Anim. Behav.* **20**, 112–118.

Petrinovich, L. and Baptista, L. F. (1987) Song development in the white-crowned sparrow: modification of learned song. *Anim. Behav.* **35**, 961–974.

Pohl-Apel, G. and Sossinka, R. (1984) Hormonal determination of song capacity in females of the zebra finch: critical phase of treatment. *Z. Tierpsychol.* **64**, 330–336.

Price, P. (1979) Developmental determinants of structure in zebra finch song. *J. Comp. Physiol. Psychol.* **93**, 260–277.

Purvis, A. (1990) *Comparative analysis by independent contrasts (C.A.I.C.). A statistical package for the Apple Macintosh.* Oxford: University of Oxford.

Purvis, A. and Rambaut, A. (1994) *Comparative Analysis by Independent Contrasts (CAIC)*, Version 2, Oxford University. Computerized algorithms and manual available through World Wide Web at http://evolve.zps.ox.ac.uk/CAIC/CAIC.html

Radesater, T., Jakobsson, S., Andbjer, N., Bylin, A. and Nystrom, K. (1987) Song rate and pair formation in the willow warbler, *Phylloscopus trochilus*. *Anim. Behav.* **35**, 1645–1651.

Reid, M. L. (1987) Costliness and reliability in the singing vigour of Ipswitch sparrows. *Anim. Behav.* **35**, 1735–1743.

Rodrigues, M. (1996) Song activity in the chiffchaff: territorial defence or mate guarding? *Anim. Behav.* **51**, 709–716.

Scharff, C. and Nottebohm, F. (1991) A comparative study of the behavioral deficits following lesions of various parts of the zebra finch song system: Implications for vocal learning. *J. Neurosci.* **11**, 2896–2913.

Schlinger, B. A. and Arnold, A. P. (1992a) Plasma sex steroids and tissue aromatization in hatchling zebra finches implications for the sexual differentiation of singing behavior. *Endocrinology* **130**, 289–299.

Schlinger, B. A. and Arnold, A. P. (1992b) Circulating estrogens in a male songbird originate in the brain. *Proc. Natl Acad. Sci. USA* **89**, 7650–7653.

Schlinger, B. A. and Arnold, A. P. (1993) Estrogen synthesis in vivo in the adult zebra finch: additional evidence that circulating estrogens can originate in brain. *Endocrinology* **133**, 2610–2616.

Searcy, W. A. (1979) Sexual selection and body size in male red-winged blackbirds. *Evolution* **33**, 649–661.

Searcy, W. A. (1992) Song repertoire and mate choice in birds. *Am. Zool.* **32**, 71–80.

Searcy, W. A. and Andersson, M. (1986) Sexual selection and the evolution of song. *Ann. Rev. Ecol. Syst.* **17**, 507–533.

Searcy, W. A. and Brenowitz, E. A. (1988) Sexual differences in species recognition of avian song. *Nature* **332**, 152–154.

Searcy, W. A. and Yasukawa, K. (1995) *Polygyny and Sexual Selection in Red-winged Blackbirds*. Princeton, NJ: Princeton University Press.

Searcy, W. A. and Yasukawa, K. (1996) Song and female choice. In Kroodsma, D. E. and Miller, E. H. (eds) *Ecology and Evolution of*

Acoustic Communication in Birds. Ithaca, NY: Cornell University Press, pp. 454–473.

Searcy, W. A., McArthur, P. D. and Yasukawa, K. (1985) Song repertoire size and male quality in song sparrows. *Condor* **87**, 222–228.

Sherman, P. (1988) The levels of analysis. *Anim. Behav.* **36**, 616–619.

Slagsvold, T. (1977) Bird song activity in relation to breeding cycle, spring weather, and environmental phonology. *Ornis Scand.* **8**, 197–222.

Slater, P. J. B., Jones, A. and TenCate, C. (1992) Can lack of experience delay the end of the sensitive period for song learning? *Neth. J. Zool.* **43**, 80–90.

Smith, D. G. (1979) Male singing ability and territory integrity in red-winged blackbirds (*Agelaius phoeniceus*). *Behaviour* **68**, 193–206.

Smith, G. T., Brenowitz, E. A., Wingfield, J. C. and Baptista, L. F. (1995) Seasonal changes in song nuclei and song behavior in Gambel's white-crowned sparrows. *J. Neurobiol.* **28**, 114–125.

Sober, E. (1998) *Reconstructing the Past: Parsimony, Evolution and Inference*. Cambridge, MA: MIT Press.

Sohrabji, F., Nordeen, E. J. and Nordeen, K. W. (1990) Selective impairment of song learning following lesions of a song control nucleus in juvenile zebra finches. *Neural Behav. Biol.* **53**, 51–63.

Spector, D. A. (1991) The singing behavior of yellow warblers. *Behaviour* **117**, 29–52.

Staicer, C. A., Spector, D. A. and Horn, A. G. (1996) The dawn chorus and other diel patterns in acoustic signaling. In Kroodsma, D. E. and Miller, E. H. (eds) *Ecology and Evolution of Acoustic Communication in Birds*. Ithaca, NY: Cornell University Press, pp. 426–453.

Steward, C.B. (1993) The posers and pitfalls of parsimony. *Nature* **361**, 603–607.

Swofford, D.L. and Olsen, G.J. (1990) Phylogeny reconstruction. In: D.M. Hillis and G. Moritz (eds). *Molecular systematics*. pp. 411–501. Sunderland, Massachusetts: Sinauer Associates.

Székely, T., Catchpole, C. K., DeVoogd, A., Marchl, Z. and DeVoogd, T. J. (1996) Evolutionary changes in a song control area of the brain (HVC) are associated with evolutionary changes in song repertoire among European warblers (Sylviidae). *Proc. Roy. Soc. Lond. B* **263**, 607–610.

Tinbergen, N. (1963) On aims and methods of ethology. *Z. Tierpsychol.* **20**, 410–433.

Vates, G. E. and Nottebohm, F. (1995) Feedback circuitry within a song-learning pathway. *Proc. Natl Acad. Sci. USA* **92**, 5139–5143.

Vates, G. E., Broome, B. M., Mello, C. V. and Nottebohm, F. (1996) Auditory pathways of caudal telencephalon and their relation to the song system of adult male zebra finches (*Taenopygia guttata*). *J. Comp. Neurol.* **366**, 613–642.

Vates, G. E., Vicario, D. S. and Nottebohm, F. (1997) Reafferent thalamo-'cortical' loops in the song system of oscine songbirds. *J. Comp. Neurol.* **380**, 275–290.

Vicario, D. S. (1993) A new brainstem pathway for bocal control in the zebra finch song system. *Neuroreport* **4**, 983–986.

Vockel, A., Pröve, E. and Balthazart, J. (1988) Changes in the activity of testosterone-metabolizing enzymes in the brain of male and female zebra finches during the post-hatching period. *Brain Res.* **463**, 330–340.

Vockel, A., Pröve, E. and Balthazart, J. (1990) Effects of castration and testosterone treatment on the activity of testosterone-metabolizing enzymes in the brains of male and female zebra finches. *J. Neurobiol.* **21**, 808–825.

Volman, S. F. (1993) Development of neural selectivity for birdsong during vocal learning. *J. Neurosci.* **13**, 4737–4747.

Vu, E. T., Mazured, M. E. and Kuo, Y.-C. (1994) Identification of a forebrain motor programming network for the learned song of zebra finches. *J. Neurosci.* **14**, 6924–6934.

Wallhausser-Franke, E., Collins, C. E. and DeVoogd, T. J. (1995a) Developmental changes in the distribution of NADPH-diaphorase containing neurons in telencephalic nuclei of the zebra finch song system. *J. Comp. Neurol.*, **356**, 345–354.

Wallhausser-Franke, E., Nixdorf-Bergweiler, B. E. and DeVoogd, T. J. (1995b) Song isolation is associated with maintaining high spine frequencies on zebra finch IMAN neurons. *Neurobiol. Learn. Mem.* **64**, 25–35.

Waser, M. S. and Marler, P. (1977) Song learning in canaries. *J. Comp. Physiol. Psych.* **91**, 1–7.

Wasserman, F. E. (1977) Intraspecific acoustical interference in the white-throated sparrow *Zonotrichia albicollis*. *Anim. Behav.* **25**, 949–952.

Welling, P., Koivula, K. and Lahti, K. (1995) The dawn chorus is linked with female fertility in the Willow Tit, *Parus montanus*. *J. Avian Biol*, **26**, 241–246.

Westcott, D. (1992) Inter- and intra-sexual selection: the role of song in a lek mating system. *Anim. Behav.* **44**, 695–703.

Wild, J. M. (1993) Descending projections of the songbird nucleus robustus archistriatalis. *J. Comp. Neurol.* **328**, 225–241.

Wiley, R. H., Hatchwell, B. J. and Davies, N. (1991) Recognition of individual males songs by female dunnocks – a mechanism increasing the number of copulatory partners and reproductive success. *Ethology* **88**, 145–153.

Williams, H. (1985) Sexual dimorphism of auditory activity in the zebra finch song system. *Behav. Neural. Biol.* **44**, 470–484.

Williams, H. (1989) Multiple representations and auditory-motor interactions in the avian song system. *Ann. N.Y. Acad. Sci.* **563**, 148–164.

Williams, H. (1990a) Models for song learning in the zebra finch: fathers or others? *Anim. Behav.* **39**, 745–757.

Williams, H. (1990b) Bird song. In Kesner, R. C. and Olton, D. S. (eds) *Neurobiology of Comparative Cognition*. Hillsdale, NJ: Erlbaum, pp. 77–126.

Williams, H. and Nottebohm, F. (1985) Auditory responses in avian vocal motor neurons: a motor theory for song perception in birds. *Science* **228**, 279–282.

Williams, H. and Staples, K. (1992) Syllable chunking in zebra finch (*Taeniopygia guttata*) song. *J. Comp. Psychol.* **106**, 272–286.

Wingfield, J. C. and Farner, D. S. (1993) Endocrinology of reproduction in wild species. In Farner, D. S., King, J. R. and Parkes, K. C. (eds) *Avian Biology*, Vol. 9. San Diego: Academic Press, pp. 163–327.

Wright, J. and Cuthill, I. (1992) Monogamy in the European starling. *Behaviour* **120**, 262–285.

Yasukawa, K. (1981) Song repertoires and density assessment in red-winged blackbirds: further tests of the Beau Geste hypothesis. *Behav. Ecol. Sociobiol.* **16**, 171–175.

Yasukawa, K., Blank, J. L. and Patterson, C. B. (1980) Song repertoires and sexual selection in the red-winged blackbird. *Behav. Ecol. Sociobiol.* **7**, 233– 238.

Zann, R. and Straw, B. (1984) Feeding ecology and breeding of zebra finches in farmland in northern Victoria. *Austral. Wildl. Res.* **11**, 533–552.

Zorumski, C. F. and Izumi, Y. (1993) Nitric oxide and hippocampal synaptic plasticity. *Biochem. Pharmacol.* **46**, 777–785.

13

The African Grey Parrot: How Cognitive Processing Might Affect Allospecific Vocal Learning

Irene Maxine Pepperberg

Department of Ecology and Evolutionary Biology, College of Arts and Sciences, Faculty of Science, The University of Arizona, Tucson, AZ 85721, USA

Introduction

The word 'parrot' brings to mind visions of brightly colored hookbills flying through a rain-forest canopy, but the term has a second equally well-known connotation. 'Parrot' is synonymous with facile, mindless mimicry – a consequence of numerous anecdotal reports in the popular press (e.g. Amsler, 1947; Hensley, 1980). In captivity, parrots reproduce everything from the sound of water gurgling down a drain to the human voice, and such random reproduction hardly suggests that these birds have some defined basis for deciding what they should or should not learn. Captivity, however, may cause natural processes to adapt in highly peculiar ways, and I propose that what we call 'mimicry' – the mere reproduction of allospecific sounds – is far too simplistic a way to describe psittacine behavior. Specifically, I believe that by examining psittacine vocal learning from a cognitive perspective, we can understand how and why these birds choose to acquire and produce allospecific vocalizations, and particularly vocalizations that are used in meaningful ways.

Few experimental studies of psittacine allospecific vocal learning exist, particularly from a cognitive perspective. In the wild, psittacine mimicry has

ANIMAL COGNITION IN NATURE
ISBN 0-12-077030-X

been described for just two species, the Grey Parrot (*Psittacus erithacus*; Cruickshank *et al.*, 1993) and the Galah (*Cacatua roseicapilla*; Rowley and Chapman, 1986). Laboratory studies have investigated allospecific vocal learning in Budgerigars (*Melopsittacus undulatus*; Gramza, 1970) and Grey Parrots (Todt, 1975; Pepperberg, 1981, 1993). Only recently, however, have studies in my laboratory begun to examine how cognitive processes might be involved in directing the acquisition of allospecific vocalizations (Pepperberg, 1994a, 1997; Pepperberg and McLaughlin, 1996; Pepperberg *et al.*, 1998).

In this chapter, I explain what I mean by a cognitive perspective, review what little is currently known about psittacine vocal behavior, and describe several studies that my students and I have performed concerning allospecific vocal learning in Grey Parrots. I then propose a paradigm for adaptive vocal learning in these birds that is based on a cognitive perspective. I close by suggesting avenues of future research.

A cognitive perspective

Cognition can be defined in many ways (e.g. Kamil, 1988; Zentall, 1993); thus I begin by explaining what I mean by a cognitive perspective. Such a perspective, I believe, proposes that we can learn most about animal capacities by hypothesizing that animals engage in extensive information processing, that is, at least to some degree, they do not simply react mindlessly to environmental stimuli, but that they actually process the stimuli and choose to react in certain ways. By extensive processing, I mean the combination of two abilities, the first being a prerequisite for the second. The first is simply the ability to use experience to solve current problems. An organism faced with green and red fruits, for instance, might recall that red indicates ripe and tasty and green indicates unripe and bitter, and therefore choose the red one. The second is the more complicated ability to choose, from among many sets of acquired information, the set appropriate to the current problem (Pepperberg, 1990b), that is, to recognize conditions under which selection of green fruit might be wise (e.g. when red indicates spoilage). This last ability often requires the capacity to transfer a skill learned in one situation or modality to another (Rozin, 1976). An organism limited to the first ability both has learned some important associations and is processing some information, but lacks the flexibility that is a hallmark of what I define as *cognitive* processing.

Based on this operative definition of cognition, I suggest how a cognitive approach might help us understand psittacine vocal behavior. A cognitive approach asks us first to determine if a bird's behavior is directed by simple associations (eat what others eat), by processing of current information based on similar past events (using memory to recognize when an item is suitable to eat), or processing that also incorporates information from a variety of

Table 13.1 Examples to demonstrate distinctions among simple associations, information processing and cognitive processing. These categories form a hierarchy: simple associations are necessary for information processing and information processing is necessary for cognitive processing. The first two examples within each category represent possible experiences of a bird in nature; the third example in each category represents what might occur in an experiment in a psychology laboratory.

Simple Associations:
  Lightning, thunder $\rightarrow\rightarrow$ take shelter
  Conspecific eats X $\rightarrow\rightarrow$ I eat X, too
  Hit button with red light $\rightarrow\rightarrow$ get food

Information Processing:
  Most holes in trees are safe shelters $\rightarrow\rightarrow$ I'll check this one out
  Round and red object in tree tasted good last time $\rightarrow\rightarrow$ I'll eat it again
  Hitting button if two objects are both red and round gives me food; avoiding button if they are both red but one is square gives me food $\rightarrow\rightarrow$ if anything is different between any two objects I should avoid the button

Cognitive Processing:
  I hear lightning and thunder, but I'm not near any tree holes $\rightarrow\rightarrow$ maybe this hollow log will be just as good; if not, I probably have time to fly back to my home range
  Round and red generally means something good to eat, but red and round in this particular tree tasted bad at this time last year $\rightarrow\rightarrow$ I'll look somewhere else, or maybe try the greenish ones
  I see two objects, one is red and round, the other is green and round; do I say I see two things, that they are different color, or that the green one is bigger? $\rightarrow\rightarrow$ I hear the question 'How many?' and based on that information, I choose to say 'two'

experiences (do I decide to eat this fruit based only on its color, or do I need to take other pieces of information into account?; see Table 13.1). The approach then asks us to use this knowledge to explain why a behavior pattern occurs as it does. I propose that the last and most complex of these processes (*cognitive* processing) may help us understand how wild parrots use some species-specific vocalizations. I then expand this proposal to suggest a connection between cognitive processing and *allospecific* vocal learning in parrots, and the worth of this connection for explaining how, why and when such learning may occur.

A brief survey of psittacine vocal behavior in the wild and in aviary settings

Few researchers have examined how wild parrots use their species-specific vocalizations. I, therefore, review vocalization studies on some parrot species with respect to 'sentinel' behavior, individual recognition and duetting. I also describe two recorded cases of interspecific mimicry.

'Sentinel' behavior

During foraging, some psittacids engage in 'sentinel' behavior: one member of the flock perches in an exposed position and calls at the approach of danger. Even if its alarm calls do not refer to specific predators, the *nature* of each call must be specific. False positives or negatives would each have serious consequences for survival; thus sentinel behavior reflects some cognitive capacity for categorization and using information flexibly. A predator observed routinely in one location, for example, must be recognized even when the location varies. Sentinel behavior has been observed in Indigo Macaws (*Anodorhynchus leari*; Yamashita, 1987), Puerto Rican Parrots (*Amazona vittata*; Snyder et al., 1987), Maroon-fronted Parrots (*Rhynchopsittica terrisi*; Lawson and Lanning, 1980) and White-fronted Amazons (*Amazona albifrons*; Levinson, 1980). A study of the Short-billed White-tailed Black Cockatoo (*Calyptorhynchus funereus latirostris*) does not mention the presence of birds specifically acting as sentinels, but does report that any individual in a flock will emit alert screams upon noting anything that is unusual (Saunders, 1983). [Note that some psychologists, e.g. Hearst (1984), would argue that detecting something 'unusual' would require a bird to have some form of representation of what is 'usual'. Given the extensive areas over which these birds forage (Saunders, 1983), such representations would require extensive memory for what was 'usual' in a particular spot; a bird would also need considerable flexibility to process 'usual' vs. 'unusual' changes with respect to each spot in the area.]

Individual recognition

Individual recognition can occur between members of mated pairs, members of a flock, and between parents and offspring. Such recognition requires cognitive processing: the ability to learn, memorize and, most importantly, the flexibility to update information and transfer it among situations. Aspects of individual recognition have been observed in a number of parrot species. Bahama Amazons (*Amazona leucocephala bahamensis*) may use calls for individual recognition of mated pairs within groups (Gnam, 1988). Individual Short-billed White-tailed Black Cockatoos can be identified by differences in the lengths of parts of their calls (Saunders, 1983). Calls that can be used to identify individuals may be part of the repertoire of Glossy Black Cockatoos (*Calyptorhynchus lathami*; Pepper, personal communication). Rowley (1980) proposes parent–offspring vocal recognition in Galahs. Wright (1996) has demonstrated the existence of dialects in Yellow-naped Amazons (*Amazona auropalliata*). Several roosts can share a dialect and some birds at roosts bordering two dialects use the calls of both neighboring dialects interchangeably; the dialects may possibly be used for flock recognition (note Schindlinger, 1995). Bradbury and Wright (personal communication) are now studying whether vocalizations are used for individual recognition in these birds.

Duetting

Some birds, particularly ones that form long-term monogamous pairs, learn duets. When dispersed in a flock, birds may use different duets than when in close contact; such behavior might mediate interactions among flock members (Gwinner and Kneutgen, 1962; Mebes, 1978; Wickler, 1980) and the appropriate set of vocalizations must be chosen for a given situation. Although only rarely recorded in the wild (e.g. Nottebohm, 1972), these duets seem more complex and seem to take longer to learn than those of shorter-lived species (e.g. wrens; Farabaugh, 1982). In general, duetting would appear to require considerable plasticity and learning capacity. Although duetting appears unrelated to pair bonding in aviary-dwelling Canary-winged Parakeets (*Brotogeris v. veriscolurus*; Arrowood, 1988), the role of duetting in the behavioral repertoire of wild, longer-lived psittacids remains unknown. Antiphonal duetting between mated pairs has been reported in the wild only for the Orange-winged Amazon, *Amazona amazonica* (Nottebohm, 1972) and the function of such behavior has not been determined.

Mimicry

Why parrots reproduce allospecific vocalizations (i.e. what I am at present calling mimicry), the extent of their mimicry, what, if any, cognitive processes are involved in mimicry and how parrots *learn* to mimic in the wild are questions that remain unanswered. Why, for example, is evidence for mimicry in the wild so rare? Allospecific mimicry in the wild has been documented for only two psittacine species. Two Grey Parrots, recorded while vocalizing in a single tree, produced 11 different mimicries representing ten species, including a bat (Cruickshank *et al.*, 1993). No explanation for the behavior was given. Two wild Galahs were recorded giving and responding to calls of the species under which they were raised, the Major Mitchell's Cockatoo (*Cacatua leadbeateri*; Rowley and Chapman, 1986). Such behavior appeared to maintain their integration within the alien flock.

The paucity of observed mimicry in the wild may have a simple explanation. Possibly parrots, like Mynahs (*Gracula religiosa*; Bertram, 1970), predominantly reproduce one another's vocalizations. I prefer, however, to categorize such behavior as conspecific learning (Nottebohm, 1972) and reserve mimicry for the behavior that results in what is defined by Baylis (1982, p. 52) as 'the resemblance of one or more vocalizations of an individual bird of one species either to the vocalizations typical of individuals of another species or to some environmental sound'.

Under that definition, captive pet psittacids apparently mimic indiscriminately (Amsler, 1947; Hensley, 1980). Few laboratory studies, however, have examined conditions under which mimicry occurs. Mowrer (1954, 1958) failed to teach a significant amount of allospecific material to any of several psittacids, and Gramza (1970) showed that some (but not all) budgerigars kept as isolates could learn pure tones, nonspecies-specific whistles and bits of music from tutor tapes. Todt (1975) demonstrated the efficacy of a modeling technique using two humans to train Grey Parrots to acquire human speech patterns. My own research (Pepperberg, 1981, 1993, 1994a; Pepperberg and McLaughlin, 1996; Pepperberg *et al.*, 1998) has shown that an adapted version of Todt's technique is more effective than various forms of noninteractive input for teaching Grey Parrots not only to reproduce human utterances but also to use these vocalizations meaningfully (see later). I suggest that 'the behavior' that results in mimicry might be affected by a constellation of conditions, and that a cognitive approach provides a means of identifying the different conditions and their various effects.

What is the basis for allospecific vocal learning in psittacids?

Although limited, data on psittacine vocal communication present a picture of a complex system. At the least, information processing capacities are likely involved in sentinel behavior, individual vocal recognition, and possibly even duetting. It is quite likely that cognitive processing (i.e. the flexibility to adapt one's knowledge to varying conditions) is also involved. Might such capacities be involved in the selection and use of allospecific sounds? Does the ability to decode ongoing speech – a *cognitive* similarity I have found between Greys and humans (Pepperberg, 1990b, 1992b; Patterson and Pepperberg, 1994; see Lieberman, 1984) – enable production not just of speech but also of other allospecific vocalizations? Is the decoding process a byproduct of, or prerequisite for, cognitive capacities? Why do captive pet psittacids appear to mimic indiscriminately, whereas birds in operant psychology studies usually fail to learn targeted speech (e.g. Mowrer, 1958)? I cannot yet answer all these questions; however, I believe that the answers are to be found by examining the extent to which cognitive processing is required for learning, that is, by using a cognitive approach in designing experiments.

Factors involved in acquiring an allospecific code

Specifically, I wonder whether wild parrots' physical capacities for imitation might somehow be tempered to prevent maladaptive mimicry. In the wild, for example, selection would presumably work against parrots that reproduced random environmental noises because such vocalizations would be indistinguishable from background sounds. Birds that could, in contrast, mimic – and thus maybe join or repel – sympatric species might fare quite well. What constraints might direct useful learning and screen out irrelevant sounds, and why do the constraints that appear to exist in the wild apparently fail under some types of captivity? My students and I believe that we have found at least some of these constraints in the Grey Parrot. The following sections describe the proposed constraints and our experimental results, and the possible reasons that parrots in different situations exhibit different types of learning.

What is true for psittacids may not, of course, hold for passerines, but some data suggest that avoidance of environmental sounds may be more widespread than was once thought. Lyrebirds (Menuridae), for example, which purportedly mimic a variety of natural and manmade environmental sounds, engage in this behavior only during subsong and apparently drop all environmental patterns except those of avian wingbeats from the adult repertoire (Robinson, 1975; Robinson and Curtis, 1996). Nevertheless, research must eventually be extended to other avian species to test the generality of the findings reported here.

Constraints on Grey Parrot mimicry: rationale for testing effects of input

If constraints do indeed exist on allospecific learning in Grey Parrots, the likely candidates are some of the same social constraints that occur for other birds. For some oscines, the extent, timing and even the presence of allospecific vocal learning are influenced by the form of input that is received (e.g. Baptista and Petrinovich, 1984, 1986). Some species may require visual and vocal interaction with a live tutor even for complete conspecific song learning (e.g. Zebra Finches, *Taeniopygia guttata*; Price, 1979[1]; see review, Slater *et al.*, 1988; cf. Adret, 1993). That the extent of social interaction may affect allospecific vocal learning in psittacids is, in fact, suggested by several studies earlier than my own. My work, however, focuses on how such social interaction and cognitive processing might be linked.

Such a link can be demonstrated only by determining which aspects of input are important for learning, whether these aspects involve social interaction or cognitive processing – or both – and also their relative importance. First, of course, those studies that failed to engender allospecific vocal learning must be noted. Comparing unsuccessful and successful training programs may suggest which aspects of input might be necessary for successful acquisition.

Prior to my studies, several researchers had attempted to teach psittacids to reproduce human speech (review in Pepperberg, 1990a). Little or nothing was learned by Budgerigars, a Yellow-headed Amazon (*Amazona ochrocephala*) and a Grey Parrot that heard repetitive human phrases and could receive food rewards for successful mimicry (Mowrer, 1954, 1958). In contrast, Greys that observed two humans interactively model specific vocal dialogues (Todt, 1975; Pepperberg, 1981, 1990a, 1993, 1994a) acquired targeted speech patterns.

Given the reputed ease with which these birds are assumed to acquire any sound in captivity (see Amsler, 1947), data on the effects of differential input were surprising. However, because different laboratories tested separate sets of conditions, the findings could have been a consequence of interlaboratory variation rather than different learning conditions (Slater, 1991). I therefore began a series of experiments to learn exactly what aspects of input enabled Grey Parrots to learn an allospecific vocal code.

Aspects of input to be tested

To demonstrate the relative importance of various aspects of input for learning, one must first identify the relevant aspects. According to a psychological paradigm called social modeling theory (Bandura, 1971, 1977), input is characterized by three main factors (reviewed in Pepperberg, 1985, 1992a, 1993, 1994a, 1997): (1) the degree to which input correlates with a specific aspect of an individual's environment (i.e. 'referentiality'; Smith, 1991); (2) extent to which input has functional meaning relevant to the individual's environment (known to psychologists as 'contextual applicability') and (3) the extent to which input is socially interactive.

Reference

Reference is, in part, what signals 'are about' (Smith, 1991). Reference concerns the direct relationship between a signal and an object or action. Reference is not always easily determined; e.g. when we say 'key', we generally mean a specific metal object [what Smith, (1991) labels an 'external' referent], but we may also mean an action, as to 'key' in data. Similarly, a bird that emits an alarm call may refer to both the predator and the action it is about to take. Thus, not all information contained in a signal involves a single referent, and determining the referent often requires cognitive processing on the part of the receiver. The receiver cannot simply process signal A, remember and interpret it as being associated with situation X, but must decide, based on additional information, among the possibilities X, Y and Z. The more explicit the referent of a signal, the more easily the signal appears to be learned.

Functionality

Functionality involves the pragmatics of signal use: when a signal is to be used and the effects of using information in the signal. Because use and effect of a signal may depend upon environmental context, functionality helps define reference – in the above example, it defines 'key' as a noun or verb. Cognitive processes are again important for extracting the function of a signal from what may be many possibilities in a given situation. The more explicit a signal's functionality, however, the more readily the signal appears to be learned.

Social interaction

Social interaction can highlight which components of the environment should be noted, emphasize common attributes – and thus possible underlying rules – of diverse actions, and allow input to be continuously adjusted to match the level of the receiver. Interaction may also provide a contextual explanation of the reasons for an action and demonstrate the consequences of an action (details in Pepperberg, 1993, 1994a, 1997). Interactive input also appears to facilitate learning, and, again, cognitive processing is likely involved in sorting out the different facets of a given interaction.

In sum, reference and functionality refer to the 'real-world' use of input, and social interaction highlights various components of the input. Researchers can specifically design input that varies with respect to these aspects and then evaluate the relative effects of such variation. To obtain information on the relative importance of these three aspects of input on learning in a mimetic species, I used several different conditions to train one adult and two juvenile Grey Parrots to produce English labels to identify various common objects. The majority of the material in the following sections, which describes this research, has been reported elsewhere (Pepperberg, 1994a, 1997; Pepperberg and McLaughlin, 1996; Pepperberg *et al.*, 1998) but is included for the convenience of the reader. Previous discussions of this material did not, however, explicitly emphasize a cognitive approach to interpreting the results, which is the point of this chapter.

The subjects and forms of input to be tested

The juvenile Grey Parrots, Alo and Kyaaro, were 10 and 6.5 months, respectively, at the beginning of the experiments, and the adult subject, Alex, was approximately 12 years old. I completed the study with Alex before I obtained the juveniles, and the birds were physically isolated from one another during the experiments with the juveniles. The juveniles had received no formal training before these experiments began and had acquired no human vocalizations. Alex, however, had had extensive training and had learned referential use of English labels for objects, shapes, colors and numbers up to six to identify, request, refuse and quantify objects (Pepperberg, 1981, 1987a, 1994b). He had been tested on concepts such as the presence or absence of sameness and difference, and on the ability to categorize objects with respect to color, shape or material (Pepperberg, 1983, 1987b, 1988). Other tests (Pepperberg, 1990b, 1992b) showed that he could comprehend as well as produce all his color, shape, material and category labels. He also had functional use of several phrases, e.g. 'Come here', 'You tickle', 'What's that?', 'I'm sorry', 'You tell me', 'Wanna go X' and 'Want Y', where X and Y are location and object labels.

Until the present experiments, Alex's training system maximized reference, functionality and social interaction. This system, called the model/rival (M/R) procedure, was adapted from the work of Todt (1975). M/R training involves three-way interactions between two humans and the avian student. M/R training primarily introduces new labels and concepts, but also aids in correcting pronunciation. Because the experiments described here are an in-depth comparison of training protocols, I provide details of the M/R procedure, although the material is available elsewhere (Pepperberg, 1981, 1983, 1990a,b,c, 1994a, 1997).

The M/R technique (Todt, 1975) uses human *social interaction* to demonstrate to a bird the targeted vocal behavior patterns. Sessions begin with a bird observing two humans handling an object in which the bird has already demonstrated some interest. One human acts as a trainer of the second human (the model/rival). The trainer presents and asks questions about the item ['What's here?', 'What matter (material)?' etc.]. The trainer rewards each correct identification with the item to which the label refers, thus demonstrating *referential* and *functional* use of labels, respectively, by providing a 1:1 correspondence between the label and the object, and modeling the use of the label as a means of obtaining the object (Pepperberg, 1981). A trainer shows disapproval for incorrect responses (errors similar to those made by a bird, such as partial identifications, unclear speech) by scolding the trainee and temporarily removing the object from sight. Thus, the second human not only acts as a model for the bird's responses and as a rival for the trainer's attention, but also illustrates the aversive consequences of errors. The model/rival is asked to speak more clearly or try again when responses are garbled or incorrect, thereby allowing a bird to observe 'corrective feedback' (see Goldstein, 1984; Vanayan *et al.*, 1985). The parrot is also included in these interactions. Because a bird is rewarded for successive approximations to a correct response, the protocol adjusts the level of training to the level of the bird. If a bird is inattentive or its accuracy regresses, trainers threaten to leave.

My model/rival (M/R) protocol requires repeating an interaction while reversing the roles of the trainer and the model/rival, and, as noted, includes the parrot in the interactions (Pepperberg, 1981). Birds thereby learn to engage in a communicative process that involves reciprocity and that can be used by either party to request information or effect environmental change. Without role reversal, birds exhibit two behavior patterns inconsistent with interactive, referential communication: they do not transfer responses to anyone other than the human who posed the questions during training, and they do not learn both parts of the interaction (Todt, 1975).

Table 13.2 Components and results of tutoring (after Pepperberg, 1997)

	Reference	Function-ality	Social interaction	Parrot tested	Learning occurred?
Model/rival	Yes	Yes	Yes	All	Yes
Model/rival-variant 1	No	No	Yes	Alex	Partial
Model/rival-variant 2	Yes	Minimal	Minimal	Alo, Kyaaro	No
Basic video	Yes	Partial	No	Alo, Kyaaro	No
Video-variant 1	Yes	Partial	Minimal	Alo, Kyaaro	Minimal
Video-variant 2	Yes	Potential	No	Alo, Kyaaro	No
Audiotape	No	No	No	Alo, Kyaaro	No

I designed the studies described here to examine how various levels of reference, social interaction and functionality might affect learning not only with respect to sound reproduction, but also with respect to comprehension and appropriate use (i.e. actions that require cognitive processing). To provide input that varied with respect to these factors, I contrasted sessions of M/R, videotape and audiotape tutoring. M/R and videotape training sessions could be designed so as to have varying components of input (see Table 13.2).

To eliminate as much reference and functionality as possible, and still retain the two-trainer method, I designed the 'M/R-variant 1' procedure (Pepperberg, 1994a). Here, the usual M/R procedure was altered so that two humans enacted the same roles as in basic M/R training, but no longer emphasized any connection between labels and specific objects or collections. In the presence of the bird, one human posed a question on a specific topic but in the absence of any objects and, in response, the other human produced a string of labels. As in the basic M/R procedure, roles were often reversed and the parrot was included in the interactions. Correct responses garnered vocal praise and the opportunity to request anything desired (Pepperberg, 1987a); errors elicited scolding and 'time-outs'.

To eliminate some functionality and as much social interaction as possible, and to examine in Grey Parrots the effect of what is known as 'joint attention' in the child language acquisition literature (e.g. Baldwin, 1991), I designed the 'M/R-variant 2' procedure (Pepperberg and McLaughlin, 1996). Here, the usual M/R procedure was amended such that the only aspects that remained were the use of a live trainer and a referential reward. A single trainer, rather than a pair, sat with her back to a bird, who was seated on a perch so as to be within reach of an object suspended by a pulley system. The trainer produced relevant phrases and sentences in which the object label was always stressed and in the final position (Pepperberg, 1981), e.g. 'You have a shiny *key*!', 'You gonna get the *key*?', etc. so as to replicate what is often heard during language-learning in young children (see de Villiers and de Villiers, 1978). Conceivably parrots, like humans, most readily remember the ends of word strings (Lenneberg, 1967; Silverstone, 1989). The trainer never made eye contact with the bird, never presented the object directly to the bird, nor did she ever focus her attention on the object while interacting with the bird. She would reward any attempt at the targeted label with vocal praise.

To provide training that closely followed the M/R procedure, but eliminated any social interaction and minimized contextual applicability, I used a 'basic video' procedure (Pepperberg, 1994a). Here, I videotaped M/R sessions of the adult trained parrot, Alex, and exposed the juvenile birds to those tapes. During taping of these training videos, Alex occasionally erred or interrupted with requests for other objects and changes of location (Pepperberg, 1983, 1987a, 1994a), which provided the opportunity to engage him in 'corrective feedback'. Thus, although Alex already knew the targeted labels (Pepperberg, 1990a,b), tapes did not present the targeted material as a review but rather recreated training sessions. As in live M/R presentations, trainers also reversed roles and also occasionally erred. The tapes furthermore retained breaks for nonvocal exchanges (e.g. when trainers preened Alex) and trainers' departures by using, respectively, scenes of such nonvocal interactions or a blank screen. A zoom lens enabled us to include life-size images of Alex and the targeted objects in addition to the somewhat smaller images of the entire training scenario (the object, Alex and two humans; Pepperberg *et al.*, 1998). While watching these tapes, the juveniles sat on a perch in front of a TV monitor in the absence of direct social interaction with trainers; no humans were present after a bird was situated on its perch. By watching a tape of a human or Alex produce a particular sound and either receive an object or be scolded, juveniles saw but did not experience directly the effect of a vocalization. Videos, therefore, demonstrated reference but lacked clear functional meaning. A previous study (Rutledge and Pepperberg, 1988) showed that Alex could respond to objects presented via a live video link; Grey Parrots thus have the capacity to recognize two-dimensional video representations.

Given that children often learn from television (e.g. 'Sesame Street') only when they view such programs with an *interactive* adult, e.g. someone who questions them about the activities being viewed (Lemish and Rice, 1986), I decided to expose the parrots to other forms of video input that involved more interaction with the human trainers. For the children, the extent of interaction seemed to be critical, because not all children learned in the presence of adults (St Peters *et al.*, 1989). My students and I tested this premise for Grey Parrots with 'video-variant 1' (Pepperberg *et al.*, 1998). We thus repeated video sessions but this time included 'co-viewers': trainers who merely ensured that the birds attended to the monitor for the entire session. Trainers provided social approbation for viewing and pointed to the screen, making comments like 'Look what Alex has!' Because we wished to separate out the effect of having a human present who interacted with the bird from the effect of having a human present who interacted with both the bird and the actions on the tape (Pepperberg *et al.*, 1998), the co-viewer did not repeat new labels, ask questions or relate the content to other training sessions. Any attempt a bird made at the label would be rewarded with vocal praise and not the object. Thus the amount of social interaction was limited and the amount of functional meaning was the same as in the basic videotape session. Note that for all video presentations, we spectrographically analysed (Kay 5500 DSP Sona-Graph) the audio portion of the video to ensure that the sound was not degraded compared to that of Alex 'live' (Pepperberg *et al.*, 1998).

In order to ensure that lack of reward for an attempt at a targeted vocalization had not been the factor that prevented learning from video, I designed the 'video-variant 2' procedure (Pepperberg *et al.*, 1998). Although neither parrot had used labels from the video sessions in the kind of vocal 'practice' that we generally heard following M/R sessions (see Pepperberg *et al.*, 1991), possibly they had attempted to produce the labels during video sessions and lack of reward had extinguished their behavior (Pepperberg, 1994a). Thus, students and I repeated the basic videotape protocol, but included an 'automatic' reward system (a pulley) so that a parrot could, in the absence of social interaction, receive the item if it attempted to produce the label. The pulley system was controlled by a student in another room who monitored the parrot's utterances through headphones. We taped sessions to test for (inter)observer reliability.

In addition, to test the effects of total absence of reference, context and social interaction, I exposed the juveniles to audiotapes (Pepperberg, 1994a). Audiotapes consisted of the audio portion of a basic videotape presentation, and thus were parallel to the M/R and video procedures but eliminated all reference and context. Juveniles were exposed to 'basic audiotape' sessions in isolation (i.e. with no social interaction), and no objects or actions were associated with the sounds presented over the speaker. Note that this procedure replicated the early studies of song learning in birds in social isolation (e.g. Marler, 1970).

Experiments with Alo and Kyaaro

Each bird received training on human labels under several conditions (Pepperberg, 1994a; Pepperberg and McLaughlin, 1996; Pepperberg *et al.*, 1998). I chose labels that the aforementioned Alex could clearly produce (Pepperberg, 1981, 1990a) to ensure that the vocalizations were within the capacity of the species. I also chose objects in which the birds had previously demonstrated interest to ensure that differential motivation to obtain an item would not affect the rate of label acquisition (e.g. Pepperberg *et al.*, 1991). Each bird received labels in M/R, M/R-variant 2, basic video, video-variant

1, video-variant 2 and audiotape sessions. Neither juvenile received training on M/R-variant 1.

I counterbalanced labels, so that, with a few exceptions, labels used for one bird with one technique were used for the other bird with another technique. So, for example, Alo received training on 'cork' in M/R sessions, whereas Kyaaro was initially exposed to 'cork' in basic video sessions. Both birds, however, were exposed to 'paper' via live tutors, to 'rock' via audiotape, and to 'key' and 'block' in M/R-variant 2 in order to compare their speeds of learning. For each bird, I repeated one of the two labels from the basic video in the video-variant 1 condition to test for possible effects of co-viewers, and repeated some labels (e.g. 'cork') that had not been learned from the nonbasic M/R procedures in subsequent M/R sessions (see Pepperberg *et al.*, 1998).

Alo's results

Alo never clearly produced, in the presence of trainers, any labels experienced via M/R-variant 2 (key, block), basic or video-variant 2 [wood, nail (initial training), chalk, chain] or audio (key, rock) training (Pepperberg, 1994a; Pepperberg and McLaughlin, 1996; Pepperberg *et al.*, 1998). Tapes of solitary sound productions also revealed a total lack of 'practice' (see Pepperberg *et al.*, 1991) of these labels, in contrast to the frequent practice of labels trained in M/R sessions (see Pepperberg, 1994a; Pepperberg and McLaughlin, 1996). Alo did attempt to produce the label trained during video-variant 1 (nail), but failed to identify the object or even produce an approximation of the correct label on formal tests for labels trained in this and all other nonbasic M/R procedures. In contrast, on tests on labels taught via the basic M/R procedure, first trial scores were 34 out of 40 for both cork and paper, 35 out of 40 for truck, and 38 out of 40 for wool (for details, see Pepperberg, 1994a; Pepperberg and McLaughlin, 1996; Pepperberg *et al.*, 1998).

Kyaaro's results

Kyaaro also did not produce, either in the presence of trainers or in private practice, labels that he experienced via audio (wood, rock) or any form of video training [cork (initial training), truck (initial training), key, block, chalk, bear] except video-variant 1 (truck). He attempted to produce labels taught via the M/R technique (paper, nail), but, at the end of his first 11 months, ran them together ('ail-er') in a manner too difficult to distinguish by trainers for testing (Pepperberg, 1994a). He did, however, produce clearly differentiated versions of nail and paper during private practice. After additional training, his labels were at the criterion for testing (for a discussion of such criteria, see Pepperberg, 1981). On identification tests for items trained under nonbasic M/R procedures and video-variant 1, Kyaaro scored 0 every trial. On tests given for labels taught via the basic M/R procedure, his first trial scores were 34 out of 40 for paper and 35 out of 40 for nail, wood, wool and cork (for details, see Pepperberg, 1994a; Pepperberg and McLaughlin, 1996; Pepperberg *et al.*, 1998).

Interestingly, in the first 11 months, Kyaaro did acquire a few extremely clear vocalizations from informal interactions with trainers: 'Hi Kyo', 'Want tickle', 'Kiss' (Pepperberg, 1994a). These utterances were generally contextually appropriate; they were used, respectively, when we entered his room but ignored him (e.g. during cleaning or a 'time-out'), while he bowed his head and stretched toward our hands, and when he stretched his beak toward our faces. As Kyaaro always accepts tickles or beak rubs, such utterances cannot be tested and no claims can be made for their referentiality.

Experiments with Alex

The results with the juveniles can be compared with my previous work with Alex. As noted earlier, Alex had learned to produce and comprehend many labels and concepts under the basic M/R condition (e.g. Pepperberg, 1990a,b, 1992b, 1994b). The question to be answered was whether a bird that had previously succeeded under M/R training procedures would fail under conditions that lacked certain aspects of input.

We thus exposed Alex to M/R-variant 1 training. In this situation he did not initially experience any modeling of the connection between labels and the objects to which they referred. He was given a sequence of eight number labels that were trained without reference either to specific objects in the laboratory or to his previously acquired English number labels (Pepperberg, 1994a, 1997). These labels were part of a study on ordinality, counting and serial learning (Pepperberg and Silverstone, unpublished data). The set, *il ee bam ba oo yuk chil gal*, was derived from Korean count labels both to permit comparisons with children (Fuson, 1988) and to be maximally different from English. *Bam* (pronounced 'baem') and *ba* were substituted for the Korean *sam* and *sa* because of Alex's occasional difficulty in producing 'ss'.

Although we attempted to perform the training in the total absence of reference, Alex would not attend to sessions until we included a minimal point of reference: a sheet of paper with the symbols 1–8 traced along the diagonal (note that he did not know that his English number labels corresponded to these symbols; Pepperberg, 1994a). In a typical session, the human acting as the trainer held the paper in front of the model and stated, 'Say number!'; all previous queries with respect to quantity had been 'How many?'. The model produced the altered Korean labels and was rewarded with the chance to request a toy or food, or erred and was scolded. Just as in basic M/R sessions, we routinely reversed roles of model and trainer; Alex was also given a turn. Although we usually reward Alex either with the object that he has labeled *or* the opportunity to request a favored item ('I want X'; Pepperberg, 1987a), here we used only the latter reward. Training, therefore, lacked the usual functional meaning and all but minimal referentiality. The procedure did, however, maintain joint attention between the bird, humans and the pictured numbers.

Alex eventually learned the string of vocal labels that were modeled, although he insisted on producing *nuk* instead of *yuk*. The results of the experiment, however, differed from those of previous studies in two important ways. First, acquisition took 9 months, which was unusually long (Pepperberg, 1981, 1994a; Pepperberg and Silverstone, unpublished data). Second, and most striking, however, was that Alex was not immediately capable of using, nor could he subsequently learn to use, these labels in a referential manner, i.e. with respect to either serial labeling or quantity. Even after we modeled 1:1 correspondences between eight objects and the string of labels, he was unable to use elements in the string to refer to smaller quantities, e.g. to say *'il ee bam ba,'* when presented with four items and asked to 'Say number'. Alex had thus learned to produce, but not comprehend the use of, these human vocalizations (Pepperberg, 1994a). Given his previous success on both production and comprehension of human labels after M/R training (e.g. Pepperberg, 1990b, 1992b, 1994b), his failure appeared to be a consequence of the training protocol and not a lack of general cognitive capacity (Pepperberg, 1994a).

Discussion

These various experiments (Pepperberg, 1994a; Pepperberg and McLaughlin, 1996; Pepperberg *et al.*, 1998) show that social interaction, reference and full functional meaning are all important factors in learning to produce and comprehend an allospecific code, even for a mimic such as the Grey Parrot. The absence of some of these factors affects whether and what type of acquisition occurs. I believe that, when such factors are missing, either of two outcomes is likely: (1) the birds fail to learn because they lack adequate information to be processed (i.e. to direct the learning process); or (2) the combination of various aspects of captivity and impoverished input corrupt the birds' processing abilities, causing them to learn in ways that would be aberrant in the wild (e.g. they learn to reproduce sounds but not in a meaningful manner). The outcome of each of the conditions my students and I tested, and how cognition may be involved in each situation, can be described in some detail.

Audiotape training, which lacked reference, functionality and social interaction, did not enable birds to acquire allospecific vocalizations (Pepperberg, 1994a, 1997). Although the juveniles whistled and squawked during audiotape sessions (monitored via an intercom), they did not attempt to reproduce the human sounds while they listened to the tapes, nor subsequently in private practice, in the presence of trainers, nor on identification tests. Possibly the human sounds were processed as background noises, maybe corresponding to what would be environmental sounds in the wild. Environmental sounds in the wild, however, would be expected to have some referential meaning relevant to their lives; in audiotape sessions, however, birds were given no opportunity to deduce explicit meanings for the sounds they heard. Furthermore, they were not shown the purpose for which the sounds could be used. The birds were essentially given no information to process. Moreover, their response to the sounds had no effect on what they subsequently heard or received, either vocally or physically. It is unclear whether the birds engaged in a cognitive evaluation of the situation and 'tuned out' the sounds because they lacked any information to process, or failed to master the labels because no detectable outcome existed between a stimulus and their response; in either case they had no reason to acquire the sounds. Their total lack of vocal learning suggests the former rather than the latter mechanism. Had their behavior entailed the latter mechanism, the following scenario would likely have occurred: the birds would have made some attempts to learn the sounds from the tapes, possibly because the sounds simply reminded them of other types of interactions with humans (Mowrer, 1954) or because an arbitrary connection could initially have been made with some irrelevant cue; the subsequent lack of effect of their vocalizations on their situation would have then extinguished the behavior. Although the overall effect would be no net learning, practice would have occurred. Had the birds engaged in other types of cognitive processing, they might have transferred skills from the M/R sessions to the audio sessions. For example, given that other human vocalizations were presented in conjunction with objects in M/R sessions, the birds might have attended to the tapes without overt learning but then made some association between the novel sound and the novel object that was subsequently presented to them in testing. They might then have attempted to produce the targeted label. They did not, however, behave in any of these ways (Pepperberg, 1994a, 1997).

The basic video condition, which included reference and limited meaning in the absence of interaction, was also not sufficient to engender allospecific vocal learning: the birds attended to the videos but did not acquire the sounds that were modeled (Pepperberg, 1994a, 1997). The juveniles could have failed to acquire vocalizations for at least three reasons: (1) they failed to realize that the interaction that they observed could be transferred to their own situation; (2) they could not determine exactly what aspect of Alex's behavior was actually causing transfer of the desired object or (3) they simply stopped responding to what they saw on tape because they received no encouragement for what could have been their first approximations to the targeted vocalization. The first two reasons suggest that inadequate information was available for processing; the third reason suggests that a potential association either did not occur or was extinguished. The birds' failure to acquire anything under video-variant 2, where attempts would be rewarded, shows that the third factor was irrelevant: no acquisition occurred that could have been rewarded (Pepperberg *et al.*, 1998). Clearly, merely watching another individual receive objects for producing particular sounds provided insufficient information for acquisition. Even the presence of a trainer to maintain the birds' interest and direct their attention to the actions on the screen did not help. Although each bird made some attempts at the labels during video-variant 1 training, neither appeared to understand what these labels represented or how these labels could be used outside of the training sessions (Pepperberg *et al.*, 1998).

Clearly, the contrast between Alex's data from M/R-variant 1 vs. basic M/R training shows that social interaction in conjunction with severely limited function and meaning engenders, at best, production but not comprehension of allospecific vocalizations (Pepperberg, 1994a). In M/R-variant 1, Alex received positive feedback merely for making particular sounds in response to a specific cue. He was given neither reason to work towards understanding what he was saying nor information about the appropriateness of his utterances. Subsequently, he was unable to transfer his learned behavior to related situations (Pepperberg, 1994a, 1997). Such results suggest that only the simplest form of processing was involved in his learning, i.e. that of forming an association between the situation and the reward, and possibly recognizing that no additional processing was needed to achieve the desired end. Such training represents most situations of mimetic birds that are pets, and explains why parrots were once thought incapable of doing more than mindlessly producing human speech sounds (e.g. Lenneberg, 1973). The pet birds did what was necessary for reward (be it the attention of their owners or a food reinforcer), but no more. In the wild, however, reward for such specific vocal associations would likely be absent and such learning improbable; otherwise many instances of psittacine mimicry of other species would have been recorded in the field. Thus, learning under the M/R-variant 1 condition was plausibly an artifact of captivity; the condition does not reflect the experience of a Grey Parrot in nature.

Although I have not yet performed experiments that involve social interaction and functional use without reference, I suggest that such training will also engender production without comprehension. Such is likely the case for pet birds that, for example, appropriately produce greeting or farewell routines ('Good night, dear', 'Good-bye, and thank you'; Amsler, 1947) but do not comprehend the use of the individual words in these routines. These birds may have a more general sense of situations in which their vocalizations can be used than do birds taught without functionality, but do not fully comprehend that part of the allospecific code they have acquired (Pepperberg, 1997). Again, they have figured out the connection between a situation, a vocalization and some form of reward from their owners, but have experienced a condition that would not occur in nature.

Given the research on M/R-variant 2, I suggest that Grey Parrots are also unlikely to acquire or comprehend elements of an allospecific code from input that is referential, fully functionally meaningful but noninteractive (see Pepperberg, 1997). Thus, the presence or absence of an item that could be considered a reward is likely to be less important than the presence or absence of social interaction. In M/R training, for example, reward is not likely to the critical factor for acquisition because a bird is rewarded only after it has attempted the targeted label, i.e. reward occurs only after some acquisition has taken place (Pepperberg, 1981, 1994a). The reward primarily reinforces referentiality. Data on nonvocal allospecific learning in a non-human primate provide some corroboration: a chimpanzee (*Pan troglodytes*) was trained through a noninteractive technique to produce symbols based on human language to answer specific questions or make requests (to signal 'M&M' in the presence of the candy); she was subsequently unable to comprehend the signal (could not choose M&M in the presence of the symbol; see Savage-Rumbaugh *et al.*, 1980a,b).

Overall, I have sought to determine the conditions that will enable Grey Parrots to acquire a referential, allospecific communication code. Although mimetic birds are characterized by their extensive capacities to acquire allospecific vocalizations, Grey Parrots (at least) seem to acquire a *meaningful* allospecific code most readily under certain environmental conditions. Although some combinations of conditions remain to be tested for these birds (e.g. reference and full functionality in the absence of social interaction; reference and limited functionality with either full or limited interaction; and the effectiveness of two- versus three-dimensional referents), input that is fully referential, functional and socially interactive ensures that these parrots will both produce and eventually comprehend allospecific vocalizations (Pepperberg, 1987a,b, 1990b, 1992b, 1994a, 1997). Lack of some or all of these aspects will affect the learning process and will be likely to prevent a subject from fully mastering the allospecific code, i.e. acquiring a code that is produced in a way that involves meaningful communication.

Conclusion

All my experiments involve teaching a referential allospecific code to subjects in a laboratory. The question remains as to the external validity of my data: can my work be related to conditions in the real world, particularly with respect to referentiality and constraints on acquisition? Furthermore, how does a cognitive approach help us understand the data?

We do not yet know if Grey Parrots use referential vocalizations in the wild. Limited data, described above for other psittacine species (duetting, sentinel behavior, individual recognition; see Pepperberg, 1994a), however, suggest that referentiality is a characteristic for which one might fruitfully search. As I have noted before (Pepperberg, 1997; Pepperberg *et al.*, 1998), a Grey Parrot is unlikely to acquire referential communication in the laboratory unless such behavior (e.g. Pepperberg, 1990a, 1992b, 1994a) was based on a pre-existent cognitive architecture (Rice, 1980; Premack, 1983) involving perception, memory and communicative intent.

If constraints found in the laboratory (i.e. the apparent need for input to involve reference, functionality and social interaction) do indeed exist in the wild, an interesting scenario emerges (Pepperberg and McLaughlin, 1996; Pepperberg, 1997). Mimicry, to be adaptive, must be both flexible and constrained: physically flexible to allow for the production of a range of sounds and constrained enough to be useful. Unconstrained, mimicry would be maladaptive. What evolutionary pathway opted for widespread mimicry in parrots yet constrained it to appropriate situations? Are specific mechanisms involved that constrain mimicry to vocalizations that are to be used in a meaningful way? Something like an innate sound detector or filter could be too limiting and lack flexibility to change with varying environmental conditions. What if, instead, psittacine mimicry (or what we might now wish to call allospecific vocal learning) occurred only in conjunction with cognitive choice or processing that relied upon meaning, function and interaction?

A cognitive mechanism that works with respect only to meaning and function would be simple and not very selective, i.e. many opportunities exist for acquisition based on an association between a sound and an object or action. The meaning and use of most auditory signals are decoded by information processing mechanisms and relatively few signals would thereby be excluded as potential sources of mimicry. For example, water sources are vital to survival, and parrots could easily associate the sound of a stream with the act of searching for or reporting about the presence of water. Yet, to my knowledge, mimicry of such sounds has not been recorded in wild parrots.

The above discussion is not meant to imply that sound–action–object associations are irrelevant to allospecific vocal learning. Interestingly, researchers who study human language acquisition argue that, in order to learn language, children must first be able to perceive the incoming signals and represent both the structural and informational content of these signals (Chomsky, 1965; Morgan and Demuth, 1996). A similar argument can be made for avian song acquisition: appropriate substitution of song terms (put in italics) for language terms leads to the following paraphrase of Morgan and Demuth (1996, p. 1) with, I believe, equivalent meaning (although to a different extent for different species; see Todt and Hultsch, this volume):

> *Songs* vary in the sounds that they include, in the sequences in which these sounds can be arranged, in the mappings of such sequences onto concepts, in the manners in which meaningful elements (*notes*) may be concatenated to form *syllable*-level units, and in the possibilities for combining *syllables* to form *phrases, songs, and song types. Song* learners

must have some means of determining which of the possible alternatives at each of these levels are manifest in the specific *songs* they are learning. This can only be provided by appropriate representation of examples drawn from those *songs*.

Such a prescription for acquisition, however, defines what is necessary but not sufficient. Further substitution of appropriate terms would result in a paraphrase appropriate to the acquisition of nonsocial background sounds. Thus it is not difficult to imagine how such sounds, e.g. rustling of leaves, might be processed for their structure, their arrangement and their information content – the approach of a predator – and one might further hypothesize a functional use for mimicking such sounds: deceiving a sympatric bird into taking cover and missing out on a food source (Pepperberg, 1997; Pepperberg *et al.*, 1998).

However, as with children, birds are likely to need social interaction for assistance in learning how to link the vocalizations that they hear with the correct objects, events and properties in the world, and, most importantly, need social interaction to direct their attention to what is worthy of learning (Bruner, 1977; Dore, 1980; Baldwin, 1995; Pepperberg and McLaughlin, 1996). Dore (1980) argues that for children the development of 'denotive symbols' (intentional communication that involves specific referents) from 'indexical signs' (intentional communication without such referents) occurs through social and emotional interaction with caretakers, specifically through interactive dialogues in which both reference and function are explicitly demonstrated. Specifically, when cognitive processes are used to understand what social interaction has demonstrated (i.e. to sort out the different facets of an interaction), a mechanism involving sound-object-action and social interaction could be maximally adaptive. In the above example, a lack of social interaction would denote reproduction of the rustling of leaves as maladaptive when compared to, for example, mimicry of actual alarm calls (i.e. rustling may have many implications whereas the alarm call has far fewer; see Munn, 1986). We know that mere temporal contiguity of a label and an object is insufficient for label acquisition by a child (e.g. Baldwin, 1991); children may, in fact, use the lack of social interaction as a specific nonvocal cue to inhibit the mapping of the label to the object (Baldwin, 1993), and our parrots may have reacted similarly in M/R-variant 2 (Pepperberg and McLaughlin, 1996). For children such a strategy would be adaptive (Baldwin, 1993): merely using temporal contiguity of a label and an object in the absence of social interaction to establish reference could cause numerous mapping errors because 30–50% of mothers' labels do not correspond to the object that a child is in the process of viewing (Collis, 1977; Harris *et al.*, 1983). I suggest a similar case is likely for Grey Parrots, particularly given the often dense foliage in which they live. Using only contiguity cues would likely result in serious acquisition errors.

Although devising a scenario is possible in which sound-object-action-interaction engenders vocal learning in the absence of cognitive processing, I suggest that this is unlikely to be the case for Grey Parrots. Arguably, a combination of cues such as hormonal levels, amount of daylight and a live tutor might engender reproduction of allospecific vocalizations (e.g. Baptista and Petrinovich, 1994, 1996) without invoking the need for cognitive processing. Here the student birds need not sort out different facets of their interaction with the live tutor, or determine the referent or the functionality of the tutor's vocalizations; the students are simply primed to learn and, because the live tutor focuses their attention, they process the information presented by the tutor (its song) as a model. Previously, I have merely stressed the need for input to include reference, functionality and social interaction (e.g. Pepperberg, 1985, 1986, 1990a, 1994a, 1997; Pepperberg and McLaughlin, 1996; Pepperberg et al., 1998) if allospecific vocal learning is to occur. Such a proposal did not, however, examine the underlying mechanisms that may be involved for *mimetic* parrots. These mechanisms become apparent only if I adopt a cognitive approach, that is, determine when cognitive processing, rather than simpler information processing or associative learning, is required. I now suggest that allospecific learning in mimetic parrots must involve cognitive processing of all the elements of the input, including that of social interaction, if more than mindless mimicry is to occur. Moreover, cognitive processing would be necessary if the parrot is to *use* the acquired vocalizations in various situations.

Although social interaction is likely to be critical for determining what is appropriate to learn with respect to parrot–parrot interactions, such interaction requires cognitive processing not only to assess the nature of the interaction, but also to target the input as worthy of processing. Humans can, by assessing whether input is coming from a dominant individual, decide whether status or acceptance might be gained through specific behavioral reproduction (Bandura, 1977). In humans, some positive correlation exists between high model status and efficacy of acquisition (rate and amount) of modeled behavior (Mischel and Liebert, 1967). Thus, social interaction in humans may facilitate or modify the course of development and passerine birds may also use such a strategy (e.g. Payne and Groschupf, 1984); parrots could respond in similar ways. [Note that social interaction might thus facilitate development of dialects, which have been observed in Amazon parrots (Nottebohm and Nottebohm, 1969; Nottebohm, 1972; Schindlinger, 1995; Wright, 1996) and which might be used to maintain flock identity. One wonders whether such dialects might include allospecific vocalizations of particular, limited-range sympatric species as a means of identifying the different dialect groups in Grey Parrots.]

Although flexibility in the use of allospecific vocalizations has not been documented in Grey Parrots in the wild, evidence, although limited, does exist in the laboratory in a study with Alex. Alex was trained to use the term 'none' to report whether 'nothing' was the same or different with respect to two exemplars, i.e. to report whether objects were identical or completely different with respect to color, shape and material (Pepperberg, 1988). In a subsequent study on relative size (i.e. questions concerning which of two objects was larger or smaller; Pepperberg and Brezinsky, 1991), Alex was, without prior training, given two objects of identical size and asked to report which was larger or smaller. He initially asked 'What's same?', and then responded to our repeated question with 'none'. Such flexibility suggests the use of cognitive processing to determine the elements of correspondence in the trained and untrained situations.

Interestingly, in captivity, all these cues that I propose that parrots use in the wild to choose what they are to learn are almost always subverted, i.e. adapted in highly peculiar ways. The pet parrot, for example, hears the microwave 'beep', sees its owners rush to the source of the signal, and processes the possibility that by reproducing this beeping noise it, too, can attract the other members of its new 'flock'. Alternatively, the vocal input given to a pet bird will often lack explicit, consistent reference and thus the bird will likely acquire some rote ability to emit the vocalizations it has heard, but will be unable to use the code productively and will lack true comprehension. The cognitive process cannot work appropriately because the relevant information is lacking, and the bird falls back on an associative mechanism. If the input lacks functionality, the subject will be unaware of the actual pragmatics of the vocalizations it has acquired, i.e. it will lack knowledge of when and how to use the vocalizations meaningfully, particularly in novel situations (see above; Pepperberg, 1997). Particularly for a pet parrot, the cognitive process will have been subverted to enable the bird to make some form of contact with its allospecific owners, who will be likely to respond to any human vocalization the bird uses.

In conclusion, learning how a particular species can produce allospecific sounds and how it comes to acquire such sounds engenders more questions than answers. My students and I have studied Grey Parrots; how similar or different is the vocal behavior of other psittacine species? Certainly an increased or decreased capacity for accurate sound reproduction would influence how vocal learning is used. Might additional data weaken the hypothesis that cognitive processing and social interaction are critical factors in vocal learning? Clearly, no shortage exists with respect to topics for further study, but a cognitive approach may lead to answers to some of these questions.

Acknowledgements

The research reported here has been supported by NSF grants BNS 91-96066 and IBN 92-21941, REU supplements, the University of Arizona Undergraduate Biology Research Program and The Alex Foundation.

References

Adret, P. (1993) Vocal learning induced with operant techniques: an overview. *Neth. J. Zool.* **43**, 125–142.

Amsler, M. (1947) An almost human Grey Parrot. *Avicult. Mag.* **53**, 68–69.

Arrowood, P. C. (1988) Duetting, pair bonding, and agonistic display in parakeet pairs. *Behaviour* **106**, 129–157.

Baldwin, D. A. (1991) Infants' contributions to the achievement of joint reference. *Child Dev.* **62**, 875–890.

Baldwin, D. A. (1993) Early referential understanding: infants' ability to recognize referential acts for what they are. *Dev. Psychol.* **29**, 832–843.

Baldwin, D. A. (1995) Understanding the link between joint attention and language. In Moore, C. and Dunham, P. J. (eds) *Joint Attention: its Origin and Role in Development*. Hillsdale, NJ: Erlbaum, pp. 131–158.

Bandura, A. (1971) Analysis of modeling processes. In Bandura, A. (ed.) *Psychological Modeling*. Chicago: Aldine-Atherton, pp. 1–62.

Bandura, A. (1977) *Social Modeling Theory*. Chicago: Aldine-Atherton.

Baptista, L. F. and Petrinovich, L. (1984) Social interaction, sensitive phases, and the song template hypothesis in the White-crowned Sparrow. *Anim. Behav.* **32**, 172–181.

Baptista, L. F. and Petrinovich, L. (1986) Song development in the White-crowned Sparrow: social factors and sex differences. *Anim. Behav.* **34**, 1359–1371.

Baylis, J. R. (1982) Avian vocal mimicry: its function and evolution. In Kroodsma, D. E. and Miller, E. H. (eds) *Acoustic Communication in Birds*, Vol. 2, *Song Learning and its Consequences*. New York: Academic Press, pp. 51–83.

Bertram, B. C. R. (1970) The vocal ability of the Indian Hill mynah, *Gracula religiosa. Anim. Behav. Monog.* **3**, 81–192.

Bruner, J. S. (1977) Early social interaction and language acquisition. In Schaffer, H. R. (ed.) *Studies in Mother–Infant Interaction*. London: Academic Press, pp. 271–289.

Chomsky, N. (1965) *Aspects of the Theory of Syntax*. Cambridge, MA: MIT Press.

Collis, G. M. (1977) Visual co-orientation and maternal speech. In Schaffer, H. R. (ed.) *Studies in Mother–Infant Interaction*. London: Academic Press, pp. 355–375.

Cruickshank, A. J., Gautier, J.-P. and Chappuis, C. (1993) Vocal mimicry in wild African Grey Parrots *Psittacus erithacus. Ibis* **135**, 293–299.

de Villiers, J. G. and de Villiers, P. A. (1978) *Language Acquisition*. Cambridge, MA: Harvard University Press.

Dore, J. (1980) Holophrases revisited: their logical development from dialog. In Barrett, M. (ed.) *Children's Single Word Speech*. New York: John Wiley & Sons, pp. 23–58.

Farabaugh, S. M. (1982) The ecological and social significance of duetting. In Kroodsma, D. E. and Miller, E. H. (eds) *Acoustic Communication in*

Birds, Vol. 2, *Song Learning and its Consequences*. New York: Academic Press, pp. 85–124.

Fuson, K. (1988) *Children's Counting and Concepts of Number*. New York: Springer-Verlag.

Gnam, R. (1988) Preliminary results on the breeding biology of Bahama amazon. *Parrot Lett.* **1**, 23–26.

Goldstein, H. (1984) The effects of modeling and corrected practice on generative language and learning of preschool children. *J. Speech Hearing Dis.* **49**, 389–398.

Gramza, A. F. (1970) Vocal mimicry in captive budgerigars (*Melopsittacus undulatus*). *Z. Tierpsychol.* **27**, 971–983.

Gwinner, E. and Kneutgen, J. (1962) Uber die biologische Bedeutung der 'zweckdienlichen' Anwendung erlernter Laute bei Vogeln. *Z. Tierpsychol.* **19**, 692–696.

Harris, M., Jones, D. and Grant, J. (1983) The nonverbal context of mothers' speech to infants. *First Lang.* **4**, 21–30.

Hearst, E. (1984) Absence as information: some implications for learning, performance, and representational processes. In Roitblat, H. L., Bever, T. G. and Terrace, H. S. (eds) *Animal Cognition*. Hillsdale, NJ: Erlbaum, pp. 311–332.

Hensley, G. (1980) Encounters with a hookbill – II. *Am. Cage Bird Mag.* **52**, 11–12, 59.

Kamil, A. C. (1988) A synthetic approach to the study of animal intelligence. In Leger, D. (ed.) *Nebraska Symposium on Motivation: Comparative Perspectives in Modern Psychology*, Vol. 7. Lincoln, NE: University of Nebraska Press. pp. 257–308.

Lawson, R. W. and Lanning, D. V. (1980) Nesting and status of the Maroon-fronted parrot (*Rhynchopsitta terrisi*). In Pasquier, R. F. (ed.) *Conservation of New World Parrots*. ICBP Technical Publication No. 1, pp. 385–392.

Lemish, D. and Rice, M. L. (1986) Television as a talking picture book: a prop for language acquisition. *J. Child Lang.* **13**, 251–274.

Lenneberg, E. H. (1967) *Biological Foundations of Language*. New York: John Wiley & Sons.

Lenneberg, E. H. (1973) Biological aspects of language. In Miller, G. A. (ed.) *Communication, Language, and Meaning*. New York: Basic Books, pp. 49–60.

Levinson, S. T. (1980) The social behavior of the White-fronted Amazon (*Amazona albifrons*). In Pasquier, R. F. (ed.) *Conservation of New World Parrots*. ICBP Technical Publication No. 1, pp. 403–417.

Lieberman, P. (1984) *The Biology and Evolution of Language*. Cambridge, MA: Harvard University Press.

Marler, P. (1970) A comparative approach to vocal learning: song development in white-crowned sparrows. *J. Comp. Physiol. Psychol.* **71**, 1–25.

Mebes, H. D. (1978) Pair-specific duetting in the peach-faced lovebird, *Agapornis roseicollis. Naturewissenschaften* **65**, 66–67.

Mischel, W. and Liebert, R. M. (1967) The role of power in the adoption of self-reward patterns. *Child Dev.* **38**, 673–683.

Morgan, J. L. and Demuth, K. (1996) Signal to syntax: an overview. In Morgan, J. L. and Demuth, K. (eds) *Signal to Syntax: Bootstrapping from Speech to Grammar in Early Acquisition.* Mahwah, NJ: Erlbaum, pp. 1–22.

Mowrer, O. H. (1954) A psychologist looks at language. *Am. Psychol.* **9**, 660–694.

Mowrer, O. H. (1958) Hearing and speaking: an analysis of language learning. *J. Speech Hearing Dis.* **23**, 143–152.

Munn, C. A. (1986) The deceptive use of alarm calls by sentinel species in mixed-species flocks of neotropical birds. In Mitchell, R. W. and Thompson, N. S. (eds) *Deception: Perspectives on Human and Nonhuman Deceit.* Albany, NY: SUNY Press, pp. 169–175.

Nottebohm, F. (1972) The origins of vocal learning. *Am. Nat.* **106**, 116–140.

Nottebohm, F. and Nottebohm, M. (1969) The parrots of Bush-Bush. *Anim. Kingdom* 19–23.

Patterson, D. K. and Pepperberg, I. M. (1994) A comparative study of human and parrot phonation: acoustic and articulatory correlates of vowels. *J. Acoust. Soc. America* **96**, 634–648.

Payne, R. B. and Groschupf, K. D. (1984) Sexual selection and interspecific competition: a field experiment on territorial behavior of nonparental finches (*Vidua* spp.). *Auk* **101**, 140–145.

Pepperberg, I. M. (1981) Functional vocalizations by an African Grey Parrot (*Psittacus erithacus*). *Z. Tierpsychol.* **55**, 139–160.

Pepperberg, I. M. (1983) Cognition in the African Grey Parrot: preliminary evidence for auditory/vocal comprehension of the class concept. *Anim. Learn. Behav.* **11**, 179–185.

Pepperberg, I. M. (1985) Social modeling theory: a possible framework for understanding avian vocal learning. *Auk* **102**, 854–864.

Pepperberg, I. M. (1986) Acquisition of anomalous communicatory systems: implications for studies on interspecies communication. In Schusterman, R., Thomas, J. and Wood, F. (eds) *Dolphin Behavior and Cognition: Comparative and Ecological Aspects.* Hillsdale, NJ: Erlbaum, pp. 289–302.

Pepperberg, I. M. (1987a) Evidence for conceptual quantitative abilities in the African Grey Parrot: labeling of cardinal sets. *Ethology* **75**, 37–61.

Pepperberg, I. M. (1987b) Acquisition of the same/different concept by an African Grey Parrot (*Psittacus erithacus*): learning with respect to color, shape, and material. *Anim. Learn. Behav.* **15**, 423–432.

Pepperberg, I. M. (1988) Comprehension of 'absence' by an African Grey Parrot: learning with respect to questions of same/different. *J. Exp. Anal. Behav.* **50**, 553–564.

Pepperberg, I. M. (1990a) Some cognitive capacities of an African Grey Parrot (*Psittacus erithacus*). In Slater, P. J. B., Rosenblatt, J. S. and Beer, C. (eds) *Advances in the Study of Behavior,* Vol. 19. New York: Academic Press, pp. 357–409.

Pepperberg, I. M. (1990b) Cognition in an African Grey Parrot (*Psittacus erithacus*): further evidence for comprehension of categories and labels. *J.*

Comp. Psychol. **104**, 41–52.

Pepperberg, I. M. (1990c) Referential mapping: a technique for attaching functional significance to the innovative utterances of an African Grey Parrot (*Psittacus erithacus*). *Appl. Psycholing.* **11**, 23–44.

Pepperberg, I. M. (1992a) What studies on song learning can teach us about playback experiments. In McGregor, P. K. (ed.) *Playback and Animal Communication: Problems and Prospects.* New York: Plenum Press, pp. 47–57.

Pepperberg, I. M. (1992b) Proficient performance of a conjunctive, recursive task by an African Grey Parrot (*Psittacus erithacus*). *J. Comp. Psychol.* **106**, 295–305.

Pepperberg, I. M. (1993) A review of the effects of social interaction on vocal learning in African Grey Parrots (*Psittacus erithacus*). *Neth. J. Zool.* **43**, 104–124.

Pepperberg, I. M. (1994a) Vocal learning in Grey Parrots (*Psittacus erithacus*): effects of social interaction, reference, and context. *Auk* **111**, 300–313.

Pepperberg, I. M. (1994b) Evidence for numerical competence in an African Grey parrot (*Psittacus erithacus*). *J. Comp. Psychol.* **108**, 36–44.

Pepperberg, I. M. (1997) Social influences on the acquisition of human-based codes in parrots and nonhuman primates. In Snowdon, C. T. and Hausberger, M. (eds) *Social Influences on Vocal Development.* Cambridge: Cambridge University Press, pp. 157–177.

Pepperberg, I. M. and Brezinsky, M. V. (1991) Acquisition of a relative class concept by an African Grey Parrot (*Psittacus erithacus*): discriminations based on relative size. *J. Comp. Psychol.* **105**, 286–294.

Pepperberg, I. M., Gardiner, L. I., and Luttrell, L.J. (1998) Limited contextual learning in the Grey Parrot (*Psittacus erithacus*): the effect of co-viewers on videotaped instruction (under review).

Pepperberg, I. M. and McLaughlin, M. A. (1996) Effect of avian–human joint attention on allospecific vocal learning by Grey Parrots (*Psittacus erithacus*). *J. Comp. Psychol.* **110**, 286–297.

Pepperberg, I. M., Brese, K. J. and Harris, B. J. (1991) Solitary sound play during acquisition of English vocalizations by an African Grey Parrot (*Psittacus erithacus*): possible parallels with children's monologue speech. *Appl. Psycholing.* **12**, 151–178.

Pepperberg, I. M., Naughton, J. R. and Banta, P. A. (1998) Allospecific vocal learning by Grey parrots (*Psittacus erithacus*): a failure of videotaped instruction under certain conditions. *Behav. Process.* **42**, 139–158.

Premack, D. (1983). The codes of man and beast. *Behav. Brain Sci.* **6**, 125–167.

Price, P. H. (1979) Developmental determinants of structure in Zebra Finch songs. *J. Comp. Physiol. Psychol.* **93**, 260–277.

Rice, M. (1980) *Cognition to Language: Categories, Word Meanings, and Training.* Baltimore, MD: University Park Press.

Robinson, F. N. (1975) Vocal mimicry and the evolution of bird song. *Emu* **75**, 23–27.

Robinson, F. N. and Curtis, H. S. (1996) The vocal displays of the Lyrebirds (*Menuridae*). *Emu* **96**, 258–275.

Rowley, I. (1980) Parent-offspring recognition in a cockatoo, the Galah, *Cacatua roseicapilla. Austral. J. Zool.* **28**, 445–456.

Rowley, I. and Chapman, G. (1986) Cross-fostering, imprinting and learning in two sympatric species of cockatoo. *Behaviour* **96**, 1–16.

Rozin, P. (1976) The evolution of intelligence and access to the cognitive unconscious. In Spragues, J. M. and Epstein, A. N. (eds) *Progress in Psychobiology and Physiological Psychology*, Vol. 6. New York: Academic Press, pp. 245–280.

Rutledge, D. and Pepperberg, I. M. (1988) *Video Studies of Same/Different.* Unpublished raw data.

Saunders, D. A. (1983) Vocal repertoire and individual vocal recognition in the short-billed white-tailed Black cockatoo, *Calyptorhynchus funereus latirostris.* Carnaby. *Austral. Wildl. Res.* **10**, 527–536.

Savage-Rumbaugh, E. S., Rumbaugh, D. M. and Boysen, S. (1980a) Do apes use language? *Am. Sci.* **68**, 49–61.

Savage-Rumbaugh, E. S., Rumbaugh, D. M., Smith, S. T. and Lawson, J. (1980b) Reference: the linguistic essential. *Science* **210**, 922–925.

Schindlinger, M. D. (1995) The evolution of vocal repertoires in parrots: evidence from the wild. Paper presented at the *XXIVth International Ethological Congress*, Honolulu, Hawaii, August.

Silverstone, J. L. (1989) Numerical abilities in the African Grey Parrot: sequential numerical tags. Senior honors thesis, Northwestern University.

Slater, P. J. B. (1991) Learned song variations in British storm-petrels? *Wilson Bull.* **103**, 515–517.

Slater, P. J. B., Eales, L. A. and Clayton, N. S. (1988) Song learning in zebra finches (*Taeniopygia guttata*): progress and prospects. In Rosenblatt, J. S., Beer, C., Busnel, M.-C. and Slater, P. J. B. (eds) *Advances in the Study of Behavior*, Vol. 18. New York: Academic Press, pp. 1–34.

Smith, W. J. (1991) Animal communication and the study of cognition. In Ristau, C. A. (ed.) *Cognitive Ethology: The Minds of Other Animals.* Hillsdale, NJ: Erlbaum, pp. 209–230.

Snyder, N. F., Wiley, J. W. and Kepler, C. B. (1987) *The Parrots of Luquillo: Natural History and Conservation of the Puerto Rican Parrot.* Los Angeles, CA: Western Foundation for Vertebrate Zoology.

St Peters, M., Huston, A. C. and Wright, J. C. (1989) Television and families: parental coviewing and young children's language development, social behavior, and television processing. Paper presented at the *Society for Research in Child Development*, Kansas City, KS, April.

Todt, D. (1975) Social learning of vocal patterns and modes of their applications in Grey Parrots. *Z. Tierpsychol.* **39**, 178–188.

Vanayan, M., Robertson, H. A. and Biederman, G. B. (1985) Observational learning in pigeons: the effects of model proficiency on observer performance. *J. Gen. Psychol.* **112**, 349–357.

Wickler, W. (1980) Vocal duetting and the pairbond. I. Coyness and the partner commitment. *Z. Tierpsychol.* **52**, 201–209.

Wright, T. (1996) Regional dialects in the contact call of a parrot. *Proc. Roy. Soc. Lond. B Biol. Sci.* **263**, 867–872.

Yamashita, C. (1987) Field observations and comments on the Indigo macaw (*Anodorhynchus leari*), a highly endangered species from northeastern Brazil. *Wilson Bull.* **99**, 280–282.

Zentall, T. R. (1993) Animal cognition: an approach to the study of animal behavior. In Zentall, T. R. (ed.) *Animal Cognition: A Tribute to Donald A. Riley.* Hillsdale, N.J: Erlbaum, pp. 3–15.

14

Cognitive Abilities of Araneophagic Jumping Spiders

R. Stimson Wilcox[1] and Robert R. Jackson[2]

[1] *Biology Department, Binghamton University, Binghamton, NY 13902-6000, USA*
[2] *Zoology Department, University of Canterbury, Christchurch 1, New Zealand*

Introduction

It is widely appreciated that natural selection acting on heritable variation is responsible for the evolution of the morphology and behavior of animals, but the relationship between natural selection and behavioral abilities tends to be more easily overlooked. Learning, for example, is sometimes viewed as generating behavior independent of natural selection but this notion does not hold up to close scrutiny. The term 'learning' has been used for a wide range of mechanisms by which previous experience adaptively alters behavior, and learning of one sort or another appears to be universal in the animal kingdom. Learning depends critically on memory, and the particular things remembered by individuals of a species will vary from circumstance to circumstance. The particular behavior that an animal might learn is not the direct product of natural selection, but an appreciation of natural selection and the species' evolutionary history is critical none the less. The goal in an evolutionary approach to animal learning is to understand how

ANIMAL COGNITION IN NATURE
ISBN 0-12-077030-X

natural selection has shaped the mechanisms by which the animal processes information from experience and files memory adaptively. We should expect species-specific biases and limitations that reflect the species' evolutionary history.

Baerends' (1939) celebrated study of sand wasps (genus *Ammophila*) illustrates this especially well. When a sand wasp female is ready to oviposit, she digs a chamber in a sand dune, plugs the hole and then flies away. Later she returns with a paralysed caterpillar. Unplugging the concealed chamber, she shoves the caterpillar inside, deposits an egg and then plugs the chamber again. Later, the egg hatches and a hungry larva begins feeding on the paralyzed caterpillar. Each morning, the sand wasp returns to the chamber, unplugs it and assesses the size of the growing larva and shrinking caterpillar. When the female wasp detects that the larva is about to eat up its food supply, she compensates by finding and paralyzing another caterpillar, bringing it to the chamber and replenishing the hungry larva's larder.

Sand wasps are especially remarkable because each female usually tends two or three chambers at the same time, each chamber being in a different location and each larva being at a different stage of feeding and development. Baerends (1939) showed experimentally that the sand wasp learns the configuration of landmarks around each concealed chamber and uses these landmarks to find, and replenish when required, the individual chambers. That is, the wasp learns not only where the chambers are but remembers what action is needed at each.

Most people might have difficulty matching the wasp's skill at nurturing larvae in sand chambers but, nevertheless, far surpass the wasp at many other learning tasks. The wasp's learning ability is specialized in a way that is understandable when we appreciate its species-specific evolutionary history. In the world in which the sand wasp evolved, the ability to monitor sand chambers has been critically important.

The sand wasp also provides an especially instructive example of why nature–nurture is a sterile distinction. Learning is not an alternative to natural selection but, instead, in its species-specific details, an evolved adaptive ability (Lorenz, 1969; Johnston, 1982; Miller, 1988; Gottlieb, 1997). Extrapolating from the sand wasp example, we should generally expect an interrelationship between learning and instinct (Fig. 14.1), with a prevalence of species-specific biases, limitations and idiosyncratic features that reflect the species' evolutionary history predominating.

Learning overlaps with a more controversial topic – animal cognition. In lay terms, cognition is reasoning, thinking and mental problem-solving. With Western philosophy's heritage from Descartes (1637), it has long been viewed as somehow disreputable even to discuss the topic of animal cognition, partly for fear that the next step would be acceptance of the notion of animal minds. For Descartes (1637), all animals are automatons, but this is a difficult position to maintain in the face of modern animal studies. For example, we

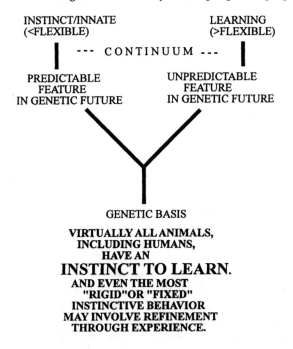

INSTINCT/INNATE   LEARNING
(<FLEXIBLE)   (>FLEXIBLE)

--- C O N T I N U U M ---

PREDICTABLE   UNPREDICTABLE
FEATURE   FEATURE
IN GENETIC FUTURE   IN GENETIC FUTURE

GENETIC BASIS

**VIRTUALLY ALL ANIMALS,
INCLUDING HUMANS,
HAVE AN**
INSTINCT TO LEARN.
**AND EVEN THE MOST
"RIGID" OR "FIXED"
INSTINCTIVE BEHAVIOR
MAY INVOLVE REFINEMENT
THROUGH EXPERIENCE.**

Fig. 14.1 Diagram showing relationships among the genome, instinctive behavior and learned behavior.

can refuse to call the problem-solving skills of African Grey Parrots (Pepperberg, 1990, 1992, 1994) avian cognition only at the risk of drastically denying the common-sense meaning of the term. However, global, all-purpose ability is not what we should expect when we study animal cognition any more than with animal learning. Instead, we should expect, with both learning and cognition, focused ability with idiosyncratic biases and limitations reflecting the species' evolutionary history.

Regardless of how useful it might be for an animal to have pronounced learning and cognitive abilities, we would expect size (more specifically brain size) to impose a ceiling on what can evolve (Gottlieb, 1997). Conceding that large-brained animals such as birds and mammals may have interesting cognitive ability is one thing, but what about spiders? The notion of a cognitive spider might seem almost ludicrous: even if some of the birds and mammals are not automatons, surely all of the spiders, insects and other arthropods are? After all, arthropods are only distantly related to *Homo sapiens* and, besides, a spider's brain is minute compared to that of birds and man. In fact, it is tempting to argue that the restriction to easily tractable (noncognitive) behavior in arthropods is a good reason to use these 'simple' animals in behavior research. The attitude of the present authors was close to this when, many years ago, we first became interested in arthropod behavior. Evidently we were wrong, and in this chapter we review recent work on *Portia*, the spiders that changed our minds.

Spiders that eat other spiders

Portia, a genus of araneophagic (i.e. spider-eating) jumping spiders (family Salticidae), appears to have the most versatile and flexible predatory strategy known for an arthropod (Jackson, 1992a, 1996). How animals incorporate deceit into their communication strategies has long been a topic of special interest in discussions of animal cognition (Mitchell, 1986), and a dominant feature of *Portia*'s predatory strategy is aggressive mimicry, a system in which the predator communicates deceitfully with its prey (Wickler, 1968; Endler, 1981).

Typical salticids do not build webs. Instead, they are hunters that catch their prey in stalk-and-leap sequences guided by vision (Forster, 1982). Salticids differ from all other spiders by having large anteromedial eyes and acute vision (Land, 1969a,b, 1985). However, the behavior of *Portia* is anything but typical for a salticid. There are some 15–20 species in this genus of African, Asian and Australian spiders (Wanless, 1984), but most of what we know comes from studies of five species, *P. africana, P. albimana, P. fimbriata, P. labiata* and *P. schultzi* (Jackson, 1992b).

Besides hunting prey cursorially, *Portia* also builds a prey-catching web (Jackson, 1986). The typical prey of the salticid is insects, but *Portia*'s preferred prey is other spiders (Li and Jackson, 1996, 1997). *Portia* frequently hunts web-building spiders from other families by invading their webs and deceiving them with aggressive-mimicry signals (Fig. 14.2). While in the other spider's web, *Portia* will also raid its victim's eggsacs, take insects ensnared in the web, or even take food directly from the mouth of the other spider (Jackson and Blest, 1982a; Jackson and Hallas, 1986a).

In the simplest instances, *Portia* makes aggressive-mimicry signals by moving legs, palps, abdomen or some combination of these to make web-borne vibrations. *Portia*'s typical victim, a web-building spider but not a salticid, typically lacks acute vision (Land, 1985) and instead perceives the world it lives in largely by interpreting tension and vibration patterns in its web (Witt, 1975). With its signals, *Portia* can gain dynamic fine control over its prey's behavior.

Different kinds of web-building spiders are most readily deceived by different web signals. As long as the web-building spider is in a suitable size range (about one-tenth to two times *Portia*'s size), *Portia* is effective at deceiving and preying on it. This is true not only for a diverse array of web-building spiders in each *Portia* species' natural habitat, but also for

Fig. 14.2 *Portia labiata*, the lower spider, deceitfully lures a member of the social spider *Stegodyphus sarasinorum* up close by signalling on the *S. sarasinorum*'s web with light palp plucks. Shortly after this photograph was taken, *Portia* lunged forward and captured the duped spider. Photograph by R. S. Wilcox.

species given to *Portia* in the laboratory that would never be encountered in nature.

Early in our research, understanding how *Portia* derives the appropriate signals for different types of prey became a primary objective. The emerging conclusion from this work, which is still in progress, is that *Portia* uses an interplay of two basic tactics (Jackson and Wilcox, 1990, 1993a,b): (1) it uses specific preprogrammed signals when cues from some of its more common prey species are detected; and (2) it also adjusts signals in a flexible fashion, as a consequence of feedback from the victims.

Next, we shall review a particularly striking example of *Portia*'s use of preprogrammed signals, and with this example also illustrate the potential for prey defense and predator–prey coevolution.

Predator–prey interactions between *Portia fimbriata* and *Euryattus* sp.

In the rain forest of Queensland, Australia, the prey of *Portia fimbriata* includes an undescribed species from the salticid genus *Euryattus*. *Euryattus* sp. is not a typical salticid and *P. fimbriata* uses a unique tactic against this one species of prey. For shelter and oviposition sites, most salticids spin small silk cocoons (Jackson, 1986), but *Euryattus* females take shelter and lay their eggs inside curled-up leaves suspended by silk strands from tree trunks, rocks or vegetation. The male of *Euryattus* courts the female by cautiously venturing onto the leaf and, by making vibratory signals on the leaf surface, luring the female out into the open (Jackson, 1985). However, *Euryattus* females also receive unwelcome visitors.

Adult females of *Euryattus* and *P. fimbriata* are comparable in size. The adult females and large juveniles, but not the smaller juveniles or the males, of *P. fimbriata* take a special interest in suspended leaves (Jackson *et al.*, 1998): even if reared in the laboratory with no prior contact with *Euryattus*, they move out on to the leaf and make signals closely resembling the calling signal of the *Euryattus* male (Wilcox and Jackson, unpublished data) (Fig. 14.3). Lured out by this counterfeit signal, the *Euryattus* female is captured by the hungry *Portia* (Jackson and Wilcox, 1990).

Interactions between *P. fimbriata* and *Euryattus* are of interest not only because they illustrate extreme focusing of preprogrammed tactics (species-specific signal imitation). These interactions also provide evidence of predator–prey coevolution. Owing to its markings, tufts of hairs and long, spindly legs, *Portia* does not have the appearance of a typical spider, resembling instead a piece of detritus. Also, *Portia*'s stepping gait is normally slow and choppy, rendering *Portia* difficult to recognize even when moving. In Queensland, *P. fimbriata* feeds on a variety of salticids in addition to *Euryattus* sp., catching these other species out in the open by stalking up behind them. If the salticid being stalked detects movement and turns to look at *Portia*, it normally peers at what appears to be no more than a piece of detritus and then turns and continues on its way, and to its doom (Jackson and Blest, 1982a).

Euryattus sp. is, among salticids, an exception. When seen, an approaching *P. fimbriata* is recognized by *Euryattus* sp. as a predator and driven away. To drive *P. fimbriata* away, *Euryattus* sp. comes out of the rolled-up leaf, then suddenly and violently leaps at or charges toward the *P. fimbriata*, sometimes banging head-on into and knocking away the unwelcome guest. Once attacked, *Portia* flees and *Euryattus* survives (Jackson and Wilcox, 1990).

The facility of *Euryattus* sp. at recognizing *Portia* is apparently pre-programmed: individuals reared from eggs in the laboratory and never exposed to a *Portia* beforehand still behave in this manner the first time they encounter the predator (Jackson and Wilcox, 1990). Also, this predisposition

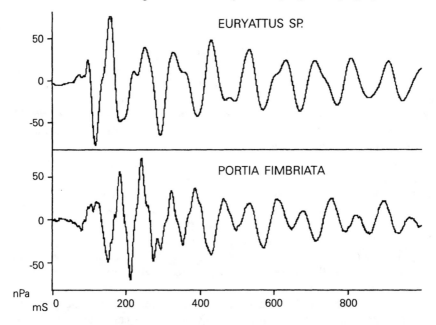

Fig. 14.3   Top: the mating signal of a male of the jumping spider *Euryattus* sp., from the rain forest in Queensland, Australia. Males make this signal while on top of a hanging, curled-up leaf. Females of *Euryattus* reside within the curl of the leaf, which they hang in the air with supporting anchor threads. This signal appears to induce the female out of the leaf, to mate with the male. Bottom: the signal made by adult female of *Portia fimbriata*, recorded from the same leaf as in the above. *P. fimbriata* lures the female to the entrance of the curl with the signal, then attacks the female and eats her. (Wilcox and Jackson, unpublished data.)

to recognize *P. fimbriata* appears to be unique to a population where *Euryattus* sp. and *P. fimbriata* are sympatric. *P. fimbriata* is absent from another population sampled about 15 km away from the habitat where *Euryattus* and *P. fimbriata* are sympatric. In tests using laboratory-reared spiders, allopatric *Euryattus* only rarely defended themselves against stalking *P. fimbriata*, and *P. fimbriata* was more effective at capturing allopatric than sympatric *Euryattus* (Jackson and Wilcox, 1993a).

These studies suggest that, in Queensland, *P. fimbriata* and *Euryattus* have been involved in a coevolutionary 'arms race' (Dawkins and Krebs, 1979), in which improvement in the predator's ability to capture the prey selected for improvement in the prey's ability to defend itself and vice versa. The potential for such arms races may partially account for the evolution of exceptional complexity in the araneophagic spider's predatory strategy (Jackson, 1992a). Next, we shall review some other examples of prey that have *Portia*-specific defenses.

Detecting *Portia*'s footsteps

The tightly strung, intertwining silk threads that make a spider' s web appear to be an extraordinarily sensitive component of the web-building spider's tactile sensory system (Masters *et al.*, 1986). When going into the other spider's web, remaining silent (i.e. making no tactile or tension cues that would be detectable by the resident spider) is probably next to impossible for *Portia*. The alternative, and the strategy *Portia* adopts, is almost the antithesis of remaining silent: *Portia* deliberately broadcasts deceitful signals.

Often there is a need for *Portia* to walk into the web, and this may present a problem because a repetitive walking gait might alert the resident spider to the presence of an intruder. *Portia* seems to compensate for this problem. Unlike that of a typical salticid, *Portia*'s walking gait is slow and choppy. Each leg tends to move out of phase with each other leg, and the speed, amplitude and phasing of each leg's movements in relation to other legs change continuously (Jackson and Blest, 1982a). Most spiders do not respond to this nonrepetitive gait, the more or less patternless signals probably registering as mere noise.

Yet, as striking exceptions, a select few of species of web-building spiders tend to react with a special kind of panic, which we call '*Portia* panic'. We have tested these species in the field and the laboratory by having, besides *Portia*, numerous other types of spiders walk across their webs. When the intruder was a spider other than *Portia*, these species normally did no more than run to the edge of the web, but when *Portia* walked on their webs, they leapt out and continued running until they were far away. For these species, there is no panic like *Portia* panic! Experimental studies in progress indicate that it is *Portia*'s slow, choppy gait that panics these special prey of *Portia*, and that prior experience with *Portia* is not necessary. For these species, the cues for panic appear to be the more or less patternless signals from *Portia*'s nonrepetitive gait (Jackson and Wilcox, unpublished data), the very features of the gait that seem to conceal *Portia* from most prey (Table 14.1).

Portia panic appears to provide additional examples, along with *Portia–Euryattus* interactions, of predator–prey coevolution. *Portia* panic also illustrates how signalling and disguise interrelate. Next, we shall examine another type of disguise in *Portia*'s repertoire, what we call 'smokescreen tactics'. Smokescreen tactics are used against a wide range of web-building spiders, but they are especially important when *Portia* attempts to catch '*Portia*-panicked' spiders.

Smokescreen tactics

We first became aware of smokescreen behavior when trying to record *Portia*'s signals in the field using a transducer connected by a stylus to the

Table 14.1 Results of introducing *Portia** and non-*Portia*[†] intruders on to webs of prey spider species known to be panicky species. Intruders were introduced on to the web of the prey spider and the response of the prey spider scored as to whether it left its web entirely (panicked) or stayed on its web, even if it only maintained contact with the web with one leg. The results show the percentage times the prey species panicked and, in parentheses, the total number of trials per prey species. The results clearly show a significantly greater number of panic responses to *Portia* than to non-*Portia* intruders χ^2-test of independence, $p < 0.001$). (Wilcox and Jackson, unpublished data.)

Panicky species	*Portia* intruders	Non-*Portia* intruders
Hygropoda dolomedes	63 (120)	0 (151)
Hygropoda sp.	50 (36)	0 (38)
Dendrolycosa sp. A	59 (81)	0 (23)
Dendrolycosa sp. B	61 (98)	0 (43)
Underleaf pholcid	58 (79)	0 (148)
Psilochorus sp.	44 (59)	0 (123)
Average %/total *n*	56 (473)	0 (526)

**Portia* intruders used: *P. africana*; *P. fimbriata*; *P. labiata*; *P. schultzi*. All are aggressive mimics.
[†]Non-*Portia* intruders used: (family Salticidae) – *Bavia aericeps*; *Cyrba ocellata*@; *Euryattus* sp.; *Jacksonoides queenslandica*; *Mopsus mormon*; *Plexippus pyakulli*; *Simaetha paetula*; *Tauala lepidus*; *Trite planiceps*; (Gnaphosidae) – *Lampona cylindrata*@; *Taieria erebus*@; (Mimetidae) – *Mimetus maculosus*@; (Pholcidae) – *Pholcus phalangoides*@.
Species denoted @ are aggressive mimics.

web. This work was frustrating on windy days because air movement caused large-scale displacement of the web which tended to mask out the signals we were trying to record from *Portia*. Eventually we realized that not only did the wind mask *Portia*'s signal but also it was when the wind blew that *Portia* was especially likely to walk across the web toward the resident spider. Later, in laboratory experiments, we demonstrated that *Portia* opportunistically times its advance across the web when there is background noise from wind or from the struggles of insects on the web (Wilcox *et al.*, 1996).

Portia is remarkably discriminating in its use of the opportunistic smokescreen tactic, reserving this tactic for when stalking a spider in a web, and not using it when stalking the web-building spider's own prey (an ensnared insect) or its eggsacs (Wilcox *et al.*, 1996), both of these being food items against which the smokescreen would be meaningless.

More recently, we have discovered that, when the wind is not blowing, *Portia* may make its own smokescreen. The self-generated smokescreen is a long train of low-frequency vibrations of the silk made by *Portia* flexing suddenly and violently, then more slowly relaxing its legs so that its body rocks up and down in the web. *Portia* proceeds to make its advance toward

Table 14.2   Analysis of signals made by ten individual *Portia fimbriata* (Q) when *P. fimbriata* was stalking *Badumna longinquus*. Data show the percentage of forward movement made by *Portia* during smokescreen signals and during an interval of 1.0 seconds after non-smokescreen signals were made. *Portia fimbriata* always moved forward during smokescreen scored for this study. In addition to the data below, we recorded 388 episodes during which *Portia* made non-smokescreen signals but no forward movement was made. Predator/prey body size = 1.0. Results show a significantly greater forward distance made during signal production than during no signal production (χ^2-test of independence, $p < 0.001$). (Wilcox and Jackson, unpublished data.)

Episodes during which *Portia* moved forward	Number of episodes	Percentage of total forward movement
Smokescreen signals	293	86.4
Non-smokescreen signals	36	10.6
Smokescreen plus non-smokescreen signals	329	97.1
No signal made	10	2.9
Total	339	100.0

the resident spider primarily while the web is reverberating with this signal (Table 14.2), and this self-generated signal appears to mask the more subtle web vibrations made by *Portia*'s footsteps.

By using smokescreens (either opportunistic or self-generated), *Portia* combines elements of stealth with aggressive mimicry, behaves with remarkable flexibility and manages to catch even '*Portia*-panicked' prey. However, another tactic of *Portia*'s, trial and error, may be an even more pronounced spider example of flexible behavior.

Flexibly adjusting signals to prey behavior

We originally viewed the trial-and-error tactic as a default tactic used by *Portia* in encounters with those prey for which it lacked preprogrammed behavior. In the field, what appeared to happen in many instances was that *Portia* entered a spider's web and began broadcasting a wide array ('kaleidoscope') of different signals. The kaleidoscope continued until the prey spider responded appropriately, after which *Portia* continued to produce the signal which worked (Jackson and Wilcox, 1993b). If, with the passage of time, the prey spider ceased to respond appropriately to the signal, *Portia* reverted back to the kaleidoscope until a new and effective signal was found.

In laboratory experiments, we confirmed that *Portia* uses feedback from prey behavior to adjust signalling flexibly (Jackson and Wilcox, 1993b). In these experiments, we controlled the way in which the prey spider responded to the signalling *Portia*. For example, by using an electromagnetic field from a wire coil to drive a magnet glued to the prey spider's dorsum, we could pair up appropriate prey movement with randomly chosen signals from *Portia*'s kaleidoscope. In these experiments, *Portia* consistently narrowed its signal production to the signals we chose at random to reward (Jackson and Wilcox, 1993b).

For how long *Portia* will remember a signal derived by trial and error is not known, but the tactic requires at least short-term memory for the period of the predatory sequence. The longer the memory period, then perhaps the more interesting the trial-and-error tactic becomes as an example of operant conditioning and learning. However, what may be of greater interest is that this tactic enables *Portia* flexibly to derive appropriate signals for just about any type of spider, even species with which it would never have had contact with any time in its evolutionary history.

Even when *Portia* has a preprogrammed tactic for a spider species, trial and error still has a role. Often *Portia* appears to use preprogrammed signals not so much to provide a solution, all by itself, for the problem of how to capture a particular spider but, instead, to get the predatory sequence off to a good start, after which *Portia* finishes the job by trial and error. The victim spider may, for instance, start approaching slowly, then lose interest, become distracted, or begin approaching too fast. When, for any reason, preprogrammed signals do not work, *Portia* switches to trial and error (Jackson and Wilcox, unpublished data).

With the trial-and-error tactic, *Portia* shows an ability to discern what happens after making different signals and to adjust subsequent signalling accordingly. Can this spider also discern and adjust to the predicted consequences of different actions without actually acting first? Doing the calculations in its head, so to speak, would be closer to the common-sense meaning of cognition or thinking.

Making detours and planning ahead

Ability to take indirect routes to a goal (detouring) has been illustrated and studied extensively in vertebrates (von Frisch, 1962; Curio, 1976; Collett, 1982; Chapuis, 1987; Rashotte, 1987; Regolin *et al.*, 1994, 1995a,b). Examples of spiders taking deliberate detours are less well known. Although there were some earlier reports that salticids make detours while in pursuit of prey (Heil, 1936; Curio, 1976), the first detailed experimental confirmation was Hill's (1979) work using North American species of *Phidippus*. The detours required in these experiments were simple and short, and Hill (1979) concluded that detouring required no great insight on the salticid's part because, in the absence of a straight path to the prey, all the salticid did was to head towards an object ('secondary goal') that would bring it closer to the prey (the 'primary goal') and continue doing this until the prey was reached.

Portia, however, takes long, complicated detours in the field (Jackson and Wilcox, 1993c), including detours in which *Portia* first moves away from the prey before heading towards it. Although detours are a feature of *Portia*'s pursuit of a wide array of prey spider species, the most vivid illustration is in interactions between *P. fimbriata* and *Argiope appensa* in Queensland (Jackson, 1992c).

A. appensa builds an orb web close up against a tree trunk. Simply to walk straight from the tree into the web may appear easy for *Portia*, but there is a problem. *A. appensa* is acutely sensitive to anything foreign in the web. When an intruder is detected, whether *Portia* or some other araneophagic predator, *A. appensa* pumps on the web by rapidly flexing its legs over and over again, setting the web into motion, and either driving or throwing the intruder out of the web (Jackson *et al.*, 1993).

Yet, *P. fimbriata* usually succeeds at capturing *A. appensa*. During typical sequences in the field, *Portia* walks up the tree trunk toward *A. appensa*, stops, looks around, then goes off in a different direction, only later to come out above the web. There are usually vines and other vegetation near the tree and often some of the vegetation extends out above the web. After looking at the web and the surrounding environment (Jackson, 1992c; Jackson and Wilcox, 1993), *Portia* moves away, often going to where the web is completely out of view, crosses the vegetation and comes out above the web. From above the web, *Portia* drops on its own silk line alongside, but without touching, the web of the *A. appensa*. Then, when parallel with the spider in the web, *Portia* swings in to make a kill.

Not only does *Portia* solve the problem of how to capture this hypersensitive prey spider without touching the web, but it also appears that *Portia* takes deliberate detours to reach an optimal approach. Some of these detours observed in nature were over 1m in length and took over 1 hour to execute (Jackson and Wilcox, 1993).

Laboratory experiments have confirmed that indirect routes taken by *Portia* against a wide range of prey are deliberate detours requiring movement to where the prey can no longer be seen and movement sometimes initially away from the prey before reaching it (Tarsitano and Jackson, 1992, 1994). In more recent experiments, *Portia* had to choose between two long and twisting paths, only one of which led indirectly to a prey spider. At the start of the test, *Portia* was on a platform high enough so that the prey was in view, but the prey went out of view once *Portia* descended the platform. In these tests, *Portia* took the route that led to the prey ('correct route') significantly more often than the route that did not lead to the prey ('incorrect route'). In some of these tests, this was despite *Portia* having to walk past the beginning of an incorrect route in order to reach the beginning of the correct route (Tarsitano and Jackson, 1997).

It is difficult to escape the conclusion that *Portia* solves detour problems in its head, makes plans and then acts on these plans. What precisely is meant by the term 'cognition' may not always be clear, but it would be contrived to deny at least the rudiments of cognition in *Portia*.

Cognitive levels

With the topic of animal cognition, as with related topics such as intelligence, awareness, minds and consciousness (Dennett, 1991), attempts to apply precise, logical definitions to examples from real animals quickly become futile Aristotelian exercises (Dennett, 1995). Generally, it is more useful to sidestep the problem of definition and focus on attributes related to cognition, discussing these in relation to interdependent stages or levels (Eysenck and Keane, 1990). From this perspective, cognitive ethology has relevance extending beyond the vertebrates.

In a framework applied initially to the behavior of Honey Bees (Dukas and Real, 1993), cognition was addressed in relation to reception, attention, representation, memory, problem-solving, communication and language. This framework differs from tradition by reducing the emphasis placed on learning and memory. It may be instructive to examine *Portia*'s predatory behavior in relation to this framework.

Reception

Considerations of an animal's sensory reception and processing systems is perhaps the most elementary level at which cognition is relevant. Generally, spiders rely heavily on chemical and tactile cues (Foelix, 1982), but most spiders have poor eyesight (Blest, 1985). Salticids are the primary exception, this family of spiders having unique complex eyes and visual acuity exceeding that known for any other animals of comparable size (Land and Fernald, 1992). Understandably, the tradition in literature on salticids has been to emphasize vision as the modality mediating interaction with prey, predators and conspecifics (Richman and Jackson, 1992). Yet, *Portia* and other salticids also make extensive use of sensory systems based on chemical cues (Pollard *et al.*, 1987; Willey and Jackson, 1993; Clark and Jackson, 1994a,b, 1995a,b) and silk-mediated tactile cues (Jackson, 1982, 1986). Salticids appear not to have substituted vision for other sensory modalities; instead, they appear simply to have added on vision with no particular detriment to their facility at using other modalities (Jackson and Pollard, 1997).

Unlike the more familiar plan of vertebrate and insect eyes, salticid principal eyes are put together very differently (Homann, 1928; Land, 1974). *Portia* has four pairs of eyes, but it is the pair of very large anterior median eyes (known as the 'principal eyes') that is responsible for acute vision (Land, 1969a,b). Three pairs of smaller secondary eyes, situated either side of the principal eyes, serve as highly proficient motion detectors (Land, 1971, 1974).

The retinae of the principal eyes have a four-layered tier arrangement (Land, 1969a). Light entering through the corneal lens passes successively through layers 4, 3 and 2 before reaching layer 1. In the central area of layer 1 (the fovea), receptors are packed especially close together (about 1 μm apart). The fovea, being the only region that receives a sharply focused image, must be primarily responsible for shape recognition (Blest *et al.*, 1990).

The eye of an average mammal is much larger than the salticid principal eye, and it would be tempting to argue on a priori grounds that the small salticid eye has to be severely limited. Yet, *Portia*'s eye has acuity rivalling that of a primate (Land, 1974, 1985; Blest *et al.*, 1990). Perhaps there is a parallel lesson regarding cognition. On a priori grounds, it is tempting to conclude that a spider's central nervous system, being so small compared to that of birds and mammals, could not possibly support more than the most rudimentary cognitive ability. Yet, as with visual acuity, there appear to be mechanisms, although poorly understood, that go a long way toward overcoming whatever limitations are imposed by small size.

We are only beginning to understand the visual discrimination abilities of *Portia*, but it is clear that a variety of different types of spiders and webs can be recognized from distances of up to about 30 body lengths away on the basis of optical cues alone (Jackson and Blest, 1982b; Clark and Uetz, 1990; Jackson and Tarsitano, 1993; Jackson, 1995; Li and Jackson, 1996, 1997) despite the fact that there are at most a few hundred receptors in the principal eye fovea (Land, 1985). The principal eye is an active eye, and this may be the key to understanding shape perception (Land, 1969b). Scanning (rapid side-to-side and rotary movement of the eye tubes) may enable the salticid to use its small retina to search for recognition cues.

The evolution of acute vision may have been critical in setting the stage for exceptional cognitive ability (Jackson, 1992a). Being able to see, locate and identify quiescent prey before entering a web, *Portia* has available distance and time in which to implement complex tactics. When interacting with an active prey, acute vision means that *Portia* can accurately track, from a distance, the prey's changing location, speed, orientation and behavior. It is difficult to envisage other sensory systems known for spiders operating in a comparable way.

Invasion of webs and use of aggressive mimicry are known for poor-sighted spiders from various families other than the Salticidae. In contrast to *Portia*, these areaneophagic species tend to specialize on a comparatively narrow range of prey spiders, and appear to have considerably simpler and less flexible predatory behavior (Jackson and Whitehouse, 1986; Jarman and Jackson, 1986; Whitehouse, 1986; Jackson and Brassington, 1987).

Attention

Cognitive attention is a many-faceted topic encompassing focused information processing in the face of multisensory input (from both internal and external sources), selective attention, attentional limitations in foraging and search imagery (Dukas and Real, 1993). Questions related to attention have not been explicit objectives in our research, but research in this realm is likely to be rewarding. For instance, while making a detour in pursuit of a prey item, *Portia* frequently moves along a path on which it can no longer see the prey and persists on this path for minutes or even hours at a time (Jackson and Wilcox, 1993a). Also, signalling sessions on webs can last for hours or even days at a time (Jackson and Hallas, 1986a,b), and more recent studies by Robert Clark (unpublished) indicate that *Portia* makes use of search imagery.

Representation

Representation, discussed in relation to cognitive (or mental) mapping, has received a great deal of attention (Gallistel, 1989). In a broad sense, a cognitive map is an internal representation of geometric relations among noticeable points in an animal's environment. In a more narrow sense, a cognitive map is computational ability, involving learning, problem-solving and memory. Demonstration of cognitive mapping requires unequivocal evidence showing that the animal computes a route between two points without having travelled along this route before (Wehner and Menzel, 1990). *Portia*'s detouring behavior appears to provide this kind of evidence. After recognizing prey for which an indirect approach is appropriate, *Portia* apparently plans a solution to the problem of how to reach the prey along a path over terrain never crossed before (Tarsitano and Jackson, 1997).

Communication and language

Perhaps this is where *Portia* is left behind. Verbal communication, being abstract and based on more or less arbitrary symbols, is an ability developed to a much greater degree in humans than known for any other animals (Dennett, 1996). Indeed, verbal communication was at one time widely regarded as uniquely human, but it has become difficult to deny that the great apes (Premack, 1986) and African Grey Parrot (see Pepperberg, 1990) have at least a rudimentary capacity for symbolic communication.

Communication is central to *Portia*'s aggressive-mimicry strategy, but *Portia*'s signals appear to function more as sensory exploitation (Proctor, 1992; Clark and Uetz, 1993; Ryan and Rand, 1993) rather than a verbal language. By walking into another spider's web, *Portia* enters the other spider's perceptual world, since the web is an extension and critical component of the web-building spider's sensory system. Once in the web, *Portia* indirectly manipulates the prey-spider's behavior by exploiting biases in how the prey spider processes web signals.

The most straightforward instances of sensory exploitation are sequences during which *Portia* makes preprogrammed or derived (by trial and error) signals to which the resident spider responds the same as it would respond to a small insect ensnared in the web. If the resident spider is relatively small and harmless, then *Portia* can capture the victim when it comes close, but the tables are likely to be turned when the resident is large and dangerous (Jackson, 1992a). Yet, *Portia* deceives and captures an enormous range of spider species, including the large and dangerous (Jackson and Hallas, 1986b). We are only beginning to understand the variety and subtlety of what *Portia* achieves during signalling bouts. For example, if the resident spider is a large and dangerous spider, *Portia* might lure it in very slowly or, instead of luring the resident spider in, stalk across the web and attack while keeping the resident spider calm but out in the open with monotonous repetition of habituating signals (Jackson and Wilcox, unpublished data).

Verbal communication in *Homo sapiens* and some other vertebrates, being based on more or less arbitrarily assigned symbols, is extraordinarily flexible. *Portia*'s signals, functioning as sensory exploitation, appear quite the opposite of arbitrary, but this does not imply inflexibility. With every appendage plus the abdomen able to move independently at different and changing rates and amplitudes, and in different and changing phase relations to each other, *Portia* appears capable of making virtually an unlimited array of different web signals (Jackson and Blest, 1982a; Jackson and Hallas, 1986a).

How *Portia*'s prey, web-building spiders, responds to signals varies considerably between species and also with the sex, age, previous experience and feeding state of the spider. Yet, *Portia* deceives and preys on just about every kind of web-building spider imaginable, as long as it is about one-tenth to twice *Portia*'s size (Jackson and Hallas, 1986a). Although we have only begun to understand how *Portia* chooses, from its large repertoire of signals, the particular signals that are appropriate for particular spiders, it is clear that this is a communication system based on a high level of flexibility.

Levels of deception

In a review of how animals use deception, Mitchell (1986) specified a classification scheme (Table 14.3) which provides an interesting perspective from which to consider *Portia*. *Portia* is a straightforward example of the first two 'levels'. Level I (deception by appearance) is illustrated by *Portia*'s camouflage (detritus mimicry). For level II, the best-known examples might be angler fish (Gudger, 1946) and firefly *femmes fatales* (Lloyd, 1986), but

Table 14.3 A summary of the levels of deception, with examples. (From Mitchell, 1986.)

Level	Deception is effected by appearance	Program	Examples of deceiver	Examples of deceived
I	Appearance	'Always do p'	Batesian mimics; butterflies with false head; plants which mimic	Not possible
II	Coordination of perception and action	'Do p given that q is so'	Firefly *femmes fatales*; birds which feign injury; angler-fish which darts lure	Males which respond to *femmes fatales* fireflies
III	Learning	'Do any p given that p resulted in q in your past'	Birds of Beau Geste hypothesis; dog which fakes a broken leg	Blue Jays which respond to Batesian mimicry of butterfly; foxes which respond to injury-feigning of birds
IV	Planning	Self-programmed	Chimp which misleads about location of food; humans who lie	Humans deceived by verbal lie

Portia's aggressive-mimicry signalling is another clear example of deception based on coordination of perception and action (Table 14.3).

Arthropod examples of Level III deception, where use of a deceptive ploy is based on learning, may be scarce, but *Portia*'s trial-and-error selection of signals appears to be a straightforward example of this. Level IV, deception based on planning ahead, is where cognition most clearly becomes relevant. We have no evidence that *Portia* plans ahead the particular signals it will use in an aggressive-mimicry sequence. Yet, with detouring, planning ahead is often a component of *Portia*'s prey-capture strategy.

Design options for animal brains

In what was freely admitted to be an 'outrageously oversimplified' framework, Dennett (1995, 1996) considered the basic methods by which animals might solve problems and specified four types of creatures: Darwinian, Skinnerian, Popperian and Gregorian. It may be instructive to consider *Portia* from the perspective of this framework.

Darwinian creatures come with preprogrammed (by natural selection) solutions to particular problems. *Portia*'s preprogrammed tactics for capturing certain of its common prey would appear to fit into this category. Natural selection can be viewed as a trial-and-error process (an algorithm) stretched over evolutionary time, those genotypes that code for successful solutions for problems persisting and those genotypes coding for the unsuccessful being filtered out. Skinnerian creatures do the trial and error within their individual lifetimes, and *Portia*'s trial-and-error tactic appears to be a spider example of this.

It is with Popperian creatures that cognition may become especially pronounced, and it is to vertebrates that we probably most often turn for examples. Unlike a merely Skinnerian creature that must try out a behavior to obtain feedback regarding success or failure, a Popperian creature might be envisaged as running a simulation in some inner environment (mind?) and planning ahead what to do. In its detouring behavior, *Portia* would seem to be Popperian.

Portia probably is left behind when it comes to the fourth type of creature, Gregorian. The Gregorian creature benefits from the problem-solving of others by importing mind tools (e.g. verbal language) from the cultural environment. Perhaps it takes more brain power to become a Gregorian animal than is feasible for *Portia*.

When we began research on *Portia*, few thoughts would have seemed more foreign to us than that one day we would seriously be discussing cognition in a spider. Yet, over and over again, *Portia* has defied the popular image of spiders as simple animals with rigid behavior. One of the challenges in this work has now become to clarify where the limits lie in *Portia*'s cognitive ability, but the greater challenge is to understand how it is that an animal with so little in the way of a brain can nevertheless do so much.

Acknowledgements

This work was supported by grants from the US National Science Foundation (BNS 8617078), the National Geographic Society (2330-81, 3226-85, 4935-92) and the Marsden Fund of New Zealand (UOC512).

References

Baerends, G. P. (1939) Fortpflanzungsverhalten und Orientierung der Grabwespe *Ammophila campestris*. *Tijdschrift voor Entomol.* **84**, 68–275.

Blest, A. D. (1985) Fine structure of spider photoreceptors in relation to function. In F. G. Barth (ed.) *Neurobiology of Arachnids*. New York: Springer-Verlag, pp. 79–102.

Blest, A. D., O'Carroll, D. C. and Carter, M. (1990) Comparative ultrastructure of Layer I receptor mosaics in principal eyes of jumping spiders: the evolution of regular arrays of light guides. *Cell Tiss. Res.* **262**, 445–460.

Chapuis, N. (1987) Detour and shortcut abilities in several species of mammals. In Ellen, P. and Thinus-Blanc, C. (eds) *Cognitive Processes and Spatial Orientation in Animals and Man*. Dordrecht: Martinus Nijhoff, pp. 97–106.

Clark, D. L. and Uetz, G. W. (1990) Video image recognition by the jumping spider, *Maevia inclemens* (Araneae: Salticidae). *Anim. Behav.* **40**, 884–890.

Clark, D. L. and Uetz, G. W. (1993) Signal efficacy and the evolution of male dimorphism in the jumping spider, *Maevia inclemens*. *Proc. Nat. Acad. Sci. USA* **90**, 11 954–11957.

Clark, R. J. and Jackson, R. R. (1994a) *Portia labiata*, a cannibalistic jumping spider, discriminates between own and foreign eggsacs. *Int. J. Comp. Psychol.* **7**, 38–43.

Clark, R. J. and Jackson, R. R. (1994b) Self recognition in a jumping spider: *Portia labiata* females discriminate between their own dragline and those of conspecifics. *Ethol. Ecol. Evol.* **6**, 371–375.

Clark, R. J. and Jackson, R. R. (1995a) Araneophagic jumping spiders discriminate between the draglines of familiar and unfamiliar conspecifics. *Ethol. Ecol. Evol.* **7**, 185–190.

Clark, R. J. and Jackson, R. R. (1995b) Dragline-mediated sex recognition in two species of jumping spiders (Araneae Salticidae), *Portia labiata* and *P. fimbriata*. *Ethol. Ecol. Evol.* **7**, 73–77.

Collett, T. S. (1982) Do toads plan detours? A study of the detour behaviour of *Bufo viridis*. *J. Comp. Physiol.* **146**, 261–271.

Curio, C. (1976) *The Ethology of Predation*. New York: Springer-Verlag.

Dawkins, R. and Krebs, J. R. (1979) Arms races between and within species. *Proc. Roy. Soc. Lond B* **205**, 489–511.

Dennett, D. C. (1991) *Consciousness Explained*. Boston: Little, Brown.

Dennett, D. C. (1995) *Darwin's Dangerous Idea*. New York: Simon and Schuster.

Dennett, D. C. (1996) *Kinds of Minds: Toward an Understanding of Consciousness*. New York: Basic Books.

Descartes, R. (1637) *Discourse on Method*.

Dukas, R. and Real, L. A. (1993) Cognition in bees: from stimulus reception to behavioral change. In Papaj, D. R. and Lewis, A. C. (eds) *Insect Learning: Ecological and Evolutionary Perspectives*. New York: Chapman and Hall, pp. 343–373.

Endler, J. A. (1981) An overview of the relationships between mimicry and crypsis. *Biol. J. Linnean Soc.* **16**, 25–31.

Eysenck, M. W. and Kean, M. T. (1990) *Cognitive Psychology.* London: Lawrence Erlbaum Associates.

Foelix, R. F. (1982) *Biology of Spiders.* Cambridge, MA: Harvard University Press.

Forster, L. M. (1982) Vision and prey-catching strategies in jumping spiders. *Am. Sci.* **70**, 165–175.

Gallistel, C. R. (1989) Animal cognition: the representation of space, time and number. *Annu. Rev. Psychol.* **40**, 155–189.

Gottlieb, G. (1997) *Synthesizing Nature–Nurture: Prenatal Roots of Instinctive Behavior.* Mahwah, NJ: Lawrence Erlbaum Associates.

Gudger, E. W. (1946) The angler-fish, *Lophius piscatorus it americanus*, use of the lure in fishing. *Am. Nat.* **79**, 542–548.

Heil, K. H. (1936) Beiträge zur Physiologie und Psychologie der Springspinnen. *Z. Vergle. Physiol.* **23**, 125–149.

Hill, D. E. (1979) Orientation by jumping spiders of the genus *Phidippus* (Araneae: Salticidae) during the pursuit of prey. *Behav. Ecol. Sociobiol.* **5**, 301–322.

Homann, H. (1928) Beträge zur Physiologie der Spinnenaugen. I. Untersuchungsmethoden, II. Das Sehvermöen der Salticiden. *Z. Vergl. Physiol.* **7**, 201–268.

Jackson, R. R. (1982) The behavior of communicating in jumping spiders (Salticidae). In Witt, P. N. and Rovner, J. S. *Spider Communication: Mechanisms and Ecological Significance.* Princeton, NJ: Princeton University Press, pp. 213–247.

Jackson, R. R. (1985) The biology of *Euryattus* sp. indet., a web-building jumping spider (Araneae, Salticidae) from Queensland: utilization of silk, predatory behaviour, and intraspecific interactions. *J. Zool. Lond. B* **1**, 145–173.

Jackson, R. R. (1986) Web building, predatory versatility, and the evolution of the Salticidae. In Shear, W. A. (ed.) *Spiders: Webs, Behavior, and Evolution.* Stanford, CA: Stanford University Press, pp. 232–268.

Jackson, R. R. (1992a) Eight-legged tricksters: spiders that specialize at catching other spiders. *BioScience* **42**, 590–598.

Jackson, R. R. (1992b) Conditional strategies and interpopulation variation in the behaviour of jumping spiders. *N. Zeal. J. Zool.* **19**, 99–111.

Jackson, R. R. (1992c) Predator–prey interactions between web-invading jumping spiders and *Argiope appensa* (Araneae, Araneidae), a tropical orb-weaving spider. *J. Zool. Lond.* **228**, 509–520.

Jackson, R. R. (1995) Cues for web invasion and aggressive mimicry signalling in *Portia* (Araneae, Salticidae). *J. Zool. Lond.* **236**, 131–149.

Jackson, R. R. (1996) Mistress of deception. *Natl Geographic Mag.*, November.

Jackson, R. R. and Blest, A. D. (1982a) The biology of *Portia fimbriata*, a web-building jumping spider (Araneae, Salticidae) from Queensland: utilization of webs and predatory versatility. *J. Zool. Lond.* **196**, 255–293.

Jackson, R. R. and Blest, A. D. (1982b) The distances at which a primitive jumping spider, *Portia fimbriata*, makes visual discriminations. *J. Exp. Biol.* **97**, 441–445.

Jackson, R. R. and Brassington, R. J. (1987) The biology of *Pholcus phalangioides* (Araneae, Pholcidae): predatory versatility, araneophagy and aggressive mimicry. *J. Zool. Lond.* **211**, 227–238.

Jackson, R. R. and Hallas, S. E. A. (1986) Capture efficiencies of web-building jumping spiders (Araneae, Salticidae): is the jack-of-all-trades the master of none? *J. Zool. Lond.* **209**, 1–7.

Jackson, R. R. and Hallas, S. E. A. (1990) Evolutionary origins of displays used in aggressive mimicry by *Portia*, a web-invading, araneophagic jumping spider (Araneae, Salticidae). *N. Zeal. J. Zool.* **17**, 7–23.

Jackson, R. R. and Pollard, S. D. (1997) Jumping spider mating strategies: sex among cannibals in and out of webs. In Choe, J. and Crespi, B. (eds) *Sexual Conflict and Cooperation*. Cambridge: Cambridge University Press, pp. 340–351.

Jackson, R. R. and Tarsitano, M. S. (1993) Responses of jumping spiders to motionless prey. *Bull. Br. Arachnol. Soc.* **9**, 105–109.

Jackson, R. R. and Whitehouse, M. E. A. (1986) The biology of New Zealand and Queensland pirate spiders (Araneae, Mimetidae): aggressive mimicry, araneophagy and prey specialization. *J. Zool. Lond. (A)* **210**, 279–303.

Jackson, R. R. and Wilcox, R. S. (1990) Aggressive mimicry, prey-specific predatory behavior and predator-recognition in the predator–prey interactions of *Portia fimbriata* and *Euryattus* sp., jumping spiders from Queensland. *Behav. Ecol. Sociobiol.* **26**, 111–119.

Jackson, R. R. and Wilcox, R. S. (1993a) Evidence of predator–prey coevolution of *Portia fimbriata* and *Euryattus* sp., jumping spiders from Queensland. *Proc. 19th Arachnol. Cong.*, Brisbane, Vol. 11, pp. 557–560.

Jackson, R. R. and Wilcox, R. S. (1993b) Spider flexibly chooses aggressive mimicry signals for different prey by trial and error. *Behaviour* **127**, 21–36.

Jackson, R. R. and Wilcox, R. S. (1993c) Observations in nature of detouring behavior by *Portia fimbriata*, a web-invading aggressive mimic jumping spider from Queensland. *J. Zool. Lond.* **230**, 135–139.

Jackson, R. R., Rowe, R. and Wilcox, R. S. (1993) Anti-predator defences of *Argiope appensa* (Araneae, Araneidae) a tropical orb-weaving spider. *J. Zool. Lond.* **229**, 121–132.

Jackson, R. R., Li, D. and Robertson, M. B. (1998) Cues by which suspended-leaf nests of *Euryattus* (Araneae: Salticidae) females are recognized by conspecific males and by an aggressive-mimic salticid, *Portia fimbriata*. *J. Zool. Lond.* (in press).

Jarman, E. A. R. and Jackson, R. R. (1986) The biology of *Taieria erebus* (Araneae, Gnaphosidae), an araneophagic spider from New Zealand: silk utilisation and predatory versatility. *N. Zeal. J. Zool.* **13**, 521–541.

Johnston, T. D. (1982) Selective costs and benefits in the evolution of learning. *Adv. Study Behav.* **12**, 65–106.

Land, M. F. (1969a) Structure of the retinae of the eyes of jumping spiders

(Salticidae: Dendryphantinae) in relation to visual optics. *J. Exp. Biol.* **51**, 443–470.

Land, M. F. (1969b) Movements of the retinae of jumping spiders (Salticidae: Dendryphantinae) in response to visual stimuli. *J. Exp. Biol.* **51**, 471–493.

Land, M. F. (1971) Orientation by jumping spiders in the absence of visual feedback. *J. Exp. Biol.* **54**, 119–139.

Land, M. F. (1974) A comparison of the visual behaviour of a predatory arthropod with that of a mammal. In Wiersma, C. A. G. (ed.) *Invertebrate Neurons and Behaviour.* Cambridge, MA: MIT Press, pp. 411–418.

Land, M. F. (1985) The morphology and optics of spider eyes. In Barth, F. G. (ed.) *Neurobiology of Arachnids.* Berlin: Springer-Verlag, pp. 53–78.

Land, M. F. and Fernald, R. D. (1992) The evolution of eyes. *Annu. Rev. Neurosci.* **15**, 1–29.

Li, D. and Jackson, R. R. (1996) Prey preferences of *Portia fimbriata*, an araneophagic, web-building jumping spider (Araneae: Salticidae) from Queensland. *J. Insect Behav.* **9**, 613–642.

Li, D. and Jackson, R. R. (1997) Influence of diet on survivorship and growth in *Portia fimbriata*, an araneophagic jumping spider (*Aranea: Salticidae*). *Canad. J. Zool.* **75**, 1652–1658.

Li, D., Jackson, R. R. and Barrion, A. (1998) Prey preferences of *Portia labiata*, *P. africana* and *P. schultzi*, araneophagic, jumping spiders (Araneae: Salticidae) from the Philippines, Sri Lanka, Kenya and Uganda. *N. Zeal. J. Zool.* (in press).

Lloyd, J. E. (1986) Firefly communication and deception: 'oh, what a tangled web'. In Mitchell, R. W. and Thompson, N. S. (eds) *Deception: Perspectives on Human and Nonhuman Deceit.* Albany, NY: State University of New York Press, pp. 113–125.

Lorenz, K. Z. (1969) Innate bases of learning. In Pribram, K. H. (ed.) *On the Biology of Learning.* New York: Harcourt Brace Jovanovich.

Masters, W. M., Markl, H. S. and Moffat, A. M. (1986) Transmission of vibrations in a spider's web. In Shear, W. A. (ed.) *Spiders: Webs, Behavior, and Evolution.* Stanford, CA: Stanford University Press.

Miller, D. B. (1988) Development of instinctive behavior: an epigenetic and ecological approach. In *Handbook of Behavioral Neurobiology*, Vol. 9, *Developmental Psychology and Behavioral Ecology.* New York: Plenum Press, pp. 415–444.

Mitchell, R. W. (1986) A framework for discussing deception. In Mitchell, R. W. and Thompson, N. S. (eds) *Deception: Perspectives on Human and Nonhuman Deceit.* Albany, NY: State University of New York Press, pp. 3–40.

Pepperberg, I. M. (1990) Some cognitive capacities of an African Grey Parrot (*Psittacus erithacus*). In Slater, P. J. B., Rosenblatt, J. S. and Beer, C. (eds) *Advances in Study of Behavior*, Vol. 19. New York: Academic Press, pp. 357–409.

Pepperberg, I. M. (1992) Proficient performance of a conjunctive, recursive task by an African Grey parrot (*Psittacus erithacus*). *J. Comp. Psychol.* **106**, 295–305.

Pepperberg, I. M. (1994) Numerical competence in an African Grey parrot. *J. Comp. Psychol.* **108**, 36–44.

Pollard, S. D., Macnab, A. M. and Jackson, R. R. (1987) Communication with chemicals: pheromones and spiders. In Nentwig, W. (ed.) *Ecophysiology of Spiders*. Heidelberg: Springer-Verlag, pp. 133–141.

Premack, D. (1986) *Gavagai! Or the Future History of the Animal Language Controversy*. Cambridge, MA: MIT Press.

Proctor, H. C. (1992) Sensory exploitation and the evolution of male mating behavior: a cladistic test using water mites (Acari: Parasitengona). *Anim. Behav.* **44**, 745–752.

Rashotte, M. E. (1987) Behavior in relation to objects in space: some historical perspectives. In Ellen, P. and Thinus-Blanc, C. (eds) *Cognitive Processes and Spatial Orientation in Animals and Man*. Dordrecht: Martinus Nijhoff, pp. 97–106.

Regolin, L., Vallortigara, G. and Zanforlin, M. (1994) Perceptual and motivational aspects of detour behaviour in young chicks. *Anim. Behav.* **47**, 123–131.

Regolin, L., Vallortigara, G. and Zanforlin, M. (1995a) Object and spatial representations in detour problems by chicks. *Anim. Behav.* **49**, 195–199.

Regolin, L., Vallortigara, G. and Zanforlin, M. (1995b) Detour behaviour in the domestic chick: searching for a disappearing prey or a disappearing social partner. *Anim. Behav.* **50**, 203–211.

Richman, D. and Jackson, R. R. (1992) A review of the ethology of jumping spiders (Araneae, Salticidae). *Bull. Br. Arachnol. Soc.*, **9**, 33–37.

Ryan, M. J. and Rand, A. S. (1993) Sexual selection and signal evolution: the ghost of biases past. *Proc. Roy. Soc. Lond. B* **340**, 187–195.

Tarsitano, M. S. and Jackson, R. R. (1992) Influence of prey movement on the performance of simple detours by jumping spiders. *Behaviour* **123**, 106–120.

Tarsitano, M. S. and Jackson, R. R. (1994) Jumping spiders make predatory detours requiring movement away from prey. *Behaviour* **131**, 65–73.

Tarsitano, M. S. and Jackson, R. R. (1997) Araneophagic jumping spiders discriminate between detour routes that do and do not lead to prey. *Anim. Behav.* **53**, 257–266.

von Firsch, O. (1962) Zur Biologie des Zwergchamäleons (*Microsaurus pumilus*). *Z. Tierpsychol.* **19**, 276–289.

Wanless, F. R. (1984) A review of the spider subfamily Spartaeinae nom.n. (Araneae: Salticidae) with descriptions of six new genera. *Bull. Br. Mus. Nat. Hist. Zool.* **46**, 135–205.

Wehner, R. and Menzel, R. (1990) Do insects have cognitive maps? *Annu. Rev. Neurosci.* **13**, 403–414.

Whitehouse, M. E. A. (1986) The foraging behaviours of *Argyrodes antipodiana* (Araneae, Theridiidae), a kleptoparasitic spider from New Zealand. *N. Zeal. J. Zool.* **13**, 151–168.

Wilcox, R. S., Jackson, R. R. and Gentile, K. (1996) Spiderweb smokescreens: spider trickster uses background noise to mask stalking movements. *Anim. Behav.* **51**, 313–326.

Willey, M. B. and Jackson, R. R. (1993) Olfactory cues from conspecifics inhibit the web-invasion behavior of *Portia*, a web-invading, araneophagic jumping spider (Araneae, Salticidae). *Can. J. Zool.* **71**, 1415–1420.

Witt, P. N. (1975) The web as a means of communication. *Biosci. Commun.* **1**, 7–23.

15

Varying Views of Animal and Human Cognition

Colin G. Beer

Institute of Animal Behavior, University Heights, 101 Warren Street, Rutgers University, Newark, NJ 07102, USA

Introduction

In this chapter I want to stand back from the splendid empirical work on animal cognitive capacities that is the focus of this book, and look at the broader context of cognitive concerns within which the work can be viewed. Indeed even the term 'cognitive ethology' currently connotes and denotes more than is represented here, as other collections of articles, such as Ristau (1991) and Bekoff and Jamieson (1996), exemplify. I include the current descendants of behavioristic learning theory, evolutionary epistemology, evolutionary psychology and the recent comparative turn that has been taken in cognitive science. These several approaches, despite their considerable overlap, often appear independent and even ignorant of one another. Like the proverbial blind men feeling the hide of an elephant, they touch hands from time to time, yet collectively have only a piecemeal and distributed understanding of the shape of the whole. Although each approach may indeed need the space to work out its own conceptual and methodological preoccupations without confounding interference from other views, a utopian spirit envisages an ultimate coming together, a more comprehensive realization of the synthetic approach to animal cognition that is this book's theme.

ANIMAL COGNITION IN NATURE
ISBN 0-12-077030-X

So I shall conduct a sort of Cook's tour of areas bordering on the ethological approaches to cognition. Although the ethological perspective penetrates into some of these areas, there are regions where the language sounds quite foreign, and the customs seem quite strange. I begin with some familiar territory, historical landmarks in the study of animal cognition, as a reminder of our joint origin.

Some nineteenth-century ideas about animal cognition

Current approaches to animal cognition can all trace their ancestry back to Darwin's evolutionary perspective in *The Origin of Species* (1859) and *The Descent of Man* (1871). In the latter volume, Darwin laid the foundation for regarding nonhuman creatures as cognitively endowed. He wrote at length about the mental powers of animals, including curiosity, attention, imagination, reason, abstraction and self-consciousness. Michael Ghiselin (1969) has argued that most of Darwin's writing in this anthropomorphic vein was merely metaphorical, but this reading cannot be sustained where Darwin was expressly seeking to establish continuities between animal and human mental capacities.

Continuity between human and animal minds offers a two-way street: contemplation of animals in human terms, or of humans in animal terms. As Donald Broadbent (1961) has put it, 'you could either humanize the brutes or brutalize humans'. Darwin's immediate successors took the first option. His younger colleague, George Romanes, is notorious for using anecdotal evidence to argue anthropomorphic conclusions. In fact, Romanes was more aware of the questionable validity of inferences of this sort than his critics acknowledge, and his justification for the 'ejective approach' of trying to imagine what it is like to be another creature, by projecting oneself into its situation, was still in effect when J. B. Watson, as a graduate student, was trying to understand the sensations experienced by a rat at a choice point in a maze.

The inflation of animal cognitive attribution to which the ejective approach was prone did not go unremarked. As a corrective Lloyd Morgan rolled out his famous canon, which requires that we should assume the minimum psychological capacity when interpreting an animal's actions. This rule continues to exert its admonitory force today, even though there is no logical law that says this is the simplest of all possible worlds as far as animal cognition is concerned. Morgan's canon is, of course, a special application of the venerable principle of parsimony, also known as Occam's razor. Once this razor was out of its sheath, however, more was in jeopardy than Morgan had envisaged.

Behavioristic learning and its aftermath

Inspired by Morgan's example, Thorndike (1898) took animal intelligence as the subject of his doctoral dissertation research. Thorndike's approach led to a psychology shorn of almost all the traditional concepts of the associationist tradition. He found that he could account for learning without recourse to thought, idea or conscious memory. According to his Law of Effect, connections between stimuli and ways of behaving are strengthened by contingent experience of satisfaction, or weakened by contingent experience of dissatisfaction. The only vestige of the traditional mentalism in Thorndike's psychology was the appeal to hedonism. Even this remnant was swept away by Watson's (1913) redefinition of psychology as 'the science of behavior'. Watson's 'psychology as the behaviorist views it', like the traditional associationistic psychology from which it in part derived, maintained that contiguity in experience was alone sufficient to forge the links of learning. This view proved to be too simple to account for learning in general, and Clark Hull revived Thorndike's law in an operationalized form as the principle of reinforcement. Reinforcement is what has to be added to contiguity to effect learning, and in Hull's monolithic system, of which it is the cornerstone, reinforcement consists in drive reduction – assuaging of a state of tissue need, as in rewarding a food-deprived animal with nourishment when it performs a targeted response (e.g. Hull, 1943).

Watson's methodological reform – his prohibition of introspection, and insistence that manipulation of circumstance and observation of overt behavior provide the data of psychology – was supposed to unify psychology and ground it as a science comparable to physics. It did nothing of the sort. Hull's was only the most prominent of numerous attempts to refine the crudities of Watson's behaviorism; the 40 years or so from the 1920s through the 1950s saw behavioristic learning theory become a highly factious, increasingly technical arena of debate. However, the theoretical divergences radiated from shared premises, such as the assumptions that there are universal laws of learning; that all the concepts entering into the expression of these laws must be empirically grounded in observational, experimental, or quantitative procedures; and that all behavior, apart from the simplest reflexes, is a product of experience. Thus, the different behavioristic schools could find a common cause in opposition to such outsiders as William McDougall, and, later, the ethologists.

McDougall's position makes for some interesting comparison. In 1980, I was rummaging in a second-hand bookshop in the Cumbrian town of Whitehaven, when I came across a little book in the Home University Library series entitled *Psychology – the Study of Behaviour*. It was written by McDougall and dated 1912, thus anticipating Watson's manifesto by a year. But McDougall's conception of behavior ostensibly set him apart from behaviorism, for where the behaviorists purportedly categorized behavior on the basis of motor pattern – 'mere movement' as Hull put it – McDougall sorted behavior by the criterion of purposiveness. So where a behaviorist might see a rat as running, McDougall would see it as fleeing, or chasing – an action recognized in relation to a functional context.

In this, and much else, McDougall resembled E. C. Tolman, who described himself as a 'purposive behaviorist'. Tolman (e.g. 1932) distinguished molecular categories of behavior – flexions and extensions, turns and runs – from molar categories such as getting to the goal box. He maintained that it is typically the latter – actions identified by their consequences – that become associated with situations, rather than the particular movements that instantiate them. The point was nicely demonstrated in an experiment by D. D. Wickens (1938, 1939). Human subjects had a forearm strapped to a board, palm down with the middle finger resting on an electrode which delivered a moderately painful shock following a signal. The subjects were readily conditioned to respond to the signal by flexing the finger upwards and so avoid the shock. What had been conditioned to the signal: the flexion movement as a stimulus–response (S–R) theorist would suppose, or the shock avoidance à la Tolman? Wickens answered the question by having his subjects turn their hands over. Most of them immediately responded to the signal by flexing the finger in the opposite direction from previously, showing that it was breaking contact with the electrode that had been conditioned, not the movement that had effected it.

Tolman was notorious among his fellow behaviorists for invoking cognitive capacities such as expectation and internal representation in his theorizing. In spite of his claim that his approach involved no more than logical inference from what he saw his animals doing, his tough-minded critics regarded him as an apostate. Guthrie (1935, p. 172), for instance, said that Tolman left his rats 'buried in thought'. Yet, it is Tolman's style of argument, rather than that of the S–R theorists, that has survived the so-called cognitive revolution in psychology. For example, his notion of a cognitive map – an internal representation of experienced spatial relations – has become commonplace in the recent learning literature, and his concept of latent learning persists in the numerous studies implying behaviorally silent learning, such as those on sensory preconditioning.

One such is an experiment by Matzel *et al.* (1988), which I shall abbreviate. In the initial part of the experiment, two stimuli, a tone and a light, were presented in succession to rats so that the tone served as a predictor of the light. Then the rats were divided into groups, which experienced shock in association with the light. For one group, the light preceded the shock (forward conditioning); for another group, the shock preceded the light (backwards conditioning). The intervals between the light and the shock were shorter than those between the tone and the light in the preconditioning phase of the experiment. When the effects of the aversive conditioning procedures were tested by seeing whether the light suppressed lever-pressing for food, only the rats in the forwardly conditioned group showed the suppression, which was consistent with previous results in comparable experiments. However, when the backwardly conditioned rats were tested with the tone, they were as strongly suppressed as the forwardly conditioned group by the light. Apparently, the backwardly conditioned rats had, in effect, mentally subtracted the shorter interval between shock and light from the time that had separated tone and light in the preconditioning phase, and deduced that the tone predicted the shock in the time remaining.

I recently heard a talk by Charles Gallistel entitled something like 'Is the S–R connection the phlogiston of psychology?'. Like T. C. Schneirla (e.g. 1959) so many years ago, Gallistel brought comparative evidence to bear on the assumption that animal learning is all of a piece. He took issue with one of the central concepts of traditional learning theory, in the light of such multifarious phenomena as the dead reckoning of desert ants, the registering of star patterns by nestling song birds, the dependence of a Honey Bee's colour/taste associations on what it perceives during the last moments before it touches down on a flower, and the remarkable memory for caching-locations displayed by birds such as Clark's Nutcracker. Among other studies supporting a representational as opposed to an instrumental theory of learning is work done by Gallistel's student Ken Cheng on place learning in rats. Cheng (1986; Gallistel, 1990) found that rats locate places on the basis of geometrical relations of environmental space, not on the basis of nongeometric distinctive features local to each place, even though they can register and use the local cues when the task is other than spatial. From these results, Cheng and Gallistel concluded that a rat's primary cognitive map is due to a central nervous module receptive to the geometry of the environ-ment but impenetrable to other potentially usable information for finding places. Although this formulation reflects the influence of the philosopher Jerry Fodor, whose book *The Modularity of Mind* (1983) started a continuing debate about how mentality is organized, it also implicates an evolutionary perspective according to which learning processes are products of and constrained by the outcomes of phylogenetic history. This kind of perspective governs the outlook of the emerging movement of evolutionary psychology, to which I now turn.

Evolutionary psychology

'Evolutionary psychology is simply psychology that is informed by the additional knowledge that evolutionary biology has to offer, in the expecta-tion that understanding the processes that designed the human mind will advance the discovery of its architecture.' This description comes from a book entitled *The Adapted Mind: Evolutionary Psychology and the Generation of Culture* (p. 3), edited by Jerome Barkow *et al.* (1992). The editors claim that the combination of modern evolutionary biology with the cognitive revolution promises 'to draw together all of the disparate branches of psychology into a single organized system of knowledge' including the 'irreducible social and cultural phenomena studied by anthropologists, sociologists, economists, and historians' (Barkow *et al.*, 1992).

This sort of claim has been made before. In the nineteenth century, Herbert Spencer developed what he called a 'synthetic philosophy' in which a conception of general evolution was supposed to integrate the whole of knowledge, including biology, psychology, ethics, sociology, economics and education. In his day, the 12 fat volumes of Spencer's opus were widely read. In our day, they stay on the shelves gathering dust. Part of the reason is that we now find Spencer's ponderous prose indigestible. Another, according to Sir Peter Medewar (1982), is that Spencer had an unworkable conception of evolution. Today, it will be claimed, we have a much sounder notion of the evolutionary process. However, there are also rumblings of disquiet with the received neoDarwinian synthesis (e.g. Grene, 1983; Ho and Saunders, 1984; Pollard, 1984; Wesson, 1991). For instance, advances in molecular biology at one extreme, and concern with the relationships between evolution and culture at another, bring critical pressure to bear on 'the tendency to reduce all explanation to a single level; and the tendency to totalize natural selection as the only operative explanatory principle' (Dyke, 1985, p. 97). If Spencer's fate is anything to go by, we should do well to keep a wary eye on the critical questioning of aspects of the Darwinian canon. (This caution, of course, applies not only to evolutionary psychology, but to any interest predicated on current evolutionary theory, including cognitive ethology.)

The more immediate inspiration for the emergence of evolutionary psychology is, no doubt, sociobiology, especially as represented in a book like E. O. Wilson's *On Human Nature* (1978). Indeed, I have heard evolutionary psychology unkindly described as no more than warmed-over sociobiology. Nevertheless, I think the enterprise more than justifies itself by the extent to which it has generated research and led to new insight about a number of aspects of human behavior and culture. The aim of achieving conceptual integration among the biological and social sciences is surely to be applauded.

Evolutionary psychology attempts to explain human psychological mechanisms as adaptively designed by natural selection pressures acting during the two million years or so that our ancestors spent as Pleistocene hunter/gatherers. Animal behavior and cognitive capacities enter in where comparative evidence promises to contribute insight into the human case. This emphasis on evolved human nature is pitted against widespread belief among social scientists that virtually everything constituting adult human intellectual and social life is imposed by culture; i.e. that the humanness of a mature human being is the emergent outcome of processes of socialization and enculturation embedded in family, educational and institutional organizations. In opposition to this 'Standard Social Science Model' (SSSM), evolutionary psychology proposes an 'Integrated Causal Model' according to which the human mind includes a number of functionally specialized or dedicated content-specific information-processing mechanisms, designed by evolution. These modular processing mechanisms, in concert with more generalized and plastic cognitive capacities, generate many of the features of culture, rather than being the product of culture. The modules are revealed by functional analysis of such universal attributes of human nature as language, preferences in mate selection and cooperative behavior.

Take cooperative behavior, for example. Cosmides and Tooby (1992) present experimental evidence supporting the view that human reasoning, rather than being a general-purpose, all-of-a-piece capacity as the SSSM assumes, consists of a number of specialized mechanisms adapted to different problems. For instance, people generally do badly on tests of logical reasoning such as the Wason selection test. This presents subjects with four cards with, say, a letter, A or B, on one side and a number, 3 or 4, on the other. If these two letters and numbers are showing, which cards should you turn over to test the truth of the proposition 'If the letter is A the number on the other side is 3?'. Most subjects pick the card with A, but few realize that they should also check the card with 4 (A and not 3 shows the proposition to be false). However, when the test refers to social situations where someone might be cheating (e.g. what questions would you ask of people in a bar to see whether they were keeping to the law about underage drinking?), these same people do much better. According to Cosmides and Tooby there appear to be specialized reasoning capacities for coping with social exchange contexts, comparable to the defences against exploitation in cooperative alliances in some primate societies.

Still on the cooperative theme, a study by William McGrew and Anna Feistner (1992) exemplifies how a more direct use of animal comparison can be brought to bear on a question of human social evolution. They have looked at food-sharing behavior in chimpanzees and callitrichid monkeys (marmosets and tamarins) to see whether there might be clues to how this behavior arose in ancestral groups of people. They found that neither presents a tidy model for the human case. Chimpanzees have tool use and primitive technology for preparing food comparable to Tasmanian aborigines, but food sharing is limited to 'tolerated scrounging' or responses to begging. Rarely is it a matter of spontaneous giving or offering. In tamarins and marmosets, tool use and food preparation are lacking, but food sharing is an important part of social exchange, and consists of active distribution, animals offering food items without solicitation, especially to infants by their parents and older siblings.

In speculating about how humans developed both the technology theme of the chimps and the social theme of the callitrichids, McGrew and Feistner suggest that, by turning to the hunting of big game, protohominids provided themselves with surplus food supplies, which, together with group attachment to a home base, fostered social exchange and hence the kinds of reciprocity relationships foundational for human society. Whether this conjecture favours a modular mechanism as opposed to the SSSM is an open question, however.

Let us look again at the topic of spatial cognition mentioned earlier. It has been known for some time that men and women differ in tests of spatial perception. While men surpass women on tests of spatial relations and mental rotation, women have better memory for objects and their locations. Moreover, these differences appear to have a hormonal basis, for they do not appear until after puberty.

Such sex differences in spatial abilities have also been found in some animals. For instance, male Meadow Voles have been found to be superior to females in tests of spatial perception, and this goes with their having larger hippocampi. No such differences were found in Pine Voles. Male Meadow Voles are polygenous and, accordingly, have relatively large home ranges calling for navigation skills which are supported by their enhanced spatial ability. Pine Voles are monogamous, with relatively modest home ranges (Gaulin and Fitzgerald, 1986; Jacobs *et al.*, 1990).

Irwin Silverman and Marion Eals (1992) argue that the human sex differences in spatial abilities have a functional correlate comparable to that distinguishing Meadow Voles and Pine Voles. Palaeontological and archaeological evidence suggests that, in Pleistocene hunter/gatherer groups, a division of labor existed in which men did most of the hunting and women did most of the gathering. Hunting calls for navigation skills such as awareness of spatial relations and a sense of direction; gathering benefits from precise memory for where and when plant foods of different sorts are to be found. Again, the conclusion is that a current aspect of human cognition has its basis in selection pressures acting on our ancestors.

Finally, a word about language, 'that quintessential human trait" as Stephen Pinker has put it. Pinker is a leading advocate of the evolutionary psychological view that language acquisition depends upon an innate language acquisition device in the brain. This conception comes from Chomsky, upon whose ideas Pinker builds, but from whom he differs in arguing that the language organ is a product of evolutionary design comparable to web-spinning in spiders and echo-location in bats. Pinker's elegant and mischievous book, *The Language Instinct* (1994), presents a powerful case for the nativist thesis. It argues, for example, that the child must start out with the ability to categorize noun phrases and verb phrases, and other basic features of grammar, to be able to process the utterances it hears. Also, so Pinker claims, the rapidity with which the child goes from imitation to competent production of sentences belies the possibility that learning is all that is involved.

However, there are other theories of language acquisition which challenge the claims of innateness and modularity. For one thing, as George Michel and Celia Moore point out in their splendid new text on *Developmental Psychobiology* (1995), the problems supposedly met by the language organ theory arise in part because the speech of children has been described in terms of the speech of adults. Hence, the developmental problem is cast 'in terms of goals rather than origins'. They argue that 'a development from perspective' provides access to developmental processes associated with the acquisition of language that are unavailable from a 'developmental to perspective' (p. 376). They describe alternative theories, such as the semantic theories of Braine (1987) and Schlesinger (1988), and the exemplar model of Chandler (1993), which I shall not attempt to describe. The following example of how facts favoring the instinct theory can be accommodated in other ways will have to suffice.

When children start forming the past tense of irregular verbs in English they do so correctly in imitation of what they hear. Then they switch to using uniformly the 'ed' ending applying to regular verbs, even in irregular cases, such as in 'runned' and 'singed', as though arriving at a grammatical rule. Only later do they adjust to using the correct forms. This U-shaped sequence has been taken as evidence of an endogenous process of rule organization independent of pattern in heard speech. However, Plunkett and Senha (1992) have simulated this development on a neural network model and obtained the same sequence without having to incorporate any rules in the system – the correct rules are emergent from general operations on input, not built in.

The example of language illustrates what I think might be an unfortunate tendency of evolutionary psychology. By talking in terms of 'developmental programs' and 'genetic determination' the possibility of accounting for adaptively designed features in developmental terms tends to be shelved. Although Tooby and Cosmides (1992), for example, appreciate that 'the genes come embedded in a matrix of cellular and developmental machinery' (p. 78), and that 'the environment is just as much the product of evolution as the genes' (p. 84), their adaptive focus somewhat slights the epigenetic perspective, with its regard for the evidence of self-organization in ontogenetic development. This perspective is well represented in the work of Brian Goodwin (e.g. 1994) and Gerald Edelman (e.g. 1987, 1988) on morphogenesis. One may argue that preoccupation with adaptive function need not concern itself with developmental issues, but evolutionary psychology purports to aim at integration, and hence coherence with current conceptions of development. Not to aim for this integration invites history to repeat itself, as happened in sociobiology.

Self-organization has also come to figure in new conceptions of the evolutionary process, as envisaged, for example, by the theories of Stuart Kauffman (e.g. 1993, 1995). In brief, Kauffman is concerned with patterns generated by complex systems, including genetic systems, when they are in states far from thermodynamic equilibrium. According to Kauffman, the order emerging from such systems presents variation for natural selection to work on 'for free'. In their recent book, *Darwinism Evolving* (1995), David Depew and Bruce Weber see Kauffman's ideas, and the work on nonlinear thermodynamics with which they are allied, as promising to bring a new Darwinian synthesis into being. Should this come to pass, evolutionary psychology, as well as the other evolutionarily informed approaches to animal and human cognition, will need to adapt to it. Remember the lesson of Herbert Spencer's synthetic philosophy. Having returned to Spencer, I can pass on to evolutionary epistemology, for he gets into the act there too.

Evolutionary epistemology

In the early pages of his magnificent *Principles of Psychology* (1890), William James wrote: 'On the whole few recent formulas have done more real service of a rough sort in psychology than the Spencerian one that the essence of mental life and bodily life are one, namely, the adjustment of inner to outer relations' (p. 6). In both the acquisition of knowledge in individual development, and in the adaptation of form to function in phyletic evolution, Spencer saw a progressive matching process shaping mind and body to the world. Indeed, as I said earlier, he thought that this process of general evolution had universal application to the material, biological, psychological and social realms.

Spencer's conception of evolution as 'continuous adjustment of internal relations to external relations' (Spencer, 1855, p. 374) anticipates a view of evolutionary epistemology, and finds current echo in the statement: 'Evolution is a process in which information regarding the environment is literally incorporated, incarnated, in surviving organisms through the process of adaptation' (Bartley, 1987, p. 23). Just as evolutionary studies divide between history and mechanism, phylogeny and selective agency, so the study of the evolution of knowing – evolutionary epistemology – divides between reconstruction of the steps through which the evolution of cognitive capacities has passed, and accounting for the means by which those steps were effected. Henry Plotkin (1994, p. 2) has described evolutionary epistemology as 'the biological study of knowledge', extending from microbial irritability to the sublimest reaches of science. In the words of Karl Popper (1972, p. 246): '. . . from the amoeba to Einstein is just one step'. Here's continuity with a vengeance.

Popper and Konrad Lorenz have been credited with launching evolutionary epistemology in its modern guise. Lorenz (1941) was first on the scene with a paper in which he joined issue with Kant. He took the position that the a priori categories and intuitions of Kant's epistemology can be regarded as a posteriori from a biological, evolutionary point of view – consequences of natural selection's having fitted the forms of thought to the forms of the world: 'Our categories and forms of perception, fixed prior to individual experience, are adjusted to the external world for exactly the same reasons as the hoof of the horse is already adapted to the ground of the steppe before the horse is born and the fin of the fish is adapted to the water before the fish hatches' (Lorenz, 1941/1982, pp. 124–125). However, adaptation is a 'satisficing' process, making do with the best that variation has so far made available, which can fall far short of ideal design (think of the human knee). So the a priori approximates the thing-in-itself (the world as it exists independently of our perception of it) only so far as it has proved functionally superior to any realized alternatives. Modern physics has shown that our intuitions about time, space and causality are anything but the last word about reality. They enable us to attain pragmatic purchase on the world by getting us to experience the world as though it were of a certain nature. Without awareness of being so, we are 'hypothetical realists' for whom 'everything is a working hypothesis' (Lorenz, 1941/1982, p. 132). Lorenz later elaborated this version of evolutionary epistemology in a book *Die Rückseite des Spiegels* (1973).

Oddly enough, Lorenz took what, on the face of it, appears to be a contradictory stance with regard to the epistemological situation of a scientist. He maintained that the scientist 'has to *begin* with pure observation, totally devoid of preconceived theory and even working hypothesis' (Lorenz, 1950, p. 233); and persisted in prescribing 'presuppositionless observation' (Lorenz, 1981, p. 47) for ethology to the end of his days. Perhaps Lorenz thought of his edict as a prudent methodological ploy to quell excessive anticipation of nature, rather than a possibility that could be literally achieved. However, even this interpretation of his continuing and unqualified advocacy of what might be called radical induction is difficult to square with Lorenz's relations with Popper.

Lorenz had known Popper since boyhood (Popper, 1974, p. 45), and quoted him with approval in later writings (e.g. Lorenz, 1981, pp. 17–18). Yet, Popper's philosophy of science was diametrically opposed to the possibility of inductive inference in the absence of presuppositions. For him all observation and description is theory-laden. Observation and description entail categorization of whatever is in question – a priori sorting of things and events into kinds. But the world can be sorted in an indefinite number of different ways. We do not do it any old how, but according to what our prior orientation vests with salience, interest, apparent significance. We may err in where we draw the lines, but without that risk of error we should never get started on the business of finding shape in the flux of phenomena. So, for Popper, science proceeds at the outset by proposing possibilities, and then testing their implications, a strategy summed up in the title of one of his books: *Conjectures and Refutations* (1963).

From this point of view, science resembles natural selection: conceptions and hypotheses are embroiled in a winnowing contest determined by trial through empirical test. Popper drew this analogy and took it seriously, extending the conception of conjecture and refutation to encompass evolution in general and the evolution of knowledge in particular (Popper, 1972). So, whereas Lorenz brought a biological perspective to bear on a theory of knowledge, Popper turned a theory of knowledge on to the process of evolution.

Important as the ideas of Lorenz and Popper have been in the emergence of evolutionary epistemology, Donald Campbell (e.g. 1974) has probably done more than anyone to develop and disseminate its themes. Indeed, it was Campbell who coined the tag 'evolutionary epistemology' (Bartley, 1987), a designation that Plotkin finds 'regrettable...because it is both pompous and portentous – it threatens people with an intellectual mugging by a philosopher' (Plotkin, 1994, p. 2). Campbell takes a very broad and inclusive view of cognition, which, like Popper's, ranges 'from the amoeba to Einstein'. He views the evolution of cognitive capacities as a cavalcade of ever more sophisticated versions of a process consisting of selective elimination or retention of blindly generated variations – trial with error or success.

In its simplest form, this process is represented by the locomotory behavior of unicellular [or, if you follow Hyman (1940), acellular] organisms such as a paramecium. This consists of random change of direction on encounter with obstacles or unfavorable conditions, until a way round or out is hit on, together with change of speed depending on whether conditions are deteriorating or improving – in the terminology of Fraenkel and Gunn (1940): 'kleinokinesis' coupled with 'orthokinesis'. Campbell (1974) calls this procedure 'non-mnemonic problem-solving', since there is only transient selective retention of the effects of successful trial behavior. This means of finding passage through a world that is discontinuous – open in this direction, closed off in that – constitutes the bottom tier of a stack of ten progressively more sophisticated ways of knowing, with science at the top.

Campbell calls his next level 'vicarious locomotor devices'. It consists of locomotion, the direction of which is governed by detection of spatial features at a distance, and hence vicarious testing of the possibilities for locomotory passage. Campbell discusses the example of receptivity to light, and begins by drawing attention to the fact that, of the full electromagnetic spectrum, from the shortest cosmic rays to the longest radio waves, only a tiny span of wavelengths constitutes the window of vision. Why this particular window between 400 and 700 nm? Campbell's answer is that it is coincident with a coincidence: for these wavelengths, transparency corresponds to penetrability and opacity corresponds to impenetrability. So, by acquiring a means of detecting and discriminating transparency and opacity at a distance, organisms were enabled to steer clear courses round obstacles without having to bump into them. There are exceptions to the crucial coincidence: clear ice and glass are transparent but solid, and fog is opaque yet can be passed through. However, Campbell points out, these exceptions were absent from the aquatic environment in which visual receptivity originated.

More recently, another coincidence has been remarked, which argues to be more fundamental than that between opacity and solidity. Günter Wächtershäuser (1987) has observed that the visible spectrum matches the range of wavelengths capable of sustaining photosynthesis: wavelengths longer than 700 nm have insufficient energy to drive the photochemistry, and wavelengths shorter than 400 nm have so much energy that they are destructive of biomolecular architecture. So Wächtershäuser speculates that the evolution of visual receptivity and its use in locomotory guidance are grounded on the discovery of the nutritive value of light. Thus, Wächtershäuser and Campbell together tell a tale of how sight as we know it had its origins in primeval protophyta: the earliest means of detecting light arose in the service of locating organisms in sunshine strong enough to effect photosynthesis, like the eyespots of present-day flagellates exemplified by *Euglena*. Subsequent elaborations of such light detectors, including addition of lenses, provided the acuity required for the vicarious locomotory probing envisaged by Campbell.

The remaining eight levels of Campbell's scheme comprise habit, instinct, visually supported thought, mnemonically supported thought, socially vicarious exploration (including observational learning and imitation), language, cultural cumulation and finally science. Without going into how he and other evolutionary epistemologists try to deal with these and allied topics, I merely list them to give an idea of the ambitious scope of this approach. The discussion of the origin of vision should give an idea of the general style of the approach: interpretive and speculative rather than experimental and quantitative. Evolutionary epistemology also involves more philosophical preoccupation with cognitive issues than either learning theory or evolutionary psychology. However, this is something it shares with the fourth and last of my varying views of animal and human cognition: the emergence of a comparative perspective in cognitive science. This is my next topic.

Comparative approaches to cognitive science

Although the beginnings of cognitive science can be traced back at least as far as the Hixon Symposium on 'Cerebral Mechanisms in Behavior' held at Cal Tech in 1948 (Jeffress, 1951), it did not emerge to public prominence until the 1970s. Then, this consortium of psychology, philosophy, linguistics, anthropology, computer science and neuroscience made bold claims to having the wherewithal, via computer modeling, for settling such age-old questions as the relation of mind to brain, the physical basis of consciousness and thought, the acquisition of knowledge and language. These claims remain largely unfulfilled, in spite of some impressive successes, such as the design of programs that can beat all but the Grandest Masters at chess. Even after most cognitive scientists have switched back from a linear symbol-manipulation conception of information processing to the kind of neural network model pioneered by McCulloch and Pitts (1943), and so built up the currently flourishing industry in connectionist models and parallel distributed processing, their achievements fall short of aspiration.

According to the editors of a recently published book, cognitive science's limited success may be due to its starting in the wrong place. In their introduction to their book *Comparative Approaches to Cognitive Science* (1995), Herbert Roitblat and Jean-Arcady Meyer liken the position of cognitive science to that of a man who wants his architect to construct the upper story of a building without bothering about the ground floor. Taking language and logic as the dominating features of human mentality, the cognitive science program has gone after the sophisticated problem-solving, theorem-proving, grammar-mastering accomplishments that depend on or constitute linguistic competence. But, say Roitblat and Meyer, this competence rests on a basis of humbler functions, such as sensory perception, sensory–motor coordination and category discrimination, which current cognitive science has made little progress in elucidating. Unlike full-blown linguistic ability, these more basic functions are shared with other animals and hence are open to comparative, or what Roitblat calls 'biomimetic' approaches. These comprise studies of animal behavior, and the design of computer simulations or robots informed by observations of how whole animals cope with their worlds – the *animat* approach.

The comparative approaches to cognitive science thus include recruitment of cognitive ethology. A clear and elegant example is a comparative study of language and animal communication by Christopher Evans and Peter Marler (1995). They discuss three basic features of human speech: partitioning of acoustic continua to yield categorical perception of vocal utterance; functional referentiality (the coding and decoding of information about external events); and the modulation of communication behavior as a function of social context (e.g. the 'audience effect'). For all three they report experimental evidence of instances in at least some birds and mammals, implying either phylogenetic antiquity or evolutionary convergence. In contrast Evans and Marler have been unable to find naturally occurring nonhuman cases of lexical syntax, and only very limited capacities for making reference to past or future times. Thus the comparative work reveals both continuities and discontinuities between human language and animal communication.

Work on perceptual control theory by Michael Bourbon (1995) illustrates the animat approach. Bourbon uses computer simulations of the behavior of bacteria in a stimulus gradient, human performance in a tracking experiment and people controlling their positions in crowds to show that the observed behavior can be achieved without resort to a cognitive map, or a top-down command system, as is so often assumed in cognitive science, but simply by keeping local sensory input within the limits of a reference value – what von Holst called a Sollwert (von Holst and Mittelstaedt, 1950). He distinguishes between behavior as viewed and interpreted by an outside observer and what an animal experiences as what it itself is doing, and argues persuasively and provocatively that, much of the time, an animal is doing no more than controlling its perceptions.

In addition to the ethological and animat approaches, the comparative version of cognitive science, as represented in the Roitblat and Meyer volume, ranges widely to include work from established fields such as animal learning theory and motivation. There are questions about whether concepts applying to ourselves can also be attributed to other animals. Can they be creative like us? Do they have intentionality? Do they have a concept of self, or any concepts at all? Some of these questions are taken up by philosophers who, as you might expect, answer that they turn on what you take the concepts to mean. Dan Dennett (1995), for example, asks 'Do animals have beliefs?' and answers: 'It all depends on what you understand by the term "belief".' He opts for a minimalist conception according to which belief obtains wherever action is influenced by information. From this perspective, it follows that the beliefs enjoined by the Apostles' Creed are on a continuum with the 'belief' a thermostat has about ambient temperature. With regard to animal behavior, Dennett would have us invoke belief whenever it helps to make sense of what an animal appears to be up to, and hence predicts its course of action.

This short way of disposing of the concerns of cognitive ethologists and philosophers of mind about animal awareness reminds me of a conference on Evolution and Cognition that I attended in France in 1994. There was much banter about what counts as cognition and what kind of creature could be cognitive. For some people, cognitive states were unimaginable unless expressible in language. For others, almost anything could he cognitive: trees, blue–green algae, perhaps even Dennett's thermostat.

John Stewart, a British cognitive scientist working in Paris, took this debate quite seriously. In a paper entitled 'Cognition = life: implications for higher-level cognition', Stewart (1995) contrasted what he called 'objectivist' and 'constructivist' conceptions of cognition. The objectivist version applies in the computational theory of mind of preconnectionist cognitive science. This assumes syntactical manipulation of symbolic representations, and an independent reality as a referential basis for semantic grounding of the symbols. Hence it is objectivist. The other paradigm, equating cognition with life, assumes an evolutionary continuity in cognitive capacities from bacteria to humanity, comparable to Campbell's evolutionary epistemology program. However, for Stewart, this latter approach is nonobjectivist in maintaining that an organism's perception 'should not be viewed as a grasping of reality but a specification of one'. Hence the constructivist conception of cognition.

On this view the organism is confined within the limits of its perceptual organization, its Umwelt to use von Uexküll's term. The animal's world is not independent of the animal itself, but a product of its sensory capacities.

This constructionist position can be linked to the skeptical tradition in philosophy, and to recent philosophical discussion of realist options (i.e. conceptions of a world apart from our perceptual experience) in, for example, the writings of Hilary Putnam (e.g. 1990). Even the creative writer and artist can be concerned about the relation between the given and the conceived. The novelist and critic A. S. Byatt expresses fear of and fascination for 'theories of language as a self-referring system of signs, which doesn't touch the world' (1991, p. 5), with the implication that we occupy 'a bounded world bearing only on the shape of our own imagination' (Byatt, 1991). The question of how artistic creativity and reality bear on one another preoccupied the poet Wallace Stevens throughout his writing life (e.g. Kermode, 1989). The objectivist view, on the other hand, connects to the program of naturalizing epistemology that has arisen in the philosophy of mind (Kornblith, 1987). This view seeks to relate belief and meaning to the natural world, as in the evolutionarily informed ideas of Ruth Millikan (1984, 1993), where biological function is the *raison d'être* of natural kind categories. The view that cognition = life thus opens on to vistas of philosophy and literature, in addition to biology and psychology. But these are topics for another essay, and this one is nearing its end.

Before ending, however, I have one final brief but circuitous excursion to make to get us back to the Roitblat and Meyer book, beginning in territory we have visited already: the question of behavioral categorization. The issue of how to describe behavior has preoccupied me ever since my graduate student days, when I saw how questions about incubation and nest-building behavior in gulls could turn on the distinction between causal and functional categorization (Beer, 1963, 1974). At about the same time, I encountered this issue in a very different context. In a book entitled *The Explanation of Behaviour* (1964) the philosopher Charles Taylor compared and contrasted two ways of describing behavior: as movement and as action, e.g. as flexing the finger upwards and as avoiding getting shocked. Taylor argued that, while movements can be explained in terms of causes, such as activity in certain neural pathways, actions require explanation in terms of intentions, and that the logical relations between causes and movements, on the one hand, and intentions and actions on the other, are profoundly different.

Taylor's book led to a great deal of discussion. In Oxford, a group of philosophers and psychologists has been meeting more or less regularly over the years to follow up the issues that have emerged, and in 1989 some of these people contributed to a book edited by Alan Montefiore and Denis Noble entitled *Goals, No-goals and Own Goals*. The centerpiece of the book is a chapter with the same title by David McFarland. In this, McFarland maintains that a scientific approach to apparent purposiveness in behavior has to distinguish critically between goal-achieving behavior, goal-seeking behavior, goal-directed behavior and intentional behavior. He argues that the purposiveness of behavior can generally be accounted for by the evolutionarily constructed design of the organism, without need for invoking goal-directedness or intention, with their implied internal representations of the goals sought and achieved by such design. In a chapter in the Roitblat and Meyer book (McFarland, 1995), he takes a similar stand, arguing that the decisions organisms make about what to do are determined by tradeoff considerations, which obviate reliance on a represented goal.

This seems to me to be a false opposition. McFarland gives no reason why goal-directedness could not implement a tradeoff decision once the decision is made. Tradeoff decisions between considerations of fuel economy and comfort affect the setting of a thermostat, but the device still works by negative feedback, which is a simple form of a goal-governed process. In the chapter immediately following McFarland's, Frederick Toates (1995) makes a similar point, and finds goal-directedness to be a central part of much motivational control. Toates compares and contrasts two forms of learning: learning based on cognitive processes and learning based on S–R processes. Acting cognitively, an animal: (a) assimilates information about its environment; (b) can utilize this information flexibly; and (c) is goal-directed, i.e. guides its behavior in accordance with an internal representation of a goal. In S–R processes, associations between stimuli and responses are strengthened by reinforcement in an inflexible way in which represented goals play no part. Past debates have been polarized between these two conceptions of learning. Toates argues that both kinds of processes play roles in learning, depending upon how their respective advantages and disadvantages, their benefits and costs, relate to the experiential context.

Conclusion

Having returned to considerations of learning, I bring this Cook's tour to a close. I think you will agree that we have covered quite a lot of country, if only in the cursory manner of Cook's tours. While there are some shared territories between the several approaches to cognition that we have visited, and between them and cognitive ethology, each also to some extent has its own preserve. Such separateness may have its advantages, at least for the time being, given the differences in questions raised, background assumptions, and orienting attitudes. Even so, there may be more scope for conversation across the borders than there has been.

In presenting his famous four questions of ethology to the world, my teacher Niko Tinbergen (1963) said of them: 'that it is useful both to distinguish between them and to insist that a comprehensive, coherent science of ethology has to give equal attention to each of them and to their integration'. I think a similar statement applies to the varying views of animal and human cognition.

Acknowledgement

I am grateful to Irene Pepperberg and another anonymous reviewer for helpful comments on an earlier version of this essay.

References

Barkow, J. H., Cosmides, L. and Tooby, J. (eds) (1992) *The Adapted Mind – Evolutionary Psychology and the Generation of Culture.* New York: Oxford University Press.

Bartley, W. W. III (1987) Philosophy of biology versus philosophy of physics. In Radnitsky, G. and Bartley, W. W., III (eds) *Evolutionary Epistemology, Rationality and the Sociology of Knowledge.* La Salle, IL: Open Court, pp. 7–45.

Beer, C. G. (1963) Incubation and nestbuilding behaviour of black-headed gulls: IV. Nest-building in the laying and incubation periods. *Behaviour* 21, 155–176.

Beer, C. G. (1974) Species-typical behavior and ethology. In Dewsbury, D. A. and Rethlingshafer, D. A. (eds) *Comparative Psychology – A Modern Survey.* New York: McGraw-Hill, pp. 21–77.

Bekoff, M. and Jamieson, D. (eds) (1996) *Readings in Animal Cognition.* Cambridge, MA: MIT Press.

Bourbon, W. T. (1995) Perceptual control theory. In Roitblat, H. L. and Meyer, J.-A. (eds) *Comparative Approaches to Cognitive Science.* Cambridge, MA: MIT Press, pp. 151–172.

Braine, M. D. S. (1987) What is learned in acquiring word classes: a step towards an acquisition theory. In MacWhinney, B. (ed.) *Mechanisms of Language Acquisition.* Hillsdale, NJ: Erlbaum, pp. 65–87.

Broadbent, D. E. (1961) *Behaviour.* London: Eyre and Spottiswoode.

Byatt, A. S. (1991) *Passions of the Mind.* London: Chatto and Windus.

Campbell, D. T. (1974) Evolutionary epistemology. In Schilpp, P. A. (ed.) *The Philosophy of Karl Popper.* La Salle, IL: Open Court, pp. 413–463.

Chandler, S. (1993) Are rules and modules really necessary for explaining language? *Psycholing. Res.* 22, 593–606.

Cheng, K. (1986) A purely geometric module in the rat's spatial representation. *Cognition* 23, 149–178.

Cosmides, L. and Tooby, J. (1992) Cognitive adaptations for social exchange. In Barkow, J. H., Cosmides, L. and Tooby, J. (eds), *The Adapted Mind.* New York: Oxford University Press, pp. 163–228.

Darwin, C. (1859) *On the Origin of Species by Means of Natural Selection, or the Preservation of Favoured Races in the Struggle for Life*. London: John Murray.

Darwin, C. (1871) *The Descent of Man, and Selection in Relation to Sex*. London: John Murray.

Dennett, D. C. (1995) Do animals have beliefs? In Roitblat, H. L. and Meyer, J.-A. (eds) *Comparative Approaches to Cognitive Science*. Cambridge, MA: MIT Press, pp. 111–118.

Depew, D. J. and Weber, B. H. (1995) *Darwinism Evolving – Systems Dynamics and the Genealogy of Natural Selection*. Cambridge, MA: MIT Press.

Dyke, C. (1985) Complexity and closure. In Depew, D. J. and Weber, B. H. (eds) *Evolution at a Crossroads*. Cambridge, MA: MIT Press.

Edelman, G. M. (1987) *Neural Darwinism – The Theory of Neuronal Group Selection*. New York: Basic Books.

Edelman, G. M. (1988) *Topobiology – An Introduction to Molecular Embryology*. New York: Basic Books.

Evans, C. S. and Marler, P. (1995) Language and animal communication: parallels and contrasts. In Roitblat, H. L. and Meyer, J.-A. (eds) *Comparative Approaches to Cognitive Science*. Cambridge, MA: MIT Press, pp. 341–382.

Fodor, J. A. (1983) *The Modularity of Mind*. Cambridge, MA: MIT Press.

Fraenkel, W. S. and Gunn, W. H. (1940) *The Orientation of Animals: Kineses, Taxes and Compass Reactions*. Oxford: Oxford University Press.

Gallistel, C. R. (1990) *The Organization of Learning*. Cambridge, MA: MIT Press.

Gaulin, S. J. C. and Fitzgerald, R. W. (1986) Sex differences in spatial ability: an evolutionary hypothesis and test. *Am. Nat.* **127**, 74–88.

Ghiselin, M. (1969) *The Triumph of the Darwinian Method*. Berkeley, CA: University of California Press.

Goodwin, B. (1994) *How the Leopard Changed its Spots*. New York: Scribner.

Grene, M. (ed.) (1983) *Dimensions of Darwinism – Themes and Counterthemes in Twentieth-Century Evolutionary Theory*. Cambridge: Cambridge University Press.

Guthrie, E. R. (1935) *The Psychology of Learning*. New York: Harper.

Ho, M.-W. and Saunders, P. T. (eds) (1984) *Beyond Neo-Darwinism – An Introduction to the New Evolutionary Paradigm*. New York: Academic Press.

Holst, E. von and Mittelstaedt, H. (1950) Das Reafferenzprinzip. *Naturwissenschaften* **37**, 464–476.

Hull, C. L. (1943) *Principles of Behavior*. New York: Appleton-Century-Crofts.

Hyman, L. H. (1940). *The Invertebrata: Protozoa through Ctenophora*. New York: McGraw-Hill.

Jacobs, L. F., Gaulin, S. J. C., Sherry, D. and Hoffman, G. E. (1990) Evolution of spatial cognition: sex-specific patterns of spatial behavior predict hippocampal size. *Proc. Natl Acad. Sci. USA*, **87**, 6349–6352.

James, W. (1890) *The Principles of Psychology*. New York: Henry Holt.

Jeffress, L. A. (ed.) (1951) *Cerebral Mechanisms in Behavior – The Hixon Symposium*. New York: Wiley.

Kauffman, S. A. (1993) *The Origins of Order – Self-organization and Selection in Evolution*. New York: Oxford University Press.

Kauffman, S. A. (1995) *At Home in the Universe – The Search for the Laws of Self-organization and Complexity*. New York: Oxford University Press.

Kermode, F. (1989) *Wallace Stevens*. London: Faber and Faber.

Kornblith, H. (ed.) (1987) *Naturalizing Epistemology*. Cambridge, MA: MIT Press.

Lorenz, K. Z. (1941) Kant's Lehre vom apriorischen im Lichte gegenwärtiger Biologie. *Blätt. Dtsche Philosophie* **15**, 94–125. [Translation: Kant's doctrine of the a priori in the light of contemporary biology. In H. C. Plotkin (ed.) (1982) *Learning, Development, and Culture – Essays in Evolutionary Epistemology*. New York: John Wiley, pp. 121–143.]

Lorenz, K. Z. (1950) The comparative method in studying innate behaviour patterns. Symposia of the Society for Experimental Biology, no. IV: *Physiological Mechanisms in Animal Behaviour*, pp. 221–268.

Lorenz, K. Z. (1973) *Die Rückseite der Spiegels*. Berlin: Piper Verlag.

Lorenz, K. Z. (1981) *The Foundations of Ethology*. New York: Springer-Verlag.

McCulloch, W. S. and Pitts, W. H. (1943) A logical calculus of the ideas imminent in nervous activity. *Bull. Math. Biophys.* **5**, 115–133.

McDougall, W. (1912) *Psychology – The Study of Behaviour*. London: Henry Holt.

McFarland, D. (1989) Goals, no-goals and own goals. In Montefiore, A. and Noble, D. (eds) *Goals, No-Goals and Own Goals*. London: Unwin Hyman, pp. 39–57.

McFarland, D. (1995) Opportunity versus goals in robots, animals, and people. In Roitblat, H. L. and Meyer, J.-A. (eds) *Comparative Approaches to Cognitive Science*. Cambridge, MA: MIT Press, pp. 415–433.

McGrew, W. C. and Feistner, A. T. C. (1992) Two nonhuman primate models for the evolution of human food sharing: chimpanzees and callitrichids. In Barkow, J. H., Cosmides, L. and Tooby, J. (eds) *The Adapted Mind – Evolutionary Psychology and the Generation of Culture*. New York: Oxford University Press, pp. 229–243.

Matzel, L. D., Held, F. P. and Miller, R. R. (1988) Information and expression of simultaneous and backwards associations: implications for contiguity theory. *Learning Motivation* **19**, 317–344.

Medewar, P. (1982) Herbert Spencer and the law of general evolution. In Medewar, P. (ed.) *Pluto's Republic*. Oxford: Oxford University Press, pp. 209–227.

Michel, G. F. and Moore, C. L. (1995) *Developmental Psychobiology – An Interdisciplinary Science*. Cambridge, MA: MIT Press.

Millikan, R. G. (1984) *Language, Thought, and Other Biological Categories – New Foundations for Realism*. Cambridge, MA: MIT Press.

Millikan, R. G. (1993) *White Queen Psychology and other Essays for Alice*. Cambridge, MA: MIT Press.

Montefiore, A. and Noble, D. (eds) (1989) *Goals, No-Goals and Own Goals*. London: Unwin Hyman.

Pinker, S. (1994) *The Language Instinct – How the Mind Creates Language*. New York: Morrow.

Plotkin, H. (1994) *Darwin Machines and the Nature of Knowledge*. Cambridge, MA: Harvard University Press.

Plunkett, K. and Sinha, C. (1992) Connectionism and developmental theory. *Br. J. Dev. Psychol.* **10**, 209–254.

Pollard, J. W. (ed.) (1984) *Evolutionary Theory: Paths into the Future*. New York: Wiley.

Popper, K. (1963) *Conjectures and Refutations*. London: Routledge and Kegan Paul.

Popper, K. (1972) *Objective Knowledge – An Evolutionary Approach*. Oxford: Oxford University Press.

Popper, K. (1974) *Unending Quest – An Intellectual Autobiography*. La Salle, IL: Open Court.

Putnam, H. (1990) *Realism with a Human Face*. Cambridge, MA: Harvard University Press.

Ristau, C. A. (ed.) (1991) *Cognitive Ethology – The Minds of Other Animals – Essays in Honor of Donald R. Griffin*. Hillsdale, NJ: Erlbaum.

Roitblat, H. L. and Meyer, J.-A. (eds) (1995) *Comparative Approaches to Cognitive Science*. Cambridge, MA: MIT Press.

Schlesinger, I. M. (1988) The origin of relational categories. In Levy, Y., Schlesinger, I. M. and Braine, M. D. S. (eds) *Categories and Processes in Language Acquisition*. Hillsdale, NJ: Erlbaum, pp. 15–51.

Schneirla, T. C. (1959) L'apprentissage et la question du conflict chez la fourmi. Comparison avec le rat. *J. Psychol. Paris* **57**, 11–44.

Silverman, I. and Eals, M. (1992) Sex differences in spatial abilities: evolutionary theory and data. In Barkow, J. H., Cosmides, L. and Tooby, J. (eds) *The Adapted Mind – Evolutionary Psychology and the Generation of Culture*. New York: Oxford University Press, pp. 533–549.

Spencer, H. (1855) *Principles of Psychology*. London: Longmans.

Stewart, J. (1995) Cognition = life: implications for higher-level cognition. *Behav. Proc.* **35**, 311–326.

Taylor, C. (1964) *The Explanation of Behaviour*. London: Routledge and Kegan Paul.

Thorndike, E. L. (1898) Animal intelligence: an experimental study of the associative processes in animals. *Psychol. Rev. Monog.*, Suppl. no. 8.

Tinbergen, N. (1963) On the aims and methods of ethology. *Z. Tierpsychol.* **20**, 410–433.

Toates, F. (1995) Animal motivation and cognition. In Roitblat, H. L. and Meyer, J.-A. (eds) *Comparative Approaches to Animal Cognition*. Cambridge, MA: MIT Press, pp. 435–464.

Tolman, E. C. (1932) *Purposive Behavior in Animals and Man*. New York: Century.

Tooby, J. and Cosmides, L. (1992) The psychological foundations of culture. In Barkow, J. H., Cosmides, L. and Tooby, J. (eds) *The Adapted Mind –*

Evolutionary Psychology and the Generation of Culture. New York: Oxford University Press.

Wächtershäuser, G. (1987) Light and life: on the nutritional origins of sensory perception. In Radnitzky, G. and Bartley, W. W. III (eds) *Evolutionary Epistemology – Rationality and the Sociology of Knowledge*. La Salle, IL: Open Court, pp. 121–138.

Watson, J. B. (1913) Psychology as the behaviorist views it. *Psychol. Rev.* **20**, 158–177.

Wesson, R. (1991) *Beyond Natural Selection*. Cambridge, MA: MIT Press.

Wickens, D. D. (1938) The transference of conditioned excitation and conditioned inhibition from one muscle group to the antagonistic group. *J. Exp. Psychol.* **22**, 101–123.

Wickens, D. D. (1939) A study of voluntary and involuntary finger conditioning. *J. Exp. Psychol.* **25**, 127–140.

Wilson, E. O. (1978) *On Human Nature*. Cambridge, MA: Harvard University Press.

Index

Printed in the United States
92616LV00001B/172/A